D0160961

HISTORICAL, THEORETICAL, AND SOCIOLOGICAL FOUNDATIONS OF READING IN THE UNITED STATES

JEANNE B. COBB

Coastal Carolina University

MARY K. KALLUS

Eastern New Mexico University

Boston   Columbus   Indianapolis   New York   San Francisco   Upper Saddle River
Amsterdam   Cape Town   Dubai   London   Madrid   Milan   Munich   Paris   Montreal   Toronto
Delhi   Mexico City   Sao Paulo   Sydney   Hong Kong   Seoul   Singapore   Taipei   Tokyo

Vice President, Editor-in-Chief: *Aurora Martinez Ramos*
Series Editorial Assistant: *Amy Foley*
Executive Marketing Manager: *Krista Clark*
Managing Editor: *Central Publishing*
Production Editor: *Paula Carroll*
Production Manager: *Laura Messerly*
Design Director: *Jayne Conte*
Cover Designer: *Suzanne Behnke*
Cover Image: *Shutterstock*
Project Manager: *Mohinder Singh, Aptara®, Inc.*
Composition: *Aptara®, Inc.*
Text Printer: *Courier/Stoughton*
Cover Printer: *Courier/Stoughton*

Credits and acknowledgments borrowed from other sources and reproduced, with permission, in this textbook appear on appropriate page within text.

Copyright © 2011 Pearson Education, Inc., 501 Boylston Street, Boston, MA, 02116. All rights reserved. Manufactured in the United States of America. This publication is protected by Copyright, and permission should be obtained from the publisher prior to any prohibited reproduction, storage in a retrieval system, or transmission in any form or by any means, electronic, mechanical, photocopying, recording, or likewise. To obtain permission(s) to use material from this work, please submit a written request to Pearson Education, Inc., Permissions Department, 501 Boylston Street, Boston, MA 02116, or e-mail permissionsus@pearson.com.

Many of the designations by manufacturers and seller to distinguish their products are claimed as trademarks. Where those designations appear in this book, and the publisher was aware of a trademark claim, the designations have been printed in initial caps or all caps.

Library of Congress Cataloging-in-Publication Data
Historical, theoretical, and sociological foundations of reading in the United States / [edited by] Jeanne B. Cobb, Mary K. Kallus.
   p. cm.
  Includes bibliographical references and index.
  ISBN-13: 978-0-13-702039-3
  ISBN-10: 0-13-702039-2
  1. Reading—United States. I. Cobb, Jeanne Beck, 1948– II. Kallus, Mary K.
  LB1050.H575 2011
  428.40973—dc22   2010017250

10 9 8 7 6 5 4 3 2 1

www.pearsonhighered.com

ISBN 13: 978-0-13-702039-3
ISBN 10:   0-13-702039-2

Dedication

For James, Dad and Mom, always my inspiration . . .

J. B. C.

For those near and dear to my heart—

M. K. K.

ABOUT THE AUTHORS

 **Dr. Jeanne B. Cobb** is Professor of Literacy Education at Coastal Carolina University. She earned her doctorate in literacy from the University of Tennessee, Knoxville, and has a combined total of 26 years in education as elementary school teacher, reading specialist, Title I teacher, university professor, and reading clinic director. Dr. Cobb's primary research interests are in the field of emergent literacy and intervention strategies for the improvement of literacy achievement of struggling readers and writers. She has published articles in *Journal of Adolescent and Adult Literacy, Journal of Students Placed at Risk, Journal of Reading Education, and the NRC Yearbook*. She has presented research papers at international, national, state, and regional conferences and conducted workshops for parents and teachers. She serves on the editorial board for educational journals and serves as conference proposal reviewer for literacy associations. A native of North Carolina, Jeanne now lives near the ocean in South Carolina with her Westie and two stray cats. She collects old basal readers and loves antique shopping and reading.

 **Dr. Mary K. Kallus** is an Associate Professor of Reading Education at Eastern New Mexico University. She completed her doctorate in curriculum and instruction with an emphasis in literacy at Texas Tech University. With 15 years of experience in K–12 and university classrooms, she continues to enjoy teaching all ages—as well as learning. Dr. Kallus has coauthored publications in *Language Arts* and the *NRC Yearbook*. Her research interests include content area literacy, adolescent literacy, intertextuality, and the use of children's literature in the classroom. Through exploring these research interests, Dr. Kallus has had the opportunity to present at several local, state, regional, and national conferences. A Texan by birth, Mary now lives in New Mexico with her dogs and enjoys reading, quilting, and horseback riding.

CONTENTS

REPRINTED PUBLICATIONS

The following articles are reprinted exactly as they appeared in the original source, except that the format of the original articles has been standardized for presentation in this text.

CHAPTER 2

Pearson, P. D. (2000). Reading in the 20th century. In T. Good (Ed.), *American Education: Yesterday, today, and tomorrow.* Yearbook of the National Society for the Study of Education (pp. 152–208). Chicago: University of Chicago Press.

Dykstra, R., & Pearson, David. (2009, May 7). What Have We Learned from and Since the First-Grade Studies? Paper presented at the International Reading Association Conference, Minneapolis, MN.

CHAPTER 5

Anderson, R. C. (1984). Role of the reader's schema in comprehension, learning and memory. In R. C. Anderson, J. Osborn, & R. J. Tierney (Eds.), *Learning to Read in American Schools: Basal Readers and Content Texts* (pp. 243–257). Mahwah, NJ: Lawrence Erlbaum Associates.

CHAPTER 6

Bransford, J. D. (1984). Schema activation and schema acquisition: Comments of Richard C. Anderson's remarks. In R. C. Anderson, J. Osborn, & R. J. Tierney (Eds.), *Learning to Read in American Schools: Basal Readers and Content Texts* (pp. 259–272). Mahwah, NJ: Lawrence Erlbaum Associates.

CHAPTER 7

Rosenblatt, L. (2004). The transactional theory of reading and writing. In Robert B. Ruddell, & Norman J. Unrau (Eds.), *Theoretical Models and Processess of Reading* (5th ed., article 48, pp. 1363–1398). Newark, DE: International Reading Association.

CHAPTER 11

Alvermann, D. E. (2001). Some 'wonderings' about literacy teacher education. *Journal of Reading Education, 27(1)*, 9–13.

CHAPTER 15

Shuy, R. (1977). Sociolinguistics. In R. Shuy (Ed.), Linguistic theory: What can it say about reading (pp. 80–94). Newark, DE: International Reading Association.

CHAPTER 16

Smith, F., & Goodman, K. (1971). On the psycholinguistic method of teaching reading. *The Elementary School Journal, 71(4)*, 177–181.

CHAPTER 17

Moll, L., Amanti, C., Neff, D., & Gonzalez, N. (1992). Funds of knowledge for teaching: Using a qualitative approach to connect homes and classrooms. *Theory into Practice, 31*(2), 132–141.

CHAPTER 19

Leu, D. J., Jr., Kinzer, C. K., Coiro, J. L., Cammack, D. W. (2004). Toward a Theory of New Literacies Emerging From the Internet and Other Information and Communication Technologies. In R. B. Ruddell & N. J. Unrau (Eds.), *Theoretical Models and Processes of Reading* (5th ed., pp. 1570–1630).

CONTRIBUTORS

JEANNE B. COBB AND MARY K. KALLUS, EDITORS

Alvermann, Donna	*University of Georgia*
Amanti, Cathy	*Tucson Arizona Unified School District*
Anderson, Richard C.	*University of Illinois at Urbana-Champaign*
Bransford, John D.	*University of Washington*
DeVivas, Romelia Hurtado	*Eastern New Mexico University*
Flores, Geni	*Eastern New Mexico University*
Gallenstein, Nancy	*Coastal Carolina University*
Galligan, Elizabeth	*Eastern New Mexico University (retired)*
Gonzalez, Norma	*University of Arizona*
Good, Kathie	*Eastern New Mexico University*
Goodman, Kenneth	*University of Arizona*
Jacobs, Walter	*University of Minnesota*
Leu, Donald	*University of Connecticut*
Moll, Luis	*University of Arizona, Professor Emeritus*
Morris, Scott Douglas	*Eastern New Mexico University*
Neff, Deborah	*University of Arizona*
Pearson, P. David	*University of California, Berkeley*
Ratliff, Phillip	*Panther Creek Consolidated Independent School District, Valera, Texas*
Rosenblatt, Louise	*Deceased*
Smith, Frank	*Independent writer/researcher*
Shuy, Roger	*Georgetown University, Professor Emeritus*
Vaden, Russell	*Coastal Carolina University*
Wilson, Amy	*University of Georgia*

Attention: Students of reading instruction! You are about to embark on an amazing adventure. Whether you are an experienced teacher of many years, a novice to the profession, or contemplating your own classroom in the near future, you will find chapters in this book that will enhance your knowledge, challenge your thinking, and provide an expanded perspective for study and for constructing your personal definition of reading.

We compare this learning journey to traveling along the reading superhighway with the destination being a richer understanding of reading instruction: how it has been taught in the past, the disciplines that have contributed to the study of reading along the way, and the new frontiers into which the field is migrating. As you travel along this superhighway, there will be the intersections of divergent disciplines, and we will venture off the main road to explore different paths. Each of these intersections or sections will provide an overview of the contributions of that discipline to your foundational knowledge of reading and will enable you to see why the teaching of reading is such a complex and controversial topic. In this book, you will find classic articles that have inspired professionals to rethink and often move in a new direction in reading instruction. You will also find the inclusion of newer and less well known voices, those who have expertise on their topics and who bring years of authentic life experiences with diverse student populations to our understandings about the teaching of reading in the 21st century. As editors, it is our belief that bringing together a sampling of the perspectives of leading reading researchers as well as practitioners from various fields of study such as educational psychology, special education, sociology, bilingual education, and linguistics yields a more comprehensive view of the current status of reading instruction.

Our intention for this text is to present a variety of perspectives about reading, its processes, and its foundations. While we designed the layout of how we planned to present this material to you, we looked closely to the International Reading Association's Standard 1 (*Standards for Reading Professionals—Revised 2003* and *Standards for Reading Professionals 2010*; Draft available at the time of publication) and have thus aligned this text closely with this standard. As well, chapters and/or activities throughout this book address IRA Standards 2, 3, 4, and 6.

Additionally, we wanted to include a variety of theoretical models and perspectives, resulting in the inclusion of top-down, bottom-up, interactive, transactional, and sociocultural frames that inform our approach to and teaching of reading. As you journey through this text, consider the intersections of these models and perspectives: How are they similar? In what ways do they differ? How will they impact your own practice as a literacy teacher?

This textbook is divided into five sections, each section containing chapters of varying lengths. Each chapter begins with guiding questions entitled "Think about. . . ." These questions are designed to focus your attention on the main themes and concepts within the chapter. A section entitled "Connecting . . ." is found at the conclusion of each chapter. The activities included in the Connections section are project oriented with hands-on opportunities to apply the knowledge gained from the chapter just read. Some of the sections also include timelines and helpful Web Sites to enrich your study of that particular aspect of reading instruction.

In the first section, *Historical Foundations of Reading*, you will delve into the trajectory of reading instruction from the earliest use of sign systems to the present. You will likely notice the cyclical nature of reading instruction, particularly the interplay between comprehension, phonics, word study, and vocabulary. Students of reading will be encouraged to draw implications from the successes and mistakes of the past in order to propose solutions to the problems faced in today's classroom contexts.

Theoretical Perspectives: Intersections of Text and Reader presents an essential foundational overview of how readers approach the text, what they bring to the text, and how the interaction and the response are influenced by this interaction. This section includes some older classic pieces that serious students of reading must analyze since the editors would be remiss if we did not include the thoughts of Rosenblatt and Anderson in a study of text and reader. Students will be challenged to draw implications for their own practice, perhaps rethinking their definition of the reading process and how that definition shapes their instruction.

In the next section, focusing on the contributions of psychology and cognitive theories, we explore educational psychology and the giants in that field whose influence has shaped not only approaches to teaching reading but also the development of commercial programs. We also present a brief overview of the reading brain and the relationships between neurological functioning and the reading process. Inquiry as it applies to reading instruction is another topic explored in this section and the differences between constructivism and constructionism are delineated.

As classrooms become increasing diverse, public schools struggle to face the challenges of linguistic and cultural differences and to navigate around the controversial views of stakeholders and their responses to changing societal norms and values. The International Reading Association Standards 2010 committee has recognized these challenges and has addressed this in creating standard 4 on diversity, which is addressed in this text's section IV. In no other content area does the changing societal landscape play such an important role as in the subject of reading. Our intent in *Theoretical Perspectives: Intersection of Language, Society, Culture, and Reader*, is to provide opportunities to explore and develop understanding, recognition, awareness, and appreciation of diversity in society.

Finally, in the fifth section, *New Frontiers: Intersections of the Past, Present, and Future in Reading Instruction and Research*, it will become increasingly evident to the student that we have only just begun to scratch the surface of the complexities and multidimensional components of reading instruction. Although the major focus of this volume has been on reading, the final section includes articles which broaden the view to include new literacies, spatial literacy, multimodal texts, and technology. It is apparent when looking toward the future of reading instruction that the new frontiers will obviously include the integration of all aspects of literacy, including reading, writing, speaking, listening, viewing, and visually representing. The future of reading instruction will be intimately intertwined with all these component areas.

Our hope, as editors, is that you enjoy the journey, that you broaden your understanding of reading, and that you draw some valuable conclusions about reading instruction that will help you to become a more knowledgeable instructor of reading. We encourage you to be reflective, to keep an open mind, to savor the new ideas, and to welcome the dissonance as a means to the end of more informed instructional practice.

Through study and reflection, teachers grow in confidence and are better equipped to articulate their views and to assume a transformative stance, vocalizing the whys and the hows of an effective reading classroom plan of action. Since we assume that all professionals in our field are committed to improving the quality of instruction for students in all classrooms, we are confident that intense reflective study throughout these chapters will enable teachers of reading to improve their practice. The ultimate goal of this book is to assure that no student is denied the right, privilege, and joy of reading. The best way to meet this goal is to invite teachers to journey along the reading superhighway with us: gazing back to where we have been, traveling through our present struggles, and envisioning a brighter, more innovative future.

ACKNOWLEDGMENTS

This project would have not come to fruition without the help and support of several people. As this is our first dip into the book-writing pool, we found Aurora Martinez and Paula Carroll of great assistance and support. Additionally, we would like to thank the editorial assistants who have worked with us throughout this project: Kara Kikel, Jacqueline Gillen, and Amy Foley. We appreciated your willingness to provide us information when it was requested as well as your cheerful attitudes.

Finally, in the concluding production stage, we acknowledge the invaluable support and assistance of Linda Thompson, Linda Clark, Laura Messerly, and Mohinder Singh.

The following reviewers provided us with different perspectives and helpful insights that guided us in our revisions and in our preparations of the final manuscript: Gary Smithey, Henderson State University, and Dr. Kenneth J. Weiss, Central Connecticut State University.

We would like to thank our colleagues who contributed to this book and were there when we needed them. P. David Pearson, Mary's hero, is owed special gratitude for allowing us the opportunity to include his research synthesis matrix. Jeanne appreciated Donna Alvermann's helpful suggestions. Additionally, our project would not have become a reality without the foundational knowledge in literacy contributed by those who paved the way for all practitioners and re-searchers in our field.

Additionally, we would like to thank our administrators, who supported us at our respective institutions. Further, we want to extend our appreciation to the graduate assistants and student workers who were willing to provide us assis-tance in our research.

Finally, special appreciation to our families and friends, as well as Toby and Bingo, for their continuous encouragement, for smiles at just the right time, for being on-call cheerleaders, and especially for understanding when we were up against hard deadlines.

JEANNE AND MARY

HISTORICAL FOUNDATIONS OF READING

INTRODUCTION

In order to know where you are going, you need to know where you have been. This first section will provide you, the reader, with the historical foundations of reading instruction, beginning with the first known documented writing all the way through the end of the 20th century. We hope this first section will provide you with the needed knowledge to travel on through the book with a deeper understanding of the historical, sociological, and theoretical foundations of reading education.

First, Kallus and Ratliff share some of the major points in the development of the written language and reading throughout history, from the cave paintings in Lascaux, France, to the publication of *The Graded Course of Instruction for the Public Schools of Chicago* in 1872.

Next, Pearson's description of reading in the 20th century provides readers with an informative overview of the major movements of reading of the last century from the top-down or bottom-up perspectives of teaching reading to theorists from other fields of study who have greatly impacted reading—nationally and internationally—over the last century. Pearson's chapter will provide you a road map for many of the other perspectives shared throughout this book. Pearson's chapter points to the intersections of the past century, providing succinct and user-friendly descriptions of the different approaches and philosophies impacting reading education.

Finally, there is a matrix of the seminal reading research conducted between the First Grade Studies, published in *Reading Research Quarterly* in 1966 to the report of the National Reading Panel in 2000. Pearson graciously gave us permission to include this summary matrix that was part of his presentation on the history of reading research at the International Reading Association Conference in Minneapolis, Minnesota, in May 2009. We believe this is an invaluable tool to assist you in navigating the reading history road map that will help you plan your itinerary for the rest of the journey through this book.

As you read through this section of the book, think about the trends in education. There is the proverbial pendulum that swings to and fro—as in any profession. Notice some "movements" or methods have come around more than once in a century or so and that the underlying philosophy or method is the same (or similar), but the packaging (and sometimes the name) is completely different.

■ ■ ■ ■ ■

Alignment of Readings in Section I to the International Reading Association's *Standards for Reading Professionals 2010* (Draft):

   Standard 1: Foundational Knowledge
      1.1; 1.2; 1.3

Standard 3: Assessment and Evaluation
   3.1 (Pearson chapter)
Standard 6: Professional Learning and Leadership
   6.3

Historical Foundations of Reading Timeline

BEGINNINGS . . .	ALL DATES ARE APPROXIMATE
20,000 BC	Cave paintings (i.e., Lacaux, France) and other logographic communications
3600 BC–3100 BC	Record keeping begins in Sumer (Mesopotamia) in the form of commodity seals (cuneiform)
3000 BC–3100 BC	Hieroglyphic writing—Egypt
2100 BC	Laws of Ur-Nammu of Ur (Mesopotamia)
ca 2000 BC	Phoenician alphabet emerges; consonant sounds only. Letter—sound correspondence versus symbol—word correspondence as in logographic or iconographic communication
Mid-1700s BC	Laws of Hammurabi—Babylon (present day Iraq)
1000 BC	Papyrus (early form of paper) used by Egyptians
850 BC	Homer's *Iliad* and *Odyssey*—first significant literature works in Greek culture
ca 750 BC	Greeks modify Phoenician alphabet to include vowels; thus the first alphabetic system emerges that includes both consonants and vowels
AD 400–1100	Dark Ages—little writing survives
AD 1100	Arabic numbers—modern calculations are possible
AD 600–1400	Priests, monks, and other religious scribe/illuminate all books by hand; many errors are present as well as limited availability of books for the population at large
ca 1446	Johann Gutenburg—moveable type printing press; first surviving Bible to be typeset and printed for the masses
1475–1500	Printing of books increases exponentially
1300s–1500s	Throughout Europe, literacy flourishes as printed materials become more available to common people
1600–1800	*Colonial Era and Early Republic*
1600–1900	Reading instruction follows two-stage model; first stage—letter sounds; second—meaning
1686	"The Church Law of 1686"—children, farm workers, and the like should learn to read for themselves to earn their own salvation
1700s	Use of hornbooks to teach reading *New England Primer* appears in Colonial America
	Schooling revolves around moral, ethical, and religious instruction; earliest materials filled with religious ideas
1731	Ben Franklin founds the first public library in the American colonies
1732	*Poor Richard's Almanac* by Ben Franklin
1798	*Blue Back Speller* created by Noah Webster
1820s	National magazines are published—i.e., *Saturday Evening Post*
1836	*McGuffy's Readers*—first "reading" textbooks

(Continued)

Historical Foundations of Reading Timeline

BEGINNINGS . . .	ALL DATES ARE APPROXIMATE
1872	*The Graded Course of Instruction for the Public Schools of Chicago* published; similar to a type of teacher's edition for teachers in the school district of Chicago
1902	Beatrix Potter's *The Tale of Peter Rabbit*; first small books that are easy for children to handle and read
1911	National Council of Teachers of English founded
1912	Ginn *Beacon Street Readers*
1914	William Gray develops first reading assessment
1920s–1960s	Reading viewed as a one-stage process; deemphasis on phonics
1940s and 1950s	

1940s	Dick and Jane utilized "look and say" method
	    Controlled vocabulary
	    Round-robin reading
	    Reading developed defined by oral reading primarily; writing = handwriting
	    Think and Do Workbooks
	    Behaviorism philosophy prevalent—sticker rewards
	    Teacher-centered classroom

1941	*Dick and Jane New Basic Readers* first published
1950	National Reading Conference (NRC) founded
1955	*Why Johnny Can't Read and What You Can Do About It* published (pro-phonics)
1956	International Reading Association (IRA) founded
1957	College Reading Association (CRA) founded
1960s and 1970s	
1960	*Dick and Jane* readers still in use Reading instruction—high, average, low groups and round-robin reading with basal readers
Early 1960s	First Grade Studies conducted by U.S. Office of Education Findings: (1) almost any approach better than look-say basal approach only (2) teacher is the key to successful reading programs
1967	Bond and Dykstra publish the First Grade Studies report in *Reading Research Quarterly* Jeanne Chall publishes *Learning to Read: The Great Debate*
Late 1960s	Skills management systems and mastery learning emerge
Early 1970s	Variety of different basals appear—linguistic, return of phonics to center stage, DISTAR
1971	Frank Smith *Understanding Reading*

(Continued)

Historical Foundations of Reading Timeline	
BEGINNINGS . . .	ALL DATES ARE APPROXIMATE
Mid to late 1970s	Emphasis on diagnosis/remediation—medical model for reading difficulties Smith, Holdaway, Goodman, Hansen advocate for throwing out basals and using children's literature solely to teach reading (whole language)
1980s	
1981	Flesch publishes *Why Johnny Still Can't Read: A New Look at the Scandal in our Schools* emphasizing phonics/opposing whole language
1983	*A Nation at Risk*
1984	*Becoming a Nation of Readers*—variety of different basals appear—linguistics, return of phonics to center stage, DISTAR Finding: first graders spend only 7 to 8 minutes reading connected text; 49 minutes doing worksheets/impetus for more independent reading
Late 1980s	Reading war rages on—phonics vs. whole language; researchers like Patricia Cunningham urge common sense and balanced approach
1990s to present	
1990	Marilyn Jager Adams publishes controversial book *Beginning to Read: Thinking and Learning about Print* Points to phonological and phonemic awareness as necessary for reading
Early 1990s	Research studies criticize whole language and point to direct, systematic phonics instruction as helpful for struggling readers
Late 1990s	Reading war is ending/most reading researchers find common ground using best of both approaches, phonics and whole language/advocate a balanced approach to literacy
1999	*Reading Excellence Act*
2002	*No Child Left Behind Act* passed by Congress—ushers in new age of reform and accountability
Mid-2000s	Focus on individualized, differentiated instruction, meeting AYP, using eclectic, commonsense-balanced approaches to help each child succeed
2008	College Reading Association (CRA) name changed to Association of Literacy Educators and Researchers (ALER)

CHAPTER 1

READING: A BRIEF HISTORY TO 1899

MARY KATHERINE KALLUS AND PHILLIP RATLIFF

THINK ABOUT **THE BEGINNINGS OF READING . . .**

1. Before you read, look at a picture of the alphabet. As you read this chapter, think about the many iterations western civilization has gone through in order for us to use our alphabet today.

2. Read to find out about the early beginnings of education in the American colonies and the early United States.

Reading, writing, and technology have always been linked, whether the technology was papyrus and ink, stamps and clay, or computers. "Historically, the nature of literacy has always changed through different historical and cultural contexts as the technologies of information and communication have changed . . ." (Leu, 2001, p. 745). Just as technology is ever changing, so too is the nature of reading and writing (literacy):

> In a world of rapidly changing technologies and new envisionments for their use, literacy appears to be increasingly deictic; its meaning is regularly redefined, not by time or space, but by new technologies and the continuously changing envisionments they initiate for information and communication. (p. 745)

Additionally, the meaning of literacy ". . . is dependent on the technologies and envisionments within many historical, religious, political, and cultural contexts" (p. 745). Literacy, as traced through time, does change meaning based on the purposes and use of reading and writing during particular periods of history.

To consider the major points of the history of reading in the United States to 1899, this chapter will provide the reader with a brief overview of the development of the alphabet in the Western world. Additionally, the focus of this chapter lies in the history of reading education in the United States rather than the development of the alphabet and the teaching of reading prior to this time.

CONTEXT

From a historical context, the ability to read (and write) determined one's lot in life. According to the discipline of anthropology, for a civilization to be considered thus, written language had to be in place within that community or group (personal communication, Phillip Shelley, July 25, 2007). A person capable of reading and writing held higher office, social status, and economic stature. Scribes and record keepers in Ancient Egypt as well as those who illuminated animal skin parchment prior to the invention of the moveable-type printing press in the 1400s were all revered members of society. They had extensive studies of learning some type of iconographic system or alphabetic communication forms to record (and pass along) information, records, and stories of the day.

THE HISTORY OF READING AND WRITING

The Earliest Foundations

To trace the history of reading is to trace the roots of writing. The ability to form and decode a system of writing suggests some members of past civilizations had the ability to "read." Tracing the development of reading and writing together is, to a certain extent, necessary. According to Smith (2002),

> The long pilgrimage of reading . . . began with the invention of characters for use in expressing and recording thought; consequently the beginnings of reading must be traced in conjunction with the development of written symbols and the materials upon which they were inscribed. (p. 1)

This "long pilgrimage" (p. 1) Smith refers to began when "[w]riting, and therefore reading, came as an aid and a necessity to early civilizations when food surpluses allowed specialization, and commerce developed to the extent that regulation was needed to avoid chaos" (Wilson, 1997–2003, ¶ 7). In these early societies, ". . . literacy was a way to record land, livestock, and crops, often for taxes or to record business transactions" (Leu, 2000, p. 745). There were various types of written records from types of shorthand and tallies to pictures and numbers (Wilson, 1997–2003, ¶ 7).

Some of the earliest written/drawn communications known came from the Paleolithic period some 17,000 to 20,000 years ago. One example of this **iconography** is the cave in

iconography—pictorial representations of a certain subject

Lascaux and other surrounding caves in the area south, south west of Lemoges, France (personal communication, Phillip Shelley, July 25, 2007; see also http://www.culture.gouv.fr/culture/arcnat/lascaux/en/).

Writing, in rudimentary record-keeping form, dates to between 3600 and 3100 BC when it first appeared in Sumer (Mesopotamia) in the form of commodity seals for tally keeping (personal communication, Phillip Shelley, July 25, 2007; see also Garraty & Gay, 1972/1981). Similar cylinders, according to Shelley, have also been found in the Indus Valley. Anthropologists, however, have not been able to positively date these cylinders (personal communication, July 25, 2007).

Hieroglyphic writing appeared in Egypt circa 3100 BC, with accounts of daily life written in Mari circa 2500 BC. The Laws of Ur-Nammu of Ur, with the earliest preserved law book, is dated 2100 BC. The Laws of Hammurabi of Babylon were recorded during his reign in the 1500s BC. (Garrity & Gay, 1972/1981).

Phoenicians and the Alphabet

The creation of the alphabet was "the most important advance in the transmission of knowledge between the invention of writing and the art of printing" (Garrity and Gay, 1972/1981, p. 87). The beginnings of our modern-day alphabet are noted by Garrity and Gay:

> The knowledge of hundreds of signs was necessary for both the hieroglyphic and the cuneiform script; this limited literacy to trained professionals. No great effort was needed to memorize two or three dozen [sic] alphabetic characters; now anyone could learn to read and write. The alphabet is democratic. (p. 87)

logographic—a symbol that represents a word

Thus, the move from a **logographic** system, where symbols represented words, to an alphabetic system, where symbols represented letters or sounds, began (Blake & Blake, 2002).

From the Phoenicians' travels around the Mediterranean Sea, the alphabet traveled with them. Rome and Greece would adopt many aspects of this alphabetic system. It was the Greeks who added the vowel sounds and symbols to this alphabet. For the Greeks, although literature was present, it was not until after the fifth century BC that ". . . signs of literacy [became] fully significant" (Graff, 1991, p. 21). Although literacy spread during the Hellenistic (Roman) and Greek periods, literacy for the masses, as will be noted later, did not become a reality until during the Renaissance.

The Middle Ages

The period from AD 400 to 1400 (the beginnings of the Renaissance), most historians refer to as the Middle or Dark Ages. In the early Middle Ages, many

". . . early and medieval Christians" (Cordasco, 1976, p. 23) tended to write antagonistically about the Greek and Roman ideas and learning.

Prior to the 10th century, monasteries were the only place to receive any schooling: "[T]hey alone offered professional training; they preserved books; they were the only libraries; they produced the only scholars; they were the sole educational institutions of the period" (Cordasco, 1976, p. 24). During this time in the Middle Ages, there were seven liberal arts offered as advanced studies in the monasteries. These included two divisions: "I. The Trivium: (1) grammar; (2) rhetoric; (3) dialectic. II. The Quadrivium: (4) arithmetic; (5) geometry; (6) astronomy; (7) music" (p. 25).

As time progressed to the late Middle Ages, from the 11th to 15th century, scholasticism—"education as an intellectual discipline" (Cordasco, 1976, p. 31)— rose. Out of scholasticism, universities were born. Universities were founded and patronized by the religious and the Church; royalty and other secular leaders alike. Scholasticism was used to promote reason of religious faith as well as to "systematize knowledge" (p. 31). During the period of scholasticism, many scholarly works in philosophy, law, and theology, for example, were produced. However, this educational system had many limitations as well. Throughout the Middle Ages, new types of schools, such as Chantry Schools (closely connected to the Church) and the Guild School (free of Church oversight) were founded. Later, these Guild Schools were run by local governments and were made into "Municipal or Burgher schools" (p. 36).

The Renaissance Era

The phenomenon of literacy for the masses is a relatively young concept, in regard to the time frame of the first literate people thousands of years ago. Before the printing press in the latter 1400s, books were scribed and illuminated mostly by monks. Since every book was scribed individually by hand, several problems arose. First was the issue of errors. Oftentimes, monks would get the wording incorrect. Another, larger issue was expense. Since each book was individually printed by hand, any form of "mass production" was out of the question. As a result, only the wealthiest people could afford to own books and, therefore, were typically the ones able to gain the necessary skills to read. Although obvious to those with a little more than a rudimentary understanding of the history of past civilizations and societies, it is important to note, at this time, typically only men were afforded the opportunity to learn to read and/or write.

The issue of availability began to gradually change with the invention of the printing press in the 1450s by a German man, Johann Gutenberg. Although the "complex prehistory of printing involved China and every region of Western Europe," (Garrity and Gay, 1972/1981, p. 485), Gutenberg, in Mainz, created what was considered one of the "most remarkable technological innovations of the Renaissance" (p. 485). The invention of printing with moveable metal type allowed for books to become more affordable to print and sell. In AD 1457, Gutenberg's son-in-law, Johann Fust ". . . printed the first surviving dated book, an edition of the Psalms in Latin" (p. 485). At this point, people who had not been able to read in the past were now learning to read, with books becoming more affordable.

Early Education in the United States

The roots of modern education in the United States centered on children learning the chores (gender specific, of course) that would assist in their daily lives once they were adults. The other important role of school, within the Puritan context, at this time was to learn to read the Bible. This continued through the early 1800s, with a shift to more advanced methods of teaching reading which included the use of hornbooks, which emphasized spelling and phonics.

Even though more people had schooling available to them, many were still left out of the education process, so many people were unable to read. Males and females were taught differently, as were persons of color, ethnicity, or social and economic status other than of European decent, receiving very little, if any, education. These were typically from **First Nation** groups and Africa (pre– and post–Civil War), as well as indentured servants from a variety of overseas locales. The issue of the lack of opportunity for *all* to receive a fair and equal education, where youth can learn to read and write—to be literate—and be contributing members of society has plagued the United States throughout her history.

First Nation—refers to indigenous peoples of North America

With the advances in technology ushered in by the Industrial Revolution and the wide variety of texts, literacy has changed greatly over our nation's past.

Reading in the United States Curriculum

Revolutionary America to the Civil War.   In Revolutionary America, rudimentary learning was prevalent (Kaestle, 1983). This early education "stressed Bible reading" (p. 3). The majority of White males could read and write, and the literacy of females was rising as well. By the time of the Revolution, schools were also becoming more available (Kaestle). Also, "some slaves received education in the Christian religion and the reading and writing of English. Although no statistics are [readily] available, there is scattered evidence of literate slaves" (p. 195). Schools, however, remained mostly accessible to the elite, with children from poorer families becoming apprentices to tradesmen. This remained the context for schooling in America until around the 1830s.

charity schools—schools established in early America for poor children who could not afford to get an education otherwise; typically set up and maintained with the idea of keeping order in society

Mass education became an issue at this time. Elite Americans, unlike their British counterparts, moved towards the idea of putting charity school in place ". . . for social stability" (Kaestle, 1983, p. 36). **Charity schools**, according to Kaestle, "taught large numbers of poor children to read, which may have enriched their lives even if it did not enhance their economic opportunities" (p. 51). During the 1830s, commerce also played a role in education. The knowledge of the written word and basic math allowed for a "reciprocal relationship between literacy and publication. The more widespread the printed word, the more schooling was encouraged; the more literacy increased, the more market there was for newspapers, almanacs, periodicals, and books" (Kaestle, p. 65). Until the eve of the Civil War, common schools did not emphasize "intellectual skills" (p. 66). Therefore, literacy may have included more Anglo people, yet did not readily allow for the improvement of one's station in life. This is particularly true for any slaves who even had any type of educational opportunity at this time, as well.

Post–Civil War.   After the Civil War, texts such as *The Art of Teaching* (Ogden, 1879) described the teaching of reading under the heading of "recitation." In Ogden's description, the teaching of reading consisted of sounding out words (similar to phonics today) and the oral reading of texts. No real consideration for the teaching of comprehension of what one "read" was made. Almost a decade later, with *The Elements of Pedagogy: A Manual for Teachers, Normal Schools, Normal Institutes, Teachers' Reading Circles, and all Persons Interested in School Education* (1886), White stated the best way to teach students to read was to use the blackboard. "No chart or primer can take the place of crayon and board in these beginning exercises, and the only wise use that can be made of chart or primer is to supplement the board lessons" (p. 221). White continues, explaining in detail, the process of teaching words in "wholes" (p. 223) as well as words being taught singularly and then eventually placed into sentences. White also discussed the importance of teaching phonics, using phonics and reading drills. White made only slight reference to a pupil's ability to actually read and comprehend the text.

In 1872, the *Graded Course of Instruction for the Public Schools of Chicago: Fourth Edition–Revised* was adopted by Chicago's Board of Education. Instructions given to teachers were very traditional. This document provided instructions on how to conduct a reading lesson. The instructions concentrated on a variety of issues for reading with prosody rather than comprehension of a text. It was noted that pupils should have an understanding of the "thoughts of the author" (p. 25). The document listed other rules the teacher should follow while teaching the lesson, which centered on breathing, pronunciation, and recitation, for example. The goal was to manufacture children into the kind of citizens the writers of the Chicago instruction manual thought they should be when they came of age. There was no free thought and no acceptance of personal feeling, which dominated much of the English/language arts at this time and even in the early 20th century.

The beginnings of reading began some 20,000 years ago, as evidenced in the cave painting in Lacaux. Throughout time, people have desired to communicate with one another and have developed the means in which to do so. This progression effected societies throughout history. Additionally, it impacted from early colonial education, through the Revolutionary and Civil Wars, to the hypertext and instant messages we read today in the United States.

CONNECTING THE HISTORY OF READING IN THE UNITED STATES TO 1899 TO YOUR CLASSROOM . . .

1. Hornbooks were the predecessor to the primer, or basal reader. Research hornbooks and create a lesson to teach your class about hornbooks and have them try to adapt 21st-century information and style to that of a hornbook from the 1700s.
2. Without the alphabet, our society would be very different. Consider a scenario of a society that no longer has a written language. What would life be like in this community? Would people be able to get along with one another? Record your answer and any additional thoughts and be prepared to share them with your professor and colleagues.

REFERENCES

Blake, B. E., & Blake, R. W. (2002). *Literacy and learning: A reference handbook.* Santa Barbara, CA: ABC CLIO.

Chicago Board of Education. (1872). *Graded course of instruction for the public schools of Chicago (4th Ed. Revised).* Chicago: Bryant, Walker, & Craig Printers.

Cordasco, F. (1976). *A brief history of education.* Totowa, NJ: Little, Adams, and Company.

Garraty, J. A., & Gay, P. (Eds.). (1981). *The Columbia history of the world.* New York City: Harper & Row, Publishers. (Original work published 1972)

Graff, H. J. (1991). *The legacies of literacy: Continuities and contradictions in western culture and society.* Bloomington: Indiana University Press.

Kaestle, C. F. (1983). *Pillars of the republic: Common schools and American society, 1780–1860.* New York: Hill and Wang.

Leu, D. J. (2001). Literacy and technology: Deictic consequences for literacy education in an information age. In M. L. Kamil, P. Mosenthal, P. D. Pearson, & R. Barr (Eds.), *Handbook of Reading Research, Volume III,* (pp. 734–770). Mahwah, NJ: Erlbaum.

Ogden, J. (1879). *The art of teaching.* Cincinnati: Van Antwerp, Bragg, and Co.

Smith, N. B. (2002). *American reading instruction: Special edition.* Newark, DE: International Reading Association.

White, E. E. (1886). *The elements of pedagogy: A manual for teachers, normal schools, normal institutes, teachers' reading circles, and all persons interested in school education.* New York: American Book Company.

Wilson, R. (1997–2003). Teaching reading—A history. Retrieved January 15, 2008, from http://www.zona-pellucida.com/wilson10.html.

CHAPTER 2

READING IN THE TWENTIETH CENTURY

P. DAVID PEARSON

***THINK ABOUT* THE HISTORY OF READING IN THE TWENTIETH CENTURY . . .**

1. As you read, make notes about the trends in reading education. Think about what ideas or theories have been renamed, or "repackaged," throughout the last century.

2. Read to find out about the "reading wars." What impact have the reading wars had on reading instruction today?

This is an account of reading instruction in the twentieth century. It will end, as do most essays written in the final year of any century, with predictions about the future. My hope is to provide an account of the past and present of reading instruction that will render predictions about the future transparent. Thus I begin with a tour of the historical pathways that have led us, at century's end, to the rocky and highly contested terrain we currently occupy in reading **pedagogy**. After unfolding my version of a map of that terrain, I will speculate about **pedagogical** journeys that lie ahead of us in a new century and a new millennium.

pedagogy—study of teaching of the methods and materials related to learning, in this case, teaching and learning how to read

pedagogical—of or pertaining to the art, science, and study of teaching, in this case teaching reading

Even though the focus of this essay is reading pedagogy, it is my hope to connect the pedagogy to the broader scholarly ideas of each period. Two factors render this task easier for the first two-thirds of the century than for the last third. First, the sheer explosion in the number of educational ideas and movements in the last thirty years makes these connections more difficult. Second, because I have lived through this last third as a member of the reading profession, I am too close to examine current practices with the critical eye of historical distance. That realization, of course, compels me to work harder at the contextualization and to be as open and as comprehensive as possible in considering alternative explanations of recent events in the history of reading instruction.

The developments in reading pedagogy over the last century suggested that it is most useful to divide the century into thirds, roughly 1900–1935, 1935–1970, and 1970–2000. This division yields two periods of enormous intellectual and curricular activity (the first and third) and a relatively quiet period at mid-century.

To guide us in constructing our map of past and present, we will need a legend, a common set of criteria for examining ideas and practices in each period. Several candidates suggest themselves. Surely, the *dominant materials* used by teachers in each period will be relevant, as will the *dominant pedagogical practices.* Both materials and pedagogy are relatively easy to witness because they lie on the surface of instruction where they are easy to see. Other important points of comparison, such as the *role* of the *teacher* and the *learner* in the process of learning to read, lie beneath the instructional surface and require deeper inferences, greater interpretation, and more unpacking for observation and analysis. Finally, for each set of practices, the most difficult task will be to understand the underlying assumptions about the *nature of reading* and *learning to read* that motivate dominant practices in each period.

THE READING SCENE AT LAST TURN OF THE CENTURY

The rhetoric of the reformers of the mid and late nineteenth century, intellectual giants such as Horace Mann and Colonel Francis Parker,[1] would lead us to conclude that the demons of drill and practice on isolated sounds and letters had been driven out of our pedagogical temples by the year 1900. So strong was their indictment, so appealing their alternative methods of reason and meaning, that one could hardly imagine the continuation of a method as painful to both student and teacher alike as was the alphabetic approach. Yet in spite of the wonderful accounts of innovative language experience activities and integrated curriculum in the laboratory schools at Columbia and the University of Chicago,[2] alphabetic approaches still dominated the educational landscape in the United States at least through World War I. These were classic **synthetic phonics** approaches (learn the parts before the whole) in which, at least in the earliest stages of learning to read, students encountered, in rapid succession, letter names, then letter sounds, then syllable blending activities that were organized into tight drill and practice sequences. The synthetic phonics traditions established much earlier in the century by Noah Webster's *Blue Back Speller* and McGuffey's *Eclectic Readers* were still strongly in evidence.[3]

synthetic phonics—part-to-whole approach in which students learn sounds represented by letters first; then blending; then phonics generalizations

Once the code had been cracked, students were expected to move right into works of literature, most of which were written for adults rather than children.

Drill and practice continued after the primer level, but moved from letter names and sounds into other aspects of the language arts, including grammar, rhetoric, and elocution.

Taking Stock: 1

The role of the learner in this period was to receive the curriculum provided by the teacher and dutifully complete the drills provided. The role of the teacher was to provide the proper kinds of drill and practice. In this period being able to read meant being able to pronounce the words on the page accurately, fluently, and, for older students, eloquently.[4] The prevailing view of reading as a cognitive process was what we have come to call the simple view of reading. In the simple view, reading comprehension is thought of as the product of decoding and listening comprehension (RC = Dec * LC), and the major task of instruction is to ensure that students master the code so that comprehension can proceed more or less by "listening to what you read."[5]

DEVELOPMENTS IN THE FIRST THIRD OF THE CENTURY

From 1900 to 1935 many new ideas emerged in the psychology and pedagogy of reading. These ideas had important and long-lasting consequences for reading instruction; many, in fact, are still with us on the cusp of a new century. I review several of these ideas in some detail because they provide a useful framework for understanding the reforms of later periods.

Early Reading Reforms

Words to letters.   Several types of reform emerged (re-emerged may be a more accurate term for there are earlier iterations of each in the historical literature) to counter the evils of what most educators regarded as the mindless drill and practice of the alphabetic approach to beginning reading instruction. Despite the flurry of reform attempts, only two gathered enough momentum to survive. The first, dubbed the words-to-letters approach by Mitford Mathews,[6] introduced words in the very earliest stages and, for each word introduced, immediately asked children to decompose it into component letters.[7] Words-to-letters is the obverse of the alphabetic, or letters-to-words, approach. However, with the alphabetic approach, it shares the goal of ensuring that children learn the sound correspondences for each letter and the same set of underlying assumptions about the nature of teaching, learning, and reading. Today we would call it analytic (whole to part) phonics.

Words to reading.   The second reform, which Mathews dubbed words-to-reading, later came to be known as the look-say or whole word method of teaching reading. Here, no attempt was made to analyze words into letter-sounds *until* a sizable corpus of words were learned as sight words. Contrary to popular opinion, which

analytic phonics—whole-to-part approach in which students first learn key sight words and are taught pertinent phonics generalizations and then apply those generalizations to particular examples in sound/symbol correspondences

would have us believe that phonics was never taught in the look-say approach,[8] some form of **analytic phonics** (a modified version of words-to-letters) usually kicked in after a corpus of a hundred or so sight words had been learned. It was different from a strict word-to-letters approach, though, because the strict requirement for decomposing each word into its component letters was dropped in favor of what might be called focused analysis. For example a teacher might group several words that start with the letter f (e.g., *farm, fun, family, fine,* and *first*) and ask students to note the similarity between the initial sounds and letters in each word. As it turned out, this approach (a combination of look-say with analytic phonics) persevered to become the "conventional wisdom" from 1930–1970.

A potpourri.   Beyond these, there were a host of specialized programs described by various scholars at the turn of the century.[9] For example, no less than six specialized alphabets appeared in this period, each designed to make the task of learning to read easier by employing a temporary alphabet that created a one-to-one letter-sound match for young readers. George Farnham designed what may have been the first truly meaning-based approach to beginning reading; it was a whole sentence approach in which a series of single pictures were matched directly to a sentence describing its content (e.g., There are three eggs on the table). Finally, numerous examples of the use of group-composed language experience stories as young readers' first texts appeared, though this approach did not gather much momentum until after World War II.[10]

Other Influential Developments

Testing and the scientific movement.   Reading was influenced by a host of developments during this period. For example, reading performance, like most other educational phenomena, became the object of scientific examination and systematic testing relatively early in the twentieth century.[11] Starting with the work of Edward L. Thorndike and William S. Gray, the period from roughly the first to the second World War witnessed the development of numerous reading assessments.[12] The first published reading assessment, circa 1914, was an oral reading assessment created by Gray (who eventually became a pre-eminent scholar in the reading field and the senior author of the country's most widely used reading series). However, most reading assessments developed in the first third of this century focused on the relatively new construct of silent reading. Unlike oral reading, which had to be tested individually and required that teachers judge the quality of responses, silent reading comprehension and rate could be tested in group settings and scored without recourse to professional judgment (only stop watches and multiple choice questions were needed). Thus it fit the demands for efficiency and scientific objectivity, themes that were part of the emerging scientism of the period. Significant developments in reading comprehension would occur in the second third of the century, but assessment would remain a psychometric rather than a cognitive construct until the cognitive revolution of the early 1970s. When comprehension was implemented in school curricula, the same infrastructure of tasks used to create test items was used to create instructional and practice materials—finding main ideas, noting important details, determining sequence of events, cause-effect relations, comparing and contrasting, and drawing conclusions.[13]

Text difficulty and readability.   Text difficulty, codified as readability, emerged as an important research area and curricular concept in the first half of this century. Unlike the developments in testing, readability was grounded in child-centered views of pedagogy dating back to theorists such as Pestalozzi, Froebel, and Herbart and championed by the developmental psychology emerging in the 1920s and 30s.[14] The motive in developing readability formulas was to present children with texts that matched their interests and developmental capacities rather than to baffle them with abridged versions of adult texts. The first readability formula, created to gauge the grade placement of texts, appeared in 1923, and it was followed by some 80 additional formulas over the next forty years until the enterprise drew to a close in the late 1960s.[15] Irrespective of particular twists in individual formulas, each more or less boiled down to a sentence difficulty factor, typically instantiated as average sentence length, and a word factor, typically codified as word frequency. These formulas were critical in the production of commercial reading materials from the 1920s through the 1980s. For reasons that will become apparent later in this chapter, readability formulas did not survive the cognitive revolution in reading instruction in the 1970s and 1980s, although there are signs of their recovery in the 1990s.

Readiness.   The third important curricular construct to emerge in the first third of the century was readiness. Like readability, it was grounded in developmental psychology rather than the scientific movement in education.[16] In research, the readiness movement was a search for the behavioral precursors to beginning reading acquisition: What skills or capacities must be in place before reading instruction can begin in earnest? What skills predict early reading success? The typical candidates for readiness skills were alphabet knowledge, auditory discrimination, visual discrimination, color and shape discrimination, following directions, language development, and, from time to time, kinesthetic and motor activities.[17] Despite the inclusion of a wide array of cognitive, perceptual, and linguistic variables in elaborate predictive studies, time and again knowledge of the names of the letters of the alphabet emerged as the best predictor of later reading achievement.[18] Scholars conducted studies with titles like "When Should Children Begin to Read?" and "The Necessary Mental Age for Beginning Reading."[19] Even though there was considerable controversy between those who wanted to delay formal instruction until maturation had a chance to do its work and those who wanted to nudge it along with specific and explicit skills instruction, both sides shared the assumption that a formal stage of readiness preceded the acquisition of reading.

Reading skills.   A fourth key curricular construct was "reading skills"—that discrete unit of the curriculum which ought to be learned by students and taught by teachers. An important related construct was the notion of a scope and sequence of skills, a linear outline of skills that if taught properly ought to lead to skilled reading. While skills have always been a part of reading instruction (witness all the bits and pieces of letter sounds and syllables in the alphabetic approach), the skill as a fundamental unit of curriculum and the scope and sequence chart as a way of organizing skills that extend across the elementary grades are twentieth century phenomena, nurtured, I would add, by the rapid expansion of commercial basal reading programs and standardized reading tests.[20]

The basal experience with skills led quite directly to two additional curriculum mainstays—the teachers' manual and the workbook. Throughout the nineteenth century and at least up through the first three decades of the twentieth century, basal programs consisted almost entirely of a set of student books. Teachers relied on experience, or perhaps normal school education, to supply the pedagogy used to teach lessons with the materials. Occasionally, for students who had progressed beyond the primer to one of the more advanced readers, questions were provided to test understanding of the stories in the readers. In the early 1900s, publishers of basals began to include supplementary teaching suggestions, typically a separate section at the front or back of each book with a page or two of suggestions to accompany each selection. In one common practice of the period, publishers provided a model lesson plan for two or three stories; for later stories, they referred the teacher back to one of the models with the suggestion that they adapt it for the new story. By the 1930s, the teachers' manuals had expanded to several pages per selection.[21] The other significant development in the 1930s was the workbook, often marketed with titles like *My Think and Do Book* or *Work Play Books.*[22]

Both of these developments were symptomatic of the expansion of scope and sequence efforts: the more skills included, the more complicated the instructional routines and the greater the need for explicit directives to teachers and opportunities for students to practice the skills. From the 1930s until at least the 1980s, this approach to skills development increased in intensity and scope. It was gradually extended beyond phonics to include comprehension, vocabulary, and study skills.[23] As I indicated earlier, the comprehension skills that made their way into basal workbooks and scope and sequence charts were virtually identical to those used to create comprehension tests. Each expansion resulted in heftier and more complex teachers' manuals and workbooks, another trend that has continued virtually unchecked since it began in the 1930s.

Remediation.   Strictly speaking, remediation is a medical or psychological construct rather than a curricular construct. I have elevated it to the status of a curricular construct in this chapter for the simple reason that it has exerted such a powerful influence on reading pedagogy over the past century. Beginning in the waning days of the nineteenth century and reaching its peak in the 1960s, the medical model has been a dominant force in our quest to meet the needs of those who struggle to learn to read. The hope is, and always was, that if we could just find the peaks and valleys in each child's profile of reading skills, we could offer focused instruction that would remedy the weaknesses and bring him or her (mostly *hims*, as our actuarial data suggest)[24] into a kind of skill equilibrium that would enable normal reading. It was, until recently, our sole approach to meeting individual needs.

Even in the classroom, the medical model, with its emphasis on diagnosis and prescription, has been the backbone of much of our instruction. After all, if filling in the valleys in children's instructional profiles works for those most in need, why wouldn't it work just as well for those less needy of instructional intervention? Don't all children deserve this sort of attention to individual needs? Note also that this diagnostic-prescriptive approach was a comfortable, maybe even a perfect, fit with the increasing emphasis on skills and scope and sequence charts in each succeeding edition of basals of this period; it is, after all, in the various skills that the performance peaks and valleys show up.

Professional Consensus.   That Colonel Parker and Horace Mann felt the need to rationalize their child-centered approaches with rhetoric detailing the evils of the dreaded alphabetic approach suggests that debate was alive and well at the beginning of the century. My account of developments in the first third of the century implies a level of consensus that is not justified. Even though most scholars accepted the new emphasis on silent reading and comprehension without much debate, they found less agreement on matters of early reading. The ubiquity of the words-to-reading approach notwithstanding, a vocal phonics lobby, complete with their own published materials, remained active throughout this period. And the concept of readiness was hotly debated, with maturationists and interventionists lining up on opposite sides.[25] That said, it must be acknowledged that the rhetoric of this period was no match for what was to come later on; the metaphor of a smoldering fire seems an apt description of the recurring curricular debate during this period. Blazes would erupt later in the century.

DEVELOPMENTS AT MID-CENTURY

The Scene in the 1960s.   The period that spans roughly 1935 to 1965 is best viewed as a time in which we engaged in fine-tuning and elaboration of instructional models that were born in the first third of the century. Most important, the words-to-reading approach that had started its ascendancy at the turn of the century gained increasing momentum throughout the century until, as has been documented in survey research conducted in the 1960s, over 90 percent of the students in the country were taught to read using one commercial variation of this approach or another.[26] So common was this approach that Jeanne Chall in her classic 1967 book, *Learning to Read: The Great Debate,* felt comfortable describing the then prevailing approach as a set of principles, which can be roughly paraphrased as follows:[27]

- The goals of reading, from the start in grade one, should include comprehension, interpretation, and application as well as word recognition.
- Instruction should begin with meaningful silent reading of stories that are grounded in children's experiences and interests.
- After a corpus of sight words is learned (somewhere between 50 and 100), analytic phonics instruction should begin. Phonics should be regarded as one of many cueing systems, including context and picture cues, available to children to unlock new words.
- Phonics instruction should be spread out over several years rather than concentrated in the early grades.
- Phonics instruction should be contextualized rather than isolated from real words and texts.
- The words in the early texts (grades 1–3) should be carefully controlled for frequency of use and repeated often to ensure mastery.
- Children should get off to a slow and easy start, probably through a readiness program; those not judged to be ready for formal reading instruction should experience an even longer readiness period.
- Children should be instructed in small groups.

While a few elements in her list are new, such as the early emphasis on comprehension and interpretation and the contextualization of phonics instruction, virtually all of the elements introduced in the early part of the century were included in her description of the conventional wisdom of the 1960s. A few things are missing when one compares Chall's list of principles underlying the conventional wisdom with our earlier account of the key developments through 1935. One is the role of skills in commercial reading programs. While skills did not make it onto her list of principles, it is clear from several chapters (specifically, chapters 7 and 8) in her 1967 book that she was mindful of their importance and curricular ubiquity. By the 1960s, skills lessons in the teachers' manual, accompanied by workbooks allowing students to practice the skills, were much more elaborate than in the 30s, 40s, or 50s. The other missing piece is the elaborate development of the teachers' manual. Earlier, I implied that they got bigger with each succeeding edition of the series. By the middle 1960s, that small teachers' guide section in the back of the children's book we found in the 20s and 30s had expanded to the point where the number of pages devoted to the teachers' guide equaled the number of student text pages in the upper grades and exceeded it in the primary grades.[28]

Taking Stock: 2

The materials of the 1960s were not fundamentally different from the materials available in the early part of the century. Students read stories and practiced skills.

Text difficulty was carefully controlled in the basal reading materials published between the 1930s and the 1960s. In the earliest readers (pre-primer through first reader at least), vocabulary was sequenced in order of decreasing frequency of word usage in everyday written and oral language. Since many of the most frequent words are not regularly spelled (*the, of, what, where,* etc.), this frequency principle provided a good fit with the whole-word or look-say emphasis characteristic of the words-to-reading approach so dominant during this period.

Students were still the recipients, and teachers still the mediators, of the received curriculum. Meaning and silent reading were more important in the 1960s version of reading curriculum than in 1900 or 1935, as evidenced by a steady increase in the amount of time and teachers' manual space devoted to comprehension activities, but it was still not at the core of the look-say approach. When all is said and done, the underlying model of reading in the 1960s was still a pretty straightforward perceptual process; the simple view—that comprehension is the product of decoding and listening comprehension ($RC = LC \times Dec$)—still prevailed. Readers still accomplished the reading task by translating graphic symbols (letters) on a printed page into an oral code (sounds corresponding to those letters) which was then treated by the brain as oral language. In both the look-say approach to learning sight vocabulary and its analytic approach to phonics, whether the unit of focus is a word or a letter, the basic task for the student is to translate from the written to the oral code. This view of reading was quite consistent with the prevailing instructional emphasis on skills. If sight words and phonics knowledge was what children needed to learn in order to perform the translation process, then decomposing phonics into separable bits of knowledge (letter-to-sound, or in the case of spelling, sound-to-letter, correspondences), each of which could be presented, practiced, and tested independently, was the route to helping them acquire that knowledge.

The Legacy of the Scholarship of the 1960s.   In beginning reading, the decade of the 1960s was a period of fervent activity. In the early 1960s, in an effort to settle the debate about the best way to teach beginning reading once and for all (this time with the tools of empirical scholarship rather than rhetoric), the Cooperative Research Branch of the United States Office of Education funded an elaborate collection of "First Grade Studies," loosely coupled forays into the highly charged arena of preferred approaches to beginning reading instruction.[29] While each of the studies differed from one another in the particular emphasis, most of them involved a comparison of different methods of teaching beginning reading. They were published in a brand new journal, *Reading Research Quarterly,* in 1966. Jeanne Chall completed her magnum opus, *Learning to Read: The Great Debate,* in 1967. It too had been funded in order to put the debate behind us, but Chall would use different scholarly tools to accomplish her goals. She would employ critical review procedures to examine our empirical research base, the content of our basal readers, and exemplary classroom practices. In 1965, Lyndon Johnson's Elementary and Secondary Education Act, one key plank in his Great Society platform, brought new resources for compensatory education to schools through a program dubbed Title I. And Commissioner of Education James Allen would, at decade's end, establish the national Right to Read program as a way of guaranteeing that right to each child in America. The country was clearly focused on early reading, and many were optimistic that we would find answers to the questions about teaching reading that had vexed us for decades, even centuries.

Chall's book and the First Grade Studies had an enormous impact on beginning reading instruction and indirectly on reading pedagogy more generally. One message of the First Grade Studies was that just about any alternative, when compared to the business-as-usual basals (which served as a common control in each of more than 20 separate quasi-experimental studies), elicited equal or greater performance on the part of first graders (and, as it turned out, second graders).[30] It did not seem to matter much what the alternative was—language experience, a highly synthetic phonics approach, a linguistic approach (control the text so that young readers are exposed early on only to easily decodable words grouped together in word families, such as the *-an* family, the *-at* family, the *-ig* family, etc.), a special alphabet (i.e., the Initial Teaching Alphabet), or even basals infused with a heavier-than-usual dose of phonics right up front—they were all the equal or the better of the ubiquitous basal. A second message, one that was both sent and received, was that the racehorse mentality of studies that compare one method against another had probably run its course. By accepting this message, the reading research community was free to turn its efforts to other, allegedly more fruitful, issues and questions—the importance of the teacher quite irrespective of method, the significance of site, and the press of other aspects of the curriculum such as comprehension and writing.[31] With the notable exception of the Follow-Through Studies in the 1970s, which are only marginally related to reading, it would take another twenty-five years for large-scale experiments to return to center stage in reading.[32]

In spite of a host of other important recommendations, most of which had some short term effect, the ultimate legacy of Chall's book reduces to just one— that early attention to the code in some way, shape, or form must be reinfused into early reading instruction. For the record, Chall recommended five broad changes: (a) make a necessary change in method (to an early emphasis on phonics of some sort), (b) re-examine current ideas about content (focus on the enduring themes in folk tales), (c) re-evaluate grade levels (increase the challenge at every grade level), (d) develop new tests (both single component tests and absolute measures with scores that are independent of the population taking the test), and (e) improve reading research (including its accessibility). Each of these recommendations will be discussed later.

The look-say basals that had experienced virtually uninterrupted progress from 1930 to 1965 never quite recovered from the one-two punch delivered by Chall's book and the First Grade Studies in 1967. Given the critical sacking they took from Chall and the empirical thrashing they took from the First Grade Studies, one might have expected one of the pretenders to the early reading throne, documented so carefully in the First Grade Studies, to assume the mantle of the new conventional wisdom in the years that followed. Ironically, it was the basals themselves, albeit in a radically altered form, that captured the marketplace of the 1970s and 1980s. They accomplished this feat by overhauling themselves to adapt to a changing market shaped by these two important scholarly efforts. Basal programs that debuted in the five years after Chall's book appeared were radically different from their predecessors. Most notably, *phonics* that had been relegated to a skill to be taught contextually after a hefty bank of sight words had been committed to memory, was back—from day one of grade one—in the series that hit the market in the late 1960s and early 1970s. Surprisingly, it was not the highly synthetic alphabetic approach of the previous century or the remedial clinics of the 1930s (which one might have expected from a reading of Chall's book). It is better described as an intensification and repositioning (to grade one) of the analytic phonics that had been taught in the latter part of grade 1 and in grades 2 to 4 in the look-say basals of the 1960s.[33] Equally significant, there was a change in *content,* at least in grade one. Dick and Jane and all their assorted pairs of competing cousins—Tom and Susan, Alice and Jerry, Jack and Janet—were retired from the first grade curriculum and replaced by a wider array of stories and characters; by the early 1970s, more of the selections were adaptations of children's literature rather than stories written to conform to a vocabulary restriction or a readability formula.

It is hard to determine how seriously educators and publishers took Chall's other three recommendations. For example, in the basals that came out after Chall, the grade 1 books (the preprimers, primers, and readers) were considerably more *challenging* than their immediate predecessors, mainly by virtue of a much more challenging grade 1 vocabulary—more words introduced much earlier in the grade 1 program.[34] One series even divided its new vocabulary words into words that ought to be explicitly introduced as sight words and those words, which they dubbed *decodable,* that should be recognized by the students by applying the phonics skills they had been taught up to that point in the program.[35] Beyond grade 1, however, changes in difficulty were much less visible, and no appreciable increase in the readability scores of these later levels occurred.

In testing, a major change toward single component tests did occur, although it is difficult to attribute this change solely to Chall's recommendation. Beginning in the early 70s and running through at least the late 80s, each successive edition of basal programs brought an increase in the number of single component tests—tests for each phonics skill (all the beginning, middle and final consonant sounds, vowel patterns, and syllabication), tests for each comprehension skill (main idea, finding details, drawing conclusions, and determining cause-effect relations) at every grade level, tests for alphabetical order and using the encyclopedia, and just about any other skill one might think of.

But other events and movements of the period also pointed toward single component tests. For one, owing to the intellectual contributions of Benjamin Bloom and John Carroll, the mastery learning movement[36] was gathering its own momentum during the late 1960s. According to proponents of mastery learning, if a complex domain could be decomposed into manageable subcomponents, each of which could be taught and learned to some predetermined level of mastery, then most, if not all, students should be able to master the knowledge and skills in the domain. Second, criterion-referenced tests were spawned during this same period.[37] The logic of criterion-referenced assessment was that some pre-determined level of mastery (say 80% correct), not the average for a group of students in a given grade level, ought to be the reference point for determining how well a student was doing on a test. A third construct from this period, curriculum-embedded assessment,[38] held that students should be held to account for precisely what was needed to march successfully through a particular curriculum—no less, no more. If one could specify the scope and sequence of knowledge and skills in the curriculum and develop assessments for each, then it should be possible to guide all students through the curriculum, even if some needed more practice and support than others. One can imagine a high degree of compatibility among all three of these powerful constructs—mastery learning, criterion-referenced assessment, and curriculum-embedded assessment. All three provide comfortable homes for single component assessments of the sort Chall was advocating.

With powerful evidence from mastery learning's application to college students,[39] publishers of basal programs and some niche publishers began to create and implement what came to be called skills management systems.[40] In their most meticulous application, these systems *became* the reading program. Students took a battery of mastery tests, practiced those skills they had not mastered (usually by completing worksheets that looked remarkably like the tests), took tests again, and continued through this cycle until they had mastered all the skills assigned to the grade level (or until the year ended). Unsurprisingly, the inclusion of these highly specific skill tests had the effect of increasing the salience of workbooks, worksheets, and other skill materials on which students could practice in anticipation of (and as a consequence of) mastery tests. Thus the basals of this period were comprised of two parallel systems: (1) the graded series of anthologies filled with stories and short non-fiction pieces for oral and silent reading and discussion, and (2) an embedded skills management system to guide the development of phonics, comprehension, vocabulary, and study skills.

Chall's last recommendation was to improve reading research. Research had been too inaccessible (to the very audience of practitioners who most needed it), too narrow in scope, and too dismissive of its past. All that needed to change, she argued. As I will detail in the next section, reading research changed dramatically, but not necessarily in a direction Chall envisioned.

One other change in basal reading programs in this period worth noting was the technology to place reduced facsimiles of student text pages onto a page where it could be surrounded by teaching suggestions and questions for guided reading. This was hailed as a major advance in the utility of manuals because teachers did not have to turn back and forth from student text to the teacher's section in order to guide the reading of a story.

This was the scene, then, in the early 1970s, just as the reading field was about to embark on a new curricular trek that continues even today. If the middle third of the century was characterized by a steady, unwavering march toward the ever-increasing prominence of a particular philosophy and set of curricular practices encapsulated in ubiquitous basals that championed a look-say approach,[41] the early 1970s brought major challenges in philosophy and pedagogy—harder texts, more phonics, and a skill development program unlike anything seen before.[42]

Taking Stock: 3

But even with some alterations in the materials available and some new peda-gogical twists, the pedagogy of the early 1970s revealed little fundamental change in the underlying assumptions about the role of the teacher and learner or the nature of reading and writing. Teachers, armed with their basal manuals, controlled the learning situation as never before, and students continued to play the role of passive recipient of the knowledge and skills mediated by the teacher. Most important, reading was still a fundamentally perceptual process of translat-ing letters into sounds. If anything, the perceptual nature of reading was made more salient than in the 1950s and 1960s by the return of phonics to center stage.

DEVELOPMENTS IN THE LAST THIRD OF THE CENTURY

Reading As the Province of Other Scholarly Traditions.[43]   Somewhere dur-ing this period—the exact point of departure is hard to fix—we began a journey that would take us through many new twists and turns on the way to different landscapes than we had visited before. Along the way we confronted fundamental shifts in our views of reading and writing and started to create a variety of serious curricular alternatives to the conventional wisdom of the 1970s. Just beyond the horizon lay even more unfamiliar and rockier territory—the conceptual revolutions in cognition, sociolinguistics, and philosophy that would have such far-reaching consequences for reading curriculum and pedagogy of the 1980s and 1990s.

Reading became an ecumenical scholarly commodity; it was embraced by scholars from many different fields of inquiry. The first to take reading under their wing were the linguists, who wanted to convince us that reading was a lan-guage process closely allied to its sibling language processes of writing, speaking, and listening. Then came the psycholinguists and the cognitive psychologists, fol-lowed soon by the sociolinguists, the philosophers, the literary critics, and the critical theorists. It is not altogether clear why reading has attracted such interest from scholars in so many other fields. One explanation is that reading is consid-ered by so many to be a key to success in other endeavors in and out of school; this is often revealed in comments like, "Well if you don't learn to read, you can't learn other things for yourself." Another is that scholars in these other disciplines thought that the educationists had got it all wrong, and it was time for another group to have their say. Whatever the reasons, the influence of these other scholarly traditions on reading pedagogy is significant; in fact, the pedagogy of the 1980s and 1990s cannot be understood without a firm grounding in the changes in world view that these perspectives spawned.

Linguistics.   In 1962, Charles Fries published a book entitled *Linguistics and Reading.* In it, he outlined what he thought the teaching of reading would look like if it were viewed from the perspective of linguistics. In the same decade, several other important books and articles appeared, each carrying essentially the same message: The perspective of the modern science of linguistics, we were told, would privilege different models and methods of teaching reading. It would tell us, for example, that some things do not need to be taught explicitly because the oral language takes care of them more or less automatically. For example, the three different pronunciations of *–ed* (as in *nabbed, capped,* and *jaded*), need not be taught as a reading skill because our oral language conventions determine the pronunciation almost perfectly. English in its oral form demands the voiced alternative /d/ after a voiced consonant such as /b/. It demands the unvoiced alternative /t/ after an unvoiced consonant such as /p/, and it requires the syllabic version /∂d/ after either /d/ or /t/. To teach these rules, which are very complex, would likely make things more confusing than simply allowing the oral language to do its work without fanfare.

Another linguistic insight came to us from the transformational generative grammars that replaced conventional structural linguistics as the dominant paradigm within the field during the 60s and 70s. Noam Chomsky published two revolutionary treatises during this period—*Syntactic Structures* in 1957 and *Aspects of a Theory of Syntax* in 1965. With these books Chomsky revolutionized the field of linguistics and paved the way, theoretically, for equally dramatic changes in the way that psychologists thought about and studied the processes of language comprehension and language acquisition.

Chomsky also provided the basis for a nativist view about language acquisition—a view that holds that humans come to the world "wired" to acquire the language of the community into which they are born. He and others drew this inference from two basic and contrasting facts about language: (a) language is incredibly complex and (b) language is acquired quite easily and naturally by children living in an environment in which they are simply exposed to (rather than taught!) the language of their community well before they experience school. Only a view that children are equipped with some special cognitive apparatus for inferring complex rules could explain this remarkable feat.

Because our prevailing views of both reading comprehension and reading acquisition were derived from the same behavioristic assumptions that Chomsky and his peers had attacked, reading scholars began to wonder whether those assumptions would hold up when we applied similar perspectives and criticisms to analyses of written language comprehension and acquisition.[44]

Psycholinguistics.   During the decade alter the publication of *Syntactic Structures*, a new field of inquiry, psycholinguistics, evolved. In its first several years of existence, the field devoted itself to determining whether the views of linguistic competence and language acquisition that had been set forth by Chomsky and his colleagues could serve as psychological models of language performance. While the effort to develop a simple mapping from Chomsky to models of language performance waned after a few unsatisfactory attempts, the field of psycholinguistics and the disposition of psychologists to study language with complex theoretical tools had been firmly established.

Particularly influential on our thinking about reading were scholars of language acquisition[45] who established the rule-governed basis of language learning. In contrast to earlier views, these psycholinguists found that children did not imitate written language; rather, as members of a language community, they were participants in language and invented for themselves rules about how oral language worked. This insight allowed researchers to explain such constructions as "I eated my dinner" and "I gots two foots." Roger Brown and his colleagues showed conclusively that children were active learners who inferred rules and tested them out. Much as Kenneth Goodman would later show with written language, "mistakes," especially overgeneralizations, in oral language could be used to understand the rule systems that children were inventing for themselves.

The analogy with oral language development was too tempting for reading educators to resist. Several adopted something like a nativist framework in studying the acquisition of reading, asking what the teaching of reading and writing would look like if we assumed that children can learn to read and write in much the same way as they learn to talk—that is, naturally. What would happen if we assumed that children were members of a community in which reading and writing are valued activities that serve important communication functions? What if we assumed that the most important factors in learning to read and write were having genuine reasons for communicating in these media and having access to a database in which there was so much print and talk about print that students could discover the patterns and regularities on their own, much as they do when they discover the patterns and regularities of oral language? While the seminal work involved in putting these assumptions to empirical tests would wait for a couple of decades, the seeds of doubt about our perceptually based views of reading acquisition were firmly planted by the middle 1960s.

syntactic—referring to grammatical relationships within a sentence and the functions of components within the sentence, as in syntactic cue

semantic—from the general sense or meaning, as in semantic cue

grapho-phonemic—referring to the relationship between phonemes, the sounds, and graphemes, the written symbols, in a language

Two influential individuals, Kenneth Goodman and Frank Smith, led the reading field in addressing these kinds of questions. In 1965, Goodman demonstrated that the errors children made while reading orally were better viewed as windows into the inner workings of their comprehension processes than as mistakes to be eradicated. He found that the mistakes that children made while reading in context revealed that they were trying to make sense of what they read. In another seminal 1967 piece, *Reading: A Psycholinguistic Guessing Game*, Goodman laid out the elements of language that he thought that readers employed as they constructed meaning for the texts they encountered. In reading, he conjectured, readers use three cue systems to make sense of text: **syntactic** cues, **semantic** cues, and **grapho-phonemic** cues. By attending to all of these cue sources, Goodman contended, readers could reduce their uncertainty about unknown words or meanings, thus rendering both the word identification and comprehension processes more manageable.[46]

Smith's revolutionary ideas were first presented in 1971 in a book entitled *Understanding Reading.*[47] In this seminal text, Smith argued that reading was not something one was *taught,* but rather was something one *learned* to do. Smith believed that there were no special prerequisites to learning to read, indeed, that reading was simply making sense of one particular type of information in our environment. As such, reading was what one learned to do as a consequence of belonging to a literate society. One learned to read from reading. The implication, which Smith made explicit, was that the "function of teachers is not so much to *teach* reading as to help children read" (pg. 3). This certainly challenged the notion of the teacher as the individual who meted out knowledge and skills to passively waiting students. For Smith, all knowing and all learning were constructive processes; individuals made sense of what they encountered based on what they already knew.[48] Even perception, he contended, was a decision-making, predictive process based on prior knowledge.

Smith also argued that reading was only incidentally visual. By that, Smith meant that being able to see was necessary but not sufficient to achieve understanding. He identified four sources of information: **orthographic**, syntactic, semantic, and visual, all of which he claimed were somewhat redundant, and argued that skilled readers made use of the three sources that were a part of their prior knowledge (the orthographic, syntactic, and semantic) in order to minimize their reliance on visual information. In fact, the danger in relying too heavily on visual information is that readers might lose sight of meaning.

> **orthographic**—pertaining to the use and nature of symbols in a writing system

The psycholinguistic perspective had a number of influences on reading pedagogy. First, it valued literacy experiences that focused on making meaning. This meant that many classroom activities, particularly worksheets and games, which focused on enabling skills such as specific letter-sound correspondences, syllabication activities, structural analysis skills, specific comprehension activities, or study skills were devalued. Second, it helped us to value texts for beginning readers, such as example 1 (see Table 2.1), in which authors relied on natural language patterns, thus making it possible for emerging readers to use their knowledge of language to predict words and meanings. This meant that texts that relied on high-frequency words in short, choppy sentences (what we have come to call basalese), as in example 2, or those based upon the systematic application of some phonics element (i.e., a decodable text), as in example 3, were correspondingly devalued.

Third, the psycholinguistic perspective helped us understand the reading process and appreciate children's efforts as readers. Errors were no longer things to be corrected; instead they were windows into the workings of the child's mind, allowing both the teacher and the child to understand more about the reading process and reading strategies. Understanding miscues also helped educators focus on comprehension and appreciate risk-taking.

TABLE 2.1   Sample Texts for Beginning Reading

1. Red Fox, Red Fox, what do you see?
   I see a blue bird looking at me.
   Blue Bird, Blue Bird, what do you see?
   I see a green frog looking at me.

2. Run, John, run.
   Run to Dad.
   Dad will run.
   Run, Dad.
   Run, John.
   See them run.

3. Nat can bat.
   Nat can bat with the fat bat.
   The cat has the fat bat.
   The rat has the fat bat.
   Nat has the fat bat.
   Bat the bat, Nat.

Fourth, psycholinguists gave us a means (miscue analysis) and a theory (reading as a constructive process) that was remarkably distinct from previous ideas about reading. The perspective made explicit links between oral and written language acquisition and helped us view reading as language rather than simply perception or behavior. In a sense, psycholinguistics continued the changes and traditions begun by the linguistic perspective; however, within the reading field, its influence was deeper and broader than its academic predecessor.

Most important, psycholinguistics affected our views of teaching and learning in a fundamental way. Reading scholars began to rethink ideas about what needed to be taught, as well as the relation between teaching and learning. So, instead of asking, "What can I teach this child so that she *will eventually become* a reader?", we began to ask, "What can I do to help this child *as* a reader?" Some teachers began to welcome all children into what Smith referred to as "The Literacy Club" as an alternative to teaching children so-called prerequisite skills.[49]

Cognitive psychology.   If psycholinguistics enabled psychologists to reexamine their assumptions about language learning and understanding by placing greater emphasis on the active, intentional role of language users, cognitive psychology allowed psychologists to extend constructs such as human purpose, intention, and motivation to a greater range of psychological phenomena, including perception, attention, comprehension, learning, memory, and executive control of all cognitive process. All of these would have important consequences in reading pedagogy.

I cannot emphasize too strongly the dramatic nature of the paradigm shift that occurred within those branches of psychology concerned with human intellectual processes. The previous half-century, from roughly the teens through the fifties, had been dominated by a behaviorist perspective in psychology that shunned speculation about the inner workings of the mind. Just show us the surface-level outcomes of the processes, as indexed by overt, observable behaviors. Leave the speculation to the philosophers. That was the contextual background against which both psycholinguistics and cognitive psychology served as dialectical antagonists when they appeared on the scene in the late 60s and early 70s.

The most notable change within psychology was that it became fashionable for psychologists, perhaps for the first time since the early part of the century, to study reading.[50] And in the decade of the 1970s works by psychologists flooded the literature on basic processes in reading. One group focused on text comprehension by trying to ferret out how it is that readers come to understand the underlying structure of texts. We were offered story grammars—structural accounts of the nature of narratives, complete with predictions about how those structures impede and enhance human story comprehension. Others chose to focus on the expository tradition in text.[51] Like their colleagues interested in story comprehension, they believed that structural accounts of the nature of expository (informational) texts would provide valid and useful models for text comprehension. And in a sense, both of these efforts worked. Story grammars did account for story comprehension. Analyses of the structural relations among ideas in an informational piece did account for text comprehension. But what neither text-analysis tradition really tackled was the relationship between the knowledge of the world that readers bring to text and comprehension of those texts. In other words, by focusing on structural rather than the ideational, or content, characteristics of texts, they failed to get to the heart of comprehension. That task, as it turned out, fell to one of the most popular and influential movements of the 70s, schema theory.

Schema theory[52] is a theory about the structure of human knowledge as it is represented in memory. In our memory, schemata are like little containers into which we deposit particular experiences that we have. So, if we see a chair, we store that visual experience in our chair schema. If we go to a restaurant, we store that experience in our restaurant schema, if we attend a party, our party schema, and so on. Clearly schema theory is linked to Piaget's theories of development and his two types of learning, assimilation and accommodation. When we assimilate new information, we store it in an existing schema; when we accommodate new information, we modify the structure of our schemata to fit the new data. The modern iteration of schema theory also owes a debt to Frederic Bartlett, who, writing in the 1930s, used the construct of schema to explain culturally driven interpretations of stories. For Bartlett, cultural schemata for stories were so strong that they prevented listeners, whether European or native Alaskan in background, from adopting the story schema of the other culture to understand its stories. Bartlett's account predates the current constructivist models of cognition and learning by sixty years; and his view is as inherently constructive as those that have succeeded him. In essence, Bartlett was saying exactly what modern constructivists say—that readers and listeners actively construct meanings for texts they encounter rather than simply "receiving" meaning from the texts.[53]

Schema theory also provides a credible account of reading comprehension, which probably, more than any of its other features, accounted for its popularity within the reading field in the 1970s and 80s.[54] It is not hard to see why schema theory was so appealing to theoreticians, researchers, and practitioners when it arrived on the scene in the 1970s. First, it provides a rich and detailed theoretical account of the everyday intuition that we understand and learn what is new in terms of what we already know. Second, it also accounts for another everyday in-tuition about why we, as humans, so often disagree about our interpretation of an event, a story, an article, a movie, or a TV show—we disagree with one an-other because we approach the phenomenon with very different background ex-periences and knowledge. Third, it accounts for a third everyday intuition that might be called an "it's-all-Greek-to-me" experience: Sometimes we just don't have enough background knowledge to understand a new experience or text.

While these insights may not sound earthshaking after the fact, for the field of reading, and for education more generally, they were daunting challenges to our conventional wisdom. Examined in light of existing practices in the 1970s, they continued the revolutionary spirit of the linguistic and psycholinguistic per-spectives. Schema theory encouraged us to ask:

> What is it that my children already know? And how can I use that to help them deal with these new ideas that I would like them to know?

rather than:

> What is it that they do not know? And how can I get that into their heads?

More specifically, with respect to reading comprehension, schema theory encouraged us to examine texts from the perspective of the knowledge and cultural backgrounds of our students in order to evaluate the likely connections that they would be able to make between ideas that are in the text and the schema that they would bring to the reading task. Schema theory, like the psycholinguistic per-spective, also promoted a constructivist view of comprehension; all readers must, at every moment in the reading process, construct a coherent model of reading for the texts they read. The most important consequence of this constructivist perspective is that there is inherent ambiguity about where meaning resides. Does it reside in the text? In the author's mind as she set pen to paper? In the mind of each reader as she builds a model of meaning unique to her experience and read-ing? In the interaction between reader and text?

Sociolinguistics.   Sociolinguistics as a discipline developed in parallel with psy-cholinguistics. Beginning with the work of William Labov, and Joan Baratz and Roger Shuy, sociolinguists had important lessons for reading scholars.[55] Mainly these lessons focused on issues of dialect and reading. Sociolinguists were finding that dialects were not ill- or half-formed variations of standard English. Instead, each dialect constituted a well-developed linguistic system in its own right, com-plete with rules for variations from standard English and a path of language de-velopment for its speakers. Speakers of dialects expressed linguistic *differences* not linguistic *deficits*. The goal of schooling was not, and should not be, to eradicate the dialect in the process of making each individual a speaker of standard English. Instead, sociolinguists stressed the need to find ways to accommodate children's use of their dialect while they are learning to read and write. Several proposals for achieving this accommodation were tried and evaluated. The first was to write special readers for dialect speakers. In the early 1960s, several examples of Black dialect readers appeared and, almost as rapidly, disappeared from major urban districts. They failed primarily because African-American parents did not want their children learning with "special" materials; they wanted their children to be exposed to mainstream materials used by other children.[56] The second equally unsuccessful strategy was to delay instruction in reading and writing until children's oral language became more standardized. Teachers who tried this technique soon found out just how resistant and persistent early language learning can be. The third, and most successful, approach to dialect accommodation involved nothing more than recognizing that a child who translates a standard English text into a dialect is performing a remarkable feat of translation rather than making reading errors. So, an African-American child who says /pōs/ when he sees *post* is simply applying a rule of Black English which requires a consonant cluster in ending position to be reduced to the sound of the first consonant. Unfortunately for children who speak a dialect, we, as a field, did not take the early lessons of the sociolinguists to heart. We continue to find schools in which children are scolded for using the oral language that they have spent their whole lives learning. We also continue to find children whose dialect translations are treated as if they were oral reading errors.

Prior to the advent of the sociolinguistic perspective, when educators talked about "context" in reading, they typically meant the print that surrounded particular words on a page. In the 1980s, and primarily because of the work of sociolinguists, the meaning of the word context expanded to include not only what was on the page, but what Bloome and Green referred to as the instructional, non-instructional, and home and community contexts of literacy.[57] From a sociolinguistic perspective, reading always occurred in a context, a context that was shaped by the literacy event at the same time as it shaped the event. The sociolinguistic versions of knowledge and language as socially and culturally constructed processes moved the constructivist metaphor to another plane, incorporating not only readers' prior knowledge in the form of schemata, but also the meanings constructed by peers and by one's cultural ancestors.

The most significant legacy of the sociolinguistic perspective was our heightened consciousness about language as a social and, therefore, cultural construction. Suddenly, reading was a part of a bigger and more complex world. Sociolinguists examined the role of language in school settings. For example, they pointed out that often success in reading was not so much an indication of reading "ability" per se, but of the success the individual experienced in learning how to use language appropriately in educational settings. Thus success, according to a sociolinguistic analysis, was more an index of how well children learned to "do school" than how well they could read. They contrasted the functions that language serves in school with the functions it serves outside of school and helped us rethink the role of language within the classroom. By studying the community outside of school, sociolinguists made us conscious of social, political, and cultural differences; as a result, we began to rethink our judgments of language and behavior. We saw that any judgment call we made, rather than reflecting the "right" way, simply reflected "our" way—the way we as teachers thought and talked and behaved because of the cultural situation in which we lived outside as well as inside school. By focusing on the role of community in learning, they caused many educators to rethink the competitive atmosphere of classrooms and of school labels and to recommend changes within schools so that children could learn from and with each other. With these contributions from sociolinguists, it was becoming more and more apparent that reading was not only not context-free but that it was embedded in multiple contexts.

Literary theory perspective.   One cannot understand the pedagogical changes in practice that occurred in the elementary reading curriculum in the 1980s without understanding the impact of literary theory, particularly reader response theory. In our secondary schools, the various traditions of literary criticism have always had a voice in the curriculum, especially in guiding discussions of classic literary works. Until the middle 1980s, the "new criticism" that had emerged in the post World War II era had dominated for several decades, and it had sent teachers and students on a search for the one "true" meaning in each text they encountered. With the emergence (some would argue the re-emergence) of reader response theories, all of which gave as much, if not more, authority to the reader than to either the text or the author, the picture, along with our practices, changed dramatically. While there are many modern versions of reader response available, the work of Louise Rosenblatt has been most influential among elementary teachers and reading educators. In the 1980s, many educators re-read (or more likely read for the first time) Rosenblatt's 1976 edition of her 1938 text, *Literature as Exploration,* and *The Reader, The Text, The poem,* which appeared in 1978. Rosenblatt argues that meaning is something that resides neither in the head of the reader (as some had previously argued) nor on the printed page (as others had argued).[58] Instead, Rosenblatt contends, meaning is created in the transaction between reader and document. This meaning, which she refers to as the poem, resides above the reader-text interaction. Meaning is, therefore, neither subject nor object nor the interaction of the two. Instead, it is transaction, something new and different from any of its inputs and influences.[59]

The Pedagogical Correlates of New Perspectives.   While the post-Chall basal tradition continued well into the decade of the 1980s, new perspectives and practices began to show up in classrooms, journal articles, and basal lessons in the early 1980s.

Comprehension on center stage.   Comprehension, especially as a workbook activity and a follow-up to story reading, was not a stranger to the reading classrooms of the 30s through the 70s. As indicated earlier, it entered the curriculum as a story discussion tool and as a way of assessing reading competence in the first third of this century.[60] Developments during mid-century were highlighted in an earlier NSSE yearbook devoted to reading;[61] by mid-century, the infrastructure of comprehension had been elaborated extensively and infused into the guided reading and workbook task. It was a staple of basal programs when Chall conducted her famous study of early reading, and had she emphasized reading instruction in the intermediate grades rather than grade one, it would undoubtedly have been more prominent in her account.

During the late 1970s and through the decade of the 1980s comprehension found its way to center stage in reading pedagogy. Just as a nationally sponsored set of research activities (i.e., the First Grade Studies and Chall's book) focused energy on reforms in beginning reading in the late 1960s, it was the federally funded Center for the Study of Reading, initiated in 1976, that focused, national attention on comprehension. Although the Center's legacy is undoubtedly bringing schema theory and the knowledge-comprehension relationship into our national conversation, it also supported much research on comprehension instruction,[62] including research that attempted to help students develop a repertoire of strategies for improving their comprehension.[63] This research was not limited to the Center; indeed many other scholars were equally involved in developing instructional strategies and routines during this period, including emphases on monitoring comprehension,[64] transactional strategies instruction,[65] KWL graphic organizers,[66] and, more recently, questioning the author.[67] Many of these new strategies found their way into the basals of the 1980s, which demonstrated substantially more emphasis on comprehension at all levels, including grade one.[68]

Literature-based reading. Even though selections from both classical and contemporary children's literature have always been a staple of basal selections dating back to the nineteenth century (especially after grade 2 when the need for strict vocabulary control diminished), literature virtually exploded into the curriculum in the late 1980s. A short burst in literary content occurred after Chall's critical account of the type of selections and the challenge of basal content; more excerpts from authentic literature appeared, even in the grade one readers. But these selections had two characteristics that had always offended those who champion the use of genuine literature—excerpting and adaptation. Rarely were whole books included; instead, whole chapters or important slices were excerpted for inclusion. And even when a whole chapter was included, it was usually adapted to (a) reduce vocabulary difficulty, (b) reduce the grammatical complexity of sentences, or (c) excise words (e.g., mild profanity) or themes that might offend important segments of the market.

Beyond basals, children's literature played an important supplementary role in the classrooms of teachers who believed that they must engage their students in a strong parallel independent reading program. Often this took the form of each child selecting books to be read individually and later discussed with the teacher in a weekly one-on-one conference. And even as far back as the 1960s, there were a few programs which turned this individualized reading component into the main reading program.[69]

But in the late 1980s, literature was dramatically repositioned. Several factors converged to pave the way for a groundswell in the role of literature in elementary reading. Surely the resurgence of reader response theory as presented by Rosenblatt was important, as was the compatibility of the reader response theory and its emphasis on interpretation with the constructivism that characterized both cognitive and sociolinguistic perspectives. Research also played a role; in 1985, for example, in the watershed publication of the Center for the Study of Reading, *Becoming a Nation of Readers,* Richard Anderson and his colleagues documented the importance of "just plain reading" as a critical component of any and all elementary reading programs.[70] This is also a period that witnessed an unprecedented expansion in the number of new children's books published annually. Finally, a few pieces of scholarship exerted enormous influence on teachers and teacher educators. Perhaps most influential was Nancie Atwell's *In the Middle.* In her account she laid out her story, as a middle school teacher, of how she invited readers, some of whom were quite reluctant, into a world of books and reading. The credibility of her experience and the power of her prose were persuasive in convincing thousands of classroom teachers that they could use existing literature and "reading workshops" to accomplish anything that a basal program could accomplish in skill development while gaining remarkable advantages in students' literary experience.[71]

In terms of policy and curriculum, the most significant event in promoting literature-based reading was the 1988 California Reading Framework. The framework called for reading materials which contained much more challenging texts at all levels. More important, it mandated the use of genuine literature, not the dumbed-down adaptations and excerpts from children's literature that had been the staple of basal programs for decades. Publishers responded to the call of California's framework and produced a remarkably different product in the late 1980s and early 1990s than had ever appeared before on the basal market.[72] Gone were excerpts and adaptations, and with them almost any traces of vocabulary control. Skills that had been front and center in the basals of the 70s and 80s were relegated to appendix-like status. Comprehension questions were replaced by more interpretive, impressionistic response to literature activities. All this was done in the name of providing children with authentic literature and authentic activities to accompany it. The logic was that if we could provide students with real literature and real motivations for reading it, much of what is arduous about skill teaching and learning will take care of itself.

Book Clubs and literature circles are the most visible instantiations of the literature-based reading movement.[73] The underlying logic of Book Clubs is the need to engage children in the reading of literature in the same way as adults engage one another in voluntary reading circles. Such voluntary structures are likely to elicit greater participation, motivation, appreciation, and understanding on the part of students. Teachers are encouraged to establish a set of "cultural practices" (ways of interacting and supporting one another) in their classrooms to support students as they make their way into the world of children's literature. These cultural practices offer students both the opportunity to engage in literature and the skills to ensure that they can negotiate and avail themselves of that opportunity.

Process writing.   In the middle 1980s, writing achieved a stronghold in the elementary language arts curriculum that it had never before held. Exactly why and how it achieved that position of prominence is not altogether clear, but certain explanations are plausible. Key understandings from the scholarship of the 70s and 80s paved the way. Functionality associated with the sociolinguistic perspective encouraged teachers to ask students to write for genuine audiences and purposes. The psycholinguistic notion of "error" as a window into children's thinking allowed us to worry less about perfect spelling and grammar and more about the quality of the thinking and problem solving children were producing. The general acceptance of constructivist epistemologies disposed us to embrace writing as the most transparently constructive of all pedagogical activities. All of these constructs allowed us as a profession to take a different developmental view on writing, one consistent with the emergent literacy perspective that was gaining strength in early childhood literacy. We came to view all attempts to make sense by setting pen to paper, however deviant from adult models, as legitimate and revealing in their own right if examined through the eyes of the child writer. Led by Donald Graves and Lucy Calkins, we revolutionized our views of early writing development.[74] Finally, we began to see reading and writing as inherently intertwined, each supporting the other.

Integrated instruction.   It is impossible to document the history of reading instruction in the twentieth century without mentioning the ways in which we have attempted to integrate reading with other curricular phenomena. Two stances have dominated our thinking about how to integrate reading into other curricula—integration of reading with the other language arts (writing, speaking, and listening) and integration across subject matter boundaries (with mathematics, science, social studies, art, and music). Like literature-based reading, both senses of integration have long been a part of the thinking about elementary reading curriculum.[75] In fact, a look back to the progressivism of Dewey and other scholars in the first part of this century reveals substantial rhetoric about teaching and learning across curricular boundaries.[76] From that early spurt of energy until the late 1980s, however, integrations assumed a minor role in American reading instruction. In basal manuals, for example, integration was portrayed almost as an afterthought until the late 1980s; it appeared in the part of the lesson that follows the guided reading and skills instruction sections, signaling that these are things that a teacher can get to "if time permits." Things changed in the late 1980s. For one, integrated curriculum fit the sociolinguistic emphasis on language in use—the idea that language, including reading, is best taught and learned when it is put to work in the service of other purposes, activities, and learning efforts. Similarly, with the increase in importance of writing, especially early writing of the sort discussed by Graves and his colleagues,[77] it was tempting to champion the idea of integrated language arts instruction. In fact, the constructivist metaphor is nowhere played out as vividly and transparently as in writing, leading many scholars to use writing as a model for the sort of constructive approach they wanted to promote in readers. The notion was that we needed to help students learn to "read like a writer."[78] Also influential in supporting the move toward integrated instruction was the work of Donald Holdaway, who, in concert with many teacher colleagues, had been implementing an integrated language arts approach in Australia for a few decades.[79]

Whole language.   Important as they are, comprehension, literature-based reading, process writing, and integrated instruction pale in comparison to the impact of whole language, which must be regarded as the most significant movement in reading curriculum in the last thirty years.[80] In fact, one might plausibly argue that whole language co-opted all four of these allied phenomena—comprehension, literature-based reading, integrated instruction and process writing—by incorporating them, problems along with strengths, into its fundamental set of principles and practices. Whole language is grounded in child-centered pedagogy reminiscent of the progressive education movement (the individual child is the most important curriculum informant).[81] Philosophically it is

> **epistemology**—a branch of philosophy having to do with the nature of knowing and knowledge; a view of knowledge

biased toward radical constructivist **epistemology** (all readers must construct their own meanings for the texts they encounter). Currically, it is committed to authentic activity (real, not specially constructed, texts and tasks) and integration (both within the language arts and between the language arts and other subject matters). Politically, it is suspicious of all attempts to mandate and control curricular decisions beyond the classroom level; as such, it places great faith and hope in the wisdom of teachers to exercise professional prerogative in making decisions about the children in their care. Whole language owes its essential character and key principles to the insights of linguistics, psycholinguistics, cognitive psychology, sociolinguistics, and literary theory detailed earlier. It owes its remarkable—if brief—appearance in the national limelight of reading instruction to its committed leaders and a veritable army of committed teachers who instantiated it in their classrooms, each with his or her own unique signature.[82]

When whole language emerged as a movement in the 80s, it challenged the conventional wisdom of basals and questioned the unqualified support for early code emphases that had grown between 1967 and the early 1980s.[83] One of the great ironies of whole language is that its ascendancy into curricular prominence is best documented by its influence on the one curricular tool it has most consistently and most vehemently opposed, the basal reader.[84] As suggested earlier, basals changed dramatically in the early 1990s, largely, I conjecture, in response to the groundswell of support within the teaching profession for whole language and its close curricular allies, literature-based reading and process writing.

Vocabulary control, already weakened during the 1970s in response to Chall's admonitions, was virtually abandoned in the early 1990s in deference to attempts to incorporate more literature, this time in unexpurgated form (i.e., without the practices of adaptation and excerpting that had characterized the basals of the 70s and 80s) into the grade 1 program.[85] Phonics, along with other skills, was backgrounded, and literature moved to center stage.

Basal programs appropriated or, as some whole language advocates have argued, "basalized" the activities and tools of whole language. Thus in the basals of the early 1990s, each unit might have a writing process component in which the rhetoric if not the reality of some version of process writing was presented to teachers and students. In the 1980s, comprehension questions, probably following a story line, might have sufficed for the guided reading section of the manual (the part that advises teachers on how to read and discuss the story), but in the 1990s, questions and tasks that supported deep probes into students' response to literature became more prevalent. Another concession to literature-based reading was the creation and marketing of classroom libraries—boxed sets of books, usually thematically related to each unit, that teachers could use to extend their lessons and units "horizontally" and enrich children's literary opportunities.

Basals also repositioned their "integrated language arts" and "integrated curriculum" strands. Dating back even to the 1920s and 1930s, basals had provided at least a "token" section in which teachers were encouraged to extend the themes or skills of the basal story into related writing (e.g., rewriting stories), oral language (e.g., transforming a story into a play and dramatizing it), or cross-curricular activities (e.g., conducting community surveys, tallying the results, and reporting them), but these forays were regarded as peripheral rather than core. In the basals of the early 1990s, as skills moved into the background,[86] these integrated language arts activities were featured more prominently as core lesson components.[87]

These changes can, I believe, be traced to the prominent position of whole language as a curricular force during this period.[88] Publishers of basals accomplished this feat of appropriation not by ridding their programs of the skills of previous eras, but by subtle repositioning—foregrounding one component while backgrounding another, creating optional components or modules (e.g., an intensive phonics kit or a set of literature books) that could be added to give the program one or another spin. Unsurprisingly, this created bulkier teachers' manuals and more complex programs.

Acceptance of whole language was not universal. To the contrary, there was considerable resistance to whole language and literature-based reading throughout the country.[89] In many places, whole language never really gained a foothold. In others what was implemented in the name of whole language was not consistent with the philosophical and curricular principles of the movement; California, whole language advocates would argue, is a case in point. Whole language got conflated with whole class instruction and was interpreted to mean that all students should get the same literature, even if teachers had to read it to them.[90]

Nor was there a single voice within the whole language movement. Whole language scholars and practitioners differ on a host of issues, such as the role of skills, conventions, and strategies within a language arts program. Some say, if we can just be patient, skills will emerge from meaningful communication activities; others spur things on by taking advantage of spontaneous opportunities for mini-lessons; still others are willing to spur spontaneity a bit.

Even so, it is fair to conclude that by the early 90s, whole language had become the conventional wisdom, the standard against which all else was referenced. The rhetoric of professional articles belies this change. As late as the mid-1980s, articles were written with the presumption of a different conventional wisdom—a world filled with skills, contrived readers, and workbooks. By 1991–92, they were written with the presumption that whole language reforms, while not fully ensconced in America's schools, were well on their way to implementation. The arguments in the 90s were less about first principles of whole language and more about fine-tuning teaching repertoires. The meetings of the Whole Language Umbrella grew to be larger than most large state conventions and regional conferences of the International Reading Association. By 1995, whole language was no longer a collection of guerrilla stories into the land of skills and basals that characterized it through the mid-1980s. It had become the conventional wisdom, in rhetoric if not in reality.

Taking Stock: 4

Returning to the lenses outlined at the beginning of this chapter (range of materials and practices, role of teacher, role of learner, and the processes of reading and learning to read), in whole language, we finally encounter major shifts in emphasis in comparison to what we found at the beginning of the century. In whole language, teachers are facilitators not tellers. They observe what children do, decide what they need, and arrange conditions to allow students to discover insights about reading, writing, and learning for themselves. Because this is truly child-centered pedagogy, learners occupy center stage. As Jerome Harste puts it, the child is the primary curriculum informant. Students must be decision makers who are involved in choices about the books they read and stories they write. The materials of reading instruction are the materials of life and living—the books, magazines, newspapers, and other forms of print that children can encounter in everyday life are the materials they should encounter in the classroom—no less, no more. Ideally, there is no need for the sort of contrived texts and tasks of the sort found in basal reading programs. Instructional practices focus not on presenting a diet of skills carefully sequenced to achieve mastery but on creating activities and tasks that support the learning students need at a particular point in time. If skills and strategies are taught, they are taught in "minilessons," highly focused forays into the infrastructure of a skill or strategy followed up by immediately recontextualizing the skill in a genuine reading or writing situation. In contrast to previous periods, reading was now regarded as a meaning-making, not a perceptual, process. The reader was an active participant in creating, not a passive recipient of, the message in a text. The process of acquiring reading was also markedly different from the "readiness" perspective so dominant in the first eighty years of the century. Emergent literacy, the alternative to traditional reading readiness views, does not specify a "pre-reading" period in which children are prepared for the task of reading. All readers, at all stages, are meaning makers, even those who can only scribble a message or "pretend" read.[91] Thus, at century's end, reading pedagogy finally developed some viable alternatives to the conventional views of teacher, learner, and process that had dominated pedagogical practice for the entire century. As it turned out, the new directions were short-lived.

The Demise of Whole Language.   At century's end, just when it appeared as if whole language, supported by its intellectual cousins (process writing, literature-based reading, and integrated curriculum), was about to assume the position of conventional wisdom for the field, the movement was challenged seriously, and the pendulum of the pedagogical debate began to swing back toward the skills end of the curriculum and instruction continuum. Several factors converged to make the challenge credible, among them (a) unintended curricular casualties of whole language, (b) questionable applications of whole language, (c) growing dissatisfaction with doctrinaire views of any sort, (d) a paradigm swing in the ideology of reading research, (e) increasing politicization of the reading research and policy agenda, and (f) increasing pressure for educators of all stripes, especially reading educators, to produce measurable results.

Unintended curricular consequences.   In its ascendancy, whole language changed the face of reading instruction, and in the process, left behind some curricular casualties, few of which were intended by those who supported whole language. Those, myself included,[92] who supported practices that were discarded in the rise of whole language, had difficulty supporting the whole language movement even though we might have been philosophically and curricularly sympathetic to many of its principles and practices. This lack of enthusiasm from curricular moderates meant that whole language failed to build a base of support that was broad enough to survive even modest curricular opposition, let alone the political onslaught that it would experience at century's turn.

What were these casualties? I see at least four: skills instruction, strategy instruction, an emphasis on text structure, and reading in the content areas. Earlier, I suggested that one of the consequences of whole language was the relegation of skills to the "appendices" of instructional programs. In accepting whole language, we tacitly accepted the premise that skills are better *caught* in the act of reading and writing genuine texts for authentic purposes than *taught* directly and explicitly by teachers. The argument is the same for phonics, grammar, text conventions, and structural elements. These entities may be worthy of learning, but they are unworthy of teaching. This position presents us with a serious conundrum as a profession. Admit, for the sake of argument, that the skills instruction of the 1970s and earlier, with decontextualized lessons and practice on "textoids" in workbook pages, deserved the criticism accorded to it by whole language advocates (and scholars from other traditions). But a retreat from most skills instruction into a world of "authentic opportunity" did not provide a satisfactory answer for teachers and scholars who understood the positive impact that instruction can have. Many young readers do not "catch" the alphabetic principle by sheer immersion in print or by listening to others read aloud. For some it seems to require careful planning and hard work by dedicated teachers who are willing to balance systematic skills instruction with authentic texts and activities.[93]

Strategy instruction was another casualty. This loss was particularly difficult for scholars who spent the better part of the early 1980s convincing basal publishers and textbook authors that the thoughtful teaching of flexible strategies for making and monitoring meaning was a viable alternative to mindless skills instruction, where skills were taught as though they were only ever to be applied to workbook pages and end-of-unit tests. But the strategy lessons that filled our basals in the middle to late 1980s—direct advice from teachers about how to summarize what one has read, how to use text structure to infer relations among ideas, how to distinguish fact from opinion, how to determine the central thread of a story, how to use context to infer word meanings, and how to make and evaluate the accuracy of predictions—were virtually non-existent in the basals of the early-to-middle 1990s. While there is no inherent bias in whole language or literature-based reading against the learning and use of a whole range of cognitive strategies, there is, as with phonics and grammar, a serious question about whether direct, explicit instruction in how to use them will help. The advice is to let them emerge from attempts to solve real reading problems and puzzles, the kind students meet in genuine encounters with authentic text. There may have been reason for concern about the strategy instruction of the 80s. But revision rather than rejection of these strategies was not a part of the rhetoric of whole language.[94]

Structural emphasis was also suspect within whole language. This suspicion extended to formal grammars, story grammars, rhetorical structures, and genre features of texts. As with skills and strategies, whole language reformers do not claim that students should not learn and develop control over these structural tools; they simply claim that, like skills, they are best inferred from reading and writing authentic texts in the process of making meaning. So, the advocates are comfortable in adopting Frank Smith's[95] admonition to encourage kids to read like a writer (meaning to read the text with a kind of critical eye toward understanding the tools and tricks of the trade that the author uses to make her points and achieve her effects on readers), but they would likely reject a systematic set of lessons designed to teach and assess children's control of story grammar elements (such as plot, characterization, style, mood, or theme) or some system for dealing with basic patterns of expository text. As with skills and strategies, many of us see a compromise alternative to both the formulaic approach of the early 1980s and the "discovery" approach of the new reforms—dealing with these structural elements as they emanate from stories that a group is currently reading can provide some guidance and useful tools for students and teachers.

Content area reading also suffered during the ascendancy of whole language and literature-based reading. Content area texts—expository texts in general, but especially textbook-like entries—were not privileged in a world of literature-based reading. This is not an implicit criticism of the literature-based reading movement; rather it is a comment about the reallocation of curricular time and energy that occurs when a movement gains momentum. There is a certain irony in this development, for it is expository reading, not narrative reading, that most concerns middle and high school teachers. The cost here has been very dear. To enter middle school and high school classrooms in order to examine the role of expository text is to conclude that it has none. Occasionally teachers assign expository texts for homework, but when students come to class the next day, clearly having avoided the assignment, teachers provide them with an oral version of what they would have gotten out of the text if they had bothered to read it. Most high school teachers have quite literally given up on the textbook for the communication of any important content. While understandable, this approach is, of course, ultimately counterproductive. There comes a time in the lives of students—either when they go to college or enter the world of work—when others expect them to read and understand informational texts on their own and in printed form rather than through oral or video transformation.[96]

Because whole language did not go out of its way to accommodate any of these curricular practices, those who were sympathetic with whole language but also champions of one or another approach were not available to help whole language respond to the criticism leveled at it in the late 1990s.

Questionable applications of whole language.   One of the dilemmas faced by any curricular challenge is sustaining the integrity of the movement without imposing the very sorts of controls it is trying to eliminate. Whole language has not found a satisfying way of managing this dilemma, and it has suffered as a consequence. Many schools, teachers, and institutions appropriated the whole language label without honoring its fundamental principles of authenticity integration, and empowerment. Basal reader publishers made the most obvious and widespread appropriation, some even positioning their basal series as "whole language" programs. Earlier, I noted another misapplication in which whole language was confounded with whole-class instruction. Nowhere was this conflation more extreme than in the implementation of the California literature framework. The logic that prevailed in many classrooms was that it was better to keep the entire class together, all experiencing the same texts, even if it meant that the teacher had to read the text to those children who lacked the skills to read it on their own. Implicit in this practice are two interesting assumptions; (1) that getting the content of the stories is the most important goal for reading instruction, and (2) that the skills and processes needed to read independently will emerge somehow from this environment in which many students are pulled through texts that far exceed the grasp of their current skills repertoire. Needless to say, whole language had enough on its hands dealing with its own assumptions and practices; these philosophical and curricular misapplications exposed the movement to a whole set of criticisms that derived from practices not of its own making.

One of the primary reasons for misapplication of whole language is, in my view, the lack of an explicit plan for professional development. Whole language gives teachers a wide berth for making curricular and instructional decisions, for whole classes and for individual children. It assumes that teachers who are empowered, sincere, and serious about their personal professional development will be able to tailor programs and activities to the needs and interests of individual children. Such an approach makes sense only when we can assume that teacher knowledge is widely and richly distributed in our profession. To offer these prerogatives in the face of narrow and shallow knowledge is to guarantee that misguided practices, perversions of the very intent of the movement, will be widespread. The puzzle, of course, is where to begin the reform—by ensuring that the knowledge precedes the prerogative, or by ceding the prerogative to teachers as a way of leveraging their motivation for greater knowledge.[97]

Growing dissatisfaction with extreme positions.   While it has reached its peak in the last five years, concern about extreme positions, be they extremely child-centered (such as the more radical of whole language approaches) or extremely curriculum-centered (such as highly structured, unswerving phonics programs) is not new. Voices from the middle, extolling balanced approaches or rationalizing the eclectic practices of teachers, began to be heard even in the earliest days of whole language's ascendancy.[98] Scholars and teachers raised a number of concerns about the assumptions and practices of the whole language movement. Most importantly, they expressed concern about the consequences of whole language outlined earlier in this essay. They questioned the assumption that skills are best "caught" during the pursuit of authentic reading activity rather than "taught" directly and explicitly. They also questioned the insistence on authentic texts and the corollary ban on "instructional" texts written to permit the application of skills within the curriculum. They questioned the zeal and commitment of the movement qua movement, with its strong sense of insularity and exclusivity. Finally, they worried that the press toward the use of authentic literature and literature-based reading would eradicate, albeit unintentionally, what little progress had been made toward the use of informational texts and teaching reading in the content areas.[99]

Ironically, in the past few years, these voices from the middle have found themselves responding not to those who hold a radical whole language position, but to those who hold steadfastly to the phonics first position. Even so, the fact that those with centrist positions were not inclined to defend whole language when the political campaign against it began in the middle 1990s undoubtedly hastened the demise of whole language as the pretender to the title of conventional wisdom.

Changing research ideology.   Prior to the 1980s, qualitative research in any form had little visibility within the reading research community. Among the array of qualitative efforts, only miscue analysis[100] and some early forays into sociolinguistic and anthropological accounts of literacy had achieved much in the way of archival status.[101] But all that changed in the 1980s and early 1990s. Qualitative research more generally, along with more specific lines of inquiry taking a critical perspective on literacy as a social and pedagogical phenomenon, became more widely accepted as part of the mainstream archival literature.[102] Treatises pointing out the shortcomings of traditional forms of quantitative inquiry, especially experimental research, appeared frequently in educational research journals.[103] In terms of curriculum and pedagogy, it is important to remind ourselves that much of the research that undergirds whole language comes from this more qualitative, more interpretive, more critical tradition. Thus the credibility of this type of research increased in concert with the influence of whole language as a curricular movement.

Somewhere in the mid-1990s, the discourse of literacy research began to take a new turn. Stimulated by research supported by the National Institute for Child Health and Human Development, a "new" brand of experimental work began to appear, beginning in the middle 1980s and gathering momentum that has reached a peak in the past year or two.[104] This is experimentalism reborn from the 1950s and 60s, with great emphasis placed upon "reliable, replicable research," large samples, random assignment of treatments to teachers and/or schools, and tried and true outcome measures.[105] This work does not build upon the qualitative tradition of the 80s and early 90s; instead, it finds its aegis in the experimental rhetoric of science and medicine and in the laboratory research that has examined reading as a perceptual process.[106] Although not broadly accepted by the reading education community (at least as of the time when this chapter was put to bed in 1999), this work has found a very sympathetic ear in the public policy arena.[107]

The political positioning of this research is important, but so is its substance. Two themes from this work have been particularly important in shaping a new set of instructional practices—phonemic awareness and phonics instruction.

The absolutely critical role played by phonemic awareness (the ability to *segment* the speech stream of a spoken word and/or to *blend* separately heard sounds into a normally spoken word) in the development of the ability to decode and to read for meaning has been well documented in the past decade and a half.[108] Irrespective of mode of instruction, the overwhelming evidence suggests that phonemic awareness is a necessary but not a sufficient condition for the development of decoding and reading. First, children who possess high degrees of phonemic awareness in kindergarten or early in first grade are very likely to be good readers throughout their elementary school careers.[109] Second, almost no children who are successful readers at the end of grade one exhibit a low level of mastery of phonemic awareness. On the other hand, a substantial proportion of unsuccessful end-of-grade-one readers possess better than average phonemic awareness; this evidence is the critical piece in establishing that phonemic awareness is a necessary but not a sufficient condition for reading success. While we can be confident of its critical role in learning to read, we are less sure about the optimal way to enhance its development. Many scholars have documented the efficacy of teaching it directly, but they also admit that it is highly likely to develop as a consequence of learning phonics, learning to read, or especially learning to write, especially when teachers encourage students to use invented spellings.[110] Research in whole language classrooms suggests that writing is the medium through which both phonemic awareness and phonics knowledge develop—the former because students have to segment the speech stream of spoken words in order to focus on a phoneme and the latter because there is substantial transfer value from the focus on sound-symbol information in spelling to symbol-sound knowledge in reading.[111]

The second consistent thread in the new experimentalism of the 1990s is the simple but undeniable emphasis on the code in the early stages of learning to read. Reminiscent of Chall's earlier conclusions, scholars in this tradition tend to advocate phonics, first, fast, and simple.[112] Less well documented, and surely less well agreed upon, is the optimal course of instruction to facilitate phonics development. Even Philip Gough, a classic bottom-up theorist, while arguing that what distinguishes the good reader from the poor reader is swift and accurate word identification, suggests that an early insistence on reading for meaning may be the best way to develop such decoding proficiency. Both Gough and Connie Juel are convinced that students can learn how to read when they have "cryptoanalytic intent" (a disposition to decipher the specific letter-to-sound codes), phonemic awareness, an appreciation of the alphabetic principle (i.e., regardless of the numerous exceptions, letters do stand for sounds), and "data" (some texts to read and someone to assist when the going gets tough).[113]

After reviewing available instructional evidence, two of the most respected scholars in this tradition, Marilyn Adams and Connie Juel, independently concluded that children can and should learn the "cipher" through a combination of explicit instruction in phonemic awareness and letter-sound correspondences, a steady insistence on invented spellings as the route to conventional spellings in writing activities, lots of opportunity to read connected text (especially when the texts contain enough decodable words to allow students to apply the phonics information they are learning through explicit instruction). Both of these reviewers, known for their sympathies toward instruction in the code, are quick to add that rich experiences with language, environmental print, patterned stories, and "Big Books" should also be a staple of effective early reading instruction.[114]

Politicization of the reading research and policy agenda.   One of the great hopes of educational researchers is that policymakers will take research seriously when they establish policy initiatives at a local, state, or national level. After all, the improvement of educational practice is the ultimate goal of educational research, and policy is our society's most transparent tool for educational improvement. Historically, however, research has been regarded as one among many information sources consulted in policy formation—including expert testimony from practitioners, information about school organization and finance, and evaluations of compelling cases. In the past half decade research, at least selective bits of research, has never been taken more seriously. Several laws in California make direct references to research. For example, in 1998 Assembly Bill 1086 prohibited the use of Goals 2000 money for professional developers who advocated the use of context clues over phonics or supported the use of inventive (sic) spellings in children's writing. The federally sponsored Reading Excellence Act of 1999, which allocated $240,000,000 for staff development in reading, requires that both state and local applications for funding base their programs on research that meets scientifically rigorous standards. The "scientifically rigorous" phrase was a late entry; in all but the penultimate version of the bill, the phrase was "reliable, replicable research," which had been interpreted as a code word for experimental research. As of early 1999, "phonics bills" (bills mandating either the use of phonics materials or some sort of training to acquaint teachers with knowledge of the English sound symbol system and its use in teaching) had been passed or were pending in 36 states.[115]

Policymakers like to shroud mandates and initiatives in the rhetoric of science, and sometimes that practice results in very strained, if not indefensible, extrapolations from research. This has happened consistently in the current reading policy arena. Two examples make the point vividly. First, California Assembly bill 1086, with its prohibition on context clues and invented spelling, represents an ironic application of research to policy. The irony stems from the fact that many of the advocates of a return to code emphasis, such as Marilyn Adams, read the research as supporting the use of invented spellings in the development of phonemic awareness and phonics.[116] Second, the mandate in several states calling for the use of decodable text (usually defined as text consisting of words that could be sounded out using a combination of the phonics rules taught up to that point in the program *plus* some instant recognition of a few highly frequent "sight" words) is based upon the thinnest of research bases. The idea is that children will learn to use their phonics better, faster, and more efficiently if the texts they read permit facile application of the principles they are learning. While it all sounds very logical, there is precious little research evidence to support the systematic and exclusive use of decodable text.[117] This lack of evidence, however, does not seem to have banked the policy fires on this matter.

Professional groups have entered the policy fray in recent years. For example, the American Federation of Teachers has endorsed a particular set of programs as scientifically validated to produce excellent results. Interestingly, each of the programs on their endorsed list is committed to early, systematic, explicit phonics instruction in a highly structured framework. The AFT influence is evident in some other professional movements, such as the Learning First Alliance.[118]

When research moves into the policy arena, one of two outcomes is most likely. If the research is widely accepted by members of the profession from which it comes, widespread acceptance and implementation usually follows. This often occurs in medical, pharmaceutical, or agricultural research. If widespread consensus on what the research says about practice is not reached, then research-based policy initiatives are likely to sharpen and deepen the schisms that already exist, and the whole enterprise is likely to be regarded as a "war" among Balkanized factions within the field. The latter scenario appears to characterize the reading field.[119]

Interestingly, the debate, accompanied by its warlike metaphors, appears to have more life in the public and professional press than it does in our schools. Reporters and scholars revel in keeping the debate alive and well, portraying clearly divided sides and detailing a host of differences of a philosophical, political, and pedagogical nature.[120] Teachers, by contrast, often talk about, and more importantly enact, more balanced approaches. For example, several scholars, in documenting the practices of highly effective, highly regarded teachers, found that these exemplary teachers employed a wide array of practices, some of which appear decidedly whole language in character (e.g., process writing, literature groups, and contextualized skills practice) and some of which appear remarkably skills-oriented (explicit phonics lessons, sight word practice, and comprehension strategy instruction).[121]

Producing measurable results.   Evaluation has always posed a conundrum for whole language supporters. First, some oppose the use of any sort of externally mandated or administered assessments as a matter of principle, holding that assessment is ultimately the responsibility of a teacher in collaboration with a student and his or her parents. Second, even those supporters who are open to external forms of accountability, or at least reporting outside the boundaries of the classroom or school, often claim that standardized tests, state assessments, and other external measures of student accomplishment do not provide sensitive indicators of the goals of curricula that are based upon whole language principles. Most appealing would be assessments that are classroom-based and individualized in nature, with the option of aggregating these sorts of data at the classroom and school levels when accountability comes knocking. During the 1990s, many felt that the increased emphasis on performance assessment and portfolios would fill this need.[122] In an age of high expectations, explicit standards, and school and classroom level accountability, none of these options is a good fit with the views and desires of policymakers and the public. Both of these constituents seem quite uneasy about the quality of our schools and our educational system, so uneasy that leaving assessment in the hands of our teachers seems an unlikely outcome. It is not at all clear to me that the proponents of at least the strong versions of whole language can, or will be willing to, hold themselves accountable to the sorts of measures that the public and policymakers find credible.

Who holds the high ground?   One other factor, both subtle and speculative (on my part) seems to be an undercurrent in the current rhetoric. Whole language has always privileged the role of the teacher as the primary curriculum decision-maker. Teachers, the argument goes, are in the best position to serve this important role because of their vast knowledge of language and literacy development, their skills as diagnosticians (they are expert "kidwatchers"), and the materials and teaching strategies they have at their disposal. And in the arguments against more structured approaches, this is exactly the approach whole language advocates have taken: "Don't make these decisions at the state, district, or even the school level. Arm teachers with the professional prerogative (and corollary levels of professional knowledge) they need in order to craft unique decisions for individual children." While this may seem a reasonable, even admirable position, it has recently been turned into an apology for self-serving teacher ideology.[123] The counter argument suggests that the broad base of privilege accorded to teachers may come at the expense of students and their parents. Thus, those who advocate a strong phonics-first position often take the moral high ground: "We are doing this for America's children (and for YOUR child!) so that they have the right to read for themselves." Even if one opposes this rhetorical move, it is hard not to appreciate the clever repositioning on the part of those who want to return to more phonics and skills.

Taken together, these factors create a policy environment in which whole language seems unlikely to flourish as the mainstream approach to teaching reading and writing. In the final analysis, however, I believe that the reluctance to own up to the "measurable results" standards is the Achilles heel for whole language. If whole language advocates were willing to play by the rules of external accountability, to assert that students who experience good instruction based upon solid principles of progressive pedagogy will perform well on standardized tests and other standards of performance, they would stand a better chance of gaining a sympathetic ear with the public and with policymakers. And as long as the criteria for what counts as evidence for growth and accomplishment are vague or left to individual teachers, the public will continue to question the movement; they will continue to wonder whose interests are being served by an unwillingness to commit to common standards.

LOOKING AHEAD: WILL WE BENEFIT FROM THE LESSONS OF HISTORY?

So where has this journey left us? And where will it take us next? We are, as Regie Routman suggests, at a crossroads.[124] Many recent developments suggest that we are retreating to a more familiar, more comfortable paradigm in which phonics, skills, and controlled text dominate our practices. Other developments suggest that we are on the verge of a new paradigm, a hybrid that weds some of the principles of whole language (integrated instruction and authentic texts and tasks) with some of the traditions of earlier eras (explicit attention to skills and strategies, some vocabulary control of early readers, and lots of early emphasis on the code) in an "**ecologically balanced**" approach to reading instruction.[125] The most cynical amongst us might even argue that we are just riding the natural swing of a pendulum that will, if we have the patience, take us back to whole language, or whatever its child-centered descendant turns out to be, in a decade or so. Before making a prediction about the direction the field will take, let me play out the first two scenarios, phonics first and balanced reading instruction.

ecologically balanced—an approach to reading instruction that pairs some of the desirable principles of the whole language movement with traditions from earlier eras (vocabulary control, phonics, essential skills)

One Alternative for the Future.   If those who have advocated most strongly for a return to phonics and a heavy skills orientation have their way—if they are able to influence federal, state, and local policy as well as the educational publishing industry—we will experience moderate to substantial shifts on most, but not all, of the criteria I put forward as lenses for tracking changes in reading pedagogy over this century (range of materials, range of pedagogical practices, role of teacher, role of student, underlying theory of reading and reading acquisition). As I read their views about policy and practice, the greatest changes will occur at the very earliest stages of learning to read—kindergarten and grade 1. They suggest explicit instruction on phonemic awareness and phonics, with a strong preference for decodable texts in the early grades. When it comes to writing, literature, response, and comprehension, they seem quite content to cede curricular authority to the practices that emerged during the 80s and early 90s, those associated with whole language, literature-based reading, and process writing.[126] Thus, looking broadly at the entire elementary reading curriculum (the range of materials and the range of pedagogical practices), things might, on the surface, look similar to the early 1990s, with some retreat to the 1980s, especially in terms of skill and strategy instruction.

But beneath that curricular surface, major changes would have occurred. For example, the role of the teacher and the learner would have reverted to what they were at the beginning of the century. The role of the teacher would be to transmit the received knowledge of the field, as reflected in research-based curricular mandates, to students. Students would eventually be regarded as active meaning makers, but only after they had received tools of decoding from their teachers. The greatest changes of all would have taken place in the underlying model of reading and reading acquisition. The simple view of reading ($RC = Dec \times LC$) would have returned in full force, and the job of young readers would be to acquire the decoding knowledge they lack when they begin to learn to read.

A Second Alternative.   If those who are pushing for ecological balance carry the day, the field will experience less dramatic shifts. A balanced approach will privilege authentic texts and tasks, a heavy emphasis on writing, literature, response, and comprehension, but it will also call for an ambitious program of explicit instruction for phonics, word identification, comprehension, spelling, and writing. A balanced approach is likely to look like some instantiations of whole language from the early 90s, but recalibrated to redress the unintended curricular consequences outlined earlier in this chapter. Major differences between a balanced approach and the new phonics are likely to manifest themselves most vividly in kindergarten and grade 1, where a rich set of language and literacy experiences would provide the context from which teachers would carve out scaffolded instructional activities to spotlight necessary skills and strategies—phonemic awareness, letter-sound knowledge, concepts of print, and conceptual development. Thus instruction, while focused and explicit, would also be highly contextualized.

Beneath the curricular surface, balanced approaches seem to share slightly more in common, at least on a philosophical plane, with whole language than with new phonics approaches. The teacher is both facilitator and instructor. The teacher facilitates learning by establishing authentic activities, intervening where necessary to provide the scaffolding and explicit instruction required to help students take the next step toward independence. The student is, as in whole language, an active meaning maker from day one of preschool. Reading is a process of constructing meaning in response to texts encountered in a specific context, and the emergent literacy metaphor, not the readiness metaphor, characterizes the acquisition process.

An Ecologically Balanced Approach.   Just in case my personal bias has not emerged, let me declare it unequivocally. I favor the conceptual map of the ecologically balanced approach. There are several reasons for favoring this stance. First, my reading of the research points to the balanced curricular position, not to the new phonics position, both at a theoretical and a pedagogical level. I do not see much support for the simple view of reading underlying the new phonics; readers do construct meaning, they don't just find it lying there in the text. Regarding pedagogical research, my reading requires me to side with Chall's view that while some sort of early, focused, and systematic emphasis on the code is called for, no particular approach can be singled out. And while I readily accept the findings of the phonemic awareness research, I do not read them as supporting drill and practice approaches to this important linguistic understanding; to the contrary, highly embedded approaches, such as invented spelling, are equally as strongly implicated in the research.[127]

Second, an ecologically balanced approach is more respectful of the entire range of research in our field. It does not have to exclude major research paradigms or methodological approaches to sustain its integrity.

Third, an ecologically balanced approach also respects the wisdom of practice. It is no accident that studies of exemplary teachers, those who are respected by their peers and nurture high student achievement, consistently find that they exhibit a balanced repertoire of instructional strategies. Teachers who are faced with the variations in achievement, experience, and aptitude found in today's classrooms apparently need, and deserve, a full tool box.

Finally, an ecologically balanced approach respects our professional history. It retains the practices that have proved useful from each era but transforms and extends them, rendering them more effective, more useful, and more supportive of teachers and students. And it may represent our only alternative to the pendulum-swing view of our pedagogical history that seems to have plagued the field of reading for most of this century. A transformative rather than a cyclical view of progress would be a nice start for a new century.

CONNECTING THE HISTORY OF READING IN THE TWENTIETH CENTURY AND YOUR CLASSROOM . . .

1. Think back carefully to your undergraduate teacher-education program. Record some of the most pivotal movements in reading education in the last 100 years, as well as the first decade of the 21st century. Why is it important for teachers of reading to know and understand these movements and their impact on reading pedagogy today? Be prepared to share your thoughts with your colleagues and professor.

2. Pearson is a self-described member of the "radical middle" in terms of reading instruction. At the end of this essay, he presents two alternatives for the future. Where would you place yourself at this point? How has your own history in the field of teaching reading as well as your history of learning to read affected you as a teacher? What alternatives would you pose in order to best facilitate the teaching of reading in today's classroom? Use your own classroom and/or learning experiences, current research trends, and policies to support your view(s) and be prepared to justify your reasoning with colleagues and the professor.

NOTES

1. See Mitford Mathews, *Teaching to Read* (Chicago: University of Chicago Press, 1996) for an account of the contributions of both these reformers.
2. See Edmund Burke Huey, *The Psychology and Pedagogy of Reading* (New York: Macmillan, 1908) for an extensive account of the methods that prevailed at the last turn of the century.
3. Noah Webster, *The American Spelling Book* (Boston: Isaiah Thomas and Ebenezer Andrews, 1798) was first published a little over two centuries ago. The first of William H. McGuffey's *Eclectic Readers* appeared between 1836 and 1840; for example, William H. McGuffey, *Eclectic Fourth Reader* (Cincinnati: Truman and Smith, 1838). Both were still available for purchase in 1900.
4. Many of the textbooks of the last half of the 19th century explicitly emphasized elocution in the textbooks for the upper elementary grades. See Mathews, *Teaching to Read*.
5. The simple view is a term coined by Philip Gough most probably as a rhetorical counter to the rampant complexity in theories and models of reading developed in the 1970s. See Philip B. Gough and M. L. Hillinger, "Learning to Read: An Unnatural Act," *Bulletin of the Orton Society* 30(1980); 171–176.
6. Matthews, *Teaching to Read*.
7. Matthews, *Teaching to Read*, documents many cases of this general approach to the reform of reading pedagogy dating back to the 1840s in the United States and to the 17th century in Germany.
8. For example, in his popular 1955 book, *Why Johnny Can't Read*, Rudolph Flesch argued that the primary cause of low reading performance during the 40s and 50s was the failure of our schools to teach phonics because of the strong grip of the look-say approach on our nation's teachers and textbook authors.
9. The very best description of the "state of the art" in early reading appears in Huey, *The Psychology and Pedagogy of Reading*.
10. A wonderful example of this approach from the University of Chicago laboratory school appears in Huey, *The Psychology and Pedagogy of Reading*.
11. See Daniel P. Resnick, "History of Educational Testing," *Ability Testing: Uses, Consequences, and Controversies, Volume 2*, eds. A. K. Wigdor and W. R. Garner (Washington, DC: National Academy Press, 1982).
12. A useful account of the assessments dominant in the first third of the century can be found in Gertrude Hildreth, *Bibliography of Mental Tests and Rating Scales* (New York: The Psychological Corporation, 1933).
13. This tradition of isomorphism between the infrastructure of tests and curriculum has been a persistent issue throughout the century. See, for example, Dale D. Johnson and P. David Pearson, "Skills Management Systems: A Critique," *The Reading Teacher*, 1975; and Resnick, "History of Educational Testing." Also see Nila Banton Smith, *American Reading Instruction* (Newark, DE, 1966): 180–186, for an account of the expansion of reading comprehension as a curricular phenomenon.

14. See Smith, *American Reading Instruction*, 259–262, for an account of the emergence of child-centered reading pedagogy. Foundational thinkers for this movement were Johann H. Pestalozzi, *How Gertrude Teaches Her Children* (Syracuse, NY: C. W. Barden Publisher, 1898); Freidrich Froebel, *The Education of Man* (New York: D. Appleton and Company, 1887), John F. Herbart, *Outlines of Educational Doctrine* (New York: Macmillan, 1990).

15. Ironically, it was the field's most ambitious effort in readability by Bormuth in 1966 that provided the closing parenthesis on this 40-year enterprise. John R. Bormuth, "Readability: A New Approach," *Reading Research Quarterly* 1 (1966): 79–132.

16. Smith, *American Reading Instruction*, 259–262.

17. Ibid., 355–56.

18. Even as recently as the influential National Academy of Science Report published in 1998, letter-name knowledge once again emerged as the best predictor of later achievement: Catherine Snow, Susan Burns, and Peg Griffith, *Preventing Reading Difficulties in Young Children* (Washington: National Academy Press, 1998).

19. M. V. Morphett and Carlton Washburne, "When Should Children Begin to Read?" *Elementary School Journal* 31 (1931): 496–501. Arthur J. Gates, "The Necessary Mental Age for Beginning Reading," *Elementary School Journal* (1937): 497–498.

20. See also Benjamin Bloom and Ralph Tyler for accounts of the influence of tests on curriculum.

21. Smith, *American Reading Instruction*, 208–209. By the 1940s, they had expanded to more than 500 pages per student book.

22. Smith, *American Reading Instruction*, 208–229.

23. Smith, *American Reading Instruction*, 231–239.

24. The first book on remedial reading was published in 1922: Clarence T. Gray, *Deficiencies in Reading Ability: Their Diagnosis and Treatment* (Boston: D. C. Heath & Company, 1922). One of the most influential scholars of disability was Arthur I. Gates, *The Improvement of Reading* (New York: Macmillan, 1935).

25. Nowhere is this tension better illustrated than in the contrast between Morphett and Washburne, "When Should Children Begin to Read?" and Gates, "The Necessary Mental Age for Beginning Reading."

26. Mary C. Austin and Coleman Morrison. *The First R.* (New York: Macmillan, 1963).

27. This account is taken from Jeanne Chall, *Learning to Read: The Great Debate* (New York: McGraw Hill, 1967): 13–15.

28. Smith, *American Reading Instruction*, 276.

29. Guy L. Bond and Robert Dykstra, "The Cooperative Research Program in First Grade Reading Instruction," *Reading Research Quarterly* 2: entire issue.

30. The reporting of data for students through grade 2 did not receive the fanfare that the first grade report did, an outcome which I find unfortunate because it was, in many ways, even more interesting. It showed stronger effects overall for code-based approaches, and it revealed the most provocative of all the findings in this entire enterprise—the project effect. The project effect was this: using analysis of covariance to control incoming performance, students were better off being in the poorest performing approach in project A than they were being in the best performing approach in Project B. This raises the whole issue of impact of contextual factors on reading achievement. See Robert Dykstra, "Summary of the Second-grade Phase of the Cooperative Research Program in Primary Reading Instruction," *Reading Research Quarterly* 4 (1968): 49–70.

31. If we were focusing on the impact of these studies on research rather than practice, these issues would occupy more of our attention. In a sense the First Grade Studies created an opening for other research endeavors; indeed, the directions that reading research took in the middle 70s—the nature of comprehension and the role of the teacher—suggest that there were groups of scholars ready to seize the opportunity.

32. When large-scale experiments returned in the early 90s, it was not the Department of Education, but the National Institute of Child Health and Human Development, that led the renaissance. For accounts of the development of the NICHD effort, see G. Reid Lyon,

"Research Initiatives in Learning Disabilities: Contributions from Scientists Supported by the National Institute of Child Health and Human Development," *Journal of Child Neurology* 10: 120–127, or G. Reid Lyon and V. Chhaba, "The Current State of Science and the Future of Specific Reading Disability," *Mental Retardation and Developmental Disabilities Research Reviews* 2: 2–9. It is also worth noting that one of the likely reasons for the demise of Method A vs. Method B experiments is that scholars in the 1960s were looking for main effects rather than interaction effects. Had they set out to find that methods are uniquely suited to particular populations in this work, they might not have rejected them so completely.

33. The impact of Chall's book, particularly the phonics recommendation, was documented by Helen Popp, "Current Practices in the Teaching of Beginning Reading," *Toward a Literate Society: The Report of the Committee on Reading of the National Academy of Education*, ed. John B. Carroll and Jeanne S. Chall (New York: McGraw Hill, 1975).

34. In an unpublished research study completed in 1978, Hansen and Pearson found two- and three-fold increases in the number of words introduced in the first grade books for the popular series published by Scott Foresman and Ginn, Jane Hansen and P. David Pearson, "Learning to Read: A Decade after Chall," unpublished manuscript, University of Minnesota.

35. The teachers' manuals of the Ginn 360 program provide the most notable example of this new trend. See Clymer et al., Ginn 360 (Lexington, Massachusetts: Ginn & Company, 1968).

36. Mastery learning can trace its intellectual roots to works of Benjamin Bloom and John Carroll Benjamin Bloom, "Learning for Mastery," *Evaluation Comment* 1 (1968): entire issue; John Carroll, "A Model of School Learning," *Teachers College Record* 64 (1963): 723–732.

37. For an account of criterion-referenced assessment as it emerged during this period, see James Popham, *Criterion-referenced Measurement.* (Englewood Cliffs, NJ: Prentice-Hall, 1978).

38. Stanley L. Deno, "Curriculum Based Measurement: The Emerging Alternative," *Exceptional Children* 52 (1985): 219–232.

39. Bloom, "Learning for Mastery."

40. The most popular of these systems was the Wisconsin Design for Reading Skill Development, followed closely by Fountain Valley. Their heyday was the decade of the 1970s, although they remained a staple, as an option, through the 80s and 90s and are still available as options in today's basals. For an account of the rationale behind these systems, see Wayne Otto, "The Wisconsin Design, A Reading Program for Individually Guided Education," *Individually Guided Elementary Education: Concepts and Practices*, eds. Herbert J. Klausmeier, Robert A. Rossmiller, and M. Saily (New York: Academic Press, 1977). For a critique of these programs during their ascendancy, see Johnson and Pearson, "Skills Management Systems."

41. This is not to say that there were no challengers to the conventional wisdom that emerged in the middle of the century. To the contrary, the alphabetic approach, now dubbed synthetic phonics, lived a healthy life as a small guerrilla force throughout the period, as did the language experience approach and a few assorted alternatives. See Chall, *Learning to Read,* and Mathews, *Teaching to Read,* for accounts of these programs.

42. It should be noted that a major child-centered reform movement, the open classroom, was creating quite a wave in educational circles and elementary schools throughout the United States in the early 1970s. It is hard, however, to find any direct impact of the open classroom movement on reading instruction. However, one could make the argument that the open classroom philosophy had a delayed impact in its influence on the whole language movement in the late 1980s.

43. Some portions of the text in this section appeared in modified form in P. David Pearson and Diane Stephens, "Learning about Literacy: A 30-year Journey," *Elementary Reading: Process and Practice 4-18*, eds. Christine J. Gordon, George D. Labercane, and W. R. McEachern (Boston: Ginn Press, 1993). (Sections adapted with the knowledge and permission of the co-author and publisher.)

44. To assert that Chomsky laid the groundwork for an essential critique of behaviorism as an explanatory model for language processes is not to assert that he drove behaviorism out of psychology or education.

45. See Roger Brown, *Psycholinguistics* (New York: Macmillan, 1970) for an account of this view of language development.

46. Kenneth G. Goodman, "A linguistic study of cues and miscues in reading," *Elementary English* 42, 639–643: Kenneth G. Goodman, "Reading: A psycholinguistic guessing game," *Journal of the Reading Specialist* 4: 126–135.

47. Frank Smith. *Understanding Reading: A Psycholinguistic Analysis of Reading and Learning to Read* (New York: Holt, Rinehart, & Winston, 1971).

48. In all fairness, it must be admitted that this contribution was not exclusively Smith's. As we shall point out in later sections, many other scholars, most notably David Rumelhart and Richard Anderson, championed constructivist views of reading. It is fair, however, to say that Smith was the first scholar to bring this insight into the reading field. David Rumelhart, "Schemata: The Building Blocks of Cognition," *Theoretical Issues in Reading Comprehension*, eds. Rand J. Spiro, Bertram C. Bruce, and William F. Brewer (Hillsdale, NJ: Erlbaum, 1980). Richard C. Anderson and P. David Pearson, "A schema-theoretic view of basic processes in reading comprehension," eds. P. David Pearson, Rebecca Barr, Michael L. Kamil, and Peter Mosenthal, *Handbook of Reading Research* (New York: Longman, 1984).

49. Frank Smith, "Reading Like a Writer," *Language Arts* 60, 558–567 (1983).

50. During this period, great homage was paid to intellectual ancestors such as Edmund Burke Huey, who as early as 1908 recognized the cognitive complexity of reading. Voices such as Huey's, unfortunately, were not heard during the period from 1915 to 1965 when behaviorism dominated psychology and education.

51. Walter Kintsch and Bonnie Meyer wrote compelling accounts of the structure of exposition that were translated by others (e.g., Barbara Taylor and Richard Beach) into instructional strategies. See Walter Kintsch, *The Representation of Meaning in Memory* (Hillsdale, NJ: Erlbaum, 1974); Bonnie J. F. Meyer, *The Organization of Prose and Its Effects on Memory* (Amsterdam: North Holland Publishing, 1975); Barbara M. Taylor and Richard Beach, "The Effects of Text Structure Instruction on Middle-grade Students' Comprehension and Production of Expository Text," *Reading Research Quarterly* 19: (134–146).

52. The most complete accounts of schema theory are provided by Rumelhart, "Schemata: The Building Blocks of Cognition," and Anderson and Pearson, "A Schema-Theoretic View of Basic Processes in Reading Comprehension."

53. Frederic C. Bartlett, *Remembering.* (Cambridge: Cambridge University Press, 1932).

54. It is not altogether clear that schema theory is dead, especially in contexts of practice. Its role in psychological theory is undoubtedly diminished due to attacks on its efficacy as a model of memory and cognition. See Timothy P. McNamara, Diana L. Miller, and John D. Bransford, "Mental Models and Reading Comprehension," *Handbook of Reading Research, Vol. 2*, eds. Rebecca Barr, Michael Kamil, Peter Mosenthal, and P. David Pearson. (New York: Longman, 1991): 490–511.

55. For early accounts of this perspective, see Joan Baratz and Roger Shuy, *Teaching Black Children to Read* (Washington, DC: Center for Applied Linguistics, 1969). William Labov, *Language of the Inner City.* (Philadelphia: University of Pennsylvania Press, 1972).

56. Baratz and Shuy, *Teaching Black Children to Read.*

57. See David Bloome and Judith Green, "Directions in the Sociolinguistic Study of Reading," *Handbook of Reading Research, Vol. 2:* 395–421.

58. Louise Rosenblatt, *Literature as Exploration.* (New York: Appleton Century Croft, 1936/1978). Louise Rosenblatt, *Reader, Text, and Poem* (Carbondale, IL: Southern Illinois University Press: 1978).

59. Rosenblatt credits the idea of transaction to John Dewey, who discussed it in many texts, including *Experience and Education* (New York: Kappa Delta Pi, 1938).

60. A very interesting, even provocative attempt to understand comprehension processes appears in Edward L. Thorndike, "Reading as reasoning: A study of mistakes in paragraph reading." *Journal of Educational Psychology* 8: 323–332. The classic reference for using tests to reveal the psychological infrastructure of comprehension is the first published factor

analysis of reading comprehension by Frederick Davis, "Fundamental Factors of Reading Comprehension," *Psychometrika* 9 (1944): 185–197.

61. *Sixty-seventh Yearbook (1968), Part II, Innovation and Change in Reading Instruction,* edited by Helen M. Robinson.

62. Dolores Durkin published an infamous study in 1978 documenting the fact that what went on in the name of comprehension was essentially completing worksheets and answering questions during story discussions. She saw almost no instruction about how to engage in any sort of comprehension task—no modeling, no demonstration, no scaffolding. Dolores Durkin, "What Classroom Observations Reveal about Reading Instruction," *Reading Research Quarterly* 14: 481–533.

63. Among the most notable efforts at the Center were the classic work on reciprocal teaching: Annemarie Palincsar and Ann L. Brown, "Reciprocal teaching of comprehension fostering and monitoring activities," *Cognition and Instruction* 1 (1984): 117–175; T. E. Raphael and P. D. Pearson, "Increasing students' awareness of sources of information for answering questions." *American Educational Research Journal* 22: 217–236; and explicit comprehension instruction as a general approach in P. D. Pearson and J. Dole, "Explicit comprehension instruction. A review of research and a new conceptualization of instruction." *Elementary School Journal* 88. no. 2: 151–165. P. D. Pearson, "Changing the face of reading comprehension instruction," *The Reading Teacher* 38: 724–738. This focus on comprehension and reasoning while reading continues even today at the Center with the work of Anderson and his colleagues.

64. The work of Paris and his colleagues is exemplary in the area of metacognitive training and comprehension monitoring (S. G. Paris, D. R. Cross, & M. Y. Lipson, "Informed strategies for learning: A program to improve children's reading awareness and comprehension," *Journal of Educational Psychology* 76: 1239–1252).

65. Michael Pressley, working in conjunction with a group of professionals in Montgomery County, Maryland, developed a set of powerful comprehension routines that, among other things, extended the four strategies of Reciprocal Teaching (questioning, summarizing, clarifying and predicting) to include more aspects of literary response (e.g., personal response and author's craft). The best resource on this line of pedagogical research is a 1993 volume of *Elementary School Journal* edited by Pressley, along with these articles, one of which is from that volume: M. Pressley et al., "Transactional instruction of comprehension strategies: The Montgomery County, Maryland, SAIL Program," *Reading and Writing Quarterly* 10: 5–19; M. Pressley et al., "Beyond direct explanation: Transactional instruction of reading comprehension strategies," *Elementary School Journal* 92: 513–555.

66. KWL, an acronym for a graphic organizer technique in which students chart, before and after reading, what they *know,* what they *want* to know, and what they *learned* is an interesting phenomenon because while it has attracted a great deal of curricular attention in basals, articles for practitioners and staff development materials, it is hard to find much research on its instructional efficacy. See Donna Ogle, "The K-W-L: A Teaching Model that Develops Active Reading of Expository Text," *The Reading Teacher* 39: 564–570.

67. Isabel Beck and Margaret McKeown have spent several years, in collaboration with a network of teachers perfecting this engaging practice which focuses on how and why authors put text together the way they do. The net result of this routine is that students learn a great deal about how to read critically (what is the author trying to do to me as a reader?) and about authors' craft (how do authors structure their ideas to achieve particular effects). See Beck et al., *Questioning the Author: An Approach for Enhancing Student Engagement with Text* (Newark, DE: International Reading Association, 1997).

68. Chall, in the 1991 edition of *Learning to Read,* documented this important increase in basal comprehension activities.

69. Chall devotes a section to individualized reading in her 1967 description of alternatives to the basal (pp. 41–42), but has little to say about it as a serious alternative to basal, phonics, or linguistic approaches. In that same period, it is undoubtedly Jeanette Veatch who served as the most vocal spokesperson for individualized reading. She published professional

textbooks describing how to implement the program in one's class (*Individualizing Your Reading Program* (New York: G. P. Putnam's Sons, 1959)). In the middle 1960s, Random House published a "series" of literature books that were accompanied (in a pocket on the inside cover) by a set of vocabulary and comprehension activities that look remarkably like basal workbook pages. The Random House materials remind one of the currently popular computer programs. Accelerated Reader, which is similarly designed to manage some assessment and skill activity to accompany trade books that children read on their own.

70. Richard C. Anderson, Elfrieda Hiebert, Judith Scott, and Ian Wilkinson, *Becoming it Nation of Readers* (Champaign, IL: Center for the Study of Reading: 1984). Anderson and his colleagues reported several studies documenting the impact of book reading on children's achievement gains.

71. Nancie Atwell, *In the Middle: Writing, Reading, and Learning with Adolescents.* (Portsmouth, NH: Heinemann, 1987). While it is difficult to locate data to document these claims about Atwell's particular influence, the rise of literature in the middle school has been documented by changes in the teacher survey portion of the National Assessment of Educational Progress of Reading.

72. Hoffman and his colleagues painstakingly documented these sorts of changes in the early 90s basals. James V. Hoffman, Sarah J. McCarthey, J. Abbott, C. Christian, L. Corman, M. Dressman, B. Elliot, D. Matheme, and D. Stable, "So what's new in the "new" basals," *Journal of Reading Behavior* 26 (1994): 47–73.

73. For a complete account of the Book Club movement, see *The Book Club Connection* by Susan L. McMahon and Taffy E. Raphael with Virginia Goatley and Laura Pardo (New York: Teachers College Press, 1997).

74. Two classic books by Donald Graves, *Writing: Teachers and Students at Work* (Portsmouth, NH: Heinemann, 1983) and *A Researcher Learns to Write* (Portsmouth, NH: Heinemann, 1984), were influential in leading the process writing movement at the elementary level, as was Lucy Calkins' classic, *The Art of Teaching Writing* (Portsmouth, NH: Heinemann, 1986).

75. Perhaps the most complete current reference on integrated curriculum is a new chapter in the third volume of the *Handbook of Reading Research* by James R. Gavelek, Taffy E. Raphael, Sandra M. Biondo, and Danhua Wang, "Integrated Literacy Instruction," in *Handbook of Reading Research*, Vol. 3, eds. Michael L. Kamil, Peter Mosenthal, P. David Pearson, and Rebecca Barr (Hillsdale, NJ: Erlbaum, in press).

76. In Chapter 10 of Huey's 1908 book on reading, two such programs, one at Columbia and one at the University of Chicago, were described in rich detail. It is Dewey's insistence that pedagogy be grounded in the individual and collective experiences of learners that is typically cited when scholars invoke his name to support integrated curriculum.

77. See Graves (1983) for an explication of his views on writing and Hansen (1987) for an account of how reading and writing support one another in an integrated language arts approach.

78. Frank Smith and Robert Tierney and P. David Pearson carried this metaphor to the extreme. All three used the reading "like a writer" metaphor in titles to papers in this period. Frank Smith, "Reading like a writer," *Language Arts* 60 (1983): 558–567; Robert J. Tierney and P. D. Pearson, "Toward a composing model of reading," *Language Arts* 60 (1983): 568–580; P. D. Pearson and Robert J. Tierney, "On becoming a thoughtful reader; Learning to read like a writer," eds. Alan Purves and Olive Niles, *Reading in the Secondary School.* National Society for the Study of Education 83rd year-book (Chicago: National Society for the Study of Education), pp. 144–173.

79. Donald Doldaway, *The Foundations of Literacy,* summarizes this perspective and work.

80. The notion of significance here is intended to capture its impact, not its validity. Even those who question its validity would have difficulty discounting its influence on practice.

81. Patrick Shannon, *The Struggle to Continue* (Portsmouth, NH: Heinemann; 1990) provides a rich account of the curricular antecedents of whole language and other progressive and critical pedagogies. See also Yetta Goodman, "Roots of the Whole-language Movement,"

Elementary School Journal 90: 113–127. The phrase, the child as curriculum informant, comes from Jerome Harste, Carolyn Burke, and Virginia Woodward, *Language Stories and Literacy Lessons* (Portsmouth, NH: Heinemann, 1984).

82. One cannot possibly name all the important leaders of the whole language movement in the United States, but surely the list will be headed by Ken Goodman, Yetta Goodman, and Jerry Harste, all of whom wrote important works explicating whole language as a philosophical and curricular initiative.

83. In the 3rd edition of *Learning to Read,* Chall makes the case that phonies instruction increased during the 1970s and began its decline in the middle 1980s at the time when comprehension became a dominant research and curricular issue. She also notes a further decline in phonics instruction in basals, based on the work of Hoffman et al., "So What's New in the New Basals" in 1993. On this issue, one should also consult Kenneth G. Goodman, Patrick Shannon, Yvonne Freeman, and Sharon Murphy, *Report Card on Basal Readers* (Katonah, NY: Richard C. Owen, 1988).

84. My understanding of the primary focus of the opposition to basals is that whole language advocates regarded basals as a pernicious form of external control on teacher prerogative, one that would lead inevitably to the "de-skilling" of teachers. In 1988, several whole language advocates and supporters wrote a monograph documenting what they took to be these pernicious effects (Goodman, Freeman, Shannon, and Murphy, 1988).

85. See Hoffman et al., "What's New in the New Basals?"

86. Perhaps the most compelling sign of the backgrounding of skills was their systematic removal from the pupil books. In the middle and even late 1980s, basal companies featured skills lessons in the pupil books on the grounds that even teachers who chose not to use the workbooks would have to deal with skills that were right there in the student materials. By the early 90s, as I noted earlier, they were out of the student books.

87. One must keep in mind that I am discussing changes in published materials, not necessarily changes in classroom practice. Whether teachers changed their actual classroom practices in a matter consistent with, or at least proportional to, the basal practices is difficult to determine given our lack of broad-based data on classroom practices. One suspects that the pendulum swings of actual classroom practice are never quite as wide as the swings in the rhetoric of policy or even the suggestions in published materials.

88. P. David Pearson, *"RT* Remembrance: The second 20 years," *The Reading Teacher* 45 (1992): 378–385. This analysis documents the increasingly dominant force of whole language, literature-based reading and process writing in the discourse of elemental reading and language arts instruction.

89. Perhaps the best documentation for the resistance to, or at least a more critical acceptance of, whole language practices comes from studies of exemplary teachers who, it appears, never bought into whole language lock, stock, and barrel but instead chose judiciously those practices which helped them to develop rich, flexible, and balanced instructional portfolios. See Ruth Wharton-MacDonald, Michael Pressley, and J. M. Hampton, "Literacy instruction in nine first-grade classrooms: Teacher characteristics and student achievement," *The Elementary School Journal* 99 (1998): 101–128.

90. Leigh Ann Martin and Elfrieda H. Hiebert, *Little Books and Phonics Texts: An Analysis of the New Alternatives to Basals* (Ann Arbor: Center for the Improvement of Early Reading Achievement/University of Michigan, in press). This analysis of the basals adopted in the early 1990s in California suggests that the vocabulary load of many of these basals was so great that most first graders could gain access to them only if they were read to them by a teacher.

91. In the late 1970s, Marie M. Clay coined the term *emergent literacy* to signal a break with traditional views of readiness in favor of a more gradual view of the shift from novice to expert reader.

92. In my own case, it was the disdain that whole language seemed to spawn regarding the implicit teaching of skills and strategies, especially those that promoted the meaning-making goals of the movement—comprehension and metacognitive strategies. See Marie

M. Clay, *Emergent reading behavior.* Unpublished doctoral dissertation, University of Auckland, Auckland, NZ (1966).

93. Elfrieda H. Hiebert and Barbara M. Taylor, eds., *Getting Reading Right from the Start: Effective Early Literacy Interventions* (Boston: Allyn and Bacon, 1994) describes several research-based interventions that balance skills instruction with authentic reading.

94. Interestingly, a recent piece in *The Reading Teacher* makes exactly this point about the comprehension strategy instruction of the 80s. See Sarah L. Dowhower, "Supporting a Strategic Stance in the Classroom: Comprehension Framework for Helping Teachers Help Students to be Strategic," *The Reading Teacher* 52(7), pp. 672–689.

95. Smith, "Learning to Read like a Writer" makes just this point.

96. For a compelling account of this "no text" phenomenon, watch for Ruth Schoenbach, Cyndy Greenleaf, Christine Cziko, and Lori Hurwitz, *Reading for Understanding in the Middle and High School* (San Francisco: Jossey-Bass, in press). In this account the staff developers and teachers of a middle school academic literacy course document the role of text in middle school as well as attempts to turn the tide.

97. Similar arguments have been made for the reform movements in mathematics, i.e., that the reforms got out ahead of the professional knowledge base; the results of the reform movement in mathematics have also been similar to the fate of the whole language movement. See Thomas Good and J. Braden. *Reform in American Education: A Focus on Vouchers and Charters* (Hillsdale, NJ: Erlbaum).

98. In 1989, a special interest group with the apocryphal label of Balanced Reading Instruction was organized at the International Reading Association. The group was started to counteract what they considered the unchecked acceptance of whole language as *the* approach to use with any and all students and to send the alternate message that there is no necessary conflict between authentic activity (usually considered the province of whole language) and explicit instruction of skills and strategies (usually considered the province of curriculum-centered approaches). For elaborate accounts of balanced literacy instruction, see Ellen McIntyre and Michael Pressley, *Balanced Instruction: Strategies and Skills in Whole Language* (Boston, MA: Christopher-Gordon, 1996); Linda B. Gambrell, Lesley M. Morrow, Susan B. Newman, and Michael Pressley, *Best Practices in Literacy Instruction.* (New York: Guilford Publications, 1999); P. David Pearson, "Reclaiming the Center," in *The First R: Every Child's Right to Read,* eds. Michael Graves, Paul van den Broek, and Barbara M. Taylor (New York: Teachers College Press, 1996).

99. Pearson details many of these concerns and arguments in "Reclaiming the Center."

100. As early as 1965, Kenneth Goodman had popularized the use of miscues to gain insights into cognitive processes. The elaborate version of miscue analysis first appeared in Yetta Goodman and Carolyn Burke, *Reading Miscue Inventory* (New York: Macmillan, 1969).

101. See Larry F. Guthrie and William S. Hall, "Ethnographic Approaches to Reading Research," and David Bloome and Judith Greene, "Directions in the Sociolinguistic Study of Reading," in *Handbook of Reading Research,* for an index of the rising momentum of qualitative research in the early 1980s.

102. As a way of documenting this change, examine the *Handbook of Reading Research,* volumes I (1984) and II (1991). Volume II contains only two chapters that could be construed as relying on some sort of interpretive inquiry. Volume II has at least eight such chapters. For an account of these historical patterns in non-quantitative inquiry, see Marjorie Siegel and Susana L. Fernandez, "Critical Approaches," in *Handbook of Reading Research,* Vol. 3, in press.

103. Starting in the mid 1980s and continuing until today, the pages of *Educational Researcher* began to publish accounts of the qualitative-quantitative divide. It is the best source to consult in understanding the terms of the debate.

104. For an account of the evolution of this line of inquiry, consult Reid Lyon, "Research initiatives in learning disabilities. Contributions from scientists supported by the National Institute of Child Health and Human Development," *Journal of Child Neurology* 10, 120–126 (1995) and Reid Lyon and Vinita Chhaba, "The current state of science and the

future of specific reading disability," *Mental Retardation and Developmental Disabilities Research Reviews* 2, 2–9 (1996).

105. The most highly touted pedagogical experiment supported by NICHD was published in 1998; Barbara R. Foorman, David J. Francis, Jack M. Fletcher, Christopher Schatschneider, and Paras Mehta, "The role of instruction in learning to read: Preventing reading failure in at-risk children." *Journal of Educational Psychology* 90 (1998): 37–55. The NICHD work in general and the Foorman et al. piece in particular has been cited as exemplary in method and as supportive of a much more direct code emphasis, even in the popular press (e.g., *Dallas Morning News*, May 12, 1998; *Houston Chronicle*, May 17, 1998: *Minneapolis Star Tribune*, August 5, 1998).

106. Much is made in this new work of the inappropriateness of encouraging young readers to use context clues as a way of figuring out the pronunciations of unknown words. The data cited are eye-movement studies showing that adult readers appear to process each and every letter in the visual display on the page and, most likely, to then recode those visual symbols into a speech code prior to understanding.

107. Richard Allington and Haley Woodside-Jiron, "Thirty Years of Research in Reading: When Is a Research Summary Not a Research Summary?" in Kenneth S. Goodman, *In Defense of Good Teaching* (York, MF.: Stenhouse, 1998). These writers document the manner in which Bonnie Grossen's unpublished manuscript *30 years of research: What we now know about how children learn to read* (Santa Cruz: The Center for the Future of Teaching and Learning Web document: http//www.cftl.org/30years/30years, 1997), which is an alleged summary of the research sponsored by NICHD, was used in several states as the basis for reading policy initiatives.

108. Classic references attesting to the importance of phonemic awareness are Connie Juel, "Beginning Reading," *Handbook of Reading Research, Vol. 2*, edited by Rebecca Barr, Michael Kamil, Peter Mosenthal, and P. David Pearson. (New York: Longman, 1991): 759–788; and Adams, *Beginning to Read*. More recently, it has been documented in Snow, Burns, and Griffith, *Preventing Reading Difficulties in Young Children*.

109. See Connie Juel, "Beginning Reading."

110. See Connie Juel, "Beginning Reading," and Adams, *Beginning to Read*.

111. The work of Linda K. Clarke, "Invented versus traditional spelling in first graders' writings. Effects on learning to spell and read," *Research in the Teaching of English* 22(3), 281–309 and Pamela Winsor and P. David Pearson, *Children at-risk: Their phonemic awareness development in holistic instruction* (Tech. Rep. No. 556), Urbana: Center for the Study of Reading, University of Illinois are most relevant on the issue of the various curricular routes to phonemic awareness development.

112. One entire issue of *American Educator* was devoted to the phonics revival in 1995 (the Summer issue: Vol. 19, no. 2). Authors of various pieces included those who would generally be regarded as leaders in moving phonics back onto center stage—Marilyn Adams, Isabel Beck, Connie Juel, and Louisa Moats, among others. A second issue was also devoted entirely to reading (Spring/Summer, 1998: Vol. 22, no. 1 and 2). The piece by Marilyn J. Adams and Maggie Bruck ("Resolving the Great Debate," *American Educator* 19 (1995), 7, 10–20 is one of the clearest expositions of the modern phonics first position I can find.

113. See Connie Juel, "Beginning Reading," in 1991, and Gough and Hillinger, 1980.

114. One of the reasons for the continuation of the debate is that few people seek common ground. Researchers who come from the whole language tradition, were they to read Adams and Juel openly, would find much to agree with about in the common privileging of big books, writing, invented spelling, and the like. They would not even disagree with them about the criminal role that phonemic awareness or knowledge of the cipher plays in early reading success. They would, however, disagree adamantly about the most appropriate instructional route to achieving early success; phonics knowledge and phonemic awareness are better viewed, they would argue, as the consequence of, rather than the cause of, success in authentic reading experiences.

115. These and other reading policy matters have been well documented in a series of pieces in *Education Week* by Kathleen Manzo Kennedy (1997, 1998, 1999).

116. Marilyn Adams (see *Beginning to Read* and Adams and Bruck, "Resolving the Great Debate") has consistently championed invented spelling.

117. Richard Allington and Hallie Woodside-Jiron, "Decodable test in beginning reading: Are mandates and policy based on research?" *ERS Spectrum,* Spring 1998, 3–11. Allington and Jiron-Ironside have conducted a pretty thorough analysis of the genesis of this "research-based" policy and concluded that it all goes back to an incidental finding from a study by Juel and Roper-Schneider in 1983. They could find no direct experimental tests of the efficacy of decodable text.

118. Learning First Alliance, *Every Child Reading* (Washington, DC: Learning First Alliance, 1999).

119. The war metaphor comes up time and again when the debate is portrayed in the public press. See, for example, Art Levine, "The Great Debate Revisited," *Atlantic Monthly,* December 1994.

120. Kathleen K. Manzo, "Study stresses role of early phonics instruction," *Education Week* 16(24), March 12, 1997, pp. 1, 24–25; Kathleen K. Manzo, "New national panel faulted before it's formed," *Education Week* 17 (23), 1998a, p. 7; and Kathleen K. Manzo, "NRC panel urges end to reading wars," *Education Week* 17(28), March 25, 1998, pp. 1, 18.

121. Several studies are relevant here. First is the work of Wharton-McDonald and Pressley, cited earlier. Also important is the work of Pressley and Allington, 1998, and Taylor, Pearson, Clark, and Walpole, in press.

122. See Pearson, DeStefano, and García, 1998, for an account of the decrease in reliance on portfolio and performance assessment.

123. An interesting aside in all of the political rhetoric has been the question of who is de-skilling teachers. As early as the 1970s, whole language advocates were arguing that canned programs and basal reader manuals were de-skilling teachers by providing them with preprogrammed routines for teaching. Recently, whole language has been accused of the de-skilling, by denying teachers access to technical knowledge needed to teach reading effectively. Elizabeth McPike, "Learning to Read: The School's First Mission," *American Educator* 19 (1995), 4.

124. Written from a somewhat centrist whole language position, Regie Routman's *Literacy at the Crossroads* (Portsmouth. NH: Heinemann, 1996) provides a compelling account of the political and pedagogical issues we confront in the current debates.

125. The *balance* label comes with excess baggage. I use it only because it has gained currency in the field. Balance works for me as long as the metaphor of ecological balance, as in the balance of nature, is emphasized and the metaphor of the fulcrum balance beam, as in the scales of justice, is suppressed. The fulcrum, which achieves balance by equalizing the mass on each side of the scale, suggests a stand-off between skills and whole language— one for skills, one for whole language. By contrast, ecological balance suggests a symbiotic relationship among elements within a coordinated system. It is precisely this symbiotic potential of authentic activity and explicit instruction that I want to promote by using the term, *balance.*

126. Adams and Bruck, "Resolving the Great Debate"; Marilyn Adams, *Beginning to Read: Thinking and Learning About Print* (Cambridge, MA: MIT Press, 1990); Jack Fletcher and G. Reid Lyon, "Reading: A research based approach," in *What's Gone Wrong in America's Classrooms?,* ed. W. Evers (Stanford, CA: Hoover Institution Press).

127. See the earlier cited studies by Clarke and Winsor and Pearson, as well as the review of phonemic awareness in Adams, *Beginning to Read.*

Summary of Early Reading Recommendations in National Research Syntheses P. David Pearson

SOURCE ISSUE/FEATURE	BOND AND DYKSTRA, FIRST GRADE STUDIES, 1967	CHALL, LEARNING TO READ: THE GREAT DEBATE, 1967	ANDERSON, HIEBERT, SCOTT, & WILKINSON, BECOMING A NATION OF READERS, 1985	ADAMS, BEGINNING TO READ: THINKING AND LEARNING ABOUT PRINT, 1990	SNOW AND BURNS, PREVENTING READING DIFFICULTIES, 1998	NATIONAL READING PANEL, 2000
Methods preference	Not explicitly mentioned BUT lots of evidence for code advantages AND Virtual all methods were superior to the Look-Say basal	Code over meaning in grades 1 and 2, BUT . . . ▪ Good teaching still needed ▪ Does not apply to all pupils or schools (believe the data) ▪ Will not cure all our ills	Not explicitly mentioned, but balance of early phonics and lots of reading/ writing is implied	Code with reading of meaningful connected text ▪ Balance all over the place	Code with reading of meaningful connected text and (by implication) decodable text	Systematic Phonics
How/when should phonics be taught	Word study skills should be taught systematically	▪ No particular preference ▪ First, fast, and out!	No one approach singled out: ▪ Should be well-designed and concentrated in Grades 1 and 2	▪ First grade conclusion: No consistent advantage for code over meaning, but non-basal is consistently superior to basal ▪ Linguistic good at word recognition but lacking in comprehension ▪ Late: Consistent advantage for code	Code over meaning in grades 1 and 2, BUT . . . ▪ Good teaching still needed ▪ Does not apply to all pupils or schools (believe the data) ▪ Will not cure all our ills	▪ Strongest effects are early on, in first grade, not much evidence for phonics beyond grade 2 ▪ In conjunction with a rich curriculum ▪ No preference for analytic vs synthetic

(Continued)

Summary of Early Reading Recommendations in National Research Syntheses P. David Pearson

SOURCE ISSUE/FEATURE	BOND AND DYKSTRA, FIRST GRADE STUDIES, 1967	CHALL, LEARNING TO READ: THE GREAT DEBATE, 1967	ANDERSON, HIEBERT, SCOTT, & WILKINSON, BECOMING A NATION OF READERS, 1985	ADAMS, BEGINNING TO READ: THINKING AND LEARNING ABOUT PRINT, 1990	SNOW AND BURNS, PREVENTING READING DIFFICULTIES, 1998	NATIONAL READING PANEL, 2000
Phonemic awareness	Not really dealt with, but phoneme discrimination was the #2 predictor	Not explicitly dealt with except as a predictor of later achievement	Implicit in K and phonics recommendations	Teach, but in conjunction with 1-s instruction	Teach, nurture, practice!!!	■ Teach it explicitly for a total of 18 hours early on ■ With letter sound instruction ■ In small groups
Preferred text for early readers	■ Lots more words lots faster; those programs that introduced a lot had better results. Better balance between HF and regular words	■ Loosen vocabulary control ■ Lots of folk/fairy tales ■ Re-evaluate grade levels	Interesting and comprehensible, with opportunity to apply phonics	Meaningful text supplemented by decodable text ■ Fairly easy to read	Seems to have been finessed in conclusion (lots of meaningful text), but some decodable text is implied	■ No evidence for the use of decodable text
Instruction before "formal" reading	Not much said	Alphabet ■ Lots of language and meaning emphasis in K	■ Letters and their sounds ■ reading ■ writing ■ oral language	■ Read alouds!!! ■ Talk about text ■ Language experience ■ Phonemic awareness ■ Letter names ■ Print Awareness	■ Read alouds!!!! ■ Oral language ■ Phonological awareness ■ Print awareness ■ Alphabetic Principle ■ Form/function relations	■ Phonemic awareness works with students before kindergarten

Role of writing in learning to read	All for it. Note the advantage of ITA and LEA and phonic-linguistic	Not a part of the scope of inquiry	Lots more needed ■ helps reading in many ways	■ Very important, in its own right and to support phonemic awareness (inv spel), phonics, and text understanding	■ Important in its own right and helps with phonemic awareness and phonics	Not a part of the scope of inquiry
Invented spelling	Note the ITA finding of greater # of words in writing sample	Not a part of the scope of inquiry	■ Implied in writing recommendation	■ Important means to discovering phonemic awareness and letter sound knowledge	■ Highly encouraged (not in conflict with goal of correct spelling) as a means of nurturing phonemic awareness and phonics knowledge	Not a part of the scope of inquiry
Role of comprehension instruction	Not a part of the scope of inquiry	■ Not too much to deal with in early readers ■ Very important later on	■ More time to direct instruction in comprehension ■ Discussion also important	Little is said, little is implied, but comprehension as a goal is central	■ Important from the outset, but do it early on with read-aloud books ■ Emphasize conceptual knowledge	Essential, especially strategy instruction and vocabulary instruction
Reading to children	Not a part of the scope of inquiry	Not a part of the scope of inquiry	Parents need to do it frequently	Parents and teachers should nurture active involvement	■ Absolutely pivotal in Pre-K and K	Not a part of the scope of inquiry
Primary forms of practice	Not a part of the scope of inquiry, but basal workbooks are criticized	Not a part of the scope of inquiry	Less time in workbooks, more time reading and writing	Read a lot. Workbooks OK if well-designed with clear purpose	■ Daily practice with easy tests plus some exposure to challenging texts	Not a part of the scope of inquiry

(Continued)

Summary of Early Reading Recommendations in National Research Syntheses P. David Pearson

SOURCE / ISSUE/FEATURE	BOND AND DYKSTRA, FIRST GRADE STUDIES, 1967	CHALL, LEARNING TO READ: THE GREAT DEBATE, 1967	ANDERSON, HIEBERT, SCOTT, & WILKINSON, BECOMING A NATION OF READERS, 1985	ADAMS, BEGINNING TO READ: THINKING AND LEARNING ABOUT PRINT, 1990	SNOW AND BURNS, PREVENTING READING DIFFICULTIES, 1998	NATIONAL READING PANEL, 2000
Just plain reading	Not a part of the scope of inquiry	Not a part of the scope of inquiry	■ Dramatic increases needed ■ Schools need better libraries	■ Very important, including independent reading, practice reading (e.g., repeated reading, pairs, etc.)	■ Critical! both easy reading to consolidate skills and challenging reading to promote new learning	Concludes the evidence for using school time is inconclusive
Teacher education	Pointed to as the most likely path to improved student learing	Not a part of the scope of inquiry	■ Five years of preparation and lots more content	Not a part of the scope of inquiry	■ LOTS of knowledge-based requirements for pre-service	Not a part of the scope of inquiry
Professional development	Implied but not specified	Yes, with an emphasis on program specific ventures	Foucs on better in-duction programs	Not a part of the scope of inquiry	■ Local programs and life-long support for personal professional development	Professional development for teaching reading comprehension works
Assessments	Not a part of the scope of inquiry	Important because they can give teachers more freedom in using methods and materials (outcome accountability) ■ Single component tests (alphabetic principle, comprehension, critical reading, appreciation) ■ Absolute, not relative, standards for cross-time comparisons	More comprehensive assessments needed ■ Fluency ■ Summarize and evaluate text ■ Amount of reading and writing	Not a part of the scope of inquiry	■ Need to conduct a lot of validity research on current tools	Not a part of the scope of inquiry

Special interventions for kids at risk	Not a part of the scope of inquiry	▪ Essential problems lie in code-knowledge, not comprehension ▪ Best remedial strategies are code-based with decodable text	Not addressed, except in Jeanne Chall's afterword	RR mentioned but topic not highlighted	▪ High on those that use highly trained professional tutors ▪ Limited role for volunteers (read to, talk to) ▪ Effective elements: Same as for garden-variety readers	Not a part of the scope of inquiry
Home literacy practices	Not a part of the scope of inquiry	Not a part of the scope of inquiry	▪ Read aloud and discuss stories ▪ Informal letter and word learning	No explicit recommendations, but lots of reading aloud and language play is implied	▪ Read alouds ▪ Language activities	Not a part of the scope of inquiry

HISTORICAL FOUNDATIONS OF READING

HELPFUL WEB SITES

Brief History

http://www.hishelpinschool.com/reading/history.html
http://www.liveink.com/whatis/history.htm
http://spencer.lib.ku.edu/exhibits/monaghan/case1.htm
http://www.zona-pellucida.com/wilson10.html
http://www.cloudnet.com/~edrbsass/educationhistorytimeline.html
http://www.indiana.edu/~reading/ieo/bibs/histread.html
http://www.reading.org/Resources/ResourcesbyTopic/HistoryOfReading/Overview.aspx
http://www.google.com/search?q=history+of+reading+instruction+in+america&hl=en&tbs=tl:
1&tbo=u&ei=n5BySpWfG4WcsgPHo7nUCA&sa=X&oi=timeline_result&ct=title&resnum=11
http://www.historyliteracy.org

History of the Alphabet

http://www.phoenician.org/alphabet.htm
http://www.ancientscripts.com/phoenician.html
http://www.guide-to-symbols.com/phoenician/
http://www.historyworld.net/wrldhis/PlainTextHistories.asp?historyid=ab33
http://www.historian.net/hxwrite.htm

Writing

http://www.viddler.com/explore/iewtv/videos/4/

Hornbook

http://thenonist.com/index.php/thenonist/permalink/the_humble_hornbook/
http://www.iupui.edu/~engwft/hornbook.html

Phoenicians Alphabet

http://phoenicia.org/alphabet.html

Alice and Jerry

http://www.tagnwag.com/alice_jerry.html
http://www.hiddenstaircase.com/new/alicejerry.html

Basal Readers

http://clarke.cmich.edu/schoolhouse/schoolsbibforbasal.htm

Dick and Jane; Think-and-Do

http://www.pan-tex.net/usr/j/julie/ju25000.htm
http://www.loganberrybooks.com/coll-dick-jane.html

Webster's Syllabary/Blue Back Speller

http://www.thephonicspage.org/On%20Reading/webstersyllabary.html
http://www.merrycoz.org/books/spelling/SPELLING.HTM
http://www.answers.com/topic/noah-webster

THEORETICAL PERSPECTIVES: INTERSECTION OF TEXT AND THE READER

INTRODUCTION

Teaching is both an art and a science. In particular, when considering the intersection of where the text and the reader meet, theory plays a pivotal role in teachers being able to successfully guide students in the process of making meaning.

Theories can help explain the reading process—to neophyte and experienced teachers alike. For our purposes here, consider a theory to be a statement or set of statements that set out to explain a certain set of widely accepted phenomena or facts (The American Heritage Dictionary of the English Language, 2003).

Therefore, the interactions between readers and texts have become elements of or entire theories in and of themselves. This interaction is at the heart of how reading and meaning-making are explained. As researchers test theories and analyze the results of the studies they conduct, models of the reading process have been proposed throughout the twentieth century. These include top-down (Smith and Goodman); bottom-up (Gough); interactive (Ruddell and Speaker; Rummelhart); transactional (Rosenblatt; Goodman); and affective (Mathewson) models.

No single theory or approach can thoroughly explain the reading process for all readers. Along that line of thought, then, the more perspective a teacher can bring to the teaching table, so to speak, the more tools that teacher can utilize, therefore giving the teacher a better chance of assisting learners in being successful readers.

One chapter in this section considers how to define text in the digital age of the 21st century. Another considers various factors that impact a reader's likelihood of being successful with his or her first experiences interacting with text.

There are also three classic pieces in this section: Anderson on schema theory; Bransford's response to Anderson, which helps amplify the concept of schema acquisition; and Louise Rosenblatt's timeless description of the transaction that results in the poem—the meaning-making that occurs between reader and text as they interact with one another.

Questions will linger, even after you finish reading this section of our book, questions about what really does constitute a text and how to teach for success, particularly when readers come to the classroom with such a potpourri of varied experiences, cultures, languages, and cognitive abilities. Critical questions will remain and new questions will be generated through the reading of these chapters. This section lays the foundation for students to formulate their own definitions of such pivotal concepts as reading, reader, and text, as well as to ponder the ways in which all these things are intricately interconnected.

REFERENCE

The American Heritage® Dictionary of the English Language, 4th ed. (2003). Retrieved January 29, 2009, from http://www.thefreedictionary.com/theory.

Alignment of Readings in Section II to the International Reading Association's *Standards for Reading Professionals 2010* (Draft):

Standard 1: Foundational Knowledge
1.1; 1.2; 1.3
Standard 2: Curriculum and Instruction
2.1; 2.2 (postreading activities); 2.3

Standard 4: Diversity
4.1; 4.2; 4.3 (postreading activities)
Standard 6: Professional Learning and Leadership
6.1 (postreading activities); 6.3

Intersection of Text and the Reader Timeline

1915	Saussure's *Course in General Linguistics* first published
1926	Piaget uses the term schema
ca 1932	Frederic Bartlett uses the terms schema in his writing in psychology and education
1938	Louise Rosenblatt's seminal work *Literature as Exploration* published; response to New Criticism
1930s–1950s	New Criticism dominant literary theory in English/language arts classrooms
1967	Smith and Goodman; *The Psycholinguistics Guessing Game*
1960s–early 1970s	Sociolinguistics (Labov, Baratz, and Shuy) and psycholinguistics (Smith and Goodman) are new, developing fields
1969	Ryan and Semmel publish "Reading as a Constructive Language Process" in *Reading Research Quarterly* Stauffer *Teaching Reading as a Thinking Process*
1970s	Schema theory movement is popular
1970s	Text theorists' publications begin to influence literary theory; later, in the 1990s become more prevalent in education (i.e., intertextualitly; Kristeva; Roland Barthes; Derrida; Fouccoult)
1970	Hal Herber publishes *Content Area Reading*—the seminal, modern textbook concerning the teaching of reading in the content areas
1971	Frank Smith's *Understanding Reading*
1973	Kenneth Goodman's *Miscue Analysis* first published through National Council of Teachers of English
1976	The Center for the Study of Reading established with U.S. Department of Education funding
1978	Louise Rosenblatt's work *The Reader, the Text, the Poem: The Transactional Theory of the Literary Work* published; discusses efferent and aesthetic reading stances as well as the *active* role of the reader Applebee's *Child Concept of Story* published
1978	Dolores Durkin's study, which was an analysis of teachers' instructional comprehension strategies; gist of study was that teachers measure comprehension rather than explicitly teach it; due to Durkin's study, a focus/increase of interest in comprehension occurred in the 1980s
Early 1980s to early 1990s	Whole language movement
1980s	Mikhail Bakhtin's works translated from Russian to English; published in the West; Bakhtin's original work first appeared in Russia in the 1920s and was brought to light in the West by French semiotician Julia Kristeva
1981	Beck and McKoewn; story mapping first developed Stanley Fish's *Is There a Text in this Class?* published; discusses the idea of interpretive communities

(Continued)

Intersection of Text and the Reader Timeline

1985	*Becoming a Nation of Readers: The Report of the Commission on Reading*
1986	Nancie Atwell's *In the Middle* first published
Late 1980s	Initial research on the DIBELS program begins at the University of Oregon
1990	M. Y. Adams' *Beginning to Read: Thinking and Learning about Print*—reaction to whole language
Mid-1990s to present	Accountability and reform movement; high-stakes testing Technology advances are starting to appear in classrooms and schools; a broader view of literacy and text begin to develop (Leu, Gee, Luke, New London Group) More teachers are incorporating technology and computer programs in their instruction and assessment of literacy Book Clubs and then Literature Circles used in teaching literature in the classroom
1997	Keene and Zimmerman's *Mosaic of Thought: Teaching Comprehension in a Reader's Workshop* published; focus on comprehension
2000	National Reading Panel asserts the five "big" components of literacy: fluency, vocabulary, comprehension, phonics, and phonemic awareness
2001	*No Child Left Behind Act*
2002	First year of funding for the Reading First Grant Program; DIBELS widely used as an assessment in RF program—deemphasize learner comprehension

CHAPTER 3

WHAT IS TEXT?
A TWENTY-FIRST CENTURY DEFINITION

MARY KATHERINE KALLUS

THINK ABOUT **DEFINING TEXT . . .**

1. What image or images come to mind when you hear the word *text*?

2. Read to find out about a view of text that can enhance your teaching and consider how this view of text can help your students connect their content learning to their lives—in and out of school.

Imagine you are a student sitting in a classroom; the teacher walks in and begins: "Good afternoon, class, please take out your text; turn to page 85, and begin reading with me. . . ." Students who live in a world where they send text messages or e-mails on cell phones and other portable devices more than they talk to their colleagues and friends face to face will have a much different view about text and how to utilize it for learning in this digital age in which we live. Is this textbook scenario what you imagine when you hear the word *text*?

Although texts used in classrooms traditionally refer to "textbooks," a text is more than just written material (Hartman, 1992). A text can be as small as an utterance, spoken or written. A text can also include visual texts such as dance, art, theatre, movies, and television shows. It can be either a linguistic or nonlinguistic sign—anything that has meaning (Bakhtin, 1986; Berger, 1984; Hartman, 1992; Hartman & Hartman, 1993; Saussure, 1915, 1974). "*Signs are things which stand for other things* or . . . *anything that can be made to stand for something else* [original italicized]" (Berger, p. 1). Saussure stated that a sign is made up of two elements, the concept (signified) and the sound-image (signifier) (see also Berger). Signs can be a text or a part of a text.

The traditional definition of text has been almost exclusively limited to written words on a page. The word *text* itself is derived from the Latin *textus,* meaning "woven" or "to weave" Many theorists (e.g., Bahktin, 1981, 1986; Barthes, 1977; Hartman, 1991a, 1991b, 1992, 1995; Kristeva, 1980) have described a text as something that is woven; with a wax and wane; a woof and a tweeter. This idea of texts weaving themselves between each other creates a beautiful mosaic as a backdrop for this discussion of what a text is.

Very rarely were some linguistic and most nonlinguistic texts considered in a traditional definition of text. Prior to the turn of the millennium and throughout the first decade of the 21st century, the definition of text has changed and continues to do so (e.g., Alvermann, Moon, & Hagood, 1999; Bean, Bean, & Bean, 1999; Hartman, 1992; Kallus, 2003; Wade & Moje, 2000). Leu (2000) states that since technology is **deictic**, so too is literacy. As the technology with which we communicate advances, so too do the texts we use to communicate—to read and comprehend. Why then is there little evidence teachers, administrators, or publishing companies are aware of and willing to adapt the curriculum to this change in what is considered a text? Rarely do they use—or value—the wide variety of linguistic and nonlinguistic texts available in the classroom (i.e., Wade & Moje, 2000).

> **deictic**—describes a word whose meaning changes with the discourse and/or context in which it is written or stated, that is, then, now, presently

Traditionally, there are many more linguistic texts used in classrooms than nonlinguistic texts (see Alvermann et al., 1999; Bean et al., 1998; Hartman & Hartman, 1993; Kallus, 2003). "Linguistic texts include written materials such as stories, chapters, articles, poems, and essays" (Hartman & Hartman, p. 203). With a broader view of text, many nonlinguistic texts should be considered and used in the classroom (see Hartman & Hartman; Short, 1992). Nonlinguistic texts include ". . . types of materials that can be 'read,' such as film, video, drama, dance, music, photography, or painting[s] . . ." (Hartman & Hartman, p. 203; see also Barthes, 1977).

The definition of text in the early 21st century encompasses the thoughts and writings of many 20th-century theorists such as Mikhail Bakhtin (1986), Roland Barthes (1977), James Paul Gee (1992), Douglas Hartman (1991a, 1991b, 1995), Julia Kristeva (1980), and Louise Rosenblatt (1974/1994, 1938/1995). These theorists set the stage; created the tone for the researchers of the late 20th century and early 21st century when concerning the ever-changing idea of what is a text.

Bakhtin (1986) stated that "[t]he text is the unmediated reality (reality of thought and experience). . . . Where there is no text, there is no object of study, and no object of thought either" (p. 103). When considering text broadly, "as any coherent complex of signs" (p. 103), then not only written texts, but also works of art, are texts. According to Bakhtin, there are also verbal texts or "utterance[s]" (p. 104), as well as "human act[s] that can [be] . . . potential text[s]" (p. 107).

Bakhtin (1986) stated: "The event of the life of the text, that is, its true essence, always *develops on the boundary between two consciousnesses, two subjects*" (p. 106; italics in the original). This is where two texts meet. The "ready-made

reactive text—the text that is created by the reader while in the process of reading the original text on paper

dialogic—relating to dialogue

heteroglossia—diversity of voices, points of view, or discourse in a type of literary work

[text] and the **reactive text** being created—and, consequently, the meeting of two subjects and two authors" (p. 107)—occurs. Further, "the text is not a thing . . ." (p. 107) and the perceiver of the text's consciousness cannot be "eliminated or neutralized" (p. 107). Therefore, the text is "an expression of consciousness, something that reflects" (p. 113) subjectively on the objective world in which we live. That is, the text is a type of juxtaposition; ". . . a reflection of a reflection" (p. 113).

Kristeva (1980) used Bakhtin's (1986) ideas of text, the **dialogic** and **heteroglossia** to build her foundation of text:

> . . . Bakhtin was one of the first to replace the static hewing out of texts with a model where literary structure does not simply *exist* but is generated in relation to *another* structure. What allows a dynamic dimension to structuralism is his conception of the 'literary word' as an *intersection of textual surfaces* rather than a *point* (a fixed meaning), as a dialogue among several writings: That of the writer, the addressee (or the character), and the contemporary or earlier cultural context. (Kristeva, pp. 64–65)

Kristeva's view of text is that it is created from "a mosaic of quotations" (p. 66). What is traditionally called a novel has a type of texture where various strands of the fabric are collected from verbal practices and previous written works (see also Barthes, 1977; Hartman, 1991a).

Barthes (1977) wrote at length about text, suggesting there are several "approaches" (p. 156) to his view of text. This first approach is that "[t]he Text [original capitalized] is not to be thought of as an object that can be computed" (p. 156) but rather ". . . a process of demonstration, speak[ing] according to certain rules (or against certain rules) . . . the text is held <u>in</u> [emphasis added] language" (p. 157). There might be "'text' in a very ancient work, while many products of contemporary literature are in no way texts" (p. 156). Barthes marks the difference as such: "the work is a fragment of substance, occupying a part of the space of books (in the library for example), the Text [original capitalized] is a methodological field" (pp. 156–157). Further, Barthes notes that a work can be seen and even held in one's hand. The text, rather, is held in language; it is a "process of demonstration" (p. 157).

Barthes (1977) differentiates between work and text. The work occupies part of a space of books, whereas the text does not necessarily occupy a physical space. A work, then, would be like what one might find in a library, for instance—"a fragment of substance" (p. 156). "Text is a methodological field" (p. 157). Barthes relates this difference to "Lacan's distinction between 'reality' and 'the real': the one is displayed, the other demonstrated . . ." (p. 157). The work, according to Barthes, can be seen; it is usually something tangible that can be held. The text, however, ". . . is . . . held in language, only exist[ing] in the movement of a discourse . . ." (p. 157). Barthes emphasizes, *"the Text is experience only in an activity of production"* (p. 157; italics in the original). Text, according to Barthes, does not stop—for example, on the shelf in a library—but rather is movement that can cut across the work or several works.

The second approach that Barthes (1977) outlines is that the text does not end at "(good) Literature [original capitalized]" (p. 157). There is no way to classify a text or even a writer under the constraints of literary manuals into a specific genre. According to Barthes, this is due to the proliferation of texts that cannot fall under one particular genre, for example. Barthes states that the text, therefore, is *"paradoxical"* (p. 158; italics in the original). The text is constrained in a sense by what it is considered to be, yet, at the same time, pushes the boundaries of general opinion of what is a text.

In his third approach, Barthes (1977) describes the difference between the work and the text, stating that the work is *"moderately* symbolic" (p. 158) and that the text is *"radically* symbolic" (p. 158). The work, then, becomes a type of "general sign" (p. 158). Further, the work is finite, "something to be sought" (p. 158). This relates to the teaching of literature with one "right" answer to or interpretation of what the author means in his or her writing—New Criticism (Rosenblatt, 1974/1994, 1938/1995; Wilhelm, 1997). The text, on the other hand, can never close and is not centered. The text is **"metonymic"** (Barthes, 1977, p. 158). The text creates associations and carryovers for the reader. It is something that is created by the reader and the **intertextual** associations that play off one another.

> **metonymic**—the substitution of one word or phrase for another; i.e., using the term "the White House" to represent "the President"

> **intertextual**—adj.—derived from the noun, intertextuality; the idea that a reader connects his or her prior experiences and knowledge with linguistic and nonlinguistic texts he or she reads

Barthes (1977) asserts that text is plural. He describes the etymological background of text as meaning a "tissue, a woven fabric" (p. 159). Barthes suggests that throughout the text, ". . . citation, references, echoes, cultural languages . . . cut across [the text] through and through in a vast stereophony" (p. 160). The meaning of a text is created through intertextual weavings of prior texts. One cannot determine the sources or influences of a text. Barthes stated:

> The intertextual in which every text is held, it itself being the text-between of another text, is not to be confused with some origin of the text; to try to find the 'sources', the 'influences' of a work, is to fall in with the myth of filiation; the citations which go to make up a text are anonymous, untraceable, and yet *already read*: they are quotations without inverted commas. (p. 160)

Text lessens the distance that exists between reading and writing, asking the reader to play the text. Comparing text to a musical score, Barthes states that there must be a collaboration that exists between the reader and the text.

Barthes's fourth approach to text relates to the plurality of the text. He describes the works and texts as unfriendly and boring without this idea of playing with the text on the part of the reader. It is the pleasure of the text, which he suggests is different from pleasure derived from reading a work. In reading a work, there is the idea of pleasure in the consumption of them, but these texts cannot be rewritten since no one writes like that any longer. Barthes cites reading authors such as Proust, as allowing the reader to gain pleasure from reading works. Text, on the other hand, is bound to a pleasure without separation (*"jouissance"*). In other words, there is a type of transparency in the language and social relations where languages circulate and meaning is created through the intertextual ebb and flow found in texts. An example of this is when someone is reading a text, then he or she creates meaning and there is a pleasure in this meaning, or internal writing, of a text. This view of text is similar to Rosenblatt's (1974, 1994) aesthetic reading as a "lived through" (p. 29) experience.

Barthes (1977), however, asserts that these approaches are in no way a "Theory of the Text" (p. 164). A "Theory of the Text" (p. 164) cannot be satisfied in a "metalinguistic exposition" (p. 164), by which he means that discourse "on the Text should itself be nothing other than text, research, [and] textual activity" (p. 164). The text then becomes a "social space" (p. 164), where no language is safe nor is any subject the analyst or decoder. There is no one single, correct way in which to "write" a text. Barthes sees the reader as the writer of a text (using intertextual connections to create meaning; see also chapter 7 in this book by Rosenblatt on transaction).

Of Barthes's (1977) discussion of text, citations, as Barthes refers to them, cannot be sourced. They are *already read* (p. 160; see also Bakhtin, 1981, 1986; Kristeva, 1980). They come from the experiences, knowledge, and understandings of the reader and the author.

One of the most overlooked, yet influential theorists in America is Louise Rosenblatt (Booth, 1995). Rosenblatt studied the transaction that occurs between a reader and a text in order to create meaning for more than 60 years. It is from this discussion and understanding of transaction that Rosenblatt (1974/1994, 1938/1995) discusses what a text is. Rosenblatt differentiates between text and poem, stating, "'text' designates a set or series of signs interpretable as linguistic symbols" (1974/1994, p. 12). In reading, "'the text' may be thought of as the printed signs in their capacity to serve as symbols" (p. 12). Her definition of text is limiting in the sense that she defines text in reading as what is present on a page, referring to print as:

> . . . a set of black marks on ordered pages or [expanding it to speech, where there is] . . . a set of sounds reverberating in the air, waiting for some reader or listener to interpret them as verbal symbols and under their guidance, to make a work of art, the poem or novel or play. (p. 13)

Therefore, a text is *anything* that stands without meaning until the reader transacts with it in order to create meaning.

Gee (1992) states that in order to give a text its meaning there is a certain amount of orality that must take place: ". . . one has to produce either out loud or 'in one's head,' *another text* where this other text is one's spoken interpretation of the original text or the mental representation of the original text one has stored in one's head" (p. 13). The second text, as described by Gee, is a type of translation of the first text into "our 'own words'" (p. 13) in order to give some meaning to the first text that had been read.

As awkward as this sounds, Gee (1992) stated that this is necessary because ". . . the original text was nothing all by itself until we interpreted it . . . translated it into another text" (p. 13). Through bringing past knowledge and experiences to a reading, the reader creates "another text" (p. 13). Gee describes this process as somewhat paradoxical because it is a process that takes place infinitely because interpretation of a text is "always just another text in 'other words'" (p. 13). Further, translation (whether it is the same language or a different language) can differ each time the text is read depending on the context in which it is read. Text has a certain structure that helps the reader create this translation.

Hartman (1991a) defined text by suggesting that text is "a flexible unit of meaning" (p. 16). Text does not have to be confined to the printed page. It can be ". . . those experiences that are 'remembered' or 'constructed' by a person in memory from physical text(s)" (p. 16). A text can be a piece of music, a piece of art (i.e., sculptures, photographs, paintings, and comic strips), drama, an utterance, or even a gesture (Hartman, 1992; Hartman & Hartman, 1993). Further, a text is "any kind of *sign* that communicates some meaning" (1991a, p. 16; see also Bakhtin, 1981, 1986; Hartman, 1992). Therefore, a text can include "both linguistic *and* nonlinguistic *signs*" (1992, p. 296). Hartman (1991a) further proposes that texts can be of various sizes and can occur at many different levels. It can be a long discourse, a single word, or idea, or concept, or structure, for example, any chunk of meaning (Hartman, 1991a, 1992; see also Rowe, 1987).

Hartman (1992) stated that text is "never an *ex-nihilo* (i.e., out of nothing) creation; it presupposes other texts and has a multiplicity of sources" (p. 296; see also Hartman, 1991a). Hartman (1992; see also Barthes, 1977; and others) describes the Latin derivation of the word text, meaning a woven structure or fabric, "suggest[ing] that the composition of any text is interwoven with previous resources that give it a particular texture, pile, and grain" (Hartman, p. 297). Here, Hartman's (1992) discussion of text suggests that texts are woven from things that are in our past, our knowledge, or our situations in life, thus creating a type of fabric where texts cut across other texts and become interconnected.

Therefore, text is more than what is written on a page; text is anything from which meaning can be created, whether it is linguistic or nonlinguistic in nature. Text can be an utterance, a conversation, a work of art, a piece of music, a gesture, or even a piece of media created for television or the movies, or the Internet. As suggested by Bakhtin (1986), Barthes (1977), Hartman (1991a, 1992), and Kristeva (1980), there is no text that stands alone; rather, texts build upon one another and through the intertextual links that readers bring to the text.

CONNECTING A BROADER VIEW OF TEXT AND YOUR CLASSROOM . . .

1. Find a lesson you are scheduled to teach soon that could lend itself to the use of a variety of texts—for example, both linguistic and nonlinguistic texts—and not just "the textbook." Plan to utilize a variety of texts to teach the lesson. How do you think this lesson was different than one based on the context of using a traditional text?
2. Once you have completed this lesson, choose three students from your class to interview. Use students whose backgrounds and ability levels differ. Inquire as to how using these various texts impacted their learning. Be prepared to report your findings to classmates and your instructor.

REFERENCES

Alvermann, D. E., Moon, J. S., & Hagood, M. C. (1999). *Popular culture in the classroom: Teaching and researching critical media literacy.* Newark, DE: International Reading Association.

Bakhtin, M. M. (1981). *The dialogic imagination: Four essays* (C. Emerson, & M. Holquist, Trans.). (M. Holquist, Ed.). Austin, TX: University of Texas Press.

Bakhtin, M. M. (1986). *Speech Genres and Other Late Essays* (V. W. McGee, Trans.). (C. Emerson & M. Holquist, Eds.). Austin, TX: University of Texas Press.

Barthes, R. (1977). *Image—Music—Text* (Selected and Trans. By Stephan Heath). New York: Hill and Wang.

Bean, T. W., Bean, S. K., & Bean, K. F. (1999). Intergenerational conversations and two adolescents' multiple literacies: Implications for redefining content area literacy. *Journal of Adolescent Literacy, 42*(6), 438–448.

Berger, A. A. (1984). *Signs in contemporary culture: An introduction to semiotics.* New York: Longman.

Booth, W. (1995). Forward. In L. Rosenblatt *Literature as exploration* (4th ed., pp. vii–xiv). New York: Modern Language Association of America. (Original work published 1938)

Gee, J. P. (1992). *The social mind: Language, ideology, and social practice.* New York: Bergin and Garvey.

Hartman, D. K. (1991a). *Eight readers reading: The intertextual links of able readers using multiple passages.* Unpublished doctoral dissertation, University of Illinois, Urbana, IL.

Hartman, D. K. (1991b). The intertextual links of readers using multiple passages: A postmodern/semiotic/cognitive view of meaning making. In J. Zutell, & S. McCormick (Eds.), *Learner factors/teacher factors: Issues in literacy research and instruction: 40th Yearbook of the National Reading Conference.* Chicago: The National Reading Conference, Inc.

Hartman, D. K. (1992). Intertextuality and reading: The text, the reader, the author, and the context. *Linguistics and Education, 4,* 295–311.

Hartman, D. K. (1995). Eight readers reading: The intertextual links of proficient readers reading multiple passages. *Reading Research Quarterly, 30*(3), 520–561.

Hartman, D. K., & Harman, J. A. (1993). Reading across texts: Expanding the role of the reader. *The Reading Teacher, 47*(3), 202–211.

Kallus, M. K. (2003). *Intertextuality and multiple text use: Three case studies of 'at-risk' middle level learners.* Unpublished doctoral dissertation, Texas Tech University, Lubbock, TX.

Kristeva, J. (1980). *Desire in language: A semiotic approach to literature and art.* (T. Gora, A. Jardine, & L. S. Roudiez, Trans.). New York: Columbia University Press.

Leu, D. J., Jr. (2000). Literacy and technology: Deictic consequences for literacy education in an information age. In M. L. Kamil, P. B. Mosenthal, P. D. Pearson, & R. Barr (Eds.), *Handbook of Reading Research: Volume III* (pp. 743–770). Mahwah, NJ: Lawrence Erlbaum Associates.

Rosenblatt, L. (1974/1994). *The reader, the text, the poem*. Carbondale and Edwardsville, IL: Southern Illinois University Press. (Original work published 1974)

Rosenblatt, L. (1938/1995). *Literature as exploration* (4th ed.). New York: Modern Language Association of America. (Original work published 1938)

Rowe, D. W. (1987). Literacy learning as an intertextual process. In J. E. Readence & R. S. Baldwin (Eds.), *Research in literacy: Merging perspectives. Thirty-sixth Yearbook of the National Reading Conference* (pp. 101–112). Rochester, NY: National Reading Conferece.

Saussure, F. (1974). *Course in general linguistics*. (C. Bally, A. Sechehaye, & A. Reidlinger, Eds.; Wade Baskin, Ed.). London: Peter Owen. (Original work published in 1915)

Short, K. G. (1992). Intertextuality: Searching for patterns that connect. In C. K. Kinzer, & D. J. Leu (Eds.), *Literacy research, theory, and practice: Views from many perspectives: 41st Yearbook of The Naitonal Reading Conference* (pp. 187–197). Chicago: The National Reading Conference, Inc.

Wade, S. E., & Moje, E. B. (2000). The role of text in classroom learning. In M. L. Kamil, P. B. Mosenthal, P. D. Pearson, & R. Barr (Eds.), *Handbook of reading research* (Vol. 3, pp. 609–627). Mahwah, NJ: Lawrence Erlbaum Associates, Pulbishers.

Wilhelm, J. D. (1997). *"You gotta BE the book": Teaching engaged and reflective reading with adolescents*. New York: Teachers College Press.

CHAPTER 4

WHO IS THE READER? COGNITIVE, LINGUISTIC, AND AFFECTIVE FACTORS IMPACTING READERS

JEANNE B. COBB AND PATRICIA WHITNEY

THINK ABOUT THE READER AND FACTORS IMPACTING THE READER . . .

1. Before you read, make a list of multiple factors impacting the success of today's readers. Add any additional factors as you read the chapter.
2. Read to find out why linguists classify all languages, including nonstandard dialects, as "good." How does the teacher's attitude toward a child's language affect the child's success in reading?
3. Read to find out about cultural collision and reading.
4. Reflect on the relationship between rewards and learning to read. In our busy schools, is it unrealistic to assume that children will be intrinsically motivated to learn?

Consider these different readers:

Reader 1:

Juan is 5 years old and can understand what people say to him in English and can communicate with the kids in his neighborhood. His mom and dad speak only Spanish and are proud of Juan's ability to speak English and to interpret for them on occasion. On the first day of school, Juan is dressed in his best outfit and is anxious to begin his new adventure. The teacher is calling out the names of the children. She stumbles because she can't pronounce Juan's last name. All the other children seem to already know the routines and what to do. Juan feels lost and alone.

Reader 2:

Terrence is a freshman in college, and it is the second day of Biology 101 class. He has read a complicated introductory chapter last night but realizes he doesn't really remember much of what he read. The professor poses a question and calls on Terrence. His heart is racing and his mind goes blank.

Reader 3:

Tara is 9 years old and in the third grade. She is excited because her dad brought home the latest *Harry Potter* book last night. He promised that they would be reading it together just as they have read all the other ones. The teacher has just announced DEAR time and Tara can't wait to begin her new book.

Reader 4:

The middle school seventh graders are finishing a social studies group project and are about to share with the class. Tony is a student with a learning disability whose task is to read aloud the introduction to the group's project. He is nervous and anxious because he knows he will stumble over the words the group has composed for him to read. He practiced and practiced at home last night until he could read it perfectly, but when he steps up in front of the class, it's a different story. He dreads the moment when giggles will come from some of his classmates, but he knows he has to step forward and do his part in order to earn a good grade for his group.

The readers in today's classrooms are diverse with unique abilities and needs, just as the students who are described in the preceding vignettes. Some of these readers are confident, mature, and quite efficient. Others are struggling beginners who laboriously sound out each word they encounter. Some of the readers are highly motivated, avid readers with specific purposes, as varied as the genres they choose. Other readers are **alliterate**; they can read well, but they choose not to read. In this chapter, the focus will be on the reader and what the reader brings to the text.

> **alliterate**—being able to read, but choosing not to read, being disinterested in reading

Public school demographics are changing rapidly. Data based on 2005 surveys from the National Center for Education Statistics (2007a) reveal that between 1972 and 2007, the percentage of public school Caucasian students decreased from 78% to 56%, while the percentage of students from other racial/ethnic groups increased from 32% to 44%. This increase reflects primarily the growth in the percentage of students who were Hispanic. Penny (2008) reiterates that the trend for young children entering public schools over the next decade is toward increasing diversity, with teachers facing classrooms in which non-Caucasian children outnumber Caucasian children by 2042.

Many of the readers in today's schools are non-Caucasian youth born in the United States of immigrant parents who do not speak English as their first language. This is particularly true in large urban areas. A University of Southern California study shows that 94% of students in the Los Angeles Unified School District are learning English as a second language ("Education taxed by non-English speaking kids," 2005). These same children and youth experience disparate treatment in medical and dental health when compared to children growing up in households where English is the primary language spoken, according to Dr. Glenn Flores, who analyzed data from the National Survey of Children's Health (Children in non-English-speaking households face many health disparities, researcher concludes, 2008). Not only do their language issues create barriers for them in receiving full access to literacy skills, but their difficulties in receiving proper health care also prevent them from arriving at school physically strong and mentally alert for learning. When reviewing 2006 statistics addressing the percentage of all students who qualify for limited-English-proficiency (LEP) services, it is evident that English language learners will be increasing over the next decade and will need special attention in today's public school classrooms. Data reveal that 9.4% of the total U.S. enrollment is qualified for LEP instructional services, with 36.3% of those students speaking Spanish as their native language (U.S. Department of Education, Office of Civil Rights, 2006).

Poverty characterizes the lives of many readers in today's elementary and high school classrooms. According to data from the National Center for Education Statistics (2007b), 15.9% of children and youth under age 18 are growing up in poverty, a number that has doubled since 1990. Children of poverty are limited in their opportunities to engage in literacy activities in their home environments due to a lack of resources and materials. Also, problematic for children of poverty is the fact that many of these households are headed by adults who have minimal literacy skills themselves. In the richest country on earth, 23% of adult Americans—44 million men and women—are functionally **illiterate** and cannot read the front page of a newspaper or the warning labels on poison bottles (Tharoor, 2002). Although low-income homes may be rich in the literacies of their cultures and possess valuable funds of knowledge, the teacher, who is often of a different ethnic and socioeconomic group, may fail to capitalize on these home literacies (Moll, Amanti, Neff, & Gonzalez, 1992).

> **illiterate**—unable to read or write at a basic level as measured by ability to read the front page of a newspaper or poison warning labels

Another characteristic of today's readers is that many are not succeeding in our public schools. More than 8 million students in grades 4–12 are struggling readers (Biancarosa & Snow, 2006). A large number of children and youth in public schools are identified as eligible for special education services. This characteristic also presents unique challenges for educators. About 12% of students receive special education in at least one of the grades kindergarten through third grade, including 16% of boys, 8% of girls, 18% of children in poverty, and 10% of children classified as nonpoverty. One in three students who receive special education in early grades will first receive special education in kindergarten ("Timing and duration of student participation in special education in the primary grades," 2007). Latest available data from the Office of Special Education, U.S. Department of Education, reports a total of 4,421,464 students ages 3 through 21 being served in special education programs, both inclusion and self-contained settings, in the fall of 2007, with 67% of those students being male and 33% female (OSEP State-Reported Data, 2007).

FACTORS THAT IMPACT THE READER

The International Reading Association *Literacy Dictionary* uses the words of Samuel Taylor Coleridge to define *reader* and to distinguish between four different types of readers (Harris & Hodges, 1995):

> The first [reader] is like the hour-glass; and their reading being as the sand, it runs in and runs out, and leaves not a vestige behind. A second is like the sponge, which imbibes everything, and returns it in nearly the same state, only a little dirtier. A third is like a jelly-bag . . . retaining only the refuse and the dregs. And the fourth . . . the slaves in the diamond mines of Golconda, who, casting aside all that is worthless, retain only pure genius. (p. 205)

All teachers would prefer to have classrooms filled with the fourth category of readers, but that is not the case. Readers come in all shapes, sizes, ages, and ability levels. From the four vignettes of readers, it is apparent that reading is a complex, multidimensional process, impacted by a number of factors. When a student fails to become an efficient reader, it is generally an issue of the convergence of a number of multiple factors. Rarely can one factor be identified as the sole cause for a reading problem (Monroe, 1932). In a classic research study conducted by Robinson (1946), it was established that the major factors contributing to reading difficulties generally fell into four major categories: physical factors, psychological factors, educational factors, and socioeconomic factors. Later researchers continued to point to this multiple causation theory and identified additional factors contributing to reading difficulties, including cognitive/intellectual, linguistic, and affective issues, with consensus that no one single factor can be pinpointed as the sole reason for a student's failure to succeed in reading (Ekwall & Shanker, 1988; Gillet, Temple, & Crawford, 2004; Harris & Sipay, 1990; Mathewson, 1994).

Often, the source of reading difficulties can be found within the reader. Ruddell and Speaker (1985) proposed one of the first comprehensive interactive models of the reading process and identified existing knowledge structures within each reader that significantly impact the message the reader gains from the text. Those structures include declarative and procedural knowledge gained about language, decoding, and worldly information. Similarly, Rumelhart (1985, 1994) recognized that the reading process was dependent on several essential knowledge sources brought to the printed page by the reader, including syntactic knowledge, lexical knowledge, semantic knowledge, and letter name knowledge. Ruddell and Speaker also pointed out that students utilize several knowledge sources while controlling and, at the same time, being under the influence of certain internal processes or states: cognitive or intellectual, linguistic, and affective. The seminal works by these researchers built on the early research of Robinson (1946) and delineated, with complex descriptions and visual flowcharts, categories of factors impacting readers and the reading process. The types and levels of information from each of these knowledge systems and the efficiency with which a reader applies the knowledge he or she brings to the text will vary with each reader who interacts with the same text. Thus, as Rosenblatt (1978) declared, in ideas revolutionary for that time, the "poem" or "literary work of art" will be a different and unique creation, depending on what each reader brings to that text and the point in time when the reader interacts with the text (p. 12).

Cognitive/Intellectual Factors Impacting the Reader

Cognition refers to knowing, thinking, reasoning, and judging. From the beginnings of reading research, cognitive issues have dominated the field, with an overemphasis on the impact of these factors on reading development and achievement (Alexander & Filler, 1976). Numerous studies have documented the relationship between intelligence and reading ability. Often, however, those studies were contradictory. On the one hand, research pointed to a lack of correlation between intelligence and success in beginning reading, except in special cases of highly gifted and/or severely mentally challenged individuals. Yet, studies revealed that competent readers tend to perform better on intelligence tests than do struggling readers. This becomes more evident with older readers when the nature of the reading task becomes closely related to comprehension and interpretive, evaluative thinking (Gillet et al., 2004; Harris & Sipay, 1990; Spache & Spache, 1977).

> Reading does not begin suddenly. . . . Reading is no one single skill alone . . . When a child has the chance to hear one good story after another, day after day, he is being taught to read. When his kindergarten year is a series of mind-stretching eye-filling trips, helping him know more solidly his world, he is being taught to read. . . . When he creates with blocks, when he communicates with paint, when he uses his body freely as a means of expression, he is being taught to read. When a child stares, fascinated, at a picture-when he looks ever so carefully . . . at the life in his aquarium, he is being taught to read . . . life doesn't stop so that the children can be taught to read. The life goes on so that the children can be taught to read. (Hymes 1965, p. 88)

The knowledge acquired through the hands-on experiences referred to in the quote by Hymes forms the essential underpinnings of reading comprehension. This knowledge is essential for readers to gain meaning from texts. "Knowledge is good" is the succinct and humorous stated motto of the mythical Faber College in the 1978 movie *Animal House*. Willingham (2006), a cognitive psychologist, uses this quote to illustrate the many benefits of knowledge. It helps students in numerous ways since knowledge actually enhances cognitive processes and ultimately empowers the brain to gain more knowledge. This happens as a student takes in more information and thinks about the new information he is gaining. Knowledge also helps improve thinking and helps in problem solving (Willingham).

Comprehension can be improved if children are taught appropriate concepts about the world around them from infancy so that there is a sufficient store of prior knowledge before they encounter written text. The importance of an enriching, nourishing and intellectually stimulating environment cannot be underestimated in the cognitive development of readers. When children are immersed and actively engaged in this literate environment where responsive and dynamic interactions are ongoing daily, then children gain the world knowledge necessary to be strong comprehenders. Vygotsky (1978) emphasized the importance of learning as a process involving cognitive and social development in interaction with others who are more experienced in the world. Similarly, research studies have linked the importance of a wide vocabulary to efficient reading, particularly comprehension abilities, with the essential vocabulary knowledge growing in direct relation to the experiences children have which broaden their view of the world and all that is in it (Brown, 1958). Early researchers pointed to the premise: when teachers intentionally work to increase vocabulary knowledge, reading comprehension will also be improved (Mezynski, 1983).

schema (pl.)—categorized, itemized knowledge stored in long-term memory that provides the base for comprehension; a theory about the comprehension process

In instructional settings, the importance of activation of prior knowledge or **schema** is of major concern (Anderson, 1984). A reader's schema, or itemized, categorized world knowledge, provides a basis for comprehension skill or contributes to the lack of comprehension ability. Children will comprehend better and more efficiently if steps are taken before reading to assure children know the concepts they will encounter in the text. Stevens (1982) stressed that comprehension would be improved if appropriate world knowledge is taught before reading a text sample. Not only is world knowledge essential for constructing a text representation, but also knowledge of text structures for fictional and nonfictional materials is important for comprehension. Applebee (1978) stressed, in pioneering research on **story grammar**, that the very young preschool child will store a representation of the text framework in memory and can use that representation when recalling the elements of a story.

story grammar—a framework of knowledge about narrative texts acquired at an early age by children whose parents read aloud to them; i.e., characters, plot, setting

Specific Cognitive Factors related to the Reading Task.   Due to the complex, multifaceted nature of the reading process, experts are not in agreement about the specific components of reading or of the aspects of cognition impacting the process. Neisser (1976) identified perception, imagery, retention, recall, problem solving, and thinking as aspects of cognition that directly relate to what happens when students read, emphasizing the active, interrelated nature of reading as process. Other experts disagree and exclude perception as a cognitive correlate in reading (Alexander & Heathington, 1988). For example, Harris and Hodges (1995) disagree with Neisser's view and define perception as merely "the extraction of information from sensory stimulation" (p. 181). Blakemore (1973) pointed to the dichotomy of visual perception versus "seeing" as a very active research area, but described it as ". . . more of a mystery than ever. The whole field is a bit like a scientific bombsite – attacked from all sides and much in need of theoretical reconstruction" (p. 674). Although significant progress has occurred in the decades since Blakemore's disparaging remark, perception, whether a cognitive correlate or a sensory function, continues to be a persistent issue for students with reading difficulties. Perception, including both visual and auditory, has played an important role in the diagnosis of specific learning disabilities related to reading.

Likewise, attention, the cognitive process related to focusing and concentrating, is often central to problems faced by students who struggle in learning to read. Attention deficit disorders are the primary identified difficulty for a significant majority of the children receiving special education services in today's classrooms under the classification of specific learning disabilities, with these LD students comprising approximately 5% of the 11% of all students classified as receiving special education services in the age group 6–17 years of age (OSEP State-Reported Data, 2007).

Neisser (1967), in his seminal work introducing the field of cognitive psychology, grouped a number of correlates under the category of thinking. Thinking, which includes recall, retention, problem solving, and imagery, has long been considered by many experts as the most important aspect of cognition impacting reading because of its influence on comprehension, unquestionably the main goal of the reading process. Retention, the act of recalling past knowledge or experiences, is directly related to comprehension. Psychologists have pointed to interference, both retroactive and proactive, as one of the main inhibiting factors for retention (Downing & Leong, 1982). Imagery also has been identified as an essential cognitive correlate for active comprehension of text (Kintsch, 1998).

Thinking and reading are closely intertwined. Otto (1971) credits Thorndike's work as having long-lasting effects on the way we view reading today and its reciprocal relationship to thinking. Thorndike (1917) concluded that reading was not a passive, mechanical act, but an analytical process of thinking and reasoning. Athey (1983) stated that "to promote thinking is to promote reading" (p. 31), agreeing with early pioneers in the reading field (Russell, 1956; Stauffer, 1969).

In an increasingly global and complex society, reading instruction cannot be separated from the critical, higher level thinking, cognitive processes necessary for survival in society. Cognition and intellectual factors play a major role in the development of those reading abilities.

Linguistic Factors Impacting the Reader

> Children learn oral language without formal instruction but are bombarded with assistance in learning to read. Ironically, oral language is actually the greater intellectual feat of the two. . . . In acquiring oral language, children must first discover the existence and purpose of language, then master its sounds and structure, and finally learn the multitude of oral symbols which constitute vocabulary. In learning to read, children can build on their previous knowledge of their language as they figure out the written symbol system used to represent it. (Fields & Lee, 1987, p. 31)

Language is the foundation for reading and writing. Children use what they have learned about language from infancy in the oral mode and gradually build a framework of knowledge about print and written language. Reading and writing, the literacy processes, emanate from oracy, the listening and speaking processes. Researchers agree that reading is primarily a linguistic process and that language knowledge is essential for success in reading. Literacy, simply explained, is regarded as a continuation of oracy and the speech continuum (Ruddell & Speaker, 1985) and language development is essential to reading comprehension (Cazden, 1965, 1979).

Goodman (1986) stresses that "language begins as a means of communication between members of a group. Through it, however, each developing child acquires the life view, the cultural perspective, the ways of meaning particular to its own culture" (p. 11). The cultural aspect of language lies at the heart of many difficulties students have when learning to read. Children adopt the language of their families and their communities. Linguists would argue that each language is "good," even nonstandard dialects, in that each has its rules, is systematic, and enables the child to function in his own sphere of influence (Kutz, 1997). It is when the child comes in contact with the standard English of his teacher and finds that his language is a mismatch that problems occur (Comber, 2000; Gee, 1996). Tonnesssen (1995) has described this as a "cultural collision" when students encounter rigid standards and expectations and do not understand the purposes behind learning the new and different version of English. Smith (1977) believes that the child's encounter with the English-speaking classroom, which may have different phonemes, different symbols, different meanings for certain words, and different grammatical rules, will appear as confronting nonsense to the child whose native language differs from the school's instructional language.

Specific Linguistic Factors Related to the Reading Task.   Early research has identified several linguistic factors at varying levels as having significant impact on the reader: phonological knowledge/decoding (Snow, Burns, & Griffin, 1998; Yopp & Singer, 1985); metalinguistic awareness (Gleitman, 1977; Singer, 1981, 1984); syntactic knowledge (Chomsky, 1972); lexical/semantic knowledge, that is, vocabulary and word meanings (Mezynski, 1983).

Young children use these components of oral language as they encounter written language. Phonological knowledge has been identified through extensive

phonological awareness—
the ability of the child to hear
and distinguish the individual
phonemes or small speech
sounds in spoken language

phonemic awareness—the
most advanced level of
phonological awareness, the
ability to manipulate and segment individual phonemes

metalinguistic awareness—
specific knowledge about
language that refers to a child's
ability to use language about
language and to understand
the explicit terms used to describe written language, that
is, word, sound, sentence,
paragraph

research as being one of the most highly predictive components
for success in beginning reading, particularly phonological
awareness (Ehri, 1991; Stahl, Duffy-Hester, and Stahl, 1998).
Phonology is the intricate system of sounds comprising a language, with each sound unit or phoneme being distinct for
each language. **Phonological awareness** refers to the ability
of the child to hear and distinguish the individual phonemes, or
small speech sounds in spoken language. **Phonemic awareness** is the most advanced level of phonological awareness and
is important in that children with this ability to manipulate and
segment individual phonemes in words are more likely to become efficient readers in the early grades (National Reading
Panel, 2000).

    Metalinguistic awareness is a specific knowledge about
language that refers to a child's ability to use language about
language and to understand the explicit terms used to describe
written language (Yaden & Templeton, 1986). Nagy and
Anderson (1995) believe that reading is a metalinguistic
process and that young children must first understand that the
print symbols carry the message and that the symbols can be labeled in a variety of ways. Before they can engage in conversations about reading, they must first understand the concepts of
sound, letter, word, and sentence. Clay (1975) was one of the first researchers to
point to the need for readers to understand the meanings of these metalinguistic
terms before they could successfully engage in beginning reading tasks.

    Syntax is defined as "the set of rules or the grammar of a language"
(Jalongo, 1992, p. 14). Children begin learning these rules from infancy and discover during their preschool years about the order and organization in spoken
language. This grammatical knowledge aids the reader in knowing the type and
function of an unknown word when it is encountered in print. Weber (1970) analyzed reading errors of first graders and found that more than 90% of the errors
were grammatically consistent, proving that even very young readers apply their
syntactic knowledge to decipher and make sense of print. Kutz (1997) believes
that literacy acquisition parallels oral language acquisition in that children build
creatively on what they know, forming and testing different hypotheses, and
eventually developing for themselves a rule-governed system that approximates
conventional standard grammar and helps them make sense of words they
encounter (p. 229).

    Although vocabulary, the lexical or semantic knowledge, is a correlate of in-
telligence, it is also directly related to the linguistic aspects of reading. The benefits of a wide vocabulary are unequally distributed among young children entering public school, with the lower socioeconomic (SES) groups entering with half
the vocabulary of children from higher SES groups (Gillet et al., 2004). By the
senior year of high school, students with larger vocabularies have continued to
build linguistic power so that the size of their vocabularies will be four times that

of their lower SES peers (Beck, McKeown, & Kucan, 2002). Another aspect of vocabulary development that impacts reading success is the research finding that children try to recognize, in print, words that they already know in speech, words for which they have a meaning in their spoken vocabulary. Children with wider speaking vocabularies are at an advantage when they encounter words in print as they begin to read (Stanovich, 1992). Poverty, not ethnicity, has been identified as one of the factors most predictive of poor literacy performance and is directly related to vocabulary power (Snow et al., 1998).

Affective Factors Impacting the Reader

> A small group of fourth graders is gathered in a circle on the rug. They are participating in literature circles and are reading aloud together from the book *Where the Red Fern Grows*. As Mary reads aloud to the group, the children are engaged and talkative. When Mary finishes her passage, the group turns to Hayden and encourages him to pick up the reading where Mary stopped. Hayden hangs his head and mumbles that he doesn't feel well. Susan picks up on his uneasiness and volunteers to read next.

Scenes like this happen daily in classrooms across the United States. Negative experiences and past failures in reading situations affect struggling readers so dramatically that often they choose to drop out of reading events and disengage from their peers and the teacher. The role of affect and the affective domain in reading, while monumental, has often been underemphasized in the research literature. This domain includes interests, motivation, values, self-esteem, feelings, beliefs, and attitudes toward school as well as reading. One possible reason for the lack of research investigating the affective domain has been the lack of valid and reliable measurement tools. Since affective measures often necessitate a self-report research technique, measurement experts point to the difficulty in gaining complete and honest answers, especially from elementary-age students.

Cognitive factors, on the other hand, have dominated the research field (Alexander & Filler, 1976; Athey, 1985; Baker & Wigfield, 1999; Barr, Kamil, Mosenthal, & Pearson, 1991; Gambrell, 1996; Hidi, 2001; McKenna & Kear, 1990; Pearson, Barr, Kamil, & Mosenthal, 1984; Ruddell, Ruddell, & Singer, 1994; Shapiro, 1993; Shapiro & White, 1991), but as measurement tools were developed and the mandate "to create lifelong readers became strong, knowledge of these factors which influence the leisure reading habit became a focus of research initiatives" (Shapiro & Whitney, 1997, p. 343).

Interest, Rewards, Values, Beliefs.   Reading researchers have traditionally viewed children's interest in reading with an eye to the strong impact interest has on the reader's engagement with text. Horace Mann (1965) decried the lack of interesting school reading material almost two hundred years ago. David Russell (1961) pointed to the benefits of teachers' focusing on the intrinsic worth of reading in their instruction since this would enable students to reap great rewards (Shapiro & Whitney, 1997; Wigfield, Guthrie, Tonks, & Perencevich, 2004).

When most children start school, they are usually looking forward to learning to read or even are already reading (Durkin, 1966). These young readers find looking at books enchanting and quickly warm to a person who will take the time to read to them. They are intrinsically interested (Condry & Koslowski, 1979; Deci, 1975; Farris & Kaczmarski, 1988) in acquiring this skill. "Intrinsic motivation is defined as doing something for its own sake rather than for external reward" (Burroughs, 1991, p. 256).

As children progress through the elementary grades, this intrinsic interest in reading begins to change (Eccles, Wigfield, & Schiefele, 1998; Kohn, 1987; Pressley, 2006; Wigfield, Eccles, & Rodriguez, 1998). Students can be found at various grade levels who will admit that either they hate reading or they do not enjoy it (Donahue, Danne, & Yin, 2005; Shapiro & White, 1991). Teachers will testify their students do not like to read (Whitney, 1986) or that their students rarely read for pleasure (Chisom 1989). For some reason, "too many students who can read choose to avoid the printed word" (Alvermann & Guthrie, 1993, p. 1). What has happened to these readers from that initial point where they were intrinsically interested in reading to the point where they hate reading? Does this shift have to do with a possible misconception on the part of teachers, principals, librarians, and educators as to what motivates a student to want to participate in the wonderful world of reading?

A person may ask, What is so wonderful about reading? The answer, of course, is very subjective. It has everything to do with one's personal experience. If one's time was filled with unsuccessful reading experiences, then one is not going to expect reading to be wonderful at all. On the other hand, if one's experience was filled with pleasurable, successful reading time, then one will expect reading to fulfill those expectations.

A disinterest in reading might be the result of rewards (Marinak & Gambrell, 2008). Although many teachers view rewards as a positive strategy for encouraging students to engage with texts, rewards often have the opposite effect and may result in a disinterest in reading. Tokens, grades, praise—all external rewards—offered in school settings have an impact on one's intrinsic interest in an activity. "A reward (a grade) encourages us to focus narrowly on a task, to do it as quickly as possible and to take few risks" (Kohn, 1987, p. 55). This is evident when one observes students rushing to complete reading assignments. Instead of reading the book, they telephone a friend who has, they hope, read the story to "please fill them in." Failing that, they examine a summary to get the gist of the story. Turning out book reports can be another example of narrowly focusing on a task in an attempt to meet the reading requirements assigned in a class. "When we work for a reward, we often see ourselves as being controlled by it; anything perceived as constraining—surveillance, deadlines, evaluation—all tend to undermine intrinsic interest in a given activity" (Kohn, p. 55). Programs that reward children with grades, prizes, and praise for the amount of reading they do may have an adverse effect on not only their responses to literature, but also on their intrinsic interest in reading. In essence, it seems to be that the conditions under which rewards are given is what increases or decreases intrinsic motivation

(Marinak & Gambrell, 2008). Contingent rewards (depending on the quality of the performance) initially undermine intrinsic motivation, whereas noncontingent rewards (performance only) tend not to undermine intrinsic motivation. However, subjects who receive rewards subsequently tend to choose easier tasks (Pressley, 2006; Tompkins, 2006; Whitney, 1994).

There seems to be an erosion of intrinsic interest in reading as some children matriculate through elementary school. Elley (1992), Foertsch (1992), and Pressley (2006) agree that regardless of the reasons, the trend seems to be getting worse. Perhaps, a child's disinterest in reading can be attributed to the child's value system. Students "learn to value some activities over others and gradually develop stable beliefs and expectations about their likes and dislikes" (Burroughs, 1991, p. 257). Disinterest in reading may also be attributed to the lack of support found within particular cultures. An International Association for the Evaluation of Educational Achievement study involving 30 countries reported that "Finnish nine-year-olds ranked first in reading books, cartoons, newspapers and magazines" (Ronnholm, 1992, 1993, p. 14). One principal and reading educator at a school within that country commented that "Finland is a highly literate society, publishing books and newspapers at a higher per capital rate than most other industrialized nations . . . leads the world in percentage of newspaper subscribers . . ." (Ronnholm, p. 14). According to the IEA study, Finns value reading highly.

Attitudes Toward Reading.   In addition to interests, motivation, values, and beliefs, the component of attitude is an integral part of the affective domain and its impact on the reader. An attitude is defined by Allport (1967) as "a mental and neural state of readiness, organized through experience, exerting a directive or dynamic influence upon the individual's response to all objects and situations with which it is related" (p. 8). Fishbein and Ajzen (1975) and Kush, Watkins, and Brookhart (2005) identified three important components of attitude: beliefs, feelings, and behaviors. Their premise points to attitude as multidimensional and more than simple feelings.

By the age of 11 pupils will have formed attitudes toward reading from their early home experiences and from their school reading encounters. These attitudes will definitely affect the ways they voluntarily use their reading skills and their free time for pleasurable reading (Gorman, White, Orchard, & Tate, 1981).

As researchers developed a variety of instruments to investigate reading attitudes and began to measure the powerful effects of these attitudes, it became increasingly apparent that reading attitude had a direct relationship to the amount of time students spent reading. The reported findings seemed to be directly linked. Factors reported to improve students' attitudes toward reading included: time spent reading (Long and Henderson, 1972; Tompkins, 2006; Whitehead, Capey, Maddren, & Wellins, 1977); having books available in a student's first language (Ivey & Broaddus, 2007; Schon, Hopkins, & Davis, 1981); teacher-student conferences (Manning & Manning, 1984; Reis, McCoach, Coyne, Schreiber, Eckert & Gubbins, 2007); peer interactions around recreational reading (Manning & Manning, 1984; Pressley, 2006); positive and engaging teaching methods (Healy, 1965; Pressley; Reis et al. Shapiro & White, 1991) versus less engaging instructional methods (McKenna, Stratton, Grindler, Rakestraw, & Jenkins, 1992; Whitney, 1994); and home literacy environments (Hansen, 1969; Shapiro & Whitney, 1997; Swalander & Taube, 2007).

FUTURE DIRECTIONS IN RESEARCH: QUESTIONS TO PONDER

Into the 21st century, these questions continue to haunt us: Why do some children struggle with reading? Why do children who are able to read choose not to read? What roles do linguistic, cognitive, and affective issues play in becoming literate in today's global societies? How do gender differences, classroom instructional practices, and high-stakes testing affect the reader? Researchers will continue to investigate the role of the reader in the complex process of becoming literate.

CONNECTING COGNITIVE, LINGUISTIC, AND AFFECTIVE FACTORS IMPACTING READERS AND YOUR CLASSROOM . . .

1. Administer a running record, miscue analysis, or informal reading inventory to one of your struggling readers. Carefully analyze the reading errors. What linguistic factors do you see impacting the reader's performance?
2. What can we do as teachers, principals, administrators, and educators to assure support for the affective factors that contribute to positive gains in reading? Work with other teachers on your team to develop a plan to do this in your school.
3. Accumulate research evidence to justify and explain the statement that language is the foundation of reading. Prepare a presentation that you could give to the faculty in your school and include activities that could be used to enhance the linguistic abilities of your students.

REFERENCES

Alexander, J. E., & Filler, R. C. (1976). *Attitudes and reading.* Newark, DE: IRA.

Alexander, J. E., & Heathington, B. (1988). Glenview, IL: Scott, Foresman.

Allport, G. W. (1967). Attitudes. In M. Fishbein (Ed.), *Readings in attitude theory and measurement* (pp. 3–13). New York: Wiley.

Alvermann, D. E., & Guthrie, J. T. (1993). *Themes and directions of the National Reading Research Center* (Perspectives in reading research, No. 1). Athens: University of Georgia and College Park: University of Maryland, National Reading Research Center.

Anderson, R. (1984). Role of the reader's schema in comprehension, learning, and memory. In H. Singer & R. B. Ruddell (Eds.), *Theoretical models and processes of reading* (3rd ed., pp. 372–384). Newark, DE: IRA.

Applebee, A. (1978). *Child's concept of story: Ages two to seventeen.* Chicago: University of Chicago Press.

Athey, I. (1983). Thinking and experience: The cognitive base for language experience. In R. Parker & F. Davis (Eds.), *Developing literacy: Young children's use of language* (pp. 19–33). Newark, DE: IRA.

Athey, I. (1985). Reading research in the affective domain. In H. Singer & R. B. Ruddell (Eds.), *Theoretical models and processes of reading* (3rd ed., pp. 527–557). Newark, DE: IRA.

Baker, L., & Wigfield, A. (1999). Dimensions of children's motivation for reading and their relations to reading activity and reading achievement. *Reading Research Quarterly, 34*, 452–477.

Barr, R., Kamil, M. L., Mosenthal, P., & Pearson, P. D. (Eds.). (1991). *Handbook of reading research* (Vol. 2). White Plains, NY: Longman.

Beck. I, McKeown, M., & Kucan, L. (2002). *Bringing words to life.* New York: Guilford.

Biancarosa, C., & Snow, C. E. (2006). Reading next—A vision for action and research in middle and high school literacy: A report to Carnegie Corporation of New York (2nd ed.). Washington, DC: Alliance for Excellent Education.

Blakemore, C. (1973). The language of vision. *New Scientist, 58*, 674–677.

Brown, R. (1958). *Words and things.* Garden City, NY: Basic Books.

Burroughs, S. G. (1991). The implications for effective education of understanding pupil motivation in schools as a multi-dimensional model. *International Journal of Adolescence and Youth, 2*(4), 251–274.

Cazden, C. (1965). *Environmental assistance to the child's acquisition of grammar.* Unpublished doctoral dissertation, Harvard University.

Cazden, C. (1979). Learning to read in classroom interaction. In C. Resnik and P. Weaver (Eds.), *Theory and practice of early reading.* Hillsdale, NJ: Erlbaum.

Children in non-English-speaking households face many health disparities, researcher concludes. (2008, June 11). *Science News.* Retrieved November 3, 2008, from http://www.sciencedaily.com/releases/2008/06/080611071033.htm

Chisom, Y. L. (1989). *Increasing literature appreciation and recreational reading behavior of intermediate grade students.* Unpublished doctoral dissertation, Nova University, Fort Lauderdale, Florida. (ERIC Document Reproduction Service No. 308 494)

Chomsky, C. (1972). Stages in language development and reading exposure. *Harvard Educational Review, 42*, 1–33.

Clay, M. (1975). *What did I write?* Portsmouth, NH: Heinemann.

Comber, B. (2000). What really counts in early literacy lessons. *Language Arts, 78*, 38–49.

Condry, J., & Koslowski, B. (1979). Can education be made "intrinsically interesting" to children? In L. G. Katz (Ed.), *Current topics in early childhood education: Vol. II* (pp. 227–260). Norwood, NJ: Ablex.

Deci, E. L. (1975). *Intrinsic motivation.* New York: Plenum Press.

Donahue, P. L., Daane, M. C., & Yin, Y. (2005). *The nation's report card: Reading 2003* (Publication No. NCES 2004-453). Washington, DC: U.S. Government Printing Office.

Downing, J., & Leong, C. (1982). *Psychology of reading.* New York: Macmillan.

Durkin, D. (1966). *Children who read early.* New York: Teachers College Press.

Eccles, J. S., Wigfield, A., & Schiefele, U. (1998). Motivation to succeed. In N. Eisenberg (Ed.), *Handbook of child psychology* (Vol. IV, 5th ed., pp. 1017–1095). New York: John Wiley.

"Education taxed by non-English speaking kids." (2005, March 19). Fox News.com. Retrieved November 3, 2008, from http://www.foxnews.com/story/0,2933,150856,00.html

Ehri, L. (1991). Development of the ability to read words. In R. Barr, M. Kamil, P. Mosenthal, & P. Pearson (Eds.), Handbook of reading research (2nd ed., pp. 395–419). NY: Longman.

Ekwall, E., & Shanker, J. (1988). Diagnosis and remediation of the disabled reader. Boston, MA: Allyn & Bacon.

Elley, W. B. (1992). *How in the world do students read?: IEA study of reading literacy.* The Hague: The International Association for the Evaluation of Educational Achievement.

Farris, P. J., & Kaczmarski, D. (1988). Whole language, a closer look. *Contemporary Education, 59*(2), 77–81.

Fields, M., & Lee, D. (1987). *Let's begin reading right*. Columbus, OH: Merrill.

Fishbein, M., & Ajzen, I. (1975). *Belief, attitude, intention, and behavior: An introduction to theory and research*. Reading, MA: Addison-Wesley.

Foertsch, M. A. (1992). *Reading in and out of school: Factors influencing the literacy achievement of American students in grades 4, 8, and 12, in 1988 and 1990*. Washington, DC: U.S. Government Printing Office.

Gee, J. (1996). *Social linguistics and literacies: Ideology in discourses* (2nd ed.). Bristol, PA: Taylor & Francis.

Gambrell, L. (1996). Creating classroom cultures that foster reading motivation. *The Reading Teacher. 50* (1), 14–25.

Gillet, J., Temple, C., & Crawford, A. (2004). *Understanding reading problems: Assessment and instruction*. Boston, MA: Pearson, Allyn & Bacon.

Gleitman, L. (1977). Discourse at the University of Victoria Conference on Linguistic Awareness. Victoria, BC, Canada.

Goodman, K. (1986). What's whole in whole language? Portsmouth, NH: Heinemann.

Gorman, T. P., White, J., Orchard, L., & Tate, A. (1981). *Language performance in schools*. London, England: Her Majesty's Stationery Office.

Hansen, H. S. (1969). The impact of the home literary environment on reading attitude. *Elementary English, 46*(1), 17–24.

Harris, A., & Sipay, E. (1990). *How to increase reading ability: A guide to developmental and remedial methods*. New York: Longman.

Harris, T. L., & Hodges, R. E. (Eds.) (1995). *The literacy dictionary: The vocabulary of reading and writing*. Newark, DE: IRA.

Healy, A. R. (1965). Effects of changing children's attitudes toward reading. *Elementary English, 42*(3), 269–272.

Hidi, S. (2001). Interest, reading, and learning: Theoretical and practical considerations. *Educational Psychology Review, 13*(3), 191–209. Retrieved June 17, 2009, from Education Research Complete database.

Hymes, J. L. (1965). Early reading is very risky business. *Grade Teacher, 82,* 88–92.

Ivey, G., & Broaddus, K. (2007). A formative experiment investigating literacy engagement among adolescent Latina/o students just beginning to read, write, and speak English. *Reading Research Quarterly, 42*(4), 512–525, 527–545. Retrieved June 16, 2009, from Education Module database. (Document ID: 1361256811).

Jalongo, M. (1992). *Early childhood language arts*. Boston, MA: Allyn & Bacon.

Kintsch, W. (1998). *Comprehension: A paradigm for cognition*. Cambridge, MA: Cambridge University Press.

Kohn, A. (1987). Art for art's sake. *Psychology Today, 21*(9), 52–57.

Kush, J., Watkins, M., & Brookhart, S. (2005). The temporal-interactive influence of reading achievement and reading attitude. *Educational Research & Evaluation, 11*(1), 29–44. Retrieved June 16, 2009, doi:10.1080/13803610500110141

Kutz, E. (1997). *Language and literacy: Studying discourse in communities and classrooms*. Portsmouth, NH: Boynton/Cook/Heinemann.

Long, B. H., & Henderson, E. H. (1972). Children's use of time: Some personal and social correlates. *The Elementary School Journal, 73*(3), 193–199.

Mann, H. (1965). *Horace Mann on the crisis in education*. Yellow Springs, OH: Antioch Press.

Manning, G. L., & Manning, M. (1984). What models of recreational reading make a difference? *Reading World, 23*(4), 375–380.

Marinak, B. A., & Gambrell, L. B. (2008). Intrinsic motivation and rewards: What sustains young children's engagement with text? *Literacy Research and Instruction, 47*(1), 9–26.

Mathewson, G. C. (1994). Model of attitude influence upon reading and learning to read. In R.B. Ruddell, M. R. Ruddell, & H. Singer (Eds.), *Theoretical models and processes of reading* (4th ed., pp. 1131–1161). Newark, DE: IRA.

McKenna, M. C., & Kear, D. J. (1990). Measuring attitude toward reading: A new tool for teachers. *The Reading Teacher, 43*(9), 626–639.

McKenna, M. C., Stratton, B. D., Grindler, M. C., Rakestraw, J. F., & Jenkins, S. (1992, December). *Differential effects of whole language and traditional instruction on reading attitudes.* Paper presented at the meeting of the National Reading Conference, San Antonio.

Mezynski, K. (1983). Issues concerning the acquisition of knowledge: Effects of vocabulary training on reading comprehension. *Review of Educationa Research, 53,* 253–279.

Moll, L., Amanti, C., Neff, D., & Gonzalez, N. (1992). Funds of knowledge for teaching: Using a qualitative approach to connect homes and classrooms. *Theory into Practice, 31*(1), 132–141.

Monroe, M. (1932). *Children who cannot read.* Chicago: University of Chicago Press.

Nagy, W., & Anderson, R. (1995). *Metalinguistic awareness and literacy acquisition in different languages.* (Technical report No. 618). Urbana, IL: Center for the Study Of Reading. (ERIC Document Reproduction Service No. ED 391147)

National Center for Education Statistics (2007a). Retrieved July 10, 2009, from http://nces.ed.gov/programs/coe/statement/s2.asp

National Center for Education Statistics (2007b). Retrieved November 4, 2008, from http://nces.ed.gov/programs/digest/d07/tables/dt07_020.asp

National Reading Panel (2000). *Teaching children to read: An evidenced-based assessment of scientific research literature on reading and its implications for reading instruction.* Washington, DC: National Institute for Literacy.

Neisser, U. (1967). *Cognitive psychology.* New York: Appleton.

Neisser, U. (1976). *Cognition and reality: Principles and implications of cognitive psychology.* San Francisco: Freeman.

OSEP State-Reported Data/Individuals with Disabilities Act (2007). Retrieved November 4, 2008, from https://www.ideadata.org/arc_toc9.asp#partbCC

Otto, W. (1971). Thorndike's Reading as Reasoning: Influence and impact. Reading Research Quarterly, *6* (4), 435–442.

Pearson, P. D., Barr, R., Kamil, M., & Mosenthal, P. (Eds.). (1984). *Handbook of research in reading.* New York: Longman.

Penny, T. (2008, August 14). U.S. white population will be minority by 2042, government says. *Bloomberg Press.* Retrieved November 19, 2008, from http://www.bloomberg.com/apps/news?pid=20601087&sid=afLRFXgzpFoY&refer=home

Pressley, M. (2006). Reading instruction that works. The case for balanced teaching. New York, NY: Guilford Press.

Rawls, W. (1961). *Where the red fern grows.* NY: Doubleday.

Reis, S., McCoach, D., Coyne, M., Schreiber, F., Eckert, R., & Gubbins, E. (2007). Using planned enrichment strategies with direct instruction to improve reading fluency, comprehension, and attitude toward reading: An evidence-based study. *Elementary School Journal, 108*(1), 3–23. Retrieved June 16, 2009, from Education Research Complete database.

Robinson, H. (1946). *Why pupils fail in reading.* Chicago, IL: University of Chicago Press.

Ronnholm, P. O. (1992, December/1993, January). The secret of their success: Many factors contribute to Finns' high scores in IEA survey. *Reading Today, 2,* 14.

Rosenblatt, L. (1978). *The reader, the text, the poem.* Carbondale, IL: Southern Illinois University Press.

Ruddell, R. B., Ruddell, M. R., & Singer, H. (Eds.). (1994). *Theoretical models and processes of reading* (4th ed.). Newark, DE: IRA.

Ruddell, R., & Speaker, R. (1985). The interactive reading process: A model. In H. Singer, & R. Ruddell (Eds.), *Theoretical models and processes of reading* (3rd ed., pp. 751–793). Newark, DE: IRA.

Rumelhart, D. (1985). Toward an interactive model of reading. In H. Singer & R. Ruddell (Eds.), *Theoretical models and processes of reading* (3rd ed., pp. 722–750). Newark, DE: IRA.

Rumelhart, D. (1994). Toward an interactive model of reading. In R. Ruddell, M. Ruddell, & H. Singer (Eds.), *Theoretical models and processes of reading* (pp. 864–894). Newark, DE: IRA.

Russell, D. H. (1956). *Children's thinking.* Boston: Ginn.

Russell, D. H. (1961). *Children learn to read.* Boston: Ginn.

Schon, I., Hopkins, K. D., & Davis, W. A. (1981, April). *The effects of books in Spanish and free reading time on Hispanic students' reading abilities and attitudes.* Paper presented at the meeting of the American Educational Research Association, Los Angeles. (ERIC Document Reproduction Service No. ED 204 096)

Shapiro, J. (1993). Affective concerns and reading. In T. V. Rasinski & N. D. Padak (Eds.), *Inquiries in literacy learning and instruction* (pp. 107–114). The 15th Yearbook of the College Reading Association.

Shapiro, J., & White, W. (1991). Reading attitudes and perceptions in traditional and nontraditional reading programs. *Reading, Research, & Instruction, 30* (4), 52–66.

Shapiro, J., & Whitney, P. (1997). Factors involved in the leisure reading of upper elementary school students. *Reading Psychology, 18,* 343–370.

Singer, H. (1981). *Review of reading research: Advance in theory and practice,* Vol. I by T. Waller & G. McKinnon. New York: Academic Press, *The Reading Teacher, 35,* 114–119.

Singer, H. (1984). Learning to read and skilled reading: Multiple systems interacting within and between the reader and the text. In J. Downing & R. Valtin (Eds.), *Language awareness and learning to read.* New York: Springer-Verlag.

Smith, E. (1977). Making sense out of reading instruction. *Harvard Educational Review, 47,* 386–395.

Snow, C., Burns, S., & Griffin, P. (Eds.). (1998). *Preventing reading difficulties in young children.* Washington, DC: National Academy Press.

Spache, G., & Spache, E. (1977). Reading in the elementary school (4th ed.). Boston, MA: Allyn & Bacon.

Stahl, S., Duffy-Hester, A., & Stahl, A. (1998). Theory and research into practice: Everything you wanted to know about phonics (but were afraid to ask). *Reading Research Quarterly, 33,* 338–355.

Stanovich, K. (1992). Are we overselling literacy? In C. Temple & P. Collins (Eds.), *Stories and readers,* Norwood, MA: Christopher Gordon.

Stauffer, R. (1969). *Teaching reading as a thinking process.* NY: Harper & Row.

Stevens, K. (1982). Can we improve reading by teaching background information? *Journal of Reading, 25.* 326–329.

Swalander, L. & Taube, K. (2007). Influences of family based prerequisites, reading attitude, and self-regulation on reading ability. *Contemporary Education Psychology. 32*(2), 206–230. Retrieved June 16, 2009, from doi:10.1016/j.cedpsych.2006.01.002

Tharoor, S. (2002, September 30). Illiterate America: 44 million American men and women are functionally illiterate. *Newsweek International.* Retrieved November 2, 2008, from http://www.shashitharoor.com/articles/newsweek/illiterate.php

Thorndike, E. L. (1917). Reading as reasoning: A study of mistakes in paragraph reading. *Journal of Educational Psychology, 8,* 323–332. Timing and duration of student participation in special education in the primary grades," (2007, March 21). *U.S. Department of Education Institute of Educational Sciences.* Retrieved November 4, 2008, from http://nces.ed.gov/pubsearch/pubsinfo.asp?pubid=2007043

Tompkins, G. (2006). Literacy for the 21st Century, a balanced approach. Columbus, OH: Prentice Hall.

Tonnessen, F. (1995). Literacy in Norway. *Journal of Adolescent and Adult Literacy, 29(3),* 244–246.

U.S. Department of Education, Office of Civil Rights (2006). Status and trends in the education of American Indians and Alaska natives: 2008. Retrieved November 4, 2008, from http://nces.ed.gov/pubs2008/nativetrends/tables/table_5_4b.asp

Vygotsky, L. (1978). *Mind in society: The development of higher psychological processes.* Cambridge, MA: Harvard University Press.

Weber, R. (1970). First graders' use of grammatical context in reading. In H. Levin and J. Williams, (Eds.), *Basic studies in reading.* NY: Basic Books.

Whitehead, F., Capey, A. C., Maddren, W., & Wellings, A. (1977). *Children and their books.* London: Macmillan Education.

Whitney, P. (1986). *Children's locus of control and intrinsically motivated reading.* Unpublished master's thesis, San Francisco State University.

Whitney, P. (1994). *Influences on grade-five students' decisions to read: An exploratory study of leisure reading behavior.* Unpublished doctoral dissertation, University of British Columbia, Vancouver, Canada.

Wigfield, A., Eccles, J. S., & Rodriguez, D. (1998). The development of children's motivation in school contexts. In P. D. Pearson & A. Iran-Nejad (Eds.), *Review of research in education* (Vol. 23, pp. 73–118). Washington, DC: American Educational Research Association.

Wigfield, A., Guthrie, J., Tonks, S., & Perencevich, K. (2004). Children's motivation for reading: Domain specificity and instructional influences. *Journal of Educational Research, 97*(6), 299–309. Retrieved June 17, 2009, from Education Research Complete database.

Willingham, D. (2006). How knowledge helps. [Electronic version]. *American Educator, 38,* 30–35.

Yaden, D., & Templeton, S. (1986). Introduction: Metalinguistic awareness – an Etymology. In D. Yaden and S. Templeton, (Eds.), *Metalinguistic awareness and beginning literacy* (pp. 3–10). Portsmouth, NH: Heinemann.

Yopp, H., & Singer, H. (1985). Toward an interactive reading instructional model: Explanation of activation of linguistic awareness and metalinguistic ability in learning to read. In H. Singer and R. Ruddell, (Eds.), *Theoretical models and processes of reading* (3rd ed., pp. 135–143). Newark, DE: IRA.

CHAPTER 5

ROLE OF THE READER'S SCHEMA IN COMPREHENSION, LEARNING, AND MEMORY

RICHARD C. ANDERSON

THINK ABOUT **SCHEMA THEORY . . .**

1. How does a culturally diverse classroom impact your teaching in terms of building and activating background knowledge?

2. As you read, create a visual representation of Anderson's Schema theory.

The past several years have witnessed the articulation of a largely new theory of reading, a theory already accepted by the majority of scholars in the field. According to the theory, a reader's *schema,* or organized knowledge of the world, provides much of the basis for comprehending, learning, and remembering the ideas in stories and texts. In this paper I will attempt to explain schema theory, give illustrations of the supporting evidence, and suggest applications to classroom teaching and the design of instructional materials.

A SCHEMA-THEORETIC INTERPRETATION OF COMPREHENSION

In schema-theoretic terms, a reader comprehends a message when he is able to bring to mind a schema that gives a good account of the objects and events described in the message. Ordinarily, comprehension proceeds so smoothly that we are unaware of the process of "cutting and fitting" a schema in order to achieve a

From Anderson, R.C., Osborn, J., & Tierney, R.J. (Eds.), *Learning to Read in American Schools: Basal Readers and Content Texts* (pp. 243–257). Copyright © 1984 by Lawrence Erlbaum Associates. Reprinted with permission of the publisher.

satisfactory account of a message. It is instructive, therefore, to try to understand material that gives us pause, so that we can reflect upon our own minds at work. Consider the following sentence, drawn from the work of Bransford and McCarrell (1974):

The notes were sour because the seam split.

Notice that all of the words are familiar and that the syntax is straightforward, yet the sentence does not "make sense" to most people. Now notice what happens when the additional clue, "bagpipe," is provided. At this point the sentence does make sense because one is able to interpret all the words in the sentence in terms of certain specific objects and events and their interrelations.

Let us examine another sentence:

The big number 37 smashed the ball over the fence.

This sentence is easy to interpret. *Big Number 37* is a baseball player. The sense of *smash the ball* is to propel it rapidly by hitting it strongly with a bat. The fence is at the boundary of a playing field. The ball was hit hard enough that it flew over the fence.

Suppose a person with absolutely no knowledge of baseball read the Big Number 37 sentence. Such as person could not easily construct an interpretation of the sentence, but with enough mental effort might be able to conceive of large numerals, perhaps made of metal, attached to the front of an apartment building. Further, the person might imagine that the numerals come loose and fall, striking a ball resting on top of, or lodged above, a fence, causing the ball to break. Most people regard this as an improbable interpretation, certainly one that never would have occurred to them, but they readily acknowledge that it is a "good" interpretation. What makes it good? The answer is that the interpretation is complete and consistent. It is complete in the sense that every element in the sentence is interpreted; there are no loose ends left unexplained. The interpretation is consistent in that no part of it does serious violence to knowledge about the physical and social world.

Both interpretations of the Big Number 37 sentence assume a real world. Criteria of consistency are relaxed in fictional worlds in which animals talk or men wearing capes leap tall buildings in a single bound. But there are conventions about what is possible in fictional worlds as well. The knowledgeable reader will be annoyed if these conventions are violated. The less-knowledgeable reader simply will be confused.

It should not be imagined that there is some simple, literal level of comprehension of stories and texts that does not require coming up with a schema. This important point is illustrated in a classic study by Bransford and Johnson (1972) in which subjects read paragraphs, such as the following, written so that most people are unable to construct a schema that will account for the material:

If the balloons popped the sound wouldn't be able to carry since everything would be too far away from the correct floor. A closed window would also prevent the sound from carrying, since most buildings tend to be well insulated. Since the whole operation depends upon a steady flow of electricity; a break in the middle of the wire would also cause problems. Of course, the fellow could shout, but the human voice is not loud enough to carry that far. An additional problem is that a string could break on the instrument. Then there could be no accompaniment to the message. It is clear that the best situation would involve less distance. Then there would be fewer potential problems. With face to face contact, the least number of things could go wrong. (p. 719)

Subjects rated this passage as very difficult to understand, and they were unable to remember much of it. In contrast, subjects shown the drawing on the left side of Figure 5.1 found the passage more comprehensible and were able to remember a great deal of it. Another group saw the drawing on the right in Figure 5.1. This group remembered no more than the group that did not receive a drawing. The experiment demonstrates that what is critical for comprehension is a schema accounting for the *relationships* among elements; it is not enough for the elements to be concrete and imageable.

Trick passages, such as the foregoing one about the communication problems of a modern-day Romeo, are useful for illustrating what happens when a

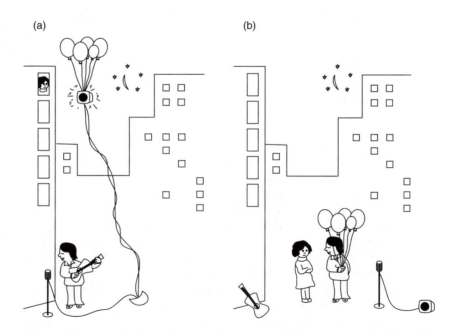

FIGURE 5.1 Version "a" represents the appropriate context and version "b" represents the inappropriate context. See text for accompanying passage.

From Bransford, J.D., & Johnson, M.K. (1972). Contextual Prerequisites for Understanding. *Journal of Verbal Learning and Verbal Behavior, 11,* 717–726. Copyright © 1972 by Academic Press, Inc. Reprinted with permission of Elsevier.

reader is completely unable to discover a schema that will fit a passage and, therefore, finds the passage entirely incomprehensible. More typical is the situation in which a reader knows something about a topic, but falls far short of being an expert. Chiesi, Spilich, and Voss (1979) asked people high and low in knowledge of baseball to read and recall a report of a half-inning from a fictitious baseball game. Knowledge of baseball had both qualitative and quantitative effects on performance. High-knowledge subjects were more likely to recall and embellish upon aspects of strategic significance to the game. Low-knowledge subjects, in contrast, were more likely to include information incidental to the play of the game.

Schema theory highlights the fact that often more than one interpretation of a text is possible. The schema that will be brought to bear on a text depends upon the reader's age, sex, race, religion, nationality, occupation—in short, it depends upon the reader's culture. This point was illustrated in an experiment completed by Anderson, Reynolds, Schallert, and Goetz (1977), who asked people to read the following passage:

> Tony slowly got up from the mat, planning his escape. He hesitated a moment and thought. Things were not going well. What bothered him most was being held, especially since the charge against him had been weak. He considered his present situation. The lock that held him was strong but he thought he could break it. He knew, however, that his timing would have to be perfect. Tony was aware that it was because of his early roughness that he had been penalized so severely—much too severely from his point of view. The situation was becoming frustrating; the pressure had been grinding on him for too long. He was being ridden unmercifully. Tony was getting angry now. He felt he was ready to make his move. He knew that his success or failure would depend on what he did in the next few seconds.

Most people think the foregoing passage is about a convict planning his escape from prison. A special group of people, however, see the passage an entirely different way; these are men who have been involved in the sport of wrestling. They think the passage is about a wrestler caught in the hold of an opponent. Notice how the interpretation of *lock* varies according to perspective. In the one case, it is a piece of hardware that holds a cell door shut; in the other it may be a sweaty arm around a neck. Males enrolled in a weightlifting class and females enrolled in a music education class read the foregoing passage and another passage which most people interpret as about several people playing cards, but which can be interpreted as about a rehearsal session of a woodwind ensemble. The results were as expected. Scores on a multiple-choice test designed to reveal interpretations of the passages showed striking relationships to the subjects' background. Physical education students usually gave a wrestling interpretation to the prison/wrestling passage and a card-playing interpretation to the card/music passage, whereas the reverse was true of the music education students. Similarly, when subjects were asked to recall the passages, theme-revealing distortions appeared, even though the instructions emphasized reproducing the exact words of the original text. For example, a physical education student stated, "Rocky was penalized early in the match for roughness or a dangerous hold," while a music education student wrote, "he was angry that he had been caught and arrested."

The thesis of this section is that comprehension is a matter of activating or constructing a schema that provides a coherent explanation of objects and events mentioned in a discourse. In sharp contrast is the conventional view that comprehension consists of aggregating the meanings of words to form the meanings of clauses, aggregating the meanings of clauses to form the meanings of sentences, aggregating the meaning of sentences to form the meanings of paragraphs, and so on. The illustrations in this section were intended to demonstrate the insufficiency of this conventional view. The meanings of the words cannot be "added up" to give the meaning of the whole. The click of comprehension occurs only when the reader evolves a schema that explains the whole message.

SCHEMA-BASED PROCESSES IN LEARNING AND REMEMBERING

According to **schema theory**, reading involves more or less simultaneous analysis at many different levels. The levels include graphophonemic, morphemic, semantic, syntactic, pragmatic, and interpretive. Reading is conceived to be an interactive process. This means that analysis does not proceed in a strict order from the visual information in letters to the overall interpretation of a text. Instead, as a person reads, an interpretation of what a segment of a text might mean is theorized to depend both on analysis of the print and

> **schema theory**—a theory that explains comprehension of text in terms of activation and construction of prior knowledge and experiences

on hypotheses in the person's mind. Processes that flow from the print are called "bottom-up" or "data driven" whereas processes that flow in the other direction are called "top-down" or "hypothesis driven," following Bobrow and Norman (1975). In the passage about Tony, who is either a wrestler or a prisoner, processing the word *lock* has the potential to activate either a piece-of-hardware meaning or a wrestling-hold meaning. The hypothesis the reader has already formulated about the text will tip the scales in the direction of one of the two meanings, usually without the reader's being aware that an alternative meaning is possible. Psychologists are at work developing detailed models of the mechanisms by which information from different levels of analysis is combined during reading (see Just & Carpenter, 1980; Rumelhart & McClelland, 1980).

The reader's schema affects both learning and remembering of the information and ideas in a text. Six functions of schemata that have been proposed (Anderson, 1978; Anderson & Pichert, 1978) are briefly explained.

> **ideational scaffolding**—framework/niche or slot provided by schema for text information

*A schema provides **ideational scaffolding** for assimilating text information.*   The idea is that a schema provides a niche, or slot, for certain text information. For instance, there is a slot for the main entree in a dining-at-a-fine-restaurant schema and a slot for the murder weapon in a who-done-it schema. Information that fits slots in the reader's schema is readily learned, perhaps with little mental effort.

A schema facilitates selective allocation of attention.   A schema provides part of the basis for determining the important aspects of a text. It is hypothesized that skilled readers use importance as one basis for allocating cognitive resources—that is, for deciding where to pay close attention.

A schema enables **inferential elaboration**.   No text is completely explicit. A reader's schema provides the basis for making inferences that go beyond the information literally stated in a text.

| inferential elaboration— basis for drawing conclusions (making inferences) provided by schema that enables the reader to go beyond what is explicitly stated in text |

A schema allows orderly searches of memory.   A schema can provide the reader with a guide to the types of information that need to be recalled. For instance, a person attempting to recall the food served at a fine meal can review the categories of food typically included in a fine meal: What was the appetizer? What was the soup? Was there a salad? And so on. In other words, by tracing through the schema used to structure the text, the reader is helped to gain access to the particular information learned when the text was read.

A schema facilitates editing and summarizing.   Since a schema contains within itself criteria of importance, it enables the reader to produce summaries that include significant propositions and omit trivial ones.

A schema permits **inferential reconstruction**.   When there are gaps in memory, a rememberer's schema, along with the specific text information that can be recalled, helps generate hypotheses about the missing information. For example, suppose a person cannot recall what beverage was served with a fine meal. If he can recall that the entree was fish, he will be able to infer that the beverage may have been white wine.

| inferential reconstruction— schema, in conjunction with text information, can enable the reader to fill in memory gaps and generate hypotheses about missing information |

The foregoing are tentative hypotheses about the functions of a schema in text processing, conceived to provide the broadest possible interpretation of available data. Several of the hypotheses can be regarded as rivals—for instance, the ideational scaffolding hypothesis and the selective attention hypothesis—and it may be that not all of them will turn out to be viable. Researchers are now actively at work developing precise models of schema-based processes and subjecting these models to experimental test.

EVIDENCE FOR SCHEMA THEORY

There is now a really good case that schemata incorporating knowledge of the world play an important role in language comprehension. We are beginning to see research on differentiated functions. In a few years it should be possible to speak in more detail about the specific processing mechanisms in which schemata are involved.

TABLE 5.1   Mean Performance on Various Measures

| | NATIONALITY | | | |
| | AMERICANS | | INDIANS | |
MEASURE	AMERICAN PASSAGE	INDIAN PASSAGE	AMERICAN PASSAGE	INDIAN PASSAGE
Time (Seconds)	168	213	304	276
Gist Recall	52.4	37.9	27.3	37.6
Elaborations	5.7	.1	.2	5.4
Distortions	.1	7.6	5.5	.3
Other Overt Errors	7.5	5.2	8.0	5.9
Omissions	76.2	76.6	95.5	83.3

From Steffensen, Joag-Dev, and Anderson (1979).

Many of the claims of schema theory are nicely illustrated in a cross-cultural experiment, completed by Steffensen, Joag-Dev, and Anderson (1979), in which Indians (natives of India) and Americans read letters about an Indian and an American wedding. Of course, every adult member of a society has a well-developed marriage schema. There are substantial differences between Indian and American cultures in the nature of marriages. As a consequence, large differences in comprehension, learning, and memory for the letters were expected.

Table 5.1 summarizes analyses of the recall of the letters by Indian and American subjects. The first row in the table indicates the amount of time subjects spent reading the letters. As can be seen, subjects spent less time reading what for them was the native passage. This was as expected since a familiar schema should speed up and expedite a reader's processing.

The second row in Table 5.1 presents the number of idea units recalled. The gist measure includes not only propositions recalled verbatim but also acceptable paraphrases. The finding was precisely as expected. Americans recalled more of the American text, whereas Indians recalled more of the Indian passage. Within current formulations of schema theory, there are a couple of reasons for predicting that people would learn and remember more of a text about a marriage in their own culture: a culturally appropriate schema may provide the ideational scaffolding that makes it easy to learn information that fits into that schema, or, it may be that the information, once learned, is more accessible because the schema is a structure that makes it easy to search memory.

The row labeled *Elaborations* in Table 5.1 contains the frequency of culturally appropriate extensions of the text. The row labeled *Distortions* contains the frequency of culturally inappropriate modifications of the text. Ever since Bartlett's day, elaborations and distortions have provided the intuitively most compelling evidence for the role of schemata. Many fascinating instances appeared in the protocols collected in the present study. A section of the American passage upon which interesting cultural differences surfaced read as follows:

> Did you know that Pam was going to wear her grandmother's wedding dress? That gave her something that was old, and borrowed, too. It was made of lace over satin, with very large puff sleeves and looked absolutely charming on her.

One Indian had this to say about the American bride's dress: "She was looking all right except the dress was too old and out of fashion." Wearing an heirloom wedding dress is a completely acceptable aspect of the pageantry of the American marriage ceremony. This Indian appears to have completely missed this and has inferred that the dress was out of fashion, on the basis that Indians attach importance to displays of social status, manifested in such details as wearing an up-to-date, fashionable sari.

The gifts described in the Indian passage that were given to the groom's family by the bride's, the dowry, and the reference to the concern of the bride's family that a scooter might be requested were a source of confusion for our American subjects. First of all, the "agreement about the gifts to be given to the in-laws" was changed to "the exchange of gifts," a wording which suggests that gifts are flowing in two directions, not one. Another subject identified the gifts given to the in-laws as favors, which are often given in American weddings to the attendants by the bride and groom.

In another facet of the study, different groups of Indians and Americans read the letters and rated the significance of each of the propositions. It was expected that Americans would regard as important propositions conveying information about ritual and ceremony whereas Indians would see as important propositions dealing with financial and social status. Table 5.2 contains examples of text units that received contrasting ratings of importance from Indians and Americans. Schema theory predicts that text units that are important in the light of the schema are more likely to be learned and, once learned, are more likely to be remembered. This prediction was confirmed. Subjects did recall more text information rated as important by their cultural cohorts, whether recalling what for them was the native or the foreign text.

Of course, it is one thing to show, as Steffensen, Joag-Dev, and Anderson did, that readers from distinctly different national cultures give different interpretations to culturally sensitive materials, and quite another to find the same phenomenon among readers from different but overlapping subcultures within the same country. A critical issue is whether cultural variation within the United States could be a factor in differential reading comprehension. Minority children could have a handicap if stories, texts, and test items presuppose a cultural perspective that the children do not share. An initial exploration of this issue has been completed by Reynolds, Taylor, Steffensen, Shirey, and Anderson (1981), who wrote a passage around an episode involving "sounding." Sounding is an activity predominantly found in the black community in which the participants try to outdo each other in an exchange of insults (Labov, 1972). In two group studies, and one in which subjects were individually interviewed, black teenagers tended to see the episode as involving friendly give-and-take, whereas white teenagers interpreted it as an ugly confrontation,

TABLE 5.2   Examples of Ideas Units of Contrasting Importance to Americans and Indians

AMERICAN PASSAGE		INDIAN PASSAGE	
IDEA UNITS MORE IMPORTANT TO AMERICANS	**IDEA UNITS MORE IMPORTANT TO INDIANS**	**IDEA UNITS MORE IMPORTANT TO AMERICANS**	**IDEA UNITS MORE IMPORTANT TO INDIANS**
Then on Friday night *they had the rehearsal at* the church *and the rehearsal dinner,* which lasted until almost midnight. *All the attendants wore dresses that were specially designed to go with Pam's.* Her mother wore yellow, which looks great on her with her bleached hair, *and George's mother wore pale green.*	*She'll be lucky if she can even get her daughter married, the way things are going.* Her mother wore yellow, which looks great on her *with her bleached hair,* and George's mother wore pale green. Have you seen the diamond she has? *It must have cost George a fortune because it's almost two carats.*	Prema's husband had to wear a dhoti *for that ceremony and for the wedding the next day.* *There were only the usual essential rituals:* the curtain removal, the parents giving the daughter away, walking seven steps together, etc., *and plenty of smoke from the sacred fire.* There must have been about five hundred people *at the wedding feast. Since only fifty people could be seated at one time, it went on for a long time.*	*Prema's in laws seem to be nice enough people.* They did not create any problem in the wedding, *even though Prema's husband is their only son.* *Since they did not ask for any dowry,* Prema's parents were a little worried about their asking for a scooter before the wedding, *but they didn't ask for one.* *Prema's parents were very sad when she left.*

Important idea units are in italics.

sometimes one involving physical violence. For example, when attempting to recall the incident, a black male wrote, "Then everybody tried to get on the person side that joke were the best." A white male wrote, "Soon there was a riot. All the kids were fighting." This research established that when written material has an identifiable cultural loading there is a pronounced effect on comprehension. It remains to be seen how much school reading material is culturally loaded.

In the foregoing research, schemata were manipulated by selecting subjects with different backgrounds. Another approach for getting people to bring different schemata to bear is by selecting different passages. Anderson, Spiro, and Anderson (1978) wrote two closely comparable passages, one about dining at a fancy restaurant, the other about a trip to a supermarket. The same 18 items of food and beverage were mentioned in the two texts, in the same order, and attributed to the same characters. The first hypothesis was that subjects who received the restaurant passage would learn and recall more food and beverage information than subjects who received the supermarket passage. The reasoning was that a dining-at-a-fine-restaurant schema has a more constrained structure than a trip-to-a-supermarket schema. That is to say, fewer food and beverage items will fit the former schema; one could choose soda pop and hot dogs at a supermarket, but these items would not be ordered at a fine restaurant. Moreover, there are more cross-connections among items in a restaurant schema. For example, a steak will be accompanied by a baked potato, or maybe french fries. In two experiments, subjects who read the restaurant text recalled more food and beverage items than subjects who read the supermarket text.

The second prediction was that students who read the restaurant text would more often attribute the food and drink items to the correct characters. In a supermarket it does not matter, for instance, who throws the Brussels sprouts into the shopping cart, but in a restaurant it does matter who orders which item. This prediction was confirmed in two experiments.

A third prediction was that order of recall of food and beverages would correspond more closely to order of mention in the text for subjects who read the restaurant story. There is not, or need not be, a prescribed sequence for selecting items in a grocery store, but there is a characteristic order in which items are served in a restaurant. This hypothesis was supported in one experiment and the trend of the data favored it in a second.

Another technique for manipulating readers' schemata is by assigning them different perspectives. Pichert and Anderson (1977) asked people to pretend that they were either burglars or home buyers before reading a story about what two boys did at one of the boys' homes while they were skipping school. The finding was that people learned more of the information to their assigned perspective. For instance, burglars were more likely to learn that three 10-speed bikes were parked in the garage, whereas home buyers were more likely to learn that the house had a leaky roof. Anderson and Pichert (1978; see also Anderson, Pichert, & Shirey, 1979) went on to show that the reader's perspective has independent effects on learning and recall. Subjects who switch perspectives and then recall the story for a second time recall additional, previously unrecalled, information important to their new perspective but unimportant to their original perspective. For example, a person who begins as a home buyer may fail to remember that the story says the side door is kept unlocked, but may later remember this information when told to assume the role of a burglar. Subjects report that previously unrecalled information significant in the light of the new perspective "pops" into their heads.

Recent unpublished research in my laboratory, completed in collaboration with Ralph Reynolds and Paul Wilson, suggests selective allocation of attention to text elements that are important in the light of the reader's schema. We have employed two measures of attention. The first is the amount of time a subject spends reading schema-relevant sentences. The second is time to respond to a probe presented during schema-relevant sentences. The probe is a tone sounded through earphones; the subject responds by pushing a button as fast as possible. The logic of the probe task is that if the mind is occupied with reading, there will be a slight delay in responding to the probe. Our results indicate that people assigned a burglar perspective, for instance, have slightly longer reading times and slightly longer probe times when reading burglar-relevant sentences. Comparable results have been obtained by other investigators (Cirilo & Foss, 1980; Haberlandt, Berian, & Sandson, 1980; Just & Carpenter, 1980).

IMPLICATIONS OF SCHEMA THEORY FOR DESIGN OF MATERIALS AND CLASSROOM INSTRUCTION

First, I urge publishers to include teaching suggestions in manuals designed to help children activate relevant knowledge before reading. Children do not spontaneously integrate what they are reading with what they already know (cf. Paris & Lindauer, 1976). This means that special attention should be paid to preparation for reading. Questions should be asked that remind children of relevant experiences of their own and orient them toward the problems faced by story characters.

Second, the teachers' manuals accompanying basal programs and content area texts ought to include suggestions for building prerequisite knowledge when it cannot be safely presupposed. According to schema theory, this practice should promote comprehension. There is direct evidence to support knowledge-building activities. Hayes and Tierney (1980) asked American high school students to read and recall newspaper reports of cricket matches. Performance improved sharply when the students received instruction on the nature of the game of cricket before reading the newspaper reports.

Third, I call for publishers to feature lesson activities that will lead children to meaningfully integrate what they already know with what is presented on the printed page. From the perspective of schema theory, prediction techniques such as the Directed Reading-Thinking Activity (Stauffer, 1969) can be recommended. The DRTA would appear to cause readers to search their store of knowledge and integrate what they already know with what is stated. It must be acknowledged, however, that the empirical evidence for the efficacy of the DRTA is flimsy at present (Tierney & Cunningham, 1984). Recently, Anderson, Mason, and Shirey (1984) have illustrated that under optimum conditions strong benefits can be obtained using a prediction technique. A heterogeneous sample of third graders read sentences such as, "The stupid child ran into the street after the ball." Children in the prediction group read each sentence aloud and then indicated what might happen next. In the case of the sentence above, a frequent prediction was that the child might get hit by a car. A second group read the sentences aloud with an emphasis on accurate decoding. A third and a fourth group listened to the sentences and read them silently. The finding was that the prediction group recalled 72% of the sentences, whereas the average for the other three groups was 43%.

Fourth, I urge publishers to employ devices that will highlight the structure of text material. Schema theory inclines one to endorse the practice of providing advance organizers or structured overviews, along the lines proposed by Ausubel (1968) and Herber (1978). Ausubel, who can be regarded as one of the pioneer schema theorists, has stated that "the principal function of the organizer is to bridge the gap between what the learner already knows and what he needs to know before he can successfully learn the task at hand" (1968, p. 148). There have been dozens of empirical studies of advance organizers over the past 20 years. Thorough reviews of this bulky literature by Mayer (1979) and Luiten, Ames, and Ackerson (1980) point to the conclusion that organizers generally have a facilitative effect. Nevertheless, from within current formulations of schema theory, there is room for reservations about advance organizers. Notably, Ausubel's insistence (cf. 1968, pp. 148, 333) that organizers must be stated at a high level of generality, abstractness, and inclusiveness is puzzling. The problem is that general, abstract language often is difficult to understand. Children, in particular, are more easily reminded of what they know when concrete language is used. As Ausubel himself has acknowledged (e.g., 1968, p. 149), "To be useful . . . organizers themselves must obviously be learnable and must be stated in familiar terms."

A final implication of schema theory is that minority children may sometimes be counted as failing to comprehend school reading material because their schemata do not match those of the majority culture. Basal reading programs, content area texts, and standardized tests lean heavily on the conventional assumption that meaning is inherent in the words and structure of a text. When prior knowledge is required, it is assumed to be knowledge common to children from every subculture. When new ideas are introduced, these are assumed to be equally accessible to every child. Considering the strong effects that culture has on reading comprehension, the question that naturally arises is whether children from different subcultures can so confidently be assumed to bring a common schema to written material. To be sure, subcultures within the United States do overlap. But is it safe simply to *assume* that when reading the same story, children from every subculture will have the same experience with the setting, ascribe the same goals and motives to characters, imagine the same sequence of actions, predict the same emotional reactions, or expect the same outcomes? This is a question that the research community and the school publishing industry ought to address with renewed vigor.

CONNECTING SCHEMA THEORY AND YOUR CLASSROOM . . .

1. Plan a lesson where your students are learning a new concept. How will you access, assess, build, and tune their schema(ta) to assist in learning this new concept? Be explicit in your description of procedures and in what types of materials you will use.
2. Recall an incident in your own teaching or learning that was not successful. How did schema or the lack thereof affect that teaching or learning event?

REFERENCES

Anderson, R.C. (1978). Schema-directed processes in language comprehension. In A. Lesgold, J. Pellegrino, S. Fokkema, & R. Glaser (Eds.), *Cognitive psychology and instruction*. New York: Plenum.

Anderson, R.C., Mason, J., & Shirey, L.L. (1984). The reading group: An experimental investigation of a labyrinth. *Reading Research Quarterly, 20,* 6–38.

Anderson, R.C., & Pichert, J.W. (1978). Recall of previously unrecallable information following a shift in perspective. *Journal of Verbal Learning and Verbal Behavior, 17,* 1–12.

Anderson, R.C., Pichert, J.W., & Shirey, L.L. (1979, April). *Effects of the reader's schema at different points in time* (Tech. Rep. No. 119). Urbana: University of Illinois, Center for the Study of Reading. (ERIC Document Reproduction Service No. ED169523)

Anderson, R.C., Reynolds, R.E., Schallert, D.L., & Goetz, E.T. (1977). Frameworks for comprehending discourse. *American Educational Research Journal, 14,* 367–382.

Anderson, R.C., Spiro, R.J., & Anderson, M.C. (1978). Schemata as scaffolding for the representation of information in connected discourse. *American Educational Research Journal, 15,* 433–440.

Ausubel, D.P. (1968). *Educational psychology: A cognitive view.* New York: Holt, Rinehart.

Bobrow, D.G., & Norman, D.A. (1975). Some principles of memory schemata. In D.G. Bobrow & A.M. Collins (Eds.), *Representation and understanding: Studies in cognitive science.* New York: Academic.

Bransford, J.D., & Johnson, M.K. (1972). Contextual prerequisites for understanding: Some investigations of comprehension and recall. *Journal of Verbal Learning and Verbal Behavior, 11,* 717–726.

Bransford, J.D., & McCarrell, N.S. (1974). A sketch of a cognitive approach to comprehension. In W.B. Weimer & D.S. Palermo (Eds.), *Cognition and the symbolic process.* Hillsdale, NJ: Erlbaum.

Chiesi, H.L., Spilich, G.J., & Voss, J.F. (1979). Acquisition of domain-related information in relation to high- and low-domain knowledge. *Journal of Verbal Learning and Verbal Behavior, 18,* 257–274.

Cirilo, R.K., & Foss, D.J. (1980). Text structure and reading time for sentences. *Journal of Verbal Learning and Verbal Behavior, 19,* 96–109.

Haberlandt, K., Berian, C., & Sandson, J. (1980). The episode schema in story processing. *Journal of Verbal Learning and Verbal Behavior, 19,* 635–650.

Hayes, D.A., & Tierney, R.J. (1980, October). *Increasing background knowledge through analogy: Its effects upon comprehension and learning* (Tech. Rep. No. 186). Urbana: University of Illinois, Center for the Study of Reading. (ERIC Document Reproduction Service No. ED195953)

Herber, H.L. (1978). *Teaching reading in content areas* (2nd ed.), Englewood Cliffs, NJ: Prentice Hall.

Just, M.A., & Carpenter, P.A. (1980). A theory of reading: From eye fixation to comprehension, *Psychological Review, 87,* 329–354.

Labov, W. (1972). *Language in the inner city: Studies in the black English vernacular.* Washington, DC: Center for Applied Linguistics.

Luiten, J., Ames, W., & Ackerson, G. (1980). A meta-analysis of the effects of advance organizers on learning and retention. *American Educational Research Journal, 17,* 211–218.

Mayer, R.E. (1979). Can advance organizers influence meaningful learning? *Review of Educational Research, 49,* 371–383.

Paris, S.G., & Lindauer, B.K. (1976). The role of inference in children's comprehension and memory. *Cognitive Psychology, 8,* 217–227.

Pichert, J.W., & Anderson, R.C. (1977). Taking different perspectives on a story. *Journal of Educational Psychology, 69,* 309–315.

Reynolds, R.E., Taylor, M.A., Steffensen, M.S., Shirey, L.L., & Anderson, R.C. (1981, April). *Cultural schemata and reading comprehension* (Tech. Rep. No. 201). Urbana: University of Illinois, Center for the Study of Reading.

Rumelhart, D.E., & McClelland, J.L. (1980). *An interactive activation model of the effect of context in perception* (Part 2: CHIP Tech. Rep.). La Jolla, CA: University of California, Center for Human Information Processing.

Stauffer, R.G. (1969). *Teaching reading as a thinking process.* New York: Harper & Row.

Steffensen, M.S., Joag-Dev, C., & Anderson, R.C. (1979). A cross-cultural perspective on reading comprehension. *Reading Research Quarterly, 15,* 10–29.

Tierney, R.J., & Cunningham, J.W. (1984). Research on teaching reading comprehension. In P.D. Pearson, R. Barr, M.L. Kamil, & P. Mosenthal (Eds.), *Handbook of reading research* (pp. 609–655). New York: Longman.

CHAPTER 6

SCHEMA ACTIVATION AND SCHEMA ACQUISITION: COMMENTS ON RICHARD C. ANDERSON'S REMARKS

JOHN D. BRANSFORD

***THINK ABOUT* SCHEMA ACTIVATION AND ACQUISITION . . .**

1. Read to find out the difference between activating and acquiring schema.

2. Read to find out what Bransford thinks are the major implications from schema theory for teachers and teaching in general.

Professor Anderson has done an excellent job of presenting the essentials of schema theory and of highlighting a number of its implications. My comments on his paper are divided into two points. First, I want to reemphasize some of Anderson's major arguments and elaborate on several of their implications. I shall then discuss some potential shortcomings of many versions of schema theory and suggest some modifications that seem relevant to the issue of understanding how people learn from texts.

> **schema activation**—
> accessing the appropriate
> background knowledge in
> order to comprehend a text

Several of Anderson's points about schema theory can be reviewed by considering the processes involved in understanding, and later remembering, a simple statement such as the following: "Jane decided not to wear her matching silver necklace, earrings, and belt because she was going to the airport." In order to

From Anderson, R.C., Osborn, J., & Tierney, R.J. (Eds.), *Learning to Read in American Schools: Basal Readers and Content Texts* (pp. 259–272). Copyright © 1984 by Lawrence Erlbaum Associates. Reprinted with permission of the publisher.

comprehend this statement, one must go beyond the information that was given and postulate a reason for the connection between airports and Jane's style of dress. People who are familiar with airports—who have a well-developed "airport schema"—might assume that Jane decided not to wear her silver jewelry because of the metal detectors in airports. In Anderson's terminology, their schemata provide a basis for interpreting and elaborating on the information they heard.

Anderson also argued that schemata affect processes at the time of output as well as at input. For example, adults who attempt to recall the original "airport" statement three days later may rely on their knowledge of airports for a selective search of memory and then state that "Jane decided not to wear some metal jewelry because it could cause unnecessary delays at the airport." Note that this type of response reveals the comprehender's assumptions about important elements. It is the fact that the jewelry was metal that was most important and not, for example, that it was expensive or pretty. Anderson also emphasized this function of schemata: They provide a basis for determining the important elements in a message or text.

Overall, Anderson discussed six functions of schemata. They provide a basis for (1) assimilating text information, (2) making inferential elaborations that fill in the gaps in messages, (3) allocating attention to important text elements, (4) searching memory in an orderly fashion, (5) formulating a summary of information, and (6) making inferences that can enable one to reconstruct an original message despite having forgotten some of the details. It may be possible to add to Professor Anderson's list of "schema functions," but the six functions he cited are sufficient to illustrate why the knowledge possessed by the learner has pervasive effects on performance. I might add that Anderson was not simply arguing that the activation of appropriate knowledge is a useful thing to do; he was asserting that it is a fundamental aspect of the act of comprehending and remembering. One clear implication of this position is that some children may appear to have poor comprehension and memory skills *not* because they have some inherent comprehension or memory "deficits," but because they lack, or fail to activate, the background knowledge that was presupposed by a message or a text.

It is instructive to note that there are many levels at which a child may lack the background knowledge necessary to understand a text. At one extreme, the child may have no information about a concept; he or she may know nothing about airports, for example. At another level, a child may know something about a concept (for example, airports) yet still fail to understand many statements that involve this concept. As an illustration, consider once again the simple statement about Jane's trip to the airport and her decision about her silver jewelry. A child may know that airports are "places where planes take off and land" yet have no knowledge that airports contain metal detectors. The child therefore knows something about airports, but his or her "airport schema" is still less articulated than that of most adults. The child's knowledge may be sufficient for understanding some types of statements about airports (e.g., John went to the airport because his aunt was coming to visit) yet insufficient for others (e.g., the earlier statement about Jane). The question of what it means for children to be "familiar" with the words used in a story is therefore more complicated than might be apparent at first glance.

Imagine another child who knows that airports are places where planes land and take off, and also knows that airports are often crowded and may be havens for thieves. This child may form the following interpretation of the statement about Jane and the airport: "Jane did not wear her expensive jewelry because she was afraid that someone might take it." This interpretation is quite different from one that focuses on the fact that airports have metal detectors. According to the "crowded airport" interpretation, the important elements are that the jewelry is valuable, visible, and easily accessible, rather than the fact that the jewelry is metal and hence may trigger a security alarm. Relatively subtle differences in people's schemata (in this case their "airport schemata") can therefore have important effects on the interpretations they make.

Consider some of the problems that can arise when two people form different interpretations of the same message. For example, imagine that a teacher forms a "metal detector" interpretation of the statement about Jane and that a child forms a "thief" interpretation. In a one-to-one conversation, these two individuals might well discover their differences in interpretation and agree that both are reasonable. However, extended one-to-one conversations are often impossible in an educational setting. Teachers are frequently forced to use assessment questions in order to evaluate students' comprehension. These questions may be supplied either by the author of a text or by the teacher. In either case, the phrasing of the question may reflect the question asker's initial interpretations of a message. For example, a question such as "Why didn't Jane wear something metal?" may stem from a "metal detector" interpretation, whereas the question "Why didn't Jane wear her expensive jewelry?" tends to reflect a "thief" interpretation. My colleagues and I have found that even relatively subtle mismatches between a learner's initial interpretations and a teacher's or a tester's way of phrasing questions can cause considerable decrements in memory performance (Barclay, Bransford, Franks, McCarrell, & Nitsch, 1974). If my phrasing of a question is not congruent with a child's initial interpretation of an event, I may erroneously conclude that the child did not learn.

Mismatches between the phrasing of questions and a child's initial interpretations affect not only teachers' assessments of children's learning abilities; I am convinced that they also affect children's assumptions about their own abilities. Several years ago, Marcia Johnson and I conducted a study with college students that is relevant to this point (Bransford & Johnson, 1973). We created a passage about a man walking through the woods; nearly all our students interpreted the story as describing a hunter. They did not realize that the passage could also be interpreted from the perspective of an escaping convict. As Anderson noted, the perspective one takes on a story affects one's interpretation of the significance of information. For example, the story included information about it being muddy, hence the man's boots sank in deeply. He then came to a little stream and walked in it for a while. From the perspective of a hunter, this information suggests that the boots may have become caked with mud and that the man tried to clean them by walking in the stream. From the perspective of an escaping convict, however, the same information suggests that the man was leaving footprints and must take precautions in order to avoid being tracked.

We asked one group of college students to read the story I have described but said nothing about the possibility of interpreting it as an escaping convict. They, therefore, assumed that it was about a hunter, and the story made sense from this point of view. After reading the story, we supplied students with questions and explained that these should help them retrieve the information they had studied. However, the questions were written from the perspective of the escaping convict interpretation. For example, one question was "What was the concern with the trail and what was done to eliminate it?" Not surprisingly, these questions did not help students remember relevant aspects of the story; instead they caused confusion. Many of the students thought about the questions for a considerable amount of time and eventually concluded that they had completely misinterpreted the story. Several apologized for having made such an error. In reality, however, they had not "misinterpreted" the story; their original interpretations had been perfectly reasonable. We eventually told the students this, of course, because it would have been unfair to let them think that they had been in error. The point I want to stress, however, is that these mismatches between initial interpretations and the phrasing of questions can occur inadvertently in almost any situation. Furthermore, learners who do not realize why their performance suffered may mistakenly attribute their difficulties to their own inabilities to learn.

The preceding examples illustrate only a few of many important implications of schema theory, but I now want to consider some possible shortcomings of many versions of this theory. I refer to these as *possible* shortcomings because I am uncertain whether they are shortcomings of the actual theory or shortcomings that stem from my personal interpretation of schema theory (i.e., my "schema theory schema" may be only partially developed). At any rate, I believe that there are some issues concerning schema theory that need to be explored, especially when one begins to ask how teachers and authors might use this theory to help themselves avoid some of the text–student mismatches and question–student mismatches that have been discussed.

One possible approach to the problem of mismatches is to analyze carefully the materials presented to children and then to simplify them so that mismatches are much less likely to occur. There are some obvious merits to this approach, but it involves some potential problems as well. These problems revolve around the issue of what it means to "simplify" texts.

Several years ago, I participated in a conference where the topic of simplifying texts arose during one of the discussion periods. One of the participants at the conference expressed some concerns about the reading materials that his children had received in the elementary grades (see Kavanagh & Strange, 1978, pp. 329–330). He felt that the content of the stories (e.g., about a milkman, mailman, etc.) was extremely dull. When he asked the teachers why the children received such uninteresting materials, he was told that the children were familiar with the "community helpers." The teachers had not read about schema theory, so they did not say, "These stories are written to be congruent with the children's preexisting schemata." Nevertheless, the teachers were emphasizing the importance of providing children with materials that were congruent with the knowledge they already possessed.

The conference participant went on to say that his children did not like to read stories about topics that were extremely familiar; they were much more interested in reading about novel situations. In addition, he asked how theories that emphasize the importance of assimilating information to preexisting knowledge can account for the fact that it is possible to understand stories about novel situations. I think that this is a crucial question to ask schema theorists. It is especially crucial for those schema theorists who argue that comprehension involves the activation of a preexisting schema that provides a coherent account of the givens in a message. Many schema theorists have very little to say about the processes by which novel events are comprehended and new schemata are acquired.

In his presentation, Professor Anderson mentioned two types of situations involving schemata. One involves the activation of preexisting schemata. The second, which he noted was more interesting, involves the construction of new schemata. Since a major goal of education is to help students develop new skills and knowledge—to help them become able to understand things that they could not understand previously—the issue of **schema construction** or schemata acquisition is extremely important. Nevertheless, nearly all the experiments used to support schema theory involve situations where students are prompted to activate preexisting schemata. For example, students may be prompted to activate a "washing clothes" schema, "prisoner" schema, "fancy restaurant" schema, "home buyer" schema, and so forth. We have seen that these schemata provide important support for both comprehension processes and memory processes. However, experiments involving these schemata "work" only because the students in the experiments have already acquired the necessary schemata. If a person knew nothing about washing clothes, for example, it would do no good to simply tell him or her that this is the topic of the washing clothes passage. Similarly, imagine that a child is told that "Jane did not wear her silver jewelry because she was going somewhere" and is then given the cue, "She is going to the airport." A child who knows only that airports are places where planes take off and land is still going to have difficulty understanding this statement. In situations such as this, we confront the problem of helping students develop new schemata or of helping them refine the structure of schemata that they have already acquired (e.g., Bransford & Nitsch, 1978; Bransford, Nitsch, & Franks, 1977; Brown, 1979).

Imagine that we want to help a child develop a more sophisticated "airport schema." We will assume that the child knows that airports are places where planes take off and land, yet is unaware that there are metal detectors in airports. A basic and time-honored procedure for helping the child acquire this new

> **schema construction—**
> acquiring new knowledge and skills based on comprehension of text

information is to tell him or her about it. One might therefore supply information such as "There are metal detectors in airports" either prior to the child's reading a text or in the text itself.

There are many reasons why a statement such as "There are metal detectors in airports" may not be helpful to a child. An obvious reason is that a child may not be familiar with the concept of metal detectors. However, assume that our child is familiar with this general concept. He or she may still not benefit from the statement that "There are metal detectors in airports." The child needs to understand what the detectors are for and who uses them. Without this information, the child may assume that there are stores in airports that sell things, and hence conclude that most airports have "metal detector" stores. This is not the interpretation we want the child to make.

It seems clear that effective teachers or writers would do much more than simply state, "There are metal detectors in airports." They would elaborate by helping the child realize that pilots guide planes to particular locations, that someone could try to force a pilot to fly to a different location, that this act may involve a gun or knife, that these objects can be detected by metal detectors, that the detectors at the airport are designed to keep people from taking knives and guns aboard the plane, and so forth. The amount of explanation needed will depend on the preexisting knowledge base of the learner (e.g., a relatively knowledgeable child may need only be told that "There are metal detectors in airports in order to discourage hijacking.") The point I want to emphasize is that the goal of this instruction is to help the child develop a more sophisticated schema rather than simply to activate a schema that already exists. The teacher or author is attempting to help the child activate various preexisting "pockets" of knowledge that previously had been unrelated, and to help the child reassemble these "pockets" of knowledge into an integrated schema. This schema should then provide support for comprehending and remembering subsequent events. For example, the child's interpretation of "the metal-detector repairman received a phone call and rushed to the airport" may now be more likely to involve the assumption that he was rushing to repair a machine rather than rushing to catch a plane or to meet someone arriving by plane.

At a general level, an emphasis on the importance of helping students activate sources of preexisting knowledge that can be reassembled into new schemata is consistent with Ausubel's (1963, 1968) theory of meaningful learning. For example, he advocates the use of "advanced organizers" in order to prepare students for texts. I think it is fair to say, however, that many aspects of this theory need greater articulation; in particular, the guidelines for writing advanced organizers are relatively vague. One of the difficulties of constructing these guidelines is that advanced organizers must differ depending on whether one is dealing with a problem of schema activation or schema construction. An advanced organizer that is relatively general can be effective if learners have already acquired the schemata necessary for understanding a text; these general statements can prime concepts that learners might fail to activate spontaneously. When one is dealing with problems of schema construction or acquisition, however, advanced organizers composed of general statements will not suffice.

Earlier, I emphasized some of the specific elaboration or explanations that may be required to help a child incorporate information about metal detectors into his or her airport schema. It seems valuable to explore this issue further by examining the processes involved in acquiring knowledge about a more complex domain. Imagine, therefore, that someone is familiar with the general terms *vein* and *artery*, yet wants to learn more about them. (This is analogous to knowing something about airports, yet needing additional information.) Assume that the person reads a passage which states that arteries are thick, are elastic, and carry blood that is rich in oxygen from the heart; veins are thinner, are less elastic, and carry blood rich in carbon dioxide back to the heart. To the biological novice, even this relatively simple set of facts can seen arbitrary and confusing. Was it veins or arteries that are thin? Was the thin one or the thick one elastic? Which one carries carbon dioxide from the heart (or was it to the heart)?

Even the biological novice who is familiar with the terms *veins* and *arteries* may have difficulty learning the information in this passage. The problem the learner faces is that the facts and relationships appear arbitrary. It is possible to create an analogous situation by using concepts that are familiar to everyone. For example, imagine reading 10 statements such as those listed below and then answering questions about them from memory:

The tall man bought the crackers.
The bald man read the newspaper.
The funny man liked the ring.
The hungry man purchased the tie.
The short man used the broom.
The strong man skimmed the book.

College students do quite poorly when they are presented with these statements and are then asked memory questions such as "Which man bought the crackers?" (Stein & Bransford, 1979; Stein, Morris, & Bransford, 1978). The students rate each sentence as comprehensible, yet have difficulty remembering because the relationship between each type of man and the actions performed seem arbitrary. The biological novice is in a similar position because he or she sees no particular reason why an artery should be elastic or nonelastic, thick or thin. Note that to a child, a statement such as "Airports have metal detectors" can also seem arbitrary. The child may therefore have difficulty retaining the new information about airports; hence it will not be available for future use. This problem of retention becomes even more acute if we make the reasonable assumption that children are introduced to a number of new ideas during the course of a day. For example, they may receive new information about airports, fancy restaurants, dinosaurs, countries, and so forth. If these new facts seem arbitrary, it can be difficult to remember which things go with what.

In order to make the facts less arbitrary, we need to give a learner information that can clarify their significance or relevance (see Bransford, Stein, Shelton, & Owings, 1980). For example, what's the significance of the elasticity of arteries?

How does this property relate to the functions that arteries perform? Note that our imaginary passage states that arteries can carry blood from the heart—blood that is pumped in spurts. This provides one clue about the significance of elasticity—arteries may need to expand and contract to accommodate the pumping of blood. It can also be important to understand why veins do *not* need to be elastic. Since veins can carry blood back to the heart, they may have less of a need to accommodate the large changes in pressure resulting from the heart pumping blood in spurts.

The process of clarifying the significance of facts about veins and arteries can be carried further. Since arteries carry blood *from* the heart, there is a problem of directionality. Why doesn't the blood flow back into the heart? This will not be perceived as a problem if one assumes that arterial blood always flows downhill, but let's assume that our passage mentions that there are arteries in the neck and shoulder regions. Arterial blood must therefore flow uphill as well. This information might provide an additional clue about the significance of elasticity. If arteries expand from a spurt of blood and then contract, this might help the blood move in a particular direction. Arteries might, therefore, perform a function similar to one-way valves.

My colleagues and I have argued that there are at least two important consequences of activities that enable a learner to understand the significance or relevance of new factual content (e.g., Bransford et al., 1980). First, people who understand the significance of facts develop knowledge structures that enable them to deal with novel situations. As an illustration, imagine that a biological novice reads a passage about veins and arteries and is then given the task of designing an artificial artery. Would it have to be elastic? A person who has merely memorized the fact that "arteries are elastic" would have little basis for answering the question. In contrast, the person who understands the significance or relevance of elasticity is in a much better position to approach the problem. For example, this person might realize the possibility of using a relatively nonelastic material that is sufficient to withstand the pressure requirements of spurting blood, plus realize the possibility of equipping the artificial artery with one-way valves that direct the flow of blood. This individual may not be able to specify all the details for creating the artificial artery, of course, but he or she at least has some appreciation of various possibilities and has an idea of the types of additional information that need to be discovered or acquired.

Activities that enable people to understand the significance of new factual content also facilitate memory. Facts that initially had seemed arbitrary and confusing become meaningful; the information is therefore much easier to retain. As an illustration, consider once again the earlier statements about the different types of men. I noted that college students have a difficult time remembering which man did what because the relationship between the type of man and the actions performed seem arbitrary. These same statements become easy to remember if students are supplied with information, or are helped to generate information, that renders these relationships less arbitrary (Stein & Bransford, 1979). For example:

The tall man purchased the crackers that had been lying on the top shelf.
The bald man read the newspaper in order to look for a hat sale.

> The funny man liked the ring that squirted water.
> The hungry man purchased the tie so that he could get into the fancy restaurant.
> The short man used the broom to operate the light switch.
> The strong man skimmed the book about weightlifting.

Elaborations such as these help people understand the significance or relevance of linking a particular type of man to a particular activity. They are therefore able to answer memory questions such as "Which man purchased the tie?" "Which man used the broom?" etc. In a similar manner, people who understand the significance of various properties of veins and arteries (e.g., the significance of the elasticity of arteries) are able to remember which properties go with what, and the child who understands the significance of having metal detectors in airports is better able to remember this fact.

It is important to note, however, that there are constraints on the type of additional information, or elaboration, that will enable students to understand the significance or relevance of new facts. As an example, consider the following list:

> The tall man purchased the crackers from the clerk in the store.
> The bald man read the newspaper while eating breakfast.
> The funny man liked the ring that he received as a present.
> The hungry man purchased the tie that was on sale.
> The short man used the broom to sweep the porch.
> The strong man skimmed the book before going to sleep.

These statements include elaborations that make sense semantically, but the elaborations do not help one understand why a particular type of man performed a particular activity. College students who receive a list of 10 sentences such as those above do *worse* than students who received the first list (the list *without* any additional elaboration; Stein & Bransford, 1979). My colleagues and I refer to elaborations such as those just noted as *imprecise* elaborations. In contrast, *precise* elaborations (such as those provided earlier) clarify the significance or relevance of facts (Stein & Bransford, 1979; Stein, Morris, & Bransford, 1978). Imprecise elaborations can make sense semantically; that is, they need not be nonsense. Nevertheless, they can actually produce poorer memory than a set of arbitrary statements that receive no elaborations at all. Note that there are many potential elaborations of facts about veins and arteries, airports, etc., that would also be imprecise. For example, a statement such as "Arteries are elastic so that they can stretch" does not help one understand why they need to be elastic, and a statement such as "There are metal detectors in airports that are used to check passengers" does not help one understand what is being checked nor why.

An emphasis on the degree of precision necessary to help people understand the significance of facts is important for analyzing the issue of what it means to "simplify" texts. A text can be composed of relatively simple words and simple syntax yet still seem quite arbitrary. My colleagues and I asked metropolitan

Nashville teachers to provide us with samples of some of the passages their elementary school students are asked to read, and found a large number that seem arbitrary. For example, one passage discussed the topic of "American Indian Houses." It consisted of statements such as "The Indians of the Northwest Coast lived in slant-roofed houses made of cedar plank. . . . Some California Indian tribes lived in simple, earth-covered or brush shelters. . . . The Plains Indians lived mainly in teepees," etc. The story provided no information about why certain Indians chose certain houses. For example, it said nothing about the relationship between the type of house and the climate of the geographical area, nor about the ease of finding raw materials to build houses depending on the geographical area. Furthermore, the story said nothing about how the style of house was related to the lifestyle of the Indians (e.g., teepees are relatively portable). If students either did not know or failed to activate this extra information, the passage was essentially a list of seemingly arbitrary facts.

Other passages we examined discussed topics such as tools, animals, machines, and so forth. In each case, the passages contained a number of facts, yet frequently failed to provide the information necessary to understand the significance of the facts. For example, a passage describing two types of boomerangs—a returning versus a nonreturning boomerang—provided information about each boomerang's shape, weight, length, function, and so forth. However, it failed to systematically help the reader understand how the structure of each boomerang was related to its function (e.g., how the shape affected whether it returned to the thrower or not, how the weight was a factor in determining whether a boomerang could be used to hunt small versus large game, and so forth). The passages about animals also failed to help students focus on relationships between structure and function. For example, camels have a number of properties that help them adapt to certain aspects of desert life, including desert sandstorms. Facts such as "camels can close their nose passages" and "camels have thick hair around their ear openings" become more significant when one understand how they reduce problems caused by blowing sand. Students who are unable to make these connections on their own experience difficulty because the facts seem arbitrary. They also fail to develop a level of understanding that can provide support for learning subsequent materials. For example, a student who realizes how various properties of camels protect them during sandstorms is in a better position to understand a subsequent story about desert travelers who wear scarves over their faces even though it is hot.

It is important to note that passages such as the ones I have described do not necessarily seem arbitrary to someone who has already developed expertise in these areas. The expert not only already knows the facts but also understands their significance or relevance. Even new facts (e.g., camels can close their nose passages) can seem meaningful to the person whose preexisting schemata provide a basis for understanding their significance (e.g., a person may already know that camels are adapted to survive in desert sandstorms). Adults who construct or evaluate passages for children are usually in a "schema activation" mode, but children who read these passages are usually confronted with the problem of constructing new schemata or of developing more detailed schemata. This is as it should be; the goal of the educator is to help children develop new skills and knowledge. However, we need to recognize that schema activation and schema construction represent two different problems. Our attempts to simplify texts can be self-defeating if we inadvertently omit the kinds of precise elaborations necessary for understanding the significance of the information. Indeed, we may sometimes need to introduce children to relatively sophisticated concepts that can provide a basis for more precise understanding. For example, the general concept of adaptation (of structure–function relationships) provides a powerful schema that supports the comprehension of new facts in a number of domains (e.g., structure–function relationships are important for understanding biological systems such as veins and arteries, tools such as different types of boomerangs, animals and environments such as camels and their desert habitats, and so forth). The careful introduction of core concepts such as this one may facilitate learning to a considerable degree.

SUMMARY AND CONCLUSIONS

I began by reemphasizing Professor Anderson's arguments about schema theory because they are extremely important. For example, Dr. Anderson's discussion of the six functions of schemata provided a powerful argument for the pervasive effects of students' preexisting knowledge. I elaborated on two implications of his argument. One implication was that students may have developed partial schemata that are sufficient for understanding some types of statements but not for understanding others. We, therefore, need a more precise analysis of what it means for students to be "familiar" with the words in a text. The second implication was that preexisting schemata affect the interpretation of teachers and authors as well as the interpretation of students, and that a person's interpretation can affect the way that he or she phrases test questions. If there is a mismatch between the phrasing of a question and a student's interpretation of a passage, decrements in performance can occur.

Most of my comments were directed at differences between schema activation and schema construction. Professor Anderson noted that these represented two different (although related) problems. Most of the experiments he discussed dealt with schema activation because this represents the current state of the experimental literature. I emphasized schema construction because a major task for the educator is to help children develop new knowledge and skills.

The concept of precision provided the framework for my discussion of schema construction. To the novice, new facts can seem arbitrary unless they are precisely elaborated in a way that clarifies their significance or relevance. New facts that are not elaborated, or that are imprecisely elaborated, are difficult to remember and hence are not available for future use. In contrast, precisely elaborated facts can be integrated into new schemata that can provide support for the comprehension of subsequent texts. I also noted that texts can be composed of simple words and syntax, yet can still seem arbitrary to the novice; the notion of what it means to "simplify" texts, therefore, warrants careful consideration. Indeed, we may need to introduce children to relatively sophisticated "core concepts" that can provide a basis for understanding the significance of a wide variety of new facts.

The final point I want to emphasize involves an issue which I have not mentioned but which I feel is extremely important. I have noted that texts which are not precisely elaborated can seem arbitrary to the novice, but I do not believe that children's materials should always be elaborated explicitly. The reason is that children must learn to identify situations where they need more information in order to understand precisely, and they must learn to supply their own elaborations. More generally, I believe that they must learn about themselves as learners. This includes an understanding of how different texts and text structures influence their abilities to comprehend new information and to remember it at later points in time.

My colleagues and I have been working with fifth graders who are proficient at decoding but who differ in their abilities to learn from texts. In contrast to the successful learners in our samples, our less-successful learners have very little insight into the factors that make things easy or difficult to comprehend and remember, and they rarely attempt to use information that is potentially available to understand the significance or relevance of new facts. Their ability to learn is therefore impaired. We have created sets of materials that enable these students to experience the effects of their own learning activities and that enable them to learn to modify their activities. We find that these exercises can improve their performance considerably. In order to do this, however, we purposely create materials that are arbitrary, help the students evaluate these materials and experience their effects on memory, and then help them learn what to do to make the same materials significant or relevant. This seems necessary in order to help the students learn to learn on their own. The learning-to-learn issue is beyond the scope of Professor Anderson's paper and mine. I simply wanted to mention the issue at this point in order to emphasize that the procedures necessary to make texts easy to learn are not necessarily identical to those necessary to help children learn to learn on their own.

CONNECTING SCHEMA ACTIVATION AND ACQUISITION TO YOUR CLASSROOM . . .

1. Describe the difference between schema activation and schema acquisition. Why is it important to understand the difference as a classroom teacher? Be prepared to share with colleagues and your professor.
2. Choose a topic or concept to create a lesson in your current classroom or in a particular grade of your choice. Describe how you would approach this topic/concept to *activate* students' schema. Depict how you would approach this topic/concept in order for students to *acquire* (for you to build) schema or background knowledge. Share with your colleagues and professor.

REFERENCES

Ausubel, D. (1963). *The psychology of meaningful verbal learning.* New York: Grune and Stratton.

Ausubel, D. (1968). *Educational psychology: A cognitive view.* New York: Holt, Rinehart.

Barclay, J.R., Bransford, J.D., Franks, J.J., McCarrell, N.S., & Nitsch, K. (1974). Comprehension and semantic flexibility. *Journal of Verbal Learning and Verbal Behavior, 13,* 471–481.

Bransford, J.D., & Johnson, M.K. (1973). Considerations of some problems of comprehension. In W. Chase (Ed.), *Visual information processing.* New York: Academic.

Bransford, J.D., & Nitsch, K.E. (1978). Coming to understand things we could not previously understand. In J.F. Kavanagh & W. Strange (Eds.), *Speech and language in the laboratory, school, and clinic.* Cambridge, MA: MIT Press.

Bransford, J.D., Nitsch, K.E., & Franks, J.J. (1977). Schooling and the facilitation of knowing. In R.C. Anderson, R.J. Spiro, & W.E. Montague (Eds.), *Schooling and the acquisition of knowledge.* Hillsdale, NJ: Erlbaum.

Bransford, J.D., Stein, B.S., Shelton, T.S., & Owings, R.A. (1980). Cognition and adaptation: The importance of learning to learn. In J. Harvey (Ed.), *Cognition, social behavior and the environment.* Hillsdale, NJ: Erlbaum.

Brown, A.L. (1979). Theories of memory and the problems of development: Activity, growth, and knowledge. In L.S. Cermak & F.I.M. Craik (Eds.), *Levels of processing and human memory.* Hillsdale, NJ: Erlbaum.

Kavanagh, J.F., & Strange, W. (Eds.). (1978). *Speech and language in the laboratory, school, and clinic.* Cambridge, MA: MIT Press.

Stein, B.S., & Bransford, J.D. (1979). Constraints on effective elaboration: Effects of precision and subject generation. *Journal of Verbal Learning and Verbal Behavior, 18,* 769–777.

Stein, B.S., Morris, C.D., & Bransford, J.D. (1978). Constraints on effective elaboration. *Journal of Verbal Learning and Verbal Behavior, 17,* 707–714.

CHAPTER 7

THE TRANSACTIONAL THEORY OF READING AND WRITING

LOUISE M. ROSENBLATT

THINK ABOUT TRANSACTIONAL THEORY . . .

1. Read to discover Rosenblatt's description of reading as a transaction between reader and text. How does Rosenblatt's view differ from the view of reading as an interaction of reader and text?
2. Read to find out about Rosenblatt's reading continuum and the difference between efferent and aesthetic reading.
3. Read to find out about the relationship between prior knowledge and comprehension according to Rosenblatt.

> Terms such as *the reader* are somewhat misleading, though convenient, fictions. There is no such thing as a generic reader or a generic literary work; there are in reality only the potential millions of individual readers of individual literary works. . . . The reading of any work of literature is, of necessity, an individual and unique occurrence involving the mind and emotions of some particular reader. (Rosenblatt, 1938/1983)

That statement, first published in *Literature as Exploration* in 1938, seems especially important to reiterate at the beginning of a presentation of a "theoretical model" of the reading process. A theoretical model by definition is an abstraction, or a generalized pattern devised in order to think about a subject. Hence, it is essential to recognize that, as I concluded, we may generalize about similarities among such events, but we cannot evade the realization that there are actually only innumerable separate transactions between readers and texts.

From Ruddell, R.B., Ruddell, M.R., & Singer, H. (Eds.), *Theoretical Models and Processes of Reading* (4th ed., pp. 1057–1092). Copyright © 1994 by the International Reading Association.

Rosenblatt, Louise M. (2004). The transactional theory of reading and writing. *Theoretical Models and Processes of Reading*, 5th edition, Robert B. Ruddell, & Norman J. Unrau, editors, International Reading Association, article 48, 1363–1398.

As I sought to understand how we make the meanings called novels, poems, or plays, I discovered that I had developed a theoretical model that covers all modes of reading. Ten years of teaching courses in literature and composition had preceded the writing of that statement. This had made possible observation of readers encountering a wide range of "literary" and "nonliterary" texts, discussing them, keeping journals while reading them, and writing spontaneous reactions and reflective essays. And decades more of such observation preceded the publication of *The Reader, the Text, the Poem* (Rosenblatt, 1978), the fullest presentation of the theory and its implications for criticism.

> **pragmatist**—philosophy developed by Charles S. Peirce and William James relating to emphasis on practicality; lessons learned from actual events

Thus, the theory emerges from a process highly appropriate to the **pragmatist** philosophy it embodies. The problem arose in the context of a practical classroom situation. Observations of relevant episodes led to the hypotheses that constitute the theory of the reading process, and these have in turn been applied, tested, confirmed, or revised in the light of further observation.

Fortunately, while specializing in English and comparative literature, I was in touch with the thinking on the forefront of various disciplines. The interpretation of these observations of readers' reading drew on a number of different perspectives—literary and social history, philosophy, aesthetics, linguistics, psychology, and sociology. Training in anthropology provided an especially important point of view. Ideas were developed that in some instances have only recently become established. It seems necessary, therefore, to begin by setting forth some of the basic assumptions and concepts that undergird the transactional theory of the reading process. This in turn will involve presentation of the transactional view of the writing process and the relationship between author and reader.

THE TRANSACTIONAL PARADIGM

Transaction

The terms *transaction* and *transactional* are consonant with a philosophic position increasingly accepted in the 20th century. A new **paradigm** in science (Kuhn, 1970) has required a change in our habits of thinking about our relationship to the world around us. For 300 years, Descartes' dualistic view of the self as distinct from nature sufficed, for example, for the Newtonian paradigm in physics. The self, or "subject," was separate from the "object" perceived.

> **paradigm**—a pattern, set of assumptions, concepts, values, and practices that constitutes a way of viewing reality

"Objective" facts, completely free of subjectivity, were sought, and a direct, immediate perception of "reality" was deemed possible. Einstein's theory and the developments in subatomic physics revealed the need to acknowledge that, as Neils Bohr (1959) explained, the observer is part of the observation—human beings are part of nature. Even the physicists' facts depend to some extent on the interests, hypotheses, and technologies of the observer. The human organism, it became apparent, is ultimately the mediator in any perception of the world or any sense of "reality."

John Dewey's pragmatist epistemology fitted the new paradigm. Hence, Dewey joined with Arthur F. Bentley to work out a new terminology in *Knowing and the Known* (1949). They believed the term *interaction* was too much associated with the old positivistic paradigm, with each element or unit being predefined as separate, as "thing balanced against thing," and their "interaction" studied. Instead, they chose *transaction* to imply "unfractured observation" of the whole situation. Systems of description and naming "are employed to deal with aspects and phases of action, without final attribution to 'elements' or presumptively detachable or independent 'entities,' 'essences,' or 'realities'" (p. 108). The knower, the knowing, and the known are seen as aspects of "one process." Each element conditions and is conditioned by the other in a mutually constituted situation (cf. Rosenblatt, 1985b).

The new paradigm requires a break with entrenched habits of thinking. The old stimulus–response, subject–object, individual–social dualisms give way to recognition of transactional relationships. The human being is seen as part of nature, continuously in transaction with an environment—each one conditions the other. The transactional mode of thinking has perhaps been most clearly assimilated in ecology. Human activities and relationships are seen as transactions in which the individual and social elements fuse with cultural and natural elements. Many current philosophy writers may differ on metaphysical implications but find it necessary to come to terms with the new paradigm.[1]

Language

The transactional concept has profound implications for understanding language. Traditionally, language has been viewed as primarily a self-contained system or code, a set of arbitrary rules and conventions that is manipulated as a tool by speakers and writers or imprints itself on the minds of listeners and readers. Even when the transactional approach has been accepted, this deeply ingrained way of thinking continues to function, tacitly or explicitly, in much theory, research, and teaching involving **texts**.[2]

text—set of signs capable of being interpreted as verbal symbols

The view of language basic to the transactional model of reading owes much to the philosopher John Dewey but even more to his contemporary Charles Sanders Peirce, who is recognized as the U.S. founder of the field of semiotics or semiology, the study of verbal and nonverbal signs. Peirce provided concepts that differentiate the transactional view of language and reading from structuralist and poststructuralist (especially deconstructionist) theories. These reflect the influence of another great semiotician, the French linguist Ferdinand de Saussure (Culler, 1982).

Saussure (1972) differentiated actual speech (*parole*) from the abstractions of the linguists (*langue*), but he stressed the arbitrary nature of signs and minimized the referential aspect. Even more important was his dyadic formulation of the relationship between "signifier and signified," or between words and concept.

These emphases fostered a view of language as an autonomous, self-contained system (Rosenblatt, 1993).

In contrast, Peirce (1933, 1935) offered a triadic formulation. "A sign," Peirce wrote, "is in conjoint relation to the thing denoted and to the mind. . . . " The "sign is related to its object only in consequence of a mental association, and depends on habit" (Vol. 3, para. 360). The triad constitutes a symbol. Peirce repeatedly refers to the human context of meaning. Because he evidently did not want to reinforce the notion of "mind" as an entity, he typically phrased the "conjoint" linkage as among sign, object, and "interpretant," which should be understood as a mental operation rather than an entity (6.347). Peirce's triadic model firmly grounds language in the transactions of individual human beings with their world.

Recent descriptions of the working of the brain by neurologists and other scientists seem very Peircean. Although they are dealing with a level not essential to our theoretical purposes, they provide an interesting reinforcement. "Many leading scientists, including Dr. Francis Crick, think that the brain creates unified circuits by oscillating distant components at a shared frequency" (Appenzeller, 1990, pp. 6–7). Neurologists speak of "a third-party convergence zone [which seems to be a neurological term for Peirce's interpretant] that mediates between word and concept convergence zones" (Damasio, 1989, pp. 123–132). Studies of children's acquisition of language support the Peircean triad, concluding that a vocalization or sign becomes a word, a verbal symbol, when the sign and its object or referent are linked with the same "organismic state" (Werner & Kaplan, 1962, p. 18).

Though language is usually defined as a socially generated system of communication—the very bloodstream of any society—the triadic concept reminds us that language is always internalized by a human being transacting with a particular environment. Vygotsky's recognition of the social context did not prevent his affirming the individual's role: The "sense of a word" is

> the sum of all the psychological events aroused in our consciousness by the word. It is a dynamic, fluid, complex whole, which has several zones of unequal stability. Meaning [i.e., reference] is only one of the zones of sense, the most stable and precise zone. A word acquires its sense from the context in which it appears; in different contexts, it changes its sense. (1962, p. 46)

Vygotsky postulated "the existence of a dynamic system of meaning, in which the affective and the intellectual unite." The earliest utterances of children evidently represent a fusion of "processes which later will branch off into referential, emotive, and associative part processes" (Rommetveit, 1968, pp. 147, 167). The child learns to sort out the various aspects of "sense" associated with a sign, decontextualize it, and recognize the public aspect of language, the collective language system. This does not, however, eliminate the other dimensions of sense. A language act cannot be thought of as totally affective or cognitive, or as totally public or private (Bates, 1979, pp. 65–66).

Bates provides the useful metaphor of an iceberg for the total sense of a word to its user: The visible tip represents what I term the public aspect of meaning, resting on the submerged base of private meaning. *Public* designates usages or meanings that dictionaries list. Multiple meanings indicated for the same word reflect the fact that the same sign takes on different meanings at different times and in different linguistic or different personal, cultural, or social contexts. In short, *public* refers to usages that some groups of people have developed and that the individual shares.

Note that *public* and *private* are not synonymous with *cognitive* and *affective*. Words may have publicly shared affective connotations. The individual's private associations with a word may or may not agree with its connotations for the group, although these connotations must also be individually acquired. Words necessarily involve for each person a mix of both public and private elements, the base as well as the tip of the semantic iceberg.

For the individual, then, the language is that part, or set of features, of the public system that has been internalized through that person's experiences with words in life situations. "Lexical concepts must be shared by speakers of a common language . . . yet there is room for considerable individual difference in the details of any concept" (Miller & Johnson-Laird, 1976, p. 700). The residue of the individual's past transactions—in particular, natural and social contexts—constitutes what can be termed a linguistic–experiential reservoir. William James especially suggests the presence of such a cumulative experiential aura of language.

Embodying funded assumptions, attitudes, and expectations about language and about the world, this inner capital is all that each of us has to draw on in speaking, listening, writing, or reading. We "make sense" of a new situation or transaction and make new meanings by applying, reorganizing, revising, or extending public and private elements selected from our personal linguistic–experiential reservoirs.

Linguistic Transactions

Face-to-face communication—such as a conversation in which a speaker is explaining something to another person—can provide a simplified example of the transactional nature of all linguistic activities. A conversation is a temporal activity, a back-and-forth process. Each person has come to the transaction with an individual history, manifested in what has been termed a linguistic–experiential reservoir. The verbal signs are the vibrations in the air caused by a speaker. Both speaker and addressee contribute throughout to the spoken text (even if the listener remains silent) and to the interpretations that it calls forth as it progresses. Each must construct some sense of the other person. Each draws on a particular linguistic–experiential reservoir. The specific situation, which may be social and personal, and the setting and occasion for the conversation in themselves provide clues or limitations as to the general subject or framework and hence to the references and implications of the verbal signs. The speaker and addressee both produce further delimiting cues through facial expressions, tones of voice, and gestures. In addition to such nonverbal indications of an ongoing mutual interpretation of the text, the listener may offer questions and comments. The speaker thus is constantly being helped to gauge and to confirm, revise, or expand the text. Hence, the text is shaped transactionally by both speaker and addressee.

The opening words of a conversation, far from being static, by the end of the interchange may have taken on a different meaning. And the attitudes, the state of mind, even the manifest personality traits, may have undergone change. Moreover, the spoken text may be interpreted differently by each of the conversationalists.

But how can we apply the conversation model of transaction to the relationship between writers and readers, when so many of the elements that contribute to the spoken transaction are missing—physical presence, timing, actual setting, nonverbal behaviors, tones of voice, and so on? The signs on the page are all that the writer and the reader have to make up for the absence of these other elements. The reader focuses attention on and transacts with an element in the environment, namely the signs on the page, the text.

Despite all the important differences noted above, speech, writing, and reading share the same basic process—transacting through a text. In any linguistic event, speakers and listeners and writers and readers have only their linguistic–experiential reservoirs as the basis for interpretation. Any interpretations or new meanings are restructurings or extensions of the stock of experiences of language, spoken and written, brought to the task. In Peircean terms, past linkages of sign, object, and interpretant must provide the basis for new linkages, or new structures of meaning. Instead of an interaction, such as billiard balls colliding, there has been a transaction, thought of rather in terms of reverberations, rapid oscillations, blendings, and mutual conditionings.

Selective Attention

William James's concept of "selective attention" provides an important insight into this process. During the first half of this century, a combination of behaviorism and positivism led to neglect of the concept, but since the 1970s psychologists have reasserted its importance (Blumenthal, 1977; Myers, 1986). James (1890) tells us that we are constantly engaged in a "choosing activity," which he terms "selective attention" (I.284). We are constantly selecting out of the stream, or field, of consciousness "by the reinforcing and inhibiting agency of attention" (I.288). This activity is sometimes termed "the cocktail party phenomenon": In a crowded room where many conversations are in progress, we focus our attention on only one of them at a time, and the others become a background hum. We can turn our selective attention toward a broader or narrower area of the field. Thus, while language activity implies an intermingled kinesthetic, cognitive, affective, associational matrix, what is pushed into the background or suppressed and what is brought into awareness and organized into meaning depend on where selective attention is focused.

The transactional concept will prevent our falling into the error of envisaging selective attention as a mechanical choosing among an array of fixed entities rather than as a dynamic centering on areas or aspects of the contents of consciousness. The linguistic reservoir should not be seen as encompassing verbal signs linked to fixed meanings, but as a fluid pool of potential triadic symbolizations. Such residual linkages of sign, signifier, and organic state, it will be seen, become actual symbolizations as selective attention functions under the shaping influence of particular times and circumstances.

In the linguistic event, any process also will be affected by the physical and emotional state of the individual, for example, by fatigue or stress. Attention may be controlled or wandering, intense or superficial. In the discussion that follows, it will be assumed that such factors enter into the transaction and affect the quality of the process under consideration.

The paradoxical situation is that the reader has only the black marks on the page as the means of arriving at a meaning—and that meaning can be constructed only by drawing on the reader's own personal linguistic and life experiences. Because a text must be produced by a writer before it can be read, logic might seem to dictate beginning with a discussion of the writing process. It is true that the writer seeks to express something, but the purpose is to communicate with a reader (even if it is only the writer wishing to preserve some thought or experience for future reference). Typically, the text is intended for others. Some sense of a reader or at least of the fact that the text will function in a reading process thus is implicit in the writing process. Hence, I shall discuss the reading process first, then the writing process. Then, I shall broach the problems of communication and validity of interpretation before considering implications for teaching and research.

THE READING PROCESS

Transacting with the Text

The concepts of transaction, the transactional nature of language, and selective attention now can be applied to analysis of the reading process. Every reading act is an event, or a transaction involving a particular reader and a particular pattern of signs, a text, and occurring at a particular time in a particular context. Instead of two fixed entities acting on one another, the reader and the text are two aspects of a total dynamic situation. The "meaning" does not reside ready-made "in" the text or "in" the reader but happens or comes into being during the transaction between reader and text.

The term *text* in this analysis denotes, then, a set of signs capable of being interpreted as verbal symbols. Far from already possessing a meaning that can be imposed on all readers, the text actually remains simply marks on paper, an object in the environment, until some reader transacts with it. The term *reader* implies a transaction with a text; the term *text* implies a transaction with a reader.

"Meaning" is what happens during the transaction; hence, the fallacy of thinking of them as separate and distinct entities instead of factors in a total situation.

The notion that the marks in themselves possess meaning is hard to dispel. For example, *pain* for a French reader will link up with the concept of bread and for an English reader with the concept of bodily or mental suffering. A sentence that Noam Chomsky (1968, p. 27) made famous can help us realize that not even the syntax is inherent in the signs of the text but depends on the results of particular transactions: *Flying planes can be dangerous.*

Actually, only after we have selected a meaning can we infer a syntax from it. Usually, factors entering into the total transaction, such as the context and reader's purpose, will determine the reader's choice of meaning. Even if the reader recognizes the alternative syntactic possibilities, these factors still prevail. This casts doubt on the belief that the syntactical level, because it is lower or less complex, necessarily always precedes the semantic in the reading process. The transactional situation suggests that meaning implies syntax and that a reciprocal process is going on in which the broader aspects guiding choices are actively involved.

Here we see the difference between the physical text, defined as a pattern of signs, and what is usually called "the text," a syntactically patterned set of verbal symbols. This actually comes into being during the transaction with the signs on the page.

When we see a set of such marks on a page, we believe that it should give rise to some more or less coherent meaning. We bring our funded experience to bear. Multiple inner alternatives resonate to the signs. Not only the triadic linkages with the signs but also certain organismic states, or certain ranges of feeling, are stirred up in the linguistic–experiential reservoir. From these activated areas, selective attention—conditioned, as we have seen, by multiple physical, personal, social, and cultural factors entering into the situation—picks out elements that will be organized and synthesized into what constitutes "meaning." Choices have in effect probably been made simultaneously, as the various "levels" transact, conditioning one another, so to speak.

Reading is, to use James's phrase, a "choosing activity." From the very beginning, and often even before, some expectation, some tentative feeling, idea, or purpose, no matter how vague at first, starts the reading process and develops into the constantly self-revising impulse that guides selection, synthesis, and organization. The linguistic–experiential reservoir reflects the reader's cultural, social, and personal history. Past experience with language and with texts provides expectations. Other factors are the reader's present situation and interests. Perusing the unfolding text in the light of past syntactic and semantic experience, the reader seeks cues on which to base expectations about what is forthcoming. The text as a verbal pattern, we have seen, is part of what is being constructed. Possibilities open up concerning the general kind of meaning that may be developing, affecting choices in diction, syntax, and linguistic and literary conventions.

As the reader's eyes move along the page, the newly evoked symbolizations are tested for whether they can be fitted into the tentative meanings already constructed for the preceding portion of the text. Each additional choice will signal certain options and exclude others, so that even as the meaning evolves, the selecting, synthesizing impulse is itself constantly shaped and tested. If the marks on the page evoke elements that cannot be assimilated into the emerging synthesis, the guiding principle or framework is revised; if necessary, it is discarded and a complete rereading occurs. New tentative guidelines, new bases for a hypothetical structure, may then present themselves. Reader and text are involved in a complex, nonlinear, recursive, self-correcting transaction. The arousal and fulfillment—or frustration and revision—of expectations contribute to the construction of a cumulative meaning. From a to-and-fro interplay between reader, text, and context emerges a synthesis or organization, more or less coherent and complete. This meaning, this "**evocation**," is felt to correspond to the text.

> **evocation**—aspects of the reading process centered on organization of a structure of components to yield the meaning of the text

Precisely because for experienced readers so much of the reading process is, or should be, automatic, aspects of the reading process tend to be described in impersonal, mechanistic terms. Psychologists are rightfully concerned with learning as much as possible about what goes on between the reader's first visual contact with the marks on the page and the completion of what is considered an interpretation of them. A number of different levels, systems, and strategies have been analytically designated, and research has been directed at clarifying their nature. These can be useful, but from a transactional point of view, it is important to recognize their potentialities and their limitations. A mechanistic analogy or metaphor lends itself especially to analyses of literal reading of simple texts. Results need to be cautiously interpreted. Recognizing the essential nature of both reader and text, the transactional theory requires an underlying metaphor of organic activity and reciprocity.

The optical studies of Adelbert Ames (1955) and the Ames–Cantril "transactional psychology" (Cantril & Livingston, 1963), which also derived its name from Dewey and Bentley's *Knowing and the Known* (1949), deserve first mention in this regard. These experiments demonstrated that perception depends much on the viewer's selection and organization of visual cues according to past experience, expectations, needs, and interests. The perception may be revised through continued transactions between the perceiver and the perceived object.

F.C. Bartlett's theory of *Remembering* (1932) (which I regret having discovered even later than did his fellow scientists) and his term *schema* are often called on to explain psychological processes even broader than his special field. It is not clear, however, that those who so readily invoke his schema concept are heeding his fears about a narrow, static usage of the term. Rejecting the image of a warehouse of unchanging items as the metaphor for schemata, he emphasized rather "active, developing patterns"—"constituents of living, momentary settings belonging to the organism" (Bartlett, 1932, p. 201). His description of the "constructive character of remembering," his rejection of a simple mechanical linear process, and his concepts of the development and continuing revision of schemata all have parallels in the transactional theory of linguistic events. His recognition of the influence of both the interests of the individual and the social context on all levels of the process also seems decidedly transactional.

The Reader's Stance

The broad outline of the reading process sketched thus far requires further elaboration. An important distinction must be made between the operations that produce the meaning, say, of a scientific report and the operations that evoke a literary work of art. Neither contemporary reading theory nor literary theory has done justice to such readings, nor to the fact that they are to be understood as representing a continuum rather than an opposition. The tendency generally has been to assume that such a distinction depends entirely on the texts involved. The character of the "work" has been held to inhere entirely in the text. But we cannot look simply at the text and predict the nature of the work. We cannot assume, for instance, that a poem rather than an argument about fences will be evoked from the text of Frost's *Mending Wall* or that a novel rather than sociological facts about Victorian England will be evoked from Dickens's *Great Expectations*. Advertisements and newspaper reports have been read as poems. Each alternative represents a different kind of selective activity, a different kind of relationship, between the reader and the text.

| stance—reader's purpose |

Essential to any reading is the reader's adoption, conscious or unconscious, of what I have termed a ***stance*** guiding the "choosing activity" in the stream of consciousness. Recall that any linguistic event carries both public and private aspects. As the transaction with the printed text stirs up elements of the linguistic–experiential reservoir, the reader adopts a selective attitude or stance, bringing certain aspects into the center of attention and pushing others into the fringes of consciousness. A stance reflects the reader's purpose. The situation, the purpose, and the linguistic–experiential equipment of the reader as well as the signs on the page enter into the transaction and affect the extent to which public and private meanings and associations will be attended to.

The Efferent–Aesthetic Continuum

The reading event must fall somewhere in a continuum, determined by whether the reader adopts what I term a *predominantly aesthetic* stance or a *predominantly efferent* stance. A particular stance determines the proportion or mix of public and private elements of sense that fall within the scope of the reader's selective attention. Or, to recall Bates's metaphor, a stance results from the degree and scope of attention paid respectively to the tip and to the base of the iceberg. Such differences can be represented only by a continuum, which I term the *efferent–aesthetic continuum.*

The Efferent Stance

The term *efferent* (from the Latin *efferre,* to carry away) designates the kind of reading in which attention is centered predominantly on what is to be extracted and retained after the reading event. An extreme example is a man who has accidentally swallowed a poisonous liquid and is rapidly reading the label on the bottle to learn the antidote. Here, surely, we see an illustration of James's point about selective attention and our capacity to push into the periphery of awareness or ignore those elements that do not serve our present interests. The man's attention is focused on learning what is to be done as soon as the reading ends. He concentrates on what the words point to, ignoring anything other than their barest public referents, constructing as quickly as possible the directions for future action. These structured ideas are the evocation felt to correspond to the text.

efferent—type of reading centered on what information is to be "carried away" after the reading event

Reading a newspaper, textbook, or legal brief would usually provide a similar, though less extreme, instance of the predominantly efferent stance. In efferent reading, then, we focus attention mainly on the public "tip of the iceberg" of sense. Meaning results from abstracting out and analytically structuring the ideas, information, directions, or conclusions to be retained, used, or acted on after the reading event.

The Aesthetic Stance

The predominantly aesthetic stance covers the other half of the continuum. In this kind of reading, the reader adopts an attitude of readiness to focus attention on what is being lived through during the reading event. The term *aesthetic* was chosen because its Greek source suggested perception through the senses, feelings, and intuitions. Welcomed into awareness are not only the public referents of the verbal signs but also the private part of the "iceberg" of meaning: the sensations, images, feelings, and ideas that are the residue of past psychological events involving those words and their referents. Attention may include the sounds and rhythms of the words themselves, heard in "the inner ear" as the signs are perceived.

The aesthetic reader pays attention to—savors—the qualities of the feelings, ideas, situations, scenes, personalities, and emotions that are called forth and participates in the tensions, conflicts, and resolutions of the images, ideas, and scenes as they unfold. The lived-through meaning is felt to correspond to the text. This meaning, shaped and experienced during the aesthetic transaction, constitutes "the literary work," the poem, story, or play. This "evocation," and not the text, is the object of the reader's "response" and "interpretation," both during and after the reading event.

Confusion about the matter of stance results from the entrenched habit of thinking of the *text* as efferent or aesthetic, expository or poetic, literary or non-literary, and so on. Those who apply these terms to texts should realize that they actually are reporting their interpretation of the writer's intention as to what kind of reading the text should be given. The reader is free, however, to adopt either predominant stance toward any text. *Efferent* and *aesthetic* apply, then, to the writer's and the reader's selective attitude toward their own streams of consciousness during their respective linguistic events.

To recognize the essential nature of stance does not minimize the importance of the text in the transaction. Various verbal elements—metaphor, stylistic conventions or divergence from linguistic or semantic norms, even certain kinds of content—have been said to constitute the "poeticity" or "literariness" of a text. Such verbal elements, actually, do often serve as cues to the experienced reader to adopt an aesthetic stance. Yet it is possible to cite acknowledged literary works that lack one or all these elements. Neither reading theorists nor literary theorists have given due credit to the fact that none of these or any other arrangements of words could make their "literary" or "poetic" contribution without the reader's prior shift of attention toward mainly the qualitative or experiential contents of consciousness, namely, the aesthetic stance.

The Continuum

The metaphorical nature of the term *the stream of consciousness* can be called on further to clarify the efferent–aesthetic continuum. We can image consciousness as a stream flowing through the darkness. Stance, then, can be represented as a mechanism lighting up—directing the attention to—different parts of the stream, selecting out objects that have floated to the surface in those areas and leaving the rest in shadow. Stance, in other words, provides the guiding orientation toward activating particular areas and elements of consciousness, that is, particular proportions of public and private aspects of meaning, leaving the rest at the dim periphery of attention. Some such play of attention over the contents of what emerges into consciousness must be involved in the reader's multifold choices from the linguistic–experiential reservoir.

> **aesthetic**—type of reading that involves a focus of attention on feelings, emotions, images in a "lived-through" experience

Efferent and **aesthetic** reflect the two main ways of looking at the world, often summed up as "scientific" and "artistic." My redundant usage of "predominantly" aesthetic or efferent underlines rejection of the traditional, binary, either–or tendency to see them as in opposition. The efferent stance pays more attention to the cognitive, the referential, the factual, the analytic, the logical, the quantitative aspects of meaning. And the aesthetic stance pays more attention to the sensuous, the affective, the emotive, the qualitative. But nowhere can we find on the one hand the purely public and on the other hand the purely private. Both of these aspects of meaning are attended to in different proportions in any linguistic event. One of the earliest and most important steps in any reading event, therefore, is the selection of either a predominantly efferent or a predominantly aesthetic stance toward the transaction with a text. Figure 7.1 indicates different readings by the same reader of the same text at different points on the efferent–aesthetic continuum. Other readers would probably produce readings that fall at other points on the continuum.

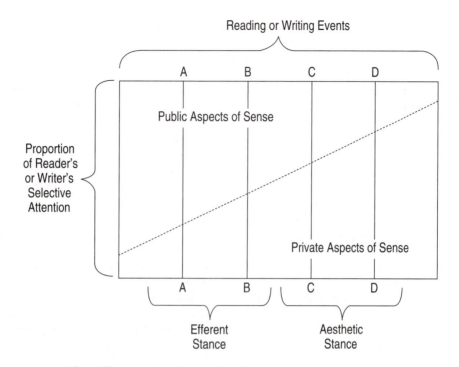

FIGURE 7.1   The Efferent–Aesthetic Continuum

Any linguistic activity has both public (lexical, analytic, abstracting) and private (experiential, affective, associational) components. Stance is determined by the proportion of each component admitted into the scope of selective attention. The efferent stance draws mainly on the public aspect of sense; the aesthetic stance includes proportionally more of the experiential, private aspect.

Reading or writing events A and B fall into the efferent part of the continuum, with B admitting more private elements. Reading or writing events C and D both represent the aesthetic stance, with C according a higher proportion of attention to the public aspects of sense.

Although many readings may fall near the extremes, many others, perhaps most, may fall nearer the center of the continuum. Where both parts of the iceberg of meaning are more evenly balanced, confusion as to dominant stance is more likely and more counterproductive. It is possible to read efferently and assume one has evoked a poem, or to read aesthetically and assume one is arriving at logical conclusions to an argument.

Also, it is necessary to emphasize that a predominant stance does not rule out fluctuations. Within a particular aesthetic reading, attention may at times turn from the experiential synthesis to efferent analysis, as the reader recognizes some technical strategy or passes a critical judgment. Similarly, in an efferent reading, a general idea may be illustrated or reinforced by an aesthetically lived through illustration or example. Despite the mix of private and public aspects of meaning in each stance, the two dominant stances are clearly distinguishable. No two readings, even by the same person, are identical. Still, someone else can read a text efferently and paraphrase it for us in such a way as to satisfy our efferent purpose. But no one else can read aesthetically—that is, experience the evocation of—a literary work of art for us.

Because each reading is an event in particular circumstances, the same text may be read either efferently or aesthetically. The experienced reader usually approaches a text alert to cues offered by the text and, unless another purpose intervenes, automatically adopts the appropriate predominant stance. Sometimes the title suffices as a cue. Probably one of the most obvious cues is the arrangement of broad margins and uneven lines that signals that the reader should adopt the aesthetic stance and undertake to make a poem. The opening lines of any text are especially important from this point of view, for their signaling of tone, attitude, and conventional indications of stance to be adopted.

Of course, the reader may overlook or misconstrue the cues, or they may be confusing. And the reader's own purpose, or schooling that indoctrinates the same undifferentiated approach to all texts, may dictate a different stance from the one the writer intended. For example, the student reading *A Tale of Two Cities* who knows that there will be a test on facts about characters and plot may be led to adopt a predominantly efferent stance, screening out all but the factual data. Similarly, readings of an article on zoology could range from analytic abstracting of factual content to an aesthetic savoring of the ordered structure of ideas, the rhythm of the sentences, and the images of animal life brought into consciousness.

EVOCATION, RESPONSE, INTERPRETATION

The tendency to reify words is frequently represented by discussions centering on a title, say, *Invisible Man* or *The Bill of Rights*. These titles may refer to the text, as we have been using the word, that is, to the pattern of inscribed signs to be found in physical written or printed form. More often, however, the intended reference is to "the work." But the work—ideas and experiences linked with the text—can be found only in individual readers' reflections on the reading event, the evocation and responses to it during and after the reading event.

Evocation

Thus far, we have focused on the aspects of the reading process centered on organizing a structure of elements of consciousness construed as the meaning of the text. I term this *the evocation* to cover both efferent and aesthetic transactions. The evocation, the work, is not a physical "object," but, given another sense of that word, the evocation can be an object of thought.

The Second Stream of Response

We must recognize during the reading event a concurrent stream of reactions to, and transactions with, the emerging evocation. Even as we are generating the evocation, we are reacting to it; this may, in turn, affect our choices as we proceed with the reading. Such responses may be momentary, peripheral, or felt simply as a general state, for example, an ambiance of acceptance or perhaps of confirmation of ideas and attitudes brought to the reading. Sometimes something unexpected or contrary to prior knowledge or assumptions may trigger conscious reflection. Something not prepared for by the preceding organization of elements may cause a rereading. The attention may shift from the evocation to the formal or technical traits of the text. The range of potential reactions and the gamut of degrees of intensity and articulateness depend on the interplay among the character of the signs on the-page (the text), what the individual reader brings to it, and the circumstances of the transaction.

The various strands of response, especially in the middle ranges of the efferent–aesthetic continuum, are sometimes simultaneous, interacting, and interwoven. They may seem actually woven into the texture of the evocation itself. Hence, one of the problems of critical reading is differentiation of the evocation corresponding to the text from the concurrent responses, which may be projections from the reader's a priori assumptions. Drawing the line between them is easier in theory than in the practice of any actual reading. The reader needs to learn to handle such elements of the reading experience. The problem takes on different forms in efferent and aesthetic reading.

Expressed Response

"Response" to the evocation often is designed as subsequent to the reading event. Actually, the basis is laid during the reading, in the concurrent second stream of reactions. The reader may recapture the general effect of this after the event and may seek to express it and to recall what in the evocation led to the response. Reflection on "the meaning" of even a simple text involves the recall, the reactivation of some aspects of the process carried on during the reading. "Interpretation" tends to be a continuation of this effort to clarify the evocation.

The account of the reading process thus far has indicated an organizing, synthesizing activity, the creation of tentative meanings, and their modification as new elements enter into the focus of attention. In some instances, the reader at some point simply registers a sense of having completed a sequential activity and moves on to other concerns. Sometimes a sense of the whole structure crystallizes by the close of the reading.

Expressed Interpretation

Actually, the process of interpretation that includes arriving at a sense of the whole has not been given enough attention in theories of reading, perhaps because reading research has typically dealt with simple reading events. For the term *interpret,* dictionaries list, among others, several relevant meanings. One is "to set forth the meaning of; to elucidate, to explain." Another is "to construe, or understand in a particular way." A third is "to bring out the meaning of by performance (as in music)." These tend to reflect the traditional notion of "the meaning" as inherent in the text.

The transactional theory requires that we draw on all three of these usages to cover the way in which the term should be applied to the reading process. The evocation of meaning in transaction with a text is indeed interpretation in the sense of performance, and transactional theory merges this with the idea of interpretation as individual construal. The evocation then becomes the object of interpretation in the sense of elucidating or explaining. The expressed interpretation draws on all these aspects of the total transaction.

Interpretation can be understood as the effort to report, analyze, and explain the evocation. The reader recalls the sensed, felt, thought evocation while at the same time applying some frame of reference or method of abstracting in order to characterize it, to find the assumptions or organizing ideas that relate the parts to the whole. The second stream of reactions will be recalled, and the reasons for them sought, in the evoked work or in prior assumptions and knowledge. The evocation and the concurrent streams of reaction may be related through stressing, for example, the logic of the structure of ideas in an efferent evocation or the assumptions about people or society underlying the lived through experience of the aesthetic reading.

Usually, interpretation is expressed in the efferent mode, stressing underlying general ideas that link the signs of the text. Interpretation can take an aesthetic form, however, such as a poem, a painting, music, dramatization, or dance.

Interpretation brings with it the question of whether the reader has produced a meaning that is consonant with the author's probable intention. Here we find ourselves moving from the reader–text transaction to the relationship between author and reader. The process that produces the text will be considered before dealing with such matters as communication, validity of interpretation, and the implications of the transactional theory for teaching and research.

THE WRITING PROCESS

The Writing Transaction

Writers facing a blank page, like readers approaching a text, have only their individual linguistic capital to draw on. For the writer, too, the residue of past experiences of language in particular situations provides the material from which the text will be constructed. As with the reader, any new meanings are restructurings or extensions of the stock of experiences the writer brings to the task. There is a continuing to-and-fro or transactional process as the writer looks at the page and adds to the text in the light of what has been written thus far.

An important difference between readers and writers should not be minimized, however. In the triadic sign–object–interpretant relationship, the reader has the physical pattern of signs to which to relate the symbolizations. The writer facing a blank page may start with only an organismic state, vague feelings and ideas that require further triadic definition before a symbolic configuration—a verbal text—can take shape.

Writing is always an event in time, occurring at a particular moment in the writer's biography, in particular circumstances, under particular external as well as internal pressures. In short, the writer is always transacting with a personal, social, and cultural environment. Thus, the writing process must be seen as always embodying both personal and social, or individual and environmental, factors.

Given the Peircean triadic view of the verbal symbol, the more accessible, the fund of organismically linked words and referents, the more fluent the writing. This helps us place in perspective an activity such as free writing. Instead of treating it as a prescriptive "stage" of the writing process, as some seem to do, it should be seen as a technique for tapping the linguistic reservoir without being hampered by anxieties about acceptability of subject, sequence, or mechanics. Especially for those inhibited by unfortunate past writing experiences, this can be liberating, a warm-up exercise for starting the juices flowing, so to speak, and permitting elements of the experiential stream, verbal components of memory, and present concerns to rise to consciousness. The essential point is that the individual linguistic reservoir must be activated.

No matter how free and uninhibited the writing may be, the stream of images, ideas, memories, and words is not entirely random; William James reminds us that the "choosing activity" of selective attention operates to some degree. Like the reader, the writer needs to bring the selective process actively into play, to move toward a sense of some tentative focus for choice and synthesis (Emig, 1983).

This directedness will be fostered by the writer's awareness of the transactional situation: the context that initiates the need to write and the potential reader or readers to whom the text will presumably be addressed. Often in trial-and-error fashion, and through various freely flowing drafts, the writer's sensitivity to such factors translates itself into an increasingly clear impulse that guides selective attention and integration. For the experienced writer, the habit of such awareness, monitoring the multifold decisions or choices that make up the writing event, is more important than any explicit preliminary statement of goals or purpose.

The Writer's Stance

The concept of stance presented earlier in relation to reading is equally important for writing. A major aspect of the delimitation of purpose in writing is the adoption of a stance that falls at some point in the efferent–aesthetic continuum. The attitude toward what is activated in the linguistic–experiential reservoir manifests itself in the range and character of the verbal symbols that will "come to mind," and to which the writer will apply selective attention. The dominant stance determines the proportion of public and private aspects of sense that will be included in the scope of the writer's attention (see Figure 7.1).

In actual life, the selection of a predominant stance is not arbitrary but is a function of the circumstances, the writer's motives, the subject, and the relation between writer and prospective reader or readers. For example, someone who had been involved in an automobile collision would need to adopt very different stances in writing an account of the event for an insurance company and in describing it in a letter to a friend. The first would activate an efferent selective process, bringing into the center of consciousness and onto the page the public aspects, such as statements that could be verified by witnesses or by investigation of the terrain. In the letter to the friend, the purpose would be to share an experience. An aesthetic stance would bring within the scope of the writer's attention the same basic facts, together with feelings, sensations, tensions, images, and sounds lived through during this brush with death. The selective process would favor words that matched the writer's inner sense of the felt event and that also would activate in the prospective reader symbolic linkages evoking a similar experience. Given different purposes, other accounts might fall at other points of the efferent–aesthetic continuum.

Purpose or intention should emerge from, or be capable of constructively engaging, the writer's actual experiential and linguistic resources. Past experience need not be the limit of the writer's scope, but the writer faced with a blank page needs "live" ideas—that is, ideas having a strongly energizing linkage with the linguistic–experiential reservoir. Purposes or ideas that lack the capacity to connect with the writer's funded experience and present concerns cannot fully activate the linguistic reservoir and provide an impetus to thinking and writing.

A personally grounded purpose develops and impels movement forward. Live ideas growing out of situations, activities, discussions, problems, or needs provide the basis for an actively selective and synthesizing process of making meaning. The quickened fund of images, ideas, emotions, attitudes, and tendencies to act offers the means of making new connections, for discovering new facets of the world of objects and events, in short, for thinking and writing creatively.

Writing About Texts

When a reader describes, responds to, or interprets a work—that is, speaks or writes about a transaction with a text—a new text is being produced. The implications of this fact in terms of process should be more fully understood. When the reader becomes a writer about a work, the starting point is no longer the physical text, the marks on the page, but the meaning or the state of mind felt to correspond to that text. The reader may return to the original text to recapture how it entered into the transaction but must "find words" for explaining the evocation and the interpretation.

The reader-turned-writer must once again face the problem of choice of stance. In general, the choice seems to be the efferent stance. The purpose is mainly to explain, analyze, summarize, and categorize the evocation. This is usually true even when the reading has been predominantly aesthetic and a literary work of art is being discussed. However, the aesthetic stance might be adopted in order to communicate an experience expressing the response or the interpretation. An efferent reading of, for example, the U.S. Declaration of Independence might lead to a poem or a story. An aesthetic reading of the text of a poem might also lead, not to an efferently written critical essay, but to another poem, a painting, or a musical composition.

The translator of a poem is a clear example of the reader-turned-writer, being first a reader who evokes an experience through a transaction in one language and then a writer who seeks to express that experience through a writing transaction in another language. The experiential qualities generated in a transaction with one language must now be communicated to—evoked by—readers who have a different linguistic–experiential reservoir, acquired in a different culture.

AUTHORIAL READING

Thus far, we have been developing parallels between the ways in which readers and writers select and synthesize elements from the personal linguistic reservoir, adopt stances that guide selective attention, and build a developing selective purpose. Emphasis has fallen mainly on similarities in composing structures of meaning related to texts. If readers are in that sense also writers, it is equally—and perhaps more obviously—true that writers also must be readers. At this point, however, some differences within the parallelisms begin to appear.

The writer, it is generally recognized, is the first reader of the text. Note an obvious, though neglected, difference: While readers transact with a writer's finished text, writers first read the text as it is being inscribed. Because both reading and writing are recursive processes carried on over a period of time, their very real similarities have masked a basic difference. The writer will often reread the total finished text, but, perhaps more important, the writer first reads and carries on a spiral, transactional relationship with the very text emerging on the page. This is a different kind of reading. It is authorial—a writer's reading. It should be seen as an integral part of the composing process. In fact, it is necessary to see that writing, or composing, a text involves *two* kinds of authorial reading, which I term *expression oriented* and *reception oriented*.

Expression-Oriented Authorial Reading

As a reader's eyes move along a printed text, the reader develops an organizing principle or framework. The newly evoked symbolizations are tested for whether they can be fitted into the tentative meanings already constructed for the preceding portion of the text. If the new signs create a problem, this may lead to a revision of the framework or even to a complete rereading of the text and restructuring of the attributed meaning.

The writer, like readers of another's text, peruses the succession of verbal signs being inscribed on the page to see whether the new words fit the preceding text. But this is a different, expression-oriented reading, which should be seen as an integral part of the composing process. As the new words appear on the page, they must be tested, not simply for how they make sense with the preceding text but also against an inner gauge—the intention, or purpose. The emerging meaning, even if it makes sense, must be judged as to whether it serves or hinders the purpose, however nebulous and inarticulate, that is the motive power in the writing. Expression-oriented authorial reading leads to revision even during the earlier phases of the writing process.

The Inner Gauge

Most writers will recall a situation that may illustrate the operation of an "inner gauge." A word comes to mind or flows from the pen and, even if it makes sense, is felt not to be right. One word after another may be brought into consciousness and still not satisfy. Sometimes the writer understands what is wrong with the word on the page—perhaps that it is ambiguous or does not suit the tone. But often the writer cannot articulate the reason for dissatisfaction. The tension simply disappears when "the right word" presents itself. When it does, a match between inner state and verbal sign has happened.

Such an episode manifests the process of testing against an inner touchstone. The French writer Gustave Flaubert with his search for *le mot juste*, the exact word, offers the analogy of the violinist who tries to make his fingers "reproduce precisely those sounds of which he has the inward sense" (1926, pp. 11, 47). The inner gauge may be an organic state, a mood, an idea, perhaps even a consciously constituted set of guidelines.

For the experienced writer, this kind of completely inner-oriented reading, which is integral to the composing process, depends on and nourishes an increasingly clear though often tacit sense of purpose, whether efferent or aesthetic. The writer tries to satisfy a personal conception while also refining it. Such transactional reading and revision can go on throughout the writing event. There are indeed times when this is the *only* reading component—when one writes for oneself alone, to express or record an experience in a diary or journal, or perhaps to analyze a situation or the pros and cons of a decision.

Reception-Oriented Authorial Reading

Usually, however, writing is felt to be part of a potential transaction with other readers. At some point, the writer dissociates from the text and reads it through the eyes of potential readers; the writer tries to judge the meaning *they* would make in transaction with that pattern of signs. But the writer does not simply adopt the "eyes" of the potential reader. Again, a twofold operation is involved. The emerging text is read to sense what others might make of it. But this hypothetical interpretation must also be checked against the writer's own inner sense of purpose.

The tendency has been to focus on writing with an eye on the anticipated reader. My concern is to show the interplay between the two kinds of authorial reading and the need, consciously or automatically, to decide the degree of emphasis on one or the other. The problem always is to find verbal signs likely to activate linkages in prospective readers' linguistic reservoirs matching those of the writer. A poet may be faced with the choice between a personally savored exotic metaphor and one more likely to be within the experience of prospective readers. Or a science writer may have to decide whether highly detailed precision may be too complex for the general reader.

Writers must already have some hold on the first, expression-oriented kind of inner awareness if they are to benefit from the second reading through the eyes of others. The first becomes a criterion for the second. The experienced writer will probably engage in a synthesis, or rapid alternation, of the two kinds of authorial reading to guide the selective attention that filters out the verbal elements coming to mind. When communication is the aim, revision should be based on such double criteria in the rereading of the text.

COMMUNICATION BETWEEN AUTHOR AND READERS

The reader's to-and-fro process of building an interpretation becomes a form of transaction with an author persona sensed through and behind the text. The implied relationship is sometimes even termed "a contract" with the author. The closer their linguistic–experiential equipment, the more likely the reader's interpretation will fulfill the writer's intention. Sharing at least versions of the same language is so basic that it often is simply assumed. Other positive factors affecting communication are contemporary membership in the same social and cultural group, the same educational level, and membership in the same discourse community, such as academic, legal, athletic, literary, scientific, or theological. Given such similarities, the reader is more likely to bring to the text the prior knowledge, acquaintance with linguistic and literary conventions, and assumptions about social situations required for understanding implications or allusions and noting nuances of tone and thought.

Yet, because each individual's experience is unique, differences due to social, ethnic, educational, and personal factors exist, even with contemporaries. The reading of works written in another period bespeaks an inevitable difference in linguistic, social, or cultural context. Here, especially, readers may agree on interpretations without necessarily assuming that their evocations from the text fit the author's intention (Rosenblatt, 1978, p. 109ff).

Differences as to the author's intention often lead to consultation of extra-textual sources. For works of the past especially, scholars call on systematic methods of philological, biographical, and historical research to discover the personal, social, and literary forces that shaped the writer's intention. The contemporary reception of the work also provides clues. Such evidence, even if it includes an author's stated intention, still yields hypothetical results and cannot dictate our interpretation. We must still read the text to decide whether it supports the hypothetical intention. The reader is constantly faced with the responsibility of deciding whether an interpretation is acceptable. The question of validity of interpretation must be faced before considering implications for teaching and research.

Validity of Interpretation

The problem of validity of interpretation has not received much attention in reading theory or educational methodology. Despite the extraordinary extent of the reliance on testing in our schools, there seems to be little interest in clarifying the criteria that enter into evaluation of "comprehension." Actual practice in the teaching of reading and in the instruments for testing of reading ability has evidently been tacitly based on, or at least has indoctrinated, the traditional assumption that there is a single determinate "correct" meaning attributable to each text. The stance factor, the efferent–aesthetic continuum, has especially been neglected; operationally, the emphasis has been on the efferent, even when "literature" was involved.

The polysemous character of language invalidates any simplistic approach to meaning, creating the problem of the relationship between the reader's interpretation and the author's intention. The impossibility of finding a single absolute meaning for a text or of expecting any interpretation absolutely to reflect the writer's intention is becoming generally recognized by contemporary theorists. "Intention" itself is not absolutely definable or delimitable even by the writer. The word *absolute*, the notion of a single "correct" meaning inherent "in" the text, is the stumbling block. The same text takes on different meanings in transactions with different readers or even with the same reader in different contexts or times.

Warranted Assertibility

The problem of the validity of any interpretation is part of the broader philosophical problem cited at the beginning of this piece. Perception of the world is always through the medium of individual human beings transacting with their worlds. In recent decades, some literary theorists, deriving their arguments from poststructuralist Continental writers and taking a Saussurean view of language as an autonomous system, have arrived at an extreme relativist position. They have developed a reading method that assumes all texts can be "deconstructed" to reveal inner contradictions. Moreover, the language system and literary conventions are said to completely dominate author and reader, and agreement concerning interpretation simply reflects the particular "interpretive community" in which we find ourselves (Fish, 1980; Rosenblatt, 1991).

Such extreme relativism is not, however, a necessary conclusion from the premise that absolutely determinate meaning is impossible. By agreeing on criteria of evaluation of interpretations, we can accept the possibility of alternative interpretations yet decide that some are more acceptable than others.

John Dewey, accepting the nonfoundationalist epistemological premises and foregoing the quest for absolutes, solved the scientists' problem by his idea of "warranted assertibility" as the end of controlled inquiry (1938, pp. 9, 345). Given shared criteria concerning methods of investigation and kinds of evidence there can be agreement concerning the decision as to what is a sound interpretation of the evidence, or "a warranted assertion." This is not set forth as permanent, absolute truth, but leaves open the possibility that alternative explanations for the same facts may be found, that new evidence may be discovered, or that different criteria or paradigms may be developed.

Although Dewey used primarily scientific interpretation or knowledge of the world based on scientific methods to illustrate warranted assertibility, he saw the concept as encompassing the arts and all human concerns. It can be applied to the problem of all linguistic interpretation (Rosenblatt, 1978, chap. 7; 1983, p. 151ff). Given a shared cultural milieu and shared criteria of validity of interpretation, we can, without claiming to have the single "correct" meaning of a text, agree on an interpretation. Especially in aesthetic reading, we may find that alternative interpretations meet our minimum criteria, and we can still be free to consider some interpretations superior to others.

In contrast to the notion of readers locked into a narrow "interpretive community," the emphasis on making underlying or tacit criteria explicit provides the basis not only for agreement but also for understanding tacit sources of disagreement. This creates the possibility of change in interpretation, acceptance of alternative sets of criteria, or revision of criteria. Such self-awareness on the part of readers can foster communication across social, cultural, and historical differences between author and readers, as well as among readers (Rosenblatt, 1983).

In short, the concept of warranted assertibility, or shared criteria of validity of interpretation in a particular social context, recognizes that some readings may satisfy the criteria more fully than others. Basic criteria might be (1) that the context and purpose of the reading event, or the total transaction, be considered; (2) that the interpretation not be contradicted by, or not fail to cover, the full text, the signs on the page; and (3) that the interpretation not project meanings which cannot be related to signs on the page. Beyond these items arise criteria for interpretation and evaluation growing out of the whole structure of shared cultural, social, linguistic, and rhetorical assumptions.

Thus, we can be open to alternative readings of the text of *Hamlet,* but we also can consider some readings as superior to others according to certain explicit criteria, for example, complexity of intellectual and affective elements and nature of implicit value system. Such considerations permit comparison and "negotiation" among different readers of the same text as well as clarification of differences in assumptions concerning what constitutes a valid interpretation (Rosenblatt, 1978, 1983). On the efferent side of the continuum, current discussions of alternative criteria for interpretation of the U.S. Constitution provide another complex example.

Criteria for the Efferent–Aesthetic Continuum

Precisely because, as Figure 7.1 indicates, both public and private elements are present in all reading, the criteria of validity of interpretation differ for readings at various points on the efferent–aesthetic continuum. Because the predominantly efferent interpretation must be publicly verifiable or justifiable, the criteria of validity rest primarily on the public, referential aspects of meaning and require that any affective and associational aspects not dominate. The criteria for the predominantly aesthetic reading call for attention to the referential, cognitive aspects but only as they are interwoven and colored by the private, affective, or experiential aspects generated by the author's patterns of signs. Especially in the middle ranges of the efferent–aesthetic continuum, it becomes important for writers to provide clear indications as to stance and for readers to be sensitive to the writer's purpose and the need to apply relevant criteria.

"Literary" Aspects of Efferent Reading

In recent decades, in one scientific field after another, the opposition between scientific and "literary" writing has been found to be illusory. Writers in the natural and social sciences have become aware of the extent to which they engage in semantic and syntactic practices that have usually been considered "literary" and that they, too, have been using narrative, metaphor, and other rhetorical devices. Examples are the importance of metaphor in writings about economics or the idea that the historian writes narrative and that he can never be completely objective in selecting his facts. Sensitivity to sexist and racist tropes has increased awareness of the extent to which metaphor permeates all kinds of texts and, indeed, all language. Sometimes the efferent–aesthetic distinction seems to be completely erased (for example, the historian is sometimes said to write "fiction").

It becomes necessary to recall that the stance reflecting the aesthetic or efferent purpose, not the syntactic and semantic devices alone, determines the appropriate criteria. For example, in a treatise on economics or a history of the frontier, the criteria of validity of interpretation appropriate to their disciplines, which involve primarily verifiability and logic, would still apply. When an economist remarks that "the scientists had better devise good metaphors and tell good stories" (McCloskey, 1985), the concept of a dominant stance becomes all the more essential. The criteria for "good" should be not only how vivid and appealing the stories are but also how they gibe with logic and facts and what value systems are implied.

The relevance of the efferent–aesthetic continuum (Figure 7.1) may be illustrated by the example of metaphor: The scientist speaks of the "wave" theory of light, and we focus on the technical concept at the extreme efferent end of the continuum. Shakespeare writes, "Like as the wave makes toward the pebbled shore / So do our minutes hasten to their end," and our aesthetic attention to the feeling of inevitability of the succeeding waves enhances the feeling of the inevitability of the passage of time in our lives. A political analysis suggested surrendering to the inevitability of fascism by calling it "the wave of the future. . . . There is no fighting it" (Lindbergh, 1940, p. 934). Despite the vividness of the metaphor, efferent attention should have remained dominant, applying the efferent criterion. Did logic and factual evidence support the persuasive appeal?

IMPLICATIONS FOR TEACHING

Reading and Writing: Parallelisms and Differences

Parallelisms between reading and writing processes have raised questions concerning their connections, especially in the classroom. The reading and writing processes both overlap and differ. Both reader and writer engage in constituting symbolic structures of meaning in a to-and-fro, spiral transaction with the text. They follow similar patterns of thinking and call on similar linguistic habits. Both processes depend on the individual's past experiences with language in particular life situations. Both reader and writer, therefore, are drawing on past linkages of signs, signifiers, and organic states in order to create new symbolizations, new-linkages, and new organic states. Both reader and writer develop a framework, principle, or purpose, however nebulous or explicit, that guides the selective attention and the synthesizing, organizing activities that constitute meaning. Moreover, every reading and writing act can be understood as falling somewhere on the efferent–aesthetic continuum and as being predominantly efferent or aesthetic.

The parallels should not mask the basic differences—the transaction that starts with a text produced by someone else is not the same as a transaction that starts with the individual facing a blank page. To an observer, two people perusing a typed page may seem to be doing the same thing (namely, "reading"). But if one of them is in the process of writing that text, different activities will be going on. The writer will be engaged in either expression-oriented or reception-oriented authorial reading. Moreover, because both reading and writing are rooted in mutually conditioning transactions between individuals and their particular environments, a person may have very different experiences with the two activities, may differ in attitudes toward them, and may be more proficient in one or the other. Writing and reading are sufficiently different to defeat the assumption that they are mirror images: The reader does not simply reenact the author's process. Hence, it cannot be assumed that the teaching of one activity automatically improves the student's competence in the other.

Still, the parallels in the reading and writing processes described above and the nature of the transaction between author and reader make it reasonable to expect that the teaching of one can affect the student's operations in the other. Reading, essential to anyone for intellectual and emotional enrichment, provides the writer with a sense of the potentialities of language. Writing deepens the reader's understanding of the importance of paying attention to diction, syntactic positions, emphasis, imagery, and conventions of genre. The fact that the sign—interpretant—object triad is, as Peirce said, dependent on habit indicates an even more important level of influence. Cross-fertilization will result from reinforcement of linguistic habits and thinking patterns resulting from shared transactional processes of purposive selective attention and synthesis. How fruitful the interplay between the individual student's writing and reading will be depends largely on the nature of the teaching and the educational context.

The Total Context

Here we return to our basic concept that human beings are always in transaction and in a reciprocal relationship with an environment, a context, a total situation. The classroom environment, or the atmosphere created by the teacher and students transacting with one another and the school setting, broadens out to include the whole institutional, social, and cultural context. These aspects of the transaction are crucial in thinking about education and especially the "literacy problem." Because each individual's linguistic–experiential reservoir is the residue of past transactions with the environment, such factors condition the sense of possibilities, or the potential organizing frameworks or schema and the knowledge and assumptions about the world, society, human nature, that each brings to the transactions. Socioeconomic and ethnic factors, for example, influence patterns of behavior, ways of carrying out tasks, even understanding of such concepts as "story" (Heath, 1983). Such elements also affect the individual's attitude toward self, toward the reading or writing activity, and toward the purpose for which it is being carried on.[3]

The transactional concept of the text always in relation either to author or reader in specific situations makes it untenable to treat the text as an isolated entity or to overemphasize either author or reader. Recognizing that language is not a self-contained system or static code on the one hand avoids the traditional obsession with the product—with skills, techniques, and conventions, essential though they are—and, on the other, prevents a pendulum swing to overemphasis on process or on the personal aspects.

Treatment of either reading or writing as a dissociated set of skills (though both require skills) or as primarily the acquisition of codes and conventions (though both involve them) inhibits sensitivity to the organic linkages of verbal signs and their objects. Manipulating syntactic units without a sense of a context that connects them into a meaningful relationship may in the long run be counterproductive.

Nor can the transactional view of the reading and writing processes be turned into a set of stages to be rigidly followed. The writer's drafts and final texts—or the reader's tentative interpretations, final evocation, and reflections—should be viewed as stopping points in a journey, as the outward and visible signs of a continuing process in the passage from one point to the other. A "good" product, whether a well-written paper or a sound textual interpretation, should not be an end in itself—a terminus—but should be the result of a process that builds the strengths for further journeys or, to change the metaphor, for further growth. "Product" and "process" become interlocking concerns in nurturing growth.

Hence, the teaching of reading and writing at any developmental level should have as its first concern the creation of environments and activities in which students are motivated and encouraged to draw on their own resources to make "live" meanings. With this as the fundamental criterion, emphasis falls on strengthening the basic processes that we have seen to be shared by reading and writing. The teaching of one can then reinforce linguistic habits and semantic approaches useful in the other. Such teaching, concerned with the ability of the individual to generate meaning, will permit constructive cross-fertilization of the reading and writing (and speech) processes.

Enriching the individual's linguistic–experiential reservoir becomes an underlying educational aim broader than the particular concern with either reading or writing. Especially in the early years, the linkage between verbal sign and experiential base is essential. The danger is that many current teaching practices may counteract the very processes presumably being taught. The organization of instruction, the atmosphere in the classroom, the kinds of questions asked, the ways of phrasing assignments, and the types of tests administered should be scrutinized from this point of view.

The importance of a sense of purpose, of a guiding principle of selection and organization in both writing and reading, is being increasingly recognized. The creation of contexts that permit purposive writing and reading can enable the student to build on past experience of life and language, to adopt the appropriate stance for selective attention, and to develop inner gauges or frameworks for choice and synthesis that produce new structures of live meaning.

Collaborative Interchange

In a favorable educational environment, speech is a vital ingredient of transactional pedagogy. Its importance in the individual's acquisition of a linguistic–experiential capital is clear. It can be an extremely important medium in the classroom. Dialogue between teacher and students and interchange among students can foster growth and cross-fertilization in both the reading and writing processes. Such discussion can help students develop insights concerning transactions with texts as well as metalinguistic understanding of skills and conventions in meaningful contexts.

Students' achievement of insight into their own reading and writing processes can be seen as the long-term justification for various curricular and teaching strategies. For example, writers at all levels can be helped to understand their transactional relationship to their readers by peer reading and discussion of texts. Their fellow students' questions, varied interpretations, and misunderstandings dramatize the necessity of the writer's providing verbal signs that will help readers gain required facts, share relevant sensations or attitudes, or make logical transitions. Such insights make possible the second, reader-oriented authorial reading.

Similarly, group interchange about readers' evocations from texts, whether of their peers or adult authors, can in general be a powerful means of stimulating growth in reading ability and critical acumen. Readers become aware of the need to pay attention to the author's words in order to avoid preconceptions and misinterpretations. When students share responses to transactions with the same text, they can learn how their evocations from the same signs differ, can return to the text to discover their own habits of selection and synthesis, and can become aware of, and critical of, their own processes as readers. Interchange about the problems of interpretation that a particular group of readers encounters and a collaborative movement toward self-critical interpretation of the text can lead to the development of critical concepts and interpretive criteria. Such metalinguistic awareness is valuable to students as both readers and writers.

The teacher in such a classroom is no longer simply a conveyor of ready-made teaching materials and recorder of results of ready-made tests or a dispenser of ready-made interpretations. Teaching becomes constructive, facilitating interchange, helping students to make their spontaneous responses the basis for raising questions and growing in the ability to handle increasingly complex reading transactions (Rosenblatt, 1983).[4]

The Student's Efferent–Aesthetic Repertory

The efferent–aesthetic continuum, or the two basic ways of looking at the world, should be part of the student's repertory from the earliest years. Because both stances involve cognitive and affective as well as public and private elements, students need to learn to differentiate the circumstances that call for one or the other stance. Unfortunately, much current practice is counterproductive, either failing to encourage a definite stance or implicitly requiring an inappropriate one. Favorite illustrations are the third-grade workbook that prefaced its first poem with the question "What facts does this poem teach you?" and the boy who complained that he wanted information about dinosaurs, but his teacher only gave him "storybooks." Small wonder that graduates of our schools (and colleges) often read poems and novels efferently or respond to political statements and advertisements with an aesthetic stance.

Despite the overemphasis on the efferent in our schools, failure to understand the matter of the public–private "mix" has prevented successful teaching even of efferent reading and writing. Teaching practices and curriculums, from the very beginning, should include both efferent and aesthetic linguistic activity and should build a sense of the different purposes involved. Instruction should foster the habits of selective attention and synthesis that draw on relevant elements in the semantic reservoir and should nourish the ability to handle the mix of private and public aspects appropriate to a particular transaction.

Especially in the early years, this should be done largely indirectly, through, for example, choice of texts, contexts for generating writing and reading, or implications concerning stance in the questions asked. In this way, texts can serve dynamically as sources from which to assimilate a sense of the potentialities of the English sentence and an awareness of strategies for organizing meaning and expressing feeling. Emphasis on analysis of the evocations, or terminology for categorizing and describing them, has no value if they overshadow or substitute for the evoked work. Such activities acquire meaning and value when, for example, they answer a writer's own problems in expression or explain for a reader the role of the author's verbal strategies in producing a certain felt response.

The developmental sequence suggested here is especially important in aesthetic reading. Much teaching of poetry at every level, including high school and college, at present takes on a continuously repeated remedial character because of the continued confusion about stance through emphasis on efferent analysis of the "literary" work. Students need to be helped to have unimpeded aesthetic experiences. Very young children's delight in the sound and rhythms of words, their interest in stories, and their ability to move easily from verbal to other modes of expression, too, often fade. They need to be helped to hold on to the experiential aspect. When this can be taken for granted, efferent, analytical discussions of form or background will not be substitutes for the literary work but become a means of enhancing it. Discussion then can become the basis for assimilating criteria of sound interpretation and evaluation appropriate to the various points on the continuum and to the student's developmental status.

IMPLICATIONS FOR RESEARCH

Research based on the transactional model has a long history (Applebee, 1974; Farrell & Squire, 1990). Until fairly recently, it has generated research mainly by those concerned with the teaching of literature in high schools and colleges, rather than by those concerned with reading per se in the elementary school (Beach & Hynds, 1990; Flood et al., 1991; Purves & Beach, 1972). It is not possible here to survey this already considerable body of research, much of it exploring aspects of response to literature; nor does space allow discussion of recent volumes dealing with applications of transactional theory in elementary school, high school, and college (Clifford, 1991; Cox & Many, 1992; Hungerford, Holland, & Ernst, 1993; Karolides, 1992). I shall instead suggest some general considerations concerning research topics and theoretical and methodological pitfalls.

The transactional model of reading, writing, and teaching that has been presented constitutes, in a sense, a body of hypotheses to be investigated. The shift it represents from the Cartesian to the post-Einsteinian paradigm calls for removal of the limitations on research imposed by the dominance of positivistic behaviorism. Instead of mainly treating reading as a compendium of separate skills or as an isolated autonomous activity, research on any aspect should center on the human being speaking, writing, reading, and continuously transacting with a specific environment in its broadening circles of context. And as Bartlett (1932) reminds us, any secondary theoretical frameworks, such as schemata or strategies, are not stable entities but configurations in a dynamic, changing process. Although the focus here will be on reading research, the interrelationship among the linguistic modes, especially reading and writing, broadens the potential scope of problems mentioned.

The view of language as a dynamic system of meaning in which the affective and the cognitive unite raises questions about the emphasis of past research. Researchers' preoccupation with the efferent is exemplified by their focus on Piaget's work on the child's development of mathematical and logical concepts and the continuing neglect of the affective by behaviorist, cognitive, and artificial intelligence psychologists. This is slowly being counterbalanced by growing interest in the affective and the qualitative (e.g., Deese, 1973; Eisner & Peshkin, 1990;

Izard, 1977). We need to understand more fully the child's growth in capacity for selective attention to, and synthesis of, the various components of meaning.

Research in reading should draw on a number of interrelated disciplines, such as physiology, sociology, and anthropology, and should converge with the general study of human development. The transactional theory especially raises questions that involve such broad connections. Also, the diverse subcultures and ethnic backgrounds represented by the student population and the many strands that contribute to a democratic culture present a wide range of questions for research about reading, teaching, and curriculum.

Developmental Processes

The adult capacity to engage in the tremendously complex process of reading depends ultimately on the individual's long developmental process, starting with "learning how to mean" (Halliday, 1975; Rosenblatt, 1985b). How does the child move from the earliest, undifferentiated state of the world to "the referential, emotive and associative part processes" (Rommetveit, 1968, p. 167)? Developmental research can throw light on the relation of cognitive and emotional aspects in the growth of the ability to evoke meaning in transactions with texts.

Research is needed to accumulate systematic understanding of the positive environmental and educational factors that do justice to the essential nature of both efferent and aesthetic linguistic behavior, and to the role of the affective or private aspects of meaning in both stances. How can children's sensorimotor explorations of their worlds be reinforced, their sensitivity to the sounds and qualitative overtones of language be maintained? In short, what can foster their capacity to apprehend in order to comprehend, or construct, the poem, story, or play? Much also remains to be understood about development of the ability to infer, or make logical connections, or, in short, to read efferently and critically.

How early in the child's development should the context of the transaction with the text create a purpose for one or the other dominant stance, or help the reader learn to adopt a stance appropriate to the situation? At different developmental stages, what should be the role or roles of reflection on the reading experience through spoken comments, writing, and the use of other media?

An overarching question is this: How can skills be assimilated in a context that fosters understanding of their relevance to the production of meaning? How can the young reader acquire the knowledge, intellectual frameworks, and sense of values that provide the connecting links for turning discrete verbal signs into meaningful constructs? The traditional methods of teaching and testing recognize the important functions of the symbolic system, the alphabetic and phonological elements (the "code"), and linguistic conventions by fragmenting processes into small quantifiable units. These are quantitatively and hence economically assessable. But do such methods set up habits and attitudes toward the written word that inhibit the process of inferring meaning, or organizing and synthesizing, that enters into even simple reading tasks? How can we prepare the way for increasingly rich and demanding transactions with texts?

Performance

Assessment of performance level is usually required as a means of assuring the accountability of the school. Whether standardized tests accurately measure the student's ability is currently being called into question. Research on correlation of reading ability with factors such as age, gender, ethnic and socioeconomic background, and so on has confirmed the expectation that they are active factors. However, such research reports a state of affairs that is interpreted according to varying assumptions, not all conducive to the development of mature readers and writers. The transactional emphasis on the total context of the reading act reinforces the democratic concern with literacy and supports the call for vigorous political and social reform of negative environmental factors. At the same time teachers must recognize that the application of quantitatively based group labels to individual students may unfairly create erroneous expectations that become self-fulfilling prophecies.

Teaching Methods

In the current transition away from traditional teaching methods, there is the danger that inappropriate research designs may be invoked to evaluate particular teaching methods. What criteria of successful teaching and what assumptions about the nature of linguistic processes underlie the research design and the methods of measurement? Any interpretations of results should take into account the various considerations concerning reader, text, and context set forth in the transactional model.

Results of research assessing different teaching methods raise an important question: Did the actual teaching conform to the formulaic labels attached to the methods being compared? The vagueness of a term such as *reader-response method* can illustrate the importance of more precise understanding of the actual teaching processes being tested in a particular piece of research. The same term has been applied to teachers who, after eliciting student responses to a story, fall back on habitual methods of demonstrating the "correct" interpretation and to teachers who make the responses the beginning of a process of helping students grow in their ability to arrive at sound, self-critical interpretations.

Much remains to be done to develop operational descriptions of the approaches being compared. Studies are needed of how teachers lead, or facilitate, without dominating or dictating. Ethnographic study of classroom dynamics, records of interchange among teacher and students, videotapes of classrooms, and analyses of text give substance to test results.

Response

Students' empirical responses to a text (mainly written protocols) form the basis of much of the research on methods generally referred to as reader response or transactional. (The term *response* should be understood to cover multiple activities.)

Protocols provide indirect evidence about the students' evocation, the work as experienced, and reactions to it. Such research requires a coherent system of analysis of students' written or oral reports. What evidence, for example, is there that the reading of a story has been predominantly aesthetic?

The problem of empirical assessment of the student's aesthetic reading of a text offers particular difficulties, especially because no single "correct" interpretation or evaluation is posited. This requires setting up criteria of interpretation that reflect not only the presence of personal feelings and associations, which are only one component, but also their relationship to the other cognitive and attitudinal components. In short, the assessment must be based on clearly articulated criteria as to signs of growing maturity in handling personal response, relating to the evoked text, and use of personal and intertextual experience vis-à-vis the responses of others.

In order to provide a basis for statistical correlation, content analysis of protocols has been used largely to determine the components or aspects of response. The purpose is to distinguish personal feelings and attitudes from, for example, efferent, analytic references to the sonnet form. This requires a systematic set of categories, such as *The Elements of Writing About a Literary Work* (Purves & Rippere, 1968), which has provided a common basis for a large number of studies. As the emphasis on process has increased, refinements or alternatives have been devised. The need is to provide for study of the relationship among the various aspects of response, or the processes of selecting and synthesizing activities by which readers arrive at evocations and interpretations (Rosenblatt, 1985a). Qualitative methods of research at least should supplement, or perhaps should become the foundation for, any quantitative methods of assessing transactions with the written word.

Experimental designs that seek to deal with the development of the ability to handle some aspect of literary art should avoid methodologies and experimental tasks that instead serve to test efferent metalinguistic capacities. For example, levels of ability to elucidate metaphor or to retell stories may not reflect children's actual sensing or experiencing of metaphors or stories so much as their capacity to efferently abstract or categorize (Verbrugge, 1979).

The dependence on single instances of reading in assessing an individual's abilities is currently being called into question. The previous reminder that we are dealing with points in a continuing and changing developmental process is especially relevant. Habits are acquired and change slowly; it may be found that the effects of a change, for example, from traditional to response methods of teaching literature, cannot be assessed without allowing for a period of transition from earlier approaches and the continuation of the new approaches over time.

Basal readers have in the past offered especially clear examples of questions and exercises tacitly calling for an efferent stance toward texts labeled stories and poems. There has been little to help students assimilate and make automatic the aesthetic mode of relating to a text. Here, preparations for reading, the teacher's questions both before and after reading, and the mode of assessment, which powerfully influences teaching, should be scrutinized.

Studies that seek to generalize about the development of abilities by simultaneous testing of the different age levels have the problem of taking into account the factor of schooling. To what extent do changes in children's ability to retell or comment on the grammar of a story reflect schooling in the appropriate way to talk about a story? Similarly, to what extent are reported changing literary interests in the middle years not a reflection of personality changes but of too narrow definitions of *literary*?

Research Methodologies

The preceding discussion has centered on suggesting problems for research implied by the transactional model. Research methods or designs have been mentioned mainly in reference to their potentialities and limitations for providing kinds of information needed and to criteria for interpretation of data. Quantitatively based generalizations about groups are usually called for, but currently there is interest in clarifying the potentialities and limitations of both quantitative and qualitative research. Empirical experimental designs are being supplemented or checked by other research approaches, such as the case study (Birnbaum & Emig, 1991), the use of journals, interviews during or after the linguistic event, portfolios, and recordings in various media. Because the single episode test has various limitations, research in which researcher and teacher collaborate—or carefully planned research carried on by the teacher—provides the opportunity for extended studies. The transactional model especially indicates the value of ethnographic or naturalistic research because it deals with problems in the context of the ongoing life of individuals and groups in a particular cultural, social, and educational environment (Kantor, Kirby, & Goetz, 1981; Zaharlick & Green, 1991). The developmental emphasis also supports the call for longitudinal studies (Tierney, 1991). Interdisciplinary collaboration, desirable at any time, seems especially so for longitudinal studies. Research will need to be sufficiently complex, varied, and interlocking to do justice to the fact that reading is at once an intensely individual and an intensely social activity, an activity that from the earliest years involves the whole spectrum of ways of looking at the world.

ACKNOWLEDGMENTS

I want to thank June Carroll Birnbaum and Roselmina Indrisano for reading this manuscript, and Nicholas Karolides and Sandra Murphy for reading earlier versions.

NOTES

1. The 1949 volume marks Dewey's choice of *transaction* to designate a concept present in his work since 1896. My own use of the term after 1950 applied to an approach developed from 1938 on.
2. By 1981, *transactional theory, efferent stance,* and *aesthetic stance* were sufficiently current to be listed and were attributed to me in *A Dictionary of Reading and Related Terms* (Harris &

Hodges, 1981). But the often confused usage of the terms led me to write "Viewpoints: Transaction Versus Interaction—A Terminological Rescue Operation" (1985).
3. The transactional model of reading presented here covers the whole range of similarities and differences among readers and between author and reader. Always in the transaction between reader and text, activation of the reader's linguistic–experiential reservoir must be the basis for the construction of new meanings and new experiences; hence, the applicability to bilingual instruction and the reading of texts produced in other cultures.
4. *Literature as Exploration* emphasizes the instructional process that can be built on the basis of personal evocation and response. Illustrations of classroom discussions and chapters such as "Broadening the Framework," "Some Basic Social Concepts," and "Emotion and Reason" indicate how the teacher can democratically moderate discussion and help students toward growth not only in ability to handle increasingly complex texts but also in personal, social, and cultural understanding.

CONNECTING TRANSACTIONAL THEORY TO YOUR CLASSROOM . . .

1. Relate the implications of Rosenblatt's transactional theory and reader response to literature to the new literacy skills of viewing and visually representing. Design an activity involving these new literacy skills and reader response to a literacy event via technology. Present your activity to your instructor and classmates.
2. Select a text (picture book, chapter from longer text) written from a different cultural perspective than your own. Note your responses, feelings, and interpretations as well as the particular cultural features, details, and themes in the text. Compare your notes with a classmate's notes. How do your interpretations and notations differ? Write about your findings and connect them to Rosenblatt's theory. Discuss implications for your own classroom literacy program.

REFERENCES

Ames, A. (1955). *The nature of our perceptions, prehensions, and behavior.* Princeton, NJ: Princeton University Press.

Appenzeller, T. (1990, November/December). Undivided attention. *The Sciences.*

Applebee, A.N. (1974). *Tradition and reform in the teaching of English.* Urbana, IL: National Council of Teachers of English.

Bartlett, F.C. (1932). *Remembering: A study in experimental and social psychology.* London: Cambridge University Press.

Bates, E. (1979). *The emergence of symbols.* New York: Academic.

Beach, R., & Hynds, S. (1990). Research on response to literature. In E. Farrell & J.R. Squire (Eds.). *Transactions with literature* (pp. 131–205). Urbana, IL: National Council of Teachers of English.

Birnbaum, J., & Emig, J. (1991). Case study. In J. Flood, J.M. Jensen, D. Lapp, & J.R. Squire (Eds.), *Handbook of research on teaching the English language arts* (pp. 195–204). New York: Macmillan.

Blumenthal, A.L. (1977). *The process of cognition.* Englewood Cliffs, NJ: Prentice Hall.

Bohr, N. (1959). Discussion with Einstein. In P.A. Schilpp (Ed.), *Albert Einstein, Philosopher-Scientist* (p. 210). New York: HarperCollins.

Cantril, H., & Livingston, W.K. (1963). The concept of transaction in psychology and neurology. *Journal of Individual Psychology, 19,* 3–16.

Chomsky, N. (1968). *Language and mind.* New York: Harcourt Brace.

Clifford, J. (Ed.). (1991). *The experience of reading: Louise Rosenblatt and reader response theory.* Portsmouth, NH: Boynton/Cook.

Cox, C., & Many, J.E. (Eds.). (1992). *Reader's stance and literary understanding.* Norwood, NJ: Ablex.

Culler, J. (1982). *On deconstruction.* Ithaca, NY: Cornell University Press.

Damasio, A.R. (1989). The brain binds entities by multilingual activities for convergence zones. *Neural Computation, 1.*

Deese, J. (1973). Cognitive structure and affect in language. In P. Pliner & T. Alloway (Eds.), *Communication and affect.* New York: Academic.

Dewey, J. (1938). *Logic: The theory of inquiry.* New York: Henry Holt.

Dewey, J., & Bentley, A.F. (1949). *Knowing and the known.* Boston: Beacon.

Eisner, E.W., & Peshkin, A. (1990). *Qualitative inquiry in education: The continuing debate.* New York: Teachers College Press.

Emig, J. (1983). *The web of meaning.* Portsmouth, NH: Boynton/Cook.

Farrell, E., & Squire, J.R. (Eds.). (1990). *Transactions with literature.* Urbana, IL: National Council of Teachers of English.

Fish, S. (1980). *Is there a text in this class?* Cambridge, MA: Harvard University Press.

Flaubert, G. (1926). *Correspondance* (Vol. 2). Paris: Louis Conard.

Flood, J., Jensen, J.M., Lapp, D., & Squire, J.R. (Eds.). (1991). *Handbook of research on teaching the English language arts.* New York: Macmillan.

Halliday, M.A.K. (1975). *Learning how to mean.* New York, Elsevier.

Harris, T.L., & Hodges, R.E. (Eds.). (1981). *A dictionary of reading and related terms.* Newark, DE: International Reading Association.

Heath, S.B. (1983). *Ways with words: Language, life, and work in communities and classrooms.* Cambridge, UK: Cambridge University Press.

Hungerford, R., Holland, K., & Ernst, S. (Eds.). (1993). *Journeying: Children responding to literature.* Portsmouth, NH: Heinemann.

Izard, C.E. (1977). *Human emotions.* New York: Plenum.

James, W. (1890). *The principles of psychology* (2 vols.). New York: Henry Holt.

Kantor, K.J., Kirby, D.R., & Goetz, J.P. (1981). Research in context: Ethnographic studies in English education. *Research in the Teaching of English, 15*(4), 293–309.

Karolides, N.J. (Ed.). (1992). *Reader response in the classroom: Evoking and interpreting meaning in literature.* White Plains, NY: Longman.

Kuhn, T. (1970). *The structure of scientific revolutions* (2nd ed.). Chicago: University of Chicago Press.

Lindbergh, A.M. (1940). *The wave of the future.* New York: Harcourt Brace.

McCloskey, D. (1985). *The rhetoric of economics.* Madison: University of Wisconsin Press.

Miller, G.A., & Johnson-Laird, P.N. (1976). *Language and perception.* Cambridge, MA: Harvard University Press.

Myers, G. (1986). *William James: His life and thought.* New Haven, CT: Yale University Press.

Peirce, C.S. (1933, 1935). *Collected papers* (Vol. 3, Vol. 6) (P. Weiss & C. Hartshorne, Eds.). Cambridge, MA: Harvard University Press.

Purves, A.C., & Beach, R. (1972). *Literature and the reader: Research in response to literature.* Urbana, IL: National Council of Teachers of English.

Purves, A.C., & Rippere, V. (1968). *Elements of writing about a literary work: A study of response to literature.* Urbana, IL: National Council of Teachers of English.

Rommetveit, R. (1968). *Words, meanings, and messages.* New York: Academic.

Rosenblatt, L.M. (1978). *The reader, the text, the poem: The transactional theory of the literary work.* Carbondale: Southern Illinois University Press.

Rosenblatt, L.M. (1983). *Literature as exploration* (4th ed.). New York: Modern Language Association. (Original work published 1938)

Rosenblatt, L.M. (1985a). The transactional theory of the literary work: Implications for research. In C. Cooper (Ed.), *Researching response to literature and the teaching of literature.* Norwood, NJ: Ablex.

Rosenblatt, L.M. (1985b). Viewpoints: Transaction versus interaction—A terminological rescue operation. *Research in the Teaching of English, 19,* 96–107.

Rosenblatt, L.M. (1991). Literary theory. In J. Flood, J.M. Jensen, D. Lapp, & J.R. Squire (Eds.), *Handbook of research on teaching the English language arts* (pp. 57–62). New York: Macmillan.

Rosenblatt, L.M. (1993). The transactional theory: Against dualisms. *College English, 55*(4), 377–386.

Saussure, F. (1972). *Cours de linguistique générate.* Paris: Payot.

Tierney, R.J. (1991). Studies of reading and writing growth: Longitudinal research on literacy development. In J. Flood, J.M. Jensen, D. Lapp, & J.R. Squire (Eds.), *Handbook of research on teaching the English language arts* (pp. 176–194). New York: Macmillan.

Verbrugge, R.R. (1979). The primacy of metaphor in development. In E. Winner & H. Gardner (Eds.), *Fact, fiction, and fantasy in childhood.* San Francisco: Jossey-Bass.

Vygotsky, L.S. (1962). *Thought and language* (F. Hanmann & G. Vakar, Eds. & Trans.). Cambridge, MA: MIT Press.

Werner, H., & Kaplan, B. (1962). *Symbol formation.* New York: Wiley.

Zaharlick, A., & Green, J. (1991). Ethnographic research. In J. Flood, J.M. Jensen, D. Lapp, & J.R. Squire (Eds.), *Handbook of research on teaching the English language arts* (pp. 205–223). New York: Macmillan.

INTERSECTIONS OF TEXT AND THE READER

HELPFUL WEBSITES

Defining Text

http://desktoppub.about.com/cs/basic/g/textcomposition.htm
http://wrt-howard.syr.edu/Handouts/Text.html
http://www.textetc.com/theory/barthes.html
http://www.textetc.com/theory.html

The Reader

http://melissawiley.com/blog/2009/06/01/how-does-e-reading-affect-the-book/
http://nces.ed.gov/
http://www.reading.org/General/AdvocacyandOutreach/SIGS/ConcernforAffectSIG.aspx
https://www.ideadata.org/default.asp
http://www.begintoread.com/research/literacystatistics.html
http://edpubs.ed.gov/Productcatalog.aspx?Item=WDkdprp/LURhWhgAUOBWih1UamZN/
hxBeD5FMVXC9yZK/O8Yrwj+zEBzG/iEZvGEbdemtHI3mDsce9KKpskUcg==

Schema Theory

http://www.sil.org/lingualinks/literacy/ImplementALiteracyProgram/
SchemaTheoryOfLearning.htm
http://www.schematherapy.com/id30.htm
http://www.analytictech.com/mb870/schema.htm
http://www.readability.biz/Reader2.html
http://www.docstoc.com/docs/35178456/%E2%80%9COrdeal-By-Cheque%E2%80%9D
http://www.nyla.org/content/user_19/Cheques.pdf

Rosenblatt

http://www.vccaedu.org/inquiry/inquiry-spring97/i11chur.html
http://scholar.lib.vt.edu/ejournals/ALAN/v32n3/karolides.pdf
http://www.tutorgig.com/ed/Louise_Rosenblatt
http://www.education.miami.edu/ep/Rosenblatt/
http://books.heinemann.com/shared/onlineresources/E00768/chapter5.pdf
http://www.poynter.org/content/content_print.asp?id=5363&custom=
http://english.ttu.edu/kairos/4.1/features/newbold/theory.htm
http://www.wisegeek.com/what-is-reader-response-criticism.htm
http://www.nyu.edu/public.affairs/releases/detail/193
http://www.education.miami.edu/ep/Rosenblatt/
http://www.phillwebb.net/History/TwentiethCentury/Pragmatism/Rosenblatt/Rosenblatt.htm
http://www.hu.mtu.edu/reader/online/20/purves20.html
http://steinhardt.nyu.edu/news/2005/9/1/louise_rosenblatt_scholar_teacher_pioneer_in_
reading_theory

Comprehension

[Free sign up required for the first three sites.]

http://www.learner.org/workshops/teachreading35/session3/index.html
http://www.learner.org/workshops/teachreading35/pdf/teachers_know_comprehension.
http://www.learner.org/workshops/teachreading35/pdf/teachers_know_comprehension.pdf
http://www.learner.org/vod/form.html
http://www.csun.edu/~hda75098/Comprehensionstrategiestable.html
http://www.csun.edu/~hda75098/NRPComprehensionReferences.html

THEORETICAL PERSPECTIVES: INTERSECTIONS OF PSYCHOLOGY, COGNITIVE THEORY, READING, AND THE READER

INTRODUCTION

At first glance, the student of reading might wonder at the inclusion of a section about theories pertaining to learning and the intersection of psychology as a discipline since learning theory was probably the topic of one of the first education courses required to become a teacher. However, it is important to revisit those cognitive and psychological contributions to the field of reading instruction since ongoing learning is as important for teachers as it is for doctors, lawyers, or mechanics. What is a theory? Simply stated, a theory is a set of guiding principles that seek to explain phenomena, that is, learning. Theory is at the heart of what drives our behaviors and practices. What we believe about how students learn best determines the types of instructional activities we will choose. If an educator subscribes to a particular theory, it will probably guide his or her instruction, whether or not the teacher can place a "label" on that theory or articulate its guiding principles. As the policy makers continue to place increased emphasis on reading assessment and accountability while pointing to the lack of improvement in reading scores, it is essential that teachers be informed about the theories that provide the foundational underpinnings for their instructional decisions and be articulate about defending their beliefs.

In this section, we will journey backward through the centuries to review the important work of psychologists and theorists such as Plato, Socrates, Thorndike, Piaget, Vygotsky, Skinner, and Bandura. We will also examine some popular reading programs and the theories from which they have evolved. We also view inquiry and will study the important contributions of Dewey, Suchman, and Thelen to consider how inquiry approaches connect to the teaching of reading. A close examination of the brain and the reading process will reveal some of the newest innovations in the field of educational psychology as applied to students with reading difficulties. Another chapter will attempt to bring some clarity to the terms *social constructionism* and *social constructivism* as topics widely used today in discussions of theories that provide an essential knowledge base for literacy teacher education.

As you begin the reading of the chapters in this section, we challenge you to be very intentional in focusing on your beliefs about how children learn and also about how reading is taught in your own classroom and local school setting. Edmund Huey (1908/1938), in his classic work, *The Psychology and Pedagogy of Reading*, first published in 1908, emphasized, "We have surely come to the place where we need to know just what the child normally does when he reads, in order to plan a natural and economical method of learning to read" (p. 9). Huey's words challenge us to continue to examine those natural behaviors of children as they learn to read. We encourage you to reflect on the mandates that require you to implement specific required curricula and instructional programs. Keeping in mind those mandates and your current practice, make note of the theories that underpin those mandates. Can you articulate a strong defense for the practices you are now implementing? If not, can you articulate a justification for changing course in your instructional reading practice?

REFERENCE

Huey, E. (1908/1938). *The Psychology and Pedagogy of Reading.* Cambridge, MA: MIT Press. (Original work published in 1908.)

■ ■ ■ ■ ■

Alignment of Readings in Section III to the International Reading Association's *Standards for Reading Professionals 2010* (Draft):

Standard 1: Foundational Knowledge
    1.1; 1.2 (timeline); 1.3
Standard 2: Curriculum and Instruction
    2.1 and 2.2 (postreading activities)

Standard 4: Diversity
    4.1; 4.2; 4.3 (postreading activities)
Standard 6: Professional Learning and Leadership
    6.1; 6.3

Intersections of Psychology, Cognitive Theory, Reading, and the Reader Timeline

BEGINNINGS . . .	
400 BC	Plato and Aristotle lay philosophical foundations for psychology; associationism
1690	Locke publishes *Essay Concerning Human Understanding;* empiricism
1748	Hume publishes *An Enquiry Concerning Human Understanding*
1824	Herbart publishes *Psychology as a Science*
1843	J. Stuart Mill publishes *A System of Logic*
1875	W. James establishes psychology laboratory at Harvard
1883	G. Stanley Hall founds child study movement
1886	First educational psychology textbook published by L. Hopkins
1890	W. James publishes *Principles of Psychology*
1892	G. S. Hall and colleagues found American Psychological Association (APA)
1898	Thorndike publishes *Animal Intelligence*
1900s–1930s	
1905	Binet and Simon begin work on scale for measuring intelligence (Binet-Simon scale)
1908	The original publication date for Huey's *The Psychology and Pedagogy of Reading*
1913	Thorndike publishes *Educational Psychology: The Psychology of Learning;* connectionism; "Law of Effect"
1916	Terman and Stanford graduate students develop *Stanford-Binet scales;* concept of IQ is developed
1920–1930	W. S. Gray and colleagues at University of Chicago publish studies on reading behavior and achievement
1929	Piaget publishes *Child's Conception of the World;* theory of cognitive development
1934	Vygotsky publishes *Thought and Language* [published in English in 1986]
1935–1938	B. F. Skinner publishes research identifying Pavlovian and term operant conditioning
1940s–1950s	
MID-1940s	Bruner's research on perception
1947	Educational Testing Service (ETS) established
1950s–1960s	
1953	B. F. Skinner publishes *Science and Human Behavior*
1955	Piaget publishes *Child's Construction of Reality*

(Continued)

Intersections of Psychology, Cognitive Theory, Reading, and the Reader Timeline

1956	Bloom's *Taxonomy of Educational Objectives* published Bruner's *Study of Thinking* published
1959	Guilford's *Three Faces of Intellect* published
1960s–1970s	
1960	Center for Cognitive Studies established at Harvard; cognitive perspectives overshadowing behaviorism
1963	S. Kirk uses term "learning disabilities" for students with perceptual disorders
1964	Association for Children with Learning Disabilities established
1966	Bruner publishes *Studies in Cognitive Growth* and *Toward a Theory of Instruction;* cognitive learning theory is popularized
1969	Bandura publishes *Principles of Modification of the Behavior*
1970	Piaget's *Science of Education* proposes Learning Cycle Model
1980s–present	
1985	H. Gardner publishes *The New Mind's Science*
1986	Bruner publishes *Actual Minds, Possible Worlds*
1998–2009	Shaywitz and colleagues research on differing patterns of processing in strong and struggling readers as revealed in neuroimaging studies
Present	Positron emission tomography (PET) and functional magnetic resonance imaging (fMRI) research ongoing with readers

INTERSECTIONS OF EDUCATIONAL PSYCHOLOGY AND THE TEACHING OF READING: CONNECTIONS TO THE CLASSROOM

KATHIE GOOD

***THINK ABOUT* EDUCATIONAL PSYCHOLOGY AND THE TEACHING OF READING . . .**

1. As you read, compile a list of major theorists and their contribution to the field of literacy.
2. Read to discover how understanding the foundational theories of learning can enhance your abilities to be a successful reading teacher.

An African proverb states, "It takes a village to raise a child." In education, there is a unique theoretical framework that builds the "learning village." The framework is filled with theorists and their theories, psychologists with their experiments and models, and researchers and the research they put forward, all laying the foundation for the educator, who must put the theoretical underpinnings and research together with the practice of teaching students. Teachers have the instructional responsibility to assure that every child is successful in learning to read. In order to achieve this goal, teachers must understand that learning does not just happen. Rather, optimal learning takes place when there is an intersection of foundational theory and everyday practice.

All educators have a personal philosophy, yet many do not know the roots from which their philosophy grew. Educators begin as students and develop their rudimentary philosophy based on the philosophies of their instructors. As the student becomes the educator, the rudimentary philosophy is reinforced by practical experience. Eventually, the educator combines the theoretical with the practical and develops his or her working educational philosophy (Noddings, 1998).

How learning occurs has been studied since the beginning of time. Early literacy is seen in the hieroglyphics left by many civilizations (Noddings, 1998). Greek philosophers posed that the mind was a muscle and, as a muscle, should be exercised to achieve maximum potential. Plato, Socrates, and other early educators believed that the more the mind was used, the more intellectual one became (Dewey, 1977). Rote memorization was viewed as acceptable as long as new knowledge was gained. After all, knowledge expanded the mind and added to the body of intellect. The more the mind was exercised, the more learning would come, efficiently and effectively. Later, Plato, and then Thorndike, would expand the theory of the mind as muscle; just learning knowledge is not enough to increase the intellectual ability of the mind. Rather, associations and connections must be made for true learning to occur (Thorndike, 1932).

The theories of how humans learn can be traced to Plato and Aristotle and their theories on associationism (Anderson & Bower, 1973). Educational psychology and, ultimately, educational behaviorism, as disciplines, are grounded in the concept of associationism, beginning with Plato and Aristotle and moving forward in time and relevancy to John Locke, David Hume, and John Stuart Mill (Leahey, 1994).

Associationism grounds all learning as associative cognitive experiences. Associationism instills the reality that learning is never completed in isolation but is dependent on previous learning and experiences. To be successful as readers, students must have the opportunity and ability to connect new words and knowledge to previous learning and experiences (Goodman, 1970). From the beginnings of associationism, all theories of learning have evolved and moved forward (Anderson & Bower, 1973).

A great deal of time could be spent combing through contributions from all the philosophers, psychologists, and researchers whose works have left a lasting impact on education and the science of learning. However, there are those philosophers, psychologists, and researchers whose work rises to the top with irrefutable, unmistaken imprints impacting education practices on a daily basis.

Plato, Aristotle, Thorndike, and Skinner all wrote of and presented theories regarding learning and cognitive processes of learning. Jean Piaget detailed his work specifically to early learning and child development. Albert Einstein called Piaget's cognitive development model a discovery "so simple that only a genius could have thought of it" (Papert, 1999). Through the study of young children, including his own, Piaget (1955) determined that the cognitive ability of children evolved in four distinct and unique stages: **sensorimotor stage**, **preoperational stage**, **concrete operational stage**, and **formal operational stage**. Historically,

sensorimotor stage—birth to about age 2; a child learns about himself or herself and his or her surroundings by using motor and reflexive actions in his or her interactions; thinking is present-minded

preoperational stage—early stages of talking through about age 7; a child can think of things not immediate or, rather, from the past; starts using symbols to represent objects; as well, objects are often personified in this stage; children in this stage must still be able to physically examine the world around them

concrete operational stage—grade 1 to early adolescence; children begin to think abstractly; can make rational judgments; may or may not need to physically examine the world around them to make judgments

formal operational stage—adolescence; the person in this stage can make decisions effectively, as well as being capable of both deductive and hypothetical thinking/reasoning; is open to a variety of ways in which to learn

Piaget has become "one of the most influential developmental psychologists" (Lourenco and Machado, 1996, p. 143).

Through Piaget's stages of development, reading teachers can glean what students are ready to learn based on the age of cognitive development. When students are unable to have success learning a new concept, teachers should ask themselves if students are not understanding because they lack the skills or associative knowledge or if the students are simply not of the cognitive maturity to understand the concept. When asking a student to engage in reader-response activities requiring inferences and conclusions or even higher level thinking, it is imperative that educators understand the cognitive maturity of students (Ogle & Lang, 2007). Understanding Piaget's theory of cognitive development is vital when moving children along the developmental continuum required to become strategic and effective readers.

Surrounding Piaget's theory of cognitive development is the encapsulating idea that children's minds are not empty vessels in which to pour knowledge, but that children are actively constructing knowledge about their world and its surroundings (Freire, 1970/2000; Lourenco & Machado, 1996). Couple the idea of children being active in the construction of knowledge with Piaget's charge that children must be taught in a social setting to truly have a holistic and well-rounded learning experience, and you, as a teacher, will believe in the importance of a classroom of active children engaging in learning. You, as a teacher, will argue against a classroom filled with desks in rows, lectures, and silent reading. Piaget's theories continue to provide a cognitive framework and one perspective on how children learn as debate continues on how children should be taught (Manning & Kamii, 2000).

Almost simultaneously with Piaget, in a different part of the world, Lev Vygotsky was also working to understand the cognitive development of learners. Though not formally trained as a psychologist or educator, the work of Vygotsky continues to greatly impact the science and processes of teaching children to read (Dixon-Krauss, 1996). Although Vygotsky's work was completed in the 1920s and 1930s, it was not until the last four decades that his work has significantly impacted education in the United States. Perhaps the primary reason is that the translation of Vygotsky's work into English did not begin until the 1960s. Almost immediately the nuisances described in Vygotsky's research began reverberating through education in the United States (Moll, 1990).

Vygotsky's theories are numerous and interconnected, with the earlier theories of associationism and connectionism. Piaget outlined in great detail the cognitive levels of learning for a child. Vygotsky unknowingly took Piaget's theories one step further through his idea of "socially meaningful activity" (Dixon-Krauss, 1996, p. 9). Socially meaningful activity is directly related to the cognitive development theory that learning is directly related to the social interactions that occur within the learning environment. Vygotsky opined that, parallel with the impact social culture had on learning, was the symbiotic idea that a valid assessment of a child could only occur when the child was actively engaged in learning in the socially culture environment. Vygotsky believed that for a child to internalize a behavior (learning), the behavior must first occur socially and only then would become part of the internal knowledge of the child, the opposite of what Piaget's theories dictated (Dixon-Krauss, 1996).

Perhaps Vygotsky's most well known and influential educational philosophy applicable to the field of reading is the zone of proximal development (ZPD). Simply defined, the ZPD is the "gap between the child's level of actual development determined by independent problem solving and her level of potential development determined by problem solving supported by an adult or through collaboration with more capable peers" (Dixon-Krauss, 1996, p. 15). The idea of scaffolding purposed by Vygotsky has the student supported with multiple layers of help as new learning is introduced. As the student moves from new information to internalized information, the layers of support are slowly removed, allowing the learning to be independent. Scaffolding is the concept behind the commonly used read-alouds with accompanying elaborate introductions and picture walks in classrooms today (Mercer & Mercer, 2005).

The ZPD is used to push children from their independent level of learning (comfort zone) to their potential level of learning. The concept of ZPD must be directed by an educator who continually has the outcome of learning in the forefront of the lesson. In reading, the ZPD is often used as the standard for measuring a student's ability to read with fluency as he or she is moved into and through more difficult material. As educators use the theory behind ZPD to encourage more advanced learning of concepts and skills, scaffolding must be used as the support required for success to occur.

> The teacher's role in supporting learning within the zone of proximal development involves three key elements:
>
> 1. The teacher mediates or augments the child's learning. She provides support for the child through social interaction as they cooperatively build bridges of awareness, understanding, and competence.
> 2. The teacher's meditational role is flexible. What she says or does depends on feedback from the child while they are actually engaged in the learning activity.
> 3. The teacher focuses on the amount of support needed. Her support can range from very explicit directives to vague [implicit] hints. (Dixon-Krauss, 1996, p. 16)

The theories of Vygotsky continue to have far-reaching implications throughout reading education in the United States. Vygotsky's work can be viewed in commonly used learning strategies and teaching methodologies such as readers' and writers' workshops, collaborative learning, literature circles, writing across the curriculum, and content area literacy strategies. Although Vygotsky's work was completed almost a century ago, many educational researchers believe the implications of his discoveries regarding learning will continue to make an imprint on education for years to come (Daniels, Wetsch, & Cole, 2007).

Always keeping the foundational theory of associationism in the back of the mind, a historical journey—and its intersections—are easy to plot and navigate. Edward L. Thorndike is commonly referred to as the "Father of Educational Psychology" (Zimmerman & Schunk, 2003, 124). Thorndike's groundbreaking work began with an experiment of placing a cat in a box and examining the length of time it took the cat to escape. Later Thorndike provided a reinforcement to the cat as it escaped the box. What impact did an experiment of cats escaping from boxes have on education? The cat and box experiment constituted the centerpiece of Thorndike's law of effect. "The Law of Effect states that responses that are closely followed by satisfying consequences become associated with the situation and are more likely to recur when the situation is subsequently encountered" (Curren, 2003, p. 265). Thorndike's work in law of effect was later reworked and presented as operant conditioning by B. F. Skinner (1968).

Thorndike's work quickly spread to the analysis of how students learn. How people learned to read remained Thorndike's focus of study throughout his career. Based on the theories of Plato and Aristotle on associationism, Thorndike extended the work to the theory of connectionism. Connectionism highlights the accepted learning practice of connecting new ideas, knowledge, or learning to existing memory in the cognitive storage. Connectionism takes the theory of associationism one step further (Hergenhahn and Olsen, 2005). Thorndike moved the theory of connectionism forward into many principles used in teaching reading. Thorndike wrote and published a series of three books, still used in schools throughout the country today. The books, known as "Thorndike's Word Books," presented educators with list of the most commonly used words (30,000 in the last book) in reading and writing (Zimmerman & Schunk, 2003). "The research of William S. Gray and E.L. Thorndike, for example, was used to design graded reading materials using controlled vocabulary, surely one of the most important developments in the teaching of reading in the 20th century" (Allington & McGill-Franzen, 2004, p. 6). Thorndike's foundational work is used in classrooms throughout the country in a variety of published and grade-leveled curricula.

Perhaps the most used theory from Thorndike's work that can be applied to today's classrooms is his idea of active learning. Active learning encourages students to become the force of their learning by interacting with not only their peers, but the learning materials as well. The crux of active learning is that the student drives the learning, using the teacher as the facilitator. The students are provided a learning environment that celebrates the risk taking necessary when trying to discover new knowledge (Thorndike, 1932).

B. F. Skinner, building on the work of Thorndike and retooling Piaget's theory of cognitive learning and experiments, proposed his own behavior theory. Through Skinner's experiments, the theory and practice of operant conditioning was founded. While many would stress that operant conditioning is a behavior-management theory and strategy, it is vital to remember that all actions of learning are, in themselves, behaviors (Kaplan & Carter, 1995). Operant conditioning is based on an almost overly simple premise.

> Operant behaviors are controlled by the central nervous system and the voluntary muscles. Operants usually occur first and are later modified or maintained by the presentation of a stimulus. Since this stimulus occurs after the operant, it is often referred to as a consequent stimulus event. The term operant means to operate, and operates means to produce an effect. (p. 31)

Vital to remember when applying the theory of operant conditioning to reading is that a response must follow the stimulus event in order to establish the pattern of behavior. Teaching students to read consists of a series of interconnected behaviors with the desired outcome of a student who can read with fluency and good comprehension. For example, each time a student pronounces a word correctly, the teacher responds with a smile or comment. The positive response encourages the student to attempt to pronounce the next word. As the stimulus-response cycle continues, the student is more apt to take risks when learning and pronouncing new words (Mercer & Mercer, 2005). Operant conditioning paved the way for the behaviorist approach to enter the classroom. Through the theory of operant conditioning, ideas such as management plans, token economies, contingency contracting, and payments for performance emerged. While there are two very distinct types of reinforcement (positive and negative) used as tools in operant conditioning, the use of positive reinforcement has proven much more successful when used in teaching students academic skills such as reading (Kaplan & Carter, 1995). Skinner's theories regarding positive reinforcement radically changed the face of education, which, at the time, prided itself on rote learning and negatively punishing discipline (Skinner, 1968).

Skinner was adamant in his belief that there were five main obstacles in learning: fear of failure, lack of directions, lack of clarity in directions, positive reinforcement was not used enough or with enough immediate feedback, and tasks contained too many large steps (Skinner, 1968.) Based on Skinner's obstacles of learning, a new instructional methodology was formed: direct instruction.

Based on Skinner's five obstacles of learning work, Siegfried Englemann developed a series of reading curriculum units. The methodology of direct instruction is used throughout classrooms today. Englemann's work focused on teaching reading and mathematics. The methodology of direct instruction has made a resurgence in education and is used for teaching the continuum of skills mandated in schools today. Direct Instruction is a very systematic and scripted curriculum. Teachers and students are directed in what to say, when to say it, and students are shown how to act while responding to the directions of the teacher. Probably the most well known curriculum developed entirely around direct instruction methodology is Englemann's Distar© reading series (Adams & Englemann, 1996). Distar© provided the foundation for well-known and commonly used published reading curricula. The most commonly used curriculum embracing the ideology of direct instruction can now been seen in the SRA (Science Research Associates) Reading Mastery series as well as in curriculum encasing math instruction. The look of direct instruction has changed with the times. The past idea of black-and-white tagboard lessons have now been replaced by up-to-date topics, vibrant pictures, and real-life connections for the new and struggling reader. Direct instruction is now presented in a programmatic package that takes nonreaders on a journey into successful reading. Important to note is that while the concept of Skinner's operant conditioning had a strong impact on education, both in behavior and academic teaching and learning, many professionals in the field of reading never embraced the behaviorist methodology. Gaffney and Anderson (2000) write:

> Interestingly, analysis of the language journal articles suggest that the reading field is not now and never has been manifestly behaviorist. The evidence for this claim is the extremely low rate of the terms reinforcement, programmed instruction, operant, behavior analysis, behavioral analysis in the *Reading Research Quarterly* or *The Reading Teacher.* Some might argue that behaviorism is or was latent, but it seems few in the reading field were ever self-conscious Skinnerians. (p. 58)

Albert Bandura's social learning theory encompasses the work of Plato and Aristotle's associationism, Thorndike's connectionism, law of effect and active learning, the human-development theories of Piaget and Vygotsky, and operant conditioning as demonstrated by B. F. Skinner (Bandura, 1986). Bandura's social learning theory extends the idea that learning does not occur in isolation. Not only does learning occur by connecting new learning to existing knowledge through cognitive processes, but learning occurs in more permanence when social interaction is involved in the learning environment (Kaplan & Carter, 1995). Bandura's social learning theory begins the moment children begin to notice that they are not alone in the universe, but part of a community. Social learning works informally and often by accident. However, the concept of social learning theory can be formally used in the classroom by educators as well.

When teaching reading, the theory of social learning begins before the student ever enters the classroom. Parents and caretakers teach young children techniques of reading when reading aloud to children and by serving as an example to children as they read materials themselves. Social learning and modeling are inseparable and often indistinguishable. Perhaps the most powerful social learning is that which is unintended or unplanned. For example, a special education teacher who is working with a Down syndrome child in reading might relate this story from her experiences:

> Carrie was an 8-year-old student with Down syndrome. Though Carrie was not a typical learner, Carrie was slowly becoming a reader. Every step in teaching Carrie to read became more structured and exaggerated. Carrie had learned how to hold a book and which side was up. However, Carrie was stuck reading the same page over and over again and never turning the page. Formal lessons were designed and taught. Teachers and parents demonstrated to Carrie over and over again how to turn the page. Carrie was not understanding the concept. Soon Carrie was

placed in a reading class with "normal" third-grade students for socialization only, or at least socialization was the only goal in the mind of the teachers and parents. Carrie joined the third-grade classroom each morning during the students' free reading time period. Carrie took a book to class with her, would find her place in the reading area, open the book, and stare at the cover or first page of the book. On the fourth day of Carrie's participation in the third-grade class, a dynamic shift in Carrie's reading behavior evolved. Carrie entered the third-grade classroom, found her place in the reading area, opened her book, and using her finger, moved her finger from left to right over each line of print. At the end of the page, Carrie would take the upper-right-hand corner of the page, easily turn the page, and then continue the left-to-right reading again.

While this may be a simple story, it is an excellent example of Bandura's social learning theory. Carrie's formal reading instruction had not changed when she began participating in the third-grade classroom. The only variable in Carrie's behavior was that she was now attending a classroom filled with readers. By watching her peers, Carrie quickly learned the basic skills of beginning reading in only 4 days. Education does not occur in isolation.

As professional educators, classroom practices are developed based on the philosophy and experiences of the teacher. Educators develop their philosophies early in their own academic careers, being influenced by university instructors and textbooks. However, when most educators are asked, they are unable to identify the philosopher, theorist, or researcher who influenced their educational philosophy or practice (Noddings, 1998). The founding principles of education proposed by psychologists and theorists must be studied and celebrated to truly understand why the art of teaching is such a complex, profound and honorable profession. Based on the work of innovative thinkers such as Plato, Aristotle, Thorndike, Piaget, Vygotsky, Skinner, and Bandura, the science and profession of teaching reading has evolved and will continue to evolve. Reading teachers continue to base their practice and instructional decisions on the sound psychological and learning base provided by the theorists of the past. As the fields of psychology and reading intersect, teachers will continue to use this knowledge to "hone their craft."

CONNECTING EDUCATIONAL PSYCHOLOGY AND THE TEACHING OF READING TO YOUR CLASSROOM . . .

1. Select a children's book and a high-frequency word list (i.e., Fry's Instant Words) and design a vocabulary lesson using high frequency words from the book. Be prepared to discuss with your classmates how your lesson is an application of Thorndike's theory.
2. Observe students during reading in your classroom. Was Bandura's social learning theory evident? What observations did you make that could be supported by Bandura's social learning theory? After observing reading in your classroom, design a lesson to emphasize social learning and reading.

REFERENCES

Adams, G. L., & Englemann, S. (1996). *Research on Direct Instruction: 25 years beyond DISTAR©.* Seattle, WA: Educational Achievement Systems. (ERIC Document Reproduction Service No. ED413575)

Allington. R. L., & McGill-Franzen, A. (2004). Looking back, looking forward: A conversation about teaching reading in the 21st century. In R. B. Ruddell & N. J. Unrau, *Theoretical models and processes of reading* (5th ed.). Newark, DE: International Reading Association.

Anderson, J. R., & Bower, G. H. (1973). *Human associative memory.* New York: Wiley.

Bandura, A. (1986). *Social foundations of thought and action.* Englewood Cliffs, NJ: Prentice Hall.

Curren, R. (2003). *A companion to the philosophy of education.* Malden, MA: Blackwell.

Daniels, H., Wetsch, J., & Cole, M. (Eds.). (2007). *The Cambridge companion to Vygotsky.* New York: Cambridge University Press.

Dewey, J. (1977). The child and the curriculum. In J. A. Boydston (Ed.), *John Dewey: The middle works. 1899–1924.* Carbondale, IL: Southern Illinois University Press.

Dixon-Kraus, L. (1996). *Vygotsky in the classroom.* White Plains, NY: Longman Publishers.

Freire, P. (1970/2000). *Pedagogy of the oppressed* (M. B. Ramos, Trans.). New York: Continuum. (Originally published in 1970).

Gaffney, J. S., & Anderson, R. C. (2000). Trends in reading research in the United States: Changing intellectual currents over three decades. In M. L. Kamil, P. B. Mosnethal, P. D. Pearson, and R. Barr (Eds.). *Handbook of reading research, Volume III.* Mahawah, NJ: Lawrence Erlbaum Associates.

Goodman, K. (1970). Reading as a psychologistic guessing game. In H. Singer and R. B. Ruddell (Eds). *Theoretical models and processes of reading.* Newark, DE: International Reading Association.

Hergenhahn, B. R., & Olson, M. H. (2005). *An introduction to the theories of learning.* Upper Saddle River, NJ: Pearson Education.

Kaplan, J., & Carter, J. (1995). *Beyond behavior modification* (3rd ed.). Austin, TX: Pro-Ed.

Leahey, T. H. (1994). Associationism. In R. J. Corsini (Ed.) *Encyclopedia of psychology* (2nd ed.). NY: Wiley.

Lourenco, O., & Machado, A. (1996). In defense of Piaget's theory: A reply to ten common criticisms. *Psychological Review, 103,* 143–164.

Manning, M. M., & Kamii, C. (2000). Whole language vs. isolated phonics instruction: A longitudinal study in kindergarten with reading and writing tasks. *Journal of Research in Childhood Education, 15*(1), 53–65.

Mercer, C. D. & Mercer, A. R. (2005). *Teaching Students with Learning Problems* (7th ed.). Upper Saddle River, NJ: Prentice Hall.

Moll, L. C. (1990). Introduction. In L. C. Moll (Ed) *Vygotsky and education: Instructional implication and applications of sociohistorical psychology.* New York: Cambridge University Press.

Noddings, N. (1998). *Philosophy of education.* Boulder, CO: Westview Press.

Ogle, D. & Lang, L. (2007). Best practices in adolescent literacy instruction. In L. B. Gambrel, L. M. Morrow, & M. Pressley (Eds.), *Best practices in literacy instruction* (3rd ed.). New York: Guilford Press.

Papert, S. (1999). The great minds of the century. *Time, 153*(12), 104–05.

Piaget, J. (1955). *The child's construction of reality.* London: Routledge and Kegan Paul.

Skinner, B. F. (1968). *The technology of teaching.* New York: Appleton-Century-Crofts.

Thorndike, E. L. (1932). *The fundamentals of learning.* New York: Teacher's College.

Zimmerman, B. J., & Schunk, D. H. (2003). *Educational psychology: A century of contributions.* Mahawah, NJ: Lawrence Erlbaum Associates.

CHAPTER 9

THE BRAIN AND READING

S. RUSSELL VADEN

THINK ABOUT **THE BRAIN AND READING . . .**

1. Have you ever wondered how the brain develops from the infant stage, where language and reading are far removed from functioning, to the early- and middle-childhood stages, where those processes are solid building blocks for learning and socialization? How is it that the human brain transforms itself into the complex machinery necessary for acquiring advanced skills in language and literacy?

2. What are the processes that "reside" in specific locations within the brain that work in concert to produce fluency in reading? Further, what do those neurological processes look like when reading fluency has become disrupted?

What is the brain? What does it do? How does it impact our ability to read? On the surface, these appear to be rather basic questions. They deal with topics that one might surmise as being primary and/or elementary within the general field of educational psychology. But, when applied directly to the study of reading, these small and basic questions open doors for a plethora of abstract discussion.

Adequate understanding of the brain—and its functions—is paramount to becoming a multidimensional instructor of reading. Not only should a teacher be sensitive to fundamental behaviors that may indicate a problem with reading (e.g., miscalling a word in a passage of text) and understanding that behavioral link to foundational elements of reading deficiency, a well-rounded teacher of reading should be able to recognize important connections to neurological functioning that often characterize a struggling reader. In this chapter, explanations will be given with regard to the links between neurological processing and the act of reading as we know it. Attention will be given to the specific functions of the brain, the locations of those functions within the brain itself, and the links between those functions and specific characteristics associated with reading. Because there is a significant, traditional belief (Gough, 1972) that reading is based on an apparent connection between neurological and cognitive processes, ultimately making reading an "automatic" process, it is imperative that teachers of reading become informed about the issues related to this premise. This chapter will explore those issues via an information-processing approach.

Before embarking upon this chapter, however, it is imperative that the reader take note that the views and beliefs about the act of reading that are described herein are but one set of theoretical assumptions about the way in which complex reading skills develop. Rather than ignoring other pertinent theoretical constructs and belief systems, this chapter simply presents the neurological foundation of reading as a valid viewpoint *in addition to* the other relevant foundations that are encountered elsewhere in the literature. Because this chapter makes no mention of social, cultural, or language-based derivatives, it is not safe to assume that the author discounts their value and worth in the grand scheme of how reading skills emerge. Rather, the author is of the belief that neurological processes are a root foundation for reading, upon which social, cultural, and language-based processes certainly do capitalize for building the structure of reading skills.

As the reader explores this chapter, he or she is encouraged to take this information as a foundational approach, supplementing his or her other knowledge and beliefs about reading. The consideration of the connection between brain processing and reading is absolutely necessary for the adequate understanding of how students learn to read, but it is only one piece of a larger puzzle concerning the ways in which skills emerge.

THE DEVELOPING BRAIN

Key Question for Exploration: *By what developmental process does the brain prepare itself for learning to read?*

What we have believed for quite some time about reading is that it is not innate (Wolfe & Nevills, 2004). People enter the world with a built-in mechanism for oral expression, but reading does not follow the same pattern. Unlike the case of spoken language, for which there is a natural evolutionary predisposal at hand (Ritchie & Bhatia, 1999; Spelke & Newport, 1998), reading must be carefully acquired through the development of targeted skills (Wolfe & Nevills, 2004). However, even before those important skills can be addressed, the brain must ready itself for reading in a way that is conducive for learning to occur (Shore, 1997). Structures and functions must be prepared within the brain itself so that reading may eventually become a facility for information processing. Although environmental issues such as ecological enrichment, social stimulation, and human interaction are known to significantly strengthen the likelihood of reading skill development (Knudsen, 1999; Molfese, Molfese, Key, & Kelly, 2003; Rosensweig, 1969), it is the organic preparation of the brain's networking system that appears to predict the greater facility of emerging literacy in young children, as complex cognitive tasks are known to require the connectedness of neuronal pathways (Blakemore & Firth, 2005).

There are numerous questions about the links between the developing brain and the act of reading that have entertained the minds of philosophers, psychologists, educators, physicians, and researchers for decades. These questions should guide the teacher's thinking about how the mechanisms and processes within the brain are related to strong reading skills:

- *Is there a set of mental activities that a person must acquire, prerequisite to reading skills?*
- *Is there a clearly defined way in which that set of mental activities or abilities takes shape within the conscious brain?*
- *Is there a developmental pattern or sequence involved in readying the brain for using those mental activities?*
- *Is there a correlation between brain activity and the acquisition of reading throughout the maturational process of early childhood?*

Those questions have been answered in countless studies devoted to understanding the ways in which the human brain develops itself into a thinking machine, designed for the process of acquiring, processing, and effectively utilizing information. Within that literature, special attention has been afforded to the ways in which the brain learns from early experiences, readying itself to gain effective reading strategies. In short, the developmental processes within the brain are key issues for the emergence of target literacy skills.

In an effort to avoid this section of the chapter reading similarly to a biology lesson, the essence of neural development will be discussed as a product rather than a process. It is the structural outcome of development that is of interest to teachers of reading rather than the minutia of what occurs chemically and physiologically within the maturational unfolding of the organic composition of the brain. As you may recall from previous learning in the biological sciences as well as in human growth and development, key elements of structural

maturation—a developmental term used to reference the biological and/or organic change of an organism, transitioning from a rather simple to a much more complex level

maturation within the brain have been shown to serve as the foundation for particular areas of learning (Bohlin, Durwin, & Reese-Weber, 2009). It is the understanding of these general brain-learning links that will be the focus of the developmental discussion within this chapter.

At birth, a typical newborn's brain is approximately 25% of the volume structure of the eventual adult brain, growing to about 75% of the adult brain volume by the end of the second year and 90% by the end of the third year. Considering this information alone, we can see that dramatic changes are occurring within the first 3 years of life with regard to brain development. As infants begin to demonstrate responses to environmental cues, neuronal connections and networks grow and solidify. Within that 3-year time frame, significant neuronal pathway development makes way for information processing and learning to occur at overwhelming rates (e.g., the stronger the neuronal connection, the faster the production and processing of information).

Such a rapid maturation of the brain's structure in a rather narrow window of time allows for heightened preparation for systematic processes of encoding or decoding of information to occur, but only once a child is exposed to information-rich environments. This is to say that only a portion of the emergence of our reading skill occurs due to a purely natural or physiological process, wherein another significant portion of that developmental preparedness occurs due to environmental stimulation and support. Obviously, the development of the brain has been characterized as a combination of both nature and nurture overtures (Edelman, 1992). However, the discussion presented within this chapter is confined primarily to the "nature" argument within that arena. It is the physical development of the brain, largely due to significant contributions from natural processes, that is of concern in establishing the connection between the act of reading and the brain as an organ (Blakemore & Firth, 2005). Thus, our focus will apply to what occurs within the brain during early childhood (i.e., after the vast neuronal expansion within the first 3 years) that typically enables the emergence of reading skills to occur.

At toddler preschool ages (30 months to 5 years), the typical brain contains almost twice as many neuronal connections as the typical adult brain. Hyperproduction of the neural network within this time is believed to occur in order to prepare the child for generic learning and adaptation in any setting, with exposure to any general set of experiences. Thus, the very young child is naturally primed for learning, regardless of the specific environmental cues. This phenomenon makes possible the fact that new skills are easier to learn at young ages as opposed to when we are older. If exposure to learning contexts takes place—and is fostered by the environment—within this critical window of time, then those **neural pathways** will remain constituted. However, if exposure to those learning contexts does not occur, then the optimum neural connectivity does not present itself for the solidification of skills. When not utilized for practice of information and skill, the neural pathways are known to dissolve away via the process of **pruning**, thereby lessening the strength and vitality with which we are able to process information. Based on the changes that occur within the toddler and preschool years, given optimum environmental cues, the brain becomes set for acquiring the information processing skills that are fundamentally necessary for reading. This sets the stage for the acquisition of an important ability to encode and decode written expression.

neural pathways—a complex set of connections among related neurons in the brain, responsible for generating and regulating brain activity; related to reading, information and skills are acquired, stored, and retrieved through the intricate networking of neuronal connections

pruning—a neurological process in which the brain regulates and alters its own form and function by reducing the number of overproduced or weak neural pathways and replacing them with more efficient configurations

Perhaps one of the human brain's most valuable properties during early development is the characteristic of being "plastic," or changeable or malleable (Greenbough, Black, & Wallace, 1987). Not necessarily related only to a change of form and structure, this property of being plastic also is important for considering the changes and alterations made with regard to function. Within the first 3 to 5 years of life, the brain undergoes many functional changes as a result of the vast neuronal connectivity described previously. Through this process, children acquire more knowledge, make more solid connections between old and new learning, and accumulate their mental processing skills that are necessary for assimilating written text into comprehension. It is this group of mental activities that is believed to contribute solidly to the development of reading.

Through development of size and shape, neuronal pathway connectivity, and functional change, the brain performs its magnificent transformation toward readiness for reading. Considering the basic premise of change described before, the brain demonstrates a natural maturation progression that allows for the development of skill sets that are fundamental to phonetic decoding, text or language assimilation, fluent word recognition, and general comprehension. It is through a developmental perspective that we are most able to appreciate the brain's activity involved in reading.

But, aside from the development of brain structure and product, there are important considerations to be made concerning the essential areas of the brain that house and support specific abilities associated with reading success. From a more structural standpoint, teachers of reading should be concerned with which mental activities and operations are occurring within different areas of the brain that allow basic reading skills to blossom. Through that awareness, brain-specific processes can be examined as correlates to a student's general capacity for reading.

THE LEARNING BRAIN

Key Question for Exploration: *What processes occur within various parts of the brain that enable it to read, and thereby to learn?*

No one part or region of the brain is solely responsible for learning to read. There is a network of areas within the brain, connecting one ability or skill with another, based on the localization of each of those aptitudes (Blakemore & Firth, 2005). Throughout the brain, many important functions occur—often simultaneously—which enable the learning process to take place in such a way that learning can occur from exposure to printed material (Begley, 2007; Shaywitz et al., 2002).

Although there are portions of the brain that specify particular functions for learning, all learning is believed to take place in much the same way, regardless of the area of the brain where the action occurs (Begley, 2007). Along those neuronal connections or pathways mentioned in the preceding developmental discussion, information is processed through the chemical and electrical signals that travel those connections. Much like a web of signals found in a telephone circuitry or within a radio signaling system, the human brain is capable of processing billions of data points every day, many of those occurring simultaneously. When this information is processed, and the neuronal connections are solidified, we are said to have "learned" (Begley, 2007). Therefore, regardless of what particular skill or ability is being considered, learning actually occurs as a complex physiological process. Considering the speed and cumulative rate of acquisition and processing, it is interesting to ponder what a busy brain we have, enabling us to learn new information all the time.

As stated, this process of signal transformation—nothing short of a modern engineering miracle—occurs within various parts of the brain. Scientists historically have considered the "thinking brain" as being divided into four separate parts, or **lobes**, across the outer **neocortex**, with each of those four lobes generating a very distinct element of activity that contributes to the process of learning. A discussion of those four lobes may be of interest to understanding the mysteries of the human brain as it is related to the act of reading. Some have reasoned that reading is a sequence or structure of several individual skills or abilities that are situated in various areas of the brain, with the general act of reading being considered an integrated sequential function of this vast system. In essence, a complex job (such as reading a passage of written text on a page) is broken into several microtasks, each of which occurs in different areas of the brain in what is believed to be simultaneous fashion. A thorough and solid explanation of the relationship between brain and reading would not be complete without considering the relationship among the brain's four predominant neocortical lobes.

The **occipital lobe**—found within the area near the lower back side of the cranium—is the portion of the brain that is responsible for significant functions such as visual integration, recognition of visual symbolic representation, and comprehension of sequential visual arrays such as groups of letters and words. This area of the brain is quite active in processing all of the visual stimulation that a person encounters when they visually scan a passage of text. For instance, all the visual features of the text that you are silently reading now from this page (e.g., shapes of letters, symbolic representation of visual text, visual combinations of letters) are being processed by your occipital region. Typically, in the field of reading instruction, we refer to this cluster of processing abilities as *orthographic* processing.

The **parietal lobe**—found within the area near the top rear quadrant of the cranium—is the portion of the brain that is responsible for important functions related to the recognition and regulation of visual and spatial elements of text. The visual orientation of text on a page (e.g., visual arrangement of letters, words, sentences, and paragraphs), the spatial array of reading (i.e., moving from left to right at a programmed speed or rate), the ability to "hold" one's visual place in reading without the use of fingers or a tool, and the general facility with translating the

lobes—areas or regions of the neocortical brain, which have specialized functions and determinants; in the activity of reading, each of the four primary lobes of the cerebral cortex is believed to contribute a particular function that adds to the cumulative gain of reading skill

neocortex—the outermost layer of the cerebral hemispheres of the brain; the part of the brain that is most involved in higher-order functions such as sensory perception, generation of motor commands, spatial reasoning, conscious thought, and in humans, language

occipital lobe—the part of the cerebral cortex region of the brain that lies in the backmost part of the head, just above the neck; the part of the brain believed to be most significantly involved in the processing and understanding of visual images and the patterns of written words

parietal lobe—the part of the cerebral cortex region of the brain that lies in the topmost center portion of the head; the part of the brain believed to be most significantly involved in regulating sensory and motor information

visual and spatial data on a written page are all pertinent examples of the specific tasks that are regulated by the parietal lobe. Teachers of reading generally refer to this set of abilities as *visuospatial* processing. When considering the impacts of the general processing abilities on reading, visuospatial processing is treated as a separate entity from orthographics, whereas orthographic processing represents the general abilities to recognize and decode visual stimuli and visuospatial processing refers to the overall visual orientation to the presentation of text in a more sensory-based capacity.

temporal lobe—the part of the cerebral cortex region of the brain that lies adjacent to the temple region of the head; the part of the brain believed to be most significantly involved in functions related to memory and speech/language

The **temporal lobe**—found within the area along the sides of the cranium, near the ears—is the portion of the brain that is concerned with functions such as regulating memory, constructing meaning from experience, interpreting auditory stimuli, and decoding receptive language. Therefore, in reading, this area of the brain processes all the auditory information that is associated with what is being read. For example, the sounds that are associated with individual visual letter symbols, blends of sounds when letters appear together, and even language inflection that is implied by written text, are all primary data that are associated with the processing that occurs in this region. On a simplified level, the temporal lobe is the region of the brain that is treating written text just as it does spoken language, actively processing the sounds associated with speech. In reading instruction, teachers generally consider this cluster of abilities as being representative of *phonetic* processing.

frontal lobe—the part of the cerebral cortex region of the brain that lies directly behind the forehead; the part of the brain believed to be most significantly involved in higher order metacognitive activities, such as planning, organizing, problem solving, selective attention, and logical reasoning

The **frontal lobe**—found within the area immediately behind the forehead—is the portion of the brain that generally is concerned with functions such as reasoning, planning, creativity, judgment, and the regulation of parts of speech. Within the task of reading, however, this lobe of the brain is an active processor of significant contextual issues that give rise to learning from what we read. Most of the overall reading comprehension skills—understanding the meaning of text, regulating one's vocabulary for constructing meaning, grasping the relationship between sentences in a paragraph, facilitating the "big picture" of what is being read—occurs in this area of the brain. Within the field of literacy instruction, teachers generally associate the frontal lobe processing abilities with what is known as *lexical* processing, wherein the global reading of words and phrases is based on the reasoning and judgment made about written ideas.

Across the four primary lobes of the neocortex, a complex task system is underway during reading. We learn from what we read based on these numerous processes that are executed within specific brain regions. Most frequently, in typically functioning brain systems, these lobe-specific tasks occur in concert, with direct influence upon one another within the process of reading. Simultaneous processing throughout the network of the brain allows for speedy and reliable acquisition of information.

PROBLEMS WITHIN THE READING BRAIN

> **Key Question for Exploration:** *What occurs within the brain that some-times complicates the process that we call reading?*

From the preceding discussion, it is evident that the neocortical lobes of the brain are active agents in processing and regulating information that is encountered during the typical "reading" task. While a significant portion of the brain, as a whole, appears to be occupied with the task, there are specific processing abilities that are of concern. Within those processing abilities, a number of concerns arise for those of us concerned with the teaching of reading. In essence, we must focus on the global issue of cognitive and behavioral byproducts of those physiological processes. The teaching of reading rests upon the observation and measurement of cognitive and behavioral skills that are secondary indicators that the primary processing abilities are reliably underway and functional. No solid foundation of literacy instruction would be complete without the cogent understanding of what the indicators of proper physiological functioning would look like and sound like within the instructional moment. However, it occasionally is easier to understand proper functioning through the lenses of what occurs within the brain that shapes underdeveloped reading skills. It is with this approach that the following discussion illustrates the process of what the brain does in order to read.

neurobiological—related to the cells of the nervous system and the organization of these cells into functional units that process information and mediate behavior

Reading disabilities are most frequently defined in a **neurobiological** fashion, pointing out that they are more likely to be explained by physiological factors than by variables associated with ecological, developmental, or instructional circumstances (Gilger & Wilkins, 2008; Hudson, High, & Al Otaiba, 2007; Snow, Burns, & Griffin, 1998). Contemporary research indicates that two primary symptoms emerge in most children with reading disabilities (Carlisle, Stone, & Katz, 2001; Shapiro, Accardo, & Capute, 1998; Thomson, Crewther, & Crewther, 2006; Torppa, Tolvanen, & Piokkeus, 2007). First, those children demonstrate significant problems with word recognition—represented by the fluent awareness of previously learned words by sight—at their target grade level. Second, they demonstrate primary difficulties with using sound-letter relationships—also known as decoding—for identifying and "sounding out" new or unknown words that are encountered in text. It is believed that those two categories of symptoms of common reading deficiency have arisen from physiological difficulties related to atypical processing within the neocortical brain. According to Shaywitz and Shaywitz (2001), these characteristics of reading disabilities are found in an estimated 17% of the school-aged population and approximately 40% of adults.

In the area of word recognition, some interesting findings have emerged from scientific studies. Pugh, Mend, and Jenner (2001) linked the fluency of associating symbols with sounds to the specific functionality of the occipital and parietal regions of the brain. Salmelin and Helenius (2004) later found that significant underactivation of those regions of the brain are consistent correlates to observed difficulties in being able to encounter written words and associate them with spoken language. Fan, Bitan, Chou, Burman, and Booth (2006) more recently have been able to isolate specific processing deficits in this same region of the brain that seem to bear direct impact on the ability to recognize previously learned words and phrases. Those three studies have an important commonality at their core—the relationship between visual and/or spatial processing abilities and the general skill of recognizing printed text. Research demonstrates that this characteristic of reading disability is reliably situated in a physiologic causal model.

The inability to process what is encountered in printed text often is attributed to significant deficiencies within the areas of the brain responsible for visual input and coding. Neurological studies have shown deficits in visual motor-detection areas of the brain that occur more frequently in persons diagnosed with dyslexia than in the nondyslexic population (Eden et al., 1996). Further investigation revealed that the visual processing of images and symbols that is centralized to the occipital and parietal regions is corelationally linked to reading abilities in both strong and weak readers—for example, more efficient processing in more skilled readers (Eden et al.).

In the area of decoding (phonological) skills, research has shown similar relationships to other areas of the brain. Boets, Wouters, Van Wieringen, and Ghequiere (2006) found that tone-in-noise detection (i.e., the neurological measurement of distinguishing ranges of tones)—which is housed within the temporal lobe—was significantly related to performance on phonological awareness tasks. King, Wood, and Faulkner (2008) have recently found that failed integrations between temporal processing and other areas of the brain are common identifiers of people with conditions similar to dyslexia. Helland, Asbjornsen, and Hushovd (2008) were able to demonstrate a range in symptom severity within dyslexia conditions based on an associated range of processing function within the temporal lobe. Given these findings, it can be concluded that phonological processing also is dependent on specific neural functioning.

Wolfe and Nevills (2004) asserted that young children, in order to begin reading, must possess the ability to process auditory sounds of their spoken language by identifying, linking, and associating those sounds in relation to text that symbolically represents those sounds. Some important research (Merzenich et al., 1996) has established that people with reading disabilities frequently do not process the sounds of their languages efficiently enough to rapidly associate them to written text. According to those researchers, children with auditory processing difficulties will most certainly be at a disadvantage when learning to read.

RESEARCH ABOUT THE BRAIN

Key Question for Exploration: *What does the primary research about the brain contribute to our contemporary understanding of reading skills and processes?*

neuroimaging—the use of a range of technologies to image and/or map the structure and functioning of the brain

positron emission tomography—a highly specialized neuroimaging technique that produces a three-dimensional view of the brain; designed to highlight the pattern of fuel uptake and regulation within sections of brain tissue during cognitive tasks, thereby contributing to the understanding of how brain tissue changes due to learning experiences

oxygenation—saturation of oxygen within the blood stream; related to neurological functioning, oxygenation boosts the power of the brain to regulate fuel uptake and use

glucose—a simple sugar that is a rather important carbohydrate for biological functioning. It is the only fuel normally used by brain cells; the brain's rate of glucose metabolism is a key indicator of neurological efficiency for cognitive tasks such as reading fluency and comprehension

functional magnetic resonance imaging—a highly specialized form of MRI scan technology; associated with the investigation of blood flow and oxygen disbursement within the brain, this type of neuroimaging technique focuses more on the functionality of the brain, rather than on its structure

In order to best understand the research about neurological contributions to reading skills, it is useful to first discuss the ways in which brain activity commonly is measured. Until the most recent three decades, the majority of brain research had been isolated to the sampling of tissue and the quantification of wave patterns in manufactured situations. Over the past 30 years, however, clear evidence of brain activity has been determined within authentic tasks through more active measures in the medical community. Two primary **neuroimaging** techniques have been utilized in the study of reading. First, **positron emission tomography** (PET) measures important functions in the brain by determining the rate at which blood flow, **oxygenation**, and **glucose** metabolism occur in response to natural stimuli. Second, **functional magnetic resonance imaging** (fMRI) measures reactivity and responsiveness in the brain by determining—via the observation of blood flow—which areas of the brain are "active" and how rapidly those activations occur given particular rates of **hemodynamic** changes within the neural tissue. Across those two primary diagnostic imaging techniques, brain researchers are able to determine which sections or regions of the brain are more and less active during a particular task, such as reading. Fletcher and associates (2000) noted that both the PET and fMRI scans are able to demonstrate clear and significant differences in neural activation patterns in children who are successful and less successful in reading.

Readers of different skill levels (i.e., strong readers versus weak readers) have been shown to demonstrate different patterns of activation and localization of processing when examined by neuroimaging techniques. Some studies have found disruption in activation/localization patterns in struggling readers (Shaywitz et al., 1998). Some substantiated greater amount and strength of activation in strong readers (Shaywitz et al., 2002). Others documented malfunctions in neuronal pathway signal exchange in readers who had been diagnosed with dyslexia (Shaywitz et al., 2003).

The newsworthy theme within these examples is that imaging techniques have provided the contemporary researcher of reading with the tools to observe and quantify the problems that are occurring within the physiological properties of the human brain when behavioral indicators of reading difficulty begin to emerge. It is with this imaging capability that the links between brain functioning and reading disability can be studied and reported. The primary research in this area promotes a physiological approach to understanding difficulties that children have

hemodynamic—the process related to the unobstructed flow of blood through the body; regarding the brain, hemodynamic balance is an important contributor to fuel uptake for neurological processing of cognitive tasks

with reading. No longer is our research confined to issues related only to motivational, intellectual, and/or attitudinal theories. Nowadays, with more scientific approaches afforded by the medical community, our reading research can take the form of brain exploration. Indeed, this is an exciting advance toward the technological investigation of reading difficulties.

Interestingly enough, the field of brain research in reading education is not limited to the fact that brain processing affects reading skill. A more promising finding over the recent years is that reading instruction, in turn, affects brain structure and function. A bidirectional relationship has been established. Not only does the degree to which our brains process critical information determine our acquired abilities to read and comprehend text, our exposure to quality reading instruction clearly impacts our neural networking that permits and facilitates complex processing.

Recent research from the University of Texas Health Science Center in Houston has demonstrated some very important phenomena. Panagiotis and associates (2007) followed a group of 15 young struggling readers over an 8-week time span during their intensive (3 hours per day) instruction in reading. Neuroimaging techniques were used as pre and post measures of brain functioning. Although all 15 of the struggling readers initially evidenced neuroimaging profiles that are consistent with poor reading, significant changes in brain activity—quantified by increased degree of activity and reduced onset latency—were found in areas of all of the children's brains that are responsible for lexical and semantic processing. The nature of this finding is rather significant in that the degree to which brain activity improved in those children was consistent with neuroimaging results of unimpaired readers. Thus, this study suggested that although there is a neurological link to reading ability, there may be a bidirectional approach. Brain structure and process affects reading ability, but intensive intervention in reading appears to impact neuropsychological functioning as well.

Similar research was introduced by the University of Louisville in Kentucky. Molfese and associates (2002) presented their findings that neuroimaging techniques longitudinally demonstrate biological or physiological connections between language-related brain functions in infancy and the reading abilities of school-aged children. They also cited their finding that those biological or physiological patterns appear to be significantly altered through intervention and training that is specified to the area of the brain that is shown to be disrupted. Again, the bidirectional relationship is clearly evidenced.

The question that this pattern brings up is one of causality. Does poor neurological processing actually cause the condition of reading disability? Does intensive intervention in reading directly cause improvement in neurological processing? The fact is that we do not have enough information in science to definitively state one perspective or another as unwaivered truth. However, we certainly have gained enough evidence from recent research to point ourselves in the direction of brain profiling as a strong and dependable correlate to reading.

CONCLUSIONS

brain-based learning—an instructional-design model based on the idea that learning activities are more effective if they occur in an atmosphere that is compatible with the way the brain naturally engages in its dynamic process in order to learn and use new information and skills

You may be asking at this point, *So what does all of this mean for me as a teacher of reading?* The answer is rather simple. We are in the age of **brain-based learning**. This concept of teaching and learning proposes that people should engage in learning through ways in which the brain is naturally designed to work. According to Jensen (2000), brain-based learning is not a discipline of its own, but rather a unique perspective. Simply, it is a way of thinking about or constituting the ways in which we teach and learn. Teaching should stimulate natural functions within the brain's complex system. Particularly in the teaching of reading skills, attention to brain function is of utmost importance.

These views and claims—as stated in this chapter—support the notion of the "bottom-up" theory of reading (Gough, 1972). Ideas that support this theory assert that readers extract information directly from the printed page and process printed text in a relatively systematic fashion rather than using a contextual system of prior knowledge and social cues for decoding and comprehension (Treiman, 2001). As stated at the onset of this chapter, such an approach does not necessarily preclude other theoretical constructs (e.g., top-down). However, this discussion merely clarifies the utility of this bottom-up approach in light of the connection between brain functioning and the act of reading.

CONNECTING THE BRAIN AND READING TO YOUR CLASSROOM . . .

1. We know that developmental changes in the brain ideally promote faster processing in basic reading skills with age. As an experiment regarding this phenomenon, administer a basic Nonsense Word Fluency test to three different children. For the most illustrative results, choose students who span across a variety of developmental stages (e.g., a 1st grader, a 4th grader, and an 8th grader). To each participant, administer a Nonsense Word Fluency probe, such as the no-cost, brief sample found at the DIBELS Web site https://dibels.uoregon.edu/measures/nwf.php. Time each child with a stopwatch as he or she proceeds through the entire probe. Record the completion time for the task as well as any distinctive behaviors that emerge during the probe. What are the differences among the performance levels of the three readers? How might those differences be explained from a developmental viewpoint? Within this rather small data set, what are the apparent trends of brain development that may be related to reading performance?
2. From the following case examples, identify the areas of the brain that are responsible for the error patterns that each student is making in reading.
   - Victor has chronic difficulties with understanding vocabulary terms that he encounters in text as well as with comprehending the general

sequence of ideas and facts within a passage. He frequently complains that reading is difficult because he does not seem to grasp the meaning of what he reads. Despite his problems with comprehension, he is strong in the areas of phonetic decoding and reading fluently.

- Demarco is a student who demonstrates classic problems with miscalling words when he reads aloud for his teacher. He consistently substitutes words and phrases for one another when they visually look alike. His errors are predictable, and the teacher frequently anticipates which words he will mistake for one another.

- Jasmine makes errors in decoding words. She does not grasp the concept that each letter—or pair of letters—represents a specific auditory sound. Her reading fluency is dramatically slowed due to her inability to rapidly associate the visual/auditory pairing of letters and their respective sounds.

- Carla takes a great deal longer than her classmates to read a passage. While reading, she frequently loses her place. Even when using her finger to underscore each line of text, her focus drops and her pace slows. Although she is skilled at phonetically decoding what she encounters in text, she is unable to skillfully follow the visual flow of the words on the page.

REFERENCES

Begley, S. (2007). *Train your mind, change your brain: How a new science reveals our extraordinary potential to transform ourselves.* New York: Ballantine Books.

Blakemore, S., & Firth, U. (2005). *The learning brain: Lessons for education.* Malden, MA: Blackwell.

Boets, B., Wouters, J., Van Wieringen, A., & Ghequiere, P. (2006). Auditory temporal information processing in preschool children at family risk for dyslexia: relations with phonological abilities and developing literacy skills. *Brain and Language, 97* (1), 64–79.

Bohlin, L., Durwin, C., & Reese-Weber, M. (2009). *Ed psych modules.* Boston, MA: McGraw-Hill.

Carlisle, J. F., Stone, C. A., & Katz, L. A. (2001). The effects of phonological transparency on reading derived words. *Annals of Dyslexia, 51,* 249–74.

Edelman, G. R. (1992). *Bright air, brilliant fire: On the matter of the mind.* New York: Basic Books.

Eden, G., Van Meter, J., Rumsey, J., Maisog, J., Woods, R., & Zeffiro, T. (1996). Abnormal processing of visual motion in dyslexia revealed by functional brain imaging. *Nature, 382,* 66–69.

Fan, C., Bitan, T., Chou, T., Burman, D., & Booth, J. (2006). Deficient orthographic and phonological representations in children with dyslexia revealed by brain activation patterns. *Journal of Child Psychology and Psychiatry and Allied Disciplines, 47* (10), 1041–1050.

Fletcher, J. M., Simos, P. G., Shaywitz, B. A., Shaywitz, S. E., Pugh, K. R., & Papanicolaou, A. C. (2000). *Neuroimaging, language, and reading: the interface of brain and environment.* Paper presented to the Research Symposium on High Standards in Reading for Students from Diverse Language Groups: Washington, DC.

Gilger, J. W., & Wilkins, M. A. (2008). Atypical neurodevelopmental variation as a basis for learning disorders. In M. Mody & E. Silliman (Eds.), *Brain, Behavior, and Learning in Language and Reading Disorders.* New York: Guilford Press.

Gough, P. B. (1972). One second of reading. In J. F. Kavanaugh & I. G. Mattingly (Eds.), *Language by Ear and by Eye.* Cambridge, MA: MIT Press.

Greenbough, W., Black, J., & Wallace, C. (1987). Experience and brain development. *Child Development, 58,* 539–559.

Helland, T., Asbjornsen, A. E., & Hushovd, A. E. (2008). Dichotic listening and school performance in dyslexia. *Dyslexia, 14* (1), 42–53.

Hudson, R. F., High, L., & Al Otaiba, S. (2007). Dyslexia and the brain: what does current research tell us? Retrieved on October 27, 2008, from http://www.ldonline.org/article/14907

Jensen, E. (2000). *Brain-based learning: The new science of teaching and training* (Revised Edition). San Diego, CA: The Brain Store.

King, B., Wood, C., & Faulkner, D. (2008). Sensitivity to visual and auditory stimuli in children with developmental dyslexia. *Dyslexia, 14* (2), 116–121.

Knudsen, E. I. (1999). Early experience and critical periods. In M. J. Zigmond (Ed.), *Fundamental Neuroscience* (pp. 637–654). San Diego, CA: Academic Press.

Merzenich, M. M., Jenkins, W. M., Johnston, P., Schreiner, C., Miller, S. L., & Tallal, P. (1996). Temporal processing deficits of language learning impaired children ameliorated by training. *Science, 271,* 77–81.

Molfese, D. L., Molfese, V. J., Key, A. F., & Kelly, S. D. (2003). Influence of environment on speech-sound discrimination: Findings from a longitudinal study. *Developmental Neuropsychology, 24* (2 & 3), 541–558.

Molfese, D. L., Molfese, V. J., Key, S., Modglin, A., Kelley, S., & Terrell, S. (2002). Reading and cognitive abilities: longitudinal studies of brain and behavior changes in young children. *Annals of Dyslexia, 52,* 99–119.

Papagiotis, G. S., Fletcher, J. M., Sarkari, S., Billingsley-Marshall, R., Denton, C., & Papanicolaou, A. C. (2007). Intensive instruction affects brain magnetic activity associated with oral word reading in children with persistent reading disabilities. *Journal of Learning Disabilities, 40* (1), 37–48.

Pugh, K. R., Mend, W. E., & Jenner, A. R. (2001). Neurobiological studies of reading and reading disability. *Journal of Communication Disorders, 34* (6), 479–492.

Ritchie, W. C., & Bhatia, T. K. (Eds.). (1999). *Handbook of child language acquisition.* Orlando, FL: Academic Press.

Rosensweig, M. R. (1969). Effects of heredity and environment on brain chemistry, brain anatomy, and learning ability in the rat. In M. Monosevitz, G. Lindzey, & D. Thiessen (Eds.), *Behavioral Genetics.* New York: Appleton-Century-Crofts.

Salmelin, R., & Helenius, P. (2004). Functional neuranatomy of impaired reading in dyslexia. *Scientific Studies of Reading, 8* (3), 257–272.

Shapiro, B. K., Accardo, P. J., & Capute, A. J. (1998). Specific Reading Disability: A View of the Spectrum. A compendium of papers presented to the Eighteenth Annual Spectrum of Developmental Disabilities course. ERIC document 417546.

Shaywitz, B. A., Shaywitz, S. E., Pugh, K., Mencl, W., Fulbright, R., & Skudlarski, P. (2002). Disruption of posterior brain systems for reading in children with developmental dyslexia. *Biological Psychiatry, 52* (2), 101–110.

Shaywitz, S. E., & Shaywitz, B. A. (2001). *The neurobiology of reading and dyslexia. Focus on Basics,* 5 (A).

Shaywitz, S. E., Shaywitz, B. A., Fulbright, R., Skudlarski, P., Mencl, W., & Constable, R. (2003). Neural systems for compensation and persistence: young adult outcome of childhood reading disability. *Biological Psychiatry, 54* (1), 25–33.

Shaywitz, S. E., Shaywitz, B. A., Pugh, K., Fulbright, R., Constable, R., & Mencl, W. (1998). Functional disruption in the organization of the brain for reading dyslexia. *Procedings of the National Academy of Sciences, USA, 95,* 2636–2641.

Shore, R. (1997). *Rethinking the brain: New insights into early development.* New York: Families and Work Institute.

Snow, C. E., Burns, M. S., & Griffin, P. (1998). Preventing reading difficulties in young children. A paper presented to the Committee on Preventing Reading Difficulties in Young Children. ERIC document 416465.

Spelke, E. S., & Newport, E. L. (1998). Nativism, empiricism, and the development of knowledge. In W. Damon (Series Ed.), D. Kuhn, & R. Siegler (Vol. Eds.), *Handbook of Child Psychology: Volume 2—Cognition, Perception, and Language* (5th ed., pp. 275–340). New York: Wiley.

Thomson, B., Crewther, D. P., & Crewther, S. G. (2006). Wots the werd? Pseudowords (nonwords) may be a misleading measure of phonological skills. *Dyslexia, 12* (4), 289–299.

Torppa, M., Tolvanen, A., & Piokkeus, A. (2007). Reading development subtypes and their early characteristics. *Annals of Dyslexia, 57* (1), 3–32.

Treiman, R. (2001). Reading. In M. Aronoff, & J. Rees-Miller (Eds.), *Blackwell Handbook of Linguistics* (pp. 664–672). Oxford, England: Blackwell.

Wolfe, P., & Nevills, P. (2004). *Building the reading brain: PreK through 3*. Thousand Oaks, CA: Corwin Press.

CHAPTER 10

INQUIRY AND LITERACY: AN UNQUESTIONABLE CONNECTION

NANCY L. GALLENSTEIN

THINK ABOUT **INQUIRY AND LITERACY . . .**

1. What relationship does the process of inquiry have to the acquisition of literacy skills?
2. How can a teacher promote the use of inquiry-based instruction while teaching literacy?
3. How does the process of inquiry relate to the constructivist theory?

INTRODUCTION

Currently, in the field of education, the term **inquiry** is often heard. This term is normally referred to during the study of science, but is there a tie to another field of study, literacy? In this chapter, the term *inquiry* will be defined in relation to the study of science. Several effective teaching methods involving inquiry will be presented. In addition, the link to literacy will be discussed in relation to the inquiry-based techniques presented, revealing an unquestionable connection between the two concepts.

> **inquiry**—involves activity and skills, with a focus on the active search for knowledge or understanding to satisfy a curiosity or solve a problem

DEFINING INQUIRY

Various dictionary definitions exist for the term inquiry, such as a question; a quest or seeking truth, information, or knowledge; an investigation; and the act of seeking information by questioning. In this chapter, the term inquiry will be discussed in relation to teaching and learning.

INQUIRY LEARNING

Incorporating inquiry into the classroom promotes a learner-centered process rather than a teacher-directed paradigm. Inquiry is a prominent feature of the National Science Education Standards (National Research Council [NRC], 1996). "The term inquiry refers to the abilities students should develop to be able to design and conduct scientific investigations and the understandings they should gain about the nature of scientific explanation" (Lind, 2005, p. 6). Students who engage in inquiry participate in similar activities and processes as scientists do when they seek to expand knowledge.

No single inquiry method invariably works for scientists. Rather, there are many methods (Bass, Contant, & Carin, 2009). "Scientists typically ask questions, find ways to investigate the questions through observations and experiments, collect and organize data, and construct models, theories, and explanations based on observational evidence, existing knowledge, and clear arguments" (Bass et al., p. 4).

Inquiry instruction supports a constructivist approach to learning, whereby learning is based on the learner's prior knowledge. According to Adams and Hamm (1998), "**constructivism** is a learning theory that suggests that knowledge is most effectively acquired by evoking personal meaning in the learner" (p. 25). Students should have various opportunities to observe, investigate, collect, sort, catalog, take notes, sketch, interview, and poll (Lind, 2005; Martin, Sexton, Franklin, & Gerlovich, 2005). Although learners are the ones who construct knowledge, in inquiry instruction teachers are active in the process by facilitating inquiry lessons or activities that address children's questions about the natural world.

> **constructivism**—the notion that people build their own knowledge and representations of new information from their own experience

"Creative engagement is one of the keys to scientific inquiry and mathematical problem solving" (Adams & Hamm, 1998, p. ix). Educators must incorporate critical and creative thinking into the classroom to do justice to the curriculum and, therefore, to their students. In the inquiry-based classroom, the learning emphasis is on thinking, not telling children what to think (Adams & Hamm 1998, p. ix). Additionally, inquiry-teaching methods focus on communities of learners whereby teachers provide instructions to students about working together successfully in groups. "Constructivists agree that students individually construct knowledge within a cultural setting with others where they have opportunities to compare knowledge, discuss with peers, ask questions, justify their position, and arrive at a consensus" (Adams & Hamm, 1998, p. 25).

According to the National Science Education Standards (NSES), "full inquiry involves asking a simple question, completing an investigation, answering the question, and presenting the results to others" (NRC, 1996, p. 122). Inquiry can take many forms, but each form generally involves some level of use of each of the following inquiry tasks listed in the Science as Inquiry Standards of the NSES Content Standards (Bass et al., 2009, p. 18).

- Ask a question about objects, organisms, and events in the environment.
- Plan and conduct a simple investigation.

- Use appropriate tools and techniques to gather and interpret data.
- Use evidence and scientific knowledge to develop explanations.
- Communicate investigation procedures, data, and explanations to others.

These strategies provide children with the ability to develop inquiry process skills and make meaning of the material learned. In addition, opportunities as such should reach children at all learning modalities—visual, auditory, and kinesthetic.

According to the NRC (2000), a number of special features characterize inquiry instruction. (1) *Learners are engaged by scientific questions.* Students should generate questions from their own real-world experiences to investigate. Initially, students may need assistance from their teacher to form questions. (2) *Learners give priority to evidence as they plan and conduct investigations.* Students determine how to collect, represent, and organize data to answer their questions. (3) *Learners connect evidence and scientific knowledge in generating explanations.* Students describe and explain their observations using prior and developing knowledge while drawing inferences from their observations. (4) *Learners apply their knowledge to new scientific problems.* In order to take ownership of their knowledge, students must have an opportunity to apply their new knowledge to relevant circumstances. (5) *Learners engage in critical discourse with others about procedures, evidence, and explanations.* Students are provided with opportunities to communicate and justify their findings and explanations in both oral and written formats. As a result, students can share what they know about their topic in relation to the current knowledge base.

Relationship of Science and Literacy Skills

Connecting science content to other subject areas, such as literacy, can also promote positive attitudes in children. Children's literature contains numerous relevant science concepts. Often, the story and pictures in a trade book trigger a child's science conceptual understandings. It is so exciting to observe a child's enthusiasm when the "light bulb finally shines."

Literacy skills can also be reinforced through hands-on science as children observe, explore, discover, and reinvent concepts. Children use science thinking skills such as comparison and classification as they discriminate between shapes, size, and amount. These skills assist children with reading and writing, such as the ability to discriminate between letters in the alphabet, syllables, and words. Additionally, children strengthen their language communication skills when discussing, drawing, and acting out their science discoveries through various forms such as recording data, using graphic aids, drama, and/or puppetry. Furthermore, sequencing and cause-and-effect relationships discovered in science can aid children when predicting story outcomes and applying information to other situations (Charlesworth & Lind, 2003).

Providing opportunities for children to write and draw pictures about what they have learned and experienced with science can provide a teacher with the necessary insights into how a child thinks and feels. Children can create their own science books and regularly record their thoughts in journals or learning logs in picture or story form. According to Shaw and Blake (1998), "children's emerging writing abilities are extended when adults take dictation of what the children say, or write experience charts as a group of children discusses a situation" (p. 10).

Martin et al. (2005) present various examples of how process skills used in science inquiry investigations are also present in the literacy curriculum. For example, they, too, support that the process skill of observation is used to discriminate shapes, sounds, syllables, and word accents when reading. Identification (identifying variables) is present in the literacy curriculum when students recognize letters, words, prefixes, suffixes, and base words. Description (defining operationally) can be demonstrated in literacy when a student isolates important characteristics, enumerates ideas, and uses appropriate terminology and synonyms. Classification involves comparing and contrasting characteristics while considering multiple attributes and arranging ideas and ordering and sequencing information. Designing an inquiry investigation relates to literacy through asking questions, investigating possible relationships, and following organized procedures. Data collection can involve literacy skills such as taking notes, using reference materials, referring to different parts of a book, recording information in an organized way, and being precise and accurate. Data interpretation is also present in the literacy curriculum when students recognize cause-and-effect relationships, vary their reading rate, organize facts, summarize new information, and think inductively and deductively. Communication of results can be demonstrated in the literacy curriculum when students arrange and sequence information in a logical format, such as a time line, or describe results clearly in graphs and/or charts. Conclusion formation (inferences are conclusions about the cause of an observation) is present in the literacy curriculum when students generalize and critically analyze What if? questions, identify main ideas, establish relationships, and use information in other situations (Martin et al., pp. 22–23). Clearly, inquiry and literacy skills are reinforced through the promotion of inquiry-based instruction across the curriculum.

Trade Books in the Inquiry Classroom

Inquiry teaching methods imitate scientists at work. Inquiry involves finding evidence and answers to questions about the world. The inquiry process adds to what is already known and can occur in various creative formats, as described in this chapter.

In an article titled "Using Science Trade Books to Support Inquiry in the Elementary Classroom," Morrison and Young (2008) reinforce the importance of both background knowledge about the topic to be investigated and initial research. Prior to designing an investigation and making observations, "The scientist might read about what is known regarding a science topic in preparation for the inquiry investigation . . . the inquiry process is not complete without a thorough analysis and evaluation of the scientist's proposed explanation in light of current scientific understanding" (p. 204). Likewise, Morrison and Young state that students should also research their chosen topic before beginning an investigation. "It is imperative that students have time to read about their topic before starting the investigation, evaluate their results and explanations, compare their ideas to accepted and published knowledge, and base their final conclusion on their findings as well as their evaluations" (p. 205). As a result, Morrison and Young recommend using quality science trade books in inquiry investigations, thus reinforcing the relationship between inquiry and literacy. They propose that quality trade books can not only strengthen students' understanding of their topics and aide in designing their investigation questions, but also that trade books can assist students to validate their findings. Furthermore, this format models how scientists in authentic research settings conduct inquiry.

INQUIRY MODELS

The inquiry teaching/learning models presented in this chapter will focus on creative and critical thinking as well as collaborative learning environments that promote knowledge acquisition and retention. The models presented will include the scientific method, learning cycle lesson plan format, inquiry training/discrepant events, and group investigation. The connection to literacy will be noted in relation to each model.

Scientific Method

The scientific method is an effective and commonly used inquiry-investigation model providing students with an opportunity to use observation skills, prediction, hypothesis testing, and experimental design. The scientific method is usually the inquiry method chosen for science fair projects. As previously mentioned, Morrison and Young (2008) strongly promote the use of trade books (literacy) when children actively engage in the scientific method. When students decide on a question to investigate, Morrison and Young reinforce the importance of reviewing the relevant literature that pertains to the question to be addressed. Once students have gathered and organized a significant amount of information (literacy), they can then proceed to design an investigation that will address their question.

The typical components of an inquiry investigation include: determining a question to be researched (literacy), developing a hypothesis, determining the if-then variables involved in the investigation, describing the exact procedures to be followed (literacy), recording the if-then results on a table, graphing the if-then results, accurately stating the operational definition (literacy), and then recording the reason for acceptance or rejection of the hypothesis (literacy). Once the inquiry-investigation procedures have been recorded, Morrison and Young (2008) suggest that students reread the information that they initially discovered in trade books in order to validate the results of their study (literacy). Clearly, a strong inquiry-literacy connection exists with this popular inquiry-investigation format.

Learning Cycle Lesson Format

The learning cycle lesson format is described as an example of an instructional model inspired by Piaget's constructivist learning theory (Kellough, Carin, Seefeldt, Barbour, & Sauviney, 1996). The learning cycle format provides children with an opportunity to learn in a "manner congruent with how they learn naturally" (Charlesworth & Lind, 2003, p. 71).

The learning cycle lesson format originated in the early 1960s as the teaching model used in the Science Curriculum Improvement Study (SCIS) program (Karplus & Thier, 1967). Of the various science programs developed during the 1960s, the SCIS program has had the greatest overall effect on student achievement (Martin et al., 2005). The SCIS program was directed by Robert Karplus, was field tested during the 1960s, was revised during the 1970s, and is still widely used today. The overall goal of this inductive instructional inquiry approach is to help learners form a broad conceptual framework for understanding science through exploration and discovery while taking ownership of concepts (Martin et al.). The SCIS program emphasizes both inquiry process skills and content as students freely explore and discover concepts. The teacher's role in the learning cycle format is to facilitate and guide learning.

The original SCIS learning cycle format consisted of three distinct phases: exploration, invention, and application. Since the learning cycle lesson format was first introduced, many renditions have been developed.

One learning cycle rendition is the 5E. The 5E learning cycle model includes five phases: engagement, exploration, explanation, expansion, and evaluation. The *engagement* phase serves as a motivator or focus for each lesson. For example, the teacher creates the environment and demonstrates enthusiasm by asking a thought-provoking question, presenting a **discrepant event** or scenario, and/or sharing a story, picture, or word that initiates thinking on the part of the students. This phase can also be used to assess students' current knowledge of the concept to be discovered or reinvented.

> **discrepant event**—an event that is at variance with what is expected

The *exploration* phase is learner centered. The intent in this phase is for children to activate all of their senses. "Firsthand inquiry experiences like the learning cycle make use of a child's natural curiosity rather than trying to suppress it" (Charlesworth & Lind, 2003, p. 59). During the exploration phase, the teacher provides concrete experiences in order to stimulate learner **disequilibrium** and foster **assimilation** (Martin et al., 2005). The teacher provides items to observe, opportunities for active learning, and basic instructions for safety and material use and then allows children to explore, discover, and reinvent concepts while constructing their own personal meaning of their experiences (literacy). For example, students may be asked to explore what happens to a set of objects in motion when a force is applied, with the target concept being inertia. During this phase, the teacher also focuses children's observations as

> **disequilibrium**—mismatch between the state of the world and one's preconceived notions

> **assimilation**—an attempt to fit new information into schemas already formed

they describe and label their thoughts (literacy) to reach conclusions and form concepts (Kellough et al., 1996).

During the third phase, *explanation*, the teacher, through focused questioning, asks children to share information (literacy) that they have discovered and collected (literacy) during the exploration phase. At this time, the teacher guides the children to make connections to their prior knowledge by processing and mentally organizing (literacy) their discovered knowledge. Children then construct the concept cooperatively and apply an appropriate label (literacy), such as inertia for the reinvented concept.

Next, during the *expansion* phase, the teacher provides children with opportunities to apply learning to meaningful situations by expanding their newly acquired concept(s) through additional explorations and experiences. Similar to the exploration phase, this phase is also learner centered. Concept labels (literacy) are used and knowledge is applied to real-world experiences and/or career awareness instilling relevancy for the reinvented concepts. For example, students would discover how the concept of inertia is relevant to their lives and how the concept of inertia is applied to various careers.

Although listed as the fifth phase, *evaluation* occurs throughout all phases of the 5E model in the form of teacher or student questions, discussions, interviews (literacy); teacher-created observation checklists, rating scales, or rubrics; student journaling, presentations or projects (literacy); and/or paper-and-pencil tests, and so on. Both informal and formal assessment can be included as part of the evaluation phase.

Although the learning cycle format originated to increase the effectiveness of teaching science concepts, it is an extremely effective inquiry model for children when learning concepts across the curriculum. Children learn best when they are actively involved in the acquisition of knowledge (National Council of Teachers of Mathematics [NCTM], 2000; NRC, 1996). Children develop a deeper understanding of concepts when they are encouraged through inquiry to construct their own knowledge.

Inquiry Training Model

The inquiry training model, developed by Richard Suchman in 1962, relies on the use of discrepant events (Joyce, Weil, & Calhoun, 2004; Martin et al., 2005). Discrepant events are described as surprising, unusual or unexpected occurrences, for example, like a sharp pin penetrating a balloon without bursting it. Discrepant events produce **cognitive dissonance** or disequilibrium and motivate the observer to "want to know." In order to maintain mental consistency, the observer strives for **cognitive equilibration** (Joyce et al., 2004; Martin et al., 2005).

cognitive dissonance—a state of mental uncertainty about the explanation of an occurrence

cognitive equilibration—a state of mental satisfaction

Discrepant events provide students with opportunities to question, learn, investigate and discover independently and interdependently as they are faced with a question or situation they will want to solve. The methods used are similar to how scientists organize knowledge and generate principles (Joyce et al., 2004). A cooperative approach is very effective with this inquiry technique, providing students with an opportunity to act as detectives in uncovering the discrepancy.

With Suchman's method, the teacher explains the inquiry procedures and then presents a discrepant event. Students then ask fact-oriented questions rather than theory (explanation) questions that the teacher can answer with a yes or no to verify the events and collect information. Intermediate and middle school students can successfully ask theory questions, whereas K–2 students often ask theory questions similar to the game Twenty Questions (Martin et al., 2005). It is very important for the teacher to assist the students in understanding the difference between fact-oriented and theory questions. Factual questions help to uncover characteristics and conditions in order to provide students the necessary details. Once enough details have been determined, students can caucus as a group and summarize what they have learned about the discrepancy. With the necessary details, students can then model how a detective processes information and eventually decides on a substantial theory (explanation) for the discrepancy. Theory questions such as, Is it a _____? or Is it because _____? are explanations for the discrepancy and do not support how a detective initially gathers the necessary data to provide a solid explanation for a discrepancy.

Similar to other inquiry techniques, the inquiry training model provides numerous benefits for learners. In addition to developing inquiry-process skills (observing, collecting and organizing data; identifying and controlling variables; formulating and testing hypotheses; and, inferring), as students uncover the reason for discrepancies, they increase their understanding of information to make meaning of the situation (literacy). Furthermore, students become more proficient in verbal expressiveness (literacy), develop and refine listening skills (literacy), become better risk takers by asking thoughtful, logical questions (literacy), become active persistent learners, experience an increase in their tolerance of ambiguity, and develop an attitude that all knowledge is tentative. After each discrepancy has been determined, students should be provided with an opportunity to analyze (literacy) their inquiry strategy and contemplate how to improve their technique for future inquiries (Joyce et al., 2004).

Group Investigation Model

Drawing upon John Dewey's educational philosophy concerning democratic problem solving, Herbert Thelen described the group investigation model (Thelen, 1960). In Thelen's model, students are provided with opportunities to experience democratic decision making and problem solving through the investigation of real problems, issues, or concerns (Eby, 1998). This model also provides educators with opportunities to integrate subject areas such as social studies, science, mathematics, and literacy (Gallenstein, 2000).

First, either students or the teacher identifies a broad topic of interest, for example, environmental, and energy concerns. Students then brainstorm subtopics that would fall under the designated topic such as recycling, global warming, population growth, and air and water pollution. During brainstorming, all ideas are accepted and included on the list of topics (literacy) for possible research.

Next, the teacher might need to narrow down the list of possible topics to a manageable four or five and invite students to vote on which topic most interests them. Learning teams of three to four members are then formed on the basis of each student's subtopic of interest. Once organized, students meet in their learning teams and determine how their subtopic could be investigated. Students are encouraged to develop a set of questions that guide their study (literacy). Depending on the age of the students, a set amount of time should be determined in advance for research. Learning teams meet according to group members' schedules with some class time allotted for periodic updates. Research can be done at the school library, on the Web, and by phone (literacy). Research can also be conducted at public libraries and museums and in parent-supervised interviews with professional and other adult citizens (literacy).

The students then organize information into a written report (literacy). When completed, each learning team shares its findings with the class in a creative format, such as a role-play, simulation, "TV interview," puppetry, or other presentation format (literacy). Last, class members evaluate each group's presentation. Evaluators comment on the quality of the form and content of the presentation. For example, was the presentation well rehearsed (literacy)? Were graphics clear and well made (literacy)? Were details presented about the topic being studied (literacy)?

The teacher also evaluates each team's written product (literacy) and group presentation (criteria should be shared with students in advance). Each student also completes a self- and peer-evaluation form, which provides class members with an opportunity to reflect on their individual contributions to their learning team's project as well as on areas for improvement. Students also evaluate each of their team members' contributions to the investigation, attendance at group meetings, and presentation skills (literacy). As noted, numerous inquiry/literacy connections are prevalent in this productive research model.

EFFECTIVENESS OF INQUIRY MODELS

Although there is no best way to teach concepts to all children, according to Bass et al. (2009), "Research indicates that students exposed to inquiry methods in science typically perform better than their peers in more traditional classes on measures of general science achievement, process skills, analytical skills, and related skills such as language arts and mathematics" (pp. 106–107). Additionally, research shows that students with learning disabilities and English-language learners (ELLs) can successfully engage in inquiry instruction (Duschl, Schweingruber, & Shouse, 2007). Likewise, Scruggs, Mastropieri, Bakken, and Brigham (1993) concluded that "Activity-based, inquiry-oriented approaches, when appropriately structured, may facilitate the acquisition of content knowledge of students with

LD" (pp. 10–11). According to Lapp (2001), "For children who are learning science by means of an inquiry-centered approach, classroom investigations and the activities surrounding them can provide context. These experiences can be springboards for growth in verbal fluency and literacy" (p. 2). Consequently, "Hands-on inquiry activities help all students span the gap between their past experiences and the development of language within their immediate environment" (Bass et al., 2009, p. 268).

CHILDREN'S LITERATURE

As demonstrated, literacy enhances scientific inquiry in a variety of ways. Children's literature should be used to extend children's inquiries, while actual inquiry should be demonstrated through the use of science process skills—observation, classification, measurement, communication, estimation, prediction, inference, and formulating hypotheses.

The National Science Teacher Association (NSTA) publishes a list of outstanding science trade books each year for grades K–12 and can be found at http://www.nsta.org/publications/ostb/. The list is assembled in cooperation with the Children's Book Council (CBC). Books in Spanish are also included.

Numerous fiction and nonfiction children's books are available that support inquiry. Martin (2009) provides a list of children's literature in Appendix B of his popular science methods textbook entitled *Elementary Science Methods: A Constructivist Approach*. Martin provides examples of how children's literature enhances inquiry. For example, mysteries can provide excellent discrepant events (inquiry training model). *Encyclopedia Brown Takes the Cake?* by Donald Sobol and Glenn Andrews and *Science Mini Mysteries* by Sandra Markle would provide exciting opportunities for children to discover and reinvent knowledge through the use of inquiry. With the scientific method, the learning cycle lesson format and the group investigation model, books can be used to introduce a lesson, provide introductory or extension information, and/or to encourage and validate children's discoveries. Titles such as *Popcorn!* by Elaine Landau; *A River Ran Wild* (river ecology) by Lynne Cherry; *My Five Senses* and *Digging Up Dinosaurs* by Aliki; and *The Very Busy Spider* by Eric Carle would be excellent resources to supplement children's inquiry. Additionally, the *Bibliography of Books for Children* published by the Association of Childhood Education International (ACEI) provides an updated list of book titles that would be appropriate for linking literacy and inquiry.

CLOSING

Inquiry instruction is an approach to teaching that focuses on understanding the world by questioning, investigating, observing, and explaining the order of the world around us (Bass et al., 2009). As mentioned, research indicates that there are numerous positive benefits for students who engage in inquiry learning. Additionally, teaching as inquiry provides many opportunities for teachers to interact with their students and to develop the abilities and attitudes children need to inquire on their own (Bass et al., 2009, p. 25). Furthermore, as presented, inquiry instruction provides many opportunities for curriculum integration, demonstrating that there is indeed an unquestionable connection between inquiry and literacy.

CONNECTING INQUIRY AND LITERACY TO YOUR CLASSROOM . . .

1. Design a discrepant event with a literacy focus, such as an age-appropriate riddle, by following Suchman's inquiry training model. Provide the opening statement and materials needed for implementation. List various theories that your students might think will apply to your focus statement. Create a list of factual questions that students might ask that could be answered by a response of yes or no. Last, based on your discrepant event, how could you extend your students' knowledge on your selected literacy concept/topic?
2. Design an inquiry-based literacy activity based on the group investigation model. A broad literacy topic of interest for pre-service and/or in-service teachers could be the "Effects of Literacy Methods." Allow students to brainstorm various subtopics such as invented spelling, whole language learning, thematic learning, phonetics-based literacy, bilingual education, and so on. Have students follow the group investigation model procedures by choosing a topic to investigate, grouping students according to their chosen topic, allowing students time to determine appropriate questions to guide their investigation, and arranging a timeline for groups to investigate and design their group's findings for whole class presentation. Once completed, have the students evaluate the outcome of their investigation.
3. Choose a direct-instruction literacy lesson and reformat it to fit the 5E learning cycle model. Be certain that both the exploration and expansion phases are student-oriented. Once completed, present your 5E learning cycle lesson to your peers or to your own classroom students. Reflect on your lesson by addressing the following questions: What worked (effective components)? What changes would you make if you had an opportunity to reteach your lesson? What did you learn about your students by implementing your literacy lesson in the 5E learning cycle format?

REFERENCES

Adams, D. M., & Hamm, M. (1998). *Collaborative inquiry in science, math, and technology*. Portsmouth, NH: Heinemann.

Bass, J. E., Contant, T. L., & Carin, A. A. (2009). *Teaching science as inquiry* (11th ed.) Boston, MA: Pearson/Allyn & Bacon.

Charlesworth, R., & Lind, K. K. (2003). *Math and science for children* (4th ed.) Albany, NY: Delmar.

Duschl, R. S., Schweingruber, H. A., & Shouse A. W. (2007). *Taking science to school: Learning and teaching science in grades K–8*. Washington, DC: National Academic Press.

Eby, J. W. (1998). *Reflective planning, teaching, and evaluation K–12*. Upper Saddle River, NJ: Prentice Hall.

Gallenstein, N. L. (2000). Group investigation: An introduction to cooperative research. *Social Studies and the Young Learner, 13*(1), 17–18.

Joyce, B. R., Weil, M., & Calhoun, E. (2004). *Models of teaching* (7th ed.) Boston, MA: Allyn and Bacon.

Karplus, R., & Thier, H. D. (1967). *A new look at elementary school science— Science Curriculum Improvement Study*. Chicago, IL: Rand McNally.

Kellough, R. D., Carin, A. A., Seefeldt, C., Barbour, N., & Souviney, R. J. (1996). *Integrating mathematics and science for kindergarten and primary children*. Englewood Cliffs, NJ: Prentice Hall.

Lapp, D. (2001). Bridging the gap. *Science Link (Newsletter of the National Science Resources Center), 12*(1), 2.

Lind, K. K. (2005). *Exploring science in early childhood education: A developmental approach* (4th ed.) Clifton Park, NY: Thomson Delmar Learning.

Martin, D. J. (2009*). Elementary science methods: A constructivist approach* (5th ed.) Belmont, CA: Wadsworth Cengage Learning.

Martin, R., Sexton, C., Franklin, T., & Gerlovich, J. (2005). *Teaching science for all children: An inquiry approach* (4th ed.) Boston, MA: Pearson Education.

Morrison, J. A., & Young, T. A. (2008, Summer). Using science trade books to support inquiry in the elementary classroom. *Childhood Education*, 204–208.

National Council of Teachers of Mathematics (2000). *Principles and standards for school mathematics*. Westin, VA: Author.

National Research Council. (1996). *National science education standards*. Washington, DC: National Academy Press.

National Research Council. (2000). *Inquiry and the national science education standards: A guide for teaching and learning*. Washington, DC: National Academy Press.

Scruggs, T. E., Mastropieri, M. A., Bakken, J.P., & Brigham, F. J. (1993). Reading verses doing: The reflective effects of textbook-based and inquiry-oriented approaches to science learning in special education classrooms. *Journal of Special Education, 27*(1), 1–15.

Shaw, J. M., & Blake, S. S. (1998). *Mathematics for young children*. Upper Saddle River, NJ: Prentice Hall.

Thelen, H. (1960). *Education and the human quest*. New York: Harper and Row.

CHAPTER 11

SOME "WONDERINGS" ABOUT LITERACY TEACHER EDUCATION

DONNA E. ALVERMANN
University of Georgia, Athens, Georgia

THINK ABOUT LITERACY TEACHER EDUCATION, SOCIAL CONSTRUCTIVISM, AND SOCIAL CONSTRUCTIONISM . . .

1. What does the author cite as reasons for differing interpretations of text by students in a classroom?
2. Read to find out about the difference between social constructivism and social constructionism.

This article grew out of an invited address to members of OTER at the 2001 annual meeting of IRA in New Orleans. Following my keynote, I had the privilege of participating in two follow-up interactive sessions that touched on some of the same issues I had raised but also extended the conversation considerably. It is from these interactions and my "talking points" at OTER that the present article began to take shape. I have chosen to frame this article as a set of "wonderings"—first, because I am less sure about the usefulness of the knowledge base for preparing literacy teachers than I was when I prepared the keynote initially, and second, because I continue to puzzle over the confusion in the field between social constructivist and social constructionist theories of learning.

WONDERING ABOUT THE STATUS
OF THE KNOWLEDGE BASE

Do we have a knowledge base for teaching others how to teach reading? To get some perspective on this question, it is necessary to consider where the field has come from and where it may be headed. When I finished writing a handbook chapter on reading teacher education more than a decade ago (Alvermann, 1990), I ended with the observation that we knew far too little about the contexts in which preservice teachers were being prepared to teach reading. Eleven years later, I could easily make the same observation. Although we have **correlational evidence** to support claims that more fully prepared and certified teachers are more successful (than those not so prepared) in producing higher student pass rates on reading performance measures (Pearson, 2001), we still do not know what accounts for their success, specifically. As Pearson noted,

> correlational evidence—
> evidence that can support, or
> correlate to, a particular claim

[Members of] the National Reading Panel (NRP Report, 2000) could not determine, from the studies they researched, which elements of teacher preparation were most effective or most desired, primarily because there is not a good database on how teachers are prepared. (p. 7)

Do we have a knowledge base for teaching others how to teach reading?

The insufficiency of the database has consequences beyond what we might imagine at first glance. For example, the lack of knowledge about which elements of literacy teacher education are most effective or most desired means that such information was unavailable to the National Board for Professional Teaching Standards, which was charged, among other things, with writing the standards for preparing teachers in the English language arts. Following a comprehensive review of the standards in the major disciplinary areas, including the English language arts, the Ford Foundation (Finn & Petrilli, 2000) reported that "Most [standards] were vague, uninspired, timid, full of dubious educational advice, and generally not up to the task at hand. Their average grade was 'D-Plus'" (no page given). This evaluation led the editors (Finn & Petrilli, 2000) to conclude that a marketplace model of teacher preparation is to be preferred over a standards-based model. In a marketplace model, anyone can be hired to teach students how to read, but if they do not produce high pass rates among their students, they are subject to being dismissed from their jobs.

Pearson (2001), among others, has taken exception to the marketplace model, warning its would-be advocates of the following:

Most salient among the many problems with the marketplace model is the question of what happens to the children and parents who must wait for this system to work. Also problematic is the question of compensation: What would be the consequences of salaries based on achievement gain from one year to the next? Although market devotees would argue that such a model would force teachers to work harder to help students learn more, it is equally as plausible to argue that teachers will work harder at selecting the students with whom they would be willing to work. (p. 10)

> *Although the term social constructivism is sometimes used synonymously with social constructionism in the literature on literacy teacher education, there are several good reasons for not conflating the two terms.*

Not everyone believes that the status of the knowledge base for literacy teacher education is as lacking in information as this article (so far) might imply. The Learning First Alliance (2001), a partnership of twelve nationally-based professional groups in education, has published a series of influential documents that claim there is a sufficient base of knowledge on how to teach reading. This claim, however, has not gone undisputed. Left out of the equation on effective teaching of reading are topics such as the comprehension process, the relationship between knowledge and comprehension, the role of context, and the composition process (Pearson, 2001). To this list of missing or marginalized topics, I would add the following: **adolescent literacy** (Alvermann, Hinchman, Moore, Phelps, & Waff, 1998), **critical literacy** (Muspratt, Luke, & Freebody, 1997), **digital/media literacy** (Alvermann, in press; Lankshear & Snyder, 2000), and the New London Group's **multiliteracies** (Cope & Kalantzis, 2000).

It is important to think multidimensionally when assessing the status of the knowledge base for preparing teachers to teach reading. Taking a narrow view of what counts as reading will not suffice, especially given the complex information and communication technologies that currently compete with print-based texts for our attention (and that of our students). Nor does it make sense to view reading and writing as neutral processes largely defined through developmental and psychological models. That more narrow view of literacy—what Street (1995) calls the autonomous model of literacy—has dominated the reading field up to the present.

Viewing literacy practices as competitive in nature and ideologically embedded does not require giving up on the cognitive dimensions of reading and writing. Rather, according to Street (1995), the ideological model subsumes the autonomous model of literacy in its attempt to understand reading and writing practices "as they are encapsulated within structures of power" (p. 161). By emphasizing the ideological nature of literacy practices, Street opens the way for seeing them as socially constructed within seemingly absent but always present power structures. It is by first recognizing such structures that teachers learn the

adolescent literacy—encompassing the in- and out-of-school literacy practices of adolescents

critical literacy—using language in any form to problem solve and communicate; to critically evaluate the world around you as a member of society

digital/media literacy—the ability to comprehend and navigate a variety of digital or multimedia texts

multiliteracies—an approach of literacy to negotiate multiple linguistic and cultural differences, which is pivotal to the various roles of students in and outside of school. In addition, attention to multiliteracies is critical for the future workforce to enable critical reading of the world in order that citizens be well versed in the pragmatics of the diverse society in which they live and work.

importance of negotiating their way through them, and in doing so, to expand their own repertoire of strategies for dealing with the multiple literacies students bring to school.

WONDERING WHAT IS MEANT BY "A SOCIAL CONSTRUCTIVIST/SOCIAL CONSTRUCTIONIST TEACHER"

Why are these labels misleading? And why is it problematic to conflate social constructivism with social constructionism? First, a point of clarification. Although the term social constructivism is sometimes used synonymously with social constructionism in the literature on literacy teacher education, there are several good reasons for not conflating the two terms (Hruby, 2001). These reasons, hopefully, will become evident in the discussion that follows (see also Alvermann & Phelps, 2002). Second, both social constructivism and social constructionism are theories of learning; they are not theories of teaching per se. Thus, it really makes no sense to speak of teachers as being either social constructivists or social constructionists.

Constructivism has become a catch-all term for a collection of theoretical approaches to learning that rely for their explanation on the cognitive developmental processes individuals use in deriving conceptual (abstract) understanding from their lived experiences. At the same time, the term has been used in very specific ways, thereby creating a situation that invariably leads to much confusion (Phillips, 2000). Literacy teacher educators generally limit their attention to four versions of constructivism: Piagetian constructivism, radical constructivism, sociohistorical constructivism, and social constructivism (Eisenhart, Finkel, & Marion, 1996; Phillips, 2000). Piagetian constructivism holds to the position that conceptual development results from an individual's ability to assimilate and accommodate new information into existing knowledge structures. To count as learning, however, this newly assimilated (or accommodated) information must correspond with an authoritative body of knowledge external to the individual. Motivation for such learning rests in the individual and in the materials (content) to be learned.

Radical constructivism also situates motivation for learning in the person and the content to be learned. However, unlike Piagetian constructivism, radical constructivism assumes that evidence of new learning rests on an individual's ability to make personal sense of her or his own experiences; that is, radical constructivists have no need to apply some sort of external litmus test to determine the "correctness" of a student's personally constructed knowledge. In short, literacy teacher educators who adhere to either Piagetian or radical constructivist theories of learning view students as "autonomous actors who learn by building up their own understandings of their worlds in their heads" (Eisenhart, Finkel, & Marion, 1996, p. 278).

Sociohistorical constructivism and social constructivism differ appreciably from the two constructivisms just discussed. Sociohistorical constructivism embraces Vygotsky's (1978) activity theory whereas social constructivism is more closely associated with Bruner (1986), at least among literacy teacher educators. Both sociohistorical and social constructivism are concerned with how factors outside-the-head, such as the culture of a classroom, the structural characteristics of schooling, and issues of social justice, form (rather than merely affect) what teachers and students do in the name of teaching and learning. Educators whose belief systems resonate with sociohistorical constructivism and social constructivism also believe that how students perceive themselves in a particular context (e.g., a content area class) mediates their motivation to learn (or not learn) the content of that class.

Social constructionism, unlike social constructivism, relies on the centrality of language to mediate what people come to understand about their lived experiences. In adhering to a social constructionist perspective on learning, literacy teacher educators are saying that they believe knowledge is based on conventions of language that members of a particular community (e.g., a social studies class, a professional organization of reading educators, an after-school book club) have constructed and agreed on. Gavelek and Raphael (1996) explain a social constructionist perspective this way:

> This perspective has the potential to shift our focus on talk about text away from seeking "facts" or "truths" toward constructing "interpretations" and offering "warranted justifications" for interpretations. From this perspective, the teacher's role would shift from asking questions to ensure that students arrive at the "right" meaning to creating prompts that encourage students' exploratory talk. Teachers would encourage talk that elicits a range of possible interpretations among individuals reading and responding at any given time. Teachers would also encourage talking about previously read texts because individuals construct different readings at different periods in life or within different contexts. Textual meaning is not "out there" to be acquired; it is something that is constructed by individuals through their interactions with each other and the world. In classrooms, these interactions take the form of discussions, and the teacher helps guide and participates in them. Underlying the processes of interpretations and justifications in discussions is language. (p. 183)

As literacy teacher educators, we need to bear in mind that while our cultural histories do not determine how we experience or respond to texts, these histories do in fact channel or help to frame our responses (Brock & Gavelek, 1998). In fact, the very idea that reading is a socially constructed practice draws on some of the most basic assumptions from cultural anthropology and sociolinguistics (Cook-Gumperz, 1986; Gee, 1988; Heath, 1983). One such assumption is that "students of different races, different social classes, and different genders may produce readings which challenge dominant or authoritative meanings because they have available to them different sets of values and beliefs" (Patterson,

Mellor, & O'Neill, 1994, p. 66). However, it will come as no surprise to most educators that readers who share common cultural backgrounds and who are contemporaries of one another may still interpret the very same text in very different ways. Given that each reader will have had unique life experiences and different ways of using language to interpret those experiences, different responses would be expected.

In sum, I believe it makes little or no sense to think about literacy practices apart from the larger social and cultural milieu in which they reside. Literacy teacher educators who conceive of literacy as critical social practice do not deny the cognitive or behavioral aspects of reading, writing, and speaking, but instead portray them as attendant processes in a much larger social context, one that is institutionally located in the political, gendered, and class-based structures of society where power is at stake daily in people's social interactions with each other and with texts of various types. In resisting the all too common urge to conflate social constructionism with social constructivism, literacy teacher educators stand to gain a better understanding of the two learning theories and the implications of those theories for their pedagogy.

CONNECTING LITERACY TEACHER EDUCATION, SOCIAL CONSTRUCTIVISM, SOCIAL CONSTRUCTIONISM, AND YOUR CLASSROOM . . .

1. Think back carefully to your undergraduate teacher-education program. Make a list of what you consider to be the essential knowledge base for a beginning teacher of reading. Be prepared to discuss why you feel your program prepared you well or why your program did not include the essential knowledge you needed to be successful. What advice would you give to university reading professors about preparing teachers of reading?
2. A social constructionist would encourage students to have a wide variety of interpretations about a text after reading. How do you encourage the students in your class to do this? Prepare a plan for improving your teaching according to this theory.

REFERENCES

Alvermann, D.E. (1990). Reading teacher education. In W. R Houston, M. Haberman, & J.P. Sikula (Eds.), *Handbook of research on teacher education* (pp. 687–704), New York: Macmillan.

Alvermann, D.E. (Ed.). (in press). *Adolescents and literacies in a digital world.* New York: Peter Lang.

Alvermann, D.E., & Phelps, S.F. (2002). *Content reading and literacy: Succeeding in today's diverse classrooms* (3rd ed.). Boston: Allyn and Bacon.

Alvermann, D.E., Hinchman, K.A., Moore, D.W., Phelps, S.F., & Waff, D.R. (1998). *Reconceptualizing the literacies in adolescents' lives.* Mahwah, NJ: Erlbaum.

Bruner, J.S. (1986). *Actual minds, possible worlds.* Cambridge, MA: Harvard University Press.

Cook-Gumperz, J. (Ed.) (1986). *The social construction of literacy.* Cambridge, England: Cambridge University.

Cope, B., & Kalantzis, M. (2000). *Multiliteracies: Literacy learning and the design of social futures.* London: Routledge.

Eisenhart, M., Finkel, E., & Marion, S.F. (1996). Creating the conditions for scientific literacy: A re-examination. *American Educational Research Journal, 33,* 261–295.

Finn, C.E., Jr., & Petrilli, M.J. (Eds.). (2000, January). The state of state standards. Retrieved September 16, 2001, from http://www.edexcellence.net/library/soss2000/2000soss.html.

Gavelek, J., & Raphael, T.E. (1996). Changing talk about text: New roles for teachers and students. *Language Arts, 73,* 182–192.

Gee, J.P. (1988). Legacies of literacy: From Plato to Freire through Harvey Graff. *Harvard Educational Review, 58,* 195–212.

Heath, S.B. (1983). *Ways with words: Language, life, and work in communities and classrooms.* Cambridge, England: Cambridge University.

Hruby, G. (2001). Sociological, postmodern, and new realism perspectives in social constructionism: Implications for literacy research. *Reading Research Quarterly, 36,* 48–62.

Lankshear, C., & Nyder, I. (with Green, B.) (2000). *Teachers and techno-literacy: Managing literacy, technology and learning in schools.* St. Leonards, New South Wales, Australia: Allen & Unwin.

Learning First Alliance. (2001, August). *Working together to improve student learning: A report on state learning alliances.* Retrieved September 16, 2001, http://www.learningnfirst.org/publications.html

Muspratt, S., Luke, A., & Freebody, P. (1997). *Constructing critical literacies.* Cresskill, NJ: Hampton.

National Reading Panel (NRP). (2000). *Report of the National Reading Panel: Teaching children to read.* Washington, DC: National Institute of Child Health and Human Development.

Patterson, A., Mellor, B., & O'Neill, M. (1994). Beyond comprehension: Poststructuralist readings in the English classroom. In B. Corcoran, M. Hayhoe, & G.M. Pradl (Eds.), *Knowledge in the making* (pp. 61–72). Portsmouth, NH: Boynton/Cook.

Pearson, P.D. (2001). Learning to teach reading: The status of the knowledge base. In C. Roller (Ed.), *Learning to teach reading: Setting the research agenda* (pp. 4–19). Newark, DE: International Reading Association.

Phillips, D.C. (Ed.). (2000). *Constructivism in education: Opinions and second opinions on controversial issues.* Chicago: University of Chicago.

Street, B.V. (1995). *Social literacies: Critical approaches to literacy in development, ethnography, and education.* New York: Longman.

Vygotsky, L.S. (1978). *Mind in society: The development of higher psychological processes.* Cambridge, MA: Harvard University.

ABOUT THE AUTHOR

Donna Alvermann teaches graduate courses at the University of Georgia. Her research interests include alternative methods of research, adolescent literacy, and critical literacy.

Constructivism: A Brief Matrix for Understanding

To assist you, the reader, this brief matrix compares the four types of constructivism, as described previously in Alvermann's chapter in this section of the text.[a]

	PIAGETIAN CONSTRUCTIVISM	RADICAL CONSTRUCTIVISM	SOCIOHISTORICAL CONSTRUCTIVISM	SOCIAL CONSTRUCTIVISM	SOCIAL CONSTRUCTIONISM
Knowledge	When someone can accommodate and assimilate new knowledge into his or her existing structures—concept development	Knowledge is actively built (von Glaserfeld, 1990); knowledge is constructed, not perceived	Closely linked with Lev Vygotsky's activity theory (1978)	Associated with Bruner (see *Actual Minds, Possible Worlds*, 1986)	Centrality of language mediates what people understand from their lived experiences; based on conventions of language agreed upon—similar to Fish's "interpretive communities" (1980)
Learning	Newly assimilated knowledge must be consistent with the body of knowledge at large	Evident only when an individual can personally understand his or her own experiences; does not need to be fact-checked with the external body of knowledge	Outside factors are considered in how they impact teaching and learning, i.e., classroom culture, social justice, etc.	Outside factors are considered in how they impact teaching and learning, that is, classroom culture, social justice, etc.	Has the potential to shift from seeking facts—seeking to interpreting a text; sense of authority lies in the learner just as in the transaction where readers are active in the meaning-making process
Motivation of the learner/motivation to learn	Within the individual and the content being learned	Within the individual and the content being learned	Perception of self as learner impacts one's learning in a particular content area	Perception of self as learner impacts one's learning in a particular content area	Triggers or other elements that catch learners' attention and sustains it

[a]See Additional Suggested Readings for full citations of all texts mentioned in the matrix.

ADDITIONAL READINGS IN CONSTRUCTIVISM
AND CONSTRUCTIONISM

Alesandrini, K., & Larson, L. (2002, January). Teachers bridge to constructivism [Electronic version]. *The Clearing House, 75.* Retrieved March 28, 2010, from http://firstsearch.oclc.org/WebZ/FTFETCH?sessionid=fsapp6-57476-g7ca92x1-z1mn7f:entitypagenum=3:0:rule=100:fetchtype=fulltext:dbname=WilsonSelectPlus_FT:recno=1:resultset=1:ftformat=PDF:format=BI:isbillable=TRUE:numrecs=1:isdirectarticle=FALSE:entityemailfullrecno=1:entityemailfullresultset=1:entityemailftfrom=WilsonSelectPlus_FT:

Boghossian, P. (2006). Behaviorism, constructivism, and Socratic pedagogy. *Educational Philosophy and Theory, 38,* 713–722.

Bruner, J. (1986). *Actual minds, possible worlds.* Cambridge, MA: Harvard University Press.

Davydov, V.V., & Radziknovskii, L.A. (1999). Vygotsky's theory and the activity-oriented approach in psychology. In P. Lloyd, & C. Fernyhough (Eds.), *Lev Vygotsky: Critical assessments: Vol. 1: Vygotsky's theory* (pp. 113–142). New York: Routledge.

Fish, S. (1980). *Is there a text in this class? The authority of interpretive communities.* Cambridge, MA: Harvard University Press.

Graffman, B. (2003). Constructivism and understanding: Implementing the teaching for understanding framework. *The Journal of Secondary Gifted Education, 15,* 13–22.

Hruby, G. (2001). Sociological, postmodern, and new realism perspectives in social constructionism: Implications for literacy research. *Reading Research Quarterly 36*(1), 48–62.

Lee, C.D., & Smagorinsky, P. (Eds.), *Vygotskian perspectives on literacy research: Constructing meaning through collaborative inquiry.* New York: Cambridge University Press.

Maurer, M.M., Bell, E.C., Woods, E., & Allen, R. (2006). Structured discovery in cane travel: Constructivism in action. *Phi Delta Kappan, 88,* 304–307.

Richardson, V. (2003). Constructivist pedagogy. *Teachers College Record, 75,* 118–121.

Ryle, A. (1999). Object relations theory and activity theory: A proposed link by way of the procedural sequence model. In P. Lloyd, & C. Fernyhough (Eds.), *Lev Vygotsky: Critical assessments: Vol. 4: Future directions* (pp. 307–318). New York: Routledge.

Seaman, J. (2006). [Review of the book *A Closer Look at Constructivism: Linking Experiential Education, Indoctrination, and the Spread of Consumerism*]. *Journal of Experiential Education, 29,* 210–212.

Smerdon, B.A., Burkam, D.T., & Lee, V.E. (1999). Access to constructivist and didactic teaching: Who gets it? Where is it practiced? *Teachers College Record, 101,* 5–34.

Sutinen, A. (2007). Constructivism and education: education as an interpretative transformational process [Electronic version]. *Studies in Philosophy and Education, 27.* Retrieved March 28, 2010, from http://lg7vy9rq6m.scholar.serialssolutions.com/?sid=google &auinit=A&aulast=Sutinen&atitle=Constructivism+and+education:+education+as+an+interpretative+transformational+process&id=doi:10.1007/s11217-007-9043-5&title=Studies+in+philosophy+and+education&volume=27&issue=1&date=2008&spage=1&issn=0039-3746

van Harmelen, M. (2008). Design trajectories: four experiments in PLE implementation. *Interactive Learning Environments, 16,* 35–46.

Von Glasersfeld, E. (1990) An exposition of constructivism: Why some like it radical. In R.B. Davis, C.A. Maher, and N. Noddings (Eds.), *Constructivist views on the teaching and learning of mathematics* (pp. 19–29). Reston, VA: National Council of Teachers of Mathematics.

Vygotsky, L.S. (1978). *Mind in society: The development of higher psychological processes.* Cambridge, MA: Harvard University Press.

Wink, J., & Putney, L. (2002). *A Vision of Vygotsky.* Boston, MA: Allyn & Bacon.

INTERSECTIONS OF PSYCHOLOGY, COGNITIVE THEORY, READING, AND THE READER

HELPFUL WEB SITES

Theorists
Plato

http://www.youtube.com/watch?v=WgPJUTltITk
http://www.crystalinks.com/plato.html
http://www.philosophypages.com/ph/plat.htm
http://www.wsu.edu/~dee/GREECE/PLATO.HTM
http://plato.stanford.edu/entries/plato/
http://www.iep.utm.edu/p/plato.htm
http://plato-dialogues.org/plato.htm
http://plato-dialogues.org/plato.htm
http://www.britannica.com/EBchecked/topic/464109/Plato
http://mally.stanford.edu/plato.html
http://scienceworld.wolfram.com/biography/Plato.html
http://library.thinkquest.org/18775/plato/biop.htm

Aristotle

http://www.philosophypages.com/ph/aris.htm
http://www.iep.utm.edu/a/aristotl.htm
http://www.wsu.edu/~dee/GREECE/ARIST.HTM
http://classics.mit.edu/Browse/browse-Aristotle.html
http://www.historyforkids.org/learn/greeks/philosophy/aristotle.htm
http://plato.stanford.edu/entries/aristotle-ethics/
http://galileoandeinstein.physics.virginia.edu/lectures/aristot2.html
http://www.answers.com/topic/aristotle
http://www-groups.dcs.st-and.ac.uk/~history/Biographies/Aristotle.html
http://www.crystalinks.com/aristotle.html
http://www.bartleby.com/65/ar/Aristotl.html
http://www.britannica.com/EBchecked/topic/34560/Aristotle
http://scienceworld.wolfram.com/biography/Aristotle.html
http://www.utm.edu/research/iep/a/aristotl.htm
http://members.tripod.com/~batesca/aristotle.html
http://www.briantaylor.com/aristotle.htm

John Locke

http://plato.stanford.edu/entries/locke/
http://oregonstate.edu/instruct/phl302/philosophers/locke.html
http://www.iep.utm.edu/l/locke.htm
http://www.blupete.com/Literature/Biographies/Philosophy/Locke.htm
http://www.philosophypages.com/ph/lock.htm
http://www.libraries.psu.edu/tas/locke/
http://www.google.com/archivesearch?q=john+locke&rls=com.microsoft:en-us&oe=UTF-
      8&um=1&ie=UTF-8&scoring=t&sa=X&oi=timeline_result&resnum=14&ct=title
http://www.island-of-freedom.com/LOCKE.HTM
http://academic.udayton.edu/gregelvers/hop/person.asp?key=13
http://cepa.newschool.edu/het/profiles/locke.htm
http://users.ox.ac.uk/~worc0337/authors/john.locke.html

http://socserv.mcmaster.ca/econ/ugcm/3ll3/locke/index.html
http://www.philosophypages.com/hy/4n.htm
http://www.essortment.com/all/whoisjohnlock_rsas.htm
http://www.trincoll.edu/depts/phil/philo/phils/locke.html

David Hume

http://plato.stanford.edu/entries/hume/
http://www.iep.utm.edu/h/humelife.htm
http://cepa.newschool.edu/het/profiles/hume.htm
http://www.philosophypages.com/ph/hume.htm
http://oregonstate.edu/instruct/phl302/philosophers/hume.html
http://www.utilitarian.net/hume/
http://www.google.com/archivesearch?q=David+Hume&rls=com.microsoft:en-us&oe=UTF-
    8&um=1&ie=UTF-8&scoring=t&sa=X&oi=timeline_result&resnum=14&ct=title
http://www.blupete.com/Literature/Biographies/Philosophy/Hume.htm
http://www.google.com/search?hl=en&rls=com.microsoft:
    en-us&q=David+Hume&start=10&sa=N
http://socserv.mcmaster.ca/econ/ugcm/3ll3/hume/index.html
http://www.youtube.com/watch?v=fvU3SrKfD9A
http://www.econlib.org/library/Enc/bios/Hume.html
http://www.epistemelinks.com/main/philosophers.aspx?philcode=hume
http://www.nndb.com/people/810/000030720/
http://www.bartleby.com/65/hu/Hume-Dav.html
http://oll.libertyfund.org/?option=com_staticxt&staticfile=show.php%3Fperson=231&Itemid=28
http://www.britannica.com/EBchecked/topic/276139/David-Hume

John Stewart Mill

http://www.iep.utm.edu/m/milljs.htm
http://plato.stanford.edu/entries/mill/
http://www.utilitarianism.com/jsmill.htm
http://cepa.newschool.edu/het/profiles/mill.htm
http://www.bartleby.com/people/Mill-JS.html
http://www.google.com/archivesearch?hl=en&rls=com.microsoft:en-
    us&resnum=1&q=John+Stewart+Mill&um=1&ie=UTF-8&scoring=t&sa=X&oi=timeline_
    result&resnum=11&ct=title
http://www.blupete.com/Literature/Biographies/Philosophy/Mill.htm
http://www.victorianweb.org/philosophy/mill/millov.html
http://www.spartacus.schoolnet.co.uk/PRmill.htm
http://www.econlib.org/library/Enc/bios/Mill.html
http://www.britannica.com/EBchecked/topic/382623/John-Stuart-Mill
http://www.john-mill.com/
http://www.librarything.com/author/milljohnstuart
http://socserv.mcmaster.ca/econ/ugcm/3ll3/mill/index.html
http://www.cpm.ehime-u.ac.jp/AkamacHomePage/Akamac_E-text_Links/Mill.html
http://www.nndb.com/people/147/000030057/
http://www.trincoll.edu/depts/phil/philo/phils/mill.html

Thorndike

http://www.muskingum.edu/~psych/psycweb/history/thorndike.htm
http://tip.psychology.org/thorn.html
http://www.indiana.edu/~intell/ethorndike.shtml
http://psychclassics.yorku.ca/Thorndike/Animal/

http://www.dushkin.com/connectext/psy/ch06/bio6a.mhtml
http://my-ecoach.com/idtimeline/theory/thorndike.html
http://www.nvc.vt.edu/alhrd/Theorists/Thorndike.htm
http://www.youtube.com/watch?v=BDujDOLre-8
http://www.skagitwatershed.org/~donclark/hrd/history/thorndike.html
http://www.answers.com/topic/edward-thorndike
http://www.coe.uh.edu/courses/cuin6373/Idhistory/thorndike_extra.html
http://www.pigeon.psy.tufts.edu/psych26/thorn.htm
http://www.bartleby.com/65/th/ThorndikE.html
http://allpsych.com/biographies/thorndike.html
http://www.coe.uh.edu/courses/cuin6373/idhistory/thorndike.html
http://www.indiana.edu/~intell/rthorndike.shtml
http://www.simplypsychology.pwp.blueyonder.co.uk/edward-thorndike.html
http://books.google.com/books?hl=en&lr=&id=MP1B8WPCrI0C&oi=fnd&pg=PA139&dq=
    Thorndike+father+of+ed.+psych&ots=ibXoCRnbtZ&sig=_DQxAXyC–8wPtPcY7KMavHHLaQ
    #PPP1,M1

Skinner

http://webspace.ship.edu/cgboer/skinner.html
http://tip.psychology.org/skinner.html
http://www.bfskinner.org/aboutbfskinner.html
http://www.sntp.net/behaviorism/skinner.htm
http://www.pbs.org/wgbh/aso/databank/entries/bhskin.html
http://www.muskingum.edu/~psych/psycweb/history/skinner.htm
http://www.youtube.com/watch?v=AepqpTtKbwo
http://ww2.lafayette.edu/~allanr/autobio.html
http://www.skagitwatershed.org/donclark/hrd/history/skinner.html
http://my-ecoach.com/idtimeline/theory/skinner.html
http://www.coe.ufl.edu/webtech/GreatIdeas/pages/peoplepage/skinner.htm

Piaget

http://www.learningandteaching.info/learning/piaget.htm
http://webspace.ship.edu/cgboer/piaget.html
http://chiron.valdosta.edu/whuitt/col/cogsys/piaget.html
http://www.edpsycinteractive.org/topics/cogsys/piaget.html
http://www.funderstanding.com/content/piaget
http://tip.psychology.org/piaget.html
http://video.google.com/videoplay?docid=-9014865592046332725
http://www.childdevelopmentinfo.com/development/piaget.shtml
http://www.indiana.edu/~intell/piaget.shtml
http://coe.sdsu.edu/eet/Articles/piaget/index.htm
http://www.crystalinks.com/piaget.html
http://honolulu.hawaii.edu/intranet/committees/FacDevCom/guidebk/teachtip/piaget.htm
http://projects.coe.uga.edu/epltt/index.php?title=Piaget%27s_Constructivism
http://www.muskingum.edu/~psych/psycweb/history/piaget.htm
http://www.mnsu.edu/emuseum/information/biography/pqrst/piaget_jean.html
http://www.newfoundations.com/GALLERY/Piaget.html
http://webspace.ship.edu/cgboer/genpsypiaget.html
http://www.nndb.com/people/359/000094077/
http://psychology.about.com/od/profilesofmajorthinkers/p/piaget.htm
https://outlook.coastal.edu/owa/redir.aspx?C=5ef23c19577c438cb92295a305baa3ac&URL=
    http%3a%2f%2fhonolulu.hawaii.edu%2fintranet%2fcommittees%2fFacDevCom%
    2fguidebk%2fteachtip%2fpiaget.htm

Einstein

http://www.westegg.com/einstein/
http://nobelprize.org/nobel_prizes/physics/laureates/1921/einstein-bio.html
http://www.humboldt1.com/~gralsto/einstein/einstein.html
http://www.britannica.com/EBchecked/topic/181349/Albert-Einstein
http://scienceworld.wolfram.com/biography/Einstein.html
http://www.time.com/time/time100/scientist/profile/einstein.html
http://www.bartleby.com/173/
http://www-groups.dcs.st-and.ac.uk/history/Biographies/Einstein.html
http://www.aip.org/history/einstein/
http://www-gap.dcs.st-and.ac.uk/~history/Mathematicians/Einstein.html
http://www.time.com/time/time100/poc/home.html
http://www.princetonhistory.org/museum_alberteinstein.cfm
http://www.amnh.org/exhibitions/einstein/

Vygotsky

http://tip.psychology.org/vygotsky.html
http://www.kolar.org/vygotsky/
http://www.funderstanding.com/content/vygotsky-and-social-cognition
http://www.newfoundations.com/GALLERY/Vygotsky.html
http://starfsfolk.khi.is/solrunb/vygotsky.htm
http://www.massey.ac.nz/~alock/virtual/trishvyg.htm
http://www.marxists.org/archive/vygotsky/
http://webpages.charter.net/schmolze1/vygotsky/
http://www.muskingum.edu/~psych/psycweb/history/vygotsky.htm
http://video.google.com/videoplay?docid=634376752589779456
http://webpages.charter.net/schmolze1/vygotsky/vygotsky.html
http://www.simplypsychology.pwp.blueyonder.co.uk/vygotsky.html

Albert Bandura

http://webspace.ship.edu/cgboer/bandura.html
http://www.des.emory.edu/mfp/bandurabio.html
http://www.des.emory.edu/mfp/self-efficacy.html
http://video.google.com/videoplay?docid=-2953790276071699877
http://www.youtube.com/watch?v=xjIbKaSXM3A
http://www.google.com/archivesearch?rls=com.microsoft:en-us&oe=UTF-
    8&q=Albert+Bandura&um=1&ie=UTF-
    8&scoring=t&sa=X&oi=timeline_result&resnum=14&ct=title
http://www.criminology.fsu.edu/crimtheory/bandura.htm
http://faculty.frostburg.edu/mbradley/psyography/albertbandura.html

Neuroscience

http://www.members.shaw.ca/hidden-talents/brain/113-left.html
http://www.learningdiscoveries.org/QuantitativeElectroencephalographQEEG.htm
http://www.learningdiscoveries.org/LearningDisabilities.htm
http://neuro.psyc.memphis.edu/neuroPsyc/np-ugp-learn.htm
http://www.dyslexia.com/science/different_pathways.htm
http://e-speec.com/functions.htm

Associationism

http://www.philosophyprofessor.com/philosophies/associationism.php

Theory of Cognitive Development

http://www.essortment.com/all/jeanpiagettheo_rnrn.htm

Zone of Proximal Development

http://tip.psychology.org/vygotsky.html

Operant Conditioning

http://tip.psychology.org/skinner.html

Radical Constructivism

https://tspace.library.utoronto.ca/citd/holtorf/3.8.html

Constructivism

www.personal.psu.edu/wxh139/construct.htm
http://dougiamas.com/writing/constructivism.html#radical

THEORETICAL PERSPECTIVES: INTERSECTIONS OF LANGUAGE, SOCIETY, CULTURE, AND THE READER

INTRODUCTION

There are probably no greater challenges facing reading teachers in classrooms than those posed by the changing nature of society and the increasing diversity of the population of the United States. Our students are likely to be youth of color, born in the United States of immigrant parents, who do not speak English as their first language. In large urban areas it is not uncommon to find classrooms with a variety of different languages spoken in one elementary, middle, or high school. A University of Southern California study shows that 94% of students in the Los Angeles Unified School District are learning English as a second language ("Education taxed by non-English speaking kids," 2005). Coupled with the rapid societal changes is the lack of preparation of many public school teachers and administrators for understanding the needs and the problems of students of color and students with different cultural and linguistic backgrounds. Often the teacher and the student have no common ground for building positive relationships and for effective communication.

In this section, the authors' voices challenge us to view language, the foundation of reading, in the context of its relationship to culture and society and to reflect on the difficulties resulting from society's failure to deal effectively with linguistic issues related to immigration and equal access to educational opportunities for all, citizens and noncitizens alike. Power and disenfranchisement are characteristic themes highlighting the struggles we face. These chapters challenge us to ponder the role of public education as advocate, as change agent, or as keeper and guard of the status quo.

Questions raised in these chapters include the following: What should teachers of reading know about language? What counts as literacy? What is most important: reading the word or reading the world? How do language and culture impact a child's success in literacy? What is the role of the reading teacher in creating a better world, where all students have equal chance for success? How can a teacher whose cultural and socioeconomic background differs from those of his or her students facilitate literacy learning for those students and capitalize on the resources they bring to school?

Sociocultural approaches to literacy instruction emphasize the coconstruction of knowledge as learners and teachers interact in positive and creative encounters through well-designed literacy events. The interdependences of individuals with their unique differences and abilities within a social network of the whole community of learners are emphasized. This section begins with two classic works from the field of linguistics in which language is the focal point or the foundation of literacy. The first, by Smith and Goodman, focuses on the intersection of psychology and linguistics. The second, by Shuy, defines sociolinguistics; the intersection of sociology and linguistics. The four chapters in this section by Hurtado de Vivas, Moll, Flores, and Galligan remind us to focus on the many resources English-language learners bring to the classroom. These include a wealth of information about other countries and their cultural perspectives and opportunities for interaction with those whose ways of thinking are different from our own. Echoes of social justice, insistence on inalienable rights, and the balancing act for teachers caught in a maelstrom of rapid societal change characterize this section, especially Morris's chapter on critical literacy. Diversity in our society has brought controversial issues to the forefront of literacy, which are highlighted in this section. The challenges are great and the responses are as varied as the teachers who struggle to cope with these challenges.

REFERENCE

"Education taxed by non-English speaking kids." (2005, March 19). Foxnews.com. Retrieved November 3, 2008, from http://www.foxnews.com/story/0,2933,150856,00.html

■ ■ ■ ■ ■

Alignment of Readings in Section IV to the International Reading Association's *Standards for Reading Professionals 2010* (Draft):

Standard 1: Foundational Knowledge
   1.1; 1.2 (timeline); 1.3
Standard 2: Curriculum and Instruction
   2.1 and 2.2 (postreading activities)

Standard 4: Diversity
   4.1; 4.2; 4.3
Standard 6: Professional Learning and Leadership
   6.1 (postreading activities); 6.3

Intersections of Language, Society, Culture, and the Reader Timeline

BEGINNINGS . . .	
1800s	Multiple languages other than English taught in public and parochial schools in 12 states, primarily in the midwestern United States
1896	*Plessy v. Ferguson,* Supreme Court ruled that segregation could be legally enforced so long as the facilities for blacks were equal to those for whites. Segregated education—*separate but equal*
Late 1800s– early 1900s	Not unusual for schools to be taught bilingually. Spanish-English in northern New Mexico and southern Colorado French-English in Maine and Louisiana German-English in North Dakota and Texas
Early 1900s	Waves of immigrants enter the United States and push for national unity
1915 to 1924	WWI results in the United States adopting an "English-only" attitude Public schools begin "sink or swim" English immersion programs Students punished for speaking other languages in public schools
1916	John Dewey publishes *Democracy and Education*; beginning of the Progressive Education Movement
1919	Nebraska passed English-only law language through the eighth grade
1920s to 1950s	Bilingual education disappears from U.S. schools
1945	WWII leads to the belief that foreign language is beneficial to USA
1954	*Brown v. Board of Education* decision, pressed by the NAACP and black parents' groups, ended legal segregation in the United States
1957	Chomsky *Syntactic Structures* published; nativist view of language acquisition
1958	*National Defense Education Act* expands foreign language teaching; created in response to Russia's successful launch of Sputnik in 1957
1959 to 1963	"Cuban boat lift"; bilingual education reintroduced with arrival of Cuban refugees, especially in Miami, FL.
1960s	
1960	Field of psycholinguistics evolves (F. Smith, Goodman) Field of sociolinguistics evolves (Labov, Baratz, Shuy)
1963	C. Fries publishes *Linguistics and Reading*
1964	Civil Rights Bill, with public accommodations and fair-employment sections, signed by President Johnson
1965	Voting Rights Bill, most effective civil rights statute enacted by Congress *Elementary and Secondary Education Act* (ESEA); initiated Title I and bilingual education programs and funding
1967	Smith & Goodman "A Psycholinguistic Guessing Game"
1968	*Bilingual Education Act*—13 states initiate bilingual education

(Continued)

Intersections of Language, Society, Culture, and the Reader Timeline

BEGINNINGS . . .	
1970s	
1970	Paulo Freire, *Pedagogy of the Oppressed*
	Office of Civil Rights Memorandum issued Schools must take steps to provide an education for students of National Origin Minority Groups who do not understand English
1971	F. Smith publishes *Understanding Reading: A Psycholinguistic Analysis of Reading and Learning to Read*
1974	*Lau vs. Nichols*—"Sink or swim" mentality ruled illegal for U.S. Supreme Court *Serna vs. Portales*—Serna family of New Mexico files on behalf of their Spanish-speaking children. Bilingual and bicultural education must be implemented *Aspira vs. Board*—Filed in New York City on behalf of Hispanic students city-wide Set guidelines for teaching in English and in Spanish
1975	National Association for Bilingual Education (NABE) established
1978	Vygotsky's *Mind in Society* translated into English
1980s	
1981	Krashen proposes second-language-acquisition hypotheses
	Castañeda vs. Pickard—Filed in Raymondville, TX; Resulted in the "Castañeda Test" for OCR guidelines: Bilingual Education programs must (1) be based on sound educational theory; (2) have adequate resources and personnel; and (3) be evaluated regularly to determine its effectiveness
1982	*Plyer vs. Doe*—Undocumented immigrants must receive a free, public education
1983	Heath's *Ways with Words* published D. Taylor coins term *family literacy* *Family Literacy: Young Children Learning to Read and Write*
1985	Vygotsky's *Thought and Language* translated into English
1990s–present	
1994	As a backlash to illegal immigration, California voters pass Proposition 187, denying benefits, including public education, to undocumented aliens in California. It is challenged by the ACLU and other groups and eventually overturned.
1997	Thomas and Collier prism model
2000s	Bilingual education under attack; English-only proponents vocal
2002	*No Child Left Behind* signed into law; ELLs and LEPs included in high stakes testing/accountability
2005	Short and Echevarria sheltered instructional observation protocol

CHAPTER 12

LANGUAGE AND CULTURE IN A DIVERSE WORLD

ROMELIA HURTADO DE VIVAS

"We aren't born just for us"
Cicero (Roman philosopher 106–43 BC)

THINK ABOUT **LANGUAGE AND CULTURE . . .**

1. Read this essay to learn about the history of bilingual education in the United States. Make note of important dates in the developmental path of bilingual education.

2. Why is it important for literacy teachers to understand second-language acquisition?

3. Historically, the United States goes through periods of conflict in relation to immigration and immigration issues. How have these periods of conflict impacted teaching literacy, especially for English-language learners?

This scenario often takes place in U.S. public schools. It is a clash of cultures and language interpretation:

Ana is 6 years old and very excited today. She is in first grade and starting school for the first time in the United States; her family moved from Mexico over the summer. She knows they speak differently here than in Mexico, but she is ready. She has a new backpack with pencils and crayons in it. Her parents have assured her she will learn to speak like the North Americans do and then she will help her parents learn as well. She can't wait! Just before she and her mother leave the house to walk to school, her father speaks to her.

"Mi hija," he says, and begins to tell her in Spanish how proud he is of her. Then he gives her the following important advice: "When you get to school, remember that you must show great respect for your teacher. You should not address her by her name. You must call her *Maestra*. That way, she will know you respect her and that you are ready to learn. She will know what a good student you are."

There is a strange, fluttery feeling in Ana's stomach as her mom says adios to her at the classroom door. The children are running in and taking seats and the teacher is saying things Ana does not understand. Nonetheless, she takes a seat as well and listens intently. She soon finds out the word for *Maestra* in this new language is "teacher." She practices saying it to herself. Then, when she gets a chance, she calls out, "Teacher, Teacher," with her hand raised.

The teacher comes to her immediately. She seems angry. She speaks in the words Ana cannot yet understand. She only hears the word *teacher* several times. Then, the teacher asks another student to explain to her and walks away, obviously upset.

The other student explains in Spanish. "You should not ever call her 'teacher.' She has a name. Her name is Mrs. Simmons. If you don't call her by her name, she will not talk to you."

The tears well up in Ana's eyes as she looks down at her lap. Why did her father tell her she should not call the teacher by her name? Why did the teacher get angry when she was trying to be respectful? Is it her father or the teacher who does not understand?

Learning language goes hand in hand with learning culture.

There is no doubt that the demographic situation of the world is constantly changing and becoming more multicultural and multilingual. Many countries in the world are experiencing massive waves of immigrants. The United States is no exception to this ever-changing situation. Seeking a better life, people move to other parts of the world for various reasons: political, economical, voluntary, or forced.

Unlike previous immigration groups, who came mainly from Europe, approximately one third of the newest groups come from Asia and another third, from Latin America countries. In fact, Hispanics will total 103 million, significantly exceeding all other ethic or racial minorities, by the year 2050 (Rumbaut, 2006). "Latinos constitute 14 percent of the U.S. population and by the year 2050 they will account for 25 percent" (Violand-Sanchez & Hainer-Violand, 2006, p. 36).

Most of the immigrant populations come from conditions and circumstances that are incomprehensible; basic needs are rarely filled. As soon as they arrive to begin a new life, they are confronted with a plethora of problems, not only social (racism, discrimination, and prejudices), but also linguistic and cultural differences. It is evident that language, literacy, and culture are linked in many ways; educators need to become knowledgeable concerning the impact that these factors affect students learning and their lives.

LANGUAGE: A HISTORICAL OVERVIEW

In the past, bilingualism was a common attribute. As a matter of fact, during the 18th and 19th centuries, multiple languages other than English were the mediums of instruction in public and parochial schools. Education was imparted in languages including German, Swedish, Norwegian, Danish, Dutch, Polish, Italian, Czech, French, and Spanish in at least in a dozen states (Ovando, Combs, & Collier, 2006). German language and culture were usually tolerated and, since they constituted a minority group and were concentrated in isolated farming areas of the Midwest, they were not considered a threat in any aspect by the rest of the population. German was taught in 52 out of 57 public schools in Saint Louis, and many Anglo-American children learned German as their second language (Kathy Escamilla, as cited in Lessow-Hurley, 2005).

By the end of 1800s, new waves of immigrants came into the country from northern and western European countries. By this time, the need and desire for national unity during the two world wars caused schools in the country to "Americanize" all immigrants: thus, an English-only law was passed in at least 15 states, and foreign language instruction was eliminated in many schools. Immigrants were forced to assimilate into one single mold. Severe punishments were inflicted to the ones who were speaking a foreign language in school environments. A second generation of immigrants stopped using their heritage (native) language and, as a consequence, bilingual education disappeared from U.S. public schools for nearly half a century (Ovando et al., 2006).

In 1958, as a result of the desire for international relations, economic development, status, power, and national security, the National Defense Education Act granted federal resources for the expansion of foreign-language teaching. By 1959, with the arrival of Cuban refugees, bilingual education was reintroduced and established into U.S. schools. The program served a middle-class population and was funded with private and public sources. The success of this type of program led to its expansion to many other schools in the country. At this time, "the nation was in the midst of an energetic movement favoring the expansion of civil rights, accompanied by a powerful affirmation of ethnic identity for minority groups" (Lessow-Hurley, 2005, p. 8). By 1968, 13 states initiated bilingual education in the country and the National Association for Bilingual Education (NABE) was established in 1975 (E. Peña, as cited in Ovando et al., 2006).

However, with the rise of progressive education at the end of 19th and early 20th centuries, bilingualism became un-American and became the target for elimination (C. Blanton, as cited in Salinas, 2006–2007). Although some states still permit bilingual education, the term *bilingual* has been stripped from federal education laws (Wright, 2006). This political attack on bilingual education programs ended with a new policy mandated in January 2002 as The No Child Left Behind Act (NCLB) signed by President George W. Bush. The NCLB mandated the education of *all* students; ELL students (ELLs) "needed to be included somehow in testing and accountability programs" (Wright, 2006). ELLs, as well as any students in the limited English proficiency (LEP) group, regardless of time of residence in the country, are expected to make adequate yearly progress (AYP) toward English proficiency. ELLs are required to achieve a proficient level of English within 3 years. By 2014, groups must pass the accountability tests. Also, the demands of NCLB even go further, punishing any school that does not meet the requirements. One difficult requirement, a direct consequence of NCLB, is that schools are to provide "reasonable accommodations" to English as a second language (ESL) students so they can attain proficiency (Wright, 2006). Research suggests that students would "pick up" the second language if "totally immersed" and become proficient. This type of philosophy, a "sink-or-swim" mentality, was ruled illegal by the U.S. Supreme Court in 1974 (*Lau vs. Nichols*).

cognitive academic language proficiency (CALP)—refers to formal academic learning; includes listening, speaking, reading, and writing about subject area content material (This level is essential for students to succeed in school.)

The new English-only advocates argue that even if bilingual education were effective, bilingualism threatens the sense of national identity and would encourage minority groups to impose their cultures and languages. This NCLB Act contradicts language research (Cummins, 1986), indicating that students need 5 to 7 years in language programs to reach academic proficiency, often called **cognitive academic language proficiency (CALP)**. As a result of this policy, many children have deficiencies in English and are placed into mainstream classrooms too soon. Language-minority students are often placed in inappropriate programs. Teachers need to recognize the difference between **linguistically diverse** and **linguistically disabled** students. At times, special support is provided in pull-out programs which have not been very effective; teachers and students struggle to continue to meet NCLB standards. Bilingual education is still under the control of those in power and their political agendas with regards to the true meaning of bilingualism.

linguistically diverse—an individual speaker who uses two or more languages

linguistically disabled—an individual with impaired linguistic abilities

Second-Language Acquisition

Research in second-language learning supports the premise that the extent to which a child is literate in the home language will determine the extent to which he or she will have a positive experience in a second language (Collier & Thomas, 1999; Cummins, 1986, 1989). A notion of transfer is mentioned by Herrera and Murry (2005), who claimed that "students will have the ability to transfer knowledge, skills, and capacities learned in the first language to learning and understandings in content-area domains taught in a second language" (p. 33). Also, Cummins (1986) comments emphatically that cognitive skills can be best acquired through the native language and then easily transferred to a second language. Trueba (1989) also claims that "the use of the native language is best because critical thinking skills and cognitive structuring are conditioned by linguistic and cultural knowledge and experiences that children usually obtain in the home and bring with them to school" (p. 80). Some of the immigrants, in particular, the Latino/Hispanic group, enter the U.S. schools with limited or even nonexistent schooling. They may lack basic critical thinking skills. They may not even read or write in their home language and are expected to perform well on high-stakes tests while mastering basic literacy and math skills in a language other than their own (DeCapua, Smathers, & Tang, 2007, p. 43).

prism model—curricular model proposed by Thomas and Collier for success of ELLs encompassing four dimensions needed to close the achievement gap

Best practices for language acquisition incorporate the four components developed by Thomas and Collier (1997) in the **prism model**: linguistic, academic, cognitive, and sociocultural. These processes influence not only first- but also second-language acquisition. According to Ovando and others (2006), the heart of the learning process with a bilingual student is the sensitivity factor. Being culturally sensitive to students' needs may be the key to learning and establishing rapport with students. In turn, students may feel comfortable in expressing themselves and can feel more at ease as they transition through different stages of learning. Through constructive learning, scaffolding, and motivational techniques, all students can discover their talents, create goals, and develop lifelong learning skills. **Basic interpersonal communication skills (BICS)** can be developed in as little as 2 years in an immersion program but can give artificial impressions of the ability to handle academic content. In a conversation setting, students have the ability to grasp meaning from body language, gestures, facial expressions, intonation, and so on. In order to develop CALP (cognitive academic language proficiency), students must participate in activities that require active learning and discussions about content and must use a high level of thinking skills.

basic interpersonal communication skills (BICS)—language skills needed in social situations; day-to-day language needed to interact socially with other people

Academic proficiency in English can take much longer since students must not only use the language for reading and writing, but also acquire information in content areas. Teachers can find ways to plan and coordinate curriculum in thematic units to optimize the practice of vocabulary and concept application by using group activities, classroom discussions, and cultural activities to strengthen the bonds between all learners, where each is a valued member of a cohesive community. Krashen (1981) argues that children do not learn a second language through direct instruction. A second language is acquired in the same way the first language was acquired, when it is understood. That is to say, teachers should provide background knowledge to make the instruction more comprehensible.

affective filter—hypothesis proposed by Krashen described as an impediment to learning new languages caused by negative emotional ("affective") responses to one's environment

Krashen's theory of the **affective filter** (1982) indicates that language acquisition takes place more efficiently when the learner experiences a low level of anxiety. On the contrary, under high stress, the learner confronts a great deal of difficulty acquiring the language. Other factors, such as lack of motivation and low self-esteem, may hinder learning a new language. Some students experience negative associations when speaking their native language. Krashen (1996) also reveals that the quality—not the quantity—of English exposure is the major factor in English acquisition. That is, the second-language input must be comprehensible. When non-English-speaking students are isolated in foreign-language classrooms, very few opportunities allow them to gain proficiency in English.

sheltered instructional observation protocol (SIOP)—research-based and validated instructional model that has proven effective in addressing the academic needs of English learners throughout the United States consisting of eight interrelated components

Short and Echevarria (2005) developed the **sheltered instruction observation protocol (SIOP)**. Sheltered instruction lesson plans provide meaningful activities to advanced students to move beyond current academic and language abilities. Through collaborative efforts, all students progress to higher levels. This method of lesson planning assists teachers in planning instruction that is available to ELLs. It includes 30 "instructional strategies grouped into eight components," with the objective of "make the content understandable for ELLs while promoting academic language growth" (p. 11). The authors argue that content-area teachers need to understand the linguistic needs of the ELLs and provide sheltered instruction to support language development. Teachers need to use "slower speech, clear enunciation, use visuals and demonstrations, targeted vocabulary development, connections to student experiences, and use of supplementary materials" (Fred Genesee, as cited in Short & Echevarria, p. 10).

Other strategies like cooperative learning, instructional conversations, multisensory instruction, and guided reading strategies are found to be useful for ELL since they will provide opportunities for listening and discussing content. Smith (2004) advocates a print-rich environment, planning for multisensory input, vocabulary, role playing, and allowing time for reading and writing for curiosity and authentic purposes. Drucker (2003) recommends using choral reading, shared reading, paired reading, books with tapes, multicultural literature, language-experience approach, total physical response, narrow reading, reading aloud, and interactive writing with texts that support cultural awareness as well as instructional objectives.

DeCapua et al. (2007) remarks that in order to achieve academic content, especially to students with interrupted formal education **(SIFE)**, effective instruction would include using visuals, charts, graphs, time lines, and Venn diagrams as well as collaborative learning activities, such as task-oriented projects and small-group activities replacing the traditional note taking and worksheet assignments (p. 43).

SIFE—students with interrupted formal education

Parents and community play a major role in the learning and schooling of children to create positive attitudes toward the educational process. Conferences and meetings must include parents of ELL students. Good rapport not only allows communication, but also makes the families feel included; motivation to do well increases when families are utilized in areas where schools need volunteers.

A suggestion comes from Moll, Amanti, Neff, and Gonzalez (2005), who recommend that teachers should identify the strengths and "funds of knowledge" (cultural artifacts and bodies of knowledge) that exist within culturally and linguistically diverse families. "These funds of knowledge represent bona fide resources for teaching and learning in classrooms" (p. 277). If parents are not included, the risk of decreasing motivation becomes a problem. However, there are many factors that hamper family's participation in schools. Most immigrant families come from low socioeconomic backgrounds, and their participation in schools is very limited. The reasons for limited school participation are varied. Some parents struggle with time for participation and feel intimidated if they do not have a "green card." Parents who do work feel afraid to ask questions. Others with a low level of formal education for helping with school work struggle with cultural or socioeconomic differences and their own negative attitudes about schools. Also, language barriers between parents and staff and possible resistance to assimilation may limit parents' participation in schools (Delpitt, 1991).

Grant and Wong (2003) point out that the barriers that exist within the literacy education profession and that may slow or prevent language-minority learners from becoming fully literate in English are "the failure of teacher-education programs to adequately prepare reading specialists to work with language-minority learners and education researchers to engage in more substantive research on English reading development for such students" (p. 386). Although some schools of education offer courses in multicultural information to the current course curriculum, it seems as if the courses are "insufficient, ineffective and potentially misleading" (p. 388). The authors advocate change at every level to ensure that students from diverse linguistic and cultural backgrounds are not left behind. Regrettably, schools with high concentrations of ELLs, are still unprepared to meet the need of these populations. This fact deprives many students of using their cultural knowledge and experience (Trueba, 1989).

CULTURE

What Is Culture?

It is almost impossible to separate the issue of culture from language. They are intertwined in complex and multidimensional ways. The issue of culture plays a significant role in people's lives and in the lives of the immigrant children who come to public schools for basic educational skills. Quite often, culture is linked to ethnic traditions of food, holidays, and folklore and "less tangible manifestations such as communication style, attitudes, values, and family relationships" (Nieto & Bode, 2008, p. 171). Nieto (2002) notes that "culture must be understood as dynamic rather than fixed, as process instead of just content, and as historically and socially contextualized rather than insulated" (p. 52). Freire and Macedo (1987) contend that culture does not function in a social vacuum, but rather as a system that is characterized by social stratification and tensions. Thus, Darder (1991) argues that there are four main classifications of culture, which overlap throughout the research on the meaning of culture. According to Darder they are "(1) cultural values or value orientation, (2) heritage and cultural artifacts, (3) language, and (4) cognitive styles." (p. 26). Each culture bases its rules and traditions around these four components. H. Giroux (in Darder) redefines culture as ". . . a dialectical instance of power and conflict . . ." and ". . . derived out of lived experiences of different social groups" (p. 29).

The effects of power and culture have created the dominant and subordinate cultures. Dominant culture refers to ideologies, social practices, and structures that affirm the central values, interests, and concerns of those who are in control of the material and symbolic wealth in society, and the subordinate culture refers to groups who exist in social and material subordination to the dominant cultures. The dominant culture in the United States is the Anglo-American culture. The subordinate culture or minority culture, as it is often called, is often the primary culture of an individual, and the dominant culture is the secondary culture. However, the secondary culture must become the dominant culture of the individual due to societal expectations and norms. As a matter of fact, in terms of Fishman (1976), the language of the dominant culture is the "unmarked language" (standard English) and the other languages will be "marked languages," associated with less social status and political power (the language of any other culture). The minority cultures in the United States are constituted by the Latinos/Hispanics, Blacks, Native Americans, and Asians. However, the Latinos constitute the biggest group among the minority.

The Culture of Power.   Students from minority cultures come to the United States with a set of beliefs different from the culture where they are going to live. They are constantly facing different challenges in order to fit in the new culture. **Acculturation, assimilation,** ethnocentrism, and stereotypes are some of the processes with which they struggle. At school, they are confronted as well with language variation, prejudice, social discrimination, and economic and political factors. Most of the students from minority backgrounds have been raised in poverty and have experiences quite different from the mainstream culture, and these differences become evident within the school environment and permeate in the students' school achievement. The belief is held that the dominant Anglo-American culture is the way to achieve success; therefore, students of different cultures have to embrace the dominant cultural norms.

> **acculturation**—exchange of cultural features that results when groups of individuals of different cultures come into continuous first hand contact; primary cultural patterns of either or both groups may be altered, but the groups remain unique

> **assimilation**—people of different backgrounds coming to see themselves as part of a larger national family

B. Benard (as cited in Violand-Sanchez, & Hainer-Violand, 2006) has found that when "positive ethnic identity is associated with high self-esteem," the result is a "commitment to doing well in school, a sense of purpose in life, confidence in one's own efficacy, and high academic achievement" (p. 36). However, students feel marginalized when they are not participating in classroom activities and their voices are not heard. If given opportunities, students can be empowered and more engaged in socializing with mainstream students rather than feeling insecure and ambivalent about the value of their own cultural identity.

Delpitt (1991) notes that, while middle-class whites might not be aware of the "culture of power" in classrooms, minority students are aware of their exclusion from certain codes and discourses. Therefore, she claims that students should be taught the implicit rules of power so they can succeed while at the same time respecting their individual cultures. Darder (1991) suggests that students, communities, and teachers alike should be empowered (p. 109).

FINAL THOUGHTS

While other countries in the world are becoming multilingual, the United States is searching for a "one-size-fits-all" plan. A need for change is necessary in the American society since it is unlikely that a-one-size-fits-all mentality will be a viable solution to the educational problems teachers are facing in diverse public school settings. Barth (2001) states that the willingness of educators and administrators to become lifelong learners affects the power of true school reforms. Schools should foster a positive ethnic identity by viewing bilingualism and biculturalism as an asset in schools today and not as a cultural deficit. Schools should promote successful programs in training teachers in ESL methodologies and encourage them to be advocates for their students and for diverse classrooms.

The future of the world will be in the hands of problem-solvers who interact effectively, make connections to new knowledge, communicate new ideas, and are flexible to changes. Suarez-Orozco and Sattin (2007) claim that "the world over needs more innovative thinking skills, cultural awareness, and higher-order thinking skills." (p. 58). Economics, energy, environment, education and e-communications interconnect the world's societies and our students must be equipped to prosper in their future global positions. The Google era demands creative and innovative skills on new sources of information and the ability to work in teams with people from different cultures, knowledgeable about the world. If schools continue to resist structural change, students will not be able to thrive amidst the abundance of information and in the proliferating media world in which they live (Crawford, 1996). Schools must nurture students who are curious, can tolerate ambiguity, and can synthesize knowledge within and across disciplines (Suarez-Orozco & Sattin, 2007). Schools are responsible for being understood within their own sociopolitical contexts (Freire, 1970; Giroux, 2004).

Schools must promote a true commitment to diversity, equity, and high levels of learning, and there is a critical need to create an environment where diversity is appreciated and every human being is valued. Schools need to develop their own vision statement so they can become more multicultural and thus more inclusive, creating exciting places for learning. In the final analysis, teachers and students need to be educated in democracy and social justice (Nieto, 2002).

Educators need to be knowledgeable about the history of their students' in- and out-of-school experiences and literacies so that they can tap into their students' perceptions and understanding of their learning (Rolon, 2005). Freire (1970) uses core stories, those stories that students bring from their native cultures, as a tool to encourage diversity. Teachers should encourage ELL students to become leaders within the school and the community so they can have a sense of belonging and identification with the culture where they are living (Violand-Sanchez & Hainer-Violand, 2006). Every child has a right to feel safe and be encouraged to learn in order to reach their highest potential. In the same way, Miller and Endo (2004) suggest that teachers should encourage student voice through activities of speaking and writing from their experiences so they can find ways to help to overcome their struggles with the new school environment. The classroom must be a validated space for *all* students.

Teachers need to be culturally sensitive to students in various aspects of their lives, and they need to reflect upon their own biases and prejudices and "overcome their misconceptions about students' intellectual capacities." (Schmoker, 2007, p. 65). Teachers must teach that there are many sides to every story, as long as every topic is discussed "with respect and in a climate of caring" (Nieto, 2002, p. 272). Teachers should provide ELL students opportunities for socialization with mainstream students so they can understand the cultural context and the use of the English language.

School authorities, stakeholders, and teachers are responsible for promoting an authentic critical democratic and educational pedagogy where the values and rights of all individuals are respected and honored. To be knowledgeable in more than one language and culture is no longer an issue in this multicultural, multilingual, globally technological interconnected world. The debate seems pointless at this juncture, because we are born, but not just for our limited worldview. After all, we live in a diverse world and an interconnected global society where language and culture are interdependent.

CONNECTING LANGUAGE, CULTURE, AND YOUR CLASSROOM . . .

1. Visit a dual-language school and interview the principal or a teacher. Prepare questions in advance that will help you understand this program, its advantages, and its disadvantages.
2. If possible, arrange a visit with a student or child and his or her family who are recent immigrants to the United States. After the visit, reflect on how the student's culture will affect their literacy learning in your classroom.
3. Prepare a presentation to share with your colleagues about the strategies you might utilize to teach English-language learners in your classroom.

REFERENCES

Barth, R. S. (2001). *Learning by heart*. San Francisco. CA: Jossey-Bass.

Collier, V. P., & Thomas, W. P. (1999). Making U.S. schools effective for English Language Learners, Part 1. *TESOL Matters, 9*(4), 1–6.

Crawford, K. (1996). Vygotskian approaches to human development in the information era. *Educational Studies in Mathematics.* (31) 43–62.

Cummins, J. (1986). Empowering minority students: A framework for intervention. *Harvard Educational* Review, *56*(1), 18–35.

Cummins, J. (1989). *Empowering minority students*. Sacramento, CA: California Association for Bilingual Education.

Darder, A. (1991). *Culture and power in the classroom: a critical foundation for bicultural education*. Westport, CT: Bergin & Garvey.

DeCapua, A., Smathers, W., & Tang, L. F. (March 2007). Schooling, interrupted. *Educational Leadership*, 40–46.

Delpitt, L. D. (November 1991). A Conversation with Lisa Delpitt. *Language Arts, 68*(7), 541–47.

Delpitt, L. (1988). The silenced dialogue: Power and pedagogy in educating other people's children. *Harvard Educational Review, 58*(3), 280–298.

Drucker, M. J. (2003). What reading teachers should know about ESL learners. *The Reading Teacher, 57*(1), 22–29.

Fishman, J. A. (1976). *Bilingual education: An international sociological perspective.* New York: Newbury House.

Freire, P. 1970. *Pedagogy of the oppressed,* New York: Seabury Press.

Freire, P., & Macedo, D. (1987). *Literacy : Reading the word and the world.* London: Routledge.

Giroux, H. A. (2004). Public pedagogy and the politics of NEO-liberalism: making the political more pedagogical. *Policy Futures in Education, 2,* 494–503.

Grant, R. A., & Wong, S. D. (2003). Barriers to literacy for language-minority learners: An argument for change in the literacy education profession. *Journal of Adolescent & Adult Literacy, 48*(5), 386–394.

Herrera, S. G., & Murry, K. G. (2005). *Mastering ESL and bilingual methods: Differentiated instruction for culturally and linguistically diverse (CLD) students.* Boston: Allyn and Bacon.

Krashen, S. D. (1981). *Second language acquisition and second language learning.* Oxford: Pergamon.

Krashen, S. D. (1982). *Principles and practices in second language acquisition.* Oxford: Pergamon.

Krashen, S. D. (1996).*Under attack: The case for bilingual education.* Culver City, CA: Language Education Associates.

Lessow-Hurley, J. (2005). *The foundations of dual language instruction.* New York: Longman.

Miller, P. C., & Endo, H. (2004). Understanding and meeting the needs of ESL students. *Phi Delta Kappan, 85*(10), 786–791.

Moll, L. C., Amanti, C., Neff, D., & Gonzalez, N. (Eds.). (2005). Funds of knowledge for teaching: Using a qualitative approach to connect homes and classrooms. In *Funds of Knowledge: Theorizing practices in households, communities, and classrooms* (pp. 71–87). Mahwah, NJ: Erlbaum Associates, Inc.

Nieto, S. (2002). *Language, culture and teaching: Critical perspectives for a new century.* Mahwah, NJ: Lawrence Erlbaum Associates, Inc

Nieto, S., & Bode, P., (2008). *Affirming diversity. The sociopolitical context of multicultural education* (4th ed.). Boston: Pearson.

Ovando C., Combs, M. C., & Collier, V. (2006). *Bilingual & ESL classroom* (4th ed.) New York: McGraw-Hill.

Rolon, C. A. (2005, November/December). Succeeding with Latino students. *Principal, 85*(2), 30–34.

Rumbaut, R. (2006). The making of a people. In M. Tienda & F. Mitchell (Eds.), *Hispanics and the future of America* (pp. 16–65). Washington, DC: National Academies Press.

Salinas, R. A. (2006–2007). "All children can learn . . . speak English." *National Forum of Educational Administration and Supervision Journal. 23,* 2.

Schmoker, M. (2007, April). Reading, writing and thinking for all. *Educational Leadership,* 63–66.

Short, D., & Echevarria, J., (2005). Teacher skills to support English Language Learners. *Educational Leadership 62*(4), 8–13

Smith, K. (2004). Language as we know it, literacy as we know it, and content area instructions: Conscious strategies for teachers. *Multicultural Education 11*(4), 46–50.

Suarez-Orozco, M., and Sattin C. (April 2007). Wanted: global citizens. *Educational Leadership,* 58–62.

Thomas, W. P., & Collier, V. P. (1997). "School effectiveness for language minority students" (NCBE Resource Collection Series No. 9) Washington, DC: National Clearinghouse for Bilingual Education.

Trueba, H. T. (1989). Raising silent voices: Educating the linguistic minorities for the 21st century. New York: Newbury House/Harper & Row.

Violand-Sanchez, E. and Hainer-Violand, J. (2006). The Power of Positive Identity. *Educational Leadership. 64*(1), 36–40.

Wright, W. E. (November 2006). A catch-22 for language learners. *Educational Leadership,* 22–27.

CHAPTER 13

IMPORTANT LINGUISTIC CONCEPTS FOR LITERACY PRACTITIONERS IN THE FIELD OF SECOND-LANGUAGE ACQUISITION

ELIZABETH ANN GALLIGAN

THINK ABOUT LINGUISTIC CONCEPTS AND SECOND-LANGUAGE ACQUISITION . . .

1. Why is it important for classroom teachers of reading to have a firm grounding in linguistic concepts?
2. Make note of Freire and Macedo's beliefs about the starting point for literacy programs and ELLs.
3. As you read, make a list of important characteristics about language that impact ELL's success in reading.

Frank Smith (1997) addresses how quickly technological revolutions in electronic media affect reading and writing. The use of the computer may in fact ". . . aid in fostering the connectedness of reading to writing and writing to reading" (p. 142), with implications for both learners and educators. In today's broad definition of literacy, boundaries among the receptive and active literacy skills are blurred. The demand for literacy skills—the ability to read, write, think, and express oneself in his or her first language—has become more critical in the 21st century. These demands are equal or even greater for learners of second or subsequent languages (L2) in a global economy. Literacy practitioners, who understand language in the broad sense, use linguistics research to inform practice. In particular, teachers who are knowledgeable in the second-language-acquisition

(SLA) perspective will be more likely to foster academic, cognitive, social, and linguistic abilities of language learners. Further, these practitioners encourage learners to reach high-achievement levels. Lack of sufficient expertise in SLA may limit the learners' potential.

LITERACY PRACTITIONERS: SECOND-LANGUAGE ACQUISITION AND CRITICAL LITERACY

Teachers are literacy practitioners whose job is to lead others to their potential to use the communicative arts. The task of a literacy practitioner in the 21st century is one broadly situated on what Freire and Macedo call "reading the word and the world":

> Reading the world always precedes reading the word, and reading the word implies continually reading the world. (T)his movement from the word to the world is always present; even the spoken word flows from our reading of the world. In a way, however, we can go further and say that reading the word is not merely preceded by reading the world, but by a certain form of *writing* it or *rewriting* it, that is, of transforming it by means of practical, conscious work. (1987, p. 35)

Their insights on the literacy process ask educators to enlarge their scope when they state:

> Reading does not consist merely of decoding the written work or language; rather, it is preceded by and intertwined with knowledge of the world. Language and reality are dynamically interconnected. The understanding attained by critical reading of a text implies perceiving the relationship between text and context. (p. 29)

The term *literacy practitioners* refers to educators at all levels: PK–16: regular classroom teachers, ESL and bilingual teachers, anyone who teaches reading and writing, special educators, tutors, coaches, speech pathologists, and all who teach any form of the communicative arts. Literacy practitioners require a deeper foundation in SLA in both general and educational (applied) linguistics to meet the demands of today's diverse, multilingual classrooms. Teachers must understand that the conjunction of experience and the act of re-visioning that experience through dialogue and critique is a central dynamic of the literacy process.

The field of critical literacy, in Freire's and Macedo's view, embraces a relational dynamic between the learner and the tangible world (1987). Literacy is an intimate connection with the perceived reality, the "real world" of the learner. Freire and Macedo argue that any literacy program should use ". . . the first language, 'the word universe' of the learners, incorporating the culture-specific expressions of their language, their anxieties, fears, demands, and dreams" (p. 25). Further, ". . . words should be laden with the meaning of the people's existential experience, and not of the teacher's experience" (p. 25).

Freire and Macedo (1987) admonish that teachers must value the experience and language of their students. This concept is particularly important due to the diverse ethnicities and backgrounds of ELLs and all students today. For literacy practitioners, a solid grounding in linguistics provides an opportunity to explore the acquisition of his or her own first language and to contrast that process with the demands of learning a second language. By comparing and contrasting aspects of L1 and L2, literacy practitioners can anticipate some of the challenges that ELLs confront and assist them more effectively.

Connecting Different Realities

The concept of a word universe and the notion of rewriting the world according to one's experience are useful concepts for literacy practitioners whose ultimate goal is to promote the full potential of a learner to read the word and the world in light of his or her own (and collective) context. Thus, the concept of literacy goes far beyond coding and decoding text.

Critical literacy demands thoughtful engagement with the world by both learner and teacher. It is essential that ELLs have teachers who make connections to students' worlds and facilitate links between students' prior knowledge and academic or school culture if ELLs are to succeed.

Relationships between school and the other worlds in which learners function should be evident in classrooms. Good teaching practice integrates language skills and removes artificial barriers created between the communicative arts. Reading and writing are like Siamese twins who should not be separated but, rather, are intertwined. Based on Freire and Macedo (1987), critical literacy is a process of engagement that uses the learners' prior knowledge and experiences in the world and incorporates that knowledge in dialogue with others, allowing learners to evaluate the forces that shape their lives.

Relevance of Second-Language Acquisition and Critical Literacy

How can literacy practitioners build their own knowledge base as well as develop ways of implementing this broad view of literacy? The more practitioners know about the various facets of human language and its power, the better prepared they are to provide bridges that help connect the real world and the "word-world" (Freire & Macedo, 1987, p. 29). Critical literacy practitioners address not only the cognitive, academic, and linguistic factors in language acquisition but also the sociocultural, political, and affective aspects of literacy.

Teachers, as literacy practitioners, glean helpful knowledge from the field of SLA. How second or subsequent languages are acquired belongs in the area of linguistics referred to as educational, or applied, linguistics. Although the term *second language* is widely used in the literature, it may be misleading in that "second" refers to all subsequent languages (third, fourth, or even preferred dialects of the first language). A better term might be *subsequent languages*. A solid background in SLA assures that teachers have a general knowledge of language and the processes by which one's first and subsequent languages are acquired.

ASPECTS OF LANGUAGE: IMPORTANT CHARACTERISTICS

One of the most compelling aspects of human language is its *generativity*, the ability to develop utterances that are not simply imitations of heard messages. Rather, they are new forms of speech echoing the complexity of the human experience. Language is a medium that is both controlled by rules and allows creativity; it is elastic. Once articulated, new forms can be transmitted to and comprehended by fellow speakers in one's speech community. Language, then, is not learned by rote memory or imitation, although at very early stages, imitation does occur to a minor degree in the first aspects of the process. If language were learned only by imitation, speakers could not ever articulate something they had not previously heard. We know this is not the case; language is effervescently generative, and we can say anything we want to.

Another significant aspect of human language is *displacement*, which allows us to talk about events in the past, present, and future. These are actions described but not currently experienced by the listener. They are carried in the narration through syntactical means. The beauty of language is that it is seemingly infinite and yet is based on rules.

The *universality* of language is another aspect of language essential for literacy practitioners to understand. Chomsky (1957) in *Syntactic Structures* described how humans generate very complicated structures from the **simple (surface)** or **deep structure** and identified the **building blocks** of language (i.e., Universal Grammar, or UG). Specific languages, such as Chinese, Swahili, or Urdu, use the same basic linguistic tools, but each specific language arises from how those tools are combined or recombined. The building blocks are the universals; the specific languages or dialects manifest various possibilities for those combinations.

The fundamental building blocks—phonology, morphology, syntax, the lexicon, pragmatics, and proxemics—exist in every language. There is no such thing as a "primitive" language; all languages are complex, rule-governed, patterned systems. All languages convey meaning.

In practical terms, when teachers apply this knowledge, they must be cognizant of their own **ethnocentricity**. It is important to recognize that all languages are "**good**." ESL teachers without a background in other languages often assume that the learner is slow or obstinate when they make errors based in their L1. Linguistic differences arise because different aspects of those blocks may be used or omitted. For example, of all the

simple (surface) structure—what is actually said or written

deep structure—meaning

building blocks—universals common to all languages

ethnocentricity—use of one's own social group in making decisions about other social/ethnic groups

"good"—linguists believe all languages or dialects are acceptable ("good") because they allow members of that group to communicate within the group

sounds available to humans, only some are selected and transmitted by specific language communities; glottal stops—for example, the stopping of sound—act as a sound in Navajo and carry meaning. Morphemes, or units of the language that affect meaning, vary widely: singular, multiple, and plural verb endings always indicate number; there may be masculine, feminine, and neuter nouns, as in English; certain features—singular subject, singular verb, adjectives, comparative forms, and so on—must always agree. These are often referred to as marked forms. Within the syntax, word order (position) may be of great importance, as it is in English syntax, or of relatively less importance, as in Spanish. Certain words or syntactical structures may be, in some societies, used only by females and not males, and vice versa. Within the **lexicon** of a speech community, a word may be marked and indicate gender (Gee, 1993).

> **lexicon**—set of words in a language

Another aspect is that one's language and culture are intertwined. As a Native American woman from Sandia Pueblo, New Mexico, once said, "If we lose our language; we lose our culture." Preservation or revitalization of native (heritage) languages is essential to maintain those cultures. Linguistic systems hold huge reservoirs of knowledge of a particular cultural worldview. This contributes to our understanding of other human beings and our world.

CONTRIBUTION OF LINGUISTIC THOUGHT IN SLA

Chomsky, the founder of contemporary theoretical linguistics, was intrigued with finding the answer to a lingering question: What is language? Chomsky became convinced that speech ability was located not outside, but inside, in the human brain. This was a revolutionary notion: that the evolution of the human brain had equipped humans with a biological capacity for acquiring language. Therefore, according to Chomsky, the ability to recognize and acquire language was innate to human beings (Gee, 1993, p. 294).

Chomsky (1957) argued that humans, through the process of evolution, were equipped with a biological capacity for acquiring language. He believed we were "hardwired" for language and that we possessed what he (infelicitously) called the Language Acquisition Device (LAD). This is a "device" in our brains that recognizes what constitutes language. Those who believe we are hardwired for language are called innatists.

Another major theoretical orientation to the understanding of human language is that of the social interactionists (Vygotsky, Krashen, Snow, and others). In contrast to Chomsky and the innatists, the social interactionists who study language emphasize on the sociocultural aspects of language development; they argue that language does not appear within a vacuum but is contextualized in specific instances of experience and is triggered by social interaction. These researchers chide Chomsky for ignoring the interaction among humans, without which, they argue, language does not develop.

As a social interactionist, the work of Lev Vygotsky (1989) demonstrated the intertwining of the relationship of thought and language in the maturation of the child's brain. His ideas, not translated into English until the 1960s, strongly influenced teaching and educational reforms of the 20th century in the United States by emphasizing opportunities for social interaction and the importance of "more competent peers" for language development in the classroom. Cooperative groups of students and the role of teacher as "coach" are direct results of the work of Vygotsky.

PEDAGOGY AND PRACTICAL APPLICATION

There are no absolutes in language pedagogy; the art of teaching evolves as new discoveries are made about language learning. The field of SLA is always evolving, and approaches to second language learning vary accordingly. In an excellent review of trends over the last 40 years, Sauvignon (2006) observes that "these trends can be seen to reflect a widely accepted mainstream view of where we are today in language pedagogy" (p. 14). She summarizes the major trends in SLA in the past 40 years as follows:

1. A decline in claims for a universal best method reflecting an increased recognition of the diversity of teaching contexts and goals;
2. Recognition of both bottom-up [meaning-focused] and top-down [form-focused] skills in the development of language proficiency;
3. An influence of our increased understanding of English-language use by both native and nonnative speakers on teaching curricula and content with new knowledge gained from corpus (analysis and comparisons of large bodies of data via electronic technology) and discourse analysis (minute analyses of actual speech acts);
4. The development of integrated and dynamic instructional models that promote meaningful communication as the means to developing the learners; communicative competence. (Sauvignon 2006, pp. 14–15)

Sauvignon observes that the extent and diversity of speakers learning second languages has increased the awareness in language pedagogy. First, language is situated in actual and/or remembered experiences. Therefore, the locus of the learning is tied to specifics. A greater emphasis on the learners' perspectives and aspirations, rather than on the teachers', has gained ascendancy.

THREE PRINCIPLES FOR LITERACY PRACTITIONERS

Three productive concepts have been selected as examples to illustrate how linguistic findings can have direct implications for classroom practice. These three principles illustrate ways in which knowledgeable practitioners have extrapolated from linguistic/SLA theory and put the implications into practice. Each principle is presented, followed by a number of implications for language teaching. Other major topics in SLA having significant impact and implications for literacy practitioners pertain to: similarities and dissimilarities between L1 and L2; effect of affect on language learning; meaning-making and semiotic systems; sequence of learning skills, cultural factors; **code mixing**; factors that affect language acquisition, including age and gender, personal factors, external conditions, external factors; personal factors, length of time in country, exposure to academic language, and the effects of various approaches and program designs.

> **code mixing**—using speech that draws to differing extents on at least two languages combined in different ways

Productive Concept 1: Interlanguage and Transfer of Skills from L1 to L2

The concept of interlanguage coined by psycholinguist Selinker (1972) delineates the processes by which transitions are made between acquiring one language and another. Before this discovery, speakers in this stage of language learning were ridiculed for their speech, or "broken English," and derogatory terms such as Tex-Mex and Spanglish were used to describe this stage of language learning. Some went so far as to refer to speakers in this intermediate stage as alingual or semi-lingual. Beginning learners (incipient bilinguals) often code mix, resulting in the combination of forms from both languages. For example, a mixture of Spanish and English might produce a sentence such as, "The car red is of mi padre." Intermediate-stage learners may still draw on rules in both languages, and this learner language conforms to universal linguistic norms of UG as postulated by Chomsky (1957).

Interlanguage indicates a transitory process. Study of interlanguage has yielded many useful insights for English-language teaching (ELT). Selinker (1974) delineated five processes central to second-language learning: language transfer, transfer of training, strategies of second-language learning, strategies of second-language communication, and **overgeneralization** of target-language linguistic material. By studying both successful L2 learners and unsuccessful attempts at L2 acquisition, Selinker's research as a psycholinguist set the agenda for many lines of further research. Although some of the terminology has changed since, Selinker's notions such as interlanguage, language transfer, examination of Lenneberg's (1967) hypothesis about a **critical period** (prepuberty) for language learning, fossilization (the "freezing" of certain incorrect usage from L1 in L2 learners' speech), error analysis, and meaningful performance still enliven the research.

> **overgeneralization**—process of extending the application of a rule to items that are excluded from it in the language norm (e.g., I "goed" or I "rided")

> **critical period**—Lenneberg's hypothesis that there is an ideal window of time to acquire language in a linguistically rich environment, after which this is no longer possible

Some Implications for Practice: Productive Concept 1

- Code mixing, *using both L1 and L2 within an utterance,* is a natural process in learning L2.
- There is no such thing as an alingual child unless there are serious physiological or psychological reasons. *A normal human being has the ability to learn language.*
- The use of L1 to facilitate L2 learning is a positive strategy because it scaffolds the knowledge from one language into the next. Teachers should allow learners to use L1 to develop ideas and thoughts as they gradually move from L1 to the target language.
- Mandates for English-only in both oral and written work in class are not advisable for early and intermediate learners because many cognitive processes still take place in the learner's brain in L1.
- Ridicule or punishment for speaking a language other than English in class is disrespectful to the learners and nonproductive for language learning.

Productive Concept 2: Language Universals

Research into the existence of universals since Chomsky proposed the concept of UG and existence of a human biological ability to process language has largely been supported. For example, research has shown that there is a very consistent order of learning the structures of one's first languages. The order of acquisition of structures in SLA seems to follow closely those in L1.

Some Implications for Practice: Productive Concept 2

- Explicit teaching of grammar and syntax should be done in the later grades.
- Trying to teach the passive voice to second graders is unwise.
- Transfer from L1 to L2 is possible after a certain threshold of competence is reached (S. Krashen).
- In upper elementary grades, attention to development of Cognitive Academic Language Proficiency (CALP) and academic reading skills must be given for ELLs.
- Particular attention should be paid to vocabulary expansion and the use of synonyms.
- The use of L1 to scaffold L2 reading and/or writing, even at more advanced levels, is perfectly acceptable and indicated.

Productive Concept 3: The Silent Period

Just as L1 learners (infants) have long exposure to a tremendous amount of linguistic input (sounds, gestures, intonation, lexical items), during which they simply imbibe language, so, too, do new language learners have a "silent period." ELLs also need substantial input from the target language and listening time before they can produce language, so, too, do second language learners. Demands from the teacher to speak may inhibit oral production. ELLs may speak very little, if at all; this may be due to the need for more listening time to make the input comprehensible; it may be caused by the cognitive overload of having too much information to process or may be due to assimilation or personal characteristics. Other factors, such as cultural norms (Don't lose face; Your answer must be perfect; Do not respond to elders) may also initially impede communication.

Some Implications for Practice: Productive Concept 3

- Teachers need to allow for nonverbal responses from ELLs, especially for new language learners.
- Teachers should not make assumptions that an ELL student is defiant or resistant based on his or her noncommunication.

Teachers feel relieved when they understand that the silent period is natural and not an indication that the teacher is not getting through to the ELL student. Mandates for use of English-only in both oral and written work in the classroom do not honor the fact that many cognitive processes are still taking place in the learner's brain in his or her L1.

COGNITIVE AND LINGUISTIC RESEARCH ESSENTIAL FOR TEACHER-EDUCATION PROGRAMS

Prominent educators (Meyer, 2000; Sauvignon, 2006; Wong-Fillmore & Snow, 2000) have addressed the importance of educational linguistics in teacher preparation, and all have noted the paucity of teacher-education programs that do provide linguistic information for teachers. Knowledge of the general field of linguistics broadens the teachers' knowledge base. Educational linguistics encourages teachers in the classroom to improve practice by means of research-based approaches, curricula, strategies, and techniques that support learners (and teachers) in providing a classroom conducive to learning for all.

For literacy practitioners, research by cognitive scientists has expanded our understanding of memory and how information is processed; in short, more is known about how humans learn. The notion of accessing prior knowledge and hanging new information on old hooks has been particularly useful in reading. In second-language learning, these insights are equally useful, or perhaps more so, with ELLs because "You only learn to read once" as Jim Cummins (1989) reminds us in his seminal book, *Empowering Minority Students.* Many second-language learners may know how to read in L1, but they still need all the help they can get about context and meaning in L2, such as mastery of different language structures, use of differing cultural assumptions, understanding elisions of thought, and the maddening use of idiomatic expressions. Prospective teachers need to be taught the use of error analyses based on learners' miscues and discourse analysis, which can lead to deeper understanding of the SLA process. Discourse analysis provides teachers with insights into how ELLs learn to make meaning from text and how they decode the immediate and cultural contexts. Meaning making in a second language challenges both the learner and the teacher.

One advocate of using discourse analysis as a teaching tool for ELLs is Dr. Lois Meyer, University of New Mexico. Meyer uses discourse analyses from actual dialogic interactions in the classroom. She then has her teacher-education students analyze the samples. This practice helps prospective educators refine their understanding of how teachers can use "teacher talk" to scaffold and extend their students' comprehension. Moreover, the students are also asked to display their own ability to do so. Meyer calls for a more active role for teachers' own [planned] discourse to model a more formal use of language. This exposure helps scaffold and develop both ELL speakers' and native speakers' language skills. She also acquaints prospective teachers with the impact of strategies such as teacher talk, student-teacher interaction, and the importance of adult support for students' oral and written skills. Teacher talk is defined by Meyer as careful and conscious (preplanned) use of language by the teacher in the classroom to shape, model, and scaffold the ELLs' literacy development by using the structures of the target language. Meyer also uses the term *language bath* to refer to the inundation of ELLs into the target language, recognizing that ELLs may not have models of effective and eloquent use of the target language in their homes or on the street (Meyer, personal communication, August 6, 2007).

Some Implications for Practice: Cognitive and Linguistic Research for Teachers

- ELLs need good models of well-spoken English.
- Teachers should prepare their discourse carefully (Meyer's teacher talk).
- Teachers should practice the skills of eliciting, leading, expanding, and elaborating teacher-student exchanges.
- Teachers should give students a "language bath" (Meyer, 2000) before new material is presented: Use high-level vocabulary in context, explain new ideas, and use graphics to scaffold the learning process and to "jump-start" ELLs' thinking and comprehension.
- Teachers should provide linguistic bridges by using a variety of structures to acquaint students with rhetorical devices in English.
- Teachers should consciously model various structures (e.g., yes-no questions, word order, intonation, metaphor, allusion) appropriate for the learners' levels.

Emphasis on the importance of current linguistic knowledge in SLA for literacy practitioners cannot be overstated. Highly qualified practitioners need current linguistic knowledge and data from action research in order to support

ELLs effectively through their approaches and to articulate their practice to all of the stakeholders, parents, administrators, the students themselves, and the local community.

SUMMARY

In closing, Dr. Robert Rumin, who was the Director of Adult Education for the Los Angeles Unified School District in the 1970s and 1980s, once stated that the essential characteristics of an ESL teacher included having "a listening ear and a listening heart" (Rumin, personal communication, 1975). This characteristic is quintessential not only for ESL teachers but for any literacy practitioner. The listening ear incorporates all the knowledge upon which one's teaching practice is based, and the listening heart incorporates the relationships that foster full growth and potential. His wisdom reverberates in the practices of today. When literacy practitioners address both the cognitive and affective domains of language, they address their students as fellow human beings and support them in their desires by creating a learning environment conducive to maximum communication and learning for all. Literacy practitioners have the distinct privilege of sharing a superb gift with English language learners, the gift of language.

CONNECTING LINGUISTIC CONCEPTS AND SECOND-LANGUAGE ACQUISITION AND YOUR CLASSROOM . . .

1. Imagine a scenario that is typical in today's classrooms. A student has entered your class and speaks little or no English. Draft a plan for supporting this student's literacy learning when no special resources are available.
2. Choose a chapter from a content area textbook in your classroom. Describe and demonstrate to your instructor and classmates how you would provide a "language bath" for a small group of ELL students. Choose a grade level for your presentation.

REFERENCES

Chomsky, N. (1957). *Syntactic Structures*. The Hague: Mouton.

Cummins, J. (1989). *Empowering minority students*. Sacramento, CA: California Association for Bilingual Education.

Freire, P., & Macedo, D. (1987). *Literacy: Reading the word and the world*. London: Bergin & Garvey.

Gee, J. P. (1993). *An introduction to human language: Fundamental concepts in linguistics*. Englewood Cliffs, NJ: Prentice Hall.

Lenneberg, E. (1967). *Biological foundations of language*. New York: Wiley.

Meyer, L. M. (2000). Barriers to meaningful instruction for English learners. *Theory into Practice*, *39*(4), 228–236.

Sauvignon, S. J. (2006). Forty years of language teaching. *Language Teaching, 40,* 1–15.

Selinker, L. (1972). Interlanguage. *International Review of Applied Linguistics in Language Teaching, 10*(3), 209–231.

Selinker, L. (1974). Interlanguage. In J. Richards (Ed.), *Error Analysis: Perspectives on second language acquisition* (pp. 31–53). Essex, England: Longman.

Smith, F. (1997). *Reading without nonsense* (3rd ed.). New York: Teachers College Press.

Vygotsky, L. S. (1989). *Thought and language.* Revised and edited by Alex Kozulin. Cambridge, MA: The MIT Press.

Wong-Fillmore, L., & Snow, C. E. (2000). What teachers need to know about language. Digest of article. U.S. Department of Educational Research and Improvement, Contract no. EDO-FL-00-06. Center for Applied Linguistics. (ERIC Clearing House on Language and Linguistics Special Report). Retrieved January 4, 2006, from http://www.cal.org/resources/digest/oo6fillmore.html

CHAPTER 14

DEVELOPING LITERACY IN ENGLISH LEARNERS: PRACTICAL "NUTS AND BOLTS"

GENI FLORES

THINK ABOUT **DEVELOPING LITERACY IN ENGLISH LEARNERS . . .**

1. Before you read, consider the steps a teacher takes when she begins a reading lesson for ELs.

2. Read to learn about sheltered instruction and its value for ELs.

One of the many difficult tasks that teachers face involves teaching reading to students who do not speak English or whose English is underdeveloped. Most public schools today are faced with educating a percentage of students for whom English is not a first language but a foreign language. These students are referred to as English learners (ELs;[1] see Collier & Thomas, 2009), and they have every potential to become productive contributors to society with excellent English and literacy skills. Their success often depends on good teachers who respect them, who see their potential, and who use strategies that aid their literacy development in a positive and nurturing atmosphere.

The very best precursor for developing English literacy in an EL is to ensure that the student is already a fluent reader in his or her native language (Peregoy & Boyle, 2005). This is fundamental to literacy development in a second language. As an example, try to remember yourself learning to read for the first time. You learned sounds and word configurations, and you attached them to objects in your environment that you already knew how to say and were familiar with. You learned that A-P-P-L-E was associated with a fruit you had often eaten. You knew

---

[1] Although ELL has been commonly used to describe English-language learners, EL (English learner) is becoming a more acceptable description of those who are learning English.

the name as well as the pronunciation before you saw the written word. Now, imagine learning to read for the first time and associating sounds and symbols to words you do not know. Imagine learning a set of symbols and being told that they mean "ging wa." Because you have no association with *ging wa*, you cannot attach meaning to the symbols you are learning to read.

If a student has already learned the process of reading in his or her native language, much of this confusion is avoided. The student already knows how symbols come together to form sounds and how those sounds represent items and ideas in the environment. The idea of reading transfers to a new language. Therefore, with that transfer, let's say you see a toothpick and under it you read the word *yáquian*. Your teacher pronounces the word *yáquian* and points to the toothpick. You will likely understand that the combination of letters and sounds that form *yáquian* is the written word for toothpick.

Because of this phenomenon, students who come to our classrooms with well-developed literacy skills in their native language tend to transition more smoothly to reading in English. With appropriate instruction, they learn to read as they learn the language. If you ever studied a foreign language after you learned to read in English, you found yourself able to transfer your knowledge of reading skills to that new language, and you may have even used your reading ability as a tool in learning words in that foreign language. Had you no understanding of the reading process in English, imagine trying to read in a foreign language!

However, not all ELs enter our classes with reading skills in their native languages. In the early years of school, kindergarten and first grade, most of the children we see are coming to us in order to learn to read for the first time. The child who does not speak English, like the child who does, is looking to the teacher for literacy development. In later school years, many ELs come to our classes having had little to no educational experiences in their background and, therefore, possess little to no reading ability. In either case, we are faced with the task of teaching reading to a student who does not speak English.

Upon receiving an EL into your classroom, the very first step should be to determine the native-language literacy level. This can be done through a review of records from the student's previous school, interviews though an interpreter that would be conducted with the student and with the family, standardized language assessments, and informal testing. If the student proves to have well-developed literacy skills in the native language, English literacy development may begin. However, if the student has underdeveloped literacy in the native language, the best approach would be to develop literacy in the native language.

Literacy development in the native language may be easy to incorporate if the student speaks a language commonly found in the public schools, such as Spanish, where teachers, programs, and resources are readily available. However, if the student speaks a language not commonly found in the schools, such as Farsi, there may be no teachers who can speak that language and no resources readily available. Also, some children are speakers of languages that are not written (for example, some Native American languages have no written form). In either case, there may be no choice but to begin literacy development in English without the benefits of the native language. However, whenever and wherever possible, literacy should be developed in the native language first. Students who do not learn to read in the native language first may struggle to develop to their full potential in English literacy (Ovando, Combs, & Collier, 2006; Wu, 2005).

There is also evidence that literacy development can occur in the native language and in English simultaneously (Haneda, 2006). This approach is used successfully in many dual-language programs at the early elementary school level. Dual-language programs, referred to as the 50-50 model, are very successful in developing literacy in the native language and the second language at the same time. Dual-literacy development may also be a good approach for students in their later years if time is an issue. Dworin (2006) reports on the *Family Stories Project*, through which a class of fourth graders improved their skills in Spanish and in English at the same time. They did so by recording and writing family stories from both language backgrounds and working with classmates in a group setting to translate them. This project used information that was interesting and personal to the students. The translation of the stories from Spanish to English and from English to Spanish provided a chance to look at spelling, vocabulary, grammar, and phonics. Through the reading of classmates' stories, the students worked on **biliteracy** and were actually developing capacity in both languages.

biliteracy—reading and writing capacity in two languages

It remains a reality, however, that many schools do not have the resources to develop native-language literacy. In this case, the teacher will have to develop the four language skills (listening, speaking, reading, and writing) in English. Even in this case, the native language should not be prohibited but rather encouraged for the comfort of the student. Teachers should keep in mind that listening and understanding in English will precede speaking, and reading will precede writing.

LITERACY DEVELOPMENT APPROACHES FOR THE EL

A child who has learned to read in the native language understands the relationship between symbols and words and is simply transferring that knowledge to a new language. One who is not literate in any language must begin by learning that symbols represent sounds and that those sounds combine to from words. Based on this, the needs of both groups may be different initially.

For the child whose literacy is developing, the use of phonics can be appropriate initially. This is because children are taught to read through phonics in many other languages. The developing reader has most likely been presented with the idea that symbols represent sounds in the native language. That child will be looking for a sound/symbol association in English.

The child with no literacy skills at all could begin to learn to read in English through a whole language approach. What becomes important here is the need to acquire some oral English first. The child sees an apple and hears the word *apple*. The child understands that apple is that fruit with the red outside and sweet, juicy, white inside. The child sees a picture of an apple and the printed word A-P-P-L-E below it. The teacher must point out that that configuration is "apple" and it is associated with the picture of the now familiar concept. The child begins the literacy process in this new language once the symbol, sounds, and object are matched up. The written word takes on meaning. Phonics and grammar can come later.

Instructional Strategies Useful for the EL

As ELs develop literacy and speaking ability in English, there are several strategies teachers can use in the classroom that will help. It is important to remember that successful EL teachers use a variety of strategies to help students to be successful.

Building Schemata. Often stories and readings deal with specific cultural issues that are not in the background understanding of students from other cultures and languages. For example, a typical American story might mention roasting hot dogs at a Fourth of July picnic. This scenario may have no meaning to a child from another country. A teacher builds schemata prior to beginning the reading (Cohen, 2007; Stott, 2001). A scan of the story ahead of time allows the teacher to "set the scene" through a preliminary discussion. In this case, the teacher can discuss patriotic celebrations in different countries and the traditions that accompany them. A quick lesson on how Americans celebrate Independence Day could follow and include a package of hot dogs and pictures of kids roasting them over a fire and eating them outside. In the best case scenario, the class might enjoy a picnic lunch before beginning to read. This will prepare the students for what they are about to read and give understanding to the story which may not have been there otherwise.

Jigsaw. For text chapter readings, students may be divided into small groups with each group being assigned a section of the chapter to read, discuss, and master among themselves (Echevarría, Vogt, & Short, 2007). Once this is accomplished, new groups are formed consisting of one member from each of the reading groups. Each person then explains the portion of the chapter that was mastered in the previous group to all the others in the new group. This cooperative learning activity allows an EL to be tutored by peers on chapter content before having to try and explain it to others. It provides opportunities for ELs to listen to English content in a supportive setting and also affords ELs time to explain content in English as a way that solidifies the learning of important concepts.

Scaffolding. Let's say the students have to write a summary of a reading. The EL may have no idea how to do this. As a whole class in a teacher-led activity, read a passage and summarize it together as the teacher writes the summary on the board or on an overhead transparency for all to see and follow. Then, divide the class in half and have each half of the class read and write a summary of a second passage. For the third passage, divide the class into groups of 4 to 6 to read and write a summary. For the fourth passage, let students work in pairs, placing each ELs with a fluent student. Finally, have students read and summarize individually. By this time, the EL should understand the process and be able to produce a summary appropriate for his or her level of English production.

Sheltered Reading.   The teacher provides an abstract of the reading, complete with vocabulary and pictures, to be read and discussed prior to tackling the actual

reading assignment. It is important to choose only the most valuable information for the **sheltered reading**. A sheltered version of this essay can be found in Figure 14.1.

> **sheltered reading instruction**—teacher provides a synopsis with vocabulary and pictures, to be read and discussed prior to tackling the actual reading assignment to scaffold the EL's reading

Sheltering a text is like creating a smaller version of the chapter or required reading so that the students can get the main idea without being overwhelmed. It can be given to the class as a whole and discussed. The reading of the entire chapter is assigned afterward. The chapter should be easier to follow and less overwhelming if a sheltered version has been provided ahead of the reading (Echevarría & Graves, 2006).

Literacy includes being able to read.

English learner (EL): a student who speaks another language but who is learning to speak, read, and write in English.

■ It is best to teach students to read in their native language <u>before</u> teaching them to read in English.

1. Native Language   2. English

■ Strategies that help:

• **Phonics**	*Letters and sounds*
• **Whole language**	*Associate words with pictures*
• **Building background**	*Talk about the story first*
• **Sheltering**	*Writing a smaller version of the big reading.*
• **Group work**	*Read together in a large group,*
	Read in a smaller group,
	Read in a very small group,
	Read in pairs,
	Read individually.

FIGURE 14.1   Helping Kids Learn to Read in English.

CONCLUSION

When a student comes to us without being able to speak English, we must first assess the student's skills in the native language. Whether the student has well-developed skills in the native language or very limited ability beyond social language in the native language, there are some things any teacher can do to better ensure success in developing English literacy. The child must be made to feel comfortable in the classroom. This means respecting the native language and its use by the student and parents and not permitting other kids to bully or make fun of the EL. Sometimes we have to provide motivation for the student to tackle the seemingly insurmountable task of learning to read in a new language. This can be done through encouragement, praise, and even by explaining (through an interpreter, if necessary) the great benefits to be had in being bilingual and biliterate. We should provide opportunity for interaction with English-speaking peers through academic grouping, sheltered lessons in the classroom, and a wealth of literature of interest at the appropriate grade level. Most importantly, we should care. Kids know when a teacher cares, and the concept of caring transcends language.

CONNECTING LITERACY DEVELOPMENT AND ENGLISH LEARNERS TO YOUR CLASSROOM . . .

1. Choose your favorite children's picture book or a chapter from a favorite chapter book at your grade level. Adapt it and create a sheltered text version of the story suitable for a new EL in your classroom.
2. Suppose a new student who speaks a language other than English enters your classroom and no other personnel or students in your school speak that language. If no ESL or bilingual classrooms are available in your school district, develop a plan for helping this student to become a reader and writer of the English language.
3. Choose a chapter from a content-area textbook at a middle school level. Design a jigsaw activity that would provide support for a middle school EL. Demonstrate your activity to your graduate class.

REFERENCES

Cohen, J. (2007). A case study of a high school English and his reading. *Journal of Adolescent and Adult Literacy, 51*(2), 164–175.

Collier, V. P., & Thomas, W. P. (2009). *Educating English learners for a transformed world.* Albuquerque, NM: Dual Language Education of New Mexico.

Dworin, J. E. (2006). The family stories project: Using funds of knowledge for writing: Students in a fourth grade biliteracy (Spanish/English) class wrote and translated family stories to improve their skills in both languages. *The Reading Teacher, 59*(6), 510–522.

Echevarría, J., & Graves, A. (2006). *Sheltered Content Instruction: Teaching English Language Learners with diverse abilities.* Boston: Pearson.

Echevarría, J., Vogt, M. E., & Short, D. J. (2007). *Making content comprehensible for English Language Learners: The SIOP Model.* Boston: Pearson.

Haneda, M. (2006). Becoming literate in a second language: Connecting home, community, and school literacy practices. *Theory into Practice, 45*(4), 337–345.

Ovando, C., Combs, M. C., & Collier, V. P. (2006). *Bilingual & ESL Classrooms: Teaching in multicultural contexts.* Boston: McGraw-Hill.

Peregoy, S. F., & Boyle, O. F. (2005). *Reading, writing, and learning in ESL: A resource book for K–12 teachers.* Boston: Pearson.

Stott, N. (2001). Helping ESL students become better readers: schema theory applications and limitations. *The Internet TESL Journal, VII(11),* retrieved January 10, 2009, from http://iteslj.org/

Wu, J. (2005). A view from the classroom. *Educational Leadership, 62*(4), 40–44.

CHAPTER 15

SOCIOLINGUISTICS

ROGER W. SHUY
Georgetown University

THINK ABOUT **SOCIOLINGUISTICS AND READING . . .**

1. As you read, make note of contributions of the field of sociolinguistics to the discipline of reading.
2. The author claims that grammar is the most stigmatizing aspect of American language dialects. As you read, think about the impact this has on the teaching of reading in public school classrooms.

WHAT IS SOCIOLINGUISTICS?

Although any effort to define a new and broad field of study such as sociolinguistics is subject to question and criticism by some of its practitioners, it will be useful to attempt at least a broad definition of the term here. Three major characteristics tend to characterize the field:

1. A concern for viewing language *variation* rather than the sort of universals upon which grammars are usually based.
2. A concern for seeing language in real *social contexts* rather than as abstract representations.
3. A high potential for relationship and application to other fields such as education, sociology, anthropology, and psychology.

In a sense, the third characteristic is really an outgrowth of the first two, but, for our purpose, these three aspects will be treated equally.

At the present time, a sociolinguist may be defined as a person who studies variation within a language or across languages with a view toward describing that variation or toward writing rules which incorporate it (rather than, as in the past, ignoring it); relating such variation to some aspects of the cultures which use it; doing large scale language surveys (macroanalysis); doing intensive studies of discourse (microanalysis); studying language function (as opposed to language forms); discovering the comparative values of different varieties of language or of different languages for the benefit of political or educational planning and decision making; studying language attitudes, values, and beliefs; and relating all the above to other fields (including education).

Although there has been a recent flurry of interest in language in real social settings, it would be foolish to claim that sociolinguistics is a new concept. It is quite likely, in fact, that man has been interested in the sorts of variation by which people set themselves off from each other since the very beginnings of speech. Humans have always lived with the cultural and linguistic paradox of needing to be like one another while, at the same time, needing to establish individuality. These needs, coupled with the multitude of complexities involved in cultural and linguistic change, motivations, attitudes, values, and physiological and psychological differences, present a vast laboratory for sociolinguistic investigation.

WHERE DID SOCIOLINGUISTICS COME FROM?

In many ways, sociolinguistics involves a putting back together, within the field of linguistics, a number of separations that have taken place over the years. For one thing, the separation of language from the realistic context in which it is used has proved very troublesome in recent years. The more traditional view of linguistics (common in the sixties), which excludes the variational and functional aspects of language from formal linguistic analysis and describes such characteristics as mere trivial performance, is finding disfavor at a rapid pace. The term **static** may be used to refer to the frameworks of both structural and transformational linguistics. A static grammar is one which excludes variation of any sort, including time, function, socioeconomic status, sex, and ethnicity, from the purview of formal linguistic analysis. Thus, when Noam Chomsky (1965:4) states, "Linguistic theory is concerned primarily with an ideal speaker/listener, in a completely homogeneous speech-community, who knows its language perfectly and is unaffected by performance variations," he is illustrating the static view of language quite succinctly. Thus linguists more or less abdicated any responsibility for studying many of the interesting, **dynamic** aspects of language in a vain effort to be "purely linguistic," whatever that might mean.

> **static language**—a grammar that excludes any variation (function, time, SES, sex, ethnicity) from analysis; remains unchanged

> **dynamic language**—continuously changing and evolving as it is spoken

> **synchronic**—study of a language as it presently exists

> **diachronic**—study of language changes over time

Another clear separation, which has been vigorously maintained in linguistics over the years, is the separation between **synchronic** and **diachronic** studies. That is, the separation of the study of language change from the analysis of a language at a given point in time. Such a notion dates back many years in the field but is perhaps most notably stated by Bernard Bloch (1948:7) when he attempted to define the goal of phonological analysis as the study of ". . . the totality of the possible utterances of one speaker at one time in using a language to interact with one other speaker. . . ." Such a theory would seem to imply that a speaker's phonological system is somehow cut off from the developments which gave it life. If, on the other hand, one were to view life as constant movement, one might also hypothesize that language is in equally constant movement in its futile effort to catch up with life. That is, life keeps moving away from the attempts of language at freezing it long enough to interact with it.

Thus, the period of linguistics called the structuralist period (the forties and fifties) was actually no different from the following transformationalist era with respect to the adherence to the study of static rather than dynamic language. But by the late sixties some fascinating new developments were taking place in several fields at the same time.

Led by William Labov, a group of scholars interested in variation in American English began to discover some new dimensions of systematic variation.[1] Past studies in American dialectology had described wide-meshed variation but had not accounted for it systematically. Using techniques borrowed largely from sociology, anthropology, and psychology, Labov clearly demonstrated that the study of a speech community was more revealing and systematic than the study of individual speakers and that instead of studying presence or absence of given features in the speech community, a great deal could be learned by seeing such features on a continuum. Such analysis began to be called gradient analysis. Thus it became important to know not just whether or not a speaker produced a given sound or grammatical structure but also the circumstances under which that form was produced (linguistic and psychosociological) as well as the frequency of occurrence of that form in relationship to consistent, comparable measures. Not all such scholars agreed with one another on the exact nature of this gradience, but the excitement generated by the notion quickly led to an alignment with linguists who had been studying creole languages such as William Stewart, who in 1964 presented his formulation of a continuum with what he called an acrolect at one end and a basilect at the other (1964:10–18). By this Stewart meant to indicate that speech communities could be plotted on a broad continuum rather than at artificial polarities such as standard or nonstandard per se. Acrolect was a person's most standard form. Basilect was his least standard. Creolists had long argued that pidgins and creoles, languages which are under construction and are therefore dynamic, offer the best opportunities to see how languages actually are developed.

At about the same time, the variationists and creolists were joined by a group of transformational linguists who were becoming disenchanted, among other things, by the static nature of their premises. James McCawley, Paul Postal, Robin and George Lakoff, Charles Fillmore, John Ross, and others began to raise objections against transformational syntax, noting its inability to accommodate real language, its failure to take into account that language is used by human beings to

---

[1]See William Labov (1963).

communicate in a social context, and its claim that syntax can be separated from semantics.[2] These scholars, currently called generative semanticists, see variation as heavily involved in grammar whenever the social context of a discourse changes. For example, one might dismiss the sentence, "Ernie thinks with a fork," as ungrammatical unless one knew that such a sentence is a response to the question, "How do you eat potatoes?" In her work on politeness, Robin Lakoff demonstrates the importance of context when she notes that when addressing a child, "You may do so-and-so" is politer than "You must do so-and-so." But in addressing a dignitary at a party, the hostess who says "You must have a piece of cake" is politer than one who says, "You may have a piece of cake" (Lakoff 1972:907–927).

All of this recent emphasis on social context by linguists was old hat to anthropologists, especially ethnographers of communication. Dell Hymes has been arguing many years for a realistic description of language, observing that institutions, settings, scenes, activities, and various sociocultural realities give order to such analysis.[3] An ethnographic approach to speech requires that the analyst have information about the relative statuses of the interlocutors, the setting of the speech act, the message, the code (including gestures), the situation, the topic, the focus, and the presuppositions that are paired with the sentences. At long last, the ethnographers of communication are beginning to get some help from linguists with other primary specializations. The upshot of all this ferment within the past few years has been an almost entirely new set of attitudes within the field of linguistics. It is difficult to describe linguistics at any point in its history as being settled with an orthodoxy; but some broad, general movements can be discerned with hindsight. In the forties and fifties we saw a structuralist emphasis, with a focus on phonology, a concern for the word, and a philosophical framework which was positivistic and empirical. In the sixties we witnessed the transformationalist era, with a focus on syntax, a concern for the sentence, and a philosophical framework which was rationalistic or idealistic, with innate knowledge and intuition playing a prominent role in analysis.

As C. J. Bailey (1973) points out, in the seventies we are entering a new period with an emphasis on discourse and a philosophical framework which is dynamic rather than individualistic or static. It is characterized by the concerns noted above by the variationists, ethnographers, generative semanticists, and creolists. Of particular concern to the interests of education is the underlying principle of the continuum. Like many such principles, it is patently obvious when noticed yet conspicuously absent from the history of language teaching.

It should be apparent, therefore, that sociolinguistics arose from a number of factors within the field of linguistics itself. A convergence of different avenues away from orthodox generative theory took place among dialectologists, creolists, semanticians, and anthropologists. Although the avenues were different, each shared a concern for variation, social reality, larger units of analysis (discourse), and a sense of continuum.

---

[2]For an account of the effects of social situation on formal grammar, see Charles Fillmore (1973).
[3]One might cite many references over a period of time. For a recent overview, see Dell Hymes (1973).

In addition, two factors outside the proper domain of linguistics also contributed heavily to the development of sociolinguistics. One was the general broadening of interests which began to develop in the sixties, leading to new kinds of interdisciplinary studies. The second was the development of interest in problems faced by minority peoples, especially in the schools. Linguists began to take an interest in urban language variation and to understand that past research methodologies were not viable for such investigation. New data-gathering techniques were required and new modes of analysis were needed. Meanwhile, linguists who had been interested in language variation as it is found in the creolization and pidginization of language also began to apply their knowledge to urban social dialect, particularly the urban, northern black, often providing important historical backgrounds for language change and offering analytical insights brought about by their perspectives. The general focus, of course, was on variability, not abstract uniformity and the critical measurement point was provided by the variability offered by Vernacular Black English. It was thought of as an area worthy of educational attention. Everything seemed ripe for this focus on Black English except for one thing—nobody in the academic world knew very much about it.

Seminal studies were done in New York by William Labov, Paul Cohen, Clarence Robbins, and K. C. Lewis; in Detroit by Roger Shuy, Walt Wolfram, and William Riley; in Washington by Ralph Fasold; and in Los Angeles by Stanley Legum. Generalizations about the findings of these studies have been made by Fasold and Wolfram in relatively non-technical language (1970). Today variability in language analysis has become a crucial issue. Thanks, at least partially, to the influence brought about by the study of Vernacular Black English.

WHAT ARE SOME IDENTIFIABLE CHARACTERISTICS OF SOCIOLINGUISTIC WORK?

A focus of study which has developed out of a diversity of interests is likely to have an equally diverse literature. Yet there are some common threads which seem to help hold sociolinguistics together. One such characteristic is the concept of gradience mentioned earlier.

Gradience

As is often the case, personal experience provides a good first example. When I was in college I had a part-time job in a wholesale grocery warehouse loading and unloading trucks and boxcars. My fellow teamsters knew that I was a college kid but also expected me to be one of them in some sense of the word. As a native speaker of their local version of nonstandard English, I found it possible to use the locally acceptable "I seen him when he done it" forms; but their linguistic expectations of a college kid made them suspicious of me every time I tried. Years ago the novelist Thomas Wolfe wrote a novel called *You Can't Go Home Again*. His thesis was that people are the products of their changing environment and that this changing environment includes the changing expectations of others. Translated to our situation this means that no matter how uneducated a person's parents may be, they expect their child to speak something other than the nonstandard English they grew up with. The child who is sensitive to his parents' wishes may respond by rattling off a locution that appears to be within the range of his parents' expectations. On the other hand, some situations may require him to not deny his heritage but to not appear uppity either. Precious few linguistic situations will require him to preserve his nonstandard dialect exactly the way it was before he was educated and elevated to some other level of expectation by those who love him. The following sentences may serve as illustrations of some of the points on such a continuum.

1. Hey! Don't bring no more a dem crates over here!
2. Hey! Don't bring no more a dose crates over here!
3. Hey! Don't bring no more a those crates over here!
4. Hey! Don't bring any more of those crates over here!
5. Please don't bring any more of those crates over here.
6. Gentlemen, will you kindly desist in your conveying those containers in this general direction?

Number 6 is surely undesirable in most communications and it is included only to extend the limits of the continuum as far as can be imagined. Most of the adjustments that an educated speaker makes to his audience are found in various modifications of numbers 4 and 5. Most certainly, there are few opportunities for him to go home to the nonstandardness of numbers 1 or 2. Those who know him will think he is patronizing them or, worse yet, making fun of them. Consequently, what the speaker does is to make subtle adjustments in his vocabulary, grammar, and phonology depending on the informality of the situation, the audience, and the topic. One safe move is to standardize the grammar, since grammar is the most stigmatizing aspect of American social dialects, while occasionally preserving a few of the less stigmatizing pronunciations and leaving in some flavor of the lexicon. This is a highly subtle and complicated linguistic maneuver which can hardly be oversimplified or under estimated.

In no way should it be implied that the specific continuum given as an example above is meant to be a right to wrong slide. Each item of the continuum has the potential for appropriateness and accuracy if the proper setting, topic, and person is discovered. But the schools would be likely to take it as a right-wrong series with a sharp line between numbers 3 and 4 with *wrong* facing one direction and *right* facing the other. Similarly, all of the *rights* would be considered good and all of the *wrongs* would be thought bad. What such an oversimplification denies are the following things:

1. That language use is more complex than any presupposed context or pseudomoral code will permit.
2. That users of language may intentionally select so-called stigmatized constructions.

3. That users of language may unintentionally select so-called constructions which, having been used, provide clear evidence of their having learned part, though not all, of the pattern.

It has been argued by linguists that people tend to be unable to perceive the fact that they are using language as they use it. One might ask, for example, if the fish see the water in which they are swimming. Much rather clear evidence seems to indicate that users of language are fairly unaware of how it is that they are giving themselves away as they speak. Studies of social stratification using only language data may well be the most accurate indices of socioeconomic status yet devised. Since people have such a hard time seeing the language they and others use (for they are after all, concentrating on understanding it, not analyzing it), they remain relatively naive about the subtle complexities they are able to engineer in using it. Contrastive norms in language production and in subjective reactions to language are a clear case in point. Many new Yorkers and Detroiters, for example, will utilize a high frequency of a stigmatized feature in their own speech despite the fact that they can clearly recognize the same features as stigmatized in the speech of others.[4]

Frequency of Occurrence

In addition to the complexities growing out of gradience and general variability, another area of complexity to which linguists have only recently attended is quantitative variability. As odd as it now may sound, it has not been the practice of linguists to note the frequency of occurrence of a given variable feature until very recently. An amusing internal argument is still going on between linguists who understand this principle and those who do not. It is said, for example, that copula deletion is a characteristic of Vernacular Black English as it is spoken in New York, Washington, D.C., and Detroit. Certain linguists violently object to this idea, noting that southern whites also say "he here" or "you gonna do it." And, of course, they are quite correct. What they fail to see, however, is that those who posit copula deletion as a characteristic of Vernacular Black English are not comparing southern whites to northern blacks but, quite the contrary, are concerned about what is considered Vernacular Black English in those specific northern contexts. But even there, we find that speakers of that dialect do not delete every copula. In fact, the frequency of occurrence of that deletion stratifies quite nicely according to socioeconomic status. Similarly, not every standard English speaker produces a copula every time it might be expected in his speech, although the frequency of occurrence is probably very high. An even clearer case is that of multiple negation which is also said to characterize Vernacular Black English, even though it is quite clear that many whites also use the form regularly. What, then, can it mean to call it Vernacular Black English? Simply that it is consistently found to occur in the continuous, natural speech of blacks at a much

---

[4]See William Labov (1966).

higher frequency than it occurs in the speech of whites from the same communities and of the same socioeconomic status (SES). Strangely enough, this sort of finding is still rather new in linguistics and, to some linguists, is quite heretical.

An example of a display of such data on the frequency of occurrence of a linguistic feature which is shared by all social groups (most of them *are* shared) is shown in Figure 15.1.

Note that the frequency of occurrence of the use of multiple negation across four SES groups in Detroit is maintained regardless of the race of the speakers, but that blacks use multiple negation at a higher frequency than do whites. Further information reveals that men use them at a rate higher than women. Such data cannot tell us that blacks use multiple negatives and that whites do not. Nor could it say that men use them and women do not. But it does offer richer information about the tendencies toward higher or lower variability usage than we could ever obtain from a methodology which offered only a single instance of such usage as evidence of its use or nonuse. The figures represent a number of informants in each of the four SES groups and a large quantity of occurrences of the feature for each informant represented in the group. In the case of multiple negation, in addition to tabulating the occurrences, it was

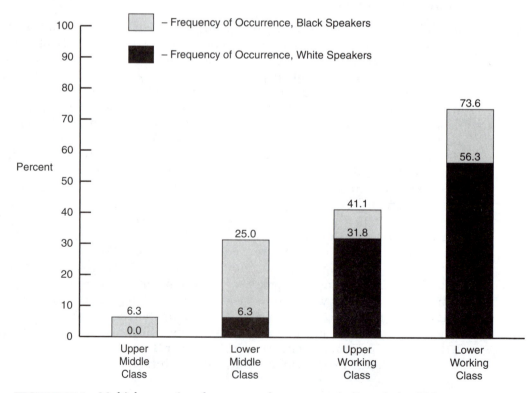

FIGURE 15.1   Multiple negation: frequency of occurrence in Detroit, by SES group.

necessary to see them in relationship to a meaningful touchstone. Thus every single negative and every multiple negative in each speaker's speech sample were added together to form a universe of potential multiple negatives. The tabulated figures display the relationship of the occurrence of multiple negatives in relationship to all potential multiple negatives.

It is reasonably safe to assume that the extent of language variation is much broader than previous research methodologies ever revealed. If an informant is asked, for example, what he calls the stuff in the London air, he may respond only once /fag/. If he should happen to use the /a/ vowel before a voiced velar stop only 50 percent of the time during all the occasions in which he refers to this concept during a ten-year period, this variability will be totally lost in this single representation in the interview. If he talks continuously for thirty minutes or so, he might use this pronunciation a dozen or more times, giving an increasingly more probable representation of his actual usage. Of course, such data gathering techniques work better for pronunciations in which the inventory of possible occurrences is very high than they do for lexicon. On the other hand, research in sociolinguistics indicates that pronunciation and grammar are more crucial indicators than vocabulary, a factor which certainly justifies highlighting them for research.

Selectional Options

Once we dispose of the notion of the right-wrong polarity evaluation and conceive of language as a continuum which operates in realistic contexts, the possibility of selectional options becomes meaningful. It is conceivable, for example, that a speaker out of a number of possible motivations, may select forms which, in some other context, would be considered stigmatized. Detailed studies of language variation have only begun to scratch the surface of such continua but several examples are suggestive of fruitful avenues of future research.

For example, I can clearly remember that as a child in a blue-collar industrial community, certain language restrictions were operational among preadolescent boys. To be an acceptable member of the peer group, it was necessary to learn and to execute appropriate rules for marking masculinity. If a boy happened to be the toughest boy in the class, he had few worries for whatever else he did would be offset by this fact. Those of us who were not the toughest could establish our masculinity in a number of ways, many of which are well recognized. Tough language (especially swearing) and adult vices (such as smoking) were sometimes effective means of obtaining such status. Likewise, if a boy were a good athlete, he could easily establish himself as masculine (in our society this was true only for football, basketball, and baseball and not for swimming, soccer, or tennis). On the other hand, a boy could clearly obtain negative points by having a nonsex-object relationship with a girl, by liking his sister, by playing certain musical instruments (especially piano and violin), and by outwardly appearing to be intelligent in the classroom. It is the latter avenue which is of interest to us here since the major instrument for adjusting one's outward appearance of intelligence was his use of oral language. Interestingly enough, what one did with written language seemed less crucial, as long as it remained a private communication between teacher and student. That is, a boy could be as smart as he wanted to on a test or an essay as long as the written document did not become public (displayed on the bulletin board).

Thus two strategies for reasonably intelligent males in this society were as follows:

a. *Keep your mouth shut in class.* If the male is white, this might be interpreted as shyness. If he is black, it usually is read as nonverbality. The strategy of keeping one's mouth shut in school is employed for different reasons at different times. In early elementary school, the child soon learns that the name of the game is to be right as often as possible and wrong as seldom as possible. One way to prevent being criticized by the teacher is to keep one's mouth shut. By preadolescence, the male's strategy for keeping his mouth shut grows out of a complex set of pressures stemming from stereotyped expectations of masculine behavior (boys are less articulate than girls and less interested in school) and the inherent dangers of appearing unmasculine to one's peers.

b. *If you give the right answer, counteract the "fink effect" by sprinkling your response with stigmatized language.* It is this strategy which boys must certainly master if they are to survive the education process in certain speech communities. Those who only keep their mouths shut tend to drop out ultimately for whatever reasons. But males who learn to adjust to the conflicting pressures of school and peer pressure are those who have learned to handle effectively the sociolinguistic continuum. In the proper context, and with the proper timing, an intelligent male can learn how to give the answer that the teacher wants in such a way that his peers will not think him a sissy. In English class he will learn how to produce the accepted forms with the subtle nuances of intonation and kinesics which signal to his peers that rather than copping out, he is merely playing the game, humoring the English teacher along. If he appears to be sufficiently bored, he can be allowed to utter the correct response. If he stresses the sentence improperly, he can be spared the criticism of selecting the accurate verb form. The six stage continuum noted earlier in this paper is a gross example of several choices available in such a situation. It is tempting to postulate that the male's need to counteract the "fink effect" by deliberately selecting stigmatized language forms is merely a working class phenomenon. Recent personal observations, however, have led me to question such a notion. My teenage son has lived his entire life in a middle-class, standard English speaking environment, but it is only since he began playing on a football team that he has developed a small number of nonstandard English features. The production of these features, which include multiple negation and *d* for *th* in words like *these* and *them*, is situationally confined to the present or abstract condition of football. He appears to use the standard English equivalents in all nonfootball contexts. Closer observation seems to indicate that not all members of the football team feel the same requirement. It would seem, in fact, that there are different pressures for different roles. My son is a defensive tackle, a position which seems to require the characteristics of an aggressive ape. Thus, apprentice apes must do everything possible to establish this condition. It is interesting to observe that pressure to select nonstandard forms seems less evident among quarterbacks and flankers.

A second recent observation has to do with the diagnosis of reading problems in an affluent Washington, D.C. suburb. A well meaning third grade teacher had diagnosed one boy's reading problem as one of "small muscle motor coordination," and she suggested that the parents send him to a neurologist. His father, a physician, objected strenuously, muttering something about teachers practicing medicine without a license. Since I knew the family, I was asked to help discover the child's real problem. After a quick examination, in which the boy evidenced little or no problem with decoding or comprehending material which was unknown to him, the only problem I discovered was that his reading was monotonous and mechanical. In the school's terminology, he did not read with "expression." A hasty survey of teachers revealed that boys tend to not read with expression, a fact which is generally accepted along with their nonverbality and dirty fingernails. Why didn't this boy read with expression? My hypothesis is that he considers it sissy. This boy is the smallest male in his class and he is using every means possible to establish his masculinity. What he lacks in athletic skill he more than makes up for with careless abandon. His voice is coarse. His demeanor is tough. He swears regularly. And so on. It would behoove the schools to do several things here. One might question the usefulness of reading with expression at all, but teachers should certainly be able to distinguish this presumed problem from other types of reading problems, particularly neurological ones. But this seems to be evidence of the same sort of pressure, this time in a middle-class community, which pits school norms against peer norms to the extent that the child is willing to deliberately select the nonstandard forms.

In addition to intentional selection of linguistic options, speakers also make unintentional selection of stigmatized language. One such selection involves the use of **hypercorrections**, a term which linguists use to refer to incorrect overgeneralization from already learned forms. Several years ago I noticed such a pattern in the development of my younger son's use of -*en* participles.

> **hypercorrection**—incorrect overgeneralization in speech from already learned forms, such as "between you and I"

Suddenly he seemed to be using the inflectional -*en* in all participle slots such as "have taughten," "have senden," and "have playen." My first reaction was to drill Joel on the proper form but I soon realized that he was actually evidencing awareness of a newly acquired pattern. What he had not yet learned was how to sort the participles out into -*en* and non-*en* forms. That would take time, but it would come. Hypercorrection is perhaps more readily recognized by English teachers in the form of the malapropism, a vocabulary item which comes close to the sound of the word intended but which clearly misses, yielding a humorous combination such as "prosecuting eternity." Grammatical hypercorrection yields equally pseudo-elegances such as "between you and I." In terms of selectional options, hypercorrections in vocabulary, pronunciation, and grammar pose an interesting problem which illustrates clearly the need to see language in a realistic social and psychological context. Hypercorrections, when detected, can count double or more in degree of stigmatization. If undetected, they are unlikely to be favored more than neutral. Thus, when people make judgments about the language used by a speaker, there are at least three areas of judgment involved: stigmatization, favoring, and hypercorrection. Detected hypercorrection probably runs the greatest risk of negative social stigmatization. Oddly enough, vocabulary hypercorrection (malapropism) is probably the most highly stigmatized, followed by pronunciation hypercorrection (the pseudo-elegance of *vahz* for *vase*, for example) and last by grammatical hypercorrection (such as "between you and I"). Stigmatization reverses this procedure, with grammatical features most stigmatized (at least in America), followed by phonological and lastly by vocabulary. This process of favoring is still relatively unknown, and it is difficult to tell whether vocabulary or grammar is the most favored condition. Within each linguistic category (pronunciation, grammar, and vocabulary), individual features can be placed and rank ordered, although the exact nature of this ordering is not totally known at this time.

Perceptual Viewpoint of the Whole

Still another characteristic of sociolinguistics is involved in the very viewpoint from which language phenomena are perceived. It is logical to believe that once the basics of language are understood, other less central features will fall into place. It has been traditional in linguistics to follow this logic. Thus linguists of various theoretical persuasions have searched for the core, the basics, and the universals of language and have paid little attention to the peripheral, the surface, or the variables. Sociolinguists do not decry an interest in universals or basics, but they feel that the peripheral variables are much more important than have ever been imagined. In fact, sociolinguists tend to treat peripheral and basic components on a par, and they believe that to understand one, they must also know a great deal about the other. Sociolinguists, therefore, stress variation, especially as it is related to sex, age, race, socioeconomic status, and stylistic varieties. They feel that by paying attention to such variables, they can better understand the exciting dynamics of language and see it as a whole.

Subjective Reactions

The development of sociolinguistics has also been paralleled by an interest in the subjective reactions of speakers to language. If speakers produce linguistic features with varying frequencies, if they make use of complex selectional options, and if they shift back and forth along a base line continuum, they most certainly also react to language produced by others. In recent years, sociolinguists have become interested in three types of subjective reactions to variation in spoken and written language:

1. Studies which compare subjective reactions to more than one language.
2. Studies which compare subjective reactions to variation within the same language.
3. Studies which compare accented speech, the production of a language by nonnative speakers.

It is felt that such studies will enable linguists to get at the threshold, if not at the heart, of language values, beliefs, and attitudes. From there it is a relatively short step to relating such attitudes to actual language teaching and planning. For example, research by Wallace Lambert and his associates (1960) attempted to determine how bilingual Canadians really felt about both English and French in that area. Therefore, several bilinguals were tape recorded speaking first one language, then the other. The segments were scrambled and a group of bilingual Canadians were asked to listen to the tape and rate the speakers on fourteen traits such as height, leadership ability, ambition, sociability, and character. The listeners were not told that they were actually rating people twice, once in French and once in English. It was somewhat surprising to the researchers that the speakers were generally stigmatized when they spoke French and favored when they spoke English. This was interpreted as evidence of a communitywide stereotype of English speaking Canadians as more powerful economically and socially.

An example of a study which compares listener reactions to variation within the same language was done in Detroit (Shuy, Baratz, & Wolfram, 1969). An equal number of black and white, male, adult Detroiters from four known socioeconomic groups were tape recorded in a relatively free-conversation mode. These tapes were played to Detroiters of three age groups (sixth grade, eleventh grade, and adult). An equal number of males and females, blacks and whites listened to the tape. These judges represented the same four socioeconomic groups as the speakers. The purpose of the study was to determine the effects which the race, sex, socioeconomic status, and age of the listener have on identifying the race and socioeconomic status of the speaker. The results of the study showed that racial identity is quite accurate for every cell except for the upper middle-class black speakers, who were judged as white by 90 percent of the listeners, regardless of their race, age, or sex. It also showed that the lower the class of the speaker, the more accurately he was identified by listeners, regardless of all other variables. The significance of this lies in the fact that listeners apparently react negatively to language more than favorably to it. That is, stigmatizing features tend to count against a speaker more than favoring features tend to help him. Such information is, of course, useful in determining how to plan a language learning curriculum, among other things.

A recent study of accented speech was done by A. Rey (1974) and contrasted the subjective reactions of Miami teachers, employers, and random adults to the accented speech of Cuban born and native white and black Miamians. Rey's interest was in the extent to which accent played a role in both employability and school evaluation. He played tape recordings of various speakers to groups of listeners and concluded that the lower status Cuban born Miamians have the least chance for success, even if the employer or teacher is also Cuban born.

WHAT ARE THE PROSPECTS FOR SOCIOLINGUISTICS IN THE FUTURE?

To date, the study of sociolinguistics can be said to have hardly begun. Variation is a vast expanse of possibilities which should keep linguists busy for years to come. A very small dent has been made in the study of variation among certain minority groups. Through an accident of history, a great deal has been learned about Vernacular Black English but very little is known about the variation used by standard English speakers, regardless of race. Little is known about the sort of variation which establishes a speaker as a solid citizen, a good guy, or an insider.

> **register**—variety in language as determined by social circumstances; most people have a repertoire of language registers

Despite some intensive research in the area, little is known about how people shift from one **register** to another or, for that matter, from one dialect or language to another. Only the barest beginnings have been made in the study of special group characteristics related to language (language and religion, law, medicine). A great deal of research needs to be done on language attitudes, values, and beliefs. Although language change has received attention in a number of recent studies, sociolinguistic research still lacks knowledge of a number of aspects of the exciting dynamics of language.

In short, the social contexts in which language can be studied have almost as many variations as there are people to vary them. In some fields of study, graduate students writing theses or dissertations often become discouraged over the fact that all the good topics for research have already been used up. This dilemma is far from a reality in sociolinguistics, where topics abound and where we are only at the beginning.

CONNECTING SOCIOLINGUISTICS AND YOUR CLASSROOM . . .

1. Choose two students in your classroom who have very different language patterns. One might be a speaker of standard English and the other might be a speaker of a nonstandard English dialect. Collect and tape-record a sample of each student retelling a story you read aloud to the class. Make a list of all grammatical variations in each student's language sample (e.g., I or me, was or were, use of the verb to be, real or really, good and well). What are the implications of this close analysis of language for ELL teachers?

2. Analyze several running records of students in your class. Make note of instances when dialect is responsible for a mispronunciation of a word. List those words. What is the role of dialect in the teaching of reading fluency? What should be a teacher's response to dialect and miscues? Be prepared to justify your position to your instructor and classmates.

REFERENCES

Bailey, Charles-James N. "Contributions of the Study of Variation to the Framework of the New Linguistics," paper presented at the International Linguistic Association, Arequipa, Peru, 1973.

Bloch, Bernard. "A Set of Postulates for Phonemic Analysis," *Language*, 24, 3 (1948).

Chomsky, Noam. *Aspects of the Theory of Syntax*. Cambridge: M.I.T. Press, 1965.

Fasold, Ralph W., & W. A. Wolfram. "Some Linguistic Features of Negro Dialect," in Ralph W. Fasold and Roger W. Shuy (Eds.), *Teaching Standard English in the Inner City*. Washington, D.C.: Center for Applied Linguistics, 1970.

Fillmore, Charles. "A Grammarian Looks to Sociolinguistics," in R. Shuy (Ed.), *Sociolinguistics: Current Trends and Prospects*. Washington, D.C.: Georgetown University Press, 1973.

Hymes, Dell. "The Scope of Sociolinguistics," in R. Shuy (Ed.), *Sociolinguistics: Current Trends and Prospects*. Washington, D.C.: Georgetown University Press, 1973.

Labov, William. "The Social Motivation of a Sound Change," *Word*, 19 (1963), 273–309.

Labov, William. *The Social Stratification of English in New York City*. Washington, D.C.: Center for Applied Linguistics, 1966.

Lakoff, Robin. "Language in Context," *Language*, 48 (1972), 907–927.

Lambert, W. E., and others. "Evaluational Reactions to Spoken Language," *Journal of Abnormal and Social Psychology*, 60 (1960), 44–51.

Rey, Alberto. "A Study of the Attitudinal Effect of a Spanish Accent on Blacks and Whites in South Florida," unpublished doctoral dissertation, School of Languages and Linguistics, Georgetown University, 1974.

Shuy, Roger W., J. C. Baratz, & W. A. Wolfram. "Sociolinguistic Factors in Speech Identification," National Institute of Mental Health Research Project No. MH-15048-01, 1969.

Stewart, William A. "Urban Negro Speech: Sociolinguistic Factors Affecting English Teaching," in R. Shuy (Ed.), *Social Dialects and Language Learning*. Champaign, Illinois: National Council of Teachers of English, 1964.

CHAPTER 16

ON THE PSYCHOLINGUISTIC METHOD OF TEACHING READING

FRANK SMITH AND KENNETH S. GOODMAN

THINK ABOUT **THE STUDY OF PSYCHOLINGUISTICS . . .**

1. Frank Smith and Kenneth Goodman discuss their fear of a commercialized "psycholinguistic method" of teaching reading. Read to find out how the study of psycholinguistics differs from a psycholinguistics approach or method to teaching reading.

2. The authors in this chapter discuss surface structure and deep structure of language. As you read, compare and contrast these structures and reflect on how they impact reading instruction in your classroom.

Our concern is with an imaginary monster—the "psycholinguistic method." At the time of this writing, it is as mythical a beast as the phoenix, the unicorn, or the hippogriff. But we have no confidence that in the near future this monster will not show its face upon the earth. In fact, we would put such a method into the same category as female presidents of the United States—a logical possibility that happens only temporarily to be an empty set.

We must declare our interest. Each of us is responsible for a book about reading that has the word "psycholinguistic" in its title (1, 2), and we are both anxious not to have the term associated with a particular instructional dogma. To be blunt, we regard the development of "psycholinguistic material" as a distinct threat, not just to us but to the entire educational community. Already we think we detect perturbations in the publishing underworld indicating that a new vogue word is about to be launched into reading pedagogy. Therefore, we have decided on this pre-emptive strike. Our objective is to destroy the phoenix of "psycholinguistic instruction" before it can arise from the methodological ashes of the 1960's, although our expectation of success is slight. Our numbers are small, and we have nothing but reason on our side.

The value of psycholinguistics lies in the insights it can provide into the reading process and the process of learning to read. As such, a "psycholinguistic approach" to reading would be the very antithesis of a set of instructional materials. As we shall argue, psycholinguistic analysis formally confirms what we have all known intuitively for years—that the key factors of reading lie in the child and his interaction with information-providing adults, rather than in the particular materials used. Materials most compatible with such interaction are those that interfere the least with natural language functioning.

Obviously we write with some feeling. This would not be the first time that the reputable name of a scientific discipline had been used with marginal justification as a label for classroom fads. The new science of psycholinguistics has much to offer the study of reading, and its contribution could be sullied by the first corner to attach its name to a souped-up package of classroom impedimenta.

Psycholinguistics, as its name suggests, lies at an intersection of psychology and linguistics. As an independent discipline, it is about fifteen years old. Its central task, according to Miller, is to describe the psychological processes that go on when people use language (3, 4). From linguistics, the new science derives insights about the system that is language—about the competence that individuals acquire when they become fluent users of their language. Some of these insights are incompatible with hypotheses about language-learning that psychologists have held for decades.

Linguistic analysis, for example, shows that it would be impossible for a child to learn to speak simply by imitating adult sentences. The number of sentences possible in a language is infinite—at least a hundred billion different grammatical twenty-word sentences could be constructed, and practically every utterance we make or hear is unique. Therefore language must be a system, a set of rules that is capable of generating an infinite number of sentences.

We are all capable of learning what these rules are, because we are all capable of distinguishing acceptable from unacceptable grammatical constructions in our language (even if our own individual grammars vary a little from one person to another). The rules must be learned; they cannot be taught, partly because no one can say what they are.

Not even linguists can describe with any adequacy the rules by which grammatical and ungrammatical sentences can be distinguished; if linguists could, we would have computers that could converse and translate with the facility of human beings.

Linguistic analysis also shows that language has two levels—a surface structure—that is, the sounds or written representation of language—and a deep structure—that is, meaning. These two levels of language are related in a complex way through the system of rules that is grammar, or syntax. Without these rules we could never understand a sentence because the meaning of a sentence is given not by the individual words, but by the manner in which the words interact with each other. (If it were not for syntax, "man bites dog" would mean the same as "dog bites man" and a Maltese cross would be indistinguishable from a cross Maltese.)

Psychology contributes insights about how language must be learned and used. Psychology shows that there are severe perceptual limitations on the amount of acoustic (or visual) "surface structure" that we can process to comprehend language. Psychology shows that our working memory is so constrained that we could not possibly comprehend speech or writing if we analyzed individual words. Psychology also provides a wealth of data about human learning, showing, for example, that negative information can be as valuable as positive information. It can be just as instructional to be wrong as to be right, although all too frequently we are conditioned to avoid the "error" of our ways. Psychological studies show that all human beings have preferred strategies that use a small and apparently innate range of capacities for acquiring new knowledge. These studies also show that learning is rarely the result of a passive exposure to "instruction" but rather the result of an active search for specific kinds of information, which is another reason why rules can be learned but not taught.

At the intersection of these areas of psychology and linguistics lies the growing and fascinating field of psycholinguistics. Already there is an imposing body of knowledge about how fluent language-users construct and perceive sentences. Psycholinguistic research confirms, for example, the linguistic insight that language is processed at deep structure levels. We remember meanings, not individual words. We distinguish elements and relationships that are not actually represented in the surface structure but are constructed from the meanings that we derive from the hidden deep structure.

Some of the most exciting advances made by psycholinguists have been in their studies of how children acquire the rules of adult language (2). Studies show that these rules are developed rapidly between the ages of eighteen months and four years, and appear to follow a similar pattern of development in all children. This pattern, so systematic and invariant, is nothing like a miniature or deformed version of adult language. This fact has led to the suggestion that children have an innate predisposition for discovering the rules of language. The view is supported by the fact that no one can verbalize these rules to tell them to a child.

Insights of the kind found in linguistics and psychology appear to be leading to a profound review of long-held beliefs about reading and how it is learned. It is becoming clear that reading is not a process of combining individual letters into words, and strings of words into sentences, from which meanings spring automatically. Rather the evidence is that the deep-level process of identifying meaning either precedes or makes unnecessary the process of identifying individual words.

Psycholingustic techniques are beginning to be applied directly to the study of learning to read. They show that the type of information a child requires is not best presented in the form of stereotyped classroom or textbook rules and exercises. Rather, a child appears to need to be exposed to a wide range of choices so that he can detect the significant elements of written language. Experiments have shown that even beginning readers look for and use orthographic, syntactic, and semantic redundancy in written language—but whoever thinks of trying to "teach" a child about that? The child learning to read, like the child learning to speak, seems to need the opportunity to examine a large sample of language, to generate hypotheses about the regularities underlying it, and to test and modify these hypotheses on the basis of feedback that is appropriate to the unspoken rules that he happens to be testing (5, 6).

None of this can, to our mind, be formalized in a prescribed sequence of behaviorally stated objectives embalmed in a set of instructional materials, programmed, or otherwise. The child is already programmed to learn to read. He needs written language that is both interesting and comprehensible, and teachers who understand language-learning and who appreciate his competence as a language-learner.

The value of psycholinguistics, we are firmly convinced, lies in the new understanding it can give us all—researchers and practitioners—about the reading process and learning to read. If we were given to slogans, we might well be among the first to assert (with the publishers and the publicists) that this is the dawn of the psycholinguistic era in reading instruction. But we appeal for caution for two reasons. First, because the discipline of psycholinguistics is new, especially in its application to reading. It is far too early to derive rigid practical conclusions from the data that have been collected. But second, because, as we have already asserted, the data clearly indicate that the "revolution" that psycholinguistics might create in reading pedagogy lies in a richer understanding of what the child is trying to accomplish and of his superb intellectual equipment.

We do not deny that there might be a psycholinguistic approach, or attitude, toward reading. In such an approach, the adjective "psycholinguistic" would be synonymous with "objective," "analytical," or "scientific." But in phrases such as "psycholinguistic primer" or "psycholinguistic kit" the adjective would be devoid of meaning.

Nor do we deny that materials for reading instruction could be improved both in their construction and use by the insightful application of psycholinguistic knowledge. Enlightened teachers do not need to wait for new materials. They can make much more effective use of existing materials simply by viewing the reading process as one in which the developing reader functions as a user of language. It may well be that such teachers will find themselves rejecting large portions of the materials and the accompanying guide books as inappropriate, unsound, and even destructive.

We stated earlier that our fears about the misuse of the word "psycholinguistic" were based on precedent. We are thinking of what has already happened to one half of the psycholinguistic partnership.

The study of reading was advanced significantly when linguists turned their attention to the subject. They contributed a number of profound and important insights that continue to serve the discriminating reading researcher and the teacher. But the name of linguistics also became associated with a particular clutch of instructional materials and that is a different kettle of fish. The attachment of the label "linguistic" to reading materials had two disadvantages. The first disadvantage was that any material or procedure that could be associated with the label gained a spurious authority, as if anything that bore the trademark "linguistic" carried a scientific seal of quality. The second disadvantage was that the word "linguistics," and the science itself, became devalued in many circles because of a kind of **Gresham's Law** that operates among instructional materials.

> **Gresham's law**—from the discipline of economics; the idea that bad money will drive out good; or in this case, bad instructional materials will drive or force out good instructional materials

We shall not speculate about reasons why no instructional materials have ever been characterized as the "psychological" method for teaching reading, although such a label would seem to be as justified as "linguistic." Whatever the reasons for the inhibitions about using the world "psychological," they do not appear to apply to "psycholinguistic," which is gaining growing prominence in the promotional literature of the education industry.

Our plea is simply that the term be used with respect.

Some teachers who read our arguments may still look forward to a psycholinguistic basal reading program. These teachers may believe that useful knowledge can come to reading teachers only in the form of a textbook series or a kit, ready for immediate application with no prior training. In fact, knowledge, however valid, can usefully influence reading instruction only if teachers have grasped its nature. When teachers understand the relevance of psycholinguistic theory and research, they will see reading materials in their true perspective.

CONNECTING **PSYCHOLINGUISTICS AND YOUR CLASSROOM . . .**

1. What is psycholinguistics? How can understanding this discipline inform your teaching of reading in the classroom? Be prepared to share your definition of psycholinguistics and its impact on your teaching of reading with your colleagues and professor.
2. Create a minilesson that utilizes some of the principles of psycholinguistics that can enhance both surface and deep structure use of the language.

REFERENCES

F. Smith. *Understanding Reading: A Psycholinguistic Analysis of Reading and Learning To Read.* New York: Holt, Rinehart and Winston, 1971.

G. A. Miller. "The Psycholinguists," *Encounter,* 23 (July, 1964), 29–37.

G. A. Miller. "Some Preliminaries to Psycholinguistics," *American Psychologist,* 20 (January, 1965), 15–20.

K. S. Goodman (editor). *The Psycholinguistic Nature of the Reading Process.* Detroit: Wayne State University Press, 1968.

K. S. Goodman, & C. Burke. "Study of Children's Behavior while Reading Orally." Final Report. United States Office of Education Project S425, 1968.

K. S. Goodman, & C. Burke. "Study of Oral Reading Miscues That Result in Grammatical Retransformation." Final Report. United States Office of Education Project 7-E–219, 1969.

CHAPTER 17

FUNDS OF KNOWLEDGE FOR TEACHING: USING A QUALITATIVE APPROACH TO CONNECT HOMES AND CLASSROOMS

LUIS C. MOLL
CATHY AMANTI
DEBORAH NEFF
NORMA GONZALEZ

THINK ABOUT FUNDS OF KNOWLEDGE FOR TEACHING . . .

1. As you read, find out what the authors mean by the term funds of knowledge.
2. Consider how teachers can make use of a family's funds of knowledge for reading instruction?
3. As you read, make note of how the authors' research contradicts long-standing views of resources within immigrant families and their relationships to the school?

We form part of a collaborative project between education and anthropology that is studying household and classroom practices within working-class, Mexican communities in Tucson, Arizona. The primary purpose of this work is to develop innovations in teaching that draw upon the knowledge and skills found in local households. Our claim is that by capitalizing on household and other community resources, we can organize classroom instruction that far exceeds in quality the rote-like instruction these children commonly encounter in schools (see, e.g., Moll & Greenberg, 1990; see also Moll & Díaz, 1987).

To accomplish this goal, we have developed a research approach that is based on understanding households (and classrooms) qualitatively. We utilize a combination of ethnographic observations, open-ended interviewing strategies, life histories, and case studies that, when combined analytically, can portray accurately the complex functions of households within their sociohistorical contexts. Qualitative research offers a range of methodological alternatives that can fathom the array of cultural and intellectual resources available to students and teachers within these households. This approach is particularly important in dealing with students whose households are usually viewed as being "poor," not only economically but in terms of the quality of experiences for the child.

Our research design attempts to coordinate three interrelated activities: the ethnographic analysis of household dynamics, the examination of classroom practices, and the development of after-school study groups with teachers. These study groups, collaborative ventures between teachers and researchers, are settings within which we discuss our developing understanding of households and classrooms. These study groups also function as "mediating structures" for developing novel classroom practices that involve strategic connections between these two entities (see Moll et al., 1990).

In this article we discuss recent developments in establishing these "strategic connections" that take the form of joint household research between classroom teachers and university based researchers, and the subsequent development of ethnographically informed classroom practices. We first present a summary of our household studies and the findings that form the bases of our pedagogical work. We then present an example of recent research between a classroom teacher and an anthropologist, highlighting details of their visit to a household, and the teacher's development of an instructional activity based on their observations. We conclude with some comments on the work presented.

SOME BASIC FINDINGS

As noted, central to our project is the qualitative study of households. This approach involves, for one, understanding the history of the border region between Mexico and the United States and other aspects of the sociopolitical and economic context of the households (see, e.g., Vélez-Ibáñez, 1993; see also Heyman, 1990; Martínez, 1988). It also involves analyzing the social history of the households, their origins and development, and most prominently for our purposes, the labor history of the families, which reveals the accumulated bodies of knowledge of the households (see Vélez-Ibáñez & Greenberg, 1989).

With our sample,[1] this knowledge is broad and diverse, as depicted in abbreviated form in Table 17.1. Notice that household knowledge may include information about farming and animal management, associated with households' rural origins, or knowledge about construction and building, related to urban occupations, as well as knowledge about many other matters, such as trade, business, and finance on both sides of the border (see, e.g., Moll & Greenberg, 1990).

TABLE 17.1   A Sample of Household Funds of Knowledge

Agriculture and Mining	*Material & Scientific Knowledge*
Ranching and farming	Construction
Horse riding skills	Carpentry
Animal management	Roofing
Soil and irrigation systems	Masonry
Crop planting	Painting
Hunting, tracking, dressing	Design and architecture
Mining	*Repair*
Timbering	Airplane
Minerals	Automobile
Blasting	Tractor
Equipment operation and maintenance	House maintenance
Economics	*Medicine*
Business	Contemporary medicine
Market values	Drugs
Appraising	First aid procedures
Renting and selling	Anatomy
Loans	Midwifery
Labor laws	Folk medicine
Building codes	Herbal knowledge
Consumer knowledge	Folk cures
Accounting	Folk veterinary cures
Sales	*Religion*
Household Management	Catechism
Budgets	Baptisms
Childcare	Bible studies
Cooking	Moral knowledge and ethics
Appliance repairs	

funds of knowledge— cultural knowledge and skills accumulated by students within their family settings that enable the household to thrive; students' strengths on which to build curriculum in diverse classrooms setting

We use the term **"funds of knowledge"** to refer to these historically accumulated and culturally developed bodies of knowledge and skills essential for household or individual functioning and well-being (Greenberg, 1989; Tapia, 1991; Vélez-Ibáñez, 1988).

Our approach also involves studying how household members use their funds of knowledge in dealing with changing, and often difficult, social and economic circumstances. We are particularly interested in how families develop social networks that interconnect them with their social environments (most importantly with other households), and how these social relationships facilitate the development and exchange of resources, including knowledge, skills, and labor, that enhance the households' ability to survive or thrive (see, e.g., Moll & Greenberg, 1990; Vélez-Ibáñez & Greenberg, 1989; see also Keefe & Padilla, 1987).

Two aspects of these household arrangements merit emphasis here, especially because they contrast so sharply with typical classroom practices. One is that these networks are flexible, adaptive, and active, and may involve multiple persons from outside the homes; in our terms, they are "thick" and "multi-stranded," meaning that one may have multiple relationships with the same person or with various persons. The person from whom the child learns carpentry, for example, may also be the uncle with whom the child's family regularly celebrates birthdays or organizes barbecues, as well as the person with whom the child's father goes fishing on weekends.

Thus, the "teacher" in these home based contexts of learning will know the child as a "whole" person, not merely as a "student," taking into account or having knowledge about the multiple spheres of activity within which the child is enmeshed. In comparison, the typical teacher-student relationship seems "thin" and "single-stranded," as the teacher "knows" the students only from their performance within rather limited classroom contexts.

Additionally, in contrast to the households and their social networks, the classrooms seem encapsulated, if not isolated, from the social worlds and resources of the community. When funds of knowledge are not readily available within households, relationships with individuals outside the households are activated to meet either household or individual needs. In classrooms, however, teachers rarely draw on the resources of the "funds of knowledge" of the child's world outside the context of the classroom.

A second, key characteristic of these exchanges is their **reciprocity**. As Vélez-Ibáñez (1988) has observed, reciprocity represents an "attempt to establish a social relationship on an enduring basis. Whether symmetrical or asymmetrical, the exchange expresses and symbolizes human social interdependence" (p. 142). That is, reciprocal practices establish serious obligations based on the assumption of "confianza" (mutual trust), which is reestablished or confirmed with each exchange, and leads to the development of long-term relationships. Each exchange with relatives, friends, and neighbors entails not only many practical activities (everything from home and automobile repair to animal care and music) but constantly provides contexts in which learning can occur—contexts, for example, where children have ample opportunities to participate in activities with people they trust (Moll & Greenberg, 1990).

> **reciprocity**—enduring social relationship based on social interdependence

A related observation, as well, is that children in the households are not passive by-standers, as they seem in the classrooms, but active participants in a broad range of activities mediated by these social relationships (see La Fontaine, 1986). In some cases, their participation is central to the household's functioning, as when the children contribute to the economic production of the home, or use their knowledge of English to mediate the household's communications with outside institutions, such as the school or government offices. In other cases they are active in household chores, such as repairing appliances or caring for younger siblings.

Our analysis suggests that within these contexts, much of the teaching and learning is motivated by the children's interests and questions; in contrast to classrooms, knowledge is obtained by the children, not imposed by the adults. This totality of experiences, the cultural structuring of the households, whether related to work or play, whether they take place individually, with peers, or under the supervision of adults, helps constitute the funds of knowledge children bring to school (Moll & Greenberg, 1990).

FUNDS OF KNOWLEDGE FOR TEACHING

Our analysis of funds of knowledge represents a positive (and, we argue, realistic) view of households as containing ample cultural and cognitive resources with great, *potential* utility for classroom instruction (see Moll & Greenberg, 1990; Moll et al., 1990). This view of households, we should mention, contrasts sharply with prevailing and accepted perceptions of working-class families as somehow disorganized socially and deficient intellectually; perceptions that are well accepted and rarely challenged in the field of education and elsewhere (however, see McDermott, 1987; Moll & Díaz, 1987; Taylor & Dorsey-Gaines, 1988; see also Vélez-Ibáñez, 1993).

But how can teachers make use of these funds of knowledge in their teaching? We have been experimenting with the aforementioned arrangements that involve developing after-school settings where we meet with teachers to analyze their classrooms, discuss household observations, and develop innovations in the teaching of literacy. These after-school settings represent social contexts for informing, assisting, and supporting the teachers' work; settings, in our terms, for teachers and researchers to exchange funds of knowledge (for details, see Moll et al., 1990).[2]

In analyzing our efforts, however, we realized that we had relied on the researchers to present their findings to the teachers and to figure out the relevance of that information for teaching. Although we were careful about our desires not to impose but to collaborate with teachers, this collaboration did not extend to the conduct of the research. In our work with teachers, at least as far as household data were concerned, we relied on a "transmission" model: We presented the information, teachers received it, without actively involving themselves in the development or production of this knowledge. But how could it be otherwise? Was it feasible to ask teachers to become field researchers? What would they get out of it? Could they develop similar insights to those developed by the anthropologists in our research team? What about methods? Could they, for example, with little experience, understand the subtleties of ethnographic observations?

In what follows we present a case example from our most recent work that addresses these questions. The goal of the study was to explore teacher–researcher collaborations in conducting household research and in using this information to develop classroom practices. As part of the work, 10 teachers participated in a series of training workshops on qualitative methods of study, including ethnographic observations, interviews, the writing of field notes, data management, and analysis.[3] Each teacher (with two exceptions) then selected for study three households of children in their classrooms. In total, the teachers visited 25 households (the sample included Mexican and Yaqui families) and conducted approximately 100 observations and interviews during a semester of study (for details, see Vélez-Ibáñez, Moll, Gonzalez, & Neff, 1991).

Rather than provide further technical details about this project, however, we present an edited transcript from a recent presentation[4] by a teacher (Cathy Amanti) and an anthropologist (Deborah Neff) who collaborated in the study. They describe their experiences conducting the research, and provide a revealing glimpse of the process of using qualitative methods to study households and their funds of knowledge.

STUDYING HOUSEHOLD KNOWLEDGE

In their presentation, Amanti and Neff first described some of their concerns in conducting the work, including how their assumptions and previous experiences may have influenced their observations. They also described their planning. Notice how they decided to divide the methodological responsibilities for conducting the interviews and observations.

> **DN:**   We are going to share with you some of our experience in working as a team doing household interviews. We have chosen the López family, a pseudonym, as the focus of this brief talk. The Lópezes are the parents of one of Cathy's students, whom we will call Carlos.
>
>   In going into the homes, we carry with us cultural and emotional baggage that tends to color our understanding of interviews and observations. We have fears and assumptions, and perhaps misunderstandings. I for one did not know exactly what to expect when I first went into the López home with Cathy. I had heard talk of dysfunctional homes, lack of discipline, lack of support systems and so forth, but remained skeptical of these negative characterizations. Having done fieldwork before, I was accustomed to this kind of uncertainty.
>
> **CA:**   I, however, was nervous because I was going out in the field for the first time with someone who's had experience doing this type of research. Deborah had experience doing ethnography, I did not, and I was concerned about balancing doing interviews and observations with establishing and maintaining rapport. I was glad, though, that she was there, and I wanted her feedback to make sure I was getting what I should from the visit.

In 2 years of teaching, I had visited only a handful of homes. So, I had been into some of these homes before but only for school-related reasons, for example, delivering a report card, but I'd only visited for a brief period of time. These research visits were to be different—I had to observe, ask questions, take notes, and establish rapport—it was a lot to assimilate, with many activities to coordinate at the same time. One problem I had, for example, was deciding how closely to stick to the questionnaires.

DN: We discussed that and Cathy decided to stick closely to the questionnaire for the time being until she got more comfortable with the procedure. She would conduct the interviews in Spanish, the language of the parents, and we decided that both of us would take notes. I would concentrate more on observations, body language, and overall context, noting suggestions to improve our interview skills and topics to follow up on in future visits. Cathy would conduct the interview and respond to the parents' questions. We decided the first interview, in particular, would be to establish rapport.

We spent a lot of time first discussing the child, for example, Carlos's performance in Cathy's class. Cathy also informed Mrs. López of school activities she might want to be involved in, such as a culminating activity to a literature unit. It took us about 10 minutes to explain the project. The Lópezes had no difficulty understanding the potential benefits to the child, although they were not quite clear about what we wanted from them. That became clear as the interviews progressed. They were glad to participate, although Mrs. López preferred not to be tape recorded.

CA: I was glad that she was able to tell us that so readily. Each time we went, we talked about the child, and tried to make astute observations. Some of these observations included, for example, noticing and asking about family photos and trophies. Encyclopedias on corner bookshelves provided a natural entrée into topics of family history and social networks of exchange, literacy, and the parents' pride in their child's achievements.

DN: At first, going into the López home, I felt a little nervous too, because it was my experience to spend an enormous amount of time living with and interacting with the families before gaining the kind of entrée we were hoping to gain in this first interview. I didn't realize then that Cathy, as Carlos's teacher, had a natural entrée into the home, and had an implicit connection with Carlos's parents. I can't emphasize this enough. She was their son's teacher, and so we were treated with a tremendous amount of respect and warmth. I was amazed at how easily and quickly Cathy gained rapport with Mrs. López, and how much the Lópezes opened up to us.

The anthropologist noticed that the teacher held a special status with the family that could help establish the trust necessary for the exchange of information. After making sure that the family understood the purpose of the visit, the teacher started the interview, and was surprised by how forthcoming the mother was with information. Cathy, the teacher, also realized that she was starting to blend her role as a teacher with her new role as researcher; as she gathered new information about the family, their history and activities, she started making connections to instructional activities she wanted to develop—a common experience among the teachers and a key moment in our work.

> **CA:** Once we began the interview, it seemed that Mrs. López was really enjoying talking about her family, her children, and her life. They had told us this in training, that people would open up once they get talking. For instance, when she got on the subject of the difference between Mexican and U.S. schools, she just kept talking, and we let her go with it, and got more out of it than if we had stayed strictly with the questionnaire. But we had to balance that with our agenda, and for the first interview the main thing was to get the family history so we would have a baseline for discussing literacy, parenting, attitudes towards school, and funds of knowledge.
>
> The issue of balancing use of the questionnaire and letting it go to probe on emergent issues was never totally resolved for me. That's why it was helpful to have an anthropologist with me. For example, during one later interview, I was prepared to accept a short answer from a parent and go on to the next question, but at Deborah's urging, I probed further and ended up with good information on religious devotion as a fund of knowledge, something that I would have missed.
>
> **DN:** Eventually, we returned to the questionnaire, moving on to discuss the family's labor history.
>
> **CA:** As we progressed asking questions about family background and labor history, I began to relax, although I was concerned with whether I was getting enough material that would be useful later in developing a learning module. Actually I never totally disengaged from my role as a teacher and when such things as cross-border trade came up, I thought this would be a great topic to use in my classroom and I tried to figure out how I could capture this resource for teaching.

SEEING BEYOND STEREOTYPES

An important aspect of the teachers' participation in the household research became the more sophisticated understanding they developed about the children and their experiences. There is much teachers do not know about their students or families that could be immediately helpful in the classroom, as the following comments illustrate:

> **DN:** One of the things that we learned about the Lópezes that we didn't know before was the depth of the multicultural experiences their son, Carlos, had in cross-border activities. It wasn't just a superficial experience for him.

CA: Half of the children in my classroom are international travelers and yet this experience is not recognized or valued because they are Mexican children going to Mexico. Anglo children may spend a summer in France and we make a big deal about it, by asking them to speak to the class about their summer activities! Carlos spends summers in Magdalena, Mexico, yet he's probably rarely been asked to share his experiences with anyone.

His visits to Mexico have been more than 1- or 2-day visits. He spends most summers there. He and his brothers are first-generation born in the U.S. but their social networks extend into Magdalena. His family's cross-border activities extend back generations. His parents were born in Magdalena. His father began coming to the U.S. during his summer vacations, when he worked as a migrant worker in California. He eventually decided to stay here permanently and moved with some friends to Tucson.

Carlos's father's parents are involved in the import/export of major appliances between Sonora and Arizona and there are regular visits of relatives back and forth. His dad says they really live in both places. I'll read some of the notes from my interview with Carlos that describe his life in Sonora:

"In Magdalena he and his family stay with different relatives. When he is there he plays with his cousins. They are allowed to wander freely around most of the town. They like to play hide-and-seek and sometimes they are taken places by older relatives. They like to visit a pharmacy that one of his aunts owns and one of his older cousins is married to someone who works on three ranches."

"Sometimes he goes to visit the ranches. Once he got to ride a horse. One thing he likes to do when he visits a ranch is play with bow and arrow. He says his cousin's husband will give him and his cousins a thousand pesos if they find the arrows." Carlos also reports playing cards when he visits Magdalena and that he has gone fishing near Santa Ana with older cousins and an uncle.

DN: It is precisely through information of these kinds of social activities that we identify funds of knowledge that can be used in the classroom to help improve his academic development.

CA: Furthermore, because of these experiences, Carlos and many of my other students show a great deal of interest in economic issues, because they have seen the difference in the two countries, in immigration law, but also in laws in general; they would ask me why there are so many laws here that they don't have in Mexico. These children have had the background experiences to explore in-depth issues that tie in with a sixth grade curriculum, such as the study of other countries, different forms of government, economic systems, and so on.

Carlos himself is involved in what we could call international commerce. He's a real entrepreneur. Not only does he sell candy from Mexico but, according to his mother, he'll sell anything he can get anyone to buy, for example, bike parts. His mother says Carlos got the idea to sell candy from other children.

We didn't uncover this only through questioning but from being there when one child came over to buy some candy from Carlos. He was really proud when he gave us each a piece to take home. Here was Carlos right in front of our eyes enacting a family fund of knowledge. This experience later turned out to be the seed for the learning module I developed for the project, which I will share with you in a few minutes.

The two presenters then discuss how the specific qualitative methods of study influenced not only the nature of the information collected from the family, yielding data about their experiences and funds of knowledge, but provided them with a more sophisticated understanding of the student, his family, and their social world. This more elaborate understanding helped the teacher transform this information into a useful instructional activity.

DN: It is so important to learn how culture is expressed in students' lives, how students live their worlds. We can't make assumptions about these things. Only a part of that child is present in the classroom. We had little idea of what Carlos's life was really like outside of the classroom, and what he knew about the world.

CA: I couldn't have done this work without the anthropological perspective and methodology I learned in the project. Ethnography is different from other forms of educational research. It's open-ended, you go in with an open mind—not prejudging—being totally receptive to everything you hear and see. I didn't want to know only if the parents read stories to their children or how many books they had. I wasn't tallying the hours of TV the children watched either. I feel that I learned much more than that with a greater breadth of knowledge because I was not narrow in my focus.

DN: Carlos is embedded in a home and world, continuous with his family's history and in a culture that is at times discontinuous from that found in school. How to take advantage of these resources in the home? This experience of going into the home, taking off your lens for a moment, trying to step outside your assumptions to see Carlos on his own terms, in his own turf, is one way to do this.

We learned a lot during these three interviews that fractured stereotypes that we had heard others say about these households. Carlos's parents not only care, but have a very strong philosophy of child-rearing that is supportive of education, including learning English. They have goals of a university education for their children, instill strong values of respect for others, and possess a tremendous amount of pride and a strong sense of identity—in addition to the more practical knowledge in which their children share on a regular basis. These values are not unique to this family. All of the households we visited possess similar values and funds of knowledge that can be tapped for use in the classrooms.

But the workshops and fieldwork experience are just the beginning. There's the extensive reflection and writing up stage, the record of the experience, from which we read segments a few minutes ago. This reflection process is not to be underemphasized, for it is not just what people say that matters, but the subtext, and our observations and interpretations; for example, the way Mrs. López's eyes lit up when she showed us the trophy her son had won in the science fair, Mr. López's pride in his philosophy of child-rearing, and so forth. And then there is the translation of this material into viable lessons for the classroom.

The presenters pointed out that it is the teacher, not the anthropologist, who is ultimately the bridge between the students' world, theirs and their family's funds of knowledge, and the classroom experience. However, teachers need not work alone. They can form part of study groups, social networks, that will provide the needed assistance and support in analyzing information and in elaborating instructional practices.

EXPERIMENTING WITH PRACTICE

The presentation concluded with a description by Cathy, the teacher, of the development of a theme study, or learning module, as we called them, based on information gathered from the households. Notice the emphasis on the inquiry process, on the students becoming active learners, and on strategically using their social contacts outside the classroom to access new knowledge for the development of their studies. Here is her summary:

CA: After we had completed our field work and written field notes for all our interviews, it truly was left up to us, the teachers, to decide how we were going to use the knowledge we had gained about our students and their families. We spent 2 days with consultants and everyone else who had been working on the project and brainstormed and bounced ideas off each other. I worked with two other teachers from my school and together we developed a learning module with a rather unusual theme—candy. You've already heard that Deborah and I witnessed Carlos selling Mexican candy to a neighbor. The fifth grade teacher I worked with also uncovered this theme. He interviewed a parent who is an expert at making all kinds of candy. In a truly collaborative effort, we outlined a week's worth of activities we could use in our classes.

To focus students' thinking on the theme, I had students free associate with the topic. I recorded their ideas on a large piece of white paper on the board. Next, I had them come up with a definition for the word candy. This was not as easy as you might think. They'd mentioned gum and sunflower seeds while brainstorming, which I wasn't sure should be included in this category. But I didn't tell them this because I wanted them to use their analytical skills to come up with their own definition.

Actually, they got stuck deciding if salty things like *picalimón* and *saladitos* (Mexican snacks that include salt and spices) were candy. Next they categorized all the candies they'd mentioned.

After that we used the KWL method to organize our unit. For those not familiar with this method, we used a three-column chart. In the first column, we recorded everything the students "know" about the topic. In the next column, we recorded what they "want" to know. The third column, the "L" column, is to be used at the end of the unit to record what the students learned during the study. After working with the project consultant, I added another W at the end of the chart—a fourth column, something new for me—to record new questions students had, to help them see that learning is ongoing, that it does not consist of discrete chunks of knowledge. We then surveyed and graphed favorite candies of the class.

With the assistance of the teacher, the students pursued their interests by focusing their inquiry on a narrower topic and by specifying a research question. As is common in research, the class relied on all their resources, including the expertise of one of the parents, to elaborate their work. Notice, however, that this was not a typical parent visit to correct or sort papers; the purpose of the parent's visit was to contribute intellectually to the students' academic activity. This parent, in effect, became a cognitive resource for the students and teacher in this classroom (see also Moll & Greenberg, 1990).

CA: Next, we became a research team. Students chose one of the questions they'd generated to answer. They chose, "What ingredients are used in the production of candy?" I framed the pursuit of the answer using the version of the scientific method we use in schools. After writing their question on the board, the students developed a procedure to answer their question; then they hypothesized what ingredients they'd find on the candy labels they brought in the next day.

The next day, after students had made a class list of ingredients in the candy samples they'd brought in, they graphed the frequency of occurrence of the ingredients they'd found. Then I had them divide the ingredients into two lists—one of ingredients they'd found in the Mexican candy samples and one of ingredients they'd found in U.S. candy samples. We all learned something that day. We were all surprised to see that fewer ingredients are used in Mexican candies and that they don't use artificial flavors or coloring—just vegetable dyes and real fruit.

The next day one of the parents of my students, Mrs. Rodríguez, came in to teach us how to make *pipitoria*, a Mexican candy treat. This turned out to be the highlight of our unit. Before she came in that morning, the students divided up to make advertising posters and labels for the candy because we were going to sell what we made at the school talent show. When Mrs. Rodríguez arrived, she became the teacher. While the candy was cooking, she talked to the class for over an hour and taught all of us not only how to make different kinds of candy but also such things as the difference in U.S. and Mexican food consumption and production, nutritional value of candy, and more. My respect and awe of Mrs. Rodríguez grew by leaps and bounds that morning. Finally, the students packaged and priced their candy.

The unit concludes, somewhat prematurely, as the teacher notes, with the students summarizing and reflecting upon their work, and by identifying further topics for future research. The teacher, in turn, has become a "mediator," providing strategic assistance that would facilitate the students' inquiry and work.

CA: The last day of the unit, students wrote summaries of what they'd learned and we recorded it on our chart. Then they began to formulate new questions. Examples of their new questions are: "What is candy like in Africa?" and "What candy do they eat in China?" As you can see, if we'd had time to continue our unit; our studies would have taken us all over the world. We did, however, cover many areas of the curriculum in one short week—math, science, health, consumer education, cross-cultural practices, advertising, and food production.

From the questions the students came up with alone, we could have continued investigating using innumerable research and critical thinking skills for a considerable part of the year. If we had continued this type of activity all year, by the end we would have been an experienced research team and my role would have been to act as facilitator helping the students answer their own questions.

CONCLUSION

We have presented a single aspect of a broader, multidimensional research project: teachers as co-researchers using qualitative methods to study household knowledge, and drawing upon this knowledge to develop a participatory pedagogy. The insights gleaned from approaching the homes ethnographically, and adapting the method to the educational goals of the project, were a result of a genuine teacher–researcher (in this case, anthropologist) collaboration. We have learned that it is feasible and useful to have teachers visit households for research purposes. These are neither casual visits nor school-business visits, but visits in which the teachers assume the role of the learner, and in doing so, help establish a fundamentally new, more symmetrical relationship with the parents of the students.

This relationship can become the basis for the exchange of knowledge about family or school matters, reducing the insularity of classrooms, and contributing to the academic content and lessons. It can also become, as illustrated above, the catalyst for forming research teams among the students to study topics of interest to them, or important to the teacher, or for achieving curricular goals.

Our concept of funds of knowledge is innovative, we believe, in its special relevance to teaching, and contrasts with the more general term "culture," or

culture-sensitive curriculum—instructional practices that rely on use of folklore-type displays and storytelling, arts, crafts, and dance and may provide only a superficial use of diverse students' cultural experiences and knowledge

with the concept of a **"culture-sensitive curriculum,"** and with the latter's reliance on folkloric displays, such as storytelling, arts, crafts, and dance performance. Although the term "funds of knowledge" is not meant to replace the anthropological concept of culture, it is more precise for our purposes because of its emphasis on strategic knowledge and related activities essential in households' functioning, development, and well-being. It is specific funds of knowledge pertaining to the social, economic, and productive activities of people in a local region, not "culture" in its broader, anthropological sense, that we seek to incorporate strategically into classrooms.

Indispensable in this scenario are the research tools—the theory, qualitative methods of study, and ways of analyzing and interpreting data. These are what allow the teachers (and others) to assume, authentically, the role of researchers in household or classroom settings. They are also what help redefine the homes of the students as rich in funds of knowledge that represent important resources for educational change.

We are currently starting the next phase of study, involving teachers in five different schools serving both Mexican and Native-American students.[5] The research design remains the same: developing our understanding of households and classrooms and collaborating with teachers in conducting the research and in developing academically rigorous instructional innovations. Now, however, we have teachers with research experience helping us organize the study groups, developing further the methodology for doing the home investigations, conceptualizing and implementing promising instructional activities, and evaluating the project. In this new study we plan to include principals, as co-researchers, and parents in the study groups, as an attempt to rethink our respective roles and develop our collective funds of knowledge about teaching and learning.

One of the hallmarks of qualitative research is that strategies often evolve within the process of doing. As teachers, administrators, and parents become more aware of the linkages that can be created utilizing this methodology, and become comfortable with the redefinition of roles that it entails, new strategies of implementation will emerge that are driven by the needs of the target community. As the research unfolds, the constitutive nature of the inquiry process becomes apparent, as teacher, researcher, parent, child, and administrator jointly create and negotiate the form and function of the exploration.

NOTES

1. Our sample includes households of students in the project teachers' classrooms, as well as students from other classrooms, but in the same general community. In total, including previous projects, we have observed in approximately 100 homes.

2. For similar ideas regarding the development of teacher "labs" or activity settings, see, for example, Berliner (1985), Laboratory of Comparative Human Cognition (1982), and

Tharp and Gallimore (1988). The creation of study groups is also a common practice among whole-language teachers and researchers (see Goodman, 1989).

3. Field notes are generally descriptive to provide context and background information, whereas interviews, usually based on a questionnaire, focus on topics of specific relevance to the project, such as the participation of children in a household activity. In the project described herein, all notes were prepared and coded using word processing programs, and lap-top computers were made available to the teachers. Anthropologists and graduate students assisted the teachers in interviewing, and provided feedback on the consistency, completeness, and depth of the field notes. Given the constraints on teachers' times, we recommend that they obtain release time from teaching to conduct observations and interviews, and record and edit field notes. Release time, we should point out, is routinely granted for other purposes, such as participating in inservice workshops, so it very well could be used for documenting the knowledge base of the students' homes.

4. The presentation (August 5, 1991) was before approximately 200 principals and other administrators (including the new superintendent) of the local school district.

5. One of our goals for 1992-1993 is to develop the project in other regions of the country through similar collaborative ventures. For example, we are currently piloting an initial teacher-anthropologist component to collect baseline and background data on target schools and communities, including demography, economy, migration, educational achievement levels, and community resources, before developing questionnaires and conducting home interviews in different regions of the country. We are also developing assessment procedures to document project success, especially the academic benefits to the students, in order to improve our accountability to the schools and communities in which we work.

CONNECTING FUNDS OF KNOWLEDGE TO YOUR CLASSROOM . . .

1. Conduct research in the neighborhoods surrounding your school. What resources are available? What funds of knowledge? Design a unit of study that will integrate these funds of knowledge. Involve the students in your planning.

2. Plan a family literacy night for your classroom's students and parents. Choose a theme that will build on the strengths of families. Involve the parents in teaching and sharing their skills and resources with one another and with their children.

REFERENCES

Berliner, D.C. (1985). Laboratory settings and the study of teacher education. *Journal of Teacher Education, 36*(6), 2–8.

Goodman, Y. (1989). Roots of the whole-language movement. *The Elementary School Journal, 92,* 113–127.

Greenberg, J.B. (1989, April). *Funds of knowledge: Historical constitution, social distribution, and transmission.* Paper presented at the annual meetings of the Society for Applied Anthropology, Santa Fe; NM.

Heyman, J. (1990). The emergence of the waged life course on the United States-Mexico border. *American Ethologist, 17,* 348–359.

Keefe, S., & Padilla, A. (1987). *Chicano ethnicity.* Albuquerque: University of New Mexico Press.

La Fontaine, J. (1986). An anthropological perspective on children in social worlds. In M. Richards & P. Light (Eds.), *Children of social worlds; Development in a social context* (pp. 10–30). Cambridge, U.K.: Polity Press.

Laboratory of Comparative Human Cognition. (1982). A model system for the study of learning difficulties. *The Quarterly Newsletter of the Laboratory of Comparative Human Cognition, 4*(3), 39–66.

Martínez, O.J. (1988). *Troublesome border.* Tucson: The University of Arizona Press.

McDermott, R.P. (1987). The explanation of minority school failure, again. *Anthropology and Education Quarterly, 18,* 361–364.

Moll, L.C., & Díaz, S. (1987). Change as the goal of educational research. *Anthropology and Education Quarterly, 18,* 300–311.

Moll, L.C., & Greenberg, J. (1990). Creating zones of possibilities: Combining social contexts for instruction. In L.C. Moll (Ed.), *Vygotsky and education* (pp. 319–348). Cambridge, U.K.: Cambridge University Press.

Moll, L.C., Vélez-Ibáñez, C., Greenberg, J., Whitmore, K., Saavedra, E., Dworin, J., & Andrade, R. (1990). *Community knowledge and classroom practice: Combining resources for literacy instruction* (OBEMLA Contract No. 300-87-0131). Tucson: University of Arizona, College of Education and Bureau of Applied Research in Anthropology.

Tapia, J. (1991). *Cultural reproduction: Funds of knowledge as survival strategies in the Mexican American community.* Unpublished doctoral dissertation, University of Arizona, Tucson.

Taylor, D., & Dorsey-Gaines, C. (1988). *Growing up literate: Learning from inner city families.* Portsmouth, NH: Heinemann.

Tharp, R., & Gallimore, R. (1988). *Rousing minds to life: Teaching, learning, and schooling in social context.* Cambridge, U.K.: Cambridge University Press.

Vélez-Ibáñez, C.G. (1988). Networks of exchange among Mexicans in the U.S. and Mexico: Local level mediating responses to national and international transformations. *Urban Anthropology, 17*(1), 27–51.

Vélez-Ibáñez, C.G. (1993). U.S. Mexicans in the borderlands: Being poor without the underclass. In J. Moore & R. Rivera (Eds.), *Issues of Hispanic poverty and underclass.* Los Angeles: Sage.

Vélez-Ibáñez, C.G., & Greenberg, J. (1989). *Formation and transformation of funds of knowledge among U.S. Mexican households in the context of the borderlands.* Paper presented at the annual meeting of the American Anthropological Association, Washington, DC.

Vélez-Ibáñez, C., Moll, L.C., Gonzalez, N., & Neff, D. (1991). *Promoting learning and educational delivery and quality among "at risk" U. S. Mexican and Native American elementary school children in Tucson, Arizona: A pilot project.* Final Report to W.K. Kellogg Foundation. Tucson: University of Arizona, Bureau of Applied Research in Anthropology.

CHAPTER 18

CRITICAL LITERACY: CRISES AND CHOICES IN THE CURRENT ARRANGEMENT

DOUG MORRIS

". . . future disasters . . . if we simply stay the current course . . . will keep coming with ever more ferocious intensity."

—Naomi Klein (2007, p. 47)

". . . it is the end of the world that is in question here . . ."

—Frederic Jameson (2003, p. 65)

THINK ABOUT CRITICAL LITERACY . . .

1. How, in this piece, is the relationship between the political nature of pedagogy and pedagogical nature of politics explored, interrogated, and revealed?

2. Henry Giroux has suggested that if education continues to participate in reproducing the present, we may be participating in reproducing a present that eliminates the future. How does this idea link to the call for extending our notions of literacy in this piece?

3. Following upon question 2, why does this piece regularly refer to a "people-centered" or "people-first" mode of literacy and pedagogy, and what can we learn from this about the current arrangement, and what needs to be altered?

Put succinctly, *critical literacy* is about creating conditions for and pursuing processes committed to learning and teaching what is needed to build and continue in a struggle to create a better world. Critical literacy sees a people-first, better world rooted in participatory democratic values that promote and solidify:

social justice; critical inquiry and a critical mentality that questions assumptions, interrogates power and authority, cultivates doubt, and is suspicious of absolutes; respect for others; intellectual and imaginative development; equality of rights, duties, and conditions; substantive freedom in which there exists the possibilities, knowledge, understanding, and resources for choosing among meaningful alternatives; substantive equity; environmental justice and rationality; production carried out to satisfy human needs and nourish human capabilities; popular sovereignty; the recognition that decisions made and policies implemented that impact the public should be under public control and management;

critical consciousness—the ongoing development of our ability to articulate and act on the complex relationships between knowledge, experience, reflection, and engagement

concern for the collective good; a central linking of theory and practice; **critical consciousness** connected to commitments to mutual concern, understanding, support, and assistance; a tolerance of differences that also builds unity and solidarity grounded in a recognition of our common humanity as well as our interdependence and interconnectedness; peaceful and nonexploitive domestic and international relations; a basic willingness to critique and challenge those social relations, institutional structures, cultural productions, and ideological formations that are hostile or antagonistic toward the preceding values, projects, and processes.

Fundamental to this critical literacy project is a striving to enhance our understanding of human needs and abilities in order to meet the needs and nourish the abilities in ways that assist in realizing our full potential and developing our multiple individualities as critical, participatory, moral, and political beings capable of building and "encouraging new cultural formations, institutional structures, and social relations of production" (McLaren, 2007, p. 208), distribution, allocation, and consumption organized and arranged through participatory associations of worker, citizen, and community councils. As such, critical literacy aims to encourage learners and teachers to investigate and analyze "power relationships inherent in language use" (Behrman, 2006, p. 490), visual images, cultural productions, and material and ideological social arrangements, "recognize that language is [and texts are] not neutral" (p. 490), that is, language, texts, culture, and social arrangements are always political in the profound sense of *the political*, or having the capacity to impact widely and vitally social life, human actions, and understanding, and shape choices and opportunities of the public. "Furthermore, [critical literacy urges that teachers and learners must] confront their own values, [conceptions and beliefs] in the production and reception of language" (p. 490) while working to broaden conceptions of the boundaries around language and text

public pedagogy—a term coined by Henry Giroux pointing to the multiple sites in society and culture in which public knowledge, values, identities, and understanding is constructed, conditioned and directed

in order to understand how, why, and for what reasons values, attitudes, beliefs, aspirations, desires, identities, and identifications are constructed through various **public pedagogical** sets of cultural and social formations. In examining the relationships between language, power, and texts surrounding public pedagogies, inside and outside classrooms, critical literacy asks, with the goal of "gaining critical consciousness and participating in the transformation of society" (Beck, 2005, p. 393): In whose interests, in what direction, with what visions and goals, under whose control and management, following what paths, and with what likely consequences are pedagogical and social projects carried forth? In other words, critical literacy requires the asking of difficult questions and the linking of complex interrelationships, not just at a theoretical level, but at a political and practical level, questions and relationships that help us critique, understand, and redirect the often highly destructive options, paths, and processes that have directed humanity over the last 70 years or so.[1] This includes questions that contribute to qualitative transformations at all levels of life that will resolve many of the political, economic, and social crises and challenges we now confront. One of the more difficult questions is, "How do we address the senses of futility, alienation, and pessimism that too often stand in the way of the kinds of transformational and sustainable thinking and acting called for in response and resistance to current arrangements?"

At the core of any serious discussion of and dialogue around critical literacy are urgent and challenging questions, concerns and actions regarding youth and the future, which must include insights into where we are and visions of where we want to go, socially and individually, inside and outside the spaces of formal education. Critical literacy recognizes that things are the way they are because they got that way, not because they have to be that way, knows that the future will be the way it is because it gets that way, not because it has to be that way (while comprehending how particular realities make particular outcomes more likely than others), and is, therefore, opposed to any form of fatalism, or what Freire (2001, p.70) calls "**finishedness**," or end-of-history narratives, in terms of human social development. This raises a number of basic questions: Why are things the way they are? How did they get to be that way? How do we want things to be in the future? How, given where we are, will we make them that way? This **problematizing** approach, which examines complex interrelationships, introduces human agency into any pedagogical practice and recognizes that "if we intend to speak of the future, then we must examine those circumstances of the past and present," and the past and present includes us (Shannon, 2000, p. 93). Critical literacy exhorts a form of human agency that perceives humans as conditioned by **interpenetrating** forces of history and culture, economics and politics, biology and society, and being and becoming and as capable of producing

finishedness—a term central to Freire's "pedagogy of freedom." Being always "unfinished," opens up possibilities for individual and social agency along with meaningful forms of participation in constructing the worlds in which we live and interact. Unfinishedness points to the dialectical relationships between our being and our becoming in that our "being" conditions our "becoming" and our "becoming" conditions our "being"

problematizing—the idea that the future is not fixed but a problem to be addressed

interpenetrating—a concept that helps us think beyond binaries or false dichotomies; feedback loops that create interpenetrating influences and transformations between our biological selves and social selves; the interpenetrating response is, we are no less biological for being social, and no less social for being biological

---

[1]For example, from a *critical literacy* perspective one might ask the question, "What is the relationship between natural gas extracted from the earth in the Middle East, blue-baby warnings in Des Moines, Iowa, and suffocating fish in the Gulf of Mexico?" See Pollan, (2006, Chapter 1), for further elaboration.

and positively transforming the conditions and circumstances in which we live, learn, teach, and struggle.

This critical literacy approach extends, and at the same time refocuses, the notion of production beyond simply that which occurs in workplaces or factories to crucially include all activities that contribute to and nurture human development. In other words, the goals and consequences of production are the social production of human beings to which we can attach the questions, "What kinds of human beings are we producing, and what kinds of human beings are we capable of producing?" The ideas and actions that inform the goals and paths undertaken in the developmental production of human beings must themselves, of course, be produced and are thus an indispensable component of any critical literacy pedagogy for the pedagogical projects will condition and characterize the ideas and actions that direct production. Societies are characterized, and conditioned, by the goals and pathways that inform and guide production processes. This includes, crucially, the pedagogical production processes that play vital roles in developing our notions and realities of "what is" and "what ought to be," of what we know and what we don't know, of what we believe is possible and what seems impossible, of the past and future, of whether we see ourselves as active participants in shaping history or merely passive recipients of and spectators on history, of what we find exciting and what we find boring, of what we view as beautiful and what we see as ugly, of how we conceive democracy, social justice, equality, economics, politics, and so on, of how we view the role of reading and literacy inside and outside formal education, of whether we see education as primarily a reproductive social enterprise or one dedicated to transformation, and how we think about and act on desires, dreams, and concepts of obligations to others. It is insufficient, however, merely to have dreams, desires, and concepts of a better society in which notions of solidarity, equality, and **democracy** develop; it is also essential to develop the willingness to critique the past and present (including self-reflection and self-criticism) and, when necessary, rupture the logic that drives current injustices, dehumanization, and inequalities and stifles the full and creative development of human beings. To adopt critical literacy's position in opposition to social suicide is not motivated by the biases of any political ideology, but by sanity, rationality, and basic human decency. To pursue critical literacy's commitment to a better future grounded in substantive economic, political, and cultural democratic practices and processes is not to surrender to a particular political ideology, but to honor a fundamental human value.

democracy—as used herein, not to be confused with corporate managed electoral forms of "democracy," but more substantive forms in which an informed, involved, inclusive and energized public is capable of meaningfully and effectively participating in, contributing to, learning from, and shaping the policies and programs that impact public life, individually and collectively

Our options and realities, limitations, and possibilities cannot be understood outside the framework of the crises and challenges we face (many starkly foreboding), nor can the tasks of production and human development, and that means we must perceive, understand, and critically address the role that militarism and its wholesale trauma, brutality, and destruction, its bleeding of vital public resources, not to mention its threats of species annihilation, has performed in defining, directing, and conditioning our recent history. There is no plausible reason to delude ourselves on these matters of human suffering, threats, and survival, and there are strong incentives to confront and overcome them. Confronting them requires widespread intellectual freedom, the courage to act on that freedom, the willingness to both encourage and persist in the work of critical inquiry, and a commitment to the possibilities of a **people-first** and better future. Overcoming will require all this, plus a general persistence in mobilizing people to collectively fight back in multiple ways against tyranny and injustice. "The question is not whether resistance to these indignities should occur but how best to express it" (Kolko, 2006a, p. 173). The tools, skills, and abilities for realizing a people-first and better world and best expressing our resistance to present injustices cannot be abstracted from the political, cultural, economic, and social processes of struggling to create it. Any stance we take against power and indignities, whether locally, nationally, or globally, must be carefully measured against not taking a stance, because both action and passivity offer sets of hazards and pitfalls. Each day we remain passive promises that the mutually reinforcing crises will make harrowing, ignoble, and deplorable future conditions more likely and far more difficult to reverse and overcome. In short, critical literacy urges that we engage in production projects at all levels of education that nurture the kinds of human development that allow us to break the chains that bind us to the irrational logic of the present dominant systems of social organization. We leave behind the chains of the past through the *activities* of the present on the path toward a better future.

> **people-first**—as opposed to profits first; an option that places the interests of human health and well-being as a priority

In brief, this people-centered mode of examining and carrying out production (seen herein as a critical form of literacy) recognizes a **dialectical relationship** between circumstances, conditions, choices, and the actions or inactions people will engage while encouraging a form of individual and social agency that calls for a commitment to change our circumstances in order to change ourselves; that is, we must create the conditions that encourage and allow students, teachers, and citizens to actively participate in the production of human development by producing the ideas, the goals, and the pathways for self-development and social development grounded in values and projects that honor the dignity, worth, and well-being of humans. Because it is a set of processes immersed in and emerging from a belief in and commitment to meaningful and energized forms of political, cultural, and economic democracy,[2] critical literacy

> **dialectical relationship**—points to the mutually influencing forces at work between and among categories represented as follows: ↔ circumstances ↔ conditions ↔ choices ↔ actions (for example); we make history; history makes us; therefore, we should be very careful about the kind of history we make

---

[2]The core of the critical literacy/critical pedagogy project as expressed through key theorists such as Paulo Freire, Bell Hooks, Henry Giroux, Patrick Shannon, Maxine Greene, Peter McLaren, Donaldo Macedo, and many others, is captured in the subtitle of Paulo Freire's important book *Pedagogy of Freedom: Ethics, Democracy and Civic Courage* (2001). For a revealing discussion of various notions of democracy see Atilio Boron, (2006) "The Truth about Capitalist Democracy," in *Telling the Truth*, Leo Panitch & Colin Keys, eds., New York: Monthly Review Press.

views as fundamental to pedagogical practice the developing of projects, experiences and structures that open up possibilities for meaningful and effective involvement by people in shaping the decisions and conditions that impact their lives, individually and collectively, economically and politically.[3] It is only through such processes of people-centered empowerment, operating at all levels of life, from the school, to the community, to the nation, to the global society, that the goals and paths that shepherd the activities of human production will reflect and realize the goals and paths of the people themselves.

While it should be clear that critical literacy is opposed to forms of determinism and reductionism, it is not so indeterminate or open-ended that it permits an anything-goes approach or a wallowing in hopeless pessimism that is the harbinger of disempowering cynicism and despair, nor is it naively optimistic, for that too can produce stultification and inaction. The former "deterministic" problem is captured in the hopeless neoliberal slogan, "there is no alternative," (Berlinski, 2008) and the latter *naively optimistic* problem is captured in the pop-psych slogans, "things always get better . . . just be happy . . . can't we all just get along." Critical literacy accepts that there is tension in any credible and functional pedagogical or social theory and practice and thus operates within and through ongoing ideological and material struggles between what is and what ought to be, the present world and the possibilities for a new world—that is, a new society that develops through processes that emerge from a present that is lacking in *essential elements* required for fully developing human potential, providing necessary services, and amply satisfying authentic, rather than artificial, human needs across a wide spectrum. Critical literacy perceives how the future is always being constructed on and conditioned by the materials of the past, and those materials include ourselves as well as our blindness and insights, limitations and possibilities, curiosities and boredoms, perceptions and misperceptions, energy and fatigue, dreams and nightmares, freedoms and subjections, needs and abilities, and so on. In these matters, critical literacy reflects the social and political ethic at the root of Dewey's admonition that we must commit to "improving the life we live in common so that the future shall be better than the past" (1966, p. 191).

In an attempt to make sense of and condition these complex relationships as well as provide the essential elements, critical literacy (to paraphrase the title of a book by Paulo Freire) is committed to projects that enhance and expand our abilities to read the world in order to read the word (Freire, 1987); read the word in order to read the world (where *read* carries with it the demand to critique in order to deepen and extend our understanding of our place, options and role in the world); write the word in order to write the world; write the world in order to write the word (where *write* carries with it the need to engage and transform and a strong sense of human agency); right the world in order to right the word; and, right the word in order to right the world, (where *right* is tied to the ways in which

---

[3]Economic democracy is essential to any project of substantive democracy. In essence, anything that is vital to the social life of people is political, and that which is arguably most vital is the way the economy is organized.

we examine, analyze, and explore the interpenetrations between power, language, ideology, culture, and institutions in learning and teaching in order to undertake activities directed toward "righting" the wrongs of the world—and the world always includes us, that is, we cannot abstract ourselves from the world in which we are living and struggling). This combination of reading, writing and righting recognizes on the one hand the **political nature of pedagogy** and the **pedagogical nature of politics**, while its "worldliness" emphasizes our common humanity and, on the other hand, apprehends how at their root, pedagogy and "politics [must be engaged] as the confrontation, of different economic, social, political, ecological, cultural and civilizational options, locally, nationally and globally" (Löwy, 2006, p. 302).

> **political nature of pedagogical and pedagogical nature of political**—how the organization of the world educates us by shaping our knowledge, visions, desires, identities, beliefs, attitudes, and so on, and how various modes of education, always political and moral, act to produce modes of discourse that in turn promote forms of human agency that allow us to reshape the world

The continuing task, therefore, of critical literacy is to develop the processes and projects necessary for fulfilling these missing essential elements intellectually, culturally, materially, and ethically in order to promote the reciprocal flourishing and fulfillment of human development within the context of our commonality amidst differences. The processes and projects operate on the understanding that there is no rational alternative to a profound commitment to both critical thought and informed social action and acknowledges no guarantees for success—but also notes no surety of failure. Absolutes on either side of this ledger result in passivity. Therefore, if we want to have any chance of righting wrongs, addressing society's urgent domestic and international predicaments, making education relevant to building fulfilling social futures, and creating a people-first (rather than profits-first), better world, the only judicious option is the regular application of generous amounts of critical thought, discerning dialogue, and well-informed action. Passivity, while always a possible option, is typically the least attractive choice, for it reduces our chances of success to near zero. We should understand that when "the question today, more than ever before, is [human] survival [. . . then] to the extent [our actions] preempt and constrain those who [. . . continue to] assault civilized society, idealism and action [follow . . .] the logic of self-interest" (Kolko, 2006a, pp. 89, 194).

Critical literacy's discussions and dialogues must be linked to critical conversations and enlightened actions in the domains of education, social responsibility, the future, distributions of power, citizenship, and energized democracy, all categories deserving of rigorous, ongoing, and interpenetrative examination and critique. Furthermore, because critical literacy, as a "reading" project, at its roots is about making sense of the world, along with our place, options, and role in the world (i.e., how we are shaped and how we shape the world—and, again, the world includes ourselves), in order to create a better world, it is essential that critical literacy skills be developed to understand and challenge power relationships in the arenas of economics, politics, ideology, technology, society, and culture and the limitations and possibilities that arise through those understandings and critiques. Here, critical literacy points to the need to expand our notions of literacy to include not only multiple literacies around linguistic, visual, aural, spatial, emotive, and gestural forms (Cope, 1999), but also literacies tied to the complex and interpenetrating relationships between those historical and social formations that have created the world as it is. These complex literacies are crucial to developing counterideologies that open up possibilities for thinking differently, in order to understand differently, in order to act differently, in order to transform our circumstances and, consequent to that, change what we are in the process of constructing alternative social futures. Critical literacy thus engages in pedagogical processes committed to understanding how, what for, and why learning and teaching emerge from and evolve into an interpenetrating vortex of social, political, and economic relations of power, knowledge, and authority. Critical literacy recognizes how schools (as well as learners and teachers) function within sets of unequal and often oppressive power relationships that operate through and out of, and are reflective of, larger material structures, historical tendencies, and ideological formations. Critical literacy works to make clear how a society that refuses to see schools as potential sites for critical, moral and political pedagogical engagements directed toward addressing and vanquishing inequalities and injustices risks losing rather than saving the future; and critical literacy struggles to make evident how a society that fails to both educate learners and teachers to develop the knowledge, skills, and abilities to participate in meaningful and effective ways as engaged citizens, empowered workers, and social agents and also to produce active subjects possessed of a critical mentality has perilously abandoned a set of crucial responsibilities to young people, to a sustainable society grounded in fairness, equality, substantive rights, and solidarity, and to the future.

Critical literacy therefore works to produce the knowledge and skills that allow people to function as social agents who recognize and act on the necessity of making power visible and accountable while interrogating and uprooting unjust and oppressive social relationships as part of an ongoing quest for understanding combined with the ongoing struggle for social justice, human dignity, well-being, and a livable future.

THE BEST ARGUMENT FOR CRITICAL LITERACY

Perhaps the best argument for critical literacy is the necessity of (1) rational discussions and critical dialogues directed toward challenging and overcoming inequalities and injustices; (2) clarity of understanding; and (3) justice and fairness-based, as well as human and environmentally friendly, economic, political, pedagogical and social transformations. That is, the best argument for critical literacy is the multiple crises, grave and growing challenges, and potentially cataclysmic problems the status quo or current power relationships have created and continue to perpetuate—that is, environmental destruction; global climate change; economic and social inequality; militarism; political authoritarianism; exploitation of labor and resources; the privatization of all things public, including public education; corporate tyranny; a profits over people economy; the criminalization of large parts of the population, especially young people of color; food shortages and hunger; attacks on ecological rationality; poverty and the concomitant threats of global disease pandemics; weapons of mass destruction, especially nuclear weapons; state and non-state terrorism; an eroding of civil and human rights; the standardizing, anti-intellectualizing and militarizing of public education; racism; sexism; and so on. In other words, one might argue that the greatest menace to the current (and future) arrangement *is* the current arrangement, and thus it is an ethical, pedagogical, intellectual and political responsibility to critique, challenge, and transform the current arrangement in the interest of human well-being, and, in Gabriel Kolko's words, "human survival," because that "is no longer an abstract notion" (2006a, p. 176).

Part of this process, emerging from critical literacy's imperatives that respect diversity while working for unity and solidarity, will require outlining, on the one hand, rational, plausible, and workable social systems emerging from "a new relation of human kind to nature" that produces "in the process a new [and energetically] democratic and participatory environmental politics," (Panitch & Leys, 2006, p. xiii) and, vitally, on the other hand, cultural formations and critical pedagogies arising from a mobilization of the collective intelligence and imagination as well as courage and commitment, of citizens, teachers, and students, which assist in undoing the authoritarian, violent, and profit-based ideological and structural legacies, damage, and monstrous calamities of the past hundred years.

Current economic, political, and education policies and arrangements in the United States threaten the future in multiple ways by undermining our opportunities for realizing critical literacy's promise of a critically educated and socially active youth as it is linked to the promise of a substantive and participatory democratic culture and society grounded in forms of critical inquiry that combine with acts of empowered social intervention. Envisioning and providing the conditions and experiences for the realization of these promises of youth and democracy is vitally linked to the possibilities and hopes for, and actions toward a better future, a future currently being disabled by the crises and challenges mentioned before. Given these multiple crises and challenges that we now face across a broad range of local, national, and global realities, expanding in the absence of, on the one hand, clear, plausible, and workable visions and goals that provide alternatives and, on the other hand, a sufficiently well-organized opposition to the policies, power relationships, and institutions currently exacerbating most, if not all, of the crises, one must ponder, at a very serious level, how much we as a culture really care about youth and the future. To the extent that we believe education *is* about youth and the future and about social justice and vibrant democracy, it is our responsibility as public intellectuals and public educators to reclaim education space as a site for struggle over ideas and material realities. If it is true that how a society views its responsibility toward youth and the future is reflected in how that society thinks about, educates toward, and acts in the direction of *living into, living through, and living out of* a social contract grounded in substantive and vibrant democratic values, visions, and structures, we must sadly conclude that U.S. culture's responsibility toward youth and the future is sorely and dangerously lacking (Giroux, 2008a).

In a society and culture dominated by profit-driven markets, the market's iron-fisted shadow, and violence against other peoples and nations, not only do the promises of youth, democracy, and the future disappear, but health and social programs are eviscerated; schools are modeled on boot camps, prisons, or malls while teachers play the role of drill instructor, guard, or sales clerk; workers are exploited, are downsized, or disappear; notions of citizenship are swallowed in a sea of commercialism and overconsumption; obesity increases as reflective of the demands of a produce-and-expand in-order-to-profit-and-survive economy; corporations capitalize on children's vulnerabilities; increasing numbers of people on a global scale are "relegated to the human waste of global neoliberalism;" and "young people [all too often are] portrayed as a generation of suspects [against whom the death penalty applies] . . . rather than as a resource for investing in the future (Giroux, 2008b, pp. 84–85). Under such conditions, accompanied by the repressive and hopeless **neoliberal** mantra "there is no alternative," a cruel set of zero-tolerance policies in schools, and an increasing criminalization of young people's behavior, a culture of fatalism, resignation, and cynicism emerges that undermines the possibilities for a vibrant and energized participatory democracy as a foundation for the resolution of the growing crises and challenges. With the increasing commercialization of youth, the evisceration of vital services and programs to support young people, assaults on the rights of youth, the failure to see youth as an investment in the future, and the escalation of youth incarceration, one might arguably conclude that care for children and youth is no longer a priority for adult society under current arrangements in the United States.

> **neoliberalism**—arguably the dominant global ideology, sometimes called "capitalism on steroids" or "market fundamentalism," dedicated to the promotion of private/ corporate wealth, power, privilege, and domination at the expense of environmental and human well-being (and perhaps survival)

Frederic Jameson advises the current arrangements suggest that "it has become easier to imagine the end of the world than the end of capitalism" or better perhaps, easier to "imagine capitalism by way of imagining the end of the world" (2003, p. 76), intimating that if we continue on the present pathways dedicated to expanding commodity boundaries that consume more energy, materials, and resources and thus generate excessive waste, we will not only erode the conditions of existence for future generations, but we will continue to eliminate the future for the present generation of peripheral people who are all too often seen as disposable (Martinez-Alier, 2006). The harsh truth of these statements is harrowing, and it points to the large-scale failure of education at all levels to develop concepts, visions, and mechanisms of alternatives to "the current arrangement," in other words, concepts, visions, and mechanisms directed toward creating egalitarian, peaceful, needs-fulfilling, and capacity-nourishing alternatives to the dominant ideologies and institutions founded in commercialism, militarism, and profiteering.

Without pedagogical projects rooted in critical literacy's injunctions, we are doomed to suffer, in the face of every new crisis under "the current arrangement," restructurings in the interests of concentrated wealth and power, and that promises the already marginalized and dispossessed (not to mention most of us outside the arenas of wealth and power) will suffer more exclusion, oppression, exploitation, poverty and despair. Critical literacy's injunctions include: advance social justice against injustice; call for critical inquiry in opposition to blind obedience; demand respect for others while battling discrimination; support equality of rights and conditions and struggle against inequality; promote substantive freedom against empty notions of freedom; elevate civic courage while antagonistic toward domestication; inspirit **solidarity** and concern for the collective good while battling to overcome forms of hyperindividualism and ruthless competition; expand our notions of and intensify our engagements with multiple literacies; and rigorously devote to the hard work necessary for developing alternative pathways grounded in involved, informed, inclusive, and energized forms of democracy that promote popular participation and civic engagement.

> **solidarity**—a concept and struggled-for reality rooted in shared sympathy community, resistance to injustice and exploitation, sociality, empowerment, and comradeship

Because public education at the primary, secondary, and university levels offers one of the few remaining sites in the culture where the critical skills, knowledge, and abilities for individual and social agency can be engaged, developed, and applied and one of the only sites through which students can develop identities grounded in democratic principles and social responsibility as a way to confront identities constructed through corporate culture that celebrate self-interest, greed, profiteering, ruthless competition, and violence, it is essential for public educators, functioning as public intellectuals, to provide the conditions, dialogues, and experiences in and through which young people can learn that the relationship between knowledge, power, and authority is not necessarily one of oppression, limitation, and domination, but potentially one of emancipation that expands the boundaries of both the possible and permissible. As part of any critical literacy project to recognize the liberatory potential of these complex relationships, students and teachers must learn the importance of their own knowledge, histories, culture, and experiences, how those relationships interpenetrate with work and life inside and outside the classroom, and how knowledge, history, culture, and experience are produced and conditioned within and through various sets of interpenetrating social forces, cultural productions, fields of language, ideological formations, institutional structures, and power relationships, as well as how they are strongly shaped by the social relations of production, distribution, allocation, consumption, and work to understand how these multiple relationships can become meaningful in ways that open up opportunities for critical (i.e., analytical, reflective, urgent, positional, and discerning) interrogations, reflections, and interventions on a path toward social, structural, and individual transformation.

Henry Giroux calls this mode of complex reading of the world and multiple texts "civic literacy," in that it is a project that revolves around and evolves out of a moral and political commitment to "enlarging the realm of critique and affirming the social; it is also about public responsibility, the struggle over democratic public life and the importance of critical education in a democratic society." (Giroux, 2009, ¶ 4). "Civic literacy" locates vital matters of social justice at the core of discourses around learning and teaching. It is in and through such lived and active projects that students and teachers, at all levels, can critically interrogate "assumptions, values and beliefs" (Bartolomé, 2007, p. 263) and examine how dominant ideologies and material relations condition and "inform, often unconsciously, their perceptions and actions" (p. 263). These critical literacy–based interrogations open opportunities for teachers and learners to become a constructive and transformative force for challenging current arrangements, evaluating and working to overcome the prerogatives of corporate power, and critically engaging institutional and interpersonal relations that engender and advance material, structural and symbolic violence and thus provide tools and inspirations that fuel both the desire and the need "to reimagine, re-enchant and recreate the world rather than [merely] adapt to it" (McLaren, 2007, p. 303).

In an age of "top-down class warfare" (Krugman, 2005, ¶ 1), increasing social and economic inequality and its concomitant poverty, homelessness, job eradication, and despair; the growing commodification of all aspects of life that reduces citizenship to consumption practices while social engagement is engulfed in hypercompetitive media spectacles; and the creeping and foreboding militarization of the globe, it is essential that critical literacy projects reexamine and take seriously the moral and political potential of a social contract rooted in notions and realities of mutual support, social justice, concern for the collective good, and investments in youth as well as global peace and international solidarity. "Taking the social contract seriously" demands "a willingness to fight for the rights of children, enact reforms that invest in their future, and provide the educational conditions necessary for [youth] to be critical citizens" (Giroux, 2008a, p. 88). Addressing ideas of a social contract in the midst of growing crises and challenges on a domestic and international scale requires probing and difficult questions about what kinds of pedagogical conditions and literacy experiences are required to ensure we save rather than lose the future. Just as "the Federal Budget . . . reflects our nation's deepest priorities," in other words, "[priorities that express] far less regard for our nation's children than for the richest most powerful Americans, and far more interest in waging war than in waging peace" (Edelman, 2008, ¶ 1), it is also true that our dreams, visions, and ideas about—and commitments to—the future reflect moral and political obligations to investments in and concerns for young people. Failing to take on the political obligations and social commitments to ensure a decent future will guarantee we continue down our current dangerous path, in which the greater evil is working to cancel out the possibilities for expressions and manifestations of the greater good.

Present trends suggest an undermining of both youth and the future reflected in the promotion of policies and the passing of legislation that eliminate crucial health, social, and education programs for young people. The current federal budget "reveals . . . a failure [to protect] the well-being of children" (Edelman, 2008, ¶ 2) by reducing vital health, juvenile justice, and education programs (including a request to eliminate 47 programs from the U.S. Department of Education) that serve the needs and interests of young people (primarily those who need assistance most), while at the same time calling for huge increases (again) for military spending and extensions of tax cuts for the wealthy and privileged ($2 trillion in lost revenue over the next 10 years). Nearly 18 million children live in poverty in the United States (according to the "official poverty line," significantly more using a more honest assessment of poverty), 9.4 million children lack health insurance, and 14 million children attend deteriorating schools every day (Shierholz, 2009). In addition, children are immersed in a culture in which notions of masculinity are produced through gruesome reveling in gun culture, constant bombardments of hypercompetitive sports, U.S. commitments to massive Pentagon spending, and spectacles of militarism and violence that regularly circulate through the various forms of corporate public pedagogy. Furthermore, "The privatization of public services and functions manifests the steady evolution of corporate power into a political form," and as a result "the remaining democratic elements of the state and its populist programs are being systematically dismantled" (Wolin, 2008, p. 284). In short, the public voice is being silenced as democracy, a basic human value, is being eliminated.

How we live into the future and whether there are possibilities for meaningful forms of democracy in that future is vitally linked to how we educate youth in the present, and present inclinations suggest that youth are now submerged in material and ideological pedagogical spheres that subvert the future rather than provide materials for creating it in sustainable, fair, and just directions. Critical literacy urges that we view education as a public rather than a private sphere if we are going to educate toward a meaningful democratic and sustainable future. Public education must engage in practices and projects dedicated to promoting the public good and public well-being, that is, the greater good, as well as public participation in shaping policies and managing how we live with one another in society. If education is surrendered to private power, schools will be reduced to training factories in which people will learn what is necessary to enable them to serve and service the interests and imperatives of society's dominant institutions, that is, the neoliberal imperatives of wealth, power, privilege, domination, and violence. Schools critical literacy argues, must instead be envisioned and realized as a public good and their legitimacy measured on how well they educate students to function as critical citizens and social agents inspired by alternative modes of social organization that create possibilities for building a better world. Schools must be sites where learners and teachers develop projects, culture, and languages that forge relationships between school life and public life. This includes linking present realities with future possibilities, social responsibility with social struggles, and individual flourishing with the imperatives of democracy.

Critical literacy attempts to make clear how education, under the guise of accountability schemes, is presently being reduced to domesticating factories of high-stakes testing linked to standardized assessment and curriculum that undermines possibilities for producing a substantive democratic culture and solidaristic society in numerous ways. For example, it "deskills teachers" by eliminating their abilities to creatively participate in the process and project of education and to engage in the radical contextualization that links what, why, and how educators teach to the knowledge, histories, and experiences teachers and learners bring to pedagogical space. In short, teachers (and students) lose their critical voice while they are distanced from the political and moral process and project of pedagogy, and democratic forms that serve and represent public interests and concerns suffer. High-stakes testing reduces learning to the lowest common denominator and, consequently, stifles students' ability to develop as critically informed citizens capable of making sense of the world outside and inside the self, essential for a functioning democracy. At best, students learn to follow rules and instructions but do not develop the interrogative tools and critical skills to evaluate whether the rules and instructions are useful, employable or legitimate (Shannon, 2007). Furthermore, it undermines the development of the sort of critical mentality necessary for a burgeoning democracy. In addition, it trains students to be docile, whereas an operational democracy demands involved, active, and vibrant citizens capable of meaningful engagement and effective participation in managing the society and shaping the future. Beyond that, high-stakes programs, combined with larger forms of corporate public pedagogy, also prepare a domesticated population of obedient consumers trained in what is necessary to maximize their consumption potential in an increasingly commercialized culture. Critical literacy would educate people to maximize their citizenship potential in an increasingly democratized culture and society geared to a future dedicated to visions of security reflective of human well-being, fulfillment, and flourishing, emerging not from a culture of fear, incarceration, and a flood of high-tech weaponry, but from a society organized around decent health, universal healthcare, vibrant public education, sustainable nutrition, creative opportunities, intellectual development, solidarity, and an empowered citizenry.

Sinking in: Crisis and Change

> *". . . the world has reached the most dangerous point in recent, or perhaps all of, history."*
> —Gabriel Kolko, *The Age of War* (2006b)

Neoliberal guru Milton Freidman (1982), in his influential tome *Capitalism and Freedom,* advised that "only a crisis—actual or perceived—produces real change. When that crisis occurs, the actions that are taken depend on the ideas that are lying around" (p. ix). That we currently face a growing number of monumental crises and foreboding challenges of a critical nature, ranging, as noted, from global climate change, to global militarism, to growing economic and social inequality, to creeping authoritarianism in the political sphere, and so on, is hardly in dispute; the most visible ideas "lying around" are unfortunately *not* designed for addressing and overcoming these crises and challenges. In fact, they are at the core of the crises, and more substantive ideas and visions, views, and pathways for alternatives to the current dominant ideologies and structures are sadly in short supply in the wider culture. Hence, there is an urgent need for and relevance of critical literacy to, on the one hand, critique the quantitative changes that regularly occur and that point more and more frequently to a gloomy and dehumanized future and, on the other hand, produce the qualitative changes necessary for advancing alternative goals and pathways through incorporating and furthering alternative practices, processes, projects, and structures in order to reenchant our humanity. It is clear how over the last 30 years of neoliberal assault and the last 60 years of increasing militarism, there has been a demolition of cultural forms, public discourses, social institutions, and noncommodified and nonmilitarized spheres vital for developing the language, ideas, and culture directed toward alternatives growing out of a dedication to public well-being, the common good, critical learning, social responsibility, and meaningfully informed and inclusive, energized, and enthused democratic politics. Absent concepts and motivations emerging from solidarity, civic responsibility, and critical thought and a clear notion of our interconnectedness and interdependence, the political sphere is robbed of its public functions and becomes at best a formal mechanism for reentrenching the current arrangement of private power and ownership structures and at worst a commercial and militarized sphere in which the public loses its capacity to dissent and resist while suffering under a growing obeisance to forms of power that rapaciously pursue profits and hegemony at the expense of a common-good centered and sustainable future.

What critical literacy makes evident, as part of its commitment to languages of hope, critique, and possibility, as well as it explorations of multiple texts, situations, and positions, is that the global public has *not* surrendered to the neoliberal and militarizing assault on public space, the public mind, public-oriented legislation, and the public good. Across the globe, workers, peasants, intellectuals, students, artists, musicians, community organizers, educators, the World Social Forum, and others unwilling to allow all aspects of existence to be bought and sold in the capitalist market have resisted and challenged the "treatment of human beings as so much garbage" by corporations, "the despotism of the capitalist workplace," the international political and business institutions that undermine the possibilities for creating "an economy and society at the service of humanity" along with "the creation of an environment that protects the earth's life-support systems" (Lebowitz, 2006, p. 12).

At a time when democratic processes are in danger of annihilation by institutions dedicated to empire building, maximizing profits, transferring wealth from the poor to the rich, and imposing fundamentalisms of various sorts (political, economic, and religious), these groups, working importantly across international borders, have extended the struggle to reclaim public space and collective life beyond control over economic resources to include forms of resistance that "focus upon practice as essential for human development" (Lebowitz, 2008; These Ideas Live Today, ¶ 3). Linking theory to practice is indispensable because "we change ourselves through our activity." In struggles for social justice and critical understanding it is crucial that the activity be grounded in a process of "protagonistic [and participatory] democracy in production [in order to] . . . ensure that the process of producing is one which enriches people and expands their capacities rather than crippling and impoverishing them" (Lebowitz,

Protagonistic Democracy, ¶ 5). These new international mobilizations emerge from an understanding of the necessity of critical popular education inside and outside schools committed to expanding public well-being by extending provisions and support networks in education, health, public transit, and the like. These groups are dedicated to imagining and creating a better world in which "issues of social justice, equity . . . poverty eradication . . . and community triumph [over] . . . material acquisition and consumption . . . as the arbiter of value" (Longfellow, 2006, p. 14), where we develop the political will to "fight for a new relation of human kind to nature . . . [while constructing] in the process a new democratic and participatory environmental politics" (Panitch & Leys, 2006, p. xiii). Mirroring critical literacy, these groups develop knowledge of the character of current arrangements and crises by elucidating how "poverty is not the fault of the poor, that exclusion is not the fault of the excluded, and wealth is the result of the chain of human activity" (Lebowitz, 2005; The Battle of Ideas, ¶ 4). And, fundamentally, these groups work to constitute a social contract that makes possible the construction and realization of meaningful democratic public spheres and international relations grounded in peace, solidarity, and equality.

Still, the prospects of a better future are in peril because the terrors emerging from current arrangements that quantitatively march on; the tens of billions of dollars in profits accrued by the major oil companies; the bloated military budget (estimated at over $1 trillion by Robert Dreyfus, 2007); the housing collapse; the global food crisis that has placed another 100 million people in conditions of food insecurity (in addition to the 800 million already living under despondent nutrition conditions; Tharamangalam, 2008); rising unemployment, outsourcing and downsizing; tax breaks for the wealthy; "the problem of food safety [that] is getting out of control [largely because of] food companies [that] put profits before all else, and government regulators . . . corrupted by that profit-driven power" (Roberts, 2008, pp. xii–xiii); growing prison populations; evisceration of civil liberties;[4] racist and sexist exclusion and oppression; schools made over in the image of corporate culture; bought and sold elections; an enormous trade deficit (nearly $70 billion for January 2008 alone); a national debt surpassing $11 trillion;[5] a growing concentration of wealth in the midst of increasing poverty; expanding power of the military-industrial-congressional-intelligence complex over life in the United States (and world); attacks on human rights; subversion of international law; aggravated assailment of people of color and immigrants; authoritarian threats evidenced in concentrated ownership of media, the corporate colonization, and privatization of public space, the rise of "newspeak," the permeation of militarism and its values, policies, and practices into the social, cultural, and political landscape of the United States, the hypercommercialization of childhood, "the unprecedented levels of secrecy, obfuscation, dissembling and downright lying that now characterize public life" (Panitch & Leys, 2005, p. vi.),

---

[4]For example, see Pamela Hess, "Bush Surveillance Program was Massive," online at http://www.commondreams.org/headline/2009/07/11.
[5]See the U.S. National Debt Clock at: http://www.brillig.com/debt_clock/.

and the power of a moralistic and anti-intellectual mode of religious fundamentalism reflected in a merging of bigoted, hateful, jingoistic, and patriarchal religion and politics; the overall disappearance of both a sense of solidarity with future generations and a set of obligations that might ensure the future will arrive in better shape than the present; a withering of vitalized democracy amidst a rising tide of cynicism, pessimism, and despair, as a consequence of the suppression of dissent and police-state tactics, material realities of life that suffer under harsh conditions of inequality, injustice, deprivation, and unpredictability, and also as a result of people lacking the means, ideological and material, along with the required time and space resources, to collectively and persistently exercise their rights and voices in ways that could make meaningful and effective forms of democracy possible.

Because public space under current arrangements has been increasingly privatized, the public mind persistently commercialized, public memory dehistoricized, and public spheres underfunded, abolished ,or corporatized, the struggle for meaningful and engaged democratic politics and forms of critical literacy that could nurture and nourish such projects has been, on the one hand, subordinated to capitalism's rapacious drive for markets and profits and, on the other hand, suppressed by the fear-inducing militarism that rears its ugliness in both the growing presence of police-state tactics and also through the violent, aggressive, and often grotesque spectacles that dominate corporate controlled media space in films, television, tabloidized news, and video games. The effect, in short, is a further undermining of energized forms of democracy, civil rights, and human dignity, all necessary, yet not sufficient, means for saving the future. Therefore, critical literacy argues, it is necessary to understand "how the horrors we see around us are not accidents but inherent in the system," and challenge "the whole system [that] revolves around profits and not human needs" (Lebowitz, 2006, p. 9), "as both an economic theory and a powerful public pedagogy and cultural politics," a position that calls for "institutional and economic struggles," supplemented with educational practices and projects that both "connect [neoliberalism's] symbolic power and its pedagogical practices with material relations of power" and engage "democracy as a site of intense struggle over matters of representation, participation and shared power" (Giroux, 2008a, pp. 11–12). In addition, critical literacy argues it is absolutely vital that public education engage in the work of learning and teaching about substantively democratic alternatives to the present authoritarian juggernaut. That project requires not only new visions, goals, plans, pathways, and actions, but also a commitment to deepen, expand, and support alternatives already under way (whether local or global) and to make them more visible in order both to tap into the hope that other possibilities provide and also to demonstrate the lie of the deadening neoliberal mantra, "there is no alternative."

Critical literacy and the Public Pedagogies of the Current Arrangement. Fundamental to critical literacy's call for an exacting analysis is the understanding that the current arrangement is more than a reflection of economic, political, and educational theories. To truly comprehend the current organization of power, we must understand the educational force of corporate culture, for it is an educational power that has superseded formal education in its ability to condition, form, and direct values, attitudes, opinions, beliefs, desires, identities and allegiances. Henry Giroux reminds us that the current arrangement functions as a form of "public pedagogy" and "has become an all encompassing cultural horizon for producing market identities, values and practices" (2008a, p. 118). The public pedagogies produced and disseminated by and through corporate power not only cancel out the possibilities of democratic practices and public

| militarism—points to both the ideological and material components of a society and culture dedicated to domestic and global militarization |

spheres and disappear from public consciousness the ugliness of **militarism**, racism, and gender oppression "by absorbing [them . . .] within narrow economic relations" and submerging them beneath hyperspectacles of commercialization that too often glorify and glamorize violence, domination and aggression, but also narrow opportunities for constructing alternative social relations, political movements, and cultural politics by grossly constraining the available "range of identities, ideologies and subject positions" (Giroux, 2008a, p. 118). The constant emphasis on individualism, privatization, and market identities narrows the social imagination, that is, it narrows the "ability to create possible reconstructions of larger social forces that affect our lives" (Shannon, 2000, p. 90) and thus subverts the possibility of any meaningful democratic politics and social agency.

Corporate public pedagogies circulate across a wide and penetrating variety of social and cultural sites ranging from schools, to college and professional sports, to multiple forms of electronic media including films, television, the Internet, and video games, to political campaigns, public relations, tabloid-style news, advertising, and so on. It includes a growing combination of sites reflective of corporate power's ability to construct and condition meaning, desires, and identities as part of a larger unrelenting attack on democracy and the public good. The permeating power of corporate public pedagogy makes the formal sites of education exceedingly more vital because schools and universities stand as some of the only sites in the wider culture in which teachers and students can critically address the commercialization and militarization of all corners of life and the attendant disappearance of democratic public spheres (including the sphere of a democratically oriented public mind that imagines beyond the present) and where they can also create opportunities for linking a critical awareness and reading of the world with meaningful and transformational interventions in the world.

In order to combat the corrupting power of corporate pedagogies, schools and universities must function as political and moral spheres in which people link the crisis of politics to a crisis of citizenship and use the power of a critical literacy–oriented pedagogy to engage in the dedicated work required to create the economic conditions, educational practices, public spaces, collective agency, political processes, and social relations to open up possibilities for social justice, peace, sustainability, and equality. It will require devoted pedagogical struggles that develop the necessary time, resources, abilities, knowledge, adventurous desires, and motivations to comprehend and overcome the disappearance of a language of commonality and a culture of solidarity, the undermining of secure social conditions and safety nets, the dismantling of links between education and struggles for social justice and global peace, the barriers to ecological rationality and environmental justice, and the evisceration of a substantively democratic social contract.

Collapsing the Social.   Critical literacy works to make clear how possibilities for producing democracy and fairness in the United States are tightly bound up with the construction of new ways to think, name, conceptualize, organize, process, experience, and transform the interpenetrating forces of power, authority, knowledge, oppression, liberation, and social justice. In order to overcome the material and symbolic realities of multiple forms of oppression, it will be necessary to overcome the tendency to collapse institutional realities of domination and exploitation into private discourses and individual pathologies. The relevance of oppression and the brutalities of structural exclusion and exploitation cannot be understood outside institutional relations of power and inequality. For example, in the category of racist oppression and exclusion, "almost 80 percent of black kids begin their adult lives with no assets whatsoever" (Oliver & Shapiro, 2007, ¶ 2). This is part of "the historical accumulation of inequality and how it continues to structure [and constrain] the lives of African Americans" (Oliver & Shapiro, 2007,¶ 4). Furthermore, "the typical white family enjoys a net worth that is more than seven times that of it black counterpart" (Conley, 2001,¶ 3). African American families earning less than $15,000 per year have a net worth of zero. In brief, "equality of opportunity cannot be achieved under unequal conditions" (Conley, 2001,¶ 6) because inequality and oppression undermine the kinds of reciprocity required for the mutual fulfillment and flourishing of human well-being in society. In addition, White students with a bachelor's degree earn $500,000 more over a lifetime than Black students with a bachelor's degree (Sanders, 2007).

Privatized discourses around individual bigotry and hateful dispositions remove iniquitous historical and social relationships from public consciousness around racism and deny public language of its possibilities for linking human agency with economic, political, and social conditions. These denials downgrade the pertinence of race and racism "as a force for discrimination and exclusion," degrade opportunities for productively engaging difference, distort our understanding of the interpenetrating relationships between public realities and private concerns, as well as between self and other, and devalue language, culture and pedagogy as "sites of contestation and struggle" (Giroux, 2008a, p. 64).

Another of the terrors of the current arrangement challenged by critical literacy is the power of its social Darwinist discourses to transmogrify our understanding of politics, history, identity, agency, and possibility, a transmutation that has impacted the character of race relations since the 1970s by undermining, through a bloated emphasis on individualism and competition, ideas and realities around mutual responsibility and common humanity grounded in compassion, concern, solidarity and respect. Under the current arrangement, corporate hegemony over all corners of life reduces politics to the protection and pursuit of wealth, subverts solidarity by reducing life to an individual struggle to see who will survive in the capitalist battle of all against all, eliminates the substance of freedom by narrowing it to forms of privatized self-interest separated from the kinds of substantive freedoms that allow for mutually enriching self and social flourishing, and creates liquid conditions of uncertainty and insecurity in daily life.

Following neoliberalism's tendencies toward privatization and its assailing of the social contract, the current arrangement's dismissal of institutional racism and its attacks on social equality as an assault on individual freedom reflects the pedagogical power of a racial and economic discourse that has been privatized and individualized. Under current arrangements the state is basically reduced to carrying out policing functions (increasingly privatized, i.e., part of the larger public subsidy/private-profit system) and transferring wealth to the privileged sectors while abandoning investments in the public good or in expanding democratic freedoms, leading to a severing of ties between individual freedom, moral responsibility and social consequences. When dominant ideologies around racism, economics, and gender relations collapse the political into the personal, the social into the individual, the historical into the immediate, and the public into the private, it allows for the reproduction of modes of structural exclusion, domination and oppression that symbolically and literally classify and order bodies along discriminatory and marginalizing lines. By rending the relationship between individual rights and the kinds of socially responsible citizenship obligatory for any form of substantive democracy, dominant ideologies not only stifle our ability to understand the repressive power of historical forms of oppression, exploitation, and injustice rooted in institutional imperatives, but it also closes options for engaging in the modes of collective struggle necessary to evolve versions of a social contract that defend the public good and extend democratic values in ways that provide social, economic and racial justice for all citizens.

Hoping and Dreaming in Hard and Dangerous Times

". . . not even the future is safe from those who envisage it as no more than the present stretching all the way to infinity."
—Terry Eagleton, *Making a Break* (2006)

Paul Epstein and Evan Mills (2007) warn, "Mega-catastrophes [are] what we can expect [. . . given] the unexpected pace and magnitude of climate change" (p. 4). Meanwhile, the *Intergovernmental Panel on Climate Change Report,* "paints a near-apocalyptic vision of Earth's future," (Zarembo & Maugh, 2007, ¶ 1) as noted in the *LA Times,* "[and] even in its softened form [. . . portends] devastating effects that will strike all regions of the world and all levels of society" (¶ 4). George Monbiot (2007) cautions, "We have a short period—a very short period—in which to prevent the planet from starting to shake us off" (p. 15), with large-scale, nonlinear disruptions in the climate system, rising sea levels, destabilizing of the ocean "conveyor belt," crop failure, accelerated thawing of permafrost, which will release large quantities of methane, spreading hunger, violence, disease, and massive displacement—in short, conditions that could quickly lead to a sinking into barbarism. Ross Gelbspan (2007) reports leading climate scientists have "declared that humanity is about to pass or already has passed a 'tipping point' in terms of global warming [. . . and scientists report] it is 'very unlikely' that we will avoid the coming era of 'dangerous climate change'" (¶ 11). Related to global climate catastrophe are "three water crises" that Maude Barlow (2008) suggests are "dwindling freshwater supplies, inequitable access to water, and the corporate control of water [that] pose the greatest threat of our time to the planet and to our survival" (¶ 1). Predictably, "the impacts will be felt by the most vulnerable, and by those who have benefited the least from . . . the hierarchized distribution of wealth." Given current tendencies, "a doomsday scenario . . . genocide by natural disaster . . . is not out of the picture" (Longfellow, 2006, pp. 2–5).

In the face of these crises, one idea that continues "lying around" (to borrow from Milton Friedman's notion of how we address crises), an idea that points to another potentially cataclysmic crisis, is a U.S. commitment to addressing problems through the Pentagon system and spreading violence around the world. Miriam Pemberton (2008), writing for the Institute for Policy Studies, even while underestimating Pentagon spending, reports that in the last 5 years, spending on military security has heavily outweighed spending on climate security. Because of the enormous commitment to militarism, Chalmers Johnson (2008) warns, "the time of reckoning is fast approaching" (¶ 2). He estimates that military expenditures are "larger than all other nations' military budgets combined" (¶ 6). Not only does this spending increase social and economic inequality by shifting wealth to elite sectors and intensify the likelihood of military aggression, and global violence, but it also moves the United States closer to economic collapse. Furthermore, massive military expenditures divert much-needed funds from a variety of public sites, including: health care—where public funds could be used to provide a publicly oriented rather than privately controlled health care system; job creation (3 million manufacturing jobs were lost between 1998 and 2003) in the midst of real unemployment figures hovering around 18% (Cox, 2009); and public and higher education (K–12). Federal spending is roughly $37 billion, roughly 3% of the real Pentagon budget); environmental protection (spending on environmental protection is less than 1% of real military spending); nutrition (one in five low-income households with elderly members is food insecure); and infrastructure repair.[6]

At the same time that trillions of dollars are diverted to military aggression, global military bases, private military contractors, debt on conflicts, and the like, the inequality in the United States is also staggering (War Resisters League, 2010).

---

[6]In measuring 15 areas of infrastructure in the United States, including drinking water, school, and aviation quality and the like, the American Society of Civil Engineers (2005) gave an average grade of D and a highest grade of C+; see American Society of Civil Engineers (2005). *Infrastructure report card, 2005.* Retrieved June 12, 2008, from http://www.asce.org.

Chris Hartman (2008) notes that between 1979 and 2005, the top 5% of American families saw their real incomes increase 81%. Over the same period, the lowest-income families saw their real incomes decline 1%, as prices continue to rise. In addition, all the income gains for 2005 accrued in the top 10% of U.S. households. At the same time, there were income declines in the bottom 90%. The richest 1% of households in the United States now own more wealth than that of the combined wealth of the bottom 90%. While a top hedge-fund manager earns more in 10 minutes than the average U.S. worker earns during an entire year (Shell, 2007), 21% of children in the United States live in poverty, and 33 million U.S. citizens live in households that do not have adequate food. William Tabb (2006) reports that from 1990 to 2002, for each additional dollar earned by the bottom 90% of the U.S. population, the top 0.01% earned an extra $18,000. In the meantime, more and more working people are forced to choose between paying for heat and paying to eat or between health care or child care; and the minimum wage, when adjusted for inflation, is more than $3.00 *less* in 2008 than it was in 1968. "The minimum wage does not provide a minimally adequate living standard," let alone a fair and just standard (Sklar, 2008, ¶ 7).

In the face of these growing challenges and grim crises, critical literacy argues that we must stand firm as public intellectuals engage in a relentless and methodologically rigorous critique of the massive injustices that follow from the terrors of the current arrangement and the horrors that accrue as a consequence of increasing militarism, privatization, fundamentalism, deregulation, inequality, racism, sexism, profiteering, environmental destruction, and so on; but crucially we must do more. We must be resolute in our commitments to social justice, critical hope, democracy, and freedom and in our belief in the potential for public-centered critical forms of pedagogy (that link critical thought to social intervention and critical dreams to new social realities) to create the conditions, knowledge, and experiences for young people (and all citizens) to develop the will and abilities to take responsibility and risks for creating an ever-evolving and substantive democratic culture and society that opens the possibility for saving the future. Necessary for taking on these tasks is "the challenge of addressing the politics and pedagogy of neoliberal common sense and . . . the educational force of [neoliberal] culture in securing widespread consent from the American people" that directs the public to comprehend life "via market mentalities and corporate paradigms" (Giroux, 2008a, p. 149).

The ongoing consequences following from the current arrangement is an abolition of those public goods, social securities, and elements of social fairness necessary for the development of individual agency, civic courage, and engaged citizenship. In order to address the powerful public pedagogical impacts of an overproductive neoliberal culture that presents itself as common sense across a wide array of cultural sites and consequently undermines notions and realities of solidarity, peace, liberty, and egalitarianism, teachers, students, and citizens, dedicated to the public good and a better future, must engage in forms of politically engaged citizenship directed toward fomenting spheres of critical public education across a wide spectrum of public spaces that produce the foundational conditions for nonviolence, racial and gender justice, equality, human dignity, ecological rationality, and meaningful freedom.

Sut Jhally (1998), in the film *Advertising and the End of the World,* argues that this generation of students may be the most important in human history because they will largely determine whether we save or lose the future. If that is the case, then this generation of educators, at the public school and university levels (and across a multitude of cultural sites), is arguably the most important generation of educators in human history, with an immense and critical responsibility to prepare the young in acquiring the tools, knowledge, and will to be change agents who critically read the word and the world. In other words, public educators as public intellectuals, along with students and citizens, must redeem education as part of an ethical and political struggle to expand democratic public life and encourage education as a political and moral project in which students, teachers, and the public are invested in and committed to the possibilities for creating a better future while rigorously and relentlessly challenging the cynical and hopeless views and realities erupting from the ravaging tendencies and nightmarish threats of the current arrangement.

In this direction, critical literacy calls on public and university educators, as well as cultural workers in all domains of public pedagogy, to take on the moral, intellectual, and social responsibility to invigorate spheres of education as sites in which adults can work with youth in developing projects dedicated to producing engaged and informed citizens, empowered and involved workers, and social and cultural agents. In short, we must develop and evolve projects dedicated to producing not only courageous and committed citizens empowered to resist political cynicism, military aggression, and economic fundamentalism but also pedagogies obliged to mobilizing the collective intellectual and imaginative potential of involved, informed, inclusive, and energized populations of people who will not allow the prospect of failure to stand in the way of attempting to achieve what appears to be impossible. In other words, we need pedagogies directed toward educating hopeful populations who dream differently in order to act differently and who are educated, and willing, to both embrace critical literacy's rational imperative to oppose social suicide, engage in rigorous social critique, pursue the demanding intellectual work required for developing the clarity necessary for transformative democratic actions of the sort that produce institutional restructurings out of which economic and social justice will emerge, and worry less about what terms we use to describe such pedagogical theories and social movements and more about what we demand, what we envision, and what we accomplish together.

Terry Eagleton (2003, p. 223) warns, ". . . unless the United States is able to do some hard thinking about the world, it is not at all certain that the world will be around for that much longer." The kind of "hard thinking" to which Eagleton refers is the kind of critical interrogation that not only helps us make sense of what is actually happening in the world, but also provides us with hopeful and imaginative insights into both where we want to go and some illumination on what it might take to get there. What critical literacy understands is that there are always contingencies and uncertainties in our understanding of complex issues, whether in history, politics, or pedagogy. This uncertainty does not mean that our insights, direction and reflections will always be shown to be incorrect, but rather they will always be incomplete. We confront this incompleteness by developing the solidaristic courage and commitment to take an active stand against all forms of injustice, discrimination, and oppression, through holding firmly to Paulo Freire's dictum "nothing can justify the degradation of human beings . . . Nothing" (2001, p. 93), accompanied by the intellectual fortitude to not stand still, to paraphrase a Giroux formulation.

The courage and fortitude emerges from the belief in and commitment to the possibilities of a better future founded in an alternative set of values in opposition to the nihilistic and hope-destroying neoliberal values that promote self-interest, profiteering, hyperindividualism, domination, rapacious greed, and ruthless competition. Those alternative values should include, but are not limited

sustainability—refers to the ongoing development of new, evolving, improving, and livable forms of social, economic, and political organization and not the reproduction of current, stultifying, dehumanizing, and destructive forms

to: **sustainability** (environmental, agricultural, ontological, epistemological); a critical mentality that educates citizens to challenge assumptions, refuse absolutes, cultivate a culture of doubt, question conventional wisdom, interrogate power, and critique prevailing notions; economic stability dedicated to the fair and equitable distribution of wealth, income, and resources as well as full and meaningful employment; a rising standard of living measured not in the accumulation of commodities but in the meeting of human needs and the fulfillment and flourishing of human abilities; concern for the collective good; participatory social, cultural, political, and crucially, economic democracy; notions of solidarity locally, nationally, and internationally; peace that works to overcome all forms of structural violence and militarism; and love, grounded in the understanding that a reciprocity of flourishing and fulfillment requires an absence of oppression and inequality.

One of our crucial tasks, then, is to pursue the hard thinking that broadens possibilities for developing a comprehension of the boundaries of our knowledge and understanding and a vision of what alternatives might look like and what will be required to achieve such alternatives. Then, we must work to expand those boundaries, while examining carefully the conditions out of which knowledge is produced, constructed, distributed, situated, assimilated, and understood, and then engage, with critical hope, the complex and too often horrifying realities we confront on a regular basis. This essentially activist stance arises from the near-truism that although passivity and inaction are always a possible response, in most circumstances, they are the worst option, particularly during this historical period in which a "dark night of despair [threatens to . . .] overcome humanity" (Kolko, 2006a, p. 175).

Engaging the world from a critical literacy stance requires serious commitment, and it is exhausting and challenging—but only in ways that are potentially invigorating and encouraging. It is at our peril that we avoid the demanding and urgent work critical literacy offers and inspires.

One is reminded of Murray Bookchin's directive that we cannot be content only to work within the options presented by the dominant system; otherwise we are forced "to choose the lesser evil rather than the greater good" (Bookchin, 1999, p. 347). Therefore, critical literacy must be vigorously committed to critiquing, transforming, and replacing the options offered by the dominant system in order to develop a different set of choices that work in the direction of the greater political, moral, social, intellectual, and common human good. In confronting the terrors of the present and the foreboding recurrence of increasingly fierce and destructive disasters, we must think, read, write, and act with an unrelenting urgency, rigor, and clarity, necessary now more than ever, that provide us with an informed hope and the critical tools for thinking hard about and acting courageously in the world. While critical literacy can offer no prescriptions or simple road maps, we can, with strong humility, offer direction rooted in a realistic hope sustained in the democratic possibilities alive in our capacities to act with a combination of civic courage, a collective spirit, critical inquiry, and local and international solidarity, (and, we might add, **social love**) so that we do not reproduce a present that cancels our future and so we do not lose our reality by abandoning our dreams.

> **social love**—recognizes that the flourishing and fulfillment of each is the condition for and the nourishment for the flourishing and fulfillment of all, and the flourishing and fulfillment of all is the condition for and the nurturing of the flourishing and fulfillment of each individual (extrapolated from Terry Eagleton, 2006)

CONNECTING CRITICAL LITERACY TO YOUR CLASSROOM . . .

This piece suggests an absence of knowledge around our interconnectedness and interdependence, now on a global scale, an absence of knowledge that increases alienation, exploitation, and human suffering. To open up a discussion about global interconnections and interdependence, we can ask a simple question in any classroom: How is the world present in this classroom? While multiple answers are possible (and should be explored), an obvious way the world is present is through our clothing. People can check the labels on their classmates' clothing or on their own clothing to see where the clothing was produced. Typically, there will be a wide range of countries (Mexico, Guatemala, Vietnam, Taiwan, Indonesia, Vietnam, Bangladesh, China, etc.). We can then ask: What do we know about the conditions of life of the people who produced our clothing? What do we know about the conditions of work for those people? What do we know about who is making our clothing? What do we know about the relationship between workers and owners in the production of our clothing (and other objects of consumption)? Then we can visit the Web site for The National Labor Committee (http://www.nlcnet.org/) to gain further insights into these questions. At this Web site people can look into the conditions of workers in the countries in which their clothing (and other objects of consumption) was made and report back to the class. We can further explore connections between economics, politics, ideologies, cultures, social structures, militarism, worker's rights, human rights, technology, globalization, and so on, in order to open up opportunities for developing multiple literacies linked to power relationships.

REFERENCES

Barlow, M. (2008, February 10). The global water crisis and the coming battle for the right to water. *Foreign Policy in Focus Policy Report*. Retrieved July 15, 2008, from http://www.fpif.org/fpiftxt/5016

Bartolomé, L. (2007). Critical pedagogy and teacher education: Radicalizing prospective teachers. In P. McLaren & J. L. Kincheloe (Eds.), *Critical pedagogy: Where are we now* (pp. 263–288). New York: Peter Lang.

Beck, A. (2005). A place for critical literacy. *Journal of Adolescent & Adult Literacy, 48*(1), 392–400.

Behrman, E. (2006). Teaching about language, power, and text: A review of classroom practices that support critical literacy. *Journal of Adolescent & Adult Literacy, 49*(6), 490–498.

Berlinski, C. (2008). *There Is No Alternative: Why Margaret Thatcher Matters*. New York: Basic Books.

Bookchin, M. (1999). *Anarchism, Marxism and the future of the left*. San Francisco: AK Press.

Conley, D. (2001). The Black-White wealth gap, *The Nation*. Retrieved July 22, 2009, from http://www.thenation.com/doc/20010326/conley

Cope, B. (1999). *Multiliteracies: Literacy learning and the design of social futures*, New York: Routledge.

Cox, J. (2009). The 'Real' Jobless Rate: 17.5% of Workers Are Unemployed. *CNBC*. Retrieved April 1, 2010 from http://www.cnbc.com/id/34040009/The_Real_Jobless_Rate_17_5_Of_Workers_Are_Unemployed

Dewey, J. (1966). *Democracy and education*, New York: Free Press.

Dreyfus, R. (2007). Financing the Imperial Armed Forces. *TomPaine.CommonSense*. Retrieved July 22, 2008, from http://www.tompaine.com

Eagleton, T. (2003). *After theory*, NY: Basic Books.

Eagleton, T. (2006). Making a break. *London Review of Books*. Retrieved July 21, 2008, from http://www.lrb.co.uk/v28/n05/eagl01_.html

Edelman, M. (2008). Where are the children in President Bush's budget? *The Huffington Post*. Retrieved July 21, 2009, from http://www.huffingtonpost.com

Epstein, P., & Mills, E. (Eds.) (2005). *Climate change futures: Health, ecological, and economic dimensions*. Cambridge: Center for Health and the Global Environment Harvard Medical School. Retrieved April 5, 2010, from http://www.climatechangefutures.org/pdf/CCF_Report_Final_10.27.pdf

Freidman, M. (1982). *Capitalism and freedom*, Chicago: University of Chicago Press.

Freire, P. (1987). *Literacy: Reading the Word and the World*. Westport, CT: Bergin & Garvey.

Freire, P. (2001). *Pedagogy of freedom*, New York: Rowman & Littlefield.

Gelbspan, R. (2007). Beyond the point of no return? *Grist Magazine*. Retrieved July 20, 2008, from http://gristmill.grist.org/story/2007/12/10/165845/92

Giroux, H. (2008a). *Against the terror of neoliberalism*. Boulder, CO: Paradigm.

Giroux, H. (2008b). Foreword. In G. Olson, & L. Worsham (Eds.), *The politics of possibility*. Boulder, CO: Paradigm.

Giroux, H. (2009). The Spectacle of Illiteracy and the Crisis of Democracy. *Z Communications*. Retrieved April 1, 2010 from http://www.zcommunications.org/the-spectacle-of-illiteracy-and-the-crisis-of-democracy-by-henry-a-giroux

Hartman, C. (2008). By the numbers. *Inequality.org*. Retrieved July 23, 2008, from http://www.demos.org/inequality/ByNumbersMay31.pdf

Jameson, F. (2003). Future city. *New Left Review, 21*, 65–79. Retrieved July 23, 2008, from http://www.newleftreview.org/?view=2449

Jhally, S. (1998). *Advertising and the end of the world*, Amherst: Media Education Foundation, DVD, Retrieved April 5, 2010, from http://www.mediaed.org/cgi-bin/commerce.cgi?preadd=action&key=101

Johnson, C. (2008). The economic disaster that is military keynesianism, *Z Communications*. Retrieved July 20, 2008, from http://www.zcommunications.org/znet/viewArticle/16444

Klein, N. (2007). Disaster capitalism: the new economy of catastrophe. *Harper's Magazine*. Retrieved July 25, 2008, from http://www.harpers.org/archive/2007/10/0081739

Kolko, G. (2006a). *After Socialism*, New York: Routledge.

Kolko, G. (2006b). *The age of war: The United States confronts the world*, Boulder, CO: Lynne Rienner.

Krugman, P. (2005). Bush's class-war budget. *Truthout*. Retrieved July 20, 2008, from https://www.truthout.org/article/paul-krugman-bushs-class-war-budget

Lebowitz, M. (2005). The knowledge of a better world. *Monthly Review*. Retrieved July 21, 2008, from http://www.monthlyreview.org/0705lebowitz.htm

Lebowitz, M. (2006). *Build it now: Socialism for the 21st century*. New York: Monthly Review Press.

Lebowitz, M. (2008). The spectre of socialism for the 21st century haunts capitalism. Retrieved July 24, 2008, from http://links.org.au/node/503

Longfellow, B. (2006). Weather report. In L. Panitch, & C. Leys (Eds.), *Coming to terms with nature* (p. 14). New York: Monthly Review Press.

Löwy, M. (2006). Eco-socialism and democratic planning. In L. Panitch, & C. Leys (Eds.), *Coming to terms with nature*. New York: Monthly Review Press.

Martinez-Alier, J. (2006). Social metabolism and environmental conflicts. In L. Panitch, & C. Leys hes (Eds.), *Coming to terms with nature* (p. 273). New York: Monthly Review Press.

McLaren, P. (2007). The future of the past. In P. McLaren, & J. Kincheloe (Eds.), *Critical Pedagogy: Where Are We Now?* New York: Peter Lang.

Monbiot, G. (2007). *Heat: How to stop the planet from burning*. Boston: South End Press.

Oliver, M., & Shapiro, T. (2007). Wealth gap between Blacks and Whites has grown larger. *Black Commentator*. Retrieved July 21, 2008, from http://www.blackcommentator.com

Panitch, L., & Leys C. (2005). *Telling the truth*. New York: Monthly Review Press.

Panitch, L., & Leys C. (2006). *Coming to terms with nature*. New York: Monthly Review Press.

Pollan, M. (2006). *The omnivore's dilemma*. New York: Penguin Books.

Pemberton, M. (2008). Military vs. climate security. *Institute for Policy Studies*. Retrieved July 20, 2008, from http://www.ips-dc.org/reports/#83

Roberts, P. (2008). *The end of food*. New York: Houghton Mifflin.

Sanders, M. (2007). The sound of opportunity. *United for a Fair Economy*. Retrieved July 24, 2008, from http://www.racialwealthdivide.org/sound_of_opportunity.html

Shannon, P. (2000). What's my name? A politics of literacy in the latter half of the 20th century in America. *Reading Research Quarterly, 35*(1), 90–107.

Shannon, P. (2007). *Reading against democracy*, Portsmouth: Heinemann.

Shell, A. (2007). Cash of the titans: Criticism of pay for fund execs grows. *USA Today*. Retrieved July 21, 2008, from http://www.usatoday.com

Shierholz, H. (2009). New 2008 poverty, income data reveal only tip of the recession iceberg. *Economic Policy Institute*. Retrieved April 1, 2010, from http://www.epi.org/publications/entry/income_picture_20090910/

Sklar, H. (2008). Minimum wage raise too little, too late. *Commondreams.org*. Retrieved July 23, 2008, from http://www.commondreams.org/archive/2008/07/24/10573/

Stiglitz, J., & Bilmes, L. (2008). $3 Trillion may be too low. *The Guardian*. Retrieved July 25, 2008, from http://commentisfree.guardian.co.uk

Tabb, W. (2006). The power of the rich. *Monthly Review Online*. Retrieved July 22, 2008, from http://www.monthlyreview.org/0706tabb.htm

Tharamangalam, J. (2008, June). Can Cuba offer an alternative to corporate control over the world's food system? Paper presented at the 20th Conference of North American and Cuban Philosophers and Social Scientists, Havana, Cuba.

War Resisters League (2010). Where Your Income Tax Money Really Goes. *War Resisters League*. Retrieved April 1, 2010 from http://www.warresisters.org/node/642

Wolin, S. (2008). *Democracy, Inc.* Princeton: Princeton University Press.

Zarembo, A., & Maugh T. (2007, April 7). Dire warming report too soft, scientists say. *Los Angeles Times*. Retrieved April 5, 2010, from http://articles.latimes.com/2007/apr/07/science/sci-warming7

INTERSECTIONS OF LANGUAGE, SOCIETY, CULTURE, AND THE READER

HELPFUL WEB SITES

Diversity and literacy

http://www.ericdigests.org/1998-1/myths.htm

Psycholinguistics

http://www.psycholinguisticsarena.com/
http://www.mpi.nl/

Sociolinguistics

The following link is from PBS. It also has a search engine on it dedicated to this topic:
http://www.pbs.org/speak/speech/sociolinguistics/sociolinguistics/
This link has a map on it where you can click to hear how people say a word differently in the United States.
http://www.utexas.edu/courses/linguistics/resources/socioling/talkmap/index.html

Other sociolinguistics Web sites

http://www.ling.upenn.edu/phono_atlas/ICSLP4.html
http://www.ncela.gwu.edu/pubs/tesol/tesoljournal/juniorhi.htm
http://www.ncela.gwu.edu/rcd/bibliography/BE020773
http://privatewww.essex.ac.uk/~patrickp/AAVE.html
http://bryan.myweb.uga.edu/AAVE/
http://www.phon.ucl.ac.uk/home/dick/SEtrudgill.htm
http://www.phon.ucl.ac.uk/home/dick/SEhogg.htm
http://www.phon.ucl.ac.uk/home/dick/SEhudson.htm
http://www.maec.org/cross/6.html
http://reese.linguist.de/English/
http://www.plastic.com/article.html;sid = 03/05/24/10202010
http://dare.wisc.edu/
http://www.clmer.csulb.edu/
http://www.usc.edu/dept/education/CMMR/home.html
http://ccat.sas.upenn.edu/~haroldfs/messeas/seabib.html
http://logos.uoregon.edu/explore/socioling/index.html

Language Acquisition

http://www.answers.com/topic/language-acquisition
http://www.ncela.gwu.edu/
http://www.ed.gov/about/offices/list/oela/index.html
http://www.carla.umn.edu/
http://www.andrew.cmu.edu/course/85-211b/language_acq.html
http://www.ascd.org/publications/books/108052/chapters/
The_Stages_of_Second_Language_Acquisition.aspx
http://www.lcsedu.net/departments/curriculum/esl/stages/
http://speech-language-therapy.com/devel2.htm
http://www.colorincolorado.org/article/26751

English Language Learners and Teaching Reading

http://www.readingrockets.org/article/291
http://www.colorincolorado.org/educators/teaching

http://www.alliance.brown.edu/tdl/elemlit/readingk3.shtml
http://www.wested.org/policy/pubs/fostering/teaching.htm
http://dww.ed.gov/topic/topic_landing.cfm?PA_ID=6&T_ID=13#
http://www.ohio.edu/linguistics/esl/
http://www.learner.org/workshops/teachreading35/session6/index.html
http://www.ers.org/CATALOG/description.phtml?II=WS-5405
http://www.cal.org/siop/about/index.html
http://docs.google.com/gview?a=v&q=cache:VclLAiotae4J:www.doe.in.gov/lmmp/pdf/refugee_
interrupted_education.pdf+&hl=en&gl=us
http://coe.sdsu.edu/people/jmora/pages/50strategies.htm
http://www.sblceastconn.org/ell.htm
http://www2.scholastic.com/browse/article.jsp?id=3749100

Language Learning

http://www.language-learning-advisor.com/
http://www.ets.org/portal/site/ets/menuitem.22f30af61d34e9c39a77b13bc3921509/?vgnextoid=
1077be3a864f4010VgnVCM10000022f95190RCRD
http://www.languageimpact.com/
http://www.llas.ac.uk/index.aspx
http://www.speakeasy.org/~dbrick/Hot/foreign.html
http://www.uebersetzung.at/twister/
http://nflrc.msu.edu/
http://iteslj.org/Articles/Lessard-Clouston-Strategy.html
http://www.cal.org/resources/digest/oxford01.html
http://www.nclrc.org/essentials/motivating/strategies.htm
http://www.plucha.info/2009/oxford%E2%80%99s-classification-of-language-learning-strategies/
http://www.allacademic.com/meta/p_mla_apa_research_citation/1/1/2/2/1/p112216_index.html
http://www.jalt-publications.org/tlt/files/98/apr/fedderholdt.html
http://eltj.oxfordjournals.org/cgi/content/abstract/61/2/91
w.actfl.org/i4a/pages/index.cfm?pageid=3394
https://www.ocps.net/cs/multilingual/Documents/PowerPoint/excellence_by_design_2006.ppt
http://homepage.ntlworld.com/vivian.c/SLA/Krashen.htm

Funds of Knowledge

http://www.learnnc.org/lp/pages/939
http://www.cal.org/resources/Digest/ncrcds01.html
http://www.ed.gov/pubs/ModStrat/pt3i.html
http://www.aaanet.org/committees/commissions/aec/fok.htm
http://repositories.cdlib.org/crede/ncrcdslleducational/EPR06/
http://www.linguistlist.org/issues/16/16-3224.html
http://classweb.gmu.edu/cip/g/gh/gh-s008.htm
http://findarticles.com/p/articles/mi_pric/is_199402/ai_185988946/
http://www.childcareresearch.org/location/1639
http://www.odemagazine.com/exchange/821/interjecting_peace_through_meaningful_home
work_strategies_to_access_rich_funds_of_knowledge
http://www.textproject.org/presentations/WVSRS-2009-keynote

Critical Literacy

http://www.learnnc.org/lp/pages/4437
http://www.lesley.edu/journals/jppp/4/shor.html
http://www.readwritethink.org/lessons/lesson_view.asp?id=23
http://wwwfp.education.tas.gov.au/english/critlit.htm
http://www.pwc.k12.nf.ca/internetliteracy/

http://www.youtube.com/watch?v=MRDp6FNynm0
http://www.slideshare.net/angelamaiers/critical-literacy-presentation
http://www.readwritethink.org/lessons/lesson_view.asp?id=1009
http://multiliteracy.wetpaint.com/page/Critical+Literacy
http://www.sil.org/lingualinks/Literacy/ReferenceMaterials/GlossaryOfLiteracyTerms/
WhatIsCriticalLiteracy.htm
http://www1.ncte.org/store/books/124348.htm
http://information-literacy.blogspot.com/2007/10/critical-literacy.html

Critical Pedagogy

http://carbon.cudenver.edu/~mryder/itc_data/crit_ped.html
http://radicalpedagogy.icaap.org/content/issue5_1/03_keesing-styles.html
http://video.google.com/videosearch?hl=en&client=firefox-a&rls=org.mozilla:en-
US:official&q=Critical+Pedagogy&um=1&ie=UTF-8&ei=PZhbSoTbLYTU8wSK_6nVBQ&sa=
X&oi=video_result_group&ct=title&resnum=10#
http://www.gseis.ucla.edu/courses/ed253a/newdk/medlit.htm
http://www.gseis.ucla.edu/courses/ed253a/dk/ML&CP.htm
http://www.questia.com/library/education/critical-pedagogy.jsp
http://library.georgetown.edu/newjour/j/msg02699.html
http://www.teachingenglish.org.uk/blogs/dilayyatkin/critical-pedagogy

Paolo Freire

http://www.youtube.com/watch?v=Q6bMBWvoPp8
http://www.youtube.com/watch?v=pVz_AOFuZ_E&NR=1
http://www.youtube.com/watch?v=UvCs6XkT3-o&NR=1
http://www.youtube.com/watch?v=Fj4SGO4iO9M&feature=fvw
http://freire.education.mcgill.ca/content/henry-giroux-interview
http://books.google.com/books?id=lr2ia2Q2i94C&dq=friere+reading+the+word+and+world&
printsec=frontcover&source=bl&ots=_aAM_PmcSt&sig=9gDmt2v2223Ec-
velr1Zx84jJNY&hl=en&ei=oWBXSrqnJJaMtgeDr4TdCg&sa=X&oi=book_result&ct=result&resn
um=2

NEW FRONTIERS: INTERSECTIONS OF THE PAST, PRESENT, AND FUTURE IN READING INSTRUCTION AND RESEARCH

INTRODUCTION

The learning journey along the reading superhighway is nearing its end. The final section in this volume is devoted to new frontiers in the study of the complex discipline of reading. The scope of the discipline has definitely broadened in recent years in ever-widening concentric circles that include the close interrelationship of reading and writing while continuing to emphasize oracy, speaking, and listening as foundational building blocks. The advent of the digital globalization of society, discussed explicitly by Leu and Kinzer in Chapter 19, has forced the addition of two "new literacies," viewing and visually representing, as teachers struggle to keep pace with the new technological advances and their impact on reading instruction and what counts as text in classroom settings. Experts in the field agree that there is one certainty with the advent of the 21st century—the premise that rapid changes will continue to occur. This continual rapid change will compel educators to continually revisit and reconstruct their instructional approaches and how they assess those approaches in order to prepare citizens for literate survival in this new technological age.

This section includes some of the newest research at the cutting edge of the field of literacy. Some may find this research troubling and unsettling. Some may question its worth and validity. The new research challenges us to rethink the boundaries of our previous definitions of what counts as literacy. Terminology such as power, space, image, teacher as text, teacher's lived experiences as text, third-space theory, learners' out-of-school literacies, multimodalities, bodies as textual representation, and new visions of assessment are just a few of the concepts investigated in new research studies in our discipline.

Another trend in reading research of the 21st century is a focus on reading behaviors across the life span to include middle-level students, adolescents, and adult readers. While previous decades yielded a plethora of research about early literacy and the early childhood years, newer research is recognizing the need for in-depth research focusing on learners who have progressed past those first literacy experiences and strategies for providing the support older students need to be lifelong readers.

Students will be challenged in this final section of *Historical, Theoretical, and Sociological Foundations of Reading in the United States* to venture beyond the last exit where the reading superhighway ends and to envision a future with limitless boundaries. Long-held beliefs and traditional values may be challenged. Keep an open mind and explore the myriad paths of creative and innovative research in a journey into the "New Frontiers of Reading Instruction."

Alignment of Readings in Section V to the International Reading Association's *Standards for Reading Professionals 2010* (Draft):

Standard 1: Foundational Knowledge
    1.1; 1.3
Standard 2: Curriculum and Instruction
    2.1; 2.2, and 2.3 (postreading activities)

Standard 3: Assessment and Evaluation
    3.1 (Cobb assessment chapter)
Standard 4: Diversity
    4.1, 4.2, and 4.3
Standard 5: Literate Environment
    5.2
Standard 6: Professional Learning and Leadership
    6.1 (postreading activities); 6.3

TOWARD A THEORY OF NEW LITERACIES EMERGING FROM THE INTERNET AND OTHER INFORMATION AND COMMUNICATION TECHNOLOGIES

DONALD J. LEU, JR., CHARLES K. KINZER, JULIE L. COIRO, AND DANA W. CAMMACK

THINK ABOUT TECHNOLOGY . . .

1. The authors discuss change in the sense of technology's impact on society and schooling. As you read, think about how technology has impacted your own life in the last decade.

2. The authors discuss change in the sense of technology's impact on society and schooling. As you read, think about how technology has impacted your classroom and the students you teach, who are "digital natives."

The essence of both reading and reading instruction is change. Reading a book changes us forever as we return from the worlds we inhabit during our reading journeys with new insights about our surroundings and ourselves. Teaching a student to read is also a transforming experience. It opens new windows to the world and creates lifetime of opportunities. Change defines our work as both literacy educators and researchers—by teaching a student to read, we change the world.

Adapted from Leu, D.J., Jr., & Kinzer, C.K. (2000). The convergence of literacy instruction with networked technologies for information and communication. *Reading Research Quarterly, 35,* 108–127. Copyright © 2000 by the International Reading Association.

Today, reading, reading instruction, and more broadly conceived notions of literacy and literacy instruction are being defined by change in even more profound ways as new technologies require new literacies to effectively exploit their potentials (Coiro, 2003; Kinzer & Leander, 2003; Lankshear & Knobel, 2003; Leu, 2000a; Smolin & Lawless, 2003). These include technologies such as gaming software (Gee, 2003), video technologies (O'Brien, 2001), technologies that establish communities on the Internet (Chandler-Olcott & Mahar, 2003), search engines (Jansen, Spink, & Saracevic, 2000), webpages, and many more yet to emerge.

Moreover, these new literacies change regularly as technology opens new possibilities for communication and information. We see this happening today as people redefine literacy practices while they communicate on a chatboard associated with a website, talk to one another using a video cam, or participate in virtual reality role-playing games (Cammack, 2002; King & O'Brien, 2002; Kinzer, 2003; Lewis & Fabos, 1999). The ability to linguistically manipulate identity as well as the norms of conversation to fit these new electronic spaces has implications for both the development of language and conceptions of the role of technology (Crystal, 2001).

All of these practices impact our conceptions of literacy and, ultimately, influence the definitions of literacies in classrooms, at home, and at work. As more and more individuals use new technologies to communicate, these linguistic activities come to shape the ways in which we view and use language and literacy. Most important, new literacies, whether intentionally or unintentionally, impact literacy instruction in classrooms (Hagood, Stevens, & Reinking, 2003; Lankshear & Knobel, 2003; Lewis & Finders, 2002).

Consider, for example, the changes experienced by students who graduate from secondary school this year. Their story teaches us an important lesson about our literacy future. Many graduates started their school career with the literacies of paper, pencil, and book technologies but will finish having encountered the literacies demanded by a wide variety of information and communication technologies (ICTs): Web logs (blogs), word processors, video editors, World Wide Web browsers, Web editors, e-mail, spreadsheets, presentation software, instant messaging, plug-ins for Web resources, listservs, bulletin boards, avatars, virtual worlds, and many others. These students experienced new literacies at the end of their schooling unimagined at the beginning. Given the increasingly rapid pace of change in the technologies of literacy, it is likely that students who begin school this year will experience even more profound changes during their own literacy journeys. Moreover, this story will be repeated again and again as new generations of students encounter yet unimagined ICTs as they move through school and develop currently unenvisioned new literacies.

While it is clear that many new literacies are emerging rapidly, we believe the most essential ones for schools to consider cluster around the Internet and allow students to exploit the extensive ICTs that become available in an online, networked environment. In an information age, we believe it becomes essential to prepare students for these new literacies because they are central to the use of information and the acquisition of knowledge. Traditional definitions of literacy and literacy instruction will be insufficient if we seek to provide students with the futures they deserve.

Precisely what are the new literacies of the Internet and other ICTs? Any realistic analysis of what we know about new literacies from the traditional research literature must recognize that we actually know very little. Far too little research has been conducted in this area for far too long. This is, perhaps, the most troublesome observation that results from any analysis of research in this area (Lankshear & Knobel, 2003; Leu, 2000a).

Another important problem is that we lack a precise definition of what new literacies are. This makes theory development as well as systematic investigation impossible. In order to move forward in this area, we have begun to frame a conception of new literacies around the following definition:

> The new literacies of the Internet and other ICTs include the skills, strategies, and dispositions necessary to successfully use and adapt to the rapidly changing information and communication technologies and contexts that continuously emerge in our world and influence all areas of our personal and professional lives. These new literacies allow us to use the Internet and other ICTs to identify important questions, locate information, critically evaluate the usefulness of that information, synthesize information to answer those questions, and then communicate the answers to others.

A more precise definition of these new literacies may never be possible to achieve because their most important characteristic is that they change regularly; as new technologies for information and communication continually appear, still newer literacies emerge (Bruce, 1997a; Leu, 2000a; Reinking, 1998). The continuous nature of these profound changes requires new theories to help us understand them and also to direct the important research agenda that lies ahead. We argue that new theoretical perspectives must emerge from the new literacies engendered by the requirements and possibilities of new technologies.

The purpose of this chapter is to explore promising lines of theoretical work and to show how a New Literacies Perspective, a theoretical perspective that has informed much of our own work, can provide important insights into the important changes taking place to literacy as the Internet and other ICTs enter our world. We begin by considering the social contexts throughout history that have shaped both the function and form of literate behavior. Next, we discuss literacy within today's social context and explain how this has produced new ICTs, such as the Internet, and the new literacies that these technologies demand. Third, we explore several theoretical perspectives that are emerging and argue why we believe a New Literacies Perspective is especially useful to understand changes taking place to the nature of reading as well as more broadly conceived notions of literacy. Then, we identify a list of 10 principles that inform a New Literacies Perspective. We conclude by considering the implications of this perspective for both research and practice.

LITERACY WITHIN SOCIAL
AND HISTORICAL CONTEXTS

The forms and functions of literacy, as well as literacy instruction itself, are largely determined by the continuously changing social forces at work within any society and the technologies these forces often produce (Boyarin, 1993; Diringer, 1968; Gee, 1996; Illera, 1997; Manguel, 1996; Mathews, 1966; Smith, 1965). Historically, the social forces affecting the nature of literacy have had diverse origins. The need to record business transactions in societies moving out of a subsistence economy, the forces of oppression and resistance, the dissemination of religious dogma, the emergence of democratic institutions, and many other disparate forces all have influenced the nature of literacy in different eras.

Often, we lose sight of these historic roots. We need to remember that social forces and the technologies they often produce define the changing nature of literacy today just as much as they have in the past. Briefly identifying previous historical contexts will remind us of how important it is to understand this point before we explore the changing nature of literacy within our contemporary context.

The manner in which social forces define the nature of literacy can be seen at the beginning of written language, which most believe took place in Sumerian society during the fourth century B.C. As agricultural technologies improved, allowing this civilization to expand, it became necessary to record business transactions and tax records. This social necessity prompted the development of the first writing technology, cuneiform tablets that were used throughout Mesopotamia to initially record economic exchanges and tax obligations (Boyarin, 1993; Diringer, 1968; Manguel, 1996).

In other cultural contexts, literacy became a way to communicate common experiences among the oppressed, often using a special symbolic system. In 11th-century Japan, the women at court developed a separate language system and Lady Murasaki used this to write the first novel, *The Tale of the Genji* (Manguel, 1996; Morris, 1964). The language system she used allowed this novel and other writing to be shared only among the women at court who could understand it.

Responses to oppression also shaped the nature of literacy in Czarist Russia among radical members of society. Revolutionaries developed *samizdat*, a secretive system for the self-publication of texts and literature prohibited by the government. From this clandestine form of writing and reading emerged a set of symbolic representations for revolution and resistance, many of which made their way past unknowing censors into officially published works of literature (Teras, 1994).

At other times, the need to spread religious dogma has shaped the form and function of literacy. In medieval Europe, for example, the Christian church used literacy as a vehicle to enforce a common religion in a world with competing religious viewpoints. A literate priesthood was used to faithfully copy, read, and interpret common religious texts. Holding literacy, the technologies of literacy, and the central texts of Christianity so tightly within a priesthood enabled this religion to survive across enormous distances, cultures, and time, while it also enforced inequities in power.

Forces of resistance inevitably emerged, however, largely due to the belief that individuals, not priests, should be responsible for their own salvation. In postreformation Europe, literacy became much more widespread as Martin Luther argued the need for individuals to read and directly access religious texts on their own. Simultaneous with this resistance, printing technologies and new book literacies emerged to enable this more individual definition of salvation and a more distributed definition of literacy.

The printing of books and the emergence of a more widely distributed literacy posed an important political threat to autocratic government. In England and her colonies, the royal government carefully restricted printing presses. Until 1695, when the Licensing Act of 1662 expired, printing was confined to London, York, and the universities at Oxford and Cambridge (Ford, 2001). Printing was completely forbidden in the royal colony of Virginia until 1730. As one Governor of Virginia, Sir William Berkeley (1642–1652 and 1660–1677) put it, "But, I thank God, there are no free schools nor printing . . . for learning has brought disobedience, and heresy, and sects into the world, and printing has divulged them, and libels against the best government. God keep us from both" (Ford, 2001, p. 6).

In the United States and other countries; the development of democracy, based on informed citizens making reasoned decisions at the ballot box, led to an even more widely distributed definition of literacy, one that included debate within a free press. The development of democracy also led to the establishment of public schools charged with developing citizens who were literate, and in their literacy might be thoughtfully informed about important national affairs in which many were expected to participate (Kaestle, Damon-Moore, Stedmen, Tinsley, & Trollinger, 1993; Mathews, 1966).

It is clear that social contexts profoundly shape the changing nature of literacy. It is also true that social contexts influence the changing nature of literacy instruction. Nila Banton Smith (1965) demonstrated how social forces at work within the United States regularly altered the nature of literacy instruction:

> The story of American reading is a fascinating one to pursue. . . . It is a story which reflects the changing religious, economic, and political institutions of a growing and progressive country. . . . This evolutionary progress in reading has been marked by a series of emphases, each of which has been so fundamental in nature as to have controlled, to a large extent, both the method and content of reading instruction during the period of its greatest intensity. (p. 1)

Smith went on to describe different periods of reading instruction and how each was shaped by the most powerful social forces of its time. These included periods during which reading instruction was influenced by religion (1607–1776), nation building and morality (1776–1840), the education of an intelligent citizenry (1840–1880), the view of reading as a cultural asset (1880–1910), the scientific investigation of reading (1910–1935), international conflict (1935–1950), and culminating, in a prescient analysis, with a period of expanding knowledge and technological revolution (1950 to the present).

Throughout history, literacy and literacy instruction have changed regularly as a result of changing social contexts and the technologies they often prompt. Clearly, the social forces in the present context will exert similar changes. Thus, any attempt to develop a theoretical framework around newly emerging technologies and new literacies must begin by exploring the important social forces at work today. Such an exploration provides the foundation for the New Literacies Perspective.

LITERACY IN TODAY'S SOCIAL CONTEXT

What are the important social forces at work today that frame the changes to literacy that we are experiencing? We believe these social forces include the following:

- global economic competition within economies based increasingly on the effective use of information and communication
- the rapid emergence of the Internet as a powerful new technology for information and communication
- public policy initiatives by governments around the world to ensure higher levels of literacy achievement including the use of the Internet and other ICTs

Global Economic Competition Within Economies Based Increasingly on the Effective Use of Information and Communication

The world of work is undergoing fundamental transformation (Bruce, 1997b; Drucker, 1994; Gilster, 1997; Mikulecky & Kirkley, 1998; The New London Group, 2000). Indeed, it is this social context that prompts many of the changes to ICTs and to literacy that we are experiencing, making the effective use of the Internet a necessary component of the literacy curriculum.

In some historical contexts, the nature of work has been defined by one's access to land, labor, or financial capital. Analyses by Bell (1977), Burton-Jones (1999), Reich (1992), and others indicate this definition has changed fundamentally within nations developing postindustrial economies. Increasingly, it is access to information and the ability to use information effectively that enables individuals to seize life's opportunities. More and more frequently, work is characterized by the effective use of information to solve important problems within a globally competitive economy. Moreover, as networked, digital technologies provide increasingly greater access to larger amounts of information, the efficient use of information skills in competitive workplace contexts becomes even more important (Gilster, 1997; Harrison & Stephen, 1996).

Because trade barriers are falling and international trade is expanding, many workplaces are undergoing a radical transformation (Bruce, 1997a; Drucker, 1994; Gilster, 1997; Mikulecky & Kirkley, 1998). In a global economy in which competition is more intense because competing organizations are more numerous and markets are more extensive, workplaces must seek more productive ways of performing if they hope to survive. Often, they seek to transform themselves into high-performance workplaces that are more productive and more responsive to the needs of their customers.

Traditionally, Industrial-age organizations were organized in a vertical, top-down fashion. Most decisions were made at the highest levels and then communicated to lower levels, thus wasting much of the intellectual capital within an organization by using tight command and control structures. Information-age organizations seeking to achieve greater productivity are organized horizontally, with teams within lower levels of the organization empowered to make important decisions related to their functioning. Members of these teams must quickly identify important problems, locate useful information related to the problems they identify, critically evaluate the information they find, synthesize this information to solve the problems, and then quickly communicate the solutions to others so that everyone within an organization is informed. These high-performance workplaces seek more fully to utilize the intellectual capital among every employee. This change has had a fundamental effect on the nature of literacy within these organizations.

Each element of change that characterizes the workplace today has important implications for the nature of literacy instruction. First, the change to a high-performance workplace requires organizations to place a premium on people who possess effective problem-solving skills. As collaborative teams seek more effective ways of working, they are expected to identify problems important to their unit and seek appropriate solutions. This has important consequences for schools that will need to provide students with greater preparation in identifying important problems and then solving them, often in collaborative situations.

Having identified important problems, members of high-performance workplace teams must then locate useful information related to those problems. Knowing how, when, and where to locate useful information on the Internet, or on an Intranet, will become an increasingly important component of the literacy curriculum, especially because the availability of information resources and search technologies is expanding rapidly, increasing the importance of effective search strategies.

Having acquired information resources, members of high-performance workplace teams must then know how to critically evaluate that information, sorting out accurate information from inaccurate information, essential information from less-essential information, and biased information from unbiased information. These critical literacies and analytic skills also will become increasingly important elements in the literacy curriculum because they are essential to the careful evaluation of any information one obtains, something that is essential in an informational space such as the Internet where anyone may publish anything.

The ability to synthesize information that one has gathered also will become increasingly important because the ability to use information to solve problems is the essential qualification of successful performance in a globally competitive information economy. We will need to pay increasing importance to informational synthesis in schools to support this important skill.

Finally, members of high-performance workplace teams need to rapidly and clearly communicate their solutions to colleagues in other organizational units. A decentralized workplace requires collaboration and communication skills so that the best decisions get made at every level in an organization and so that changes at one level are clearly communicated to other levels. Because each unit is empowered to identify and solve problems, one must keep others informed of changes that are taking place and negotiate these changes with others who might be affected by them. We need to support the development of effective collaboration and communication skills using new communication technologies if we wish to prepare children for their futures in a world where these skills are so important.

It is not surprising that the Internet and other ICTs have appeared and become such a prominent part of our lives during the transition from an industrial to a postindustrial society. These new information and communication tools allow us to identify important problems, quickly gather information, critically evaluate the information we locate, synthesize that information into a solution, and then communicate the solution to others. The new literacies required to effectively use ICTs to accomplish these functions are central to success in an information age.

It is important, however, to recognize that new literacies do not simply create more productive workers and workplaces. Just as important, the new literacies of the Internet and other ICTs provide individuals with opportunities to make their personal lives more productive and fulfilling. This might happen while refinancing a home, selecting a university, advocating for social justice, purchasing books, or any one of hundreds of other tasks important to daily life. In addition, we are beginning to see that the new literacies of the Internet and other ICTs permit greater civic engagement in democratic institutions. Increasingly, national and local politics are changing as more citizens discover important information about candidates, participate online in campaign efforts, organize online communities to support various political agendas, and communicate more frequently with their representatives via e-mail. Expertise in the new literacies of the Internet and other ICTs helps individuals have more satisfying personal lives, more engaged civic lives, as well as more productive professional lives.

The Rapid Emergence of the Internet as a Powerful New Technology for Information and Communication

The appearance of the Internet is not a spontaneous, arbitrary event. It has appeared and become a central part of our lives because the nature of the workplace and other social institutions is changing.

In the workplace, survey data from the United State show recent rapid increases in Internet use, revealing changes taking place from the restructuring process described in the previous section. In just one year (August 2000 to September 2001), use of the Internet at work among all employed adults 25 years of age and older increased by nearly 60%, from 26.1% of the workforce to 41.7% (U.S. Department of Commerce, 2002). If this rate of increase continues, nearly everyone in the workforce will be using the Internet at work within just a few years. Currently, workers in positions with the highest levels of education report the highest levels of Internet use in the United States. In managerial positions with some professional specialty, 80.5% of workers report using the Internet. But even in technical, sales, and administrative support positions, 70.5% of workers report using the Internet (U.S. Department of Commerce, 2002). Clearly the Internet is rapidly becoming central to full participation in the workplace.

Statistics on Internet usage at home in the United States parallel these changes in the workplace. Nearly 60% of all households report that they had Internet access in 2002. Among those who had not previously used the Internet, 47% report that they are somewhat likely or very likely to go online during 2003 (Lebo, 2003). Moreover, the percentage of U.S. households with broadband Internet access has been doubling each year from 1998 to 2001, an adoption rate in households exceeding that of any previous technology including telephones, color televisions, videocassette recorders, cellular phones, and pagers (U.S. Department of Commerce, 2002). Most interesting, perhaps, is that Internet users report an increase in time they spend on the Internet and a decrease in the time they spend viewing television (Lebo, 2003). Internet users report watching about 10% fewer hours of television per week in 2002 (11.2 hours per week) compared to 2001 (12.3 hours per week). This pattern also holds true for U.S. children: Nearly 33% of children reported in 2002 that they are viewing less television than before they started using the Internet; this frequency is up nearly 50% from just one year earlier (Lebo, 2003).

The Internet also is appearing in school classrooms in the United States and other countries at a rate that parallels its appearance in the workplace and at home. In only eight years (1994 to 2002), the percentage of classrooms in the United States possessing at least one computer with Internet access has gone from 3% to 92% (National Center for Education Statistics [NCES], 2003a). This is an adoption rate that is unprecedented in schools for any previous technology including televisions, radios, telephones, videocassette recorders, and even books. The availability of Internet access has had a demonstrated impact on students. In 2001, 94% of children ages 12–17 who had Internet access said that they used the Internet for school-related research (Lenhart, Simon, & Graziano, 2001).

The quality of Internet access in schools has also undergone a rapid transformation. In 1996, three quarters of U.S. public schools with Internet connections reported using phone modem access (Heaviside, Riggins, & Farris, 1997), while in 2002, 94% of schools reported having broadband access (NCES, 2003a), permitting faster access to richer, more memory intensive media. The rate at which schools have moved from phone modem access to broadband access in the United States is even faster than this same migration in homes (cf. Lebo, 2003).

Thus, it is clear that the Internet is rapidly finding its way to a central location in the workplace as well as in home and school contexts. We believe that the appearance of the Internet in the workplace as well as in home and school contexts is one of the most powerful social revolutions taking place today. At the heart of this revolution are the new literacy skills and strategies demanded by the Internet and other ICTs.

Public Policy Initiatives by Governments Around the World to Ensure Higher Levels of Literacy Achievement

Governments around the world are keenly aware of the consequences of global economic competition for their citizens. They have responded by implementing public policies to raise literacy achievement in an attempt to better prepare their children for the challenges that lie ahead. Simultaneously, they have responded with initiatives that provide new ICTs resources to schools in an effort to prepare children for the new literacies of their future. These simultaneous steps by nations around the world are the beginning of a convergence we anticipate for literacy instruction with networked technologies for information and communication (Leu & Kinzer, 2000).

In the United Kingdom, for example, education has been identified as a top priority of the Labour government. The first white paper of this government, *Excellence in Schools*, explains in detail how higher standards for literacy are to be developed and achieved in England, Wales, and Northern Ireland (U.K. Secretary of State for Education and Skills, 1997). The reason for this is clearly linked to global competition in an information age and the implications of a restructured economy: "We are talking about investing in the human capital in the age of knowledge. To compete in a global economy . . . we will have to unlock the potential of every young person" (p. 3).

The U.K. Department for Education and Skills (formerly Department of Education and Employment) has published other papers such as this at "The Standards Site" (www.standards.dfee.gov.uk). Both the national standards and the new national curriculum have included ICTs for the first time (U.K. Department for Education and Skills, 1998). Finally, a National Grid for Learning (www.ngfl.gov.uk) was launched in 1998 to provide an online national portal for teacher and student learning.

Similar policy initiatives are taking place in Finland, one of the first nations to begin this work. The Finnish government appointed an expert committee in 1994 to prepare a national strategy for education, training, and research in an information society. This report, *Education, Training and Research in the Information Society: A National Strategy* (Finland Ministry of Education, 1995), outlines the important role the educational system can play in helping Finland to compete in a global information economy. The report served as the impetus for a number of initiatives from the Ministry of Education, including a three-year program launched in 1996 to teach students effective use of ICTs in schools. This program included developing new teaching methods for the use of ICTs, connecting all schools to the Internet before the year 2000, and providing new computers to schools. Most important, the program also provides every teacher with five weeks of paid release time for professional development in the instructional use of new information technologies (Finland Ministry of Education, 1998; R. Svedlin, personal communication, January 8, 1998).

Ireland, like many other nations, also launched two policy initiatives: a National Reading Initiative and a Schools IT 2000 initiative. The National Reading Initiative included the appointment of a national coordinator, provision for remedial services in every school, a tripling of adult literacy funding, increased funding for remedial teachers, and a program of development for literacy related software (Ireland Department of Education and Science, 1998).

The Schools IT 2000 initiative (Ireland Department of Education and Science, 1998) was implemented because "knowledge and familiarity with new technologies will be an important dimension of employability in the information society" (Ireland Department of Education and Science, 1998). Schools IT 2000 encompassed a number of policy initiatives intended to prepare children for a competitive, global, information economy. These included (a) a Technology Integration Initiative to provide more than 15,000 computers and Internet connections in 1998 with additional funds available during subsequent years; (b) a Teacher Skills Initiative to provide training in ICTs for more than 8,000 teachers; (c) a Schools Support Initiative to develop ScoilNet (www.scoilnet.ie), an Internet portal site to provide information and support for educators; and (d) a School Integration Project to provide funding for at least 40 model schools that will demonstrate the effective use of ICTs in the classroom.

Important policy initiatives also are underway in Australia. In April 1999, the federal government approved *The Adelaide Declaration on National Goals for Schooling in the Twenty-First Century* (Australia Department of Education, Science and Training, 2004), which included an emphasis on both literacy and IT. In particular, the goals noted that "When students leave school, they should . . . be confident, creative and productive users of new technologies, particularly information and communication technologies." Moreover, the federal government has developed *A Strategic Framework for the Information Economy: Identifying Priorities for Action* (Australia National Office for the Information Economy, 1999), which outlines a national strategy and 10 action priorities for becoming more competitive in a global information economy. The second priority focuses on the role of schools in preparing children in information technology: "Deliver the education and skills Australians need to participate in the information economy."

Finally, the federal government along with commonwealth, state, and territory education departments has developed an online Internet portal, Education

Network Australia (www.edna.edu.au). This extensive resource provides a range of information resources for children, teachers, professors, researchers, and policymakers.

New Zealand is also beginning public policy initiatives to raise literacy achievement and to integrate ICTs into the curriculum. At the end of 1998, the government announced that it intended to develop a National Literacy and Numeracy Strategy to enable every 9-year-old to become proficient in reading, writing, and mathematics by 2005 (Literacy Strategy Underway, 1999). As part of this effort, the government appointed a National Literacy Taskforce to assist in developing this strategy. In addition to the need to be competitive in the global economy, the impetus for this is the need to close the gap between good and poor readers (Literacy Strategy Underway, 1999).

Simultaneous with these initiatives in literacy education, the New Zealand national government released a policy paper titled *Interactive Education: An Information and Communication Technologies (ICTs) Strategy for Schools* (New Zealand Ministry of Education, 1998) which describes strategies for supporting the use of ICTs in the nation's schools. This document defines the focus for national initiatives in ICTs: building infrastructure and improving the capability of schools to use ICTs effectively in the curriculum. It describes several new initiatives the national government took in 1999: developing an online portal site for schools, teachers, and children (*Te Kete Ipurangi*, available at www.tki.org.nz/e/tki); providing support for professional development so schools can plan for and implement the use of ICTs more effectively; and supporting model ICTs professional development schools. The reason for these initiatives again was related to global economic competition: "New Zealand schools aim to create a learning environment that enables students to develop the attitudes, knowledge, understandings, and skills to enable them . . . to succeed in the modern competitive economy" (New Zealand Ministry of Education, 1998, Introduction).

The United States has a long history of state and local control over educational policies and a recent past characterized by intense partisanship at the federal level over educational issues. As a result, national policy initiatives have been difficult to implement in education. Prior to 2002, most of the public policy initiatives for raising literacy achievement took place at the state level. Many states established standards or benchmarks, often in conjunction with new statewide assessment instruments. Many states also initiated polices to infuse more IT and ICTs in the classroom.

At the federal level, educational policy initiatives had been more diffuse in origin, and many were implemented only after bitter partisan debates. Nevertheless, several important initiatives at the federal level have focused on literacy issues. These initiatives produced legislation such as The Reading Excellence Act, the appointment of a National Reading Panel, and the development of Standards for the English Language Arts (International Reading Association [IRA] & National Council of Teachers of English [NCTE], 1996). Each of these initiatives, designed to improve reading achievement, was marked by substantial controversy. The controversy has continued with the passage of the No Child Left Behind Act in 2002.

The No Child Left Behind Act enacts an extensive list of public policy initiatives, many of which are also designed to increase student achievement in reading. These provisions include several requirements: that all students are proficient in reading and math within 12 years; that assessment in both reading and math be conducted annually for all students in grades 3–8 and be conducted at least once in grades 10–12; that reading programs be funded only if they are based on scientifically based reading research; and that all teachers be highly qualified, with state certification.

Similar to other nations, this major policy initiative in reading also contains a technology component. Title II, Section D, of the No Child Left Behind Act is devoted to technology with the stated goal, "To assist every student in crossing the digital divide by ensuring that every student is technologically literate by the time the student finishes the eighth grade, regardless of the student's race, ethnicity, gender, family income, geographic location, or disability." In order to promote the goals of this section, the U.S. federal government plans to provide $1 million each year, most of which will go for state and local technology grants. States must provide a long-range plan for implementing this initiative, and all local units must devote a minimum of 25% of the funds to professional development in the instructional use of the Internet and other ICTs. In addition, the Secretary of Education is charged with developing a national educational technology plan.

In addition to the No Child Left Behind Act, a major policy initiative has been the establishment of the Universal Service Support Mechanism for Schools and Libraries, a policy initiative known informally as the "E-rate program." This program is funded by Congress under the Telecommunications Act of 1996 and is administered by the Schools and Libraries Division (SLD) of the Universal Service Administrative Company (www.sl.universalservice.org), a nonprofit organization established by the Federal Communications Commission for this purpose. Starting in 1998, the program began to annually distribute up to $2.25 billion in financial support to schools and libraries for Internet access based on indicators of financial need. This program has contributed in important ways to the rapid infusion of Internet-connected computers within the K–12 classrooms of the United States.

In summary, many nations around the world, aware of the need to prepare students for the challenges of a competitive global economy, are developing public policy initiatives to raise literacy standards and infuse ICTs into the curriculum. While each nation approaches the issue in its own fashion, what is striking is the common effort in this direction. Especially salient is the federal response from those nations, like Australia and the United States, with a long tradition of local control and little previous history of federal intervention. Even these countries are beginning to develop important national initiatives to raise literacy levels and prepare children in the use of ICTs.

THE IMPORTANCE OF AN EXPANDED DEFINITION OF LITERACY: EMERGING THEORETICAL PERSPECTIVES[1]

We have seen how three important social forces in today's world are shaping both the forms and functions of literacy:

1. global economic competition within economies based increasingly on the effective use of information and communication
2. the rapid emergence of the Internet as a powerful new technology for information and communication
3. public policy initiatives by governments around the world to ensure higher levels of literacy achievement, including the use of the Internet and other ICTs

It is clear that the nature of literacy is changing rapidly as new ICTs appear, requiring new literacies to fully exploit their potential in what Reinking (1998) has called our **"post-typographic" world**. These changes make it increasingly impossible to function in the worlds of research, theory, and practice if we define literacy in ways that ignore the reality of the new literacies of the Internet and other ICTs. Questions and issues about types of texts, types of literacies, assessment, curriculum, and teacher education, and how these are impacted by present and emerging technologies, must be addressed if we are to shape theories and pedagogies of literacy that dynamically respond to social and technological change.

> **post-typographic world**—a world in which printed text is no longer the dominant format of text/information

Yet to address these issues in a cogent manner, we must begin to develop an adequate definition of what it means to be literate. To develop such a definition, one must ask whether *literacy* as a term presupposes print, whether it presupposes text. Does literacy mean comprehension of print or comprehension of a message that has permanence in ways that a nonrecorded oral message does not? Does reading children's literature presuppose a printed children's book, or can children's literature exist on a CD-ROM or website? Does text presuppose only print, or does it include all aspects in an author's toolbox, which allows meaning to be preserved for later reading and response by an audience?

In addition, definitions and theories of literacy also must consider the rapid changes we are experiencing today as new ICTs regularly emerge. We have argued that the definition of literacy has always changed over historical periods but that it is changing today at a pace we have never before experienced as new technologies for information and communication appear rapidly and continuously (Leu, 2000a; Leu & Kinzer, 2000). Literacy, therefore, may be thought of as a moving target, continually changing its meaning depending on what society expects literate individuals to do. As societal expectations for literacy change, and as the demands on literate functions in a society change, so too must definitions of literacy change to reflect this moving target.

Current definitions of literacy have moved well beyond earlier definitions of literacy as the ability to sound out words and/or copy accurately what is dictated. Definitions of reading, for example, have moved far beyond Flesch's (1955, 1981) views that "[we should teach the child] letter-by-letter and sound-by-sound until he knows it—and when he knows it, he knows how to read" (1955, p. 121) and "learning to read is like learning to drive a car . . . The child learns the mechanics of reading, and when he's through; he can read" (1981, p. 3). Definitions by Dechant (1982), Goodman (1976), Rumelhart (1994), and others include one's interaction between the text and the reader and include comprehension of the message in addition to decoding the printed page. These authors recognized that the ability to communicate, to present one's message, and to understand and evaluate another's message is part of reading, and that an interaction and transaction into one's experiences as well as personal response and meaning-making is part of the goal for literacy instruction (Harste, 1990; Rosenblatt, 1994; Shanahan, 1990). Yet all these definitions come from a perspective of print and owe their historical roots and conceptions of literacy to a largely print-based world.

Of course, these definitions can be applied to literacy in technological environments to the extent that the symbol systems available to readers and writers when the definitions were conceptualized also exist in electronic environments. However, to the extent that there are additional demands and capabilities of literacy in electronic environments beyond those available at the times respective definitions were conceptualized, current definitions may be less applicable. And, perhaps, the greatest shortcomings of current definitions can be seen in the requirements of interactions between traditionally available literacy resources and new ones, and in the demands on readers and writers that were previously not required for authorship, comprehension, and response to occur. We argue that, as the medium of the message changes, comprehension processes, decoding processes, and what "counts" as literacy activities must change to reflect readers' and authors' present-day strategies for comprehension and response.

Clearly, definitions of literacy must change to include electronic environments. In some ways, however, incorporating technology into definitions of literacy becomes less an argument about whether or not such changes are needed or are effective and more a recognition that schools must incorporate technology or be viewed as out of touch or even irrelevant (see, Hagood, Stevens, & Reinking, 2003; Lewis & Finders, 2002). Even though many are calling for more research on the efficacy of technology in learning, there is increasing recognition that technology is here to stay; the demand from businesses, parents, and society at large is such that technology will continue to appear in schools even before research outcomes are known.

In sum, the significance of the increasing availability of technology within and beyond schools relates to their situated use in literacy practice, and perhaps relates just as much to the symbolic capital (Bourdieu, 1991) of the technologies in relation to the social spaces of schooling (Bromley & Apple, 1998; Bruce, 1997a). Technology availability in schools both changes literate signifying practices and signifies change in and of itself. The material and ideological meanings of the computer, as with any tool (Cole, 1996), are deeply intertwined. While this double relation of meaning is true across the subject areas of schooling, it may be particularly true for language arts given the significant construction of a discourse on *technological* knowledge as a form of literacy. In this sense, *literacy* might index a very broad range of knowledge and practice (e.g., having technical skill across programs and platforms, knowing how to install and upgrade software) with developing technologies.

Within such a web of practice and representation, schools and districts lacking technology could well be imagined as only "partially literate" spaces. This, of course, is not an argument for the proliferation of technology in schooling. Rather, it is an argument that, in many ways, the meaning of schooled literacy has already been (and will continue to be) articulated with the availability and meaning of technology. As Cammack (2003) points out in her review of Alvermann's (2002) edited volume, "differences in technology use and perceptions of value between teachers and students can effectively act to block change in the integration and use of technology in literacy pedagogy."

Definitions of literacy must move beyond being located in only paper printed media. Children's literature cannot be limited only to the pages in a paper-based book of printed pages, but must include books in electronic formats as well. The added information and capabilities that electronic formats provide for authors and readers necessitate an expanded view of literacy, what it means to be literate, and what it means to be a teacher (and learner) in the language arts.

Consider, for example, that "decoding" in a print context involves decoding the alphabetic characters as well as any pictures, charts, maps, and graphs that are included on the page. In this sense, the decoding and interpretation of graphics and other forms of media as literacy practice is certainly not a new development, and over the last decade or so researchers have been giving increasing attention to the significance of images, television, drama, and other forms of media in the literate lives of children (Alvermann, Hinchman, Moore, Phelps, & Waff, 1998; Dyson, 1999; Flood & Lapp, 1995). Such work provides an important research base from which to analyze literacy practices in the multimedia environment of the Internet.

At the same time; the nature and relationships of Internet multimedia also pose unique problems that the study of offline multimedia forms cannot address adequately. For example, forms of decoding are developing that were either relatively minor or simply not possible offline. In an electronic environment, decoding for comprehension includes decoding the strategic use of color; various clues that indicate hyperlinked texts and graphics; the possible actions of meaning-bearing icons and animations; and pictures, maps, charts, and graphs that are not static, but that can change to address questions that an interactive reader can pose to informational text during the reading act. Although definitions of literacy still must include concepts of composition, decoding, comprehension, and response, in order to understand how each of these definitional factors play out in electronic environments we must take into account current uses as indicators of current definitions of literacy.

With personal computers' and the Internet's graphical interfaces, it is no longer possible to position the print text as the focal text in all instances, with images serving only a supporting role in meaning construction. As many webpages are overwhelmingly an assemblage of images, understanding reading across these images significantly decenters print-based reading (Flood & Lapp, 1995). **Hypermedia** reading practices have at least as much to do with the multiple relations between images as they do with the paths among segments of print text. Importantly, the nature of images also permits writers and readers to link them in ways other than paper-based texts. For instance, while typically a term or phrase of text is linked in linear sequence, an image may be divided into an "image map" in which diverse topological parts of the image are linked to other various images, text, video, or media objects. Running a mouse pointer over an image, for example, often "pops up" text without the mouse being clicked, or causes expansion of an image or graphic. Part of a pie chart might expand with new information when the pointer is moved over its slices, yet no overt clue exists that this would occur, presenting a serendipitous and differential experience across readers who might or might not have moved the mouse pointer over the image.

> **hypermedia**—a nonlinear medium of information that is created by an author's use of a variety of text, hyperlinks, and other graphic tools or representations

Perhaps more significant, changing definitions must acknowledge the expanded presence of multimedia, which has led to a proliferation of new combinations of authoring (e.g., voice-annotated websites, video clips with **hypertextual analysis**). Lemke (1998), from a semiotic perspective, argues convincingly that a central problem is that meanings are not fixed and additive, but multiplicative. That is, in the electronic environment what must be interpreted is not a complementary relation of separately developed texts but the expansive signification of an entire sign system. The literacies necessary to understand multiple, interdependent meanings index the need for complex understandings of literacy "toolkits" (Gee, 1990; Wertsch, 1991) for interpreting and producing meaning in hypermedia that includes but extends traditional texts.

> **hypertextual analysis**—an avenue in which a reader can establish and create meaning across a variety of texts

Despite all these changes, our understanding of the new literacies required by ICTs is not well advanced. No single theoretical perspective has yet to explain the full range of the changes to literacy brought about by the Internet and other ICTs. Nevertheless, several useful perspectives are beginning to evolve from various quarters. These include perspectives that focus on critical literacies (Luke, 1997; Muspratt, Luke, & Freebody, 1998), multiliteracies (The New London Group, 2000), media-literacy (Tyner, 1998), and others that provide us with insights about the new literacies of ICTs.

Some, for example, have argued that a literacy curriculum during an age of information needs to include new, critical literacies that enable children to adequately evaluate messages from individuals and corporations that shape the information they provide (Muspratt et al., 1998). These authors argue that it is impossible to discuss literacy without considering who is using it and for what purposes. They describe the essential need to understand the stance of the person producing a message, the motive behind the message, and the need to critically evaluate these messages. They foreground the important need to develop critical literacies as an essential element of any instructional program because new media forms, globalization, and economic pressures engender messages that increasingly attempt to persuade individuals to act in ways beneficial to an economic or political unit but not necessarily beneficial to the individual. During an age of information, any theoretical perspective that seeks to capture the changes taking place to literacy must include these essential critical literacies. As the Internet quickly becomes both an important source for information and an important commercial and political context, critical literacies become even more important to our lives.

> **heuristic**—method or procedure of learning or discovery based on the use of inquiry to find a solution through various avenues, such as trial and error, experimentation, and evaluation

A second **heuristic** that is useful comes from the work of The New London Group (2000). Emerging from sociolinguistic traditions, the group uses the construct *multiliteracies* to capture changes taking place in two dimensions central to literacy: (1) the multiple modalities of communication in a world where many new communication technologies have appeared and (2) the growing diversity of culture and language within an increasingly global community. Instead of defining literacy as a unitary construct, this group recognizes the inherent diversity that constructs literacy in a world defined by new technologies of communication and new cultural and linguistic contexts that become more visible with globalization. Within this type of theoretical framework, one might view reading, writing, and communication on the Internet as including a set of multiliteracies, emerging as individuals from different cultural contexts encounter one another within different communication technologies.

Still others (Silverblatt, Ferry, & Finan, 1999; Tyner, 1998) take a media literacy perspective, which focuses on the new literacies required from new media forms. Media literacy perspectives often are closely aligned with critical literacy perspectives, though they focus more on media forms beyond text such as video and the images that often drive a culture. Like those who take a critical literacy perspective, proponents of a media literacy perspective stress the importance of analyzing an author's stance and motives as well as the need for a critical evaluation of the message itself. This perspective is important to include when considering literacy within Internet technologies because these technologies make possible a panoply of media forms within a single message, thus increasing the importance of understanding how each may be used by an author to shape a reader's interpretation. And, because locations on the Internet often are populated with commercial, political, and economic motives, it becomes essential to be able to carefully evaluate these while gathering information (Kinzer & Leander, 2003).

Other theoretical orientations, too, are possible when considering new literacies appearing on the Internet. These include feminist perspectives (Hawisher & Selfe, 1999), perspectives that draw from postmodernist interpretations of popular culture (Alvermann, Moon, & Hagood, 1999), or perspectives that come from work in cultural transformations (Warschauer, 1999). Each has important insights to contribute to understanding the changes that are taking place.

Although each of these perspectives provides essential insights, we believe they are limited for at least two reasons. First, they fail to place the Internet and other ICTs at the center of their perspective. Instead of emerging from the new literacies of the Internet and other ICTs, these theoretical perspectives have evolved from other contexts and have then been applied to the ICTs landscape. We believe the new literacies of the Internet, because they are more encompassing and because they change more rapidly and in more profound ways than traditional print literacies, require their own theoretical framework in order to adequately understand them and the role they should play in a literacy curriculum.

A second limitation also exists. Other theoretical orientations frequently suffer from a narrower theoretical grounding, often because each has emerged from a more limited tradition of inquiry. For example, while a multiliteracies perspective is a most useful one, its sociolinguistic grounding somewhat limits its ability to predict any of the more cognitive and ontological aspects of new literacies that students must develop in order to become literate with the Internet and other ICTs (Lankshear & Knobel, 2003). We believe that any theory must bring multiple perspectives (Labbo & Reinking, 1999) to bear on framing the totality of the new literacies emerging from the Internet and other ICTs if it is to be useful in informing the complex teaching and learning issues within school contexts.

In short, we believe that a theoretical framework for the new literacies of the Internet and other ICTs needs to be grounded in these technologies themselves, taking advantage of the insights that a variety of different perspectives might bring to understanding the complete picture of the new literacies emerging from these technologies.

IDENTIFYING CENTRAL PRINCIPLES OF NEW LITERACIES EMERGING FROM THE INTERNET AND OTHER ICTS

Although it is too early to define a comprehensive theory of new literacies emerging from these technologies, we are convinced that it is time to begin this process by identifying the central principles on which this theory should be built. Our work is pointing us to these principles of a New Literacies Perspective:

1. The Internet and other ICTs are central technologies for literacy within a global community in an information age.
2. The Internet and other ICTs require new literacies to fully access their potential.
3. New literacies are deictic.
4. The relationship between literacy and technology is transactional.
5. New literacies are multiple in nature.

6. Critical literacies are central to the new literacies.
7. New forms of strategic knowledge are central to the new literacies.
8. Speed counts in important ways within the new literacies.
9. Learning often is socially constructed within new literacies.
10. Teachers become more important, though their role changes, within new literacy classrooms.

The Internet and Other ICTs Are Central Technologies for Literacy Within a Global Community in an Information Age

From a sociolinguistic perspective, Gee (1996) and The New London Group (2000) have argued that literacy is embedded in and develops out of the social practices of a culture. We agree and, from a historical perspective, have demonstrated how different literacies have emerged from different social contexts and the technologies they often prompt.

For the past 500 years, literacy has emerged from a variety of social contexts but has been shaped largely by the technologies of the book and the printing press. Today, both the social context and the technologies of our age are rapidly changing. We believe the Internet and other ICTs are quickly becoming the central technologies of literacy for a global community in an information age. As a result, these technologies are quickly defining the new literacies that will increasingly be a part of our future. Literacy theory, research, and practice must begin to recognize this important fact.

Looking briefly at how reading comprehension takes place on the Internet will illustrate how we need to rethink our assumptions about literacy. Traditionally, reading comprehension has often been defined by the construction of meaning from a fixed body of text. On the Internet, reading comprehension takes on a very different and broader definition. New skills and strategies are required in this context to successfully comprehend information such as how to search for appropriate information; how to comprehend search engine results; how to make correct inferences about information that will be found at any hyperlink; how to determine the extent to which authors "shape" information presented on a webpage; how to coordinate and synthesize vast amounts of information, presented in multiple media formats, from a nearly unlimited set of sources; and how to know which informational elements require attention and which ones may be ignored. Perhaps we can best recognize this fundamentally different conception of reading comprehension when we understand that two students, with an identical goal, will construct meaning differently, not only because they bring different background knowledge to the task but also because they will use very different search strategies, follow very different informational paths, read very different sets of information, draw very different critical conclusions about what they have read, and attend to very different informational elements. Reading comprehension has a very different meaning on the Internet (Coiro, 2003).

The Internet and Other ICTs Require New Literacies to Fully Access Their Potential

New literacies include the skills, strategies, and disposition that allow us to use the Internet and other ICTs effectively to identify important questions, locate information, critically evaluate the usefulness of that information, synthesize information to answer those questions, and then communicate the answers to others. We encounter new literacies nearly every time we try to read, write, and communicate with the Internet and other ICTs. Examples of new literacies include

- using a search engine effectively to locate information;
- evaluating the accuracy and utility of information that is located on a webpage in relation to one's purpose;
- using a word processor effectively, including using functions such as checking spelling accuracy, inserting graphics, and formatting text;
- participating effectively in bulletin board or listserv discussions to get needed information;
- knowing how to use e-mail to communicate effectively; and
- inferring correctly the information that may be found at a hyperlink on a webpage.

It is essential, however, to keep in mind that new literacies, such as these, almost always build on foundational literacies rather than replace them. Foundational literacies include those traditional elements of literacy that have defined almost all our previous efforts in both research and practice. These include skill sets such as phonemic awareness, word recognition, decoding knowledge, vocabulary knowledge, comprehension, inferential reasoning, the writing process, spelling, response to literature, and others required for the literacies of the book and other printed material. Foundational literacies will continue to be important within the new literacies of the Internet and other ICTs. In fact, it could be argued that they will become even more essential because reading and writing become more important in an information age. While foundational literacies become more important, they also will be insufficient if one is to fully utilize the Internet and other ICTs (Coiro, 2003; IRA, 2002; Leu, 2000b; RAND Reading Study Group, 2002; Spires & Estes, 2002; Sutherland-Smith, 2002). Reading, writing, and communication will assume new forms as text is combined with new media resources and linked within complex information networks requiring new literacies for their effective use.

New Literacies Are Deictic

Leu (1997a, 2000a) and Leu and Kinzer (2000) have argued that we are entering a period of literacy as technological deixis. During this period, the forms and functions of literacy change rapidly as new technologies for information and communication emerge and as individuals construct new envisionments for their use.

The term *deixis* (dike-sis) is a word used by linguists and others (Fillmore, 1972; Murphy, 1986) for words such as *now, today, here, there, go,* and *come.* These are words whose meanings change quickly depending on the time or space in which they are uttered. If we say "now" as we write this draft, it means our current moment during the spring of 2003. If you say "now" when you encounter this example, it means the moment in time when you read these lines. While to Gertrude Stein "A rose is a rose, is a rose," *now* is not *now,* is not *now.* Rather, its meaning depends on the temporal context when it is uttered or written.

Literacy also is deictic (dike-tic). We have seen how both the forms and functions of literacy have changed regularly over time, but because technological change happened slowly, the changes to literacy occurred over extended historical periods. Today, technological change happens so rapidly that the changes to literacy are limited not by technology but rather by our ability to adapt and acquire the new literacies that emerge. Deixis is a defining quality of the new literacies of the Internet and other ICTs. This will continue into the future but at a much faster pace as new technologies repeatedly appear, requiring new skills and new strategies for their effective use. As literacy increasingly becomes deictic, the changing constructions of literacy within new technologies will require all of us to keep up with these changes and to prepare students for a vastly different conception of what it means to become literate.

There are three sources for the deictic nature of literacy: (1) transformations of literacy because of technological change, (2) envisionments of new literacy potentials within new technologies, and (3) the use of increasingly efficient technologies of communication that rapidly spread new literacies. Each source contributes to the fundamental changes taking place in the nature of literacy.

The rapid transformations in the nature of literacy caused by technological change are a primary source for the deictic nature of literacy. New technologies regularly and repeatedly transform previous literacies, regularly redefining what it means to become literate. Consider, for example, the new writing skills required to effectively use a word processor like Microsoft Word. Each time one upgrades to a new version (Word 6, Word 2001, Word 2003, etc.) one must develop new composing and communication skills to take full advantage of the new potentials within each new version. While one might have needed the ability to save documents in different formats in an early version of this program, later versions require additional composing skills such as inserting photographic images from one's photo files or editing a graphic image that is placed within a document. Subsequent generations of this single program will require even newer literacies as new technologies generate new communication and information potentials.

The deictic nature of literacy also is caused by the envisionments we construct as we use new technologies for literate acts. Individuals who use new technologies often envision new ways of using them and, in their envisionments, change the nature of literacy (Leu, Karchmer, & Leu, 1999). Envisionments take place when individuals imagine new possibilities for literacy and learning, transform existing technologies to construct this vision, and then share their work with others. This happens regularly within technologies that permit users to create new visions for their use, something that defines the Internet and most other ICTs.

Consider a person who wishes to send a specially designed and formatted message via e-mail, but she has an e-mail program containing very limited design and format tools. This person might think to use a word processor with more powerful design tools to compose the message, knowing that she could then paste the formatted message into the e-mail message window. Thus, a word processor can be transformed into a tool for composing e-mail messages, a purpose for which it was not designed, but a function it fills admirably. This potential only comes to life when a person envisions a new function for a technology and enacts this envisionment. In essence, we can say that she envisioned how to repurpose a technology for a new and different function. Envisionments such as this happen regularly as individuals encounter new problems and seek solutions in new and creative uses of existing technologies. They contribute to the deictic nature of literacy.

The third factor that prompts the deictic nature of literacy is the use of increasingly efficient technologies of communication that rapidly distribute new literacies. The Internet and other ICTs not only change themselves, but they also provide the central vehicle for exchanging new technologies for information and communication. Increasingly, for example, we simply download new technologies from the Internet when these appear rather than receive a CD or other storage medium through the traditional mail system. Because we can now immediately download a new technology from the Internet or send it to millions of individuals with just a keystroke, the changes to literacy derived from new technologies now happen at a faster pace than ever before. This increases the already rapid pace of change in the forms and functions of literacy, increasing the complexity of the challenges we face as we consider how best to prepare students for their literacy futures. Thus, the rapid pace of change in the forms and functions of literacy are exacerbated by the speed with which new technologies and new envisionments are communicated (Leu, 2000a).

In summary, we believe that the deictic nature of literacy will increase in the years ahead, limited only by our own ability to adapt to the new literacies that emerge. People, not technology, will limit the speed with which new literacies appear.

The Relationship Between Technology and Literacy Is Transactional

Technology transforms the forms and functions of literacy (Reinking, 1998), but literacy also transforms the forms and functions of technology. Thus, the relationship between literacy and technology is transactional. We have argued above, and most would agree, that new technologies for information and communication require new literacies to fully exploit their potential. It is important to recognize, however, that when we use technology in new ways, we also transform the technology itself, creating additional new literacies in the process.

The most common mechanism by which users transform a technology through their literate behavior is what we have referred to earlier as an envisionment. When individuals imagine new possibilities for literacy, transform the function or the structure of existing technologies to construct this vision, and then share their work with others, an envisionment has occurred.

In addition, though, technology is transformed through instructional practices in literacy classrooms. This happens every day on the Internet when educators construct new curricular resources with Internet technologies and then share their work with others (Leu et al., 1999). Examples include the following:

- Harriet Tubman & The Underground Railroad (www2.lhric.org/pocantico/tubman/tubman.html), a site developed by Patty Taverna, Terry Hongell, and Patty's second-grade class at Pocantico Hills School in Sleepy Hollow, New York
- Earth Day Groceries Project (www.earthdaybags.org), an environmental project developed by Mark Ahlness, a third-grade teacher in Seattle, Washington
- SCORE Cyberguides (www.sdcoe.k12.ca.us/score/cyberguide.html), a collection of Internet resources for individual works of literature contributed by teachers and coordinated by the San Diego schools
- Book Rap (http://rite.ed.qut.edu.au/old_oz-teachernet/projects/book-rap), literature discussion groups run over the Internet from Australia

While these new instructional tools, and thousands of others that are appearing, provide important resources for the literacy classroom, each also requires additional new literacies for their effective use.

New Literacies Are Multiple in Nature

A New Literacies Perspective recognizes that a singular label, literacy, fails to capture the complexity of the changes that can only be captured by a plural label. Increasingly, scholars are beginning to recognize that changes taking place result in multiple new literacies required in different social contexts. For example, The New London Group (2000) defines *multiliteracies* as a set of open-ended and flexible multiple literacies required to function in diverse contexts and communities. We believe the same multiplicity of literacy is emerging because of multiple technological contexts. We believe that the Internet and other ICTs require that we develop a systematic understanding of the multiple literacies that exist within these many different contexts. This multiplicity of new literacies is apparent on at least three different levels.

The first level of multiplicity that characterizes the new literacies of Internet technologies is that meaning is typically represented with multiple media forms. Unlike traditional text forms that typically include a combination of two types of media—print and two-dimensional graphics—Internet texts integrate a range of symbols and multiple-media formats including icons, animated symbols, audio, video, interactive tables, virtual reality environments, and many more (Brunner & Tally, 1999; Lemke, 1998). Also, Web designers often use nontraditional combinations of font size and color, with little uniformity in style and design from one website to another (Ciolek, 1996). As a result, we confront new forms and combinations of texts and images that challenge our traditional understandings of how information is represented and shared with others. The multiplicative effects of these unique combinations of multiple-media forms (Lemke, 1998) demand that students "understand how various literacies and various cultural traditions combine these different semiotic modalities to make meanings that are more than the sum of what each could mean separately" (p. 288). For traditional language arts curriculums that tend to focus on the process of making meaning from text as opposed to critically analyzing and interpreting the messages within images, Internet technologies require literacy educators to broaden their definitions of literacy to encompass these new, complex, and multiple forms of Internet literacies.

The second level of multiplicity is that the Internet and other ICTs offer multiple tools for constructing multiple forms of communication. Literate individuals will be those who can effectively assess their individual purposes for using the Internet and then seek out, from the Internet's many offerings, the particular tool and form that best meet their needs. For example, when seeking particular information, readers will need to know procedures for using key-words within the most appropriate type of search engine while those hoping to browse online resources for the sake of open-ended exploration should be familiar with the hierarchical categories of information indexed by many search engines. Similarly, when hoping to communicate asynchronously with others, Internet users should be literate in tools such as e-mail, listservs, and discussion boards. When seeking more real-time interactive forms of information, Internet users need to have an understanding of how to access instant messaging technologies, communicate effectively with video conference technologies, participate in chat rooms, and enter virtual environments. A New Literacies Perspective assumes that proficient users of the Internet also will understand how to construct, design, manipulate, and upload their own information to add to the constantly growing and changing body of knowledge that defines the Internet.

A final level of multiplicity that characterizes the new literacies of Internet technologies consists of the new skills demanded by our students as they more frequently encounter information from individuals in different social contexts. In schools, at home, and in the workplace, the Internet provides opportunities for individuals to meet and exchange ideas, yet it is important to realize that each of these ideas is not an isolated piece of information but, rather, is shaped by the social and cultural contexts in which each of us exists. Typically, students are accustomed to exchanging information with others within their own classroom, school, or neighborhood and usually are not surprised by what they learn through these exchanges. However, the global sharing of information permitted by the Internet introduces new challenges for students now expected to interpret and respond to information from multiple social and cultural contexts that share profoundly different assumptions about our world. These multiple contexts for new literacies have important implications for educators preparing students to critically understand and interpret the meaning of text and images they find on the Internet.

Critical Literacies Are Central to the New Literacies

Another central principle of the new literacies is that they demand new forms of critical literacy and additional dependence on critical thinking and analysis as one encounters information. Open networks such as the Internet permit anyone to publish anything; this is one of the opportunities this technology presents. However, this open access also is one of the Internet's limitations; information is much more widely available from people who have strong political, economic, religious, or ideological stances that profoundly influence the nature of the information they present to others. As a result, we must assist students in becoming more critical consumers of the information they encounter (Alvermann et al., 1999; Muspratt et al., 1998). Although the literacy curriculum (and assessment programs) have always included items such as critical thinking and separating fact from propaganda, richer and more complex analysis skills will need to be included in classrooms where the Internet and other ICTs begin to play a more prominent role.

As we begin to study the new literacies of the Internet we will depend greatly on work from the communities of critical literacy and media literacy and will be informed by research that targets higher-order thinking about what is being communicated. Multiple, critical literacies populate the new literacies of the Internet, requiring new skills, strategies, and insights to successfully exploit the rapidly changing information and media technologies continuously emerging in our world.

New Forms of Strategic Knowledge Are Central to the New Literacies

Mayer (1997) has reminded us that each technology contains different contexts and resources for constructing meanings and requires somewhat different strategies for doing so. New technologies for networked information and communication are complex and require many new strategies for their effective use. Hypertext technologies, for example, embedded with multiple forms of media and unlimited freedoms of multiple navigational pathways, present opportunities that may seduce some readers away from important content unless they have developed strategies to deal with these seductions (Lawless & Kulikowich, 1996; Lawless, Mills, & Brown, 2002). Other cognitive and aesthetic changes to text on the Internet present new challenges to comprehension (Coiro, 2003; Spires & Estes, 2002), inquiry (Eagleton, 2001), and information seeking (Sutherland-Smith, 2002) as well. Moreover, as we have argued, the technologies of the Internet will continue to change regularly and rapidly, presenting us with even newer technologies of literacy that demand more (and more sophisticated) strategies to effectively exploit them. Thus, the new literacies will be largely defined around the strategic knowledge central to the effective use of information within rich and complexly networked environments.

There will be many types of strategic knowledge important to the new literacies. We can be certain, though, that they will include the new forms of strategic knowledge necessary to locate, evaluate, and effectively use the extensive resources available within the Internet. The extent and complexity of this information is staggering. Moreover, these already extensive resources increase each day as new computers are connected to networks and as people create new information and publish it for others to use. They require new forms of strategic knowledge in order to exploit them effectively. How do we best search for information in these complex worlds? How do we design a webpage to be useful to people who are likely to visit? How do we communicate effectively with video-conference technologies? How do we function in the virtual worlds that are being developed as social learning environments? What are the rules for participating on listservs, chatrooms, bulletin boards, and other electronic communication environments? These questions highlight the central role that strategic knowledge will play for people who communicate using the new literacies of the Internet and other ICTs.

Speed Counts in Important Ways Within the New Literacies

In a world of vast information resources, the new literacies of the Internet will be defined in important ways around the rate at which one can read, write, and communicate. Within competitive information economies where problem identification and solution are critical, the rate at which one can acquire, evaluate, and use information to solve important problems becomes central to success. The speed it takes to acquire information will become an important measure of success within various technologies. Quickly finding, evaluating, using, and communicating information will become central instructional issues.

As speed becomes essential for the effective use of the new literacies of the Internet and other ICTs, it will be critical to solve the equity issues that result from children who process and communicate information at different rates. Slow readers and writers are challenged within traditional literacies; within the new literacies of the Internet these individuals will be left far behind. The gap between highly literate and literacy challenged individuals will be exacerbated by the new literacies of the Internet. Highly literate individuals will skim webpages, link to other webpages, and generally sift through large amounts of information in a short time. Individuals who read slowly and haltingly will still be evaluating the first screen of information by the time a more rapid reader has already completed the informational task. If we truly seek to enable every student to succeed in a society defined by information and the speed with which it may be accessed, we will need to devote substantial resources to discover solutions to this important issue.

Learning Often Is Socially Constructed Within New Literacies

We expect that social learning strategies will be central to literacy instruction in the future, and here we highlight two dimensions that are important to recognize within our current framework of a New Literacies Perspective.

First, social learning plays an important role in the exchange of new skills and strategies needed to interact within increasingly complex and continually changing technologies for information and communication. Models of literacy instruction often have focused on an adult whose role is to teach the skills he or she possesses to a group of students who do not know those skills. This is no longer possible, or even appropriate, within a world of multiple new literacies framed by the Internet and other ICTs. In fact, today, many young students possess higher levels of knowledge about some of these new literacies than most adults. It is simply impossible for one person to know all the new literacies and teach these directly to others. Each of us, however, will know something unique and useful to others.

Consequently, effective learning experiences will be increasingly dependent on social learning strategies and the ability of a teacher to orchestrate literacy learning opportunities between and among students who know different new literacies. This will distribute knowledge about literacy throughout the classroom, especially as students move above the stages of foundational literacy. One student, for example, may know how to edit digital video scenes in the hope of including these within a webpage, but another may know how best to compress the video so that it can function optimally in a Web-based environment. In a student-centered, social learning environment, this knowledge can be exchanged, ironically, in a classroom where the teacher may not know either of these skills as well as the students. By orchestrating opportunities for the exchange of new literacies, both teachers and students may enhance their literacy skills and their potential for effective communication and information use. This social learning ability may not come naturally to all students, however, and many will need to be supported in learning how to learn about literacy from one another (Labbo, 1996; Labbo & Kuhn, 1998).

If, as we believe, literacy learning becomes increasingly dependent on social learning strategies, socially skilled learners will be advantaged while "monastic learners," children who rely solely on independent learning strategies, may be disadvantaged. This will be an important change in many classrooms because individual learning often has been the norm, privileging children who learn well independently. In classrooms where the acquisition of new literacies is important, children who are better at independent learning experiences will be disadvantaged. Increasingly, we must support children who are unfamiliar or ineffective with social learning strategies.

On a second dimension, social learning is not only important for how information is learned, but it also plays a vital role in how information is constructed within the technologies themselves. Much of the Internet is built on the social knowledge constructions of others (e.g., telecollaborative learning projects, threaded discussions, interactive chats, and collaborative databases). Every day, many new websites are developed and serve to expand the global knowledge base shared through Internet technologies. In both the workplace and at home, the new technologies of literacy allow us to take advantage of the intellectual capital that resides in others, enabling us to collaboratively construct solutions to important problems by drawing from the expertise that lies outside ourselves.

Thus, the construction of knowledge will increasingly be a collaborative venture within the learning spaces defined by the Internet and other ICTs. These new technologies will introduce important new instructional challenges for educators, especially with content area contexts. As the Internet and other ICTs bring us closer together, students will need to be prepared for the important, collaborative co-construction of new information and the learning that results (Jonassen, in press; Jonassen, Howland, Moore, & Marra, 2003).

Teachers Become More Important, Though Their Role Changes, Within New Literacy Classrooms

The appearance of the Internet and other ICTs in school classrooms will increase, not decrease, the central role that teachers play in orchestrating learning experiences for students. Teachers will be challenged to thoughtfully guide students' learning within information environments that are richer and more complex than traditional print media, presenting richer and more complex learning opportunities for both themselves and their students. Moreover, in a world of literacy as deixis, new literacies will continuously emerge from even newer technologies, requiring teachers to be (a) aware of emerging technologies for information and communication, (b) capable of identifying the most important new literacies that each requires, and (c) proficient in knowing how to support their development in the classroom.

The teacher's central role will change in a fundamental way, however. Teachers will increasingly need to orchestrate complex contexts for literacy and learning rather than simply dispense literacy skills, since they will no longer always be the most literate person in the classroom. Increasingly, students are coming to school more literate in the new literacies of ICTs than their teachers (Chandler-Olcott & Mahar, 2003). This is a historic change. As a result, roles between student and teacher will sometimes be reversed. Skilled teachers will take advantage of this by constructing contexts for learning in which students who possess new literacies are valued and are supported in sharing their expertise with others. Instead of being the single source for all literacy knowledge, teachers will become orchestrators of literacy learning environments, where members of a classroom community exchange new literacies that each has discovered.

Students with teachers who make thoughtful decisions about what needs to be learned and how it should be learned in new literacies will be privileged; those with teachers who have not yet figured these things out will be disadvantaged, perhaps even more so than with foundational literacies. Because teachers become even more important to the development of literacy in a world of new literacies, greater attention will need to be placed on teacher education and professional development.

A NEW LITERACIES PERSPECTIVE: IMPLICATIONS FOR RESEARCH AND PRACTICE

A New Literacies Perspective tells us that the Internet and other continuously emerging ICTs will be central to literacy in both our personal and professional lives and that these technologies require new literacies in order to effectively exploit their potential (IRA, 2002; Kinzer & Leander, 2003; Leu, 2002). It also tells us that it is essential to begin to integrate these new literacies into classrooms if we hope to prepare all students for the literacy futures they deserve (Leu & Kinzer, 2000). In addition, this theoretical perspective suggests that complexity and change define the new literacies of the Internet and other ICTs (Cammack, 2003; Coiro, 2003). Most important, it suggests that the literacy curriculum and assessment practices have not begun to recognize the important new literacies these technologies require (Leu, 2000a; Leu & Ataya, 2002). What is clear from a New Literacies Perspective is that there are important aspects to the literacy curriculum that require our immediate attention for both research and practice.

As we begin to consider the implications of a New Literacies Perspective, we want to make three important points. First, it is important to understand that simply using technology in the classroom does not assure that students are acquiring the new literacies they require. Using technologies such as Accelerated Reader (Topping & Paul, 1999) or other software packages designed to support the acquisition of foundational literacies will not prepare students for the new literacies of the Internet and other ICTs. Using these instructional technologies does nothing to develop the essential skills, strategies, and dispositions that define the new literacies. This type of thinking has been one reason why the field has not moved faster at integrating new literacies into classroom instruction; using software programs to teach foundational literacies is the only vision many have for integrating literacy and technology in classrooms.

Second, a central challenge for both research and practice emerges from the inherently deictic nature of any new literacy. Because new literacies continuously change as even newer technologies require even newer literacies, we require new epistemologies and new instructional practices that keep up with the rapid changes we anticipate. How, for example, can we keep up with new ideas about what to teach within research and dissemination paradigms that require four years or more between the conception of a research problem and the wide dissemination of results through research journals that rely on printed volumes? How can we keep up with new ideas about how to teach with these technologies when the technologies themselves regularly change? How can we assess students on their ability to use the Internet and other ICTs when the very skills we assess will change as soon as new technologies appear? While a New Literacies

Perspective does not provide complete answers to these questions, it does suggest that these are critical questions for both research and practice.

Third, and most important, we believe that implementing a New Literacies Perspective in classrooms is essential if we hope to avoid societies in which economic advantage is sustained by the wealthy and denied to the poor. Because of the compounding effect of differences in reading achievement and access to Internet resources by advantaged members of society, we are in danger of developing two classes of citizens: one that is largely poor, minority, and challenged by the new literacies required for reading and learning on the Internet and another that is largely advantaged, white, and excels with the new literacies required for reading and learning on the Internet. Such a development presents fundamental challenges to any society that professes egalitarian ideals and equal opportunities for all its citizens.

According to data from the National Assessment of Educational Progress (NAEP), reading comprehension in the United States has been generally resistant to efforts at improvement (NCES, 2003b). Of particular concern, white fourth-grade students scored at or above the "basic" level of reading at nearly twice the rate as many minority groups (NCES, 2003b). Just as troubling, economically advantaged students at the fourth-grade level scored at or above the "basic" level of reading at nearly twice the rate compared to disadvantaged students (NCES, 2003b). Most troublesome of all, the achievement gap is increasing between high- and low-performing students. Since 1992, NAEP average reading scores for high-performing students have increased, while those for low-performing students have dropped (NCES, 2003b). Given the powerful connection between reading comprehension ability and learning (Alexander & Jetton, 2000; Bransford, Brown, & Cocking, 2000), it is clear that the United States is developing two classes of learners.

As challenging a picture as the NAEP data present, they do not yet reflect students' ability to read and comprehend within the complex, networked, informational spaces of the Internet. The Internet requires new literacies to achieve high levels of reading comprehension in this context, but we know very little about what these literacies are or how best to teach them. The report of the RAND Reading Study Group (2002), *Reading for Understanding: Toward an R&D Program in Reading Comprehension,* captures the essence of the problem: "Accessing the Internet makes large demands on individuals' literacy skills; in some cases, this new technology requires readers to have novel literacy skills, and little is known about how to analyze or teach those skills" (p. 4).

The Internet is also a reading context where digital divide issues abound (Solomon, 2002). It is clear that advantaged and white students have far greater Internet access at home than disadvantaged and minority students (Lebo, 2003). Because the skills necessary to achieve high levels of reading comprehension on the Internet are seldom taught in schools (Padron & Waxman, 1996; Warschauer, 2003; Wenglinski, 1998), the skills are more often acquired at home by those economically advantaged members of society who have the greatest access to the Internet and more extensive learning opportunities (Warschauer, 2003).

Before we can expect all students to be prepared to read and comprehend at high levels on the Internet, we must provide scientific data to demonstrate what these skills are, how to assess them, and how best to teach them (Coiro, 2003; RAND Reading Study Group, 2002). Despite the perceived importance of the Internet as a context for teaching and learning (Web-Based Education Commission, 2000; U.S. Department of Education, 1999), relatively little research exists on the new literacies the Internet requires for achieving high levels of reading comprehension (National Institute of Child Health and Human Development, 2000). This situation must change.

Issues of What Should Be Taught and Learned Within a Context of Continuous Change

A New Literacies Perspective suggests that an aggressive agenda of research must be launched immediately in order to better understand the new skills, strategies, and dispositions required to effectively use the Internet and other ICTs. Little work, especially by the literacy research community, has been conducted in this area. And, it is the literacy research community that needs to bring powerful insights about literacy, instruction, and learning to these issues. The task is so large, involves literacy in such profound ways, and must be accomplished so quickly that it is not possible to vest the responsibility for this work solely in the hands of those who have traditionally explored issues of technology or even literacy and technology. Each of us must bring our special area of expertise to the study of literacy within the new worlds of the Internet and other ICTs.

Scholars who study reading comprehension, for example, need to examine the various components of meaning construction to help us understand the extent to which comprehension processes are similar or different within the multimedia, hyperlinked contexts of the Internet and other ICTs (Coiro, 2003). Reading comprehension is likely to be a major area of investigation because the Internet and other ICTs focus so much on information and learning from text. However, given recent models (RAND Reading Study Group, 2002) that define reading comprehension in terms of reader, text, and task, the parameters of reading comprehension on the Internet are likely to expand to include problem identification, search strategies, analysis, synthesis, and the meaning construction required in e-mail messages and other communication technologies. Many questions await investigation: What new aspects of comprehension are required when reading information on the Internet? Are inferential processes and strategies similar or different on the Internet? How do other aspects of the comprehension process change? Reading comprehension strategies within this context are likely to be especially important, and we need to know what these are.

Scholars doing work in early literacy must bring their special insights to help us understand when and in what ways young children should begin to read, write, and communicate with ICTs. We have always viewed the early years as critical to literacy development. These scholars must now turn their attention to the new literacies emerging from new technologies, helping us to understand how best to teach these new literacies in ways that answer the call for technology use that is developmentally appropriate, equitable, and integrated into the regular literacy learning environment of young children (National Association for the Education of Young Children, 1996).

Media literacy scholars, too, need to bring their understanding of critical literacies to the study of what students need to learn within the new literacies of the Internet and other ICTs. Earlier we argued that critical literacies are essential to reading on the Internet because issues of stance, information shaping, and information validity become so important within an information space where anyone may publish anything. Consequently, there is new sense of urgency in ensuring that students develop an awareness of the diverse perspectives around any question they investigate. Literacy educators will need to incorporate more strategies like those suggested by Brunner and Tally (1999) to foster deeper student insight into the various ways of looking at the same event, for example, viewing a historical event from the perspective of the different people involved (e.g., viewing a Civil War video series while "looking for evidence of the way average soldiers, in contrast to generals, or men in contrast to women, or white in contrast to blacks, experienced the war" [p. 46]).

Scholars in the areas of composition and communication also have much to contribute to this work. They must bring their powerful lenses to bear on issues of e-mail communication, webpage and multimedia composition, and the many other important issues we need to understand in these areas. Clear, rapid, and effective communication that takes advantage of the networked information contexts of ICTs will be central to our students' success. We need to know how to support students in achieving these abilities.

Although many of us have not yet recognized it, insights from multicultural and cross-cultural education also are going to be especially critical to our effective use of ICTs (Leu, 1997b). We need the finest minds in this area to help us understand the important experiences taking place as classrooms link to other classrooms from different cultural contexts, engaging in cooperative projects and seeking to understand one another's cultural context. As we engage in this important work, enormous potential exists to understand the advantages that diversity bestows by bringing multiple perspectives to bear on important problems that face us all. The Internet permits us to construct new definitions of multicultural education and broadens the definition of diversity in the classroom to global dimensions. If we take full advantage of these new opportunities the Internet will allow us to construct a truly global village among classrooms that shows students how to take full advantage of the many benefits that diversity bestows.

A central challenge for each of us is how to use these new technologies to support students with special needs. It is quite possible that the gap between proficient readers and less-proficient readers will increase within the world of rich, complexly structured information networks as the effects of differences in reading rate and accuracy become magnified. If we do not wish to leave a single child behind, we must focus on the issue of how best to support students with special needs with the powerful new technologies that are available to us.

Our colleagues who conduct research on teacher education also have an enormous agenda ahead. They need to apply their finest heuristics, helping us to better understand how to prepare new and experienced teachers to support children in the new literacies of ICTs in the classroom. Increasingly the challenge for classrooms is one that is changing from access to the thoughtful use of powerful new technologies for literacy. We need important new models and clear data to direct us in this area.

Scholars exploring important agendas in adolescent literacy and content area literacy may have the most to contribute. Research in these areas can help us to better understand ways to support information acquisition, develop the critical evaluation skills essential to effective use of Internet resources, and develop strategies for the effective use of information to solve important problems.

Scholars in the area of teacher research also have important work ahead of them. We know that some exceptional teachers are developing new insights and new models of instruction on the Internet (Karchmer, 2001). We need to know how to take advantage of these learning experiences and use the insights developed by these exceptional teachers to support our work in teacher education and staff development.

We also need to invite scholars in the areas of adult literacy to the research table. We cannot afford to abandon adults who have not had the advantage of being prepared for the new literacies required of an information economy. It may be a special challenge to broaden the literacy skills of this population because they do not have the advantage of growing up in a rich multimedia and technology world the way many children have. But, if we succeed in involving adults, it will provide us with special opportunities to take advantage of their many years of experience. Intellectual capital is important to all of us in a networked information context. We cannot afford to lose any of it.

Family literacy scholars are essential, as well, to the research that must be done. Networked information resources provide special opportunities to connect schools with families. How can we best take advantage of information networks to support a collaborative effort in students' education? How can we ensure access to ICTs in the home? We need answers to these questions if we seek to provide the best learning environment possible for every child.

Additionally, scholars in the areas of children's and adolescent literature have much to contribute. New forms of literature, written by students themselves, are beginning to emerge as the Internet makes possible new publishing opportunities. We need to know how best to support the integration of these new opportunities for literacy and learning into school classrooms.

Finally, while considering the contributions we require in all these areas, we also may wish to consider the important consequences resulting from a deictic vision of new literacies for what students need to learn. The continuously changing technologies of literacy mean that we must help children "learn how to learn" new technologies of literacy. In fact, the ability to learn continuously changing technologies for literacy may be a more critical target than learning any particular technology of literacy itself.

In this section, we have presented just some of the areas that require the attention of our brightest minds, our most talented scholars, and all our teachers. The work ahead is immense and requires us to pool all our talents if we are to understand the new skills, strategies, and dispositions that students must acquire in the new literacies of the Internet and other ICTs.

Issues of How to Teach Within a Context of Continuous Change

As we consider issues related to how to teach and learn the new literacies of the Internet and other ICTs, it is likely that our focus will turn to understanding the social and constructivist nature of learning strategies that new literacies demand. We indicated earlier that social and constructive perspectives would be important to the construction of new information within the technologies themselves. Both of these areas are important to research and practice within a New Literacies Perspective. We need to study how best to support the development of new literacies within classrooms where students will know more than teachers about some new literacies and seek new ways in which to organize and orchestrate classroom learning to take advantage of the new literacy knowledge others are acquiring. In short, we need to determine the most effective ways to manage learning experiences in the new literacies when these literacies are distributed throughout a classroom. As we do this, we also need to understand how best to collaboratively construct new information with the Internet and other ICTs, a potential that is at the very heart of most new literacies.

The lessons that classroom teachers are acquiring about both of these issues are important to understand. In fact, we believe that teachers who integrate the Internet and other ICTs into their classrooms will contribute as much—and perhaps more—than traditional researchers to understanding the most effective instructional practices for supporting the development of new literacies. The Internet and other ICTs permit teachers to rapidly connect with other teachers to share successes and exchange insights about how best to teach the new literacies (Karchmer, 2001) and it will be important to study how classroom teachers connect with others, exchange information, and construct new visions of best practices. Resources such as RTEACHER (see www.reading.org), a listserv sponsored by the International Reading Association, where teachers and others can exchange ideas about successful practices, are just the beginning of new epistemologies that will be required to keep up with the rapidly changing nature of information about instructional practice that is a part of the changing nature of the new literacies.

What seems certain is that Internet resources will increase the central role that teachers play in orchestrating learning experiences for students as literacy instruction converges with Internet technologies. Teachers will be challenged to thoughtfully guide students' learning within information environments that are richer and more complex than traditional print media, presenting richer and more complex learning opportunities for both themselves and their students. This alone should make teacher education and professional development issues important priorities. In addition, however, we must recognize that as the new literacies continually change, new professional development and teacher education needs will emerge. It is safe to say that our educational systems have never before faced the professional development needs that will occur in our future. The Internet, however, provides us with new opportunities to rapidly disseminate new models of effective instruction. Models of dissemination that take advantage of the communication potential in these new technologies, such as those developed by the Case Technologies to Enhance Literacy Learning (CTELL) group (Teale, Leu, Labbo, & Kinzer, 2002) may become increasingly important.

Issues of Assessment Within a Context of Continuous Change

A fundamental challenge to the integration of new literacies into the curriculum, at least in the United States, is that we currently do not include these important literacy skills on national and state assessments. Given the evidence that teachers emphasize literacy skills appearing on important assessments (Linn, Graue, & Sanders, 1990), there is little incentive for teachers to make new literacies a central part of the curriculum until these are included in state and national standards and on literacy assessments.

The best evidence that educational systems ignore the new literacies of Internet technologies, at least in the United States, can be seen in the state assessment programs that evaluate children's performance in reading and writing. New literacies, such as reading on the Internet or within other ICTs, are not included on any state assessments, and most states have no immediate plans to include these within literacy assessments (Leu & Ataya, 2002). Moreover, most states have seen the assessment of new literacies, such as comprehending text on the Internet, composing e-mail messages, or writing with a word processor, as a technology assessment issue, not a reading or writing assessment issue. This continues to occur even though the ability to locate, read, and evaluate information on the Internet is increasingly a part of our daily lives (Lebo, 2003). In addition, not a single state permits any student who prefers to use a word processor to do so during state writing assessments, unless this is formally specified in a special education student's Individualized Educational Plan. This continues to occur despite evidence that nearly 20% more students are able to pass the Massachusetts state writing assessment when permitted to use word processors (Russell & Plati, 2000).

There are other challenges we face in the assessment of new literacies. The most prominent one, perhaps, is that literacy assessments, to date, are always assessments of an individual working alone. Given the importance of social learning and collaborative meaning construction on the Internet and other ICTs, we will need to begin to assess how well students can learn new literacies from others and how well they can co-construct meaning and collaborate in constructing written information with others. As we have pointed out, learning how to learn from others and learning how to collaboratively construct meaning will be increasingly important. It seems clear that new technologies will require new approaches to both what is assessed and how we go about the assessment (Pellegrino, Chudowsky, & Glaser, 2001).

CONCLUDING THOUGHTS ABOUT A NEW LITERACIES PERSPECTIVE

Change increasingly defines the nature of literacy and the nature of literacy learning. New technologies generate new literacies that become important to our lives in a global information age. We believe that we are on the cusp of a new era in literacy research, one in which the nature of reading, writing, and communication is being fundamentally transformed. To inform this journey, we have defined a New Literacies Perspective, which provides a useful starting point to inquiry in this area. We have explained how literacy has changed regularly throughout time, influenced by important social forces and technologies. We explored the social context of the current period including global economic competition, the rise of the Internet and other ICTs, and educational policies from nations around the world that emphasize higher achievement in literacy and the effective use of information technologies. Then, we reviewed emerging theoretical perspectives in this area and explained why we believe a New Literacies Perspective is especially useful to understand the changes that are taking place. Finally, we presented a set of principles that inform our research in this area and discussed some of their more challenging implications to both research and practice.

It will be up to each of us to recognize the continually changing nature of literacy and to develop a rich understanding of these changes. We hope that you will bring your own expertise to the important work that lies ahead as we all seek to prepare students for the new literacies of the Internet and other ICTs that define their future. They deserve nothing less.

NOTE

1. Portions of this section are an expansion of work that appeared originally in Kinzer and Leander (2003), and quotations from this section should reference that work.

CONNECTING TECHNOLOGY AND YOUR CLASSROOM . . .

1. Survey several colleagues in your school about their use of technology in instruction. Record what technologies and new literacies they use in their teaching. Ask them to comment on how this use has impacted their teaching.

2. Create a lesson that utilizes and/or teaches some new technology. Make sure to consider the national technology standards from the International Society for Technology in Education (ISTE; see www.iste.org).

REFERENCES

Alexander, P.A., & Jetton, T.L. (2000). Learning from text: A multidimensional and developmental perspective. In M.L. Kamil, P.B. Mosenthal, P.D. Pearson, & R. Barr (Eds.), *Handbook of reading research* (Vol. 3, pp. 285–310). Mahwah, NJ: Erlbaum.

Alvermann, D.E. (Ed.). (2002). *Adolescents and literacies in a digital world.* New York: Peter Lang.

Alvermann, D.E., Hinchman, K.A., Moore, D.W., Phelps, S.F., & Waff, D.R. (Eds.). (1998). *Reconceptualizing the literacies in adolescents' lives.* Mahwah, NJ: Erlbaum.

Alvermann, D.E., Moon, J.S., & Hagood, M.C. (1999). *Popular culture in the classroom: Teaching and researching critical media literacy.* Newark, DE: International Reading Association; Chicago: National Reading Conference.

Australia Department of Education, Science and Training. (2004). *The Adelaide declaration on national goals for schooling in the twenty-first century.* Canberra, Australia: Author. Retrieved March 7, 2004, from http://www.dest.gov.au/schools/adelaide/adelaide.htm

Australia National Office for the Information Economy. (1999). *A strategic framework for the information economy: Identifying priorities for action.* Canberra, Australia: Author. Retrieved January 30, 1999, from http://noie.gov.au/projects/framework/reports/dec98_strategy.htm

Bell, D. (1977). *The coming of post-industrial society.* New York: Basic Books.

Bourdieu, P. (1991). *Language and symbolic power* (G. Raymond & M. Adamson, Trans.). Cambridge, MA: Harvard University Press.

Boyarin, J. (Ed.). (1993). *The ethnography of reading.* Berkeley: University of California Press.

Bransford, J.D., Brown, A.L., & Cocking, R.R. (Eds.). (2000). *How people learn: Brain, mind, experience, and school.* (Expanded ed.). Washington, DC: National Academy Press.

Bromley, H., & Apple, M.W. (1998). *Education, technology, power: Educational computing as a social practice.* Albany: State University of New York Press.

Bruce, B.C. (1997a). Current issues and future directions. In J. Flood, S.B. Heath, & D. Lapp (Eds.), *Handbook of research on teaching literacy through the communicative and visual arts* (pp. 875–884). New York: Simon & Schuster Macmillan.

Bruce, B.C. (1997b). Literacy technologies: What stance should we take? *Journal of Literacy Research, 29,* 289–309.

Brunner, C.B., & Tally, W. (1999). *The new media literacy handbook: An educator's guide to bringing new media into the classroom.* New York: Anchor Books.

Burton-Jones, A. (1999). *Knowledge capitalism: Business, work and learning in the new economy.* Oxford, UK: Oxford University Press.

Cammack, D. (2002). Literacy, technology, and a room of her own: Analyzing adolescent girls' online conversations from historical and technological literacy perspectives. In D.L. Shallert, C.M. Fairbanks, J. Worthy, B. Maloch, & J.V. Hoffman (Eds.), *51st year-book of the National Reading Conference* (pp. 129–141). Oak Creek, WI: National Reading Conference.

Cammack, D. (2003). Book review: *Adolescents and literacies in a digital world. Reading Online,* 6(10). Retrieved December 15, 2003, from http://www.readingonline.org/electronic/elec_index.asp?HREF=cammack/index.html

Chandler-Olcott, K., & Mahar, D. (2003). "Tech-savviness" meets multiliteracies: Exploring adolescent girls' technology-related literacy practices. *Reading Research Quarterly, 38,* 356–385.

Ciolek, T.M. (1996). The six quests for the electronic grail: Current approaches to information quality in WWW resources. *Review Informatique et Statistique dans les Sciences Humaines*

(RISSH), 1–4, 45–71. Retrieved March 15, 2003, from http://www.ciolek.com/PAPERS/ six-quests1996.html

Coiro, J. (2003). Reading comprehension on the Internet: Expanding our understanding of reading comprehension to encompass new literacies. *The Reading Teacher, 56,* 458–464.

Cole, M. (1996). *Cultural psychology: A once and future discipline.* Cambridge, MA: Belknap Press of Harvard University Press.

Crystal, D. (2001). *Language and the Internet.* Cambridge, UK: Cambridge University Press.

Dechant, E. (1982). *Improving the teaching of reading* (3rd ed.). Englewood Cliffs, NJ: Prentice Hall.

Diringer, D. (1968). *The alphabet: A key to the history of mankind.* New York: Funk and Wagnalls.

Drucker, P.F. (1994). The age of social transformation. *Atlantic Monthly, 278*(5), 53–80.

Dyson, A.H. (1999). Coach Bombay's kids learn to write: Children's appropriation of media material for school literacy. *Research in the Teaching of English, 33*(4), 367–402.

Eagleton, M. (2001, December). *Factors that influence Internet inquiry strategies: Case studies of middle school students with and without learning disabilities.* Paper presented at the annual meeting of the National Reading Conference, San Antonio, TX.

Fillmore, C.J. (1972). How to know whether you're coming or going. In K. Huldgaard-Jensen (Ed.), *Linguistik 1971* (pp. 369–379). Amsterdam: Athemaiim.

Finland Ministry of Education. (1995). *Education, training and research in the information society: A national strategy.* Helsinki, Finland: Author. Retrieved January 1, 1999, from http://www. minedu.fi/infostrategy.html

Finland Ministry of Education. (1998). *The information strategies of the Ministry of Education and their implementation.* Helsinki, Finland: Author. Retrieved December 15, 2003, from http://www.minedu.fi/eopm/strategi/alku.html

Flesch, R. (1955). *Why Johnny can't read.* New York: Harper & Brothers.

Flesch, R. (1981). *Why Johnny still can't read.* New York: Harper & Row.

Flood, J., & Lapp, D. (1995). Broadening the lens: Toward an expanded conception of literacy. In K.A. Hinchman, D.J. Leu, & C.K. Kinzer (Eds.), *Perspectives on literacy research and practice* (44th yearbook of the National Reading Conference, pp. 1–16). Chicago: National Reading Conference.

Ford, T.K. (Ed.). (2001). *The printer in eighteenth-century Williamsburg.* Williamsburg, VA: Colonial Williamsburg.

Gee, J.P. (1990). *Social linguistics and literacies.* London: Falmer.

Gee, J.P. (1996). *Social linguistics and literacies: Ideology in discourses.* London: Taylor & Francis.

Gee, J.P. (2003). *What video games have to teach us about learning and literacy.* New York: Palgrave Macmillan.

Gilster, P. (1997). *Digital literacy.* New York: John Wiley.

Goodman, K.S. (1976). Reading: A psycholinguistic guessing game. In H. Singer & R.B. Ruddell (Eds.), *Theoretical models and processes of reading* (2nd ed., pp. 497–508). Newark, DE: International Reading Association.

Hagood, M.C., Stevens, L.P., & Reinking, D. (2003). What do THEY have to teach US? Talkin' 'cross generations! In D. Alvermann (Ed.), *Adolescents and literacies in a digital world* (pp. 68–83). New York: Peter Lang.

Harrison, T.M., & Stephen, T. (Eds.). (1996). *Computer networking and scholarly communication in the twenty-first-century university.* Albany: State University of New York Press.

Harste, J.C. (1990). Jerry Harste speaks on reading and writing. *The Reading Teacher, 43,* 316–318.

Hawisher, G.E., & Selfe, C.L. (Eds.). (1999). *Passions, pedagogies and 21st century technologies.* Logan: Utah State University Press.

Heaviside, S., Riggins, T., & Farris, E. (1997). *Advanced telecommunications in U.S. public elementary and secondary schools, Fall 1996* (NCES No. 97–944). Wasington, DC: U.S. Department of Education.

Illera, J.L.R. (1997). De la lectura en papel a la lectura multimedia. In Fundalectura (Ed.), *Lectura y nuevas tecnologías: 3er congresso nacional de lectura* (pp. 69–88). Bogotá, Colombia: Fundación para el Fomento de la Lectura.

International Reading Association. (2002). *Integrating literacy and technology in the curriculum: A position statement of the International Reading Association.* Newark, DE: Author.

International Reading Association & National Council of Teachers of English. (1996). *Standards for the English language arts.* Newark, DE: International Reading Association; Urbana, IL: National Council of Teachers of English.

Ireland Department of Education and Science. (1998). *Schools IT 2000.* Retrieved January 1, 1999, from http://195.7.52.179/overview/it2k.htm

Jansen, B.J., Spink, A., & Saracevic, T. (2000). Real life, real users, and real needs: A study and analysis of user queries on the web. *Information Processing and Management, 36,* 207–227.

Jonassen, D.H. (Ed.). (in press). *Handbook of research for educational communications and technology* (2nd ed.). Mahwah, NJ: Erlbaum.

Jonassen, D.H., Howland, J., Moore, J., & Marra, R.M. (2003). *Learning to solve problems with technology: A constructivist perspective* (2nd ed.). Columbus, OH: Merrill/Prentice Hall.

Kaestle, K., Damon-Moore, H., Stedmen, L.C., Tinsley, K., & Trollinger, W.V., Jr. (1993). *Literacy in the United States: Readers and reading since 1880.* New Haven, CT: Yale University Press.

Karchmer, R.A. (2001). The journey ahead: Thirteen teachers report how the Internet influences literacy and literacy instruction in their K–12 classrooms. *Reading Research Quarterly, 36,* 442–466.

King, J., & O'Brien, D. (2002). Adolescents' multiliteracies and their teachers' needs to know: Toward a digital detente. In D.E. Alvermann (Ed.), *Adolescents and literacies in a digital world.* (pp. 40–50). New York: Peter Lang.

Kinzer, C.K. (2003). *The importance of recognizing the expanding boundaries of literacy. Reading Online, 6*(10). Retrieved December 13, 2003, from http://www.readingonline.org/electronic/elec_index.asp?HREF=/electronic/kinzer/index.html

Kinzer, C.K., & Leander, K. (2003). Technology and the language arts: Implications of an expanded definition of an literacy. In J. Flood, D. Lapp, J.R. Squire, & J.M. Jensen (Eds.), *Handbook of research on teaching the English language arts* (2nd ed., pp. 546–566). Mahwah, NJ: Erlbaum.

Labbo, L.D. (1996). A semiotic analysis of young children's symbol making in a classroom computer center. *Reading Research Quarterly, 31,* 356–385.

Labbo, L.D., & Kuhn, M. (1998). Electronic symbol making: Young children's computer-related emerging concepts about literacy. In D. Reinking, M. McKenna, L.D. Labbo, & R.D. Kieffer (Eds.), *Handbook of literacy and technology: Transformations in a posttypographic world* (pp. 79–92). Mahwah, NJ: Erlbaum.

Labbo, L.D., & Reinking, D. (1999). Negotiating the multiple realities of technology in literacy research and instruction. *Reading Research Quarterly, 34,* 478–492.

Lankshear, C., & Knobel, M. (2003). *New literacies: Changing knowledge in the classroom.* Buckingham, UK: Open University Press.

Lawless, K.A. & Kulikowich, J.M. (1996). Understanding hypertext navigation through cluster analysis. *Journal of Educational Computing Research, 14,* 385–399.

Lawless, K.A., Mills, R., & Brown, S.W. (2002). Children's hypermedia navigational strategies. *Journal of Research on Computing in Education, 34*(3), 274–284.

Lebo, H. (2003). *The UCLA Internet report: Surveying the digital future, year three.* Los Angeles: UCLA Center for Communication Policy. Retrieved December 15, 2003, from http://www.ccp.ucla.edu/pdf/UCLA-Internet-Report-Year-Three.pdf

Lemke, J.L. (1998). Metamedia literacy: Transforming meanings and media. In D. Reinking, M.C. McKenna, L.D. Labbo, & R.D. Kieffer (Eds.), *Handbook of literacy and technology: Transformations in a posttypographic world* (pp. 283–301). Mahwah, NJ: Erlbaum.

Lenhart, A., Simon, M., & Graziano, M. (2001). *The Internet and education: Findings of the Pew Internet & American life project.* Retrieved December 13, 2003, from http://www.pewinternet.org/reports/toc.asp?Report=39

Leu, D.J., Jr. (1997a). Caity's question: Literacy as deixis on the Internet. *The Reading Teacher, 51,* 62–67.

Leu, D.J., Jr. (1997b). Internet en el aula: Nuevas oportunidades para la educación, el apren-dizaje y la enseñaza. In Fundalectura (Ed.), *Lectura y nuevas tecnologias: 3er congresso nacional de lectura* (pp. 47–68). Bogotá, Colombia: Fundación para el Fomento de la Lectura.

Leu, D.J., Jr. (2000a). Literacy and technology: Deictic consequences for literacy education in an information age. In M.L. Kamil, P.B. Mosenthal, P.D. Pearson, & R. Barr (Eds.), *Handbook of reading research* (Vol. 3, pp. 743–770). Mahwah, NJ: Erlbaum.

Leu, D.J., Jr. (2002b). Our children's future: Changing the focus of literacy and literacy instruc-tion. *The Reading Teacher, 53,* 424–431.

Leu, D.J., Jr. (2002). The new literacies: Research on reading instruction with the Internet and other digital technologies. In A.E. Farstrup & S.J. Samuels (Eds.), *What research has to say about reading instruction* (3rd ed., pp. 310–337). Newark, DE: International Reading Association.

Leu, D.J., Jr., & Ataya, R. (2002, December). *Assessing assessment strategies among the 50 states: Evaluating the literacies of our past or the literacies of our future?* Paper presented at the annual meeting of the National Reading Conference, Miami, FL.

Leu, D.J., Jr., Karchmer, R., & Leu, D.D. (1999). The Miss Rumphius effect: Envisionments for literacy and learning that transform the Internet. *The Reading Teacher, 52,* 636–642.

Leu, D.J., Jr., & Kinzer, C.K. (2000). The convergence of literacy instruction and networked technologies for information and communication. *Reading Research Quarterly, 35,* 108–127.

Lewis, C., & Fabos, B. (1999). *Chatting on-line: Uses of Instant Messenger among adolescent girls.* Paper presented at the annual meeting of the National Reading Conference, Orlando, FL.

Lewis, C., & Finders, M. (2002). Implied adolescents and implied teachers: A generation gap for new times. In D.E. Alvermann (Ed.), *Adolescents and literacies in a digital world* (pp. 101–113). New York: Peter Lang.

Linn, R.L., Graue, M.E., & Sanders, N.M. (1990). Comparing state and district results to national norms: The validity of the claims that "everyone is above average." *Educational Measurement: Issues and Practice, 9*(3), 5–14.

Literacy Strategy Underway. (1999). *New Zealand Education Gazette, 78*(1). Retrieved January 1, 1999, from http://www.edgazette.govt.nz/articles/show_articles.cgi?id=5024

Luke, C. (1997). Media literacy and cultural studies. In S. Muspratt, A. Luke, & P. Freebody (Eds.), *Constructing critical literacies: Teaching and learning textual practice* (pp. 19–49). Cresskill, NJ: Hampton.

Manguel, A. (1996). *A history of reading.* New York: Viking.

Mathews, M. (1996). *Teaching to read: Historically considered.* Chicago: University of Chicago Press.

Mayer, R.E. (1997). Multimedia learning: Are we asking the right questions? *Educational Psychologist, 32,* 1–19.

Mikulecky, L., & Kirkley, J.R. (1998). Changing workplaces, changing classes: The new role of technology in workplace literacy. In D. Reinking, M.C. McKenna, L.D. Labbo, & R.D. Kieffer (Eds.), *Handbook of literacy and technology: Transformations in a post-typographic world* (pp. 303–320). Mahwah, NJ: Erlbaum.

Morris, I. (1964). *The world of the shining prince: Court life in ancient Japan.* London: Oxford Press.

Murphy, S.M. (1986). Children's comprehension of deictic categories in oral and written lan-guage. *Reading Research Quarterly, 21,* 118–131.

Muspratt, A., Luke, A., & Freebody, P. (Eds.). (1998). *Constructing critical literacies: Teaching and learning textual practice.* Cresskill, NJ: Hampton.

National Association for the Education of Young Children. (1996). *Position statement: Technology and young children.* Retrieved December 15, 2003, from http://www.naeyc.org/resources/position_statements/pstech98.htm

National Center for Education Statistics. (2003a). *Internet access in public schools and classrooms: 1994–2002.* Retrieved December 15, 2003, from http://nces.ed.gov/surveys/frss/publica-tions/2004011

National Center for Education Statistics. (2003b). *The nation's report card: Reading highlights 2003.* Washington, DC: U.S. Department of Education. Retrieved March 7, 2004, from http://nces.ed.gov/pubsearch/pubsinfo.asp?pubid=2004452.

National Institute of Child Health and Human Development. (2000). *Report of the National Reading Panel. Teaching children to read: An evidence-based assessment of the scientific research literature on reading and its implications for reading instruction* (NIH Publication No. 00-4769). Washington, DC: U.S. Government Printing Office.

New London Group, The. (2000). A pedagogy of multiliteracies: Designing social futures. In B., Cope & M. Kalantzis (Eds.), *Multiliteracies: Literacy learning and the design of social futures* (pp. 9–38). London: Routledge.

New Zealand Ministry of Education. (1998). *Interactive education: An information and communication technologies (ICTs) strategy for schools.* Wellington, NZ: Author. Retrieved January 1, 1999, from http://www.tki.org.nz/r/ict/curriculum/stdoc_e.php

O'Brien, D. (2001, June). "At-risk" adolescents: Redefining competence through the multiliteracies of intermediality, visual arts, and representation. *Reading Online, 4*(11). Retrieved December 15, 2003, from http://www.readingonline.org/newliteracies/lit_index.asp?HREF=/newliteracies/obrien/index.html

Padron, Y., & Waxman, H. (1996). Improving the teaching and learning of English language learners through instructional technology: *International Journal of Instructional Media, 23*(4), 341–354.

Pellegrino, J.W., Chudowsky, N., & Glaser, R. (Eds.). (2001). *Knowing what students know: The science and design of educational assessment.* Washington, DC: National Academy Press.

RAND Reading Study Group. (2002). *Reading for understanding: Toward an R&D program in reading comprehension.* Santa Monica, CA: RAND.

Reich, R. (1992). *The work of nations.* New York: Vintage Books.

Reinking, D. (1998). Synthesizing technological transformation of literacy in a post-typographic world. In D. Reinking, M.C. McKenna, L.D. Labbo, & R.D. Kieffer (Eds.), *Handbook of literacy and technology: Transformations in a post-typographic world* (pp. xi–xxx). Mahwah, NJ: Erlbaum.

Rosenblatt, L.M. (1994). The transactional theory of reading and writing. In R.B. Ruddell, M.R. Ruddell, & H. Singer (Eds.), *Theoretical models and processes of reading* (4th ed., pp. 1057–1092). Newark, DE: International Reading Association.

Rumelhart, D.E. (1994). Toward an interactive model of reading. In R.B. Ruddell, M.R. Ruddell, & H. Singer (Eds.), *Theoretical models and processes of reading* (4th ed., pp. 864–894). Newark, DE: International Reading Association.

Russell, M., & Plati, T. (2000). *Mode of administration effects on MCAS composition performance for grades four, eight, and ten.* Retrieved February 1, 2001, from http://www.bc.edu/research/nbetpp/statements/WE052200.pdf

Shanahan, T. (1990). Reading and writing together: What does it really mean? In T. Shanahan (Ed.), *Reading and writing together: New perspectives for the classroom* (pp. 1–18). Norwood, MA: Christopher-Gordon.

Silverblatt, A., Ferry, J., & Finan, B. (1999). *Approaches to media literacy: A handbook.* Armonk, NY: Sharpe.

Smith, N.B. (1965). *American reading instruction.* Newark, DE: International Reading Association.

Smolin, L.I., & Lawless, K.A. (2003). Becoming literate in the technological age: New responsibilities and tools for teachers. *The Reading Teacher, 56,* 570–577.

Solomon, G. (2002). Digital equity: It's not just about access anymore. *Technology and Learning, 22*(9), 18–26.

Spires, H.A., & Ester, T.H. (2002). Reading in Web-based learning environments. In C.C. Block & M. Pressley (Eds.), *Comprehension instruction: Research-based best practices* (pp. 115–125). New York: Guilford.

Sutherland-Smith, W. (2002). Weaving the literacy Web: Changes in reading from page to screen. *The Reading Teacher, 55,* 662–669.

Teale, W.H., Leu, D.J., Labbo, L.D., & Kinzer, C. (2002). The CTELL project: New ways technology can help educate tomorrow's reading teachers. *The Reading Teacher, 55,* 654–659.

Teras, V. (1994). *A history of Russian literature.* New Haven, CT: Yale University Press.

Topping, K.J., & Paul, T.D. (1999). Computer assisted assessment of practice at reading: A large scale survey using Accelerated Reader. *Reading & Writing Quarterly, 15,* 213–231.

Tyner, K. (1998). *Literacy in a digital world: Teaching and learning in the age of information.* Mahwah, NJ: Erlbaum.

U.K. Department for Education and Skills. (1998). *The standards site: Welcome to schemes of work.* Retrieved January 1, 1999, from http://www.standards.dfee.gov.uk/schemes3/?view=get

U.K. Secretary of State for Education and Skills. (1997). *Excellence in schools.* Suffolk, UK: Author.

U.S. Department of Commerce, National Telecommunications and Information Administration. (2002). *A nation online: How Americans are expanding their use of the Internet.* Washington, DC: U.S. Department of Commerce.

U.S. Department of Education. (1999). *Getting America's students ready for the 21st century: Meeting the technology literacy challenge.* Retrieved January 30, 1999, from http://www.ed.gov/about/offices/list/os/technology/plan/national/index.html

Warschauer, M. (1999). *Electronic literacies: Language, culture, and power in online education.* Mahwah, NJ: Erlbaum.

Warschauer, M. (2003). *Technology and social inclusion: Rethinking the digital divide.* Cambridge, MA: MIT Press.

Web-Based Education Commission. (2000). *The power of the Internet for learning: Moving from promise to practice: The report of the Web-Based Education Commission.* Washington, DC: U.S. Government Printing Office. Retrieved December 15, 2003 from http://interact.hpcnet.org/webcommission/index.htm

Wenglinski, H. (1998). *Does it compute? The relationship between educational technology and student achievement in mathematics.* Princeton, NJ: Educational Testing Service. (ERIC Document Reproduction Service No. ED425191)

Wertsch, J. V. (1991). *Voices of the mind: A sociocultural approach to mediated action.* Cambridge, MA: Harvard University Press.

CHAPTER 20

THE COLLEGE CLASSROOM AS PENSIEVE: PUTTING LANGUAGE, POWER, AND AUTHORITY TO PRODUCTIVE USE

WALTER R. JACOBS

***THINK ABOUT* THE COLLEGE CLASSROOM AS PENSIEVE . . .**

1. Read to consider how the concept of the Pensieve might reframe relationships between teachers and students.
2. Think about the types of unique experiences you can share with students to help them become more engaged learners.
3. While reading, discover the kinds of media products teachers can use to enable students to construct informed critiques of society.

> *Toward the end of the class I asked the students if "the opportunity to get rid of the niggas" was a possible justification for the trade. It is the first time I used that term this semester. It slipped off the tongue pretty easily, especially as (at that point) I was pretty frustrated at them being firmly entrenched in their Whiteness in all its erased glory. Perhaps they were a bit scared to voice opinions, even after repeated comments from me that it's ok to disagree with me, that it would not count against them. Moreso, though, it is Whiteness as absence: don't see racial implications, would vote no 'cause it's "the right thing to do."*
>
> —Walt, field note (FN), 1997

Should potentially explosive language and perspectives such as expressed in the preceding ethnographic field note be used in introductory college courses? What happens when teachers do so, in an effort to more fully engage students on multiple levels, as I did in the field note regarding the film *Space Traders*, in which the citizens of the United States vote to trade all African Americans (like me) in exchange for new technologies from extraterrestrial aliens? What happens when we use ethnography to both create and study contexts where teachers deploy theory to complicate and extend lived understandings of social realities? In short, we theorize and empirically create the classroom as a context in which both students and instructor(s) attempt to comprehend and use language, power, and authority productively in democratic and humane forms in the physical classroom, and beyond. We create **Pensieves**, classrooms where the participants implode public and private ideas and experiences of who they were, are, and could be. In such a classroom teacher/researchers construct themselves as objects as well as subjects of study, helping individuals and groups negotiate the ever-expanding complexities of life in hyperdimensional societies.

> **Pensieve**—term introduced in one popular book in the *Harry Potter* children's series; a stone basin that stores human ideas and experiences. In this article the college classroom acts as a Pensieve, where excess thoughts from professor's and students' minds are extracted and poured into a siphon (research/field notes) and later examined and analyzed

If we are to make the classroom more democratic and, by extension, encourage students to be more critical and engaged citizens, we must experiment with new course forms and processes along lines expressed earlier (Grossberg, 1997; Kumar, 1997; Lee, 2000). We must attempt to use the cultural studies dicta of "the necessary detour through theory" and "engaging the concrete in order to change it" to more critically explore everyday life (Morley & Chen, 1996; Turner, 1996). The concept of the Pensieve—introduced in one popular book in the *Harry Potter* children's series—may offer one possibility:

> "At these times," said Dumbledore, indicating the stone basin, "I use the Pensieve. One simply siphons the excess thoughts from one's mind, pours them into the basin, and examines them at one's leisure. It becomes easier to spot patterns and links, you understand, when they are in this form." (Rowling, 2000, p. 597)

Rowling describes the Pensieve as a stone basin that stores human ideas and experiences. Harry Potter and others can then enter the basin to critically examine their ideas and experiences. I believe that the concept of the Pensieve can be used as a metaphor for a particular type of class experience, one where the instructor deconstructs the participants' (instructor and students) understandings in a way that makes invisible components visible.[1] Specifically, instructors establish themselves as models for possible articulation of ideas and experiences in a particular time and place, in such a way that students can explore these ideas and experiences in other times and places. This revolves around what I call "the three

---

[1] I am indebted to Guy Trombley (2001) for the notion of the Pensieve as a metaphor for the classroom.

EXs": teachers *expose* students to multiple narratives that involve the teachers' own lived experiences, *explode* those narratives into their constitutive parts based on structural locations (race, class, gender, sexual orientation, etc.), and *explicate* possible new narratives that explore implications of combinations of the constitutive parts. In other words, teachers center ourselves (share articulations) in order to encourage students to displace us (create dis-articulations) and center themselves (generate rearticulations) to explore their own understandings, identities, and practices (Jacobs, 1998).

I used ethnographic methods to simultaneously teach and research 1997–1998 freshman-level sociology of the media classes at Big State University, a large midwestern public research institution. I used multiple texts to illustrate theoretical concepts and to stimulate personal reflection and sociological analysis (Jacobs, 2005). In this article I will focus on one such text I used in 1997 (the film *Space Traders*) and classes that were centered on the film.

THE CONTEXT: CLASSLESS SOCIETY, CORPORATE-MODEL COLLEGES, HOSTILE CAMPUSES

In all my sociology classes I use the movie *Space Traders* as a teaching tool. It is the HBO film adaptation (Hudlin & Hudlin, 1994) of Derrick Bell's "The Space Traders" short story (in Bell, 1992). Both versions depict the United States in the near future. The nation is burdened economically with a deficit, faces energy problems, suffers from severe environmental hazards, and continues to struggle with the issue of race. However, all these social ills can be solved if the country surrenders its African American citizens to a group of extraterrestrial travelers—"space traders"—who will turn the Statue of Liberty into gold, clean up polluted waterways, and provide the country with a source of unlimited energy in exchange. The U.S. government is given a set time period (5 days in the film, 17 in the story) to decide whether or not to accept the offer. It decides to let the public determine the outcome, establishing two telephone numbers for citizens to vote yes or no in the privacy of their homes. What happens on judgment day is far less important, however, than what is revealed over the course of the time period about the country and Americans of all persuasions. As the U.S. government leaves the final decision to its citizens through a national telephone referendum, the story explores responses to the trade offer from the country's political and judicial establishment, its commercial culture industries, and its citizens, particularly its African Americans. As African American people mount traditional strategies of resistance—sit-ins, rallies, and boycotts—American captains of industry wage a massive campaign (largely though the media) to shape the consciousness of Americans. Despite these efforts, the majority of the citizens vote to surrender African Americans to the space traders (see Brooks & Jacobs, 1996, for a more complete analysis).

Bell (1992) argues that African Americans were, are, and will be sacrificed when such sacrifices serve the nation's interests. These sacrifices, he continues, are based on a racism that is a permanent component of American life, and he emphasizes the urgency to move beyond the belief that time and altruism of Americans will solve the country's racial problems. At the end of the short story, "there was no escape, no alternative. Heads bowed, arms now linked by slender chains, black people left the New World as their forebears had arrived" (Bell, 1992, p. 194). The video adaptation, however, does not make such a strong articulation. For instance, while at the end of the film African Americans are also beamed above the traders' ships, this is not done in chains, and, further, they are allowed one piece of carry-on luggage, suggesting that they are guests going to a better place. Indeed, it is such rich textual polysemy that makes the film version an excellent text for debate in the project of constructing college classrooms as Pensieves.

When I screen *Space Traders* I reserve the end of that day's class for discussion about ambiguous and confusing parts of the film only; the following class is for debate about implications. An initial question usually concerns the space traders' use of the image of former president Ronald Reagan to deliver the proposition to the current vice president. One student in 1997, for example, responded that Reagan didn't do much for African Americans, and, further, that their group position deteriorated during his administration, so it meant that this was a bad sign for African Americans' immediate future. In a field note, one of my research assistants wrote, "I was surprised TOM[2] said what he did. I didn't expect him to admit that Reagonomics exploited urban Blacks. He didn't really say it, but he acknowledged it. What does this mean?" Rob's field note expressed surprise that TOM would make such a statement, primarily given that throughout the semester TOM was our most persistent and ardent supporter of free-market big-business-as-usual and rarely acknowledged any problem with this state of affairs. He articulated the dominant understanding of the American dream: that through hard work and patience any individual can achieve success (a comfortable middle-class position) and that categorizing people in groups impedes the dream.

I am not arguing that students are cultural and ideological dupes, passively accepting truth and knowledge claims disseminated by authority figures and formations. On the contrary, "in the postmodern, hegemony is won not simply through the transmission of ideas and the control of the population through centralization and homogenization; it operates also through the *abundance of choice* and the resulting fragmentation of the populace" (Sholle & Denski, 1993, p. 300; emphasis in original). Students know the codes of the operation of difference in media and understand themselves through ubiquitous construction of the Other (McLaughlin, 1995), but they are less likely to admit that these understandings are the result of struggle within unevenly occupied terrain or struggle in which some groups have more power to construct favorable representations of themselves and unfavorable accounts of others and that these social constructions have very real material and cultural effects beyond the personal (Fiske, 1994;

[2]This is pseudonym, as are all names of referenced students. Students' pseudonyms are in ALL CAPS; the first names of research assistants and the author are lowercase.

Giroux, 1994, 1996; Kellner, 1995). One of the tasks of a Pensieve is to construct alternative representations as a means toward leveling social and cultural conditions; members can learn to organize new ways of thinking into new ways of doing. This project involves constant discussion of how specific connections of elements of societal issues and personal beliefs serve particular interests and powers and that these connections are not "natural," that they are created through discourse and can be broken through discourse and replaced with different understandings (Hall, 1996; Hebdige, 1996; Slack, 1996).

| hegemonic—predominant influence and/or power, as of a group within in a state, region, or nation, over another or others |

This, of course, is a description of the United States as a **hegemonic** society, wherein articulations about who and what our society was, is, and should be are subject to continual debate . . . on an uneven playing field. With regard to higher education, the dominant model being increasingly applied to the pubic university is that of a corporation: it should become a leaner and trimmer operation, one that is more accountable to both owners (the citizens of the states) and students, the "customers" (Aronowitz, 2000; Dellucchi & Korgen, 2002; Kolodny, 1998; Nelson, 1997a, 1997b). One manifestation of this trend is students' expectations to be prepared with immediately marketable skills rather than to be taught the joys of learning for its own sake. As described by Prashad:

> The contemporary university is no longer a cloister to which the youth retire to "play" with ideas away from the cares of the world; these few postadolescent days cannot be spent without an eye to the prospects of each student in a world in which the gains of increased productivity (due to technology) have been monopolized by transnational corporations. (1997, p. 249)

Instructors can create classrooms as spaces where students can experiment with ideas of who they are and can be. Instructors and students alike can explore "the various ways in which representations are constructed as a means of comprehending the past through the present in order to legitimate and secure a particular view of the future" (Giroux, 1994, p. 87). Creating classrooms as Pensieves allows us to put this ideal into practice.

The Pensieve in Action: Big State University, 1997

> Very briefly discussed color-blindness and valuing diversity as broad approaches to race relations. Man, I miss s335 and more sophisticated discussion.
>
> —Walt, FN, 1997

> This class makes me nauseous with their apathy.
>
> —Beeta, FN, 1997

> Walt getting frustrated that nobody is responding to his questions . . . most of them legitimate and well posed. I'm getting annoyed too.
>
> —Lori, FN, 1997

> Ultimately, I think today's poor discussion had little to do with Walt
> and a lot to do with "generation-I-don't-give-a-fuck."
>
> —Rob, FN, 1997

As can be deduced from the preceding selections from our field notes, the assistants and I were frustrated with the initial in-class discussion of the film *Space Traders* in our s101 Media Culture class. Each of the assistants, however, had been in at least one other sociology s335 Race and Ethnic Relations class in which the text was very enthusiastically and sophisticatedly discussed. s335 classes were mainly populated by junior and senior sociology majors, as opposed to the majority freshman and sophomore (and undeclared major) s101 class (in all, 24 freshmen, 22 sophomores, 8 juniors, 11 seniors). Part of our disappointment, then, was the result of an unfair comparison with a class that was older and motivated more by the subject matter in and of itself.

Constructing a classroom as Pensieve, however, involves reflexively investigating the effects of researchers' own frustrations and disappointments as well as their joys and hopes and aspirations. Kleinmann and Copp (1993, p. 52) argue that "if we incorporated the idea that emotions encompass the research process, we would begin to use all our feelings, even the ones we now consider inappropriate, as tools for analysis." By making sociological sense of our affective perspectives and experiences by thinking, talking, analyzing, and writing about them, we further the project of the Pensieve as a heuristic for helping others explore analogous complex social worlds. Pensieves create "teachers as text," where instructors establish themselves as models for possible articulations of the common good in a particular time and place, in such a way that students can explore the common good in other times and places (Jacobs, 1998).

In order to facilitate the creation of a rich set of experiences (affective and otherwise), I choose assistants who would bring diversity to a predominantly White, traditional college-aged, middle-class, and politically middle-of-the-road student body. Lori is White, a single mother, was 3 years older than most other Big State seniors, working class, and bisexual. More important than just possessing several subaltern identities, Lori constantly evaluated what these identities mean, in and of themselves, and how they fit together (in accordance with McLaren's [1995, pp. 126–128] **resistance multiculturalism**).

resistance multiculturalism— when growing numbers of students are resistant to multicultural awareness classes and activities (as opposed to when these courses were purely voluntary)

She was a participant in two of my race and ethnicity classes, first as a student and then as my very first teaching assistant. She was, then, used to my "teacher-as-text" project and—most importantly—willing to speak up and challenge me when necessary, thereby adding another level to the project's heuristic: Authority can and should be challenged in an effort to figure out how it can and does work in other contexts and how challenges may be received and negotiated (see Jacobs, 1998).

Beeta is Iranian American, upper middle class, heterosexual, and double majored in economics and sociology. As was the case with Lori, the articulation of these (and other) identities is more important than the identities themselves (see

critical multiculturalism— also known as Giroux's "border pedagogy," a new view of multiculturalism tied to an agenda of progressive education that does not see diversity in itself as a goal but sees the need for diversity as advancing toward a commitment to social justice

vulgar multiculturalism— fraudulent use of the term multiculturalism in which the fundamental principles are grossly perverted and society is viewed through a loose and oversimplified lens, that is, a mindset in which the world is divided into a privileged set of victims and their alleged oppressors

also the Bad Subjects Production Team's (1998, p. 12) distinction of **critical multiculturalism** from **vulgar multiculturalism**. The students perceived Beeta as the most "normal" of the assistants, so she shared the closest bond with them, eliciting thoughts about many subjects—class and nonclass alike— throughout her research notes.

Rob is Mexican American, working class, heterosexual, and very sympathetic to Marxist analysis. As were Beeta and Lori, he was a senior, was in one of my previous s335 courses, and stood out as one of the few who questioned received wisdom from the beginning of class. In a 1997 field note, for example, Rob wrote, "PAM starts talking about [student organization]. It's basically a 'helping people' thing. You know, like soup kitchens, canned goods, donations, etc. If she's trying to make me feel guilty, it's not going to work. [Student organization] is microcosmic, man, I'm more concerned with macrolevel solutions. Like revolution."

Finally, a brief biographical note about me. I majored in electrical engineering as an undergraduate, and my first and only postgraduation engineering job took me from the metropolis of Atlanta, Georgia, to a Department of Defense facility in rural south-central Indiana. I expected and was prepared for the drastic change in the racial composition of my environment but was stunned to find that I was truly an Other in the workplace: in a building of hundreds I was one of the very few African Americans, urbanites, Democrats, profeminists, non-Christians, and the like. In my second year, however, I realized that my interest in studying my coworkers vastly outweighed my engineering interests and skills. For instance, I designed and administered surveys to try to figure out connections between our disparate perspectives and social locations and to ascertain why we got along so well (in the first year, that is!) given that we were so very different. After being told that I was doing "sociology without a license," I enrolled in a Ph.D. program to earn the license, writing about my "unofficial" experiences along the way (Jacobs, 1994).

Regardless of our personal biographies, in the classroom the instructor's task is not to allow their positions (of whatever form: emotional, political, theoretical, etc.) to police politically correct thought and rigidly manipulate ideas of desirable social and spatial utopias. That is what Giroux (1996, p. 127) calls "politicizing education," which "silences in the name of a specious universalism and denounces all transformative practices through an appeal to a timeless notion of truth and beauty." No, the challenge is to adopt "political education," which decenters power and calls attention to and critiques efforts to unjustly stratify groups and reify inequality:

> Politicizing education perpetuates pedagogical violence, while a political education expands the pedagogical conditions for students to understand how power works on them, through them, and for them in the service of constructing and deepening their roles as engaged thinkers and critical citizens. (Giroux, 1996, p. 53)

We must, in other words, teach to transgress (hooks, 1994), but we can not proscribe the results of those transgressions.

It is the instructor's job, then, to use his or her frustrations productively—to find ways to get students motivated by course texts and the overarching project of becoming critical social agents, but without telling them exactly what positions to take. Returning to the class discussion of *Space Traders*, we find an example of students and instructors exploring their frustrations in the classroom as a Pensieve. After 20 minutes of relatively bland discussion I tried a "radical" idea:

> Whoa!!! Walt gets bold . . . he asks us to anonymous vote on trade.
> —Lori, FN, 1997

> Wow! I never thought he would do something so radical . . . I mean, that's pretty radical for Walt.
> —Beeta, FN, 1997

The class thought so too, as there were numerous gasps of surprise and shocked expressions when I asked the class to simulate the vote taken in the film and anonymously disclose whether they would vote yes or no to this question: If the space traders asked for all African Americans today, how would *you* vote? Each student wrote yes or no on a slip of paper, folded it so that neighbors could not discern their vote, and passed the slips to the front of the room. The students were astonished when I announced, "Most of these are yes votes" halfway through the ballot count and breathed a collective sigh of relief when I said "just kidding" 10 seconds later. Then, just before I got to the end of the count I said, "This one says 'yes, and I would start with you first, Walt.'" This time the class knew that I was joking right off and laughed immediately. Later, however, Lori told me that she dared JASON to write that down and that when I "read" it, she told him that she was only joking, to which he insisted that he didn't write it. The upshot was that JASON did become more vocal (and more critical) in the ensuing debate, perhaps to prove that he wasn't racist. At any rate, he was one person who responded well to the radical move.

Why was it termed *radical*? Operating in the teacher-as-text project, I usually present numerous fragments of issues and ideas and make temporary articulations in the effort to try to get students to make their own flexible, complex articulations. In other words, I force students into the gray in order to negotiate the increasing grays of our lives. The mock vote, however, forced students into a Black-White situation. Rob, though, preferred this. Here he commented on my repeated efforts to get the 2 students who actually wrote yes (compared to 50 no votes) to identify themselves:

> There were some things I would have done differently, and on a few occasions I was frustrated with Walt's methods and strategies. That's very easy for me to say as an objective observer from the outside, however. . . . Nonetheless, I would not have asked the 2 yes people to identify themselves so many times. I understand that had one of those people stepped forward, the discussion would have exponentially increased in vitality, but the cost of appearing desperate was too great.

This note illustrates three points about the dynamics of language, power, and authority in a classroom as Pensieve. First, Kamala Visweswaran (1994) reminds us that silences can be just as theoretically and empirically informative as audible discourse. Theoretically, it supports Collins's (1991) arguments that we resist full entry into the "matrix of domination": the 99% White class (1 Asian American in a class of 65) was reluctant to examine aspects of White privilege with their African American instructor. Empirically, we see the silences were strategic, as the class became more vocal in the more impersonal medium of the electronic classroom (EC) and more private medium of the essay:

> The fact that the story was written by African-Americans may say something about the way whites and blacks want to deal with racial issues. This is exclusively my opinion, but I believe that white people think that there is little racism left in the world and would like to ignore the racism that there is. On the other hand, I believe that because racism effects blacks more than whites, black people don't want the issue ignored.
>
> —EC response

> As an audience member the comparison allowed me to feel the intense pressure and frustration felt by the blacks. I was able to connect with the minority group, as I am sure others did as well.
>
> —Essay response

> This story was a great wake up call.
>
> —Essay response

> I think a problem with widely broadcasting a text like this as a learning tool rather than a source of entertainment is that it could create a lot of paranoia and heightened tension and resentment between whites and blacks.
>
> —EC response

> I would have to agree with [3 students]. Shows like *Space Traders* cause a lot of uproar, a lot of uproar we don't need.
>
> —EC response

> I never asked my black acquaintances [about group treatment in America] because that doesn't make for polite conversation.
>
> —Essay response

> Little did I know that I would experience one of the worst realizations of my life.
>
> —Essay response

Overall, 37 students posted messages concerning *Space Traders* in the EC (compared with a normal 15 to 20 per topic) and all 65 students completed an essay assignment that compared short-story and film versions of the text. The preceding responses indicate that one way or another, most students did engage the issues, in a variety of ways and from a variety of perspectives. Again, it is not the job of instructors to police politically correct thought in Pensieves, but rather to foster an environment "in which a spectrum of plausible ideas come into play, so that class members—as well as the person deemed the 'teacher'—might enter a collective experience to sort things out anew each term" (Wald, 1997, p. 133). Note, also, the extension of the previous point concerning authority: Teachers deconstruct their positions as well as students, as "excitement is generated through collective effort" (hooks, 1994, p. 8). Some students resist such collective effort, but hooks argues that a certain amount of resistance is desirable, as it indicates that teachers are challenging deeply held (yet often un- or underanalyzed) convictions. We must teach students that "joy can be present along with hard work. . . . And sometimes it's necessary to remind students that pain and painful situations don't necessarily translate into harm. We make that very fundamental mistake all the time. Not all pain is harm, and not all pleasure is good" (Ron Scapp, in a conversation with bell hooks [1994, p. 154]).

Second, I feel Rob's field note points to the difficulty of striking a balance between asking too much and too little of students with regards to critical thinking. When students' taken for granted understandings are displaced and when they are confronted with multiple complexities about societal haves and have-nots, students often become angry, blaming the teacher for making them "think" (hooks, 1994; McLaughlin, 1996). Some wrestle with the challenge constructively, but some yearn for simpler days in which they were comfortably oblivious to the operation of power at the level of the everyday, and resist complex analysis. According to Takata (1997, p. 200), "Learning is messy. . . . There are often frustrating detours, temporary setbacks, and latent learning," but adopting the teacher as text position is one method of alleviating this form of resistance. By "emphasiz[ing] the partiality of any approach to challenging oppression and the need to constantly rework these approaches" (Kumashiro, 2001, p. 4), and by demonstrating that *teachers* are as deeply immersed in the complex muck as are the students—yet somehow manage to survive and, indeed, thrive in chaotic and disorienting spaces—teachers can help instill a sense of hope in students and encourage them to tackle tough questions (Jacobs, 1998).

Third, the issue of "objectivity" raises its head. In other field notes, Rob describes how his note taking suffered a bit as he became frustrated with the (lack of) responses by the class. In Pensieves, researchers can chart the operation of power as knowledge (Foucault, 1980), of which objectivity claims are of prime interest, often effacing recognition of complexity and inequality (Gieryn, 1994; Haraway, 1991). In this effort, capturing the researchers' *own reactions as affected by the space under study* is extremely valuable. In a way, objectivity here parallels that of the responsible use of authority, as detailed by Giroux (1996, p. 136): "By allowing their own forms of authority to be held up to critical scrutiny, authority itself becomes an object of social analysis and can then be viewed as central to the conditions necessary for ownership and production of knowledge." Participation

hyperreflexivity—
excessive response to
stimuli; overactive or
overresponsive reflexes

in postmodern spaces involves **hyperreflexivity**; a study of the classroom as Pensieve demands that instructors or researchers and their practices be as much an empirical object or subject as the students.

In this effort I reflexively put more frustrations on the table in the last 15 minutes of class:

> Walt says something about "would vote not pass, or would everybody just say fuck the niggas??? Whoa . . . never heard him react so passionately. Maybe that's needed today.
>
> —Lori, FN, 1997
>
> Walt says "fuck 'em." I bet he really wants to say this to the class.
>
> —Rob, FN, 1997
>
> JASON asks me if Walt just said "fuck" but skips the "nigga" part. I say "fuck yea he did."
>
> —Lori, FN, 1997

I went on to say that I would not fully articulate my personal thoughts on the trade but asked the students to think about the implications of the statement, given who was saying it. I asked the class what they would think if I told them I thought the trade would pass in 1997. Forty percent thought I was just being a "devil's advocate," while 60% thought I was serious. Many people raised their hands to comment, including several who had not spoken to that point, and the class left in a buzz.

Throughout the discussion I wanted to call attention to the complex operation of power and its consequences, rather than building a rigid, doctrinaire hierarchy of power that effaces the very pertinent traces of its construction. Articulations slide, collide, and mutate; I wanted the students to begin to think about what particular elements of their experiences they will foreground and which they will push into the background, based on the dynamics of particular contexts in which those articulations are made.

The use of language is an important consideration in that effort. For instance, the use of terms such as "fuck" and "nigger" can be extremely volatile and reinforce systems of domination if left unmarked. On the other hand, we can use such language to encourage our students and ourselves to investigate how language works in circuits of power, and how it may be redeployed to serve alternative interests (such as the term "queer"; see Warner, 1993). It may take time to develop sufficient rapport in order to conduct this project, but it is an integral component in the attempt to create the classroom as Pensieve. In my classes I do not receive any complaints about the use of potentially disturbing language. On the contrary, this seems to enhance classroom experiences for some students, as suggested by this comment on a 1997 course evaluation: "[Walt is] the type of guy you'd want as a friend. Sometimes he swears or uses expressions like college kids do. That is what helps people learn and makes it fun." So, through a combination of exposure to new texts and the creation of connections (for both students and instructors) between those texts and larger contexts (social issues and personal experiences), and signaling that it is OK—and, in fact, encouraged!—to take risks and articulate potentially unpopular ideas and beliefs, I was able to create the 1997 s101 Media Culture class as a Pensieve.

CONCLUSION: EVOKING THE FUTURE

In a classroom as Pensieve the participants seek to explore the processes and products of a postmodern form of pedagogy in which they use mass-marketed images, sounds, words, material artifacts, and built environments to create and live in social worlds with other similarly constructed subjects and issues. In Pensieves instructors want to "evoke," using a definition that is "not a presence that calls into being something that was absent; it is a coming to be of what was neither there present nor absent, for we are not to understand 'evocation' as linking two differences in time and place, as something that evokes and something else evoked" (Tyler, 1986, p. 130). That is, the ideas and experiences that the participants put into the Pensieve have invisible traces attached; we want to illuminate these traces and investigate implications of various combinations of the new complexities.

Thomas McLaughlin (1996) argues that today's college students do the "theory" of making connections of media and their own experiences, but that this is often nonsystematic and can (and should) be more rigorous; they are critical of media as pertaining to their individual lives only. When I taught and researched my sociology of the media classes as Pensieves, the students, assistants, and I all became more aware of how media products (such as *Space Traders*) are structured by and structure larger cultural systems of social life. We explored how we can resist, transform, and appropriate mediated understandings instead of passively absorbing messages of who we should be and how we should act within social categorization (race, gender, class, sexual orientation, etc.). Although some students resisted this effort, many others greatly appreciated the lessons learned.

> critical social agent—one who lives with uncertainty about what is true and possesses the courage to take a stand on issues of human suffering, domination, and oppression

Creating a college classroom as Pensieve involves planning, conducting, and studying the results of deliberate "controlled chaos," the introduction of multiple perspectives, experiences, texts, emotions, dreams, fears, hopes and desires in an effort to help all involved think differently about their social worlds. It invites all to become **critical social agents** (McLaren, 1995, pp. 15, 56):

Living as a critical social agent means knowing how to live contingently and provisionally without the certainty of knowing the truth, yet at the same time with the courage to take a stand on issues of human suffering, domination, and oppression. . . . As postmodern dreamers, it has become our burden as well as our responsibility to transform our despair into compassion and commitment, to challenge our feelings of disorientation and hopelessness with an ethics of risk and refusal.

Michael Apple (2000, p. 5) argues: "being critical means something more than simply fault-finding. It involves understanding the sets of historically contingent circumstances and contradictory power relationships that create the conditions in which we live." In a Pensieve we confront the too-common circumstance wherein "the unwillingness to approach teaching from a standpoint that includes awareness of race, sex, and class is often rooted in the fear that classrooms will be uncontrollable, that emotions and passions will not be contained. . . . Making the classroom a democratic setting where everyone feels a responsibility to contribute is a central goal of transformative pedagogy" (hooks, 1994, p. 39). An active negotiation of both teacher and student passions and perspectives concerning language, power, and authority can be very empowering when a college classroom is created as Pensieve. It conjures pedagogical tools for use under expanding postmodern conditions of life, in which representing ourselves and others is fraught with contradictions and tensions (Clifford & Marcus, 1986; Clough, 1992, 2000; Harvey, 1989; McLaren & Lankshear, 1993). When we can no longer be certain that what we know is what we know (and that who we are is who we are), we need processes in which we can attempt to shape the postmodern rather than letting the postmodern indiscriminately shape us. Creating college classrooms as Pensieves can be an important part of this project.[3]

[3]See Kavoori (2007) for an additional example of creating a college classroom as Pensieve.

CONNECTING THE PENSIEVE CONCEPT TO YOUR CLASSROOM . . .

1. On the first day of class, ask students to prepare a "Top 10" list (for example, 10 favorite children's books) as a form of self-introduction. Share your list with the students as well. Ideally, include items that you might be a bit embarrassed to share. In class discuss *why* you hesitated about including some entries. Include a mechanism students can use to share their lists with others (post a list to the course Web site, exchange lists in class, etc.).

2. To begin a discussion of assigned readings, ask students to underline two or three passages in the readings; then direct the students to write these underlined sections on the board. These passages can address either aspects of the text that the students liked or issues that were confusing or disagreeable. You should acknowledge a few of the listed passages that you also underlined. Additionally, you can write more passages on the board.

3. If you have any nontraditional literacy practices, share them with your fellow graduate students. For example, I sometimes tell my class that the following question is just for the men: How many of you read short stories

aloud for fun to other men? In response to the nervous laughter this question always generates, I discuss the pleasure I take in this activity, despite pressure from some peers that the activity is not a legitimate one for a heterosexual man, and analyze the reasons behind such cultural policing.

REFERENCES

Apple, M. (2000). *Official knowledge: Democratic education in a conservative age* (2nd ed.). New York: Routledge.

Aronowitz, S. (2000). *The knowledge factory: Dismantling the corporate university and creating true higher learning*. Boston: Beacon.

Bad Subjects Production Team. (1998). *Bad subjects: Political education for everyday life*. New York: New York University Press.

Bell, D. (1992). *Faces at the bottom of the well*. New York: Basic Books.

Brooks, D. E., & Jacobs, W. R. (1996). Black men in the margins: Space Traders and the interpositional fight against b[l]acklash. *Communication Studies, 47*, 289–302.

Clifford, J., & Marcus, G. (Eds.). (1986). *Writing culture*. Berkeley: University of California Press.

Clough, P. (1992). *The end(s) of ethnography: From realism to social criticism*. Newbury Park, CA: Sage.

Clough, P. (2000). Comments on setting criteria for experimental writing. *Qualitative Inquiry, 6*(2), 278–291.

Collins, P. H. (1991). *Black feminist thought*. New York: Routledge.

Dellucchi, M., & Korgen, K. (2002). "We're the customer—we pay the tuition": Student consumerism among undergraduate sociology majors. *Teaching Sociology, 30*(1), 100–107.

Fiske, J. (1994). *Media matters: Everyday culture and political change*. Minneapolis: University of Minnesota Press.

Foucault, M. (1980). *Power/Knowledge*. New York: Pantheon.

Gieryn, T. (1994). Objectivity for these times. *Perspectives on science, 2*(3), 324–349.

Giroux, H. (1994). *Disturbing pleasures*. New York: Routledge

Giroux, H. (1996). *Fugitive cultures*. New York: Routledge.

Grossberg, L. (1997). *Bringing it all back home: Essays on cultural studies*. Durham, NC: Duke University Press.

Hall, S. (Ed. by L. Grossberg). (1996). On postmodernism and articulation: An interview with Stuart Hall. In D. Morley & K-H Chen (Eds.), *Stuart Hall: Critical dialogues in cultural studies* (pp. 131–150). New York: Routledge.

Haraway, D. (1991). *Simians, cyborgs, and women*. New York: Routledge.

Harvey, D. (1989). *The condition of postmodernity*. Cambridge, MA: Blackwell.

Hebdige, D. (1996). Postmodernism and "the other side." In D. Morley & K-H Chen (Eds.), *Stuart Hall: Critical dialogues in cultural studies* (pp. 174–200). New York: Routledge.

Hooks, B. (1994). *Teaching to transgress*. New York: Routledge.

Hudlin, R., & Hudlin, W. (Producers). (1994). *Space Traders*, in *Cosmic Slop* (Video Recording). New York: Home Box Office.

Jacobs, W. R. (1994). Off the margin: The interpositional stranger. *Symploke, 2*(2), 177–194.

Jacobs, W. R. (1998). The teacher as text: Using personal experience to stimulate the sociological imagination. *Teaching Sociology, 26*(3), 222–228.

Jacobs, W. R. (2005). *Speaking the lower frequencies: Students and media literacy*. Albany, NY: State University of New York Press.

Kavoori, A. (2007). Media literacy, "thinking television," and African American communication. *Cultural Studies ↔ Critical Methodologies, 7*(4), 460–483.

Kellner, D. (1995). *Media culture*. New York: Routledge.

Kleinmann, S., & Copp, M. (1993). *Emotions and fieldwork*. Newbury Park, CA: Sage.

Kolodny, A. (1998). *Failing the future: A dean looks at higher education in the twenty-first century*. Durham, NC: Duke.

Kumar, A. (Ed.). (1997). *Class issues: Pedagogy, cultural studies, and the public sphere*. New York: New York University Press.

Kumashiro, K. (2001). "Posts" perspectives on anti-oppressive education in social studies, English, mathematics, and science classrooms. *Educational Researcher, 30*(3), 3–12.

Lee, A. (2000). *Composing critical pedagogies: Teaching writing as revision*. Urbana, IL: National Council of Teachers of Education.

McLaren, P. (1995). *Critical pedagogy and predatory culture*. New York: Routledge.

McLaren, P., & Lankshear, C. (1993). Critical literacy and the postmodern turn. In C. Lankshear & P. McLaren (Eds.), *Critical literacy: Politics, praxis, and the postmodern* (pp. 379–419). Albany, NY: State University of New York Press.

McLaughlin, T. (1996). *Street smarts and critical literacy*. Madison, WI: University of Wisconsin Press.

Morley, D., & Chen, K-H (Eds.). (1996). *Stuart Hall: Critical dialogues in cultural studies*. New York: Routledge.

Nelson, C. (1997a). *Manifesto of a tenured radical*. New York: New York University Press.

Nelson, C. (Ed.). (1997b). *Will teach for food: Academic labor in crisis*. Minneapolis: University of Minnesota Press.

Prashad, V. (1997). Other worlds in a Fordist classroom. In A. Kumar (Ed.), *Class issues: Pedagogy, cultural studies, and the public sphere*. New York: New York University Press.

Rowling, J. K. (2000). *Harry Potter and the goblet of fire*. New York: Scholastic.

Sholle, D., & Denski, S. (1993). Reading and writing the media: Critical media literacy and postmodernism. In C. Lankshear & P. McLaren (Eds.), *Critical literacy: Politics, praxis, and the postmodern* (pp. 297–321). New York: State University of New York Press.

Slack, J. (1996). The theory and method of articulation in cultural studies. In D. Morley & K-H Chen (Eds.), *Stuart Hall: Critical dialogues in cultural studies* (pp. 112–127). New York: Routledge.

Takata, S. (1997). The chairs game—competition versus cooperation: The sociological uses of musical chairs. *Teaching Sociology, 25*, 200–206.

Trombley, G. (2001). Interactive class websites as research tools: Student-driven meta-analysis and evaluation of students' learning process. Paper presented at the "Classrooms of the future" conference, Minneapolis, Minnesota.

Turner, G. (1996). *British cultural studies* (2nd Ed.). New York: Routledge.

Tyler, S. (1986). Post-modern ethnography: From document of the occult to occult document. In J. Clifford & G. Marcus (Eds.), *Writing culture* (pp. 122–140). Berkeley: University of California Press.

Visweswaran, K. (1994). *Fictions of feminist ethnography*. Minneapolis: University of Minnesota Press.

Wald, A. (1997). A pedagogy of unlearning. In A. Kumar (Ed.), *Class issues: Pedagogy, cultural studies, and the public sphere* (pp. 125–147). New York: New York University Press.

Warner, M. (Ed.). (1993). *Fear of a queer planet*. Minneapolis: University of Minnesota Press.

CHAPTER 21

LITERACY INSTRUCTION ON MULTIMODAL TEXTS: INTERSECTING PAST, PRESENT, AND FUTURE

AMY ALEXANDRA WILSON

THINK ABOUT MULTIMODAL TEXTS AND INSTRUCTION . . .

1. As you read, make note of the varied ways that adolescents use literacy in their daily lives.
2. Why it is important to value adolescents' out-of-school literacies in today's classrooms?
3. What is text? What constitutes a multimodal text?
4. Why is it important to plan a literacy curriculum that includes multimodal texts?

A Navajo and Piute student dons the roach and regalia that he and his grandmother made together in preparation for his upcoming grass dance. Moving his feet carefully to the beat of the drums, he competes in powwows, wearing geometric beaded designs that he secretly created in school on graphing paper. "My heritage dates back basically to the beginning of time," he writes in the first chapter of his autobiography in his eighth-grade language arts class. "I am Native American; my tribes that I am from are the Navajo and Paiute tribes of Utah." He brings Cree music to school for his teacher to play for others, along with videos detailing the symbolism of grass dancing. He repeatedly uses words such as *traditions, ancestors, heritage,* and *old-school ways,* terms that apply to his affinity for grass dancing.

Four adolescents e-mail family members, friends, coaches, fellow church members, girl scout troops, teachers, and more on their MySpace and Hotmail accounts. Not only are their audiences varied, but their e-mails encompass a variety of genres as well: links to computer games; proverbs with accompanying images; optical illusions; slide shows of recent events; multicolored font and emoticons; pictures of new haircuts; links to sites with videos and music; animated e-cards, and more. With rapidly multiplying advances in technology, these adolescents have increasingly easy access to designing **multimodal** digital texts, and they inevitably encounter a hybrid of textual forms daily as they read their computer screens. This trend shows no sign of slowing.

> **multimodal**—modes of communication; such as speaking, reading, writing, body language, and so forth

In a sixth-grade earth science class, the teacher designs a unit that addresses the state's curriculum standard on land breezes and sea breezes. Plotting two line graphs on one chart, students record the temperature of sand and water at specific points in time as both are concurrently heated. After determining which of them heats and cools more quickly, the students then draw a diagram showing the directionality of the land breezes and sea breezes as hot air rises and cool air sinks during different times of day. The teacher asks students, all of whom live close to the coast, to visualize times they had been to the beach themselves. She uses these experiences as a backdrop for discussion as the students then read about coastal breezes from their textbook.

Where do these past traditions, future advances in technology, and current teaching practices converge? At the intersection of literacy and modality, where words and dance, graphs and digital animation, and photos and music offer adolescents multiple avenues for fuller understanding and self-expression than printed text alone could provide. Each mode of communication has its own unique affordances (Kress & van Leeuwen, 2006). For instance, the diagram of coastal breezes allowed students to think of the phenomenon in terms of a spatial relationship between the sea and the land, whereas the overlapping line graphs allowed students to see comparative and contrastive relationships in temperatures.

Other examples indicate the affordances of modalities as well. One Web site that an adolescent recommended to her friends via e-mail contained subdued colors, "papyrus" fonts, and somber worship music, all of whose respective affordances combined together in a multimodal text that encouraged the reverent attitude its words recommended. The geometric beaded designs on graph paper enabled the Navajo and Piute student mentioned earlier to design his regalia in specific, mathematically precise ways that words alone could not have afforded him. In sum, each mode (and combination of modes) contains its own set of affordances; therefore, limiting definitions of literacy to the ability to read and write printed words may not prepare students for the variety of communicative modes that they encounter and use as integral parts of their lives.

This expanded definition of literacy is necessarily concomitant with an expanded definition of text. Witte (1992) defined a text as "organized sets of symbols or signs" (p. 237), claiming that a conception of *text* as words alone is not a defensible position. Likewise, Kress (2003) defined a text as "any instance of communication in any mode or in any combination of modes, whether recorded or not" (p. 48). Accordingly, grass dances, lab demonstrations, spoken words with gestures, and animated e-cards are all texts. In turn, each of these texts contains potential visual, kinesthetic, and auditory components, none of which should be ignored in discussions on overall meanings (Kress & van Leeuwen, 2001). Understanding these various textual forms has become ever more important for today's adolescents as the world witnesses unprecedented contact among people from different cultures (Appadurai, 1996), each with historically distinctive ways of designing texts (Jewitt, 2006), and as digital media enables these diverse users to share a multiplicity of hybrid textual forms. For people who are uncertain about why and how they might incorporate multimodal instruction as part of their curricula—especially in political climates wherein students take high-stakes tests dominated by printed words—this essay offers beginning insights, suggestions, and justifications for the inclusion of multimodal texts in classrooms.

WHY IT IS IMPORTANT TO INCORPORATE MODALITY AS A PART OF LITERACY INSTRUCTION IN CLASSROOMS

A curriculum that includes multimodal texts may be more *culturally responsive* than curricula that privilege words alone. The term *culture* does not necessarily refer to reified practices and beliefs of an ethnic group, although some cultures certainly are related to one's geographical position and how people in that location have developed social positions and shared understandings over time. Instead, in this definition, culture refers to the multiple cultural worlds that people inhabit, which may range from dating life at a university to the expectations held of lower caste women in Nepal (Holland, Lachicotte, Skinner, & Cain, 1998). Cultural worlds are often maintained in part through the exchange of texts.

Consider, for example, the cultural world of various adolescent online gamers, who develop expertise with words, still images, and moving images as they learn and influence the social norms of a particular gaming community. Too often, teachers may view these adolescents' Internet activities as being detrimental to their understanding of printed words (Luke, 2002), instead of recognizing their online activities as legitimate uses of multimodal texts. When teachers expand their literacy instruction to include discussions of multiple forms of representation as valid ways of communicating, then they begin to build bridges between many students' lived-in cultural worlds at home and their academic worlds at school.

Consider, too, the Navajo and Piute grass dancer who wanted to "express myself in dance and not in words." This mode—grass dancing—is a form of communication with its own unique affordances and historical connotations. As Jewitt (2006) has explained, modal affordance is a "complex concept connected to the material and the cultural, social historical use of a mode. In other words, how a mode has been used, what it has been repeatedly used to mean and do, and the social conventions that inform its use in context shapes its affordance" (p. 26). In practice, this student participated in grass dancing as a form of expression that he considered to be distinctively Native American, as informed by the historical connotations of grass dancing in powwow communities. As such, this mode afforded him a means of communication distinct from speaking or writing in English. To deny grass dancing as a distinguished and significant form of communication—and to exclusively privilege reading and writing in a dominant language at school—may be culturally *un*responsive, indeed. Thus, when teachers acknowledge that texts include multimodal representations, they may more fully honor the cultural worlds of individual students.

As the screen replaces the page as the dominant medium of communication (Kress, 2003), another important reason to teach multimodal texts is to prepare students for *powerful participation in an age of digital communication.* The computer screen is fundamentally different from the page; whereas the latter may contain still images and words at best, the former may include videos, images, music, sounds, changing colors, words, and any combination of these on a single page. Consequently, to prepare students to read and write in new communicative mediums, teachers must provide explicit instruction on the affordances and uses of multiple representational systems. Furthermore, as Kress and van Leeuwen (2006) have pointed out, text designers often embed conflicting messages within different modes, and if students do not learn how to critically read all modes, then they may not understand the full implications of a given text. Therefore, students must learn to attend to the various modes that confront them as they read texts on the screen, and they need to explicitly question the messages that inhere in each mode both individually and as a whole.

To be sure, teachers may not be able to provide instruction on all the textual forms that students encounter as they watch television and surf the Internet. Rapid technological advances ensure that multimodal, digital texts are always changing: in the world of technology, *"now* is not *now,* is not *now"* (Leu, Kinzer, Coiro, & Cammack, 2004, p. 1591). Despite these swift developments, however, one constant remains certain: New technologies will continue to communicate using mediums other than only printed words (Murray, 1997). As a result, though today's instruction may not fully prepare students to use the all the technologies of tomorrow, **metacognitive** discussions and evaluations of various modes can help students critically read and design texts that will be prevalent in the future.

> **metacognitive**—an internal dialogue or thought process during an activity; such as when one is reading

Along with preparing students for the future, literacy instruction on multiple types of texts may also help students *understand content* more fully. According to Shulman (1987), a key component of pedagogical content knowledge is the ability of teachers to take complex concepts, often found in printed texts, and to transform them into multiple representations that are comprehensible to their specific students. Vygotsky (1978) has shed light on why using these different representations may help students comprehend content more fully: Modes and **semiotic** resources mediate thought and prompt internal activity. It follows that different semiotic resources—such as videos, science labs, and printed texts—could mediate thought and prompt internal representations in different ways. Thus, the science teacher

> **semiotic**—from semiotics; the study of signs, their functions, and relationships

who used a graph, demonstration, and textbook may have helped students understand scientific concepts more fully by creating multiple internal representations of them.

Researchers (e.g., Pressley, 2001) have shown that giving students a printed text and simply telling them to read it does not ensure that they understand it. Instead, students deserve explicit instruction on comprehension strategies—such as monitoring their comprehension, summarizing, visualizing, asking questions, and more—to extract meanings from the text and to critically read it. Though less is known about how to teach comprehension strategies for multimodal texts, perhaps giving students a diagram, a video, or a demonstration and simply telling them to make sense out of it is just as ineffective as distributing printed words without further instruction. Just as students can access the content in printed texts more fully if they apply comprehension strategies, so, too, can they access the content in multimodal texts when they learn explicit strategies for reading multiple representations.

HOW MODALITY CAN BE INCORPORATED INTO LITERACY INSTRUCTION

The question remains: If literacy instruction on multimodal texts is vital for many reasons, how do teachers incorporate it into their curricula? Research on the reading of printed words points in some promising directions. Many previous studies have focused on *metacognition*, or making students aware of their thinking processes as they read (Pressley, 2001). Some types of thinking—such as identifying text patterns, summarizing, using text features to determine the importance of information, and so on—promote better comprehension than other types of thinking. By extension, metacognitive discussions on the reading of multimodal texts may also help students be more critical and sophisticated readers of them.

For instance, just as a teacher may help students identify the main ideas in a text with printed words by attending to textual features such as headings, so, too, can teachers help students find the main idea in images by attending to the components of the image are central and dominant compared to components that are marginal (Kress & van Leeuwen, 2006). In narrative pictures that depict some sort of action, students may also identify the "actor" who acts upon the "goal" of the image to promote critical reading. Often in Western cultures, actors in images are males, while those who are acted upon are females (Berger, 1972). Promoting metacognition in the reading of multimodal texts—or making students aware that they should attend to the components and implicit meanings of all modes—can help them to understand, question, and challenge these images.

Unfortunately, all too often teachers ignore diagrams, pictures, and other **nonlinguistic** representations as they read texts with students and grade their work (e.g., Kress, Jewitt, Ogborn, & Tsatsarelis, 2001). Indeed, adults may actually dissuade or discourage students from using some types of

nonlinguistic—describes a type of "text" where meaning is conveyed by communicative avenues other than print

representations under the misguided belief that pictures are the province of young children or that words are superior to other communicative forms (Kress, 1997). By even granting a legitimate space for multimodal representations in the classroom and by holding metacognitive discussions in which teachers explicitly attend to these modes, teachers can help their students to think critically about the textual forms that surround them as a part of their lives within and without school.

As part of ongoing discussions that promote metacognition, teachers can also make students aware of the various *affordances* of these texts. For instance, after the aforementioned Navajo and Piute student performed grass dances for his school, students could compare this text to the reading of stories or historical accounts by Native Americans and discuss the affordances of each. Following this discussion, students could be asked to imagine that they were creating a Web site on one aspect of the history of Native Americans. Music of mourning, videos of dances, graphs depicting declining populations, spoken words, and historical edicts all are characterized by singular affordances with distinctive social connotations. After the creation of this real or imagined Web site, students could reflect on why they chose each mode, why they made certain modes more prominent than others, and what they hoped to convey with each.

Some teachers—especially those in the content areas—may assert that they teach their subject matter, and not reading. With the advent of proliferating multimodal texts, the challenge of explicit literacy instruction is compounded, and these teachers may by extension believe that it is not their job to directly teach the reading and writing of multiple representations as well. However, just as literacy instruction on printed texts is a means to improve comprehension of content, so, too, can instruction on multimodal texts enhance students' understanding of key disciplinary ideas.

Consider again the lesson on coastal breezes described earlier. As Lemke (1998) has noted of semiotic resources in science, "No verbal text can construct the same meaning as a picture, no mathematical graph carries the same meaning as an equation . . . no verbal description makes the same sense as an action performed" (p. 110), and so forth. Since representational practices constitute the discipline of science (Pauwels, 2006), if students are going to learn to communicate as scientists, they need to become aware of how they might best convey scientific concepts. Since major concepts in earth science often depend on spatial reasoning (Orion & Ault, 2007), students can be made aware of when images, videos, 3-D models, or other textual forms might be appropriate to convey ideas along with words. If students were asked to design a representation of coastal breezes, they might draw a diagram with arrows indicating the directionality of the breeze and colors representing the relative temperatures of the land and the sea. Students could then explain why they chose this form of representation over other modes (such as actual photographs or videos of the coast). Alternatively, teachers could show several more-or-less effective ways of communicating scientific concepts, ask students which they think is best for the purposes of conveying a particular concept, and ask them to explain why. As students develop a repertoire of effective representational practices, they in essence learn to think and communicate like experts within a given discipline.

MULTIMODAL LITERACY INSTRUCTION: INTERSECTING PAST, PRESENT, AND FUTURE

The push of "traditional" literacy instruction—which is often exclusively page based and word based—need not be at odds with the pull of future literacy instruction, which of necessity should encompass the hybrid textual forms that students now encounter on screens (Labbo, 2006). On the contrary, teaching students about different representational forms may help them comprehend printed words more fully as they understand how and when to use them and how they relate to other modes (Kress, 2003). Moreover, the ability to communicate in nonprint forms extends back prior to the advent of the written word. Teachers who provide literacy instruction on multimodal texts thus can look both backward and forward: back to communicative forms such as music, speaking, and drawing that are vital to the maintenance of deep-rooted cultural worlds and forward to a new multiplicity of digital texts. As these types of multimodal texts converge together in present-day classrooms, they can help students develop rich understandings as they learn how to read and communicate content using a variety of mediums. Instruction on multimodal texts is thus a vital part of curricula as students develop multiliteracies (New London Group, 2000) that empower them to be more understanding of dissimilar cultures, more cognizant of communicative possibilities, and more critical participants in society.

CONNECTING **MULTIMODAL TEXTS, INSTRUCTION, AND YOUR CLASSROOM . . .**

1. How would you justify to your middle school principal the use of multimodalities and a variety of texts in your eighth-grade language arts class when the curriculum is focused on "high-stakes" tests? Write a letter to your principal, including references to "best practices," to explain why you think this will be a constructive learning experience.
2. Develop a plan for teaching comprehension strategies for multimodal texts. Choose a multimodal text and create a lesson plan for helping students to understand that text.
3. In light of this reading, consider your own understanding of text. How has your view of what is a text changed? Be prepared to share your views with your colleagues and the professor.

REFERENCES

Appadurai, A. (1996). *Modernity at large: Cultural dimensions of globalization.* Minneapolis, MN: University of Minnesota Press.

Berger, J. (1972). *Ways of seeing.* London: British Broadcasting Corporation and Penguin Books.

Holland, D., Lachicotte, W., Skinner, D., & Cain, C. (1998). *Identity and agency in cultural worlds.* Cambridge, MA: Harvard University Press.

Jewitt, C. (2006). *Technology, literacy, and learning: A multimodal approach.* New York: Routledge.

Kress, G. (1997). *Before writing: Rethinking the paths to literacy.* London: Routledge.

Kress, G. (2003). *Literacy in the new media age.* London: Routledge.

Kress, G., Jewitt, C., Ogborn, J., & Tsatsarelis, C. (2001). *Multimodal teaching and learning: The rhetorics of the science classroom.* New York: Continuum.

Kress, G., & van Leeuwen, T. (2001). *Multimodal discourse: The modes and media of contemporary communication.* London: Arnold.

Kress, G., & van Leeuwen, T. (2006). *Reading images: The grammar of visual design* (2nd ed.). London: Routledge.

Labbo, L. (2006). Literacy pedagogy and computer technologies: Toward solving the puzzle of current and future classroom practices. *Australian Journal of Language & Literacy, 29*(3), 199–209.

Lemke, J. L. (1998). Multiplying meaning: Visual and verbal semiotics in scientific text. In J. R. Martin & R. Veel (Eds.) *Reading science: Critical and functional perspectives on discourses of science* (pp. 87–113). London: Routledge.

Leu, D. J., Jr., Kinzer, C. K., Coiro, J. L., & Cammack, D. W. (2004). Toward a theory of new literacies emerging from the Internet and other information and communication technologies. In R. B. Ruddell & N. Unrau (Eds.), *Theoretical models and processes of reading* (5th ed., pp. 1570–1613). Newark, DE: International Reading Association.

Luke, A. (2002). What happens to literacies old and new when they're turned into policy? In D. Alvermann (Ed.), *Adolescents and literacies in a digital world* (pp. 186–203). New York: Peter Lang Publishing.

Murray, J. H. (1997). *Hamlet on the Holodeck: The future of narrative in cyberspace.* Cambridge, MA: MIT Press.

New London Group. (2000). A pedagogy of multiliteracies: Designing social futures. In B. Cope & M. Kalantzis (Eds.), *Multiliteracies: Literacy learning and the design of social futures* (pp. 9–37). London: Routledge.

Orion, N., & Ault, C. R. (2007). Learning earth sciences. In S. K. Abell & N. G. Lederman (Eds.), *Handbook of research on science education* (pp. 653–687). Mahwah, NJ: Lawrence Erlbaum Associates.

Pauwels, L. (2006). Introduction: The role of visual representation in the production of scientific reality. In L. Pauwels (Ed.), *Visual cultures of science: Rethinking representational practices in knowledge building and science communication* (pp. vii–xix). Hanover, NH: Dartmouth College Press.

Pressley, M. (2001). Metacognition and self-regulated comprehension. In A. E. Farstrup & S. J. Samuels (Eds.), *What research has to say about reading instruction,* (pp. 291–309). Newark, DE: International Reading Association.

Shulman, L. S. (1987). Knowledge and teaching: Foundations of the new reform. *Harvard Educational Review, 57,* 1–22.

Vygotsky, L. (1978). *Mind in society: The development of higher psychological processes.* (M. Cole et al., Eds.). Cambridge, MA: Harvard University Press.

Witte, S. (1992). Context, text, intertext: Toward a constructivist semiotic of writing. *Written Communication, 9,* 237–308.

CHAPTER 22

READING ASSESSMENT: REVISITING THE PAST, LIVING IN THE PRESENT ACCOUNTABILITY CLIMATE, CRAFTING A VISION FOR THE FUTURE

JEANNE B. COBB

THINK ABOUT **READING ASSESSMENT . . .**

1. As you read, find out about advantages and disadvantages of standardized tests.
2. Find examples of the ways that reading instruction and reading assessment have changed since the inception of the reform movement.
3. As you read, think about why a beginning teacher would describe his or her job as being a "pressure cooker."
4. As you read, make notes about future directions in reading assessment.

A small group of fourth-grade teachers are gathering in the media center after school waiting for a faculty meeting to begin. The conversation turns to the upcoming state standardized-test days. There is frustration, anxiety, and concern in their voices as they lament the loss of teaching time that must be devoted to preparing their students to do well on the tests. An experienced teacher of 20 years relates how she has seen the detrimental effects of the reform movement and the impact of these testing practices on the learning environment in her classroom. She laments, "The high-stakes tests have robbed me of all my joy in teaching!" Another teacher remarks that she is concerned because her fourth graders are very low in their reading abilities, much lower than groups she has had in the past. A beginning first-year teacher exclaims, "My professors never told me I would be teaching in a pressure cooker!"

accountability—the justification of educational programs or instructional practices in terms of student achievement; usually tied to the reform movement and standardized testing

high-stakes testing—standardized tests mandated by local, state, or federal governments with important decisions concerning student placement, promotion and/or retention made on the basis of that single test score

The reform movement has swept across the United States, fueled by the fire of political agendas, and has impacted teachers' classroom instructional practices as well as the learning environment for students. This movement and the focus on **accountability** have resulted in a dramatic shift in the way reading is assessed and how reading is taught. Johnston and Costello (2005) express dismay at the unfortunate reality in today's schools that "what gets assessed is what gets taught" (p. 256). This undesirable consequence of the **high-stakes testing** movement has drastically changed the ways teachers assess the needs of their students, how they select assessments to evaluate those needs, and how they plan instruction. Cheng (2000) pointed to the resulting measurement-driven instruction as one of the most serious consequences of mandated high-stakes testing since teachers reach the point at which they are teaching only to the test. Some teachers lose their motivation to be creative thinkers, using the scripted, mandated curriculum materials and focusing only on what is needed to achieve the desired end of students' passing the test. Critical thinking skills, problem solving, aesthetic appreciation of literature, the visual arts, drama, creative movement, and music have been crowded out of the school day as the curriculum has been narrowed to focus mainly on the basic skills of "readin', writin', and 'rithmetic." (Allington, 2002; Darling-Hammond & Wise, 1985).

HISTORICAL OVERVIEW OF STANDARDIZED TESTING AND CURRICULAR STANDARDS

Many researchers who have studied the historical context of reading instructional practices would say that the philosophical pendulum has swung back and forth in opposite directions for many years (Reutzel & Mitchell, 2005). These shifts in instructional practice were not tied to policy decisions even up to the late 1980s. Hursh (2005) points out that the oversight responsibilities for educational policy had traditionally been left to local governments, with curriculum and assessment decisions being made within districts. Under this system, state education departments set the basic standards and minimum requirements for graduation and teacher preparation. In fact, prior to 1980, fewer than 12 states in the United States mandated standardized testing or standard curriculum objectives for all students. However, in a brief period of 15 years, 42 states had developed content standards to inform instruction. The shift from local control to state control was spurred on in part due to the publication of *A Nation at Risk* (1983; Jennings, 1995). State curricular frameworks would soon follow and would later become the underpinnings of statewide testing programs.

In the mid-1990s, President Bill Clinton began the push for nationwide testing programs in reading and mathematics to assess his Goals 2000: Educate America legislation (U.S. Department of Education, 1994). With the release of the National Assessment of Educational Progress (NAEP, 1995) data showing marked declines in fourth-grade reading scores across the United States, the public became increasingly discouraged and distrusting of public schools and the methods being used to teach reading, primarily "whole language" (Reutzel & Mitchell, 2005).

By the end of the decade of the 1990s, Congress had approved the Reading Excellence Act in 1998 targeting high poverty and low-reading-achieving schools. The reform and accountability movement was advanced with the election of George W. Bush in 2000 so that by 2001, mandatory assessments, known as "high-stakes tests" could be found in the majority of states (Hoffman, Assaf, & Paris, 2001). The passing of the *No Child Left Behind (NCLB)* legislation by Congress in 2001 mandated that all 50 states require some form of testing program to meet federal accountability guidelines (No Child Left Behind [NCLB], 2002).

Freebody (2007) deplored the shift in thinking and the targeting of literacy education as the central focus of the reform movement:

> Literacy education has become the scapegoat of choice for the economic, social, moral and intellectual fragilities and failings of our society, or at least its immediately impending fragilities and failings, or, at the very least, the fragilities and failings of some groups within the society. (p. 70)

When a Standardized Test Becomes a High-Stakes Test

Standardized tests can be defined as assessments that measure student knowledge and progress in academic areas and then compare individual student progress to some desirable average standard, either local, state, or national performance. The tests become "high stakes" when decisions concerning student placement, promotion, and/or retention are made on the basis of that one test score. Additionally, the tests significantly impact teachers and principals when incentives are offered to schools based on the students' performance and when punishments for educators are tied to lack of adequate progress based on students' test scores. This accountability system has been touted as the means to reaching the desired end of improving student achievement, and no one content area has been targeted more intensively than reading. Adams (1990) concurs with the accountability movement's overemphasis on reading achievement when she points out that "literacy education is the most politicized topic in the field of education" (p. 1). Apple (1987) and Freebody (2005) have argued that blaming literacy education for all that is wrong with schooling has provided a respite from society's harsh realities and our inability to resolve the complex issues of economic, moral, intellectual and social inequalities.

Politicians Point to Benefits of Standardized Testing

Some of the research pointing to the advantages and positive benefits of standardized, high-stakes testing has stressed that more attention to a uniform statewide curriculum results in clearer understandings on the part of educators as to what skills should be mastered and assessed at each grade level. Administrators often cite this standardization of curriculum, linked to high-stakes testing, as a positive for their districts since transient students who move from school to school within the district or across a state can make the transition more easily. Those who favor high-stakes tests believe that this standardization of curriculum keyed to standardized testing also results in more instructional support for low-performing schools and more consistency across and within school districts with respect to what is being taught at each grade level (McColskey & McMunn, 2000).

The high-stakes testing movement has gained momentum since its proponents believe that it motivates teachers to improve their instruction in order to receive accolades for high student achievement on test day and to avoid negative consequences of low student performance. The stakeholders of local public schools and their insistence on quantified comparisons have pushed the reform movement to such extremes that realtors use school test scores to rate the quality of neighborhoods, and parents even use test scores published in newspapers to make relocation and real estate decisions (Amrein & Berliner, 2002).

RESEARCH ON HIGH STAKES TESTING AND ITS IMPACT ON STRUGGLING READERS

Can it be assumed that higher achievement for low-performing, struggling readers is a logical byproduct of high-stakes, standardized testing? Struggling readers are the students targeted by policy makers as reaping the most benefits from the high-stakes testing and reform movement. Surprisingly, there is scant research to support the idea that the use of high stakes tests assures that "no child is left behind" (Cobb & White, 2006) or how assessment contributes to student learning and enhanced achievement (Black & William, 2005; Crooks, 1988).

The few research studies that have investigated the impact of statewide testing programs and mandated reading curricula on children with serious reading difficulties point to the opposite. Gillborn and Youdell's (2000) research documented questionable practices of administrators who often instruct teachers to focus on the students with the best chance of passing the standardized tests. This practice negatively impacts the struggling readers, leaving them to fall farther behind their peers. Johnson, Treisman, and Fuller (2000) reported that the high-stakes testing and accountability movement in Texas resulted in some schools spending too much time on test-taking routines with the consequences being that at-risk students were not adequately taught the essential skills and concepts.

In direct contrast to the views of many legislators and politicians who point to standardized testing as essential for improving the quality of instruction for all children, particularly those who struggle, many researchers, teachers, and social critics contend that high-stakes testing policies have actually made educational quality worse. Meisels (2000), in a treatise on the damaging effects of standardized testing for young children, reported that there is significant damage to children's self-esteem and particularly to the self-concepts of low-SES, male, minority children. Kohn (2000) echoed this theme and warned: States that persist in determining students' promotions, as based on a single standardized test score, will reap the consequences of higher dropout rates tantamount to an "educational ethnic cleansing" (p. 325).

Research informs us that high-stakes testing policies have had a disproportionate negative impact on students from racial minority and low-socioeconomic backgrounds. In Arizona, Louisiana, and Georgia it has been noted that African American and Hispanic students fail high-stakes tests in disproportionate numbers to their white or affluent counterparts. In 1997 in the state of Texas, half the African American, Hispanic, or economically disadvantaged sophomores that took the test failed it, while four out of every five White sophomores passed (Amrein & Berliner, 2002).

Teachers point to the fact that mandated-testing and test-practice routines rob them of valuable instructional time needed to remediate the deficits of the struggling students. In a documented North Carolina research study, 67% of teachers interviewed reported modifying instructional methods as a direct result of testing mandates. More than 70% of teachers reported that they now spend more time practicing for tests with their students than before the mandates were implemented. Nearly 50% of these same teachers reported that high-stakes tests and the intense preparation for testing had negatively impacted students' love of learning (Jones et al., 1999).

Rising Concerns and Mounting Criticism

The preoccupation of the past several years on raising student test scores at all costs has resulted in a number of educators, parents, and, now, even politicians speaking out about the erosion of quality in education. Mounting criticism has been the object of editorials and news clips on television and radio. The discussion has heightened because Congress has continued to debate the need for major revisions to the NCLB legislation, a primary source of the federal mandates on public schools (NCLB, 2002). Kahlenberg (2008) stated that the first order of educational business under the Obama administration in 2009 should be to come up with a new name for NCLB. U.S. Rep. George Miller, D-California., a proponent and crafter of the legislation, has joked that the mere mention of the NCLB brand evokes fiery discontent (Kahlenberg, 2008). In response to public complaints, President Obama has called for new assessments that track students' progress over time rather than relying on the results of a single standardized test, and $18 billion has been earmarked for the nation's schools to help districts meet the NCLB expectations (Arado, 2008). At the beginning of Obama's term in office, economic issues have diverted attention from pressing educational issues.

Representative Lois Capps, D-California, 23rd California District, in an opinion piece, has also called for a close reexamination of the NCLB legislation after visiting educators throughout her district. She stated that her teachers and administrators welcome accountability but feel a better system is needed. She stated that educators are questioning the fairness of the present system being mandated by the federal government. Representative Capps, a grandmother and mother, disagrees with the "failing" labels that NCLB applies to low performing schools. She has also criticized the use of one standardized test score for making important decisions that affect children's lives in such a permanent way. In summary, Representative Capps has echoed what the educational research literature has documented for more than 20 years, the questionable use of standardized "high-stakes" tests ("It's Time to Reevaluate No Child Left Behind," 2007).

A sampling of newspaper articles and editorials across the United States reveal the growing anti-high-stakes test sentiment and have repeated the claims that the accountability and reform movement is failing those it has claimed to assist (Wolf, 2007). In April 2007, the Houston School Board entertained proposals to drop standardized testing in favor of end-of-course exams (Mellon, 2007). Similar proposals have been presented to Nevada lawmakers to limit the time spent on standardized tests and the number of tests a student must take per year (Whaley, 2007). Following recommendations from South Carolina's new State Superintendent of Education, Dr. Jim Rex, the legislature in that state has voted to abolish the Palmetto Achievement Challenge Test (PACT) in favor of a revised diagnostic test known as PASS (Adcox, 2008). Dropout statistics reported from Massachusetts revealed that the dropout rate has risen to its highest rate in nine years after implementation of high-stakes state testing, with Latino and African American students composing almost 45% of these dropouts, a percentage disproportionate to the demographics of the state (Ullucci, 2008).

READING ASSESSMENT: WHAT DOES THE FUTURE HOLD?

Do the advantages and benefits of mandated standardized testing outweigh the concerns and override the negative consequences of this system? As literacy professionals we must pose the essential questions: Is this the best way to improve student achievement for the struggling readers, those "left behind"? How can we provide evidence that our students are successful in reading without an overemphasis on formal testing? What if standardized tests were replaced tomorrow? What would we propose as a replacement? The public has become accustomed to measurable comparisons and will not be satisfied without an understandable, viable substitute. Educators, armed with an arsenal of reasons to eliminate the use of high-stakes tests, must be informed, equally prepared, and fortified with solid proposals for how schools and teachers can demonstrate that they have alternatives and that they will still remain accountable for children's learning. As educators, we are quick to identify the problems of standardized tests, but we must be equally articulate in proposing solutions and in defending our solutions as viable replacements.

Critical Literacy, New Literacies and Increasingly Diverse and Polarized Global Society

When the stakes are high and test time looms on the horizon, educators feel the pressure and often resort to raising scores in any way possible. This practice results in the elimination of the very skills needed for survival in today's complex, digital, global economy. Taylor and Walton (1997) reported that the use of mandated tests results in a curriculum shaped by test questions, rather than by a curriculum emanating from a clear and proactive vision of what is good for children of the 21st century.

What are the nonnegotiable literacy skills necessary for the children who will be the adult citizens of the 21st century? Educators believe that today's students will face an increasingly multicultural, multilingual society coupled with rapid change in the parameters defining text, media, and technology (Gee, Hull, & Lankshear, 1996; Johnston, 2005). Any vision of curricula for the 21st century must include recognition of the impact of these new literacies, technology, and the media as well as methods to assess them (Leu, 2000; Leu & Kinzer, 2003). It seems as if educators now accept as fact the evolving communication landscape and its resulting new literacy practices, irrevocably changed from the traditional literacy skills by these new technologies, such as the Internet, blogs, wikis, instant messaging, text messaging, e-mail, and popular new Web sites such as http://www.myspace.com, http://www.facebook.com, and http://twitter.com.

Kalantzis, Cope, and Harvey (2003) have outlined several literacy skills and dispositions that will be needed to cope with the demands of the 21st century: resilience, flexibility, openness, reciprocity, self-directing behaviors, and collaborative skills. The changing nature of society and the types of literacy skills needed to survive in this society will also necessitate new types of assessments to measure whether or not students have acquired these essential skills.

Educators must craft a vision for a future that takes into consideration the varied demands that will be placed on students, by setting forth a progressive, dynamic curriculum to include critical thinking, problem solving, and evaluative reading comprehension and viewing skills to cope with an increasingly complex society.

An equally daunting challenge facing future reading educators involves assessing these new literacy skills. Can these skills be assessed with paper-and-pencil, multiple-choice examinations? Absolutely not—most reading experts would agree. There is an intersection of technology and critical literacy as society becomes increasingly complex, polarized, and digitized. Students of the 21st century must be critical consumers of information bombarding them from the media, Internet, and printed texts. Many conflicting viewpoints are being presented simultaneously every minute of every day, and students must be critical thinkers to absorb and evaluate these diverse viewpoints.

Reading Assessment for the Future: What Steps Do We Take?

Reading professionals can count on one certainty, the certainty of change, as they embrace the challenge of crafting a new vision for reading curricula for the future citizens of the 21st century. Reading instruction, assessment of curricula, and the improvement of instruction will continue to be moving targets and the major foci of educators, politicans, and community stakeholders. Contemporary society and life in it will continue to change just as language is dynamic and ever changing (Barton, 2001).

If we expect continual improvement in students' reading achievement in such a climate of change, then instruction must be continually refined, improved, and frequently assessed. Calfee and Hiebert (1996) pointed to the dichotomy of two strands of assessments in reading. One has been external, based on standardized test scores and the second, internal to the classroom setting, has been grounded in teachers' informal assessments, observations, and daily interactions with students. The first strand has increasingly become the main source of information about student progress; yet, the second strand yields the valuable diagnostic clues about instructional decisions. Given the fact that the needed future literacy skills and dispositions do not lend themselves to assessment in a multiple-choice, standardized test format, a new model of reading assessment is needed with equal emphasis on both strands of assessment (Calfee & Hiebert, 1996).

Afflerbach (2007) also emphasized the importance of the ongoing classroom-based assessments and pointed to the need for these **formative** measures in reading to improve teaching and learning. He echoed the premise of Calfee and Hiebert and declared that there is an imbalance in reading assessment in the following areas: (1) overemphasis on reading product, not process; (2) overemphasis on skills, not on how students use the information they gain from texts; (3) lack of emphasis on cognitive and affective factors; (4) lack of emphasis on student self-assessments; and (5) lack of professional development monies spent for teacher expertise in assessment while budgets are expanding for purchasing and scoring of tests, and for purchasing test-preparation materials.

> **formative**—assessment of an instructional practice as it is taking place to monitor progress of learners (e.g., informal classroom measures, running records)

There is much evidence that classroom teachers often fail to recognize instruction as the key to improving student performance. In a study surveying classroom teachers, Wade and Moore (1993) noted that 65% of teachers pointed to student characteristics as the main problem when students failed to learn or performed poorly on standardized tests. Home factors were the primary reason given for students' failure to learn by 32% of the teachers. Only 3% of teachers in this study believed that the education system was the most important factor impacting student achievement. It is essential that educators recognize the importance of their own instruction and how classroom formative assessments inform their instruction. In addition, teachers must identify the factors that prevent schools from assuring that students achieve critical literacy skills and intentionally assess and address those factors. Ultimately, it is the day-to-day instruction

summative—a final
assessment to measure the
degree to which instructional
goals or objectives have been
met or the progress learners
have made (e.g., end-of-year
standardized tests)

that must be assessed if dramatic change in student achievement is to occur (Hempenstall, 2001). Herein lies one of the major problems with high-stakes testing. The assessment of regular ongoing classroom instruction is not measured by most standardized tests. If the **summative** mandated high-stakes tests are replaced, they must be replaced by formative assessments and a regular ongoing process for monitoring of instruction. Black and William (1998a, 1998b) are insistent, based on their research findings, that improving formative assessments will improve student achievement.

Guiding Principles: Replacing or Supplementing Standardized Tests in Reading

Davis (1998) has underscored the need to be intentional in our focus on the development of reading assessments that gauge the full complexities of the reading process and what we already know about it. This researcher describes our present standardized tests as "thin" because the results we receive only describe a small part of what students know about reading.

Afflerbach (2004), writing for The National Reading Conference, has outlined a series of reading-assessment principles that are based on a complete definition of the reading process and that can be used to guide future decisions with respect to replacing high-stakes standardized tests or supplementing them with more appropriate measures. Some of the most salient considerations are discussed here. The first principle would ensure that reading assessments reflect a child's performance over several time periods and include a variety of tests given for a variety of purposes. A second important principle would be the use of a variety of formats and types of responses, measuring a wide range of reading skills. A third important consideration would be the necessity of following ethical guidelines as set forth by the American Educational Research Association, the International Reading Association, and the American Psychological Association. Any assessments used should provide students and their parents with useful information about their strengths and suggestions for improvement (Black & William, 1998b). An equally important principle for redesigning reading assessments would be providing teachers with useful diagnostic information that can be directly linked to classroom instructional practice. Finally, reading assessments must provide administrators with valuable data for program evaluation for comparison to district and state standards and goals.

Some Innovative Examples of Supplementary Assessments

Afflerbach (2008) reiterated that accountability is measured on one single day by one single test score, but teachers accomplish accountability with daily, authentic, practical assessments that inform instruction. Accomplished reading teachers are already using combinations of informed teacher assessments, regular progress monitoring, teachable moments, running records and informal reading inventories, student self-assessments, observational checklists, metacognitive responses, and skillful questioning to supplement the single test score and to accomplish accountability (Afflerbach, 2008).

Johnston (2005) discussed a promising assessment strategy piloted by the National Educational Monitoring Project (NEMP) in New Zealand. On one of the sample NEMP test items, children work as a group within a set time frame and are instructed to pretend that they are a library committee for their classroom. The children evaluate a set of books individually and then together as a group, with each member being required to justify their selections and their reasons (Flockton & Crooks, 1996). This activity, based on an authentic, meaningful literacy task, yields valuable assessment data about children and their problem-solving and collaborative skills, which are essential for survival in a global, interdependent society.

Damico (2005) proposed a comprehensive view of literacy and accountability based on Green's (1988) three-dimensional sociocultural model, including operational, cultural, and critical literacies. The model encourages juxtaposition of texts and promotes intertextual connections across texts as readers gain understandings that are socially relevant to their own lives. As readers engage with texts and interact with their peers, the teacher is able to observe and document students' higher level thinking abilities and critical reading behaviors.

> **portfolio assessment**—a way of documenting a learner's progress over time by assembling a collection of student work that exhibits the student's efforts, progress, and achievements

Portfolio assessment, widely supported in the early to mid-1990s, offers a viable substitute or supplement for standardized testing and focuses on the involvement of the student in his or her own learning process. Specifically defined, "a portfolio is a purposeful collection of student work that exhibits the student's efforts, progress, and achievements in one of more areas" (Paulson, Paulson, & Meyer, 1991, p. 60). Portfolios have been successfully used to document student literacy learning over a period of time and offer promise as a supplemental assessment strategy to be used in conjunction with high-stakes tests to provide a comprehensive view of a student's progress in reading and writing.

> **reciprocal teaching**—a type of formative assessment and instructional strategy using teacher and peer modeling to teach important cognitive strategies leading to improved comprehension

Reciprocal teaching (Palinscar & Brown, 1984) is an instructional strategy that has been used for decades but has recently received new focus as holding promise for improving students' comprehension test scores (Oczkus, 2003). It is built on four strategies that good readers use to comprehend text: predicting, questioning, clarifying, and summarizing. Reciprocal teaching has been proven by research studies to be effective in teaching and assessing students' use of multiple comprehension strategies. The National Reading Panel (National Institute of Child Health & Human Development, 2000) advocated the use of cooperative learning with multiple reading strategies and highly recommended reciprocal teaching as an effective teaching practice.

The use of reciprocal teaching as a type of formative assessment provides teachers with the opportunity to observe firsthand a student's reading behaviors and comprehension strategy use while combining an instructional technique with an assessment strategy. In addition, it offers a method for teacher modeling of the literate disposition of reciprocity (Kalantzis, Cope, & Harvey, 2003). Reciprocity, a desirable disposition for citizens of 21st-century democracies, has been defined as "a willingness to engage in joint learning tasks, to express uncertainties, and ask questions, to take a variety of roles in joint learning . . ." (Carr & Claxton, 2002, p. 16).

CONCLUSIONS

As we engage in the challenging task of designing new reading curricula for the demands of a 21st-century democratic society, we must set goals to foster the literacy skills and dispositions we hope to instill in our future citizens. If we hope to encourage lifelong learners who are resilient, flexible, critical thinkers and problem solvers, as well as collaborative workers who are consumers of the printed page as well as the digital text, then we need an innovative curriculum with an assessment system that is equally progressive.

In spite of the overwhelming data in the research literature claiming the detrimental effects of high-stakes testing on teachers and students, most reading experts will sadly agree that it is highly unlikely that the external, standardized assessments will be replaced. The politicians' and the public's hunger for quantitative comparisons, that is, **norm-referenced** and **criterion-referenced tests**, will continue to justify the existence and implementation of these standardized tests. But, as it becomes increasingly evident that the assessment imbalance and overemphasis on these measures has not resulted in significant gains in reading achievement, it is hoped that changes will be made in the present accountability system.

norm-referenced tests—a type of assessment of learner performance in which a student's performance is compared to the norming group, students in the sample population used in standardization of the test

criterion-referenced tests—a type of assessment of learner performance which translates students' test scores into a statement about the mastery behavior expected of a person on a particular objective or goal

By viewing the future through an optimistic lens, we can look forward to the time when needed changes in reading assessment will take place. Teachers can become change agents by insisting on a balanced and efficient approach to reading assessment that combines formative assessments with the external, summative demands. The needed change in reading assessment can take place if researchers and teachers respond to the challenge by demonstrating to stakeholders that diagnostic classroom assessment strategies are valid, reliable measures of reading progress and by providing evidence that use of formative assessments results in improved student literacy achievement.

CONNECTING READING ASSESSMENT TO YOUR CLASSROOM . . .

1. How has the reform and accountability movement impacted your district, school, classroom, and children? Interview public school teachers in your community and collect data from their responses. Prepare a presentation for your class based on your findings.
2. Share an example of an informal reading assessment that you use or would like to use in your classroom. What information does it provide that is not available from your state mandated standardized test results?
3. If you could replace the standardized tests required by your district, what would you choose? Explain how your plan would assure accountability for student learning to the stakeholders in your local community, the state, and the nation. Could you justify it to your state legislature or local school board?

REFERENCES

Adams, M. (1990). *Beginning to read: Thinking and learning about print*. Cambridge, MA: MIT Press.

Adcox, S. (2008, May 15). SC Senate OKs replacing end-of-the-year student tests. *Rock Hill Herald*. Retrieved August 15, 2008, from http://0www.lexisnexis.com.library.coastal.edu/us/lnacademic/results/docview/docview.do?docLinkInd=true&risb=21_T8984967389&format=GNBFI&sort=RELEVANCE&startDocNo=1&resultsUrlKey=29_T8984967397&cisb=22_T8984967396&treeMax=true&treeWidth=0&csi=304481&docNo=3

Afflerbach, P. (2004). *National Reading Conference Policy Brief on High Stakes Testing and Reading Assessment*. Retrieved October 10, 2008, from http://www.nrconline.org/

Afflerbach, P. (2007). Best practices in literacy assessment. In L. Gambrell, L. Morrow, M. Pressley, & J. Guthrie (Eds.), *Best practices in literacy instruction* (pp. 264– 284). New York: Guilford Press.

Afflerbach, P. (2008, May). Assessment and accountability: From teachable moments to tests. Paper presented at the annual Reading Research Conference of the International Reading Association, Atlanta, GA.

Allington, R. (2002). *Big brother and the national reading curriculum: How ideology trumped evidence*. Portsmouth, NH: Heinemann.

Amrein, A., & Berliner, D. (2002). The impact of high-stakes tests on student academic performance: An analysis of NAEP results in states with high-stakes tests and ACT, SAT, and AP test results in states with high school graduation exams. Tempe, AZ: Educational Policy Research Unit, College of Education, Arizona State University.

Apple, M. (1987). Foreword, in C. Lankshear, *Literacy, schooling and revolution*. London: Falmer.

Arado, M. (2008, November 19). Educators expect Obama will alter No Child Left Behind rules. *Daily Herald*. Retrieved July 29, 2009, from http://www.dailyherald.com/story/?id=251777

Barton, D. (2001). Directions for literacy research: Analyzing language and social practices in a textually mediated world. *Language and Education, 15*(2–3), 92–104.

Black, P., & William, D. (1998a). Assessment and classroom learning. *Assessment in Education: Principles, Policy, & Practice, 5*(1), 7–74.

Black, P., & William, D. (1998b). Inside the black box. *Phi Delta Kappan, 79*, 139–148.

Black, P., & William, D. (2005). Assessment for learning in the classroom. In J. Gardner (Ed.), *Assessment and learning*. London: Sage.

Calfee, R., & Hiebert, E. (1996). Classroom assessment of reading. In R. Barr, P.D. Pearson, & M. Kamil (Eds.), *Handbook of Reading Research* (pp. 281– 309). Mahweh, NJ: Lawrence Erlbaum Associates.

Carr, M., & Claxton, G. (2002). Tracking the development of learning dispositions. *Assessment in Education, 9*(1), 9–37.

Cheng, L. (2000). *Washback or backwash: A review of the impact of testing on teaching and learning.* Ontario, Canada (ERIC Document Reproduction Service No. ED422280).

Cobb, J., & White, A. (2006). High stakes testing, accountability, and prescribed direct phonics instruction: A comparison of struggling readers attending a university reading clinic before and after state mandated testing. *Journal of Reading Education, 32*(1), 31–37.

Crooks, T. (1988). The impact of classroom evaluation practices on students. *Review of Educational Research, 58,* 438–481.

Damico, J. (2005). Multiple dimensions of literacy and conceptions of readers: Toward a more expansive view of accountability. *The Reading Teacher, 58*(7), 644–652.

Darling-Hammond, L., & Wise, A. (1985). Beyond standardization: State standards and school improvement. *The Elementary School Journal, 85,* 315–336.

Davis, A. (1998). *The limits of educational assessment.* Oxford, UK: Blackwell.

Flockton, L., & Crooks, T. (1996). National education monitoring project: Reading and speaking, assessment results, 1996 (No. 6). Dunedin, New Zealand: Educational Assessment Research Unit.

Freebody, P. (2005). Critical literacy. In Beach, R., Green, J., Michael, M., & Shanahan, T. (Eds.), *Multidisciplinary perspectives on literacy research* (pp. 433–454). Cresskill, NJ: Hampton Press.

Freebody, P. (2007). *Literacy Education in School: Research perspectives from the past, for the future.* Camberwell, Victoria: Australian Council for Educational Research.

Gee J., Hull, G., & Lankshear, C. (1996) *The new work order: Behind the language of the new capitalism.* St Leonards: Allen and Unwin.

Gillborn, D., & Youdell, D. (2000). *Rationing education: policy, practice, reform, and equity.* Buckingham, UK: Open University Press.

Green, B. (1988). Subject-specific literacy and school learning: A focus on writing. *Australian Journal of Education, 32*(2), 156–179.

Hempenstall, K. (2001). School-based reading assessment: Looking for vital signs. *Australian Journal of Learning Disabilities, 6,* 26–35.

Hoffman, J., Assaf, L., & Paris, S. (2001). High-stakes testing in reading: Today in Texas, tomorrow? *The Reading Teacher, 54,* 482–492.

Hursh, D. (2005). The growth of high-stakes testing in the USA: Accountability markets, and the decline in educational equality. *British Educational Research Journal, 31*(5), 605–622.

It's time to reevaluate *No Child Left Behind.* (2007, July 1). *Christian Science Monitor.* Retrieved August 1, 2007, from http://www.csmonitor.com

Jennings, J. (1995). School reform based on what is taught and learned. *Phi Delta Kappan, 76,* 765–769.

Johnson, J., Treisman, U., & Fuller, E. (2000). Testing in Texas. *The School Administrator,* 20–26.

Johnston, P. (2005). Literacy assessment and the future. *The Reading Teacher, 58*(7), 684–686.

Johnston, P., & Costello, P. (2005). Principles for literacy assessment. *Reading Research Quarterly, 40*(2), 256–267.

Jones, M. G., Jones, B. D., Hardin, B., Chapman, L. Yarbrough, T., & Davis, M. (1999). The impact of high-stakes testing on teachers and students in North Carolina. *Phi Delta Kappan, 81,* 199–203.

Kahlenberg, R. (2008, October 13). What to Do With No Child Left Behind? *Education Week.* Retrieved October 16, 2008, from http://www.edweek.org/

Kalantzis, M., Cope, B., & Harvey, A. (2003). Assessing multiliteracies and the new basics. *Assessment in Education: Principles, Policy, & Practice, 10*(1), 15–26.

Kohn, A. (2000). Burnt at the high stakes. *Journal of Teacher Education, 51,* 315–327.

Leu, D. (2000). Our children's future: Changing the focus of literacy and literacy instruction. *The Reading Teacher, 53*(5), 424– 429.

Leu, D. J., & Kinzer, C. K. (2003). Toward a theoretical framework of new literacies on the Internet: Central principles. In J. C. Richards & M. C. McKenna (Eds.), *Integrating multiple literacies in K-8 classrooms: Cases, commentaries, and practical applications* (pp. 18–37). Mahwah, NJ: Erlbaum.

McColskey, W. H., & McMunn, N. (2000). Strategies for dealing with high stakes state tests. *Phi Delta Kappan, 82*(2), 115–120.

Meisels, S. (2000). On the side of the child. *Young Children, 55*(6), 16–19.

Mellon, E. (2007, April 12). TAKS ban wouldn't end standardized tests. *The Houston Chronicle.* Retrieved August 16, 2008, from http://www.chron.com/disp/story.mpl/front/4707430.html

NAEP 1994 Reading: A first look—Findings from the National Assessment of Educational Progress (rev. ed.). (1995). Washington, DC: U.S. Government Printing Office.

National Institute of Child Health and Human Development. (2000). *Report of the National Reading Panel. Teaching children to read: An evidenced-based assessment of scientific research literature on reading and its implications for reading instruction.* (NIH Publication No. 00-4769). Washington, DC: U.S. Government Printing Office.

A nation at risk: An imperative for educational reform. (1983). Washington, DC: U.S. Department of Education.

No Child Left Behind Act of 2001, Pub. L. No. 107-110, 115 Stat. 1425 (2002).

Oczkus, L. (2003). *Reciprocal teaching at work: Strategies for improving reading comprehension.* Newark, DE: International Reading Association.

Palincsar, A. S., & Brown, A. (1984). Reciprocal teaching of comprehension-fostering and comprehension monitoring activities. *Cognition and Instruction, 1*(2), 117–175.

Paulsen, F., Paulson, P., & Meyer, C. (1991). What makes a portfolio a portfolio? *Educational Leadership, 48*(5),60–63.

Reutzel, R., & Mitchell, J. (2005). High-stakes accountability themed issue: How did we get here from there? *The Reading Teacher, 58*(7), 606–608.

Taylor, K., & Walton, S. (1997). Co-opting standardized tests in the service of learning. *Phi Delta Kappan, 79*(1), 66–70.

Ullucci, K. (2008, October 14). MCAS: Rhetoric or results? Retrieved October 19, 2008, from http://www.southcoasttoday.com/apps/pbcs.dll/article?AID=/20081014/OPINION/810140308

U.S. Department of Education (1994). *Goals 2000: Educate America Act.* (1994). Washington, DC: U.S. Department of Education.

Wade, B., & Moore, M. (1993). *Experiencing special education.* Buckingham: Open University Press.

Whaley, S. (2007, March 10). Lawmakers debate imposing limitations on school testing. Retrieved August 16, 2007, from http://www.reviewjournal.com/lvrj_home/2007/Mar-10-Sat-2007/news/13084430.html

Wolf, P. (2007). Academic improvement through regular assessment. *Peabody Journal of Education, 82*(4), 690–702.

CHAPTER 23

LIVING A LITERATE LIFE IN THE "THIRD BUBBLE": A CASE STUDY OF A HIGH SCHOOL DROPOUT IN SOLITARY CONFINEMENT IN A MAXIMUM SECURITY PRISON

JEANNE B. COBB

THINK ABOUT ADULT LITERACY AND THIRD-SPACE THEORY . . .

1. As you read, construct your own definition of third-space theory.

2. Consider the role power plays in literacy learning in a classroom setting. As you read, consider the similarities in the disenfranchisement of Iceman as an adult literacy learner in the prison environment and the feelings of a struggling reader in today's public school classroom.

3. Reflect, as you read, on the intimate relationship between art and literacy.

counterhegemonic—
movement to push against
oppressive and discriminatory
boundaries set by race, class,
gender

As a radical standpoint, perspective, position, "the politics of location"
necessarily calls those of us who would participate in the formation of
counterhegemonic *cultural practice to identify the spaces where we*
begin . . . that movement requires pushing against oppressive boundaries
set by race, sex, and class domination . . . a defiant political gesture. . . .

(hooks, 1990, p. 145)

> **third space**—a hybrid type of in-the-middle space where people may move, live, and construct their own identities and where new knowledge may be constructed

Although bell hooks is referring here, in her volume *Yearning*, to her disenfranchisement by virtue of her ethnicity and her gender, this creation of a real and imagined **third space** in which to reenvision identity can also be applied to the lives of prisoners. This research investigation, a 4-year case study of the literacy life of one Hispanic/Asian American prisoner placed in solitary confinement, explores the complexities of his attempts to create an organized and orderly literate and artistic third space within the physical confines of a 9½ × 4½-foot prison cell.

It seems that a common misconception exists in contemporary society today that prisons are largely populated by functionally illiterate inmates who have little interest in literacy or in engaging in literate or artistic activities. Meatheringham, Snow, Powell, and Fewster (2007) concur that there is an erroneous, stereotypical view that all prisoners are illiterate and that illiteracy accounts for their criminal activity. Their research shows that there is little evidence to support these stereotypical views. Perhaps the stereotypes are fueled by persistent reports that funding for prison education programs is minimal. A recent report from the Institute for Higher Education Policy stated that fewer than 5% of prisoners nationwide are enrolled in any college coursework. This is unfortunate, since mounting evidence shows that education can be a cost-effective approach to reducing recidivism (Erisman & Contardo, 2005).

The present study attempts to look closely at this apparent stereotypical view of prison life as devoid of literate and artistic daily activities. A close investigation of the literate life of one male prisoner placed in solitary confinement in the maximum security unit of a state penitentiary in the Southwest contradicted the stereotypes.

THEORETICAL FRAMEWORK—THIRD-SPACE THEORY AND IMAGE BASED RESEARCH

This study was framed in two theoretical perspectives that have only recently been applied to literacy research: third-space theory and **image-based research**. Soja (1996), a pioneer in third-space theory, has challenged scholars to reframe the concept of space and how it is understood in human interaction and social situations. He proposed a concept of third space as a hybrid type of in-the-middle space where people may move, live, and construct their own identities. Soja credits Henri Lefebvre (1991) as having more influence than any other scholar on broadening our views of social spatiality and our ways of viewing complex social interrelationships in the modern world. Lebebvre views space as a social product and points out that society grants more space to the affluent and higher class citizens, while less space is given to those who are less wealthy. He broadens space to include not only the obvious physical form or real geographic space, but also the imagined space, a

> **image-based research**—innovative research technique emphasizing analysis of images and their accompanying verbal or written messages

mental construct. He defines the third space as space that is modified through use and over time to become the space of the real and the imagined, where new knowledge may be constructed.

Moje and others (2004) describe two other views of third space based on their research in secondary school settings. One conceptual view of third space is based on Bhabha's (1994) definition, which proposes that third space can be formed when people come together through use of language and sign systems to resist cultural and political authority. Third space, then, becomes a newly formed cultural space in which new knowledge is generated (pp. 37–38). Another view of third space as applied by Moje and others is that of the educational perspective in which students can appropriate differing discourses they encounter in learning situations and use them as resources for gaining a more complete understanding of their world and for becoming highly literate. This connotation of third space is particularly applicable to minority youth and to the prisoner in this case study because the creation of a third space opens up opportunities for literacy success for those whose voices are marginalized or silenced (Warren, Ballenger, Ogonowski, Roseberry, & Hudicourt-Barnes, 2001).

Third-Space Theory as Applied to Prisoners

There has been limited application of third-space theory to the lives of prisoners in the research literature. Muth (2005) used qualitative research to investigate six prisoners' views of literacy and learning within the confining first space of a prison's educational classroom setting. The most comprehensive research to date connecting third-space theory to the literate lives of incarcerated adults in prison environments is the work of Wilson (1996, 1998, 2000, 2003). She integrates themes of power, disenfranchisement, sociocultural theory, and Bhabha's (1994) work while pursuing a research agenda investigating prisoners' literate lives over a 12-year period. Her ethnographic work applies third-space theory to the prison environment in Northern England. Her findings confirm that the prison rules, regulations, and strict governance of all aspects of daily living are often prohibitive of literacy practices due to prisoners' access to resources. This restrictive environment, fueled by increased security issues, is one of imposition of a rigid power structure.

Prisons are also social environments, even for those who are placed in solitary confinement. Wilson (2000) found that prisoners would break the rules in order to have some small contact with the outside world they left behind or with their fellow inmates, who often have tidbits of news about current events. In spite of the strict regulatory environment of prisoners, which limits their access to resources for advancing their own literacy, there is still a multitude of writing being done within this setting by some inmates (Wilson, 1993). Her experience demonstrates that prisoners create a "third space," in which literacy thrives between the first space of prison regulations and the second space of the outside world and its often tormenting memories of regret and guilt for the prisoners (Wilson, 2000, p. 67).

Theoretical Framework—Image-Based Research

The second theoretical perspective underpinning this study is that of image-based research. Luke and Elkins (1998) have challenged reading researchers to reframe thinking and to investigate new literacies in order to discover what it will mean to be a reader or writer in the 21st century. Image-based research is one approach to the study of new literacies and has been confirmed by Prosser (1998) as having just appeared in the past 30 years. He believed that images linked with verbal responses provide researchers new ways of viewing reality and of investigating the way in which participants see themselves and their world. Prosser states that the additional analysis of images and the accompanying verbal or written messages can enhance our understandings of phenomena, particularly as related to human situations. Eisner (1985) has stressed broadening the lens of literacy to include different sensory systems to afford literacy users opportunities to construct meaning about the world in unique ways. Gardner (1982) also proposed more comprehensive cognitive views in his pioneering work on multiple intelligences. Silverman (1993) supports image-based work and states that images are neglected data sources for literacy field studies.

The investigation of art can offer unique insight into literacy as meaning making (Albers, 1997). Short, Harste, and Burke (1996) encouraged educators to move from written language to the arts when grappling to understand how meaning is constructed. Greene (1973) purports that art's function is for seeing and, inherent in that, is seeing new perspectives and gaining new understandings.

There is some precedence for using image-based research in educational studies. Wetton and McWhirter (1998) utilized a "draw-and-write" strategy in health education to inform researchers and teachers about the way children perceive health and safety-related concepts. Webber and Mitchell (2000) used students' drawings of teachers to understand the children's perceptions of the teaching profession and student–teacher relationships. McKay and Kendrick (1999, 2001a, 2001b) were among the first to use image-based research in the field of literacy to study young children's drawings of reading and writing.

Image-Based Research as Applied to Prisoners

A review of the literature yields limited evidence of the use of image-based research and literacy in prison studies. However, art has historically been one of the ways prisoners cope with their captivity (Kornfeld, 1997; Ursprung, 1997). Gussak and Ploumis-Devick (2004) found that "creativity and artistic expression are naturally inherent in correctional settings" (p. 35). Johnson (2008) believes, from his work, that art can be a valuable tool in the prison system, but support for these programs is declining. Art can have positive effects on quality of life, emotional health, and prisoner rehabilitation. Although the research base is minimal, Prosser (1998) believes that images provide researchers with new ways of viewing reality and of investigating the ways in which participants (i.e., prisoners) see themselves and others, giving credence to the use of image as a medium for study. It appears that there is a theoretical foundation for incorporating art and representational drawing into research-based inquiry in literacy learning, particularly with adults, such as prisoners, who have had limited opportunity to further their literacy skills after being incarcerated.

METHOD/RESEARCH TECHNIQUES

Case study research was the method for this study utilizing a qualitative, interpretative, analytic research technique. All data were reviewed initially according to categories of relevance. The researcher then looked across categories for themes relating to the prisoner's use of reading, writing, and art. A constant comparative method was used to identify themes apparent from the data (Bogdan & Biklen, 1982; Ryan & Bertrand, 2000).

Three research questions were the focus of this study: (1) How does one prisoner, a bilingual Hispanic/Asian American high school dropout, describe his use of literacy to create a third space within the confines of solitary confinement? (2) How does one prisoner, a bilingual Hispanic/Asian American high school dropout, describe his use of art and visual imagery to create a third space within the confines of solitary confinement? (3) In what ways do literacy and art work together to help this prisoner survive his solitary confinement and to construct a new identity for himself in the third space?

Data Sources

Data sources included transcriptions of interviews with the prisoner, 25 drawings, his verbal and written descriptions of his drawings, his poetry, daily logs of literate activities, samples of literacy artifacts, and his written correspondence with the researcher over a 4-year period.

FINDINGS RESEARCH QUESTION 1: A LITERATE LIFE

> Writing bridged my divided life of prisoner and free man. I wrote of the emotional butchery of prisons, and of my acute gratitude for poetry. Where my blind doubt and spontaneous trust in life met, I discovered empathy and compassion. The power to express myself was a welcome storm rasping at tendril roots, flooding my soul's cracked dirt. Writing was water that cleansed the wound and fed the parched root of my heart. I wrote to sublimate my rage, from a place where all hope is gone, from a madness of having been damaged too much, from a silence of killing rage. I wrote to avenge the betrayals of a lifetime to purge the bitterness of injustice (Baca, 1993, p. 11).

Jimmy Baca, Chicano poet and former prisoner, has won numerous awards for his gripping poetry, which is intensely lyrical and poignant, as evident in the preceding excerpt. His poetic words are illustrative of the creation of a third space in prison. Poetry helped him to bridge the gap between the confines of the physical space imposed by society's incarceration and the abstract mental space of the torments of a life gone bad. The in-between third space was his created haven of literate activity, of which poetry was the creative product.

Like Baca, "Iceman" [the pseudonym the prisoner gave himself for purposes of this study] has used literacy as a third-space respite from the demeaning and monotonous routines of prison life. Iceman is a 55-year-old Hispanic male with Asian ancestry. Spanish is his native language, but he speaks fluent English. He has been in a state prison in the Southwestern United States for 10 years and has a projected parole date of 2011. He dropped out of school in the ninth grade and is a self-educated man. He has been in solitary confinement for 8 years. One hour of daily outside recreation is mandated but does not happen on a regular basis.

He believes that reading, writing, and art are all important ways by which he copes with prison life. Literacy helps him to exercise his mind, he reports. It also helps him to use his imagination for the reconstruction of images. He knows that he has learned to read and write better on his own and resents the fact that the prison system has not helped him to improve his literacy. He has applied to take college correspondence courses in the past, but the warden has forbidden it. This has been a great disappointment to him. He states that the hardest thing about being in prison is not being able to put his ideas to work. Equally hard is not being able to obtain information. He wants to know and to learn. When released from prison, he would like to expose all the injustices done to inmates through writing articles or creation of a Web site.

Reading

Analysis of the data revealed that literacy plays an active role in Iceman's daily routine, with reading and writing being the primary ways he spends his time. Table 23.1 displays the ways he has reported that he uses literacy. He is very interested in reading, writing, and learning new things. He describes himself as a voracious reader who averages reading 1 to 3 books per week, and approximately 50 to 70 books per year. Figure 23.1 shows his reading log for one month. Some of the books are checked out through the prison library. Others are obtained from inmates whose families send them literary care packages. He described a unique "fishing pole" system used by the inmates in his pod, all of whom are placed in single cells in solitary confinement. There is a very small opening at the top of each cell wall. The inmates pass reading materials, newspapers, paperback books, and other reading materials along the cell block by using a fishing pole–type device. Of course, this is against the rules, but Iceman's hunger for access to the outside world and for literacy resources outweighs the fear of punishment. Some of the guards overlook these activities as relatively innocent, while others may force a lockdown or a required menu of peanut butter

TABLE 23.1   Ways in Which Iceman Uses Literacy in His Daily Life

Writing letters to researcher (he has no other friends or family that correspond with him)

Writing letters to organizations addressing prisoner rights

Taking notes/doing legal research

Preparing legal documents for his own appeal to Fifth Circuit Court of Appeals

Preparing legal documents for other inmates in his role as writ writer

Filling out property request forms

Reading court cases

Making law library request for material forms

Filing court briefs

Filling out grievance complaints about prison abuse/no daily recreation

Requesting free materials seen in magazines and catalogs

Requesting information on topic he's interested in

Helping other inmates prepare papers for parole package

Mailing off sketches and descriptions of inventions to mechanical magazines

Entering contests for free giveaways

Reading newspapers (sometimes 3 to 4 weeks old)

Filling out visitation request forms (for me and my daughter/no other visitors in 9 years)

Writing poetry

Reading books, magazines, and comic strips

Making library card requests with book titles

Reading his Bible and devotional material provided by prison church ministries

Reading government and state documents requested through the mail—reports on prison studies, Ford Foundation commission reports on safety and abuse in prisons

Creating get-well, birthday, and holiday cards

Reading official prison documentation and notices

Writing undercover notes to fellow pod mates

Reading correspondence from undergraduate writing class—critiques on his poetry writing

Keeping a journal

Writing prayers in his letters

Reading third-space theory articles

Reading poetry from Jimmy Santiago Baca

Writing a book—Survival Manual for Inmates in Solitary Confinement

Writing an article—Daily Life in Solitary Confinement

Reading religious organization's monthly magazines

Reading grammar books, thesaurus

Reading pamphlets

Reading Activities (Books)		Date — STUDY Practical	Law Library cases (Law)	Minutes - total spent Bible	Battle	Other
MAY 3						
4	NUMEROLOGY 2 hrs	1 hr		1½ hrs		3 hrs
5	" 4 hrs		2	1½	1 hr	—
6	" 2 hrs	1 hr		—		2 hrs
7	Augustine(?) 4 hrs			—		2 hrs
8	" 1 hrs	1 hr	2	1½	1 hr	1 hr
9	" 2 hrs			1½		2 hrs
10	" 1 hrs	1 hr	2	1½		—
11	DEAD SEA SCROLLS 4 hrs			1½		—
12	" 2 hrs	1 hr	2	1½	1 hr	—
13	2 hrs			—		4 hrs
14	The Hiding Place 4 hrs			—		2 hrs
15	" 4 hrs	1 hr	2	1½	1 hr	—
16	— —			1½		6 hrs
17	— —		2	1½		2 hrs
18	SPEAKING CHINESE 3 hrs	1 hr		1½		
19	" 3 hrs		2	1½	1 hr	
20	" 4 hrs	1 hr		1½		2 hrs
21	— —			—		
22	100 ORATIONS 4 hrs		2	1½	1 hr	
23	" 1 hrs	1 hr		1½		4 hrs
24	— —		2	1½		
25	IQ BOOK 7 hrs		●	1½		
26	" 2 hrs	1 hr	2	1½	1 hr	
27	— —			—		
28	Present Darkness 3 hrs			—		4 hrs
29	1 hrs	1 hr	X	1½	1 hr	
30	1 hrs			1½		
31	— —			1½		2 hrs
JUNE 1	Journey 3 hrs	1 hr	2	1½	1 hr	2 hrs
2	2 hrs			1½		1 hrs
3	2 hrs	1 hr	2	1½	1 hr	1 hrs

① Books as named.
② Study Grammar a study guide by A.J. Thompson + A.V. Martinet
③ Bible—I listen to two programs ½ hr, ½ hr, two ½ hr solo every day except Sat + Sun
④ Battle field of the mind with study Guide by Joyce Meyers
⑤ Other is newspapers and magazines or pamphlets.
Even Actions or Thesauras, Puzzles or Soduko's
Religious organizations monthly magazines.

FIGURE 23.1 Iceman's Reading Log—One Month.

and jelly sandwiches for a week as punishment. Iceman reports that being able to read even a scrap of a newspaper article, 3 or more weeks old, is a treat for him. The Bible is also his constant companion and one of his primary daily reading activities.

Iceman has repeatedly stressed that he loves to read and that he often rereads texts for better understanding. He immerses himself in law books, reviewing legal cases. He has become a "self-proclaimed" legal advisor, or "writ writer," for many inmates who are working through the system to secure early paroles and releases. Much of his energy these days goes into writing a legal brief that he will file on his own behalf to seek an early release from prison. He requests the law books he needs from the prison library system and pours over the cases daily. He trades his legal work for supplies from the prison store. Sometimes families of his fellow inmates will send him legal paper, pads, or other materials he needs in return for the legal work he does for their incarcerated relatives.

Writing

Data analysis revealed that Iceman also engages in a number of writing activities. One of those activities is his filing of complaints against the penal system for its violation of rules. He explained that often prisoners are denied medical attention and or access to drugs. Also, it is a common occurrence that the inmates in solitary confinement are denied their 1 hour of outside exercise and walks in the fresh air. There are always a number of excuses given, he complains—excuses that range from a guard's feeling sick that day to the weather as being too hot or too cold. Iceman's perception is that the denial of this outside privilege is done "on a whim," and the prisoners are powerless to claim that right. The only recourse, he explains, is to lodge a formal complaint. He is seen by guards, the warden, and his fellow inmates as a literate, articulate advocate and a prison reformer. He believes it is his calling to stand firm for his rights and the rights of his fellow inmates. He has learned the discourse of "righteous indignation" through his indoctrination over time into a rigid power system in which his voice is marginalized. The ability to have a "voice" is critical to his survival, for maintaining his own sense of worth and dignity as an individual. Literacy plays a significant role in this identity he has crafted for himself within the prison walls.

The data provided much evidence of Iceman's use of process writing. In his letters to me, he frequently made reference to his use of all five steps of the writing process. He also discusses his sense of the audience for which he is writing.

> I will go back to the draft for R. later. I don't like to push myself to [sic] much then it defeats the purpose of retaining the knowledge. Somehow the last sentence does not sound right. I'll figure it out later. I know it's wrong. OK I'll leave this page for now . . .
>
> Write! Write I do. When I am not working on the portraits I add on to the draft of the survival manual that you got me started on. But I'm learning a lot. I have to think back to write it in a laymans [sic] level. Especially since I have found that a lot of folks are illiterate in the system.

It is apparent from the data that his great desire to improve his own literacy overrides his concern or embarrassment at what others will think of his grammar or spelling. He is open to peer editing and to editing by the researcher.

> I told you that I have some problems with composition. To me that means saying what I mean to say. On the draft I had W. edit it for me. I met him on the recreation yard and he struck me as a sort a educated type guy. I took a chance in showing him the draft. He told me how to restructure it and I did. Mind you that I wrote that thing four times first. He corrected some typos and suggested some changes of words.

He writes in a letter to me, with a poem enclosed, "Like always please critic anything I send you. I welcome it. It would help me in expanding my knowledge." As a result, with his permission, I read aloud a poem he had written to my

MORNINGS

In the quiet before dawn, when all is still,
This is the time, when just for a while, all hearts can heal.
A time for lovers to share their love and release their passion,
A time to feel God's compassion.
It's the time I like the most, a time of gentle peace,
When all the haste, sometimes even the hate, seems to cease.
Mornings are special times for renewal or to just sit on a lake shore,
A time when nature comes to life once more.
In the morning, before the first rays of the sun pierce the sky,
Or before the first dove spreads its wings to fly.
You can almost see, and even feel, God's hand shape the day,
And, if you listen real close, you can even hear the angels at play.
God gave us mornings not only to renew the day, but also the soul,
If you've ever sat to watch a sunrise, then you too must know.
The awe of the start of another day which God has made,
And the love he sends and says will not ever fade.

GLG © 03/06

[Handwritten critiques:]

This is a wonderful poem that points out all the beautiful things that arrive with a new morning. GP

Great imagery! Keep it up! ST

Wow!
Your words are beautiful and inspiring. You use your words in such a way that I could feel what you were portraying. Wonderful job. MB

Use of imagery is wonderful. Very creative poetic m m
- Be confident in yourself because you have a great talent. Keep your head up! BL

Good job! This is amazing. I can't truly see what you were describing. God Bless KW

Great writing. I am also a poet myself. Keep up the wonderful writing. TH

Love the insight, great job! God Bless and may He (God) keep you in his care. RW

FIGURE 23.2   Iceman's Poem with Critique from College Writing Class.

undergraduate writing class. The students wrote comments on his poem which I returned to him. He was elated and excited to receive the positive and constructive feedback they gave him (see Figure 23.2).

He appears to have a fear of losing his intelligence if he does not work to exercise his mind, and he believes literacy is crucial in those efforts. "I use my creativity to keep from squirrel caging the mind," he states. On another occasion, he wrote to me, "I try to work the mind 'cause it is a muscle that deteriorates if you don't put it to work." These statements by Iceman confirm conclusions from Wilson's (2000) research. The longer an inmate remains in prison, the more fearful he or she becomes about losing some of their intelligence. Iceman related to me that there is a widespread fear of "losing one's mind" among the prisoners and that he has seen inmates "go completely crazy" in the solitary confinement pod (see Figures 23.1 and 23.3).

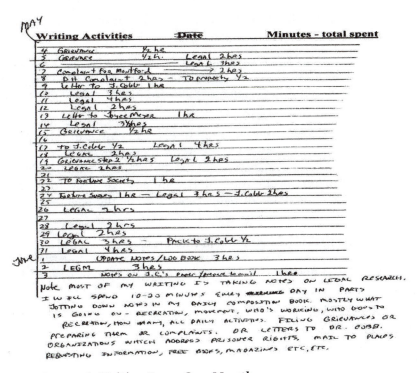

FIGURE 23.3   Iceman's Writing Log—One Month.

FINDINGS RESEARCH QUESTION 2: AN ARTISTIC LIFE

> I guess that . . . God has some purpose for me. I really believe that the future holds good things for all of us. I hope my drawing gets better, my memory . . . Drawing is a way of reasoning on paper.

With respect to art and the use of images, data analysis revealed that drawing and artistic endeavors occupy a primary place in Iceman's daily routine. As is the case with his literate life, his artistic life exists in an oasis, a third space he has created, a world where he can escape from the hardships he faces in solitary confinement. Iceman refers to his drawing as one of the important ways he has learned to cope with prison life and mentions that he feels lucky that he has the gift of art. He reveals that he started doing art to relax his mind. He likes to focus on beautiful images and lovely memories of the days before his incarceration as opposed to morbid, depressing prison themes in his artwork. Iceman states that he longs for links to the outside world and that he uses art for that link through imagery that conjures up powerful memories and pleasant images:

> I can do anything, I would guess. I ain't no Picasso. I think my work is pretty good and getting better. I could do a lot of stuff here but the people around me don't like my art cause they are into prison type work. I don't like to do that cause it is depressing.

It is apparent from analysis of his drawings in Table 23.2 that Iceman makes conscious choices to avoid painful memories, thoughts, or activities and to use positive, lovely imagery to lift his spirits and to remain calm. Although there are a few somber images, the majority are positive, peaceful, and upbeat. There is also a celebration of his Hispanic culture, while the Asian culture is noticeably absent.

TABLE 23.2   Images Displayed in Iceman's Art

Christian symbols—Christ, crown of thorns, cross, Christ carrying a sinner (man)

Portraits of researcher and her family

Culture symbols—Mexican sombrero, mariachis, guitar, Native American blanket

Mother holding a baby

Halloween symbols—ghosts, jack-o'-lanterns, bats, spiderwebs, spider with witch hat, cat, frog with witch hat

Patriotic symbols—flag, "United We Stand" lettering red, white, and blue

Female subjects—Caucasian, not Hispanic, with long blonde hair

Sad male clown

Rose with thorns

Orchid

Antique car—four-door coupe

Musical staff with notes and treble clef

Female subject—Hispanic with sombrero

Male subject—Hispanic with headband and cigarette

Small blonde female child dressed in pajamas with stuffed rabbit and blanket

Small blonde male child dressed in diaper and patched shirt with melting ice cream cone

Christmas symbols—Santa Claus, holly with berries, jingle bell

Large vehicle tires with Goodyear label

Female soldier scantily dressed in headband labeled "Beat Me" and military-type, heavy black lace-up shoes with machine gun (inspired by Jessica Lynch rescue)

War backdrop—black, burned images, metal pipes and chains/military images

Parrots, tropical background

Mayan ruins, Mexican sun

Another prominent theme in his art is his faith and use of Christian symbolism. Although raised a Catholic, he confessed that he had "lost his faith" in young adulthood but reclaimed it upon entry into prison life:

> Honestly, this understanding [faith] has not been for too long. I had not picked up a bible [cap?] for some time. Since I did, I have learned a lot. . . . You see since we are cast in the image of the Lord, I believe we are just a small part of the whole picture, like just one little bloodcell in a huge body.

Iceman's artistic talents provide him with a marketable skill that he uses to purchase supplies, stamps, and much-needed daily necessities to make life more bearable. Figure 23.4 is one example of the kinds of greeting cards he creates for inmates who want to send a special card to a child or spouse. In the same letter with the card, he also sent me a unique poem he had written entitled, "Lesson of Halloween." The poem captures a poignant memory of a fall conversation between 8-year-old Iceman and his elderly Asian grandfather, who questions American children's tradition of trick or treat. In this way art evokes memories of childhood events, and the imagery inspires literate responses, that is poetry.

FINDINGS RESEARCH QUESTION 3: CREATING A NEW IDENTITY

When I first proposed to Iceman that he become the subject of a research study, he was intently curious. As we discussed the concept of third space, he was intrigued. He asked to read all articles I could send him. On another visit, he

FIGURE 23.4   Sample Halloween Greeting Card Designed by Iceman.

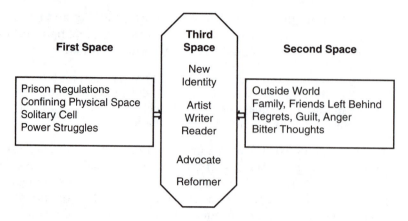

FIGURE 23.5   Iceman's New Identity in the Third Bubble.

laughed and rephrased the name of the theory, "I can see it, 'cause you could say that I live in the third bubble here." Iceman has created a new identity within his third bubble. The visual in Figure 23.5 illustrates his positive identity, carved out between the first and second spaces of his prison existence. Wilson (2000) refers to this construction of identity as creating an "identity kit" (p. 68). Iceman's new identity includes links to the outside world as well as a social network of fellow inmates who value him and perceive him as mentor, advisor, and role model. This affords him a mechanism for maintaining some aspects of freedom and outside contacts so that he can avoid being totally absorbed by the authoritarian power structure of prison life.

CONCLUSION

Iceman's world, the prison world of a single cell in solitary confinement, is a very restrictive *first space*, physically limiting his educational opportunities, his activities, and his desire for meaningful work as well as his desire to become a literate and creative individual. His *second space*, intense internal feelings and emotions resulting from negative past experiences with family and friends who have all deserted him, present him with a painful and depressing reality of unwise choices, significant mistakes, and the resulting "black hole" of sadness and regret. In an effort to escape the painful and restrictive confines of the *first-* and *second-space* realities in his life, Iceman has constructed his own *third space* through his literacy and his art, enabling him to cope with prison life and to "live and move" within a more desirable, happy space. His third-space reality enables him to construct a more positive self-image and transform himself, reshaping his identity as a literate, educated man. This third-space reality is one where he is redeeming himself, finding a new and empowered voice, and gaining a more positive sense of his own self worth, pursuing his "lost dreams," and envisioning a future for himself, a future filled with hope and joy.

LOST DREAMS

As a child, I had many dreams,
In each, I'd become something great.
A fireman, a doctor, a baseball star,
Even the governor of a state.

....

Then the journey of life took its turns,
My dreams were lost among the fray.
Paying little heed to the paths I chose,
Suddenly, I had lost my way.

....

I began to run at a faster pace,
Never knowing which way to turn,
At every stop,
Whispers, "One day that boy will learn."

....

Every stop must come to a close. Yet,
Mine has not reached its end.
I have chosen a path with fewer turns,
So that hearts I've broken can mend.

....

It wasn't as hard as I had once thought,
To make the changes from old to new,
Education is the best map of life,
Its direction always proves true.

....

So, when dreams get lost, as mine were,
Just teach yourself another way.
By learning, learning, and learning more,
I'll accomplish my dreams one day!!

Iceman 02/05

CONNECTING THIRD-SPACE THEORY TO YOUR CLASSROOM . . .

1. Visit an adult literacy class in your community. Interview the teacher. What conclusions can you draw from your interview and observations that confirm or disconfirm the creation of a third space within that learning environment?
2. Spatial analysis in literacy research implies change, and change involves power. Sketch your classroom and analyze carefully the distribution of space within your physical arrangement. What conclusions can you draw about power relationships within your class based on your analysis of space?

3. Develop a new curriculum plan for teaching a unit in social studies for your classroom that integrates literacy and art while keeping in mind the social practices and lived experiences of your students. Keep third-space theory in mind as you create the unit.

REFERENCES

Albers, P. (1997). Art as literacy. *Language Arts, 74*(5), 338–350.

Baca, J. (1993). *Working in the dark: Reflections of a poet of the barrio.* Santa Fe, NM: Red Crane Books.

Bhabha, H. (1994). *The location of culture.* London: Routledge.

Bogdan, R., & Biklen, S. (1982). *Qualitative research for education.* Boston: Allyn & Bacon.

Eisner, E. (1985). *The art of educational evaluation: A personal view.* London: Falmer Press.

Erisman, W., & Contardo, J. (2005). *Learning to reduce recidivism: A 50-state analysis of postsecondary correctional education policy.* Washington, DC: Institute for Higher Education Policy.

Gardner, H. (1982). *Art, mind, and brain: A cognitive approach to creativity.* New York: Basic Books.

Greene, M. (1973). *Teacher as stranger.* Belmont, CA: Wadsworth Publishing Company.

Gussak, D., & Ploumis-Devick, E. (2004). Creating wellness in correctional populations through the arts: An interdisciplinary model. *Visual Arts Research 29*(1), 35–43.

hooks, b. (1990). *Yearning: Race, gender, and cultural politics.* Cambridge, MA: South End Press.

Johnson, L. (2008). A place for art in prison: Art as a tool for rehabilitation and management. *The Southwest Journal of Criminal Justice, 5*(2), 100–120.

Kornfeld, P. (1997). *Cellblock visions: Prison art in America.* Princeton, NJ: Princeton University Press.

Lefebvre, H. (1991). *The production of space.* Malden, MA: Blackwell.

Luke, A., & Elkins, J. (1998). Reinventing literacy in "New Times." *Journal of Adolescent and Adult Literacy, 42*(1), 4–8.

Meatheringham, B., Snow, P., Powell, M., & Fewster, M. (2007). Literacy and assessment in prison. In S. Dawe (Ed.), *Vocational education and training for adult prisoners and offenders in Australia: Research readings* (pp. 177–203). Adelaide SA: Australia: NCVER.

McKay, R., & Kendrick, M. (1999). Young children draw their images of literacy. *The Reading Professor, 22*(1), 8–34.

McKay, R., & Kendrick, M. (2001a). Children draw their images of reading and writing. *Language Arts, 78*(6), 529–533.

McKay, R., & Kendrick, M. (2001b). Images of literacy: Young children's drawings about reading and writing. *Canadian Journal of Research in Early Childhood Education, 8*(4), 7–22.

Moje, E., Ciechanowski, K., Kramer, K., Ellis, L., Carrillo, R., & Collazo, T. (2004). Working toward third space in content area literacy: An examination of everyday funds of knowledge and Discourse. *Reading Research Quarterly, 39*(1), 38–70.

Muth, W. (2005, December). *Exploring third space within a federal prison.* Paper presented at the annual meeting of National Reading Conference, Miami, FL.

Prosser, J. (1998). *Image-based research.* London: Falmer Press.

Ryan, G., & Bertrand, H. (2000). Data management and analysis methods. In N.K. Denzin & Y.S. Lincoln (Eds.), *Handbook of qualitative research* (2nd ed.). Thousand Oaks, CA: Sage Publications.

Short, K., Harste, J., & Burke, C. (1996). *Creating classrooms for authors and inquirers.* Portsmouth, NH: Heinemann.

Silverman, D. (1993). *Interpreting qualitative data.* London: Sage.

Soja, E. (1996). *Thirdspace: Journeys to Los Angeles and other real-and-imagined places.* Cambridge, MA: Blackwell.

Ursprung, W. A. (1997). Insider art: The creative ingenuity of the incarcerated artist. In D. Gussak & E. Virshup (Eds.), *Drawing time: Art therapy in prisons and other correctional settings* (pp. 13–24). Chicago: Magnolia Street Publishers.

Warren, B., Ballenger, C., Ogonowski, M., Roseberry, A., & Hudicourt-Barnes, J. (2001). Rethinking diversity in learning science. The logic of everyday languages. *Journal of Research in Science Teaching, 38,* 1–24.

Webber, S., & Mitchell, C. (2000). *That's funny, you don't look like a teacher.* London: Falmer Press.

Wetton, N., & McWhirter, J. (1998). Images and curriculum development in health education. In J. Prosser (Ed.), *Image-based research* (pp. 263–283). London: Falmer Press.

Wilson, A. (1993). A creative story about prison writing. *Research and Practice in Adult Literacy Bulletin, 21,* 3.

Wilson, A. (1996). 'Speak up, I can't write what you're reading.' *Journal of Correctional Education, 47*(2).

Wilson, A. (1998). 'Three days and a breakfast.' *Research and Practice in Adult Literacy Bulletin, 37,* 2–4.

Wilson, A. (2000). There is no escape from third-space theory: Borderland discourse and the 'in between' literacies of prisons. In D. Barton, M. Hamilton, & R. Ivanic (Eds.), *Situated literacies: Reading and writing in context* (pp. 54–69). London: Routledge.

Wilson, A. (2003). Researching in the third space: Locating, claiming, and valuing the research domain. In S. Goodman, T. Lillis, J. Maybin, & N. Mercer (Eds.), *Language, literacy, and education: A reader* (pp. 293–307). Stoke on Trent, UK: Open University Trentham Press.

INTERSECTIONS OF THE PAST, PRESENT, AND FUTURE IN READING INSTRUCTION AND RESEARCH

HELPFUL WEB SITES

Technology

http://www.readingrockets.org/
http://www.nsba.org/sbot/toolkit/tiol.html
http://classroom.jc-schools.net/read/electronicpen_files/v3_document.htm
http://classroom.jc-schools.net/read/writing.html
http://www.literacy.uconn.edu/writing.htm (Resources for teachers)
http://www.thenewsliteracyproject.org/
http://literacy.alltop.com/
http://www.courant.com/features/booksmags/hc-readingrise1.artjan18,0,2748298.story
http://www.frankwbaker.com/rebooting_news_standards.htm
http://eduscapes.com/sessions/doors/index.htm
http://eduscapes.com/sessions/experience/readwrite1.htm
http://www.theapple.com/benefits/articles/6082-book-punch-a-reading-writing-teaching-tool
http://eduscapes.com/sessions/doors/index.htm
http://eduscapes.com/sessions/experience/readwrite1.htm
http://www.nsba.org/sbot/toolkit/tiol.html
http://classroom.jc-schools.net/read/writing.html

Multiliteracies

http://changingminds.org/explanations/behaviors/body_language/body_language.htm
http://multiliteracies.com/
http://www.brendanpauljacobs.com/education.htm

Multimodal Texts

http://www.norcalwp.org/multimodal/
http://www.readwritethink.org/lessons/lesson_view.asp?id=1139
http://www.ncte.org/topics/assessment
http://www.ceosyd.catholic.edu.au/cms/Jahia/site/curriculumonline/pid/78
http://www.equinoxpub.com/books/showbook.asp?bkid=10
http://www.everybodywrites.org.uk/projects/details/more-than-words-multimodal-texts-in-the-classroom/
http://www.accessmylibrary.com/coms2/summary_0286-13842714_ITM
http://wordandimage.wpmued.org/2008/02/16/5-valuing-multimodal-texts/

Multimodalities

http://amys-excogitation.blogspot.com/2007/04/multimodal-literacy.html
http://www.academiccommons.org/library/multi-modal-literacy
http://l05.cgpublisher.com/proposals/305/index_html
http://www.compositionstudies.tcu.edu/bookreviews/online/32-2/morris.html

Reading Assessment

http://www.questia.com/library/education/reading-assessments.jsp
http://literacyencyclopedia.ca/index.php?fa=items.show&topicId=226
http://wwhttp://www.pbs.org/newshour/indepth_coverage/education/no_child/testing.htmlw.fairtest.org/facts/howharm.htm
http://www.ed.gov/policy/elsec/reg/proposal/index.html
http://www.wrightslaw.com/heath/read.prevent.failure.htm

http://nces.ed.gov/nationsreportcard/reading/
http://nces.ed.gov/pubsearch/pubsinfo.asp?pubid=2007496
http://www.wrightslaw.com/info/read.programs.frcc.htm#ready
http://www.wrightslaw.com/nclb/4defs.reading.htm
http://www.wrightslaw.com/bks/nclb/nclb.htm
http://www.fcrr.org/assessment.htm
http://www.ed.gov/parents/read/resources/goodprogram.html
http://www.wrightslaw.com/info/nclb.parent.guide.heath.htm
http://www.wisegeek.com/what-is-high-stakes-testing.htm
http://www.fairtest.org/arn/caseagainst.html
http://www.researchchannel.org/prog/displayevent.aspx?fID=568&rID=3444
http://www.youtube.com/watch?v=amkmxbRn5tk
http://www.youtube.com/watch?v=WFSN5AttlGk&feature=related
http://www.youtube.com/watch?v=bapQpAB0ZBY&feature=related
http://www.youtube.com/watch?v=10SetbvhFro&feature=related

Third-Space Theory

http://scholar.google.com/scholar?hl=en&lr=&q=cache:KKL7s1WIl-kJ:coeweb.fiu.edu/
research_conference/2007_SUIE_Proceedings_files/Pane.FINAL.pdf+related:MeoPj7aYJJcJ:
scholar.google.com/
http://librarianinterrupted.wordpress.com/2007/12/18/a-third-space-for-teens/
www.easyprague.cz/eecera2007/download/files/11.00%20Levy.pps
http://www.instep.net.nz/change_for_improvement/a_common_theory_of_improvement/
joint_inquiry_in_the_third_space
http://www.ite.org.uk/ite_topics/popular_culture_primary_english/009.html
http://docs.google.com/gview?a=v&q=cache:9vjDjKUrUaIJ:www.eastmidlandscpd.co.uk/
casestudies/38.pdf+third+space+theory+literacy&hl=en&gl=us
www.bera.ac.uk/files/2008/10/BERA-ZEICHNER.ppt

INDEX

Note: Page numbers followed by *f* indicate figures.